# Out of the Black Patch

## The Autobiography of
## Effie Marquess Carmack
## Folk Musician, Artist, and Writer

Volume 4
**LIFE WRITINGS OF FRONTIER WOMEN**

A Series Edited by
Maureen Ursenbach Beecher

Effie M. Carmack, ca. 1910. Courtesy of Hazel Bushman.

# Out of the Black Patch

*The Autobiography of*
*Effie Marquess Carmack*
*Folk Musician, Artist, and Writer*

Edited by

## Noel A. Carmack

and

## Karen Lynn Davidson

UTAH STATE UNIVERSITY PRESS
Logan, Utah
1999

Utah State University Press
Logan, Utah 84322-7800

Publication of this book was supported by a subvention from John K. and Shirley A. Carmack.


Typography by WolfPack
    Dust jacket design by Michelle Sellers

Library of Congress Cataloging-in-Publication Data

Carmack, Effie Marquess, 1885-1974.
    Out of the black patch : the autobiography of Effie Marquess Carmack, folk musician, artist, and writer / [edited by Noel A. Carmack and Karen Lynn Davidson].
        p.   cm. — (Life writings of frontier women ; v. 4)
Includes bibliographical references and index.
    ISBN 0-87421-279-0
    1. Carmack, Effie Marquess, 1885-1974. 2. Farm life—Kentucky. 3. Mormons—Kentucky—Biography. 4.  Folk singers—United States—Biography. 5.  Painters—United States—Biography. 6.  Authors, American—Biography. 7.  Kentucky—Social life and customs. 8. Kentucky—Biography. I. Carmack, Noel A., 1967- II. Davidson, Karen Lynn. III. Title. IV. Series.
    CT275.C2976 A3  1999
    973.9'092—dc21

                                99-006901

For Harry
1919–1923

# CONTENTS

# Illustrations

# Foreword

## Maureen Ursenbach Beecher

In recognition of the importance to literature of biography and autobiography, the Association for Mormon Letters in 1987 was offering a new prize in life writing. I was asked to help in identifying appropriate candidates for the prize. Elder John Carmack, then managing director of the Historical Department of the Church of Jesus Christ of Latter-day Saints in Salt Lake City shared with me a rare mimeographed volume of the memoirs of his grandmother Effie Marquess Carmack. I was charmed. The committee, however, considered the manuscript as yet unpublished, so the AML prize went to another book. But I never forgot Effie's story.

My history-writing colleagues and I, researchers in the LDS Church Historical Department and the Joseph Fielding Smith Institute for Church History and beyond, had long been accustomed to reading, as resources for our historical inquiries, the life writings of frontier women. We loved the diaries, the letters, and the autobiographies, but had not thought them a literature of their own. With Effie's text, however, I felt a new compunction: with or without historical research as motivation, others might well read this raw material with as much relish as we. I passed the manuscript on to a literature-sensitive friend whose judgment I trusted.

She agreed—it was a delightful read. Would she consider editing it for publication? Not just now, she replied. But certainly it deserved a place among American autobiographies available for general readers.

Not a "written for publication" autobiography, this text grew, as such memoirs often do, out of a mother's wish to share her life and its meaning with her children. Much more, however, than the testimonials of the religious faithful which were its literary precedents, Effie's account provides in vibrant colors a richly detailed background for her testimony. Every sense is enlivened—the taste of Postum that brings back her first summer in Arizona; "this mixture of smells, cedar smoke, greasewood, and sour dock greens"; the roughness of the ground under a wire fence as she escaped from a crazed cow and the squeak of the wires through the staples as she pulled herself through. The text is laced through with Effie's awareness of beauty: "roses, jonquils, and honeysuckle"; "a sweet-toned guitar with twelve strings"; her first child, born too small but then "fattened like a little pig, . . . a perfect roly poly of a baby." Effie explains that as a child "I surely must have had an unnatural love for pretty things, especially flowers." That she became a painter of note in the Southwest is not surprising.

But there was ugliness, too, in Effie's world. The "black patch" that is Kentucky's tobacco country becomes tactile in Effie's words: "Worming and suckering tobacco was a terrible, backbreaking job, and the gum from the sticky green leaves would soon be all over our hands and clothing, so thick that when a garment became folded and stuck, it was hard to pull it apart again. The sickening smell of the hot sun on the green tobacco usually gave me a headache."

But for the most part there is joy in Effie's text, and love, and faith, and achievement. Effie accepts herself, warts and all, with a candor which inspires trust. "I was a thin, scrawny child," she writes, "ugly and small for my age." But at the dances, the sing-alongs, the parties, she was popular: "I usually got a partner of some kind." And admirers a-plenty.

There is candid disclosure in Effie's account, but there is mystery in what she leaves unspoken. The reader is caught between the lines with unanswered questions: why, for instance, after page-long descriptions of Effie's young loves is her marriage so bluntly and abruptly stated: "Edgar (Carmack) went to work for Evert, and we were soon married, and moved to the old Birchfield Marquess place." No courtship, no in-and-out-of-love, no suspense, just "we were soon married." One wonders.

In her later life, honors came to Effie Marquess Carmack for her good works in the community, for her art, for her memory of the folklore and the folk music of her past, for her service to her church. She hardly mentions those; her focus is on others, her family of origin at first and then her own eight children. For them she composed her life into the text her grandson gave me. It made me want to know her, and to share her story.

Years passed, and Effie's text sat patiently on my shelf waiting for its time to come. When I compiled a list of publishable texts for this present series, Effie's book was at the top for its appeal to general readers and scholars alike. Karen Lynn Davidson, former professor of English and chair of the Honors Program of Brigham Young University, accepted the invitation to prepare the manuscript. She was then living in Southern California near the final residence of Effie Carmack and the current home of some of her family, a coincidence which would prove fortuitous. With Carmack family members as resources, Karen transcribed the mimeographed volume, researched its provenance, and began the process of documenting Effie's genealogy. She researched the folk song repertoire and examined the poetry of the multi-talented Effie.

Karen's manuscript languished while the Life Writings of Frontier Women series proved its worth. Its first three volumes each won a prize for excellence in its field. By the time senior editor John Alley and Utah State University Press were ready for the next text, however, Karen had moved to Princeton, so Noel Carmack, Effie's great grandson, the preservation librarian at Utah State University and the author of a journal article on Effie Carmack's career as an artist, undertook further documentation of the manuscript and the writing of a new introduction. His research brought out the historical context and folkways that influenced Effie's life and writing. Noel also provided copies of the paintings and photographs reproduced here. With undiluted enthusiasm we now present the completed text to the series and to the reading public.

Out of Kentucky's Black Patch came this bright rainbow, this cheerful, affable, resourceful, honest, diligent achiever. Effie lived a splendid life; more than that, she also wrote it with the same vigorous splendor with which she lived it. We are proud to present her now, in the fourth volume of the series Life Writings of Frontier Women.

# PREFACE

## The Manuscript

The autobiography of Effie Carmack, covering a period of some eighty-seven years, was written as a gift to her children and grandchildren. She was driven to write her story out of a desire to leave them something of worth, an account of her unusual life experience. Having lost her mother at a young age, Effie learned the value of the written record. "How I do wish my mother had kept a diary, or a book of remembrance," she wrote. "I realize now what a priceless thing they can be" (p. 105, herein). Her own autobiography reflects this valuation of family history. First printed under the title *Down Memory Lane*, it recounts her experiences as a young girl, adolescent, and adult woman and mother; it shows her persistence in establishing an identity and a place in her extended family lineage.

Effie did not, however, begin writing her story until her fifties. Even then, though decades had passed, Effie's youth in rural Kentucky was more to her than a vague recollection. Her autobiography is a story rich with memories of childhood pastimes, rural domesticity, and folklife. With sharp detail, she recounts the day-to-day life of the Marquess family: Christmas gifts, the use of medicinal herbs, the steps taken in a typical housecleaning, the sad events of the typhoid epidemic of 1898–1899, the songs she and her family played and sang. Beyond brief references to her childhood schooling, she describes the benches, playtime games, spelling bees, and even what she took for lunch. She doesn't simply allude to the fiddler's contest; she describes the pieces that were played, who performed them, and the prizes they won.

Personal narratives, based on memory, are often laden with inaccuracies. Constructing believable characters and settings from real events can cause authors to depart from historical fact. Embellishment for the sake of a good story might easily have driven Effie's work, but her story seems to avoid such pitfalls.[1] The strength of Effie's writing lies in her unmistakable ability to recall specific events in detail. She dredged up the past and let it flow with ease, much like an oral telling or performance.

Effie's desire to preserve such memories was an endeavor that spanned several decades. Beginning in the mid-1940s, she worked on her autobiography and other projects until the last months of her life. All told, she spent nearly thirty years writing and compiling her story for publication.

The literary success of her story may be due, in part, to its being carefully written in several installments. Although *Down Memory Lane* was printed in typescript format in 1973, the first half (or so) had actually been finished in 1948 and covered Effie's life through that year. Simply called "Autobiography," this earlier memoir was typed by her daughter, Hazel Carmack (Bruchman) Bushman, and then circulated privately in the family. Twenty years later, Effie added an update, for the most part leaving the 1948 version as originally written. Hazel Bushman was again the typist. Any small alterations were made for clarity (such as substituting a proper name for a pronoun) or to add details that were not included earlier. Effie aids the reader by parenthetically dating the various times she added to her document. A photocopy of this longer, combined typescript was privately printed by Atascadero News Press in 1973 and circulated among friends and family. It is this version from which the present edition is taken.

## Editorial Methods

The usual practice in editing an autobiography is to preserve all spelling, usage, and punctuation of the original. However, the handwritten manuscripts from which Hazel Bushman typed the two installments of the journal no longer exist. Because Hazel had extensive training and experience as a secretary, her natural tendency was to amend and regularize any nonstandard spelling or usage, especially because the family intended the second typed version to be photocopied and bound. Since for all practical purposes Effie's writing had already been edited, the best choice for this edition seemed to be to normalize the few remaining instances of nonstandard spelling and apostrophe use. A few colloquial pronoun cases and verb forms have been left as written as it seemed officious and unnecessary to change them. There are a few instances in which Effie, in keeping with southern folk speech, referred to her African American neighbors using racial slurs. Effie was sensitive to these offensive terms and tried to remove

---

1.  See, for example, John E. Miller, "Narrative Rules and the Process of Storytelling," chap. 6 in *Laura Ingalls Wilder's Little Town: Where History and Literature Meet* (Lawrence: University Press of Kansas, 1994), 81–95.

them from later versions of the text. The few that were overlooked, though, have been left unchanged by the editors.

It should be pointed out, however, that there is no reason to conclude that any regularized version would be very different from Effie's original. Although her formal schooling ended by the eighth grade, Effie was an excellent student. She tells of being spelling champion, of playing word and map games with her family, of reading and studying, and of "memorizing whole chapters of the Bible"; and she comments frequently on the "perfect" (or less than perfect) English of various relatives or friends. She was interested in language and writing her entire life, and various handwritten documents that do exist show that she was a competent writer of standard English. Thus, the reader can be confident that this is not a radically different autobiography from the one that came from Effie's pen.

It is our intention to present the document as faithfully to the copy-text source as possible. We have sought to keep emendations to a minimum. However, to provide meaningful breaks in the text, we have divided the narrative into six numbered chapters and an epilogue. Each chapter has been given a title and epigraph. Some items printed with the post-1948 additions were in fact family updates or newsletters written by people other than Effie. Because these family news items hold more significance for friends and relatives than the general reader, they have been omitted in this edition. Effie's own writing in the post-1948 section tends to be more fragmented; as various topics came to mind, she would simply introduce them by adding a subtitle. We have chosen to eliminate these subtitles to allow more continuity and uniformity in the narrative. Substantial selections from this post-1948 portion appear as the epilogue. Each omission is noted by bracketed ellipses and a note describing the omitted material.

Although *Down Memory Lane* appeared in typescript format, it was printed with a number of hand corrections and additions. In several instances, Effie added words or names to spaces she left blank. Considering such emendations, it was necessary to devise a clear editorial method and use standardized apparatus.[2] To best provide an honest representation of Effie's emendations in the final document, the following methods were employed:

---

2. The standard by which this copy-text was edited is Mary-Jo Kline's *A Guide to Documentary Editing*, 2d ed. (Baltimore: Johns Hopkins University Press, 1998). For a pioneering work on editorial method, the reader should consult G. Thomas Tanselle, "The Editing of Historical Documents," in *Textual Criticism and Scholarly Editing* (Charlottesville: University Press of Virginia, 1990), 218–73.

1. Clarifications, identifications, and other editorial expansions of the original text appear in square brackets in roman type: driv[ing].
2. Editorial comments, in the editors' voice, appear in italics between brackets: [*The autobiography does not include this picture*].
3. Canceled material is shown with a strikeout as in the original: ~~good~~
4. Material underlined for emphasis has been standardized to italics.
5. Interlined words are enclosed in carets at the place of insertion: ^gone^. Their placement in the original is indicated in a note.
6. Portions of text repeated elsewhere in the document are enclosed in angle brackets and described in a note.
7. Editorially omitted material is indicated by three ellipses enclosed in brackets: [ . . . ]. The substance of the edited material is described in a note.
8. Biographical references to individuals are noted at the first appearances of their names in the text or when an individual is most conspicuous in the narrative. When possible, biographical references include a full name with years of birth and death. In many cases, only an estimated birth date, based on census returns, is provided. Unidentifiable persons are left unnoted.

## Annotations and Sources

In order to clarify or add insight to obscure references, we have used explanatory notes. We have avoided extensive interpretation of the writing to allow the text to stand on its own, affording an unencumbered reading of the document. The length or brevity of a note usually depends upon the availability of relevant sources. Standard biographical dictionaries and reference works are rarely cited. If a source adds meaningful insight to the text, it is discussed at reasonable length. Otherwise, the reader is supplied a brief comment and directed to other sources for further study.[3]

Attempting to provide biographical information for all individuals mentioned by Effie would be painstaking, if not impossible. Many names have been left undocumented, but where available, birth and death years have been supplied in a note. Luckily, Effie was a dedicated genealogist. She collected photographs, scraps of family lore, histories, and vital records. She is to be credited for much of the information provided in this edited work. A number of general historical sources proved helpful nonetheless, including recently published biographical works by the

---

3. See G. Thomas Tanselle, "Some Principles for Editorial Apparatus," in *Textual Criticism*, 119–76.

Christian County Genealogical Society and indexed county census returns for 1870, 1880, and 1900. Genealogical records preserved at the Family History Library of the Church of Jesus Christ of Latter-day Saints were also invaluable sources of biographical information. A chart is provided to better identify Effie's family members and her place among them. For additional sources, the reader should consult the bibliography.

## Acknowledgments

Many individuals have contributed their time and expertise in preparing this important document. First, we must thank Maureen Ursenbach Beecher for including Effie's writings in this award-winning series on frontier women and for allowing us the opportunity to edit the autobiography for general readership. We are also grateful to John Alley, editor of Utah State University Press, for his interest in this project and advice on producing a quality manuscript.

Our heartfelt thanks go out to the members of the Carmack family who assisted in providing photographs, newspaper clippings, and personal accounts of their experiences with Effie. They include Violet Carmack Mattice, Dona Bruchman Harris, Robert M. Carmack, Betty Carmack Hendrickson, Donna Bess Carmack Musto, Itha V. Carmack, Thomas W. Carmack, and Olitha Carmack. Our thanks go to John Wesley Marquess and Mary Ann Willis for providing Marquess family information.

We express special gratitude to Hazel Carmack Bushman, John Kay Carmack, and Shirley Carmack, who provided many documentary sources and were tremendously supportive from the start of this project. John and Shirley Carmack also provided a generous subvention to the publisher of this book. Moreover, their and Hazel Bushman's desire to share Effie's story was the motivation for getting this book published.

We are especially grateful for the untiring work of Austin Fife and his wife, Alta, in preserving the ballads of common people. Without their efforts, Effie's record would be incomplete.

A number of individuals deserve our thanks for providing expert advice and assistance. These include Barre Toelken, who kindly answered questions about the folkloristics of the text and ballads; W. Lynwood Montell, formerly of Western Kentucky University, and William T. Turner of Hopkinsville Community College, who answered questions on local history and folklore; Betty McCorkle of the Christian County Genealogical Society, who offered advice on relevant sources; Richard A. Smath of the Kentucky Geological Survey, who helped locate Christian County landmarks; Michael C. Sutherland of the Special Collections division at Occidental College, who generously helped uncover material on Dr. Austin Fife; Marian Hart, Susan Beatie, and Olive Doellstedt of the

Atascadero Art Association (formerly the Atascadero Art Club), who provided clippings on the Art Club and Effie's art activities; Randy Williams and the rest of the staff of the Fife Folklore Archives at Utah State University; the search room staff at the Historical Department Archives of the Church of Jesus Christ of Latter-day Saints, especially Ronald G. Watt, who offered kind and helpful reference assistance; John Walters of the Documents Department at the Utah State University Libraries; and the staff of the Special Collections and Archives at Utah State University, especially April Haws, who helped with the photographs and maps. We are grateful to Charles M. Hatch for his heroic efforts in copy editing.

Without the Joseph Fielding Smith Institute for Church History at Brigham Young University and the encouragement it has provided from the outset, the series Life Writings of Frontier Women would not have appeared. General editor Maureen Ursenbach Beecher and secretary Marilyn Rish Parks were supported in their work on the texts with the blessing of Ronald K. Esplin, director of the Institute; the collegiality of the rest of the historical staff provided a nurturing environment for the ongoing work of preparing and publishing life writings.

We thank John W. Welch, Doris Dant, and the editorial staff of *BYU Studies* for allowing us to use portions of a previously published article for the introductory essay.

We also thank Mary C. and Gerald O. Lynn for spending many patient hours assisting in proofreading. Kenneth and Audrey Godfrey gave encouragement and advice; Jason McCraw, Heber Manire, Flora Manire Schuller, and other members of the Hopkinsville, Kentucky, LDS Ward deserve our thanks for providing genealogical assistance and for locating sites in northern Christian County.

Thanks go to our many friends and colleagues who shared our excitement over Effie's narrative. We are most grateful to our spouses and families for their encouragement and support in this project.

Last of all, we appreciate the opportunity to have been a part of Effie's story. Our lives, like many others, have been enriched by learning a little bit more about her.

# INTRODUCTION

Too often, social history reduces women's life writings to mere resources for broader analysis and interpretation. Historians and demographers may overlook the richness of the women's voices that emerge from uninhibited, reflective writing. Vernacular works by ordinary women provide grounded history that fills and colors gaps left by bean counters and theoreticians. The immediacy of unhampered words written by a woman in private often can do more for our understanding of gender roles, class distinctions, and race relations than formal, necessarily reductive interpretations. Only now are we beginning to acknowledge the imprints left by women writers such as Agnes Miner, May Cravath Wharton, Marietta Palmer Wetherill, and others whose lives remained unnoticed until perceptive editors and biographers brought them to light.[1]

Writings by Mormon women in the rural South are scarce, even virtually unknown. The autobiography of Effie Marquess Carmack, a convert to the Church of Jesus Christ of Latter-day Saints from southwestern Kentucky, contributes well to our understanding of rural white women in the post–Civil War South. It is a rare expression of a woman's vernacular, yet artful, voice and provides an unusual glimpse into the world of ordinary—though in this case Mormon—southern women, revealing the domestic life of a wife and mother as it recounts the customary and material lore of Kentucky's Black Patch and the turbulent economic changes affecting the region. Effie Carmack's preservation, and celebration, of folkways may be her most significant contribution. Her manifest devotion to them appears not only in her lively autobiographical descriptions of

---

1.　These women's writings can be found in May Cravath Wharton, *Doctor Woman of the Cumberlands: The Autobiography of May Cravath Wharton, M.D.* (Pleasant Hill, TN, 1953; reprint, Nashville: Parthenon Press, 1972), and Sharon Niederman, *A Quilt of Words: Women's Diaries, Letters & Original Accounts of Life in the Southwest, 1860–1960* (Boulder: Johnson Books, 1988).

1

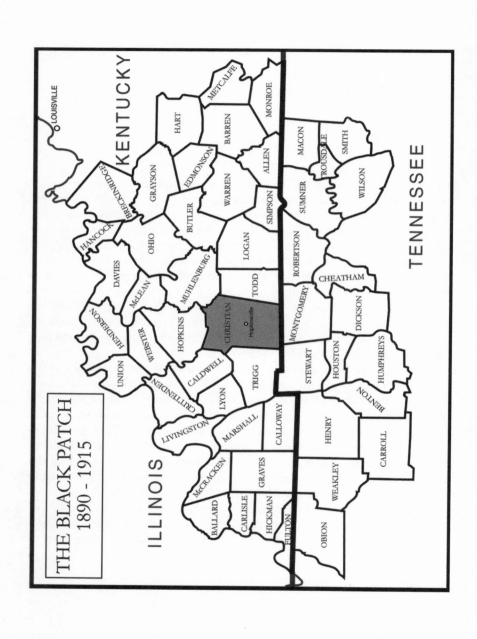

THE BLACK PATCH
1890 - 1915

KENTUCKY

LOUISVILLE

BRECKINRIDGE

HANCOCK

DAVIES

McLEAN

HENDERSON

WEBSTER

UNION

CRITTENDEN

LIVINGSTON

McCRACKEN

BALLARD

CARLISLE

HICKMAN

FULTON

OHIO

GRAYSON

HART

METCALFE

BARREN

MONROE

EDMONSON

BUTLER

WARREN

ALLEN

SIMPSON

MUHLENBURG

LOGAN

HOPKINS

CALDWELL

LYON

MARSHALL

GRAVES

CHRISTIAN

Hopkinsville

TODD

TRIGG

CALLOWAY

WEAKLEY

OBION

MACON

SUMNER

TROUSDALE

SMITH

WILSON

ROBERTSON

CHEATHAM

MONTGOMERY

DICKSON

STEWART

HOUSTON

HUMPHREYS

BENTON

HENRY

CARROLL

TENNESSEE

ILLINOIS

traditions but also in her painting, poetry, and, especially important, her phenomenal folksong repertoire, preserved by Austin Fife and the Library of Congress.

The rural landscape of Kentucky's Pennyrile Region has changed little after a century of industry and southern turmoil. In the heart of Christian County, where this story begins, a patchwork of tobacco and sorghum farms sits in contour upon the area's gently rising hills.[2] The ghosts of white and black tenant farmers bent over tobacco leaves for harvest, can be sensed among the furrows. Hopkinsville, the county seat and center of the dark-fired tobacco district, was where farmers brought their large hogsheads of leaf crop to market. Abandoned smoke barns remind us of an earlier age, when women and children toiled in the fields, bundling the leaves on loading sticks, after which men and boys hung the tobacco inside the barns on fire tiers to cure. Despite advances in agricultural technology, the people hold fast to deeply rooted traditions and continue many of the same domestic routines practiced by their pioneer forebears.

Today's tobacco growers of Christian County descend from an underprivileged lot, a people brought low by toil and economic hardships. A homestead for rural families in postbellum Kentucky often consisted of little more than a cabin, a few horses and chickens, a log-hewn smoke barn, and a plot of ground on which to grow tobacco and "truck." There resided individuals who lived and breathed the southern tobacco culture. They exhibited, as did others in the American South, a common dependence on frontier ideals, much like those who migrated west. As sociologist Howard W. Odum observed, the South "retains in its folk culture threads of the frontier struggle and reflects the costs that went into building a frontier society."[3] The autobiography of Effie Marquess Carmack is a vivid portrayal of a woman's faith and perseverance through the economic hardships that gripped the dark-fired tobacco region during the late nineteenth and early twentieth centuries.

---

2.    For descriptions of the geography in the Crofton and Hopkinsville areas, see Carl Ortwin Sauer, *Geography of the Pennyroyal: A Study of the Influence of Geology and Physiography upon the Industry, Commerce and Life of the People* (Frankfort: Kentucky Geological Survey, 1927), 36–45, 199, 247–48; and U.S. Department of Agriculture, *Soil Survey of Christian County, Kentucky,* comp. Ronald D. Froedge, et al. (Frankfort: U.S. Department of Agriculture, Kentucky Department for Natural Resources and Environmental Protection, and Kentucky Agricultural Experiment Station, 1980), 1–4, 9. See also Charles Mayfield Meacham, *A History of Christian County, Kentucky: From Oxcart to Airplane* (Nashville: Marshall & Bruce Co., 1930), 14.

3.    Howard W. Odum, *The Way of the South: Toward the Regional Balance of America* (New York: Macmillan, 1947), 21.

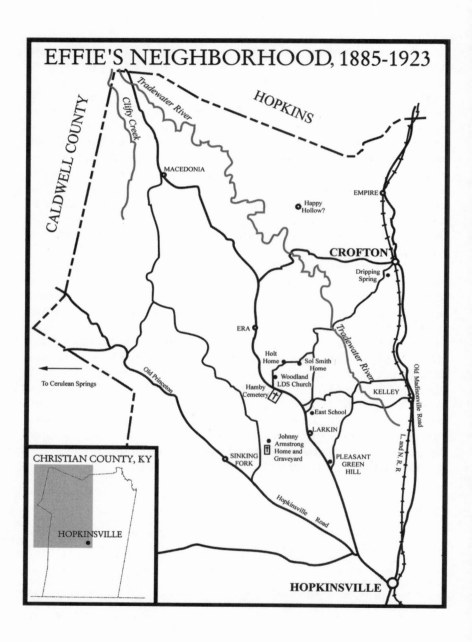

# EFFIE'S NEIGHBORHOOD, 1885-1923

HOPKINS

CALDWELL COUNTY

Tradewater River

Cliffy Creek

MACEDONIA

EMPIRE

Happy
Hollow?

CROFTON

Dripping
Spring

ERA

Tradewater River

Holt
Home

Sol Smith
Home

Woodland
LDS Church

Hamby
Cemetery

KELLEY

East School

Old Princeton

LARKIN

To Cerulean Springs

Johnny
Armstrong
Home and
Graveyard

SINKING
FORK

PLEASANT
GREEN
HILL

Old Madisonville Road

L. and N. R. R

Hopkinsville Road

CHRISTIAN COUNTY, KY

HOPKINSVILLE

HOPKINSVILLE

Effie Lee Marquess was born on September 26, 1885, in Crofton, Christian County, Kentucky, the sixth child of Boanerges "Bo" Robert Marquess and Susan John "John Susan" Armstrong.[4] Effie's birthplace was nestled in the Black Patch, a tobacco farming region covering western Kentucky and northwestern Tennessee. Black Patch farmers grew a regionally distinct, dark, olive-colored variety of tobacco that was cured in smoke-filled barns.[5] Growing up on a dark-fired tobacco farm was not a carefree existence. According to Suzanne Marshall Hall, "Men, women, and children worked in the tobacco patch, the barnyard, the garden, the chicken pen, and the house. Play, in this culture, often imitated work, and provided valuable schooling for children."[6] Effie's family was no exception. "Even though we were poor, as far as money was concerned, and lived in a crude log hut," she wrote, "we were rich in a few things, such as a fervent appreciation for the beauties of nature around us. We possessed a stretch of stream that was far more entertaining, as a playground, than the most expensive of parks" (p, 58, herein). In describing the people of the region in her unpublished novel, "Tobacker," Effie wrote that "they are different from the mountain folks. They are just common people, hardened to toil as all tobacco growers must be. A mixture of honest and dishonest, good and bad, religious and irreligious, educated and illiterate, sensible and ignorant."[7]

Effie was resolute in her effort to preserve the traditions of her western Kentucky environs. In the preface to her autobiographical work of poetry, *Backward Glances* (ca. 1945), Effie declared her intent to vernacularize the work. "I tried to keep it right down in the clods of Kentucky," she wrote.

> We were of the soil, common and unsophisticated, and I wanted this story of our lives to be kept in tune with our log cabin and true to our home life. If judged by a literary critic, I am sure it is full of errors . . . but I am also sure it will strike a responsive chord in the hearts of other commoners like myself who have experienced many of the things I have mentioned here. Many things will soon be forgotten if

---

4. See pages 190–91, herein; vital dates are from copies of LDS family group sheets in Noel Carmack's possession.

5. See John Morgan, "Dark-Fired Tobacco: The Origin, Migration, and Survival of a Colonial Agrarian Tradition," *Southern Folklore* 54 (1997): 145–84.

6. Suzanne Marshall Hall, "Working the Black Patch: Tobacco Farming Traditions, 1890–1930," *Register of the Kentucky Historical Society* 89 (summer 1991): 267.

7. Effie Marquess Carmack, "'Tobacker': A Tale of the Night Riders of Kentucky," 1, copy of undated and unfinished MS in the possession of John K. Carmack, Salt Lake City, Utah.

they are not put down by someone that cherishes the memory of them—things such as running down the lye in the ash hopper to make soap, pulling straw from the straw stack for the straw beds, carding and spinning, grinding sausage and storing it in corn shucks. Many customs and habits of the people of Western Kentucky are fast being forgotten as the new age pushes the old ways back.[8]

Although her formal education did not extend beyond eighth grade, Effie was in fact highly literate and impressively self-educated. She was competent not only in the mechanics of language but in illustrative description and metaphor as well. Her accounts of home life shed light on the way of life in the Black Patch. She sketches colorful vignettes that expose the southern tobacco economy and depict the individuals who lived it. In "Tobacker" she gives this bleak but vivid description of the hard times in the tobacco district:

The dawn of the twentieth century marked a time in this section of tobacco growers which resembled in a small way the age described by Charles Dickens in his "Tale of Two Cities," the age just preceding the French Revolution, when he said "it was the best of times" for a certain, satisfied class. In this case it was the tobacco buyers who had shut the ears of their conscience toward the feeble protest of helpless farmers and towards the look of hopeless, dumb despair in the faces of pitiful hard-worked women, who, with their stunted offspring at their breast, came year after year, each time expectant and hopeful, only to see again and again the product of the long year's toil taken for a pitifully meager sum. In fact often there was not even enough money left to buy shoes for their scrawny brood, and they must keep them in by the fire until some other plan could be devised.

Yes, it was the best of times for the buyers of the crops, who were quickly accumulating fortunes, but it was the worst of times for the tiller of the soil who was risking his luck on the gamble of raising tobacco, risking and losing.[9]

Effie was not alone in her allegiance to the Kentucky frontier heritage. A sampling of fine writers from the Bluegrass State includes such

---

8.    Effie Marquess Carmack, "Foreword," in *Backward Glances: An Autobiography in Rhyme* (n.p.: author, n.d. [ca. 1945]). The original manuscript was first written as a Mother's Day gift for her sister, Lelia, and was entitled "My Old Kentucky Home." It is typed and bound in a scrapbook cover and contains handwritten corrections and insertions (original MS in Noel Carmack's possession).

9.    Carmack, "Tobacker," 3.

literary figures as James Lane Allen, Allen Tate, Rebecca Caudill, Jesse Stuart, Elizabeth Madox Roberts, and Harriette Simpson Arnow. All enlivened their writing by drawing upon their "Kentucky experience." The first poet laureate of the United States, Robert Penn Warren, was born and raised in Guthrie, Kentucky. Warren wrote vividly of the turmoil during western Kentucky's tobacco wars in his story "Prime Leaf" (1931) and in *Night Rider* (1939), his first published historical novel.

While its setting is the same, Effie's work contains none of the idealism and allegory of Warren's *Night Rider*. Effie's is a real, tangible account of rural life in a primitive region of the post–Civil War South. One can detect her clear attachment to a familiar landscape. Effie often records her life story like a folklorist recording practices or performances. At times, her narrative and dialogue approach what linguists call "literary dialect."[10] Although she may not have intended an accurate reconstruction of dialect, she clearly infused her writing with regionalisms and folk motifs.[11] And even though she came from a state where strong Unionist sentiments prevailed, Effie inherited racial expressions and attitudes that permeated Kentucky as much as they did the rest of the slaveholding South. Her anecdotal use of such terms harkens back to a time when the boundaries dividing men, women, and children by race and economic class were hardened by decades of violent hostility.[12]

Effie's narrative is written with remarkable clarity. Her attention to detail invokes a strong sense of presence. The sights, sounds, smells, and dialogue do more than simply provide a colorful backdrop to a common rural experience; they serve as sensory cues that draw the reader into a human drama. Her story comprises cyclical struggles, personal tragedies, and significant changes, paradoxically intertwined with persistence and hope.

Effie's sense of community was based, in large part, upon her familial connections as well as her physical surroundings. The Marquess household fit within a larger family network of friends, neighbors, and extended relatives. Social orientation was fixed by affirming kinships with

---

10. See Sumner Ives, "A Theory of Literary Dialect," in *A Various Language: Perspectives on American Dialects*, ed. Juanita V. Williamson and Virginia M. Burke (New York: Holt, Rinehart and Winston, 1971), 145–77.

11. Such literary constructs are discussed in Roger D. Abrahams, "Folklore and Literature as Performance," *Journal of the Folklore Institute* 9 (August-December 1972): 75–94. See also Elizabeth C. Fine, "The Development of the Text in American Folkloristics," chap. 6 in *The Folklore Text: From Performance to Print* (Bloomington: Indiana University Press, 1984), 16–56, esp. 28–30; and Sandra K. Dolby Stahl, *Literary Folkloristics and the Personal Narrative* (Bloomington: Indiana University Press, 1989).

12. See Rebecca Sharpless, "Southern Women and the Land," *Agricultural History* 67 (spring 1993): 38.

those individuals who were part of the local landscape.[13] Consider, for example, her periodic wagon rides to Hopkinsville with her parents and siblings. The journey was marked by familiar homes and landmarks and by calling to mind the personalities associated with them. "One would think that a long jolt over rough roads in an old two horse wagon, usually in the hot summer, would leave unpleasant impressions, but not so," she wrote. "Those trips to town stand out as glorious monuments in my memory. I asked who lived in every house along the way, and our patient father usually told us" (p. 93, herein). These "topophilic sentiments," as Daniel Rolph calls them, are indicative of the southern sense of place. People are bound together by the land and community. Homes and farms are rarely discussed without tying them to an individual or a family who resided there.[14]

The folklife in Effie's writings bespeaks the well-rooted traditions of western Kentucky and other regions of the American South. Descriptive memories of playtime, wooden toys, and family activities reveal that her childhood, although economically deprived, was enriched by simple, time-honored customs. And yet, while Effie's family was deeply religious, her father was not superstitious and did not believe in the preternatural. "Some of our neighbors were quite superstitious and told spooky tales about graveyards and ghosts," Effie wrote.[15] But her father refused to allow his children to be exposed to such a belief system—an unusual restriction, since supernatural lore pervaded southern culture. On the other hand, her family's use of herbs and folk remedies demonstrated a pragmatic frontier heritage dependent on human skills and natural resources.

Nature is not a harsh element in Effie's story. She evokes the environment's capacity to sustain life and the curative value of its useful plants and herbs. "I am thankful," she wrote, "for all my parents told me of the use of herbs, etc., for healing: white walnut bark as a safe laxative; slippery elm bark for the stomach; blackberries and briar root for teething babies—dozens of simple remedies that are effective, yet leave no bad

---

13. According to Barbara Allen, ". . . the southern sense of place is constructed, maintained, and articulated in a distinctively regional conversational pattern that emphasizes placing people within a social and geographical frame. . . . In these conversations, the landscape becomes a symbolic one, with historical and social as well as physical dimensions, a complex structure of both kinship networks and land-ownership patterns." See "The Genealogical Landscape and the Southern Sense of Place," in *Sense of Place: American Regional Cultures*, ed. Barbara Allen and Thomas J. Schlereth (Lexington: University Press of Kentucky, 1990), 152–53.

14. Daniel N. Rolph, "Folklore, Symbolic Landscapes and the Perception of Southern Culture," *Journal of Southern Studies* 1 (summer 1990): 117–26.

15. Carmack, "The Hant," in *Backward Glances*, 38.

after-effects."[16] When recounting natural calamities, she accepts them as god sent, as manifestations of divine influence, or as part of the normal course of things. One season, a flood took "the best part" of their farm holdings: "I can't remember now that we suffered any extra want because of the loss of crops and livestock," she wrote. "We were used to financial calamities. Often, when they had worked all year, and made a good crop of tobacco, they got nothing for it when selling time came" (p. 55, herein). Raising tobacco to satisfy smokers she viewed as a foolhardy enterprise. "The foolish thing was to keep on raising it, when they were not getting anything for it," she commented. "It would have been far more intelligent to have raised food for the winter months" (p. 151, herein).

Effie's respect for nature and the physical world shaped her play and learning. Her creativity grew out of the emotions, impressions, and discoveries produced by what she called her "enchanted woodland." Her childhood playground included a plum thicket and field of wildflowers near a lush forest of dogwoods, white oak, and hickory. The forest floor was carpeted by moss beds and sassafras. "When I was alone," she remembered, "and no one to play with me, I would find certain places in the banks where there were great cracks where there was beautiful, moist, bluish white clay that was wonderful for modeling. Many long happy hours I have spent making horses, dogs, heads, pitchers, whole sets of dishes, and hundreds of marbles of all sizes" (pp. 39–40, herein).[17]

The art and music of family and friends also stimulated Effie. She seldom entered the home of Marion and Ailsee Moore, her nearest neighbors, but remembered one item in it for the rest of her life: "One thing that charmed me, above all others (in that house) was a lifesized painting of a young girl, which stood on an easel in one corner of the room. It was the first hand painted portrait I had ever seen. It must have been good work, it certainly charmed me, and when I got a chance I gazed in awe and wonder to think that anyone could make a picture look as much like life as that one did" (p. 82, herein). During the coal boom, Effie's father, Bo, a full-time tobacco farmer and occasional fiddle player, regularly joined his brother, Lycurgus or "Curg," to entertain at dance halls and resorts in the Cumberland Gap. Sounds of her father's violin or her mother's singing voice often filled winter evenings, fostering an appreciation of music that continued all her life. Homemade dancing dolls, wooden toys, and pegboard games also engendered an atmosphere of learning and creative imagination, and "drawing pictures on a

---

16. Effie Marquess Carmack, *Down Memory Lane: The Autobiography of Effie Marquess Carmack* (Atascadero, Calif.: Atascadero News Press, 1973), 181.

17. See also Carmack, "Springtime," in *Backward Glances*, lines 45–52, p. 9.

big old double slate was something that never lost its charm," she recalled (p. 42, herein).

Had she been able to complete her education and then obtain more formal art instruction, Effie might have looked forward to a distinguished, perhaps prosperous, career in art. Instead, because of her obligations at home, she only finished the eighth grade and was content to learn under the motivating influence of her father. "Sometimes father would point out pictures in the cloud formations. A long level cloud, with one upright, made a perfect ship at sea, and, if you were going to paint those thunderheads, over there, you would need to put the halo of white light on the side next to the sun, with a soft gray on the shadow side" (pp. 195–96, herein). These treasured moments with her father encouraged the inquisitive young Effie, cultivating her budding interest in art. An ability to express herself artistically would help sustain her through life.

Despite her humble circumstances, Effie never let a lack of art supplies discourage her. She sometimes resorted to clever alternatives. On one occasion she converted a roll of toilet paper into useful material: "Aunt Fannie gave me one roll, but it was never used for the purpose for which it was intended. It was used as tracing paper, to put over pretty pictures, and trace them. It was placed on the old wall plate of the attic at home with my other treasured possessions, chalk box and trinkets, and was kept for years, a roll of my favorite pictures traced carefully" (p. 46, herein). If sketch pads and standard painting surfaces were unavailable, she used whatever materials she found: cardboard, the reverse sides of wall coverings, or wrapping paper. To make brushes, she sometimes chewed the ends of matchsticks to fray them.[18]

During this time, young Effie's encounters with outside influences were few but significant. By all accounts, her introduction to Mormonism changed her life. By the late nineteenth century, Latter-day Saint (LDS) missionaries were a noticeable presence in southern rural communities. The affable young men traveled the backcountry, relying on the hospitality of receptive families for a home-cooked meal and a warm bed. Often, they secured a one-room schoolhouse, dance hall, or bowery in which to preach their message.

Mormon membership grew in Kentucky after the Civil War. Until that time, missionaries had sporadically entered the upper Cumberland and southern Appalachia, converting pockets of mountain families and creating small member branches in the region. From about 1832 until

---

18.  "Mrs. Carmack Speaker at Art Club Meeting," *Atascadero News*, May 16, 1957, 2; Diane Gustafsen Gouff, "My Most Unforgettable Character" (a personal essay based on Effie's autobiography and interviews), in *Down Memory Lane* by Effie Marquess Carmack, 237.

the coming of the rebellion, the Mormon presence in the South was limited to a handful of traveling missionaries, including Samuel H. Smith, Reynolds Cahoon, Wilford Woodruff, Orson Pratt, Warren Parrish, Lorenzo Barnes, James Emmett, and Peter Dustin. As early as 1836, Kentucky was a part of the LDS Church's Tennessee Conference, which consisted of Tennessee's Benton, Henry, and Weakley Counties and Kentucky's Calloway County. In 1876, Kentucky became a part of the LDS Southern States Mission, where it remained until the fall of 1928. In the late 1890s, proselyting forces in the mission tripled from 167 at the end of 1894 to a peak of 501 in 1897. Between 1877 and 1899, some 2,087 Mormon missionaries (51 percent of all the church's missionaries in the United States and Canada) were sent to the South. This resulted in rapid increases in church membership in the South, from 1,200 in 1890 to 2,800 in 1895 and over 10,000 in 1900.[19]

It is little wonder that travel author Horace Kephart included Latter-day Saint proselytizing in his observations of the southern susceptibility to evangelism. He wrote that "many mountaineers are easily carried away by new doctrines extravagantly presented. Religious mania is taken for inspiration by the superstitious who are looking for 'signs and wonders.'" Kephart saw the Mormon missionaries as more threatening, as a danger to fundamental rules of connubial conduct: "At one time, Mormon prophets lured women from the backwoods of western Carolina and eastern Tennessee."[20] Historian Gene Sessions has observed that the missionaries

> taught a system of collectivism inherently inimical to the individualistic traditions which had grown up with the slave society in the South among the religions particularly. Not only this, but the dedicated army of elders encouraged their converts to abandon their homeland to settle in the deserts of the West. . . . They often converted a single member of such basic southern community units as the family, extended family, or church, drawing its members apart

---

19. Leonard J. Arrington, "Mormon Beginnings in the American South," *Task Papers in LDS History*, no. 9 (Salt Lake City: Historical Department of the Church of Jesus Christ of Latter-day Saints, 1976), 7, 10, 12. See also LaMar C. Barrett, "History of the Southern States Mission, 1831–1961" (master's thesis, Brigham Young University, 1960), 80–87, 121.

20. Horace Kephart, *Our Southern Highlanders: A Narrative of Adventure in the Southern Appalachians and a Study of Life among the Mountaineers*, enlarged edition (New York: Macmillan, 1922), 344. For more on itinerant preaching in the South, see Roy West, "Pioneer Preachers: Religion in the Upper Cumberland," in *Lend an Ear: Heritage of the Tennessee Upper Cumberland*, ed. Calvin Dickinson, et al. (New York: University Press of America, 1983), 21–32.

and menacing to disrupt with philosophical and even geographic distance the basic unit of the hierarchical system of the South.[21]

As a result, Mormon missionaries suffered a number of attacks and lynchings. Between 1879 and 1900 some fifteen missionaries and church members were killed in acts of mob violence. A young missionary named Joseph Sanding was shot and killed in 1879 by a mob near Varnell's Station, Georgia. In 1884, two Mormon missionaries and three local members were murdered during the "Cane Creek Massacre" in Lewis County, Tennessee. In November 1899, two Mormon elders in Butler County, Kentucky, were cruelly whipped and driven from the area; Effie saw the wounds these missionaries suffered.[22]

Such violence did not occur in Christian County, though, where several families embraced Mormonism with enthusiasm. When LDS missionaries entered the Hopkinsville area in 1897, the Marquess family was one of the first to accept their message. "A lot of people 'round were interested," Effie remembered. "It looked like the whole county was a goin' to join the Church. But finally it simmered down to four or five families."[23] Indeed, the Marquesses' conversion was a culmination of many years of honoring Christianity but rejecting formal religions. Effie remembered that "although not contented with our homespun religion, we read the Bible and waited for a time when maybe the right religion would come along" (p. 163, herein).

The message the missionaries brought was curiously different from the fiery preaching common among traveling evangelicals. After the young men obtained permission to preach in the Larkin schoolhouse, Effie's father read their calling cards and said, "You know, this sounds different. I think we'd better go hear them."[24] They preached a gospel unlike anything the Marquesses had heard before. They told of a church founded by one Joseph Smith, Jr., and how he had a vision of God and

21. Gene A. Sessions, "Myth, Mormonism, and Murder in the South," *South Atlantic Quarterly* 75 (spring 1976): 219–20. See also David Buice, "Chattanooga's *Southern Star:* Mormon Window on the South, 1898–1900," *BYU Studies* 28 (spring 1988): 5–15.

22. See Sessions, 212–25. Also, William Whitridge Hatch, *There Is No Law . . . : A History of Mormon Civil Relations in the Southern States, 1865–1905* (New York: Vantage Press, 1968) and Daniel N. Rolph, "A Prophecy of 'Woodpeckers and Unnatural Deaths,'" chap. 3 in *"To Shoot, Burn, and Hang": Folk-History from a Kentucky Mountain Family and Community* (Knoxville: University of Tennessee Press, 1994), 49–67.

23. Effie Carmack, undated recording, ca. 1958. For more on these proselyting activities in Christian County, see Daniel N. Rolph, "Kentuckians and Mormonism: An Historical Overview, 1831–1931" (master's thesis, University of Kentucky, 1985), 74–76.

24. Carmack, undated recording, ca. 1958.

Jesus Christ, who called him to organize the church based on a restored priesthood that had been lost since the days of the New Testament. "We couldn't get enough of it. We were just thrilled with it," Effie recalled.[25]

In mid-March 1898, during a late winter snowfall, Effie entered the frigid waters of a nearby creek to be baptized a Mormon, only a month after her parents and older sisters, Etta and Lelia. "The Elders brought a new way of life," she wrote. "Everything we heard and read fit in perfectly with Christ's teachings."[26] Young Mormon elders would always have a welcome place at Effie's hearth or table because, as she put it, they had brought the "pure joy" of their gospel message into her life.

Religious conversion, however, was not the only heartfelt change for Effie and the rest of her family. Only a year after their baptism, her mother, Susan John, died of yellow fever. One month later, Effie's sister Etta succumbed to typhoid. More changes came in quick succession when her two older brothers moved away and her father had to sell the farm. After her sister Sadie married, Effie's father took a new wife, Serena Long, a woman whom Effie unaffectionately addressed as "Miss Serena." Although Effie tells of growing to love Miss Serena through serving her, the relationship was not intimate. Increasingly, Effie turned to her sisters Lelia and Sadie as confidantes and mother figures.

In 1901, the Marquess family—now reduced to Effie and her father, stepmother, and ten-year-old brother, Autie—moved to Franklin, Arizona, where they lived for a short time on the farm of Joseph Wilkins. Their short move to Arizona was pleasant, but her father's longing for home hastened their return before Effie could fully enjoy the open skies of the Southwest. "Back in Kentucky papa was happy again; to hear the birds sing, the babble of water over rocks, the soft grass under the shade trees, and the mellow sunshine that filtered through the leaves was all he needed, but not to me—I was lonesome for the west" (p. 234, herein).

After returning to Kentucky, Bo Marquess began chewing tobacco. This continued until the addiction took hold and damaged his digestive system. He died a short time later in 1903 with his children at his bedside and a host of neighbors to bid him farewell.

That same year, Effie married Henry Edgar Carmack, the nineteen-year-old son of a neighboring farmer. Edgar, as he was commonly addressed, was a descendant of Irish emigrants who had migrated to the middle Tennessee Cumberlands from Maryland and Virginia. Although his father, Thomas Green Carmack, and stepmother, Mattie Olivia Hale,

---

25. Ibid.
26. Carmack, *Down Memory Lane*, 185.

had converted to Mormonism in 1897, he was not as concerned about religious matters. Effie noted the irony in the fact that despite her wish to marry a Latter-day Saint, "I married a fellow who was not a Mormon, and had a difficult time converting him" (p. 237, herein).

Effie wrote little about her courtship, wedding, and forty-nine-year relationship with Edgar. In marriage, her creative endeavors took lower priority to the challenges of mothering and household responsibilities. "I had care of the children and the farm and hired hands, I milked cows, tended garden etc.," she recalled.[27] Still, Edgar was a capable, hard-working husband and father. "He was a kind father and loved the children, especially when they were small," Effie remembered. "He would take one on each knee and sing 'Two Little Children' and he liked to tell them about his grandmother and the songs she would sing for him and the things she cooked when he would go there" (pp. 340–41, herein). However, he was not as supportive as he might have been of the religious and artistic activities that meant so much to Effie. She recalled that despite his earnest commitment to work, his penchant for horses brought hardships. "My husband's money went for fine horses, harness[es], feed etc.," she wrote. "But I managed to keep the children clothed."[28] "Not that their father was lazy, he worked hard all the time; but the money he earned never seemed to do the children or I any good, and I know it was my own fault. If I had demanded more, I'm sure I could have had more" (p. 340, herein). Effie's self-disparagement raises more questions about her relationship with Edgar than perhaps can be answered by available sources.

Never openly critical of her husband, Effie in her memoir shows restraint on the subject of Edgar's spousal qualities. She more often casts Edgar as a stoic than as a man of sensitive disposition. It appears that typical dynamics of patriarchy affected Effie's life as they did those of other women in the agricultural South. Her unmet demands for adequate food and clothing for the children, her difficulties in getting Edgar to share her religious zeal, and her deferential references to her father-in-law, as "Mr. Carmack," are all symptoms of this southern family order. It is not surprising, then, that she memorialized her own pleasant filial experience. Effie's high estimation of her widowed father and his nurturing qualities goes against the prevailing belief that all southern rural families were oppressively paternal.

Suzanne Marshall Hall observed that in the Black Patch, "as in most agricultural societies, men's power superseded women's."[29] Women's

---

27. Carmack, "Autobiography," a 12 page autobiographical sketch, March 1971, 1.
28. Ibid.
29. Hall, "Working the Black Patch," 267.

roles on a tobacco farm included caring for the children, laundering, cooking, watching over the livestock, stripping and grading the tobacco, and selling corn and eggs for extra income. "Men oversaw the tobacco patch and controlled the household economy. Women contributed to the household coffers by raising poultry and selling or trading eggs and chickens at the community general store. The remuneration for hours of work with the hens came in the form of due bills redeemable at the store. This income, although restricted, gave women the satisfaction of providing a crucial weekly sum that supplied the family with grocery staples, clothing, and even luxuries."[30]

Aside from housework and field labor, mothering was most often the chief responsibility of Kentucky farm women. The demands of farm labor largely dictated the number of children born to rural wives. In economically depressed areas, such as the dark tobacco district, where farm acreage was low and it was less feasible to employ hired hands, high fertility was common.[31] As part of their daily routine, rural mothers, in addition to keeping their children fed and clothed, were often the principal providers of love and nurturing in the home. In Kentucky's impoverished Black Patch region, it was difficult to feel resilient bearing and

30. Ibid., 270. Suzanne Marshall Hall's work is most informative on the roles of women in the Black Patch. See Suzanne Marshall, *Violence in the Black Patch of Kentucky and Tennessee* (Columbia: University of Missouri Press, 1994), 31–32, 64–85, 93–94. However, several works shed light on women's work in Kentucky. See Helen Deiss Irvin, *Women in Kentucky* (Lexington: University Press of Kentucky, 1979); Nancy Disher Baird and Carol Crowe-Carraco, "'A True Woman's Sphere': Motherhood in Late Antebellum Kentucky," *Filson Club History Quarterly* 66 (July 1992): 369–94; Margaret Ripley Wolfe, "Fallen Leaves and Missing Pages: Women in Kentucky History," *Register of the Kentucky Historical Society* 90 (winter 1992): 64–89; and Shaunna L. Scott, "Drudges, Helpers and Team Players: Oral Historical Accounts of Farm Work in Appalachian Kentucky," *Rural Sociology* 61 (summer 1996): 209–26. For an informative examination of women's roles in the rural south, see Margaret Jarman Hagood, *Mothers of the South: Portraiture of the White Tenant Farm Woman* (Chapel Hill: University of North Carolina Press, 1939). See also Anne Firor Scott, *The Southern Lady: From Pedestal to Politics, 1830–1930* (Chicago: University of Chicago Press, 1970); Pamela Tyler, "The Ideal Rural Southern Woman as Seen by 'Progressive Farmer' in the 1930s," *Southern Studies* 20 (fall 1981): 278–96; Rebecca Sharpless, "Southern Women and the Land," *Agricultural History* 67 (spring 1993): 30–42; and Margaret Ripley Wolfe, *Daughters of Canaan: A Saga of Southern Women* (Lexington: University Press of Kentucky, 1995), esp. 126–29.

31. For example, Margaret Jarman Hagood's survey of white southern tenant farm women in a subregion of the Piedmont South and in the Deep South states of Georgia, Alabama, Mississippi, and Louisiana reveals patterns of gender and fertility. Of the 117 mothers surveyed in the Piedmont subregion, 115 married mothers had been married an average of 18.9 years and had given birth to a mean number of 6.4 children per mother. See Hagood, *Mothers of the South*, 108–10 and 231–34. See also Harriet A. Byrne, "Child Labor in Representative Tobacco-Growing Areas," U.S. Department of Labor Children's Bureau, publication no. 155 (Washington, D.C.: G.P.O., 1926).

caring for a young family. But Effie was unequivocally fond of her children.[32] She remembered that the thing for which she was most thankful was that although she struggled to provide for her children's physical needs, she "didn't neglect to teach them the important things they needed to know. It didn't take money to do that, just precious time and patience" (p. 341, herein).

Unfortunately, all of Effie's children seemed alarmingly prone to accidents and infirmities. Cecil Eugene, her first child (1904–1984), was born prematurely after an accidental fall sent Effie into early labor. Although he had a normal infancy, Cecil's troubled birth foreshadowed the adversities of child-rearing to come. In the ensuing years, Effie bore seven more children: Violet (b. 1908), Noel Evans (1911–1980), Grace (1913–1984), Hazel Marguerite (b. 1914), Lenora Bernice (1915–1950), David Edgar (1917–1952), and Harold Grant (1919–1923). Each experienced physical challenges which varied in severity; a ninth child was stillborn. Effie saw her children through injuries, whooping cough, influenza, and near-drownings. A long-term but rewarding challenge was the extra attention her youngest daughter, Bernice, required; her intellectual development was slowed by slight mental retardation. The demands of such arduous caregiving must have been disheartening at times, but Effie persevered.

One incident involving Cecil tested both her endurance and her faith. At the age of two, Cecil had a bout with pneumonia that nearly took his life. The neighbor's children had taken him outside to play and kept him out in a cold February rain. By late evening, he was hot with fever and short of breath. Some time later, after Effie's considerable effort to clear his lungs and treat his temperature with medication, Cecil fell into a deep, unresponsive slumber. After twenty minutes of close observation, the doctor, unable to detect breathing or a heartbeat, pronounced Cecil dead. Effie, however, refused to allow her baby's life to slip away. Through the night and into the morning hours, she massaged her son's cold, lifeless body with hot water and rubbing alcohol. She "longed for someone with the authority to administer to him" in accordance with Latter-day Saint practice. Edgar was not a member of the church and could not give priesthood blessings, and at this particular time, the Mormon elders were unavailable. "Not wanting to leave a thing undone that might help," she later wrote, "I got a small bottle of olive oil, asked the Lord to bless and

---

32. Effie's feelings of affection for her children were not unusual. However, Hagood wrote that "the [southern] mother is proud of having borne the children she has although she may not have wished for another before she became pregnant each time." See Hagood, *Mothers of the South*, 125.

purify it, and to recognize a mother's anointing and blessing on her child, and to bring him back to life." In her prayer, she promised to raise the child to the best of her ability and dedicate her life to God. During the hours she continued to work over her son, her "whole body was a living, working prayer." Just before dawn, a faint heartbeat could be heard, and Cecil revived and asked for something to eat. The boy regained all of his faculties, and within days, word traveled from the hills west of Crofton that the Carmack boy had risen from the dead (pp. 248–49, herein). It wasn't long after this miraculous experience that Edgar was baptized on a "momentous day" in 1908. From then on he took churchgoing more seriously. Friends who earlier had not responded to Effie's attempts to tell them of Mormonism also became more interested.

In 1911, Edgar and Effie moved to the farm of Francis McDonald in Holladay, Utah. While there, Edgar found employment working for Joseph Andrus putting up hay on his ranch near Park City. In Edgar's absence, Effie picked currants with the McDonalds' seventeen-year-old son, Howard, who later became president of Brigham Young University (1945–1949). After haying was done, Edgar began working in the canyon, assisting in the excavation of a waterline trench. At the end of September, when the work was finished, Edgar and some of the other men got wet while returning home in an open truck bed during a cold rainstorm. Within a short time, he began complaining of inflammation and pain in his foot; this was followed by a severe case of rheumatic fever. For almost six months, Edgar lay sick and unable to work. One of his few activities during rehabilitation came when, in a sacred Mormon ordinance making their marriage eternal, he was sealed to Effie in the Salt Lake Temple, along with children Cecil, Violet, and infant son Noel. When a full recovery appeared doubtful, it was recommended that Edgar move to a lower altitude, prompting the family to move back to Kentucky, where he could resume his farming in a more healthy environment.

As it turned out, the change did not prove therapeutic. The years following their return from Utah were the darkest for Effie and her family. While Edgar was suffering from rheumatic heart disease, Effie contracted an unidentified but debilitating illness that lingered several years. The symptoms were similar to those of tuberculosis—coughing blood, continuing fatigue, and fever spells, all of which Effie believed were the result of a poor diet. During her illness, Effie gave birth to three more children. Two, Grace and Hazel, were born without complications, but Bernice's birth came with some difficulty. The three girls were born in close succession, and Effie's sickness inhibited her ability to manage day-to-day responsibilities in the home.

Busy dealing with the demands of tobacco farming and with its fluctuating yields and returns, Edgar did not offer additional domestic support.

He entrusted his crop to an association of dark-fired tobacco planters but made little profit. By 1920, Kentucky leaf-crop prices dropped to their lowest point in ten years.[33]

At the doctor's admonition, Edgar tried to alleviate Effie's burdens by doing laundry and light housework. But even with his first effort, he found the extra chores overtaxing and hired a young woman named Lola Jones to take over. The doctor had also recommended that Effie do something enjoyable but not laborious. "Dr. Lovell," Effie remembered, "told him that he had better let me do it, as it would be far better to have a mother doing easy things I enjoyed than not to have any mother at all." Thus about 1915, while Effie had help, she took up painting again. "I had done lots of little things," she wrote. "I knew that I could paint, if only I had the time and material" (p. 267, herein). Her friend and neighbor Bernice Allington had been a helpful art tutor while they lived in Utah, and with some assistance from her longtime friend Bernice Pollard Walker, Effie received additional instruction in watercolor painting. "I was interested in painting, and enjoyed it, and was surprised that it was so easy for me, and I tackled hard subjects" (p. 268, herein). Most of these works consisted of candid watercolor sketches of her children, neighbors, aunts, and uncles; one of them was awarded a red ribbon at the 1915 Christian County Fair. With her childhood pastime regained, Effie found a sense of healing and peace of mind.

Nevertheless, ill health, Edgar's unpredictable income, and the care of eight dependent children (by this time, David and Harold had been added to the family) weighed heavily upon Effie. Her most painful challenge came so suddenly, and so tragically, it outweighed anything she had previously faced. In the spring of 1923, just two days after Easter Sunday, her two eldest sons, Cecil and Noel, were burning saw briers and grass in the fields just prior to plowing. In another part of the clearing, near an embankment, four-year-old Harry was playing stick horses in the tall sage grass with his brother David, who was celebrating his sixth birthday. Without warning, a sudden change in wind direction sent the blaze into

---

33.   These turbulent cycles of depression in the Kentucky tobacco market are discussed in Tracy Campbell, *The Politics of Despair: Power and Resistance in the Tobacco Wars* (Lexington: University Press of Kentucky, 1993), 152–54, and W. F. Axton, *Tobacco and Kentucky* (Lexington: University Press of Kentucky, 1975), 82–105. See also John G. Miller, *The Black Patch War* (Chapel Hill: University of North Carolina Press, 1935); James O. Nall, *The Tobacco Night Riders of Kentucky and Tennessee, 1905–1909* (Louisville: Standard Press, 1939); Bill Cunningham, *On Bended Knees: The Night Rider Story* (Nashville: McClanahan Publishing House, 1983); Christopher Waldrep, *Night Riders: Defending Community in the Black Patch, 1890–1915* (Durham: Duke University Press, 1993); and Marshall, *Violence in the Black Patch.*

the grass where the two boys were playing. Before Harry could outrun the flames, they overtook him, burning through his long underwear and thick overalls. By the time Cecil and Noel responded to David's cries for help, the fire had consumed nearly all of Harry's tender skin. For the next few hours, Effie remained near her little boy's blackened body until he took his final breath. Effie was forever changed by the experience. This time, unlike Cecil's miraculous revival, neither prayer nor cure brought Harry's precious life back.[34]

Harry's death was the most traumatic of Effie's incessant confrontations with adversity. Although she learned to adapt to the loss, her emotional and physical well-being never fully recovered. Her intense grief triggered a number of bodily ailments, including facial eczema and a pain in her heart that she claimed plagued her continually. Reminded of the sufferings of Job, Effie tried to remain patient, consoling herself with scriptures. "Sometimes," she said, "I felt like I was getting more than my share, but I never felt rebellious nor did I blame the Lord for my affliction" (p. 293, herein).

In the midst of physical infirmities, Effie's ability to cope was made more difficult by daily reminders of Harry and unreciprocated expressions of grief between her and Edgar. Like many other bereaved parents, Effie and Edgar's inability to communicate feelings of loss impaired their ability to adjust and find comfort.[35]

Although Effie seemed to bear no guilt or feelings of responsibility for Harry's death, losing her role as his mother seemed to haunt her in later years. Her only regret was that she did not adequately expose him to the joyful music she had experienced as a child. "Children need music and songs and laughter," she wrote. After determining that she had been remiss, she "tried to make up for lost time" with her other children. The intimate relationship between mother and child also became a recurring theme in Effie's paintings, often as the Madonna and Christ child or a Navajo mother and baby. Thoughts of children must have pressed upon

---

34. The foregoing narrative is drawn from Effie's own poignant account found on pages 287–88.

35. The difficulties of parental communication have been addressed in R. Schwab, "Paternal and Maternal Coping with the Death of a Child," *Death Studies* 14 (1990): 407–22, and N. Feeley and L. Gottlieb, "Parents' Coping and Communication Following Their Infant's Death," *Omega: Journal of Death and Dying* 19 (1988–1989): 51–67. See also Harriet Sarnoff Schiff, *The Bereaved Parent* (New York: Crown, 1977), and the various issues discussed in Therese A. Rando, ed., *Parental Loss of a Child* (Champaign, Ill.: Research Press, 1986), esp. Catherine M. Sanders, "Accidental Death of a Child," 181–90.

her mind; their names and faces appeared in her creative works and, as her writings reveal, even in her dreams.

Harry's death marked other pivotal changes in Effie's life. In February 1924, she and Edgar moved their family to Joseph City, a small Mormon settlement on the Little Colorado in northern Arizona.[36] At first, they lived in a house tent that her brother John and son Cecil, who had both been living in the area, prepared for them before they arrived. Despite her circumstances, she wasted no time finding her place in front of easel and canvas. By mid-1927, Edgar was successfully running a dairy and delivery route between Joseph City and Winslow.[37] Shortly thereafter, they took up permanent residence in Winslow, where Effie cultivated with even greater energy the talent that had been evident in her early works. "After we had been in Arizona a long time, I went back to Kentucky, and I was astonished to see many of the watercolors that I had done in the homes of friends and kinfolks. They were as good as the oil colors that I did later" (p. 268, herein).

Effie now taught lessons in the LDS Sunday School and Mutual Improvement Association and theology in its Relief Society, and after school and in the evenings, she gave art lessons to the children at the local elementary school. Each week she had the youngsters choose a subject, usually a simple landscape, to teach them the rudiments of linear perspective, the placement of subjects, and techniques to create the illusion of space. As an integral part of her assignments, she emphasized the importance of drawing from observation: "I had them draw from nature—a small picture of a tree and rocks, or a sunset sky, or whatever they chose to do" (p. 300, herein). As the popularity of her art lessons increased, the school teachers began to receive instruction as well. Although Effie enjoyed the association with her adult peers, the children's joy and excitement in learning seemed to gratify her most.

It can be argued that Effie's expressive works—artistic, poetic, and autobiographical—were of purgative value, that the acts of writing and painting were therapeutic. Besides being a source of personal fulfilment, her art may have been, in many respects, a cathartic response to the tragedy and hardship that had affected her life. Artistic expressions often contain covert symbols or images of extreme emotional stress that

36. "Joseph City Notes," *Winslow Mail*, October 3, 1924, 4.

37. "Joe City Dairy Opens New Milk Station in Winslow," *Winslow Daily Mail*, March 16, 1927, 3; Adele B. Westover and J. Morris Richards, *A Brief History of Joseph City* (Winslow, Ariz.: The Winslow Mail, n.d.), 22; Adele B. Westover and J. Morris Richards, *Unflinching Courage* (Joseph City, Ariz.: John H. Miller, 1963), 27.

may have occurred many years earlier.[38] Hence, Harry's unexpected death could have triggered increased artistic activity as one of Effie's few consoling outlets for bereavement. Perhaps art assured her that out of ugliness she could express beauty, out of tragedy she could express hope. The events surrounding Effie's artistic reawakening were consistent with experiences of other folk artists, most typically women, who, according to a recent study, used their art "to help overcome a stressful life experience."[39]

Effie's early efforts certainly fall within a long tradition of American folk painting. Folk art, often defined analogously with primitive, self-taught, or outsider art, is generally produced by individuals who are untrained and have had little or no familiarity with formal art theory. Most important, however, folk art emerges out of the cultural environment in which it is created. These self-taught artistic expressions reflect the world views of the artist and his or her culture. Folk art incorporates distinctive regional, ethnic, and cultural patterns that reveal the artist's sense of place and personal identity. Just as colloquial communication often emphasizes a distinct geographic relationship between a community and its inhabitants, folk artists create for purposes of identity and self-realization, closely tying themselves to the places or subjects represented in their art.

Effie's creative work can be divided into three thematic categories at the root of her identity—namely, kinship, place, and religion. These themes follow those of other self-taught Kentucky artists who created personal visual statements with their art. Effie's early drawings and watercolors often portrayed physical surroundings, farm life, and family and neighbors

---

38. See, for example, Rita Simon, "Bereavement Art," *American Journal of Art Therapy* 20 (July 1981): 135–43; Gregg M. Furth, "The Use of Drawings Made at Significant Times in One's Life," in *Living with Death and Dying*, ed. Elizabeth Kübler-Ross (New York: Macmillan, 1981), 63–94; Harvey Irwin, "The Depiction of Loss: Uses of Clients' Drawings in Bereavement Counseling," *Death Studies* 15 (1991): 481–97; and Christina Mango, "Emma: Art Therapy Illustrating Personal and Universal Images of Loss," *Omega: Journal of Death and Dying* (1992): 259–69.

39. "Characteristics of Folk Art, A Study Presented at the American Psychological Association Conference" (by Jules and Florence Laffal), *Folk Art Finder* 5 (September 1984): 2, 4. According to Roger Manley, "outsider artist's [*sic*] life stories frequently reveal traumatic events that threw them onto their own resources and triggered responses that led to art making: the loss of a job through illness, injury, or retirement; the death of a spouse or elderly parent; religious doubt; social ostracism; imprisonment. These events precipitate their transformation from 'ordinary' farmers, loggers, or textile workers into artists as well." See *Signs and Wonders: Outsider Art inside North Carolina* (Raleigh: North Carolina Museum of Art, 1989), 9.

in informal settings.[40] She combined these visual depictions of Kentucky folklife with written ones, illustrating childhood memories of worming the tobacco, milking cows, soapmaking, and carding and spinning.[41] She drew several works for her book of autobiographical poetry, *Backward Glances*, to pass on images of the traditional home life of western Kentucky in the 1890s. Otherwise, as she wrote, "many things will soon be forgotten if they are not put down by someone who cherishes the memory of them."[42]

As Effie's interests shifted toward subjects outside her own personal experience, her work took on themes and attributes more consistent with sophisticated studio traditions than folk genres. Her interest in New Testament subjects inspired a number of religious paintings. Her favorite religious subjects seemed to be gospel narratives, including scenes of the Nativity and depictions of Christ and the apostles at the Sea of Galilee. Besides recalling her own religious upbringing, Effie was inspired by Protestant instructional art, on which the Mormon Church relied heavily during this period.

A high point in Effie's creative experience came during the summer of 1936, when she had the pleasure of accompanying a tour group of artists over the Mormon pioneer trail. Her daughter Hazel, who was at that time a missionary in the East Central States Mission, had read a prospectus on the tour in the (Salt Lake City) *Deseret News* and, with her brother Noel's assistance, conspired to send their mother on the trip, providing money for tuition and travel expenses. Headed by BYU art professor B. F. Larsen and his wife Geneva, the group of fifteen traveled by bus to important pioneer sites and landmarks, documenting the historic route through sketches, paintings, and photographs.[43] The two-week art

---

40. For more on Effie's art, see Noel A. Carmack, "'A Memorable Creation': The Life and Art of Effie Marquess Carmack," *BYU Studies* 37 (1997–1998): 101–35. An informative treatment of frontier women and their artistic pursuits is found in Sandra L. Myres, *Westering Women and the Frontier Experience, 1800–1915* (Albuquerque: University of New Mexico Press, 1982), 245–48.

41. In order to control the destructive effects of tobacco worms, each worm had to be plucked from the leaf and destroyed by hand. Naturally, this was an unpleasant and tedious job for women and children who worked in the tobacco fields.

42. Carmack, "Foreword," in *Backward Glances*, 2.

43. "Local Woman with 17 Artists Making University Tours," *Winslow Mail*, June 12, 1936, 1; "Winslow Woman Is Member of Artist Group Making Tour," *Winslow Mail*, August 14, 1936, 1. See also H. R. Merrill, "While Yet the Old Trail Lasts, "*Deseret News* (Church section), February 22, 1936, 1, 8; Carlton Culmsee, "Spiritual Significance of an Art Tour," *Deseret News* (Church section), August 15, 1936, 1, 8. For more background on the tour, see Noel Carmack, "'The Yellow Ochre Club': B. F. Larsen and the Pioneer Trail Art Tour, 1936," *Utah Historical Quarterly* 65 (spring 1997): 134–54. Seventeen of Effie's art tour paintings are in the possession of her grandson and LDS Church authority John K. Carmack, Salt Lake City, Utah.

tour was an emotional peak of which Effie spoke fondly throughout her remaining years. Always grateful to Hazel and Noel for providing her the means, she later wrote, "It was one of the most wonderful experiences of my life" (p. 328, herein). During a round of successful traveling exhibitions of the group's work throughout Utah and Idaho, Effie wrote to B. F. Larsen, saying, "I experience a happy thrill when I think of a reunion of our group" and she hoped all would be present.[44]

Although relatively unpublicized, the reunion took place the following summer, and the group, including Effie, toured New Mexico. This trip included visits to pueblo sites on the Rio Grande, near Albuquerque and Santa Fe, where the group sketched and painted weathering Zuni and other Pueblo adobes. On the Arizona side of the border, the artists painted scenes at Navajo National Monument such as the ancient cave dwellings of Betatakin and Keet Seel.[45] These two tours under Larsen's supervision were the closest Effie came to academic art instruction. Once introduced to Native American dwellings, Effie frequently returned to the subject, painting Navajo and Hopi sites in the nearby Four Corners region, such as Walpi and Wupatki. In addition to depicting Indian earthen dwellings on the Colorado Plateau, she featured in a number of paintings mission and Spanish provincial architecture seen along Sonora's west coast highway and California's Highway 101. In 1939, when American self-taught painters and regionalists were gaining national recognition, Effie entered a painting depicting an old village, Tzin Tzun Tzan, in the New York World's Fair hobby division and won second place (p. 318, herein).

Over the next two decades, Effie repeatedly returned to the Arizona landscape for inspiration. As further motivation for producing desert subjects, a circumstantial engagement to exhibit her work at the Bruchman Curio Store in Winslow provided a new venue for making her talent known. The store's owner, R. M. Bruchman, had generously provided financial support for one of Edgar's catastrophic medical expenses, and Effie intended to sell her work to repay him. Works produced during and after this period in Winslow reveal Effie's enthusiasm for such subjects as

44. Effie M. Carmack to B. F. Larsen, December 29, 1936, B. F. Larsen Papers, University Archives, Harold B. Lee Library, Brigham Young University, Provo, Utah.

45. "Artist Tells Rotary of New Mexico Tour," *Winslow Mail*, August 13, 1937, 8; Gouff, "My Most Unforgettable Character," in *Down Memory Lane* by Effie Marquess Carmack, 238. A painting of San Ildefonso, New Mexico, is in the possession of John K. Carmack, Salt Lake City, Utah; a painting of Betatakin is in the possession of Itha Carmack, Atascadero, California.

the towering redrock buttes of Monument Valley, the rainbow sands of the Painted Desert, and the windswept landscape of the Arizona Strip.

In about 1942, sometime after she began exhibiting work at the curio store, an unidentified man representing the Southwest Museum in Los Angeles entered the store and examined Effie's display with considerable interest. Visiting the Carmack home next, he told Effie that the institution's curator would like to exhibit her paintings, since their illustrations of Native American life were compatible with other artistic works and artifacts at the museum. A short time later, Effie received a letter from the museum requesting about twenty-five paintings for a scheduled exhibition. To fill the museum's order, Effie completed more than two dozen oils depicting all facets of Navajo and Hopi culture. These paintings proved successful. During the exhibition, curator M. R. Harrington reportedly noted that Effie's paintings were "the best coloring of Indian life he had ever had in his museum" (p. 316, herein).

In the spring of 1946, Effie and Edgar moved to Atascadero, California, so that Edgar, his health still failing, could convalesce near their children. Edgar benefitted from California's lower altitude and fresh coastal air. Nevertheless, it pained Effie to leave her home of more than twenty years and longtime associations and friendships. She also missed the warmth and solitude of her self-made studio, a building she described as a "shanty" with a fireplace (pp. 320–21, herein).[46]

Yet, she was as resilient and eager to excel as ever. Two months after relocating, Effie was introduced as "a new artist in Atascadero" at the Music and Arts Fellowship, where she "delighted her audience with an exhibit of some of her historical paintings, including a pony express station and Pioneer Trail in Wyoming, old Indian ruins in Arizona, with the portrait of an old Indian in northern Arizona, and an ancient church in Old Mexico."[47] Four months later, in January 1947, Effie had her first formal exhibit at Atascadero's Carlton Hotel. After this successful show, Effie was among fourteen local artists, including Frances Joslin and Al Johnson, who sparked the idea of an art club. The following year, on April 2, 1948, the Atascadero Art Club was organized with Johnson as president.[48] Soon the organization became an important component of

---

46. See also Effie M. Carmack, "The Long Road from Winslow, Arizona to Atascadero" (a travel diary in rhyme, April 1946), copy of typescript in Noel Carmack's possession.

47. "Music and Art Group Enjoy Fine Program," *Atascadero News*, September 27, 1946, 3.

48. Atascadero Art Club, Inc., "Effie Carmack," announcement, 14th Annual Fall Festival (September 15–16, 1973); "History of Atascadero Art Club," *Snapshot Magazine*, April 1951, 6–7; "Full of Pep and Go at 84," *Atascadero News*, February 19, 1970, 3; "Atascadero Art Club . . . Keeping the Arts Alive in Atascadero," *Atascadero News* (Colony Days edition), October 17, 1990, 12.

Atascadero's community activities, sponsoring monthly workshops and art festivals on the central coast. Effie was always an active supporter of the group in the years that followed. Fellow art club members remembered her as a natural artist and musician. Charter member Marian Hart recalled that she was an "outstanding member of the Art Club. We all admired and enjoyed her many talents."[49]

By this time, however, Edgar's poor health required that Effie find employment. At the urging of her old friend Bernice Walker, Effie began performing in Knotts Berry Farm stage shows. Clothed in dresses from a bygone era, she played guitar and sang with other nostalgic personalities from the South. Through these performances, she not only gained a source of income but received considerable attention for the repertoire of folk songs she had learned as a child. Impressed with her collection of songs, the popular country-western entertainer Tennessee Ernie Ford, with whom Effie had occasion to perform, once reportedly asked, "Where in the world did you get them?"—even though she had learned them only a "spittin' distance" from where he had lived (p. 335, herein).[50] Fortunately, through the efforts of western folklorists Austin and Alta Fife, many of these important folk songs were recorded between 1947 and 1952 for the Library of Congress.[51] Recordings were made in her home and, on at least one occasion, at Occidental College in Los Angeles, where Austin Fife was professor of languages. Later, when Dr. Fife was teaching in France, he featured Effie on a *Voice of America* radio broadcast (p. 194, herein).

Despite the encouragement she garnered from these performances, Effie always returned to painting, writing, family, and church service as her primary sources of gratification. To her credit, she was recognized in 1945 as one of six most notable individuals in northern Arizona and featured in *Who's Who in the South and Southwest* for the year 1947. Selections of her poetry were included in a nationally published anthology, *Poetry Broadcast* (1946), as well as in other small publications and magazines.[52] At one point, she completed a number of religious paintings for LDS church buildings in Globe, Phoenix, St. Johns, Holbrook, Winslow, and Taylor, Arizona. Others were completed for LDS

---

49. Marian Hart to Noel Carmack, September 15, 1996; "Honored at Studio Warming by Artist Friends," *Atascadero News*, March 19, 1964, 2.

50. See Bill Barton, "The Latchstring is Always Out to the Fellowmen of Effie Carmack," *Deseret News* (Church section), January 15, 1966, 5.

51. For more information concerning these recordings, see appendix one.

52. *Poetry Broadcast: An Anthology Compiled for Radio Programs* (New York: The Exposition Press, 1946), 56.

churches in St. George, Utah; Overton, Nevada; and Hollyfield, North Carolina. While many of Effie's paintings are still hanging on the walls of aging Winslow and Atascadero residents, a number of them are in the possession of her grandchildren and great-grandchildren.[53]

Effie's years in Atascadero marked a period in which she grew closer to Edgar and reconciled the problems they experienced many years before. Edgar's difficulty in showing affection or providing support in the early years of their marriage weighed heavily on his conscience. Feeling regretful, he made a confession the night before he died in February 1952. According to Effie's account, he said "'Mom, I coulda done 'lot better than I did.' He said 'I worked and made good wages but you never got much of it.' He said 'I spent it all on the horses an wagons an harnesses an stuff. You scratched 'round and patched the children's shoes and managed to scrimp and buy material to make their clothes with.' He says 'since I've been sick an had time to think of it, I was a pretty poor daddy.'" Effie "told him I thought it was kinda good for him to confess it." But, despite his shortcomings, she concluded that "he was a good man."[54]

After Edgar's death, Effie continued her art club activities and self-motivated missionary work. Seldom did a day pass that she wasn't painting in her studio, attending an art club workshop, or preparing work for the club's annual art show. Never too busy for a visit from the LDS missionaries, she often hosted them to a meal or a cottage meeting in her parlor. On Sunday evenings, she entertained grandchildren and great-grandchildren with songs sung to the strum of her guitar and by popping corn in the fireplace. A special honor came in 1971 when she was one of five women nominated as California's Mother of the Year.[55]

That she would have credited her parents for this high honor is apparent from her autobiographical writings. Effie was deeply grateful for her inauspicious but exemplary upbringing. Respect for parents and

---

53. Barre Brashear, "County Art Show Sketches," (San Luis Obispo, Calif.) *Telegram-Tribune*, February 19, 1952, 1. The largest collection of Effie's paintings is in the possession of John K. Carmack, Salt Lake City, Utah. Several paintings are among the families of Effie's daughters: Grace Bushman, Hazel Bushman (formerly Bruchman), and Violet Mattice. Some are owned by families of her deceased sons: Cecil E. Carmack, Noel E. Carmack, and David E. Carmack. Of the many other scattered holdings, a few paintings are reportedly in the Barry Goldwater Collection.

54. Effie Carmack, undated interview by John K. Carmack, ca. 1969.

55. "Hobbies Bring Enjoyment to This Lady," *Atascadero News*, October 24, 1957, 9; Doreen Saylor, "Retired Pair Leads Busy, Peaceful Life," *Atascadero News*, May 28, 1964, 4; "Full of Pep and Go at 84," *Atascadero News*, February 19, 1970, 3; "Honors for Atascadero Mother," *Atascadero News*, May 6, 1971, 1.

predecessors was a major theme of her writings. Effie expressed her high regard for ancestry in the following stanzas from *Backward Glances*:

> And now since I've studied the problem profoundly
> And searched out the sources from which we descend,
> I see many whys and can guess many wherefores,
> To show why our lives take some definite trend.
> Our Marquess forefathers were lovers of music,
> And lovers of beauty, religion and art.
> And though we were raised in a patch of tobacco
> These things in our beings still held a rich part.[56]

Until age forced her to surrender her pen and brush, Effie carried on this heritage through her autobiographical writings and her art. In January 1974 she became ill, and although she was reluctant to go to the hospital, the doctor insisted that she be hospitalized so she could be treated for fluid on her lungs and other problems.[57] After about six weeks in the hospital, Effie Carmack passed away on March 5, 1974, at the age of eighty-eight. The obituary that followed her death recognized her as one of the area's most talented artists, as both a writer and a painter.[58]

Effie's life was shaped by a wide range of events and circumstances—idylls of childhood, religious conversion, poverty, loss of parents, illness, maternal anguish and grief, and creative solitude. Those who read her autobiography will notice a shift from the enchantment of youth to the melancholic autumn of adulthood. Pleasant memories of playtime and family are subjugated to recurring pensiveness and longing for that simple life she experienced as a child in Kentucky, revealing a strain of sadness she continually tries to rectify. In spite of this, she emerges as a survivor and, by recreating those pleasant memories for her children, finds a form of reconciliation.

Although she seemed satisfied with the autobiography, Effie expressed some trepidation that it might not be received the way she wished. Often portraying herself with reticence, Effie was slow to characterize her life as anything more than appreciable. "Not that there has been anything very extraordinary or wonderful in it, but one thing for sure, it is different from that of any other" (p. 31, herein). And yet, her life story attests to her remarkable perseverance and stamina. A body of creative works also shows her prolific efforts to better her intellectual and

---

56. Carmack, "Concerning Our Father and Mother," *Backward Glances*, lines 17–24, p. 31.
57. In conversation with Karen Lynn Davidson, December 3, 1994.
58. "Death Summons Mrs. Effie Carmack," *Atascadero News*, March 7, 1974, A8.

socioeconomic situation. Her work often brought unsolicited praise, for which she expressed modest gratitude. "But," she wrote, "the thing I am proudest of is my children and grandchildren. I had 8 children—five living—I have 19 grand children and 67 great grand children. All clean honorable and religious, a posterity that any mother could be proud of."[59]

The importance of Effie Carmack's autobiography can be appreciated on several levels. It is one of a few which illuminate late nineteenth-century Mormon activities outside the boundaries of "Zion"— the core area of membership in Utah. More specifically, it brings to light the remarkable odyssey of a woman who was significantly changed by the influence of Mormonism on the southern frontier. Much of Effie's life was far removed from the distinctively Mormon frontier experience, but her encounters with the distresses of motherhood, emotional disruptions of successive change, and tests of personal faith were not unlike those of many of her LDS counterparts. The autobiography provides an unusual glimpse into domesticity for Mormon and non-Mormon women in the South and Southwest.

Another valuable aspect of Effie's autobiography is her record of Kentucky folkways. Her observations of rural life should be appealing to both folklorists and general readers. She describes at length the conventions of children's games, play parties or "moonlights," herbal remedies, and various crafts and practices in Black Patch tobacco culture. Effie places these traditions in the daily routines of living, providing an opportunity to view the folkways of her home region in context. Her self-described "mania" of collecting folk music as a child resulted in an impressive repertoire, for which she was recognized. The autobiography frequently mentions music and the settings in which it was performed or played. Her accounts of farm life and agrarianism in western Kentucky are particularly descriptive. Such passages will undoubtedly be of interest to social historians and students of tobacco culture.[60]

Whatever its historical and cultural value, Effie's personal story remains compelling, partly because of the emotional release she gained through written and visual expression. These appealing reversions to childhood were a means of containment, a way to resolve her episodic encounters with adversity. Effie's memorialization of family folkways—

---

59. Carmack, "Autobiography," March 1971, 8.
60. For another example of these kinds of observations, see Austin E. Fife, "Virginia Folkways from a Mormon Journal," *Western Folklore* 9 (October 1950): 348–58.
61. Barbara Allen, "Family Traditions and Personal Identity," *Kentucky Folklore Record* 28 (January–June 1982): 1–5.

historical and customary—provided a sense of well-being difficult to attain during her years of maturity.[61] The act of documenting happy memories of youth and adolescence provided a cathartic outlet for the pain of losing children, discord within her family, emotional stresses of motherhood, and unresolved conflicts in marriage. While not bereft of happiness, Effie seemed to be searching for peace in an adult life that contained too much tragic emotion. But the sad voice that whispers through Effie's writing may not be always apparent. By thoughtfully drawing inferences from the narrative, the reader may come to appreciate Effie Carmack, not for her public accomplishments, but for her private and somewhat ritualized acts of survival.

"Uncle Robert Marquess, son of Martha A. Pettypool, and his sisters Mayes and Emma from an old tintype." Courtesy of Itha Carmack.

# Chapter One

# Pictures Of Childhood

*While pictures of childhood are still in my memory,*
*Before life's short candle burns low and grows dim,*
*There's a picture of home that must not be forgotten,*
*Though kept by the poor halting words of my pen.*
*The poets have told of old homes in Kentucky*
*And songs have been sung of its sunshine and rain,*
*But none have described the sweet home of my childhood*
*With half of its gladness, nor half of its pain.*
                    —"Prologue" in *Backward Glances*, 5

I thought that maybe some of my children, or grandchildren, might just appreciate a story of my life. Not that there has been anything very extraordinary or wonderful in it, but one thing sure, it is different from that of any other.

My great grandfather, Benjamin Armstrong, came to Christian County, Kentucky from Greenville County, South Carolina shortly after 1800. He took up several hundred acres of land which was later divided among his several children. On one of these small divisions of land, in a humble log hut, I was born, on September 26, 1885.

I like the words of a Prophet of God who said, "Having been born of goodly parents. . . ."[1]

We had a wonderful spiritual heritage, but my physical heritage was not so good. My mother had a serious case of a disease like cholera, a violent purging and vomiting, just before I was born. The doctor came, but

---

1. The allusion is to the Book of Mormon prophet Nephi, quoted in the opening words of the Book of Mormon: "I Nephi, having been born of goodly parents . . ." (I Nephi 1:1).

none of his remedies were effective, and he said that it looked as if they were going to lose both the mother and the baby.

An old friend heard of mother's sickness, walked a long way, brought some hard cider and gave mother small doses of it often.[2] She soon got all right, but when I was born, shortly after this, they said that I was a sorry specimen of humanity. Just a skeleton, and of course, mother had no milk for me because of her serious illness.

In those days there were no nursing bottles, so they fed me with a spoon, chewed food, and made sugar tits, and managed to keep me alive.[3] I must have come out of it O.K. as they said that I walked early, though I was small. I was a scrawny child for several years.

We feel shocked nowadays when we think of grownups chewing food for a baby, but I have heard on good authority that it was about the only way that you could raise a baby in those days without a mother's milk, and without a nursing bottle. The saliva from the one who chewed the food helped it to digest.

I knew of a boy, in Utah (1913), who was sick and delirious, went for a drink, drank some lye that was in a glass above the sink, and it ate his swallowing apparatus out. They had to feed him through a tube below his throat, but it would not digest unless someone furnished saliva with the food. So I guess the chewing for the babies was sort of a scientific operation.

Anyway I survived, and if my older sisters are correct about my age when we moved to grandpa Armstrong's old place (my brothers and sisters say that I was only a little over one year old—1887) I can remember one or two happenings distinctly.[4]

A certain rocky stretch of road leading from the house we were moving from, to the creek. We had just started out, our father was driving the team to the loaded wagon, and my mother was walking and driving a flock of geese. I insisted on walking with her and carrying a cat to boot. She endured that for a short distance, but, when I demanded the long stick with which she was guiding the geese, she lost all patience with me, jerked the cat out of my arms, causing it to scratch me, picked me up and soused me down into a bunch of bedding in the back end of the wagon, and in no uncertain tones demanded that I shut up, which I did.

---

2. Compare with remedies in Gordon Wilson, "Swallow It or Rub It On: More Mammoth Cave Remedies," in Gordon Wilson, *Folklore of the Mammoth Cave Region*, edited by Lawrence S. Thompson (Bowling Green: Kentucky Folklore Society, 1968), 67–74.

3. Sugar tits are cloths containing sugar and dampened with water, used as pacifiers.

4. John Armstrong (1803–1885) was the son of Benjamin Armstrong (b. 1778) and Jane Brasher (b. 1783). He was married to Susan Croft (b. 1807), Martha "Patsy" Boyd (1813–1853), and Drewsilla (Druscilla) Wooldridge (b. 1817).

Children know when their mother means business. This episode must have made a profound impression on my mind, as it is indelibly stamped there.

I also remember how the old house looked that we moved into. There was one big log room with an attic, and a smaller room about twelve feet from it, with an open hall between them. We called it a porch.[5]

Not long after we moved in my father took the old boards of the porch floor up (preparing to put a new floor in), leaving the old log sleepers standing there naked and ugly.

The old Seth Thomas clock probably needed oiling, anyway, in the night it started going *squeak*-squeak, *squeak*, squeak![6] I heard it in my sleep and dreamed it was a monkey sitting on one of those old log sleepers *hollering*.

I remember how my father and mother laughed when I told them of my dream. My dad asked me how a monkey looked, as he knew I had never seen one, and doubted that I had ever seen a picture of one, either. I told him that its head was like a coconut and it was a little bigger than a cat. There was more laughter, but I couldn't see the joke.

Next morning when we went out, there was an old mother cat lying under the sleepers dead, and several little kittens were trying desperately to find some breakfast. So much for my very earliest recollections.

This old log house, where my childhood was spent, was as crude and primitive as a home could be. It was the same type of dwelling the pioneers built when they landed in America.

---

5.  Based on Effie's description and her drawing of John Armstrong's cabin, she is referring to what is traditionally known as a dog-trot house. The open hallway being the defining characteristic, dog-trot houses are sometimes called dog-run, possum-trot, turkey-trot, double-log, two-pens-and-a-passage, two-P, three-P, open-hall, hallway, double-pen-and-passage houses, or occasionally double-pen or saddle-bag houses. In his excellent study of Kentucky architecture, Lynwood Montell states, "As we now know it in Kentucky, the dogtrot house probably originated in Virginia. By 1820 it was fairly common in southeastern Tennessee through the influence of the central passage house described elsewhere. It is known in the mountains of eastern Kentucky, but it is far more common in central, western, and southern Kentucky, especially along the headwaters of the Barren and Green rivers. It is usually of log construction, infrequently of frame, but almost never of brick." See William Lynwood Montell and Michael Lynn Morse, *Kentucky Folk Architecture* (Lexington: University Press of Kentucky, 1976), 21. See also Richard Hulan, "Middle Tennessee and the Dogtrot House," *Pioneer America* 7 (July 1975): 44–45, and Jerah Johnson, "The Vernacular Architecture of the South: Log Buildings, Dog-Trot Houses, and English Barns," in *Plain Folk of the South Revisited*, edited by Samuel C. Hyde, Jr. (Baton Rouge: Louisiana State University Press, 1997): 46–72.
6.  Seth Thomas (1785–1859) was an American clock manufacturer. Some of his most popular models were mantel clocks, often constructed with elegantly marbled wood. They had an 8-day, half-hour strike, with a cathedral gong bell.

Grandpa Armstrong's cabin, where Effie lived as a child. Note the eyebrow window just below the eaves and the "dogtrot" passage through the middle. From *Down Memory Lane*. Drawing by Effie Carmack.

*Milking Time*, by Effie Carmack. Oil on canvas, n.d., 11" x 14". "When we were through, we'd walk home in the twilight"; quotation from "Milking Time" in *Backward Glances*, p. 7. Original painting in the possession of Noel A. Carmack.

The logs were hewn out with a broad axe, notches were chopped in the ends to make them fit closer together, the cracks were filled with chinks and mud (called dobbin). The chinks and mud were usually whitewashed on the outside, and *always* whitewashed on the inside, making it look clean and fresh, and helping to reflect the dim coal oil lamp-light of evenings.[7] In winter the open fireplace helped the light problem too. And in summer we usually worked as long as we could see, and were ready to lay our tired bodies down by the time it was dark.

To one who has been brought up with all the modern conveniences: bright electric lights at the touch of a switch, hot and cold running water

7.  For the various types of corner notching in Kentucky log cabin construction, see Montell and Morse, *Kentucky Folk Architecture*, 8–11. For more on log cabin construction, see Henry Glassie, "The Appalachian Log Cabin," *Mountain Life and Work* 39 (winter 1963): 5–14, his "The Types of the Southern Mountain Cabin," in Jan Harold Brunvand, *The Study of American Folklore*, 2d ed. (New York: W.W. Norton & Company, 1978), Appendix C, 391–420, esp. 398–99, and Clinton A. Weslager, *The Log Cabin in America; from Pioneer Days to the Present* (New Brunswick: Rutgers University Press, 1969).

*in* the house, gas heat, refrigerators, washers that require only a small amount of labor, candy every day, toys and beautiful picture books all through the year, and all the many things we have today that makes life easy and pleasant, I am sure it would be difficult for them to see how children could find very much happiness in such a drab old home as the old log house I have just pictured.

Somehow, though, even with all the inconveniences, with only a very few cheap toys at Christmastime, with a little stick candy at rare intervals; with the only cold drinks in summer cool water from the well, and sometimes homemade cider, we seemed to appreciate the small things that came our way with a keener thrill of joy than children of today do with the multiplicity of things they have to enjoy.

In the springtime, when the grass came up, the daffodils blossomed, the early windflowers and tiny bluets started opening along the path to the spring where we went for water.[8] The beauty of it all was almost more than I could contain.

These flowers came in March with the first breath of spring. Later, the bluebirds came and made nests in the bird boxes the boys put up out by the woodpile. When the purple martins came it was a pretty sure sign that there would be no more killing frost. This was usually around the first of May. *That* was a red letter day in our young lives. *Then* we could take off our wool petticoat and our home knit yarn stockings. They were made of pure sheep wool, and so thick and sturdy they would almost stand alone. I could hardly stand them when it got the least bit warm. They always scratched my legs and made me uncomfortable. So we rejoiced when the time came to shed them for awhile.

When shoes, yarn stockings, and heavy petticoats were off I felt as if I could nearly fly. We raced down the smooth path to the big old tobacco barn, climbed the orchard trees, made hickory whistles, pop guns, and squirt guns from the bamboo canes and the alders that grew down by the creek.[9]

I remember every foot of the path that led to the spring that was about a quarter of a mile west of the house. It led out between the stables and the plum thicket, across the little foot bridge that spanned the big gulley, across a little stretch of worn out field where nothing but sassafras

---

8.  Windflowers are any plant of the genus *Anemone*; they are also related to rue anemone (*Anemonella thalictroides*). Bluets (*Houstonia caerulea*, L.) refer to a delicate plant native to the United States with 4-parted bluish flowers and tufted stems; also called innocence, quaker-ladies, etc.

9.  Alders are trees or shrubs of the genus *alnus*. They usually grow in moist ground, often forming thickets. The wood is used by turners and the bark in dyeing and tanning.

bushes and tiny bluets could grow, then through a stretch of enchanted woodland.[10]

There was not a time in the year but what that woodland held some magic charm. Even in deepest winter, when the trees were loaded with snow, or the branches were glistening with sleet or frozen rain, it was a fairyland.

There were also the interesting tracks of wild animals, when snow was on the ground. It furnished us our winter wood, and the Christmas tree when that happy hallowed time arrived.

In springtime that woodland was a never ending source of delight. Early wild flowers, beds of moss, the sweet tender oak balls that grew on the young whiteoaks, the stems of the tender young hickory leaves to be peeled and eaten, the succulent young sassafras sprouts that grew slimy when we chewed them, but they tasted good anyway, and we liked them.

Then there were the dogwoods that really put on a show with their wealth of big white blossoms, the end of each leaf tipped with a little puckered up place of reddish wine color, with a center of tiny green balls.[11] After the white leaves dropped off the green berries grew large and sturdy, finally turning a bright red. They then furnished dandy ammunition for our pop guns, and with a number one gun with a barrel that was long enough, you could just about raise a blister on a fellow, if you dared the risk of getting your gun taken from you for keeps.

The red bud trees bloomed about this time of year also, adding their color to the white of the dogwoods.

In the spring branch there were water dogs, tadpoles, bullfrogs, and water mocassins, which made it interesting *and* dangerous. At rare intervals we would hear of someone killing a rattlesnake, and the deadly copperheads were quite common.

Blackberry briars flourished along the spring branch too, and down in the edge of the woods the luscious dewberrys grew. There were mulberry trees scattered around too.

It was in the fall of the year, though, when the woods *really* paid off. There were wild grapes, huckleberries, hickory nuts, walnuts, hazelnuts, and down along the creek banks the sugar haw trees and the black

---

10.  Sassafras (*Sassafras albidum*) has long been used medicinally and has many useful applications. The oil of the sassafras contains a great deal of mucilage. It is often used as a diaphoretic and a diuretic. Sassafras is also helpful in abating fever, pneumonia, bronchitis, catarrth, mumps, etc.

11.  Dogwood (*Cornus Florida*, L.) is a tree with small greenish flowers surrounded by showy white or pink petallike bracts; it is well known in the southern states and has tonic and anti-intermittent properties.

Untitled, by Effie Carmack. Oil on plywood panel, n. d., 17½" x 38⅞". Original in the possession of Noel A. Carmack.

haw trees thrived. The leaves would all fall from the sugar haw trees leaving only the big clusters of red haws, which were as sweet as sugar. They were clean and shiny looking, and there was nothing to prevent us from just cramming all we could hold, which we usually did, when we ran across them.[12]

The black haws must have contained some magic vitamin that my poor scrawny body was starved for. They were oblong, flat and oval, and hung down from the limbs in different sized clusters. They had big flat seeds in them, but I didn't even bother to spit them out, just swallowed seeds and all. If they ever caused any bad effects I have no remembrance of it.

I must have had a pretty good digestive system, as nothing seemed to upset me except the fresh pork at hogkilling time, when I would get a sour stomach and spit up clear grease. If I spat it into the fireplace it would blaze up a foot high. Sometimes I would belch it up on the way to the well, and when I would come back with my bucket of water there would be the big white dab of clear grease, cold and solid in the path.

It's a wonder we lived through it. Mother nature must have foreseen that her children would not have very good judgment, and arranged many ways to help our bodies adjust themselves to all kinds of crazy conditions.

On the farm we children had never heard of parks or playgrounds, or playrooms where children have modeling clay to work with, and swings and teeter totters, seesaws and scooters. We didn't really need them, for we *had* most of these things, maybe in rather a crude form, but still very entertaining. We made seesaws of everything, and all kinds of swings.

The great washes, or gulleys as we called them, must have been a source of sorrow and regret to the owners of a farm, for they signified worn out soil, but the joy and entertainment they furnished we children would compensate in part for the loss of the soil.

We built bridges across these gulleys, made cellars and fireplaces in the sides of them. Made mills down their steep banks. We played like the dirt was our grist, and hauled it up the steps in the bank and galloped gallantly over the bridge on our sycamore horses. (We had made them ourselves.) Then we poured our grinding down the smooth trench we had made, and the coarse and fine meal was separated perfectly.

When I was alone, and no one to play with me, I would find certain places in the banks where there were great cracks where there was beautiful, moist, bluish white clay that was wonderful for modeling. Many long

---

12.  Sugar haws or black haws are the fruit of a spring-flowering shrub called hawthorn, of the genus *Crataegus* especially the American *C. Coccinea*, L. They have shining, often lobed, leaves and white or pink fragrant flowers.

happy hours I have spent making horses, dogs, heads, pitchers, whole sets of dishes, and hundreds of marbles of all sizes.

Summertime brought its share of joys. When the berries were ripe, the melons and vegetables were plentiful, the peaches were ripened, *and* the swimming in the creek was fun.

*But,* there were serious drawbacks to it, too. The chiggers, ticks, and fleas; the terrible heat, when even the beds at night were as hot as if they had been exposed to the hot sunshine.

Then there were also the swarms of terrible flies, and the troublesome mosquitoes that came humming in the night, bringing chills and fever accompanied by terrific headaches.

No one in the country ever thought of having screen on the doors and windows at that time, and it had not been determined yet just what the cause of the chills and fever was. Some claimed they were caused by eating overripe melons; others thought that breathing the night air was responsible. Doctors claimed that they were caused from biliousness, and administered rounds of calomel as well as quinine. Groves chill tonic was sometimes an effective remedy, but often the chills persisted in spite of everything.[13]

There was one good thing; we were not easily daunted. We were accustomed to all kinds of unpleasant necessities, and took them as a part of life, never thinking of complaining, if there was no way of remedying it.

We didn't give up supinely, though, and put up with *every*thing. I can remember when I would see the light from the old coal oil lamp suddenly appear about midnight. I would know that my mother was chasing a flea out of her shimmy,[14] and if there was a cat in the house it would usually catch fury at the same time.

We burned wool rags and old shoes in a vain effort to scare the mosquitoes away. We finally learned that the smell of coal oil was offensive to them, and as that was one thing we usually had a supply of we would sprinkle it on the bed, or put it on a cloth and hang the cloth on the headboard of the bed.

Nature is a kind mother, and as far as it is possible for her to do, she builds up a resistance to those things that are harmful to our bodies; but I suppose in our case we did so *many* things against the laws of health that she could not possibly cope with all of it.

---

13. This probably refers to Grove's Bromo-Quinine tablets, a preparation for the cure of colds, manufactured and sold by Edwin Wiley Grove (1850–1927), a philanthropist and pharmacist.
14. Chemise.

We were just emerging into that period when the best of the food was being removed from the wheat, and was being fed to the pigs, cattle and horses.

When farmers fattened great pens full of hogs; killed them in the fall, and made lard, sausages, hams, middlings and shoulders; to be eaten the remainder of the year.

When the best of the food from the sugar was being refined away, leaving only a predigested dead sweet.

When it was thought that vegetables were not fit to eat unless they had been cooked several hours with a great chunk of fat bacon to season them, and when hot bread was eaten three times a day, winter and summer.

When it was the popular thing for women and girls to wear a corset as tight as she could possibly stand it, and then to swear it was not the least bit tight; and with long pointed shoes, so tight it was a misery to walk in them.

No wonder we had terrible sick headaches. No wonder we suffered toothache, and lost our teeth early in life. No wonder our eyesight failed us, and we aged prematurely.

*But,* despite sickness and toil, we managed to get a great deal of joy out of life. Hardships and privation seemed to strengthen our love for one another, and to make us appreciate more keenly the few joys that came our way.

It is no wonder that we appreciated the different seasons when they came. Winter arrived when we had endured the heat, flies, chiggers, chills, and unceasing labor about as long as we could. Springtime, with its turnip greens, came as a welcome relief from the monotonous diet of bread and meat, beans and molasses. That is expressing the dead letter of it, but the spirit of it was joyous and happy.

It seems to me, as I remember it now, that no one in any station of life could have been happier than we were. The long winter evenings around a roaring fire were never dull. There was always something interesting and pleasant to do. We popped corn, ate walnuts and hickory nuts, read, sang, made music, or even danced.

My father played the fiddle and there was always a guitar or banjo for accompaniment, as most of the family could play either of them. Our father and mother had both been excellent dancers, and dancing in their day was really an art, and they took a delight in teaching it to us. The Lancers, the Minuet, the Virginia Reel, the Mazourka, the Polka, the Schottische, the Waltz, and the intricate changes of the quadrilles.

Often Lelia or Sadie would read a story aloud to an attentive audience, often we would have spelling matches, or have map questions from the geography book.[15] And drawing pictures on a big old double slate was something that never lost its charm.

One thing has been a source of wonder to me. It is the way that our mother managed to do all the work so smoothly and pleasantly for the vast amount of visitors we had. There was no commercial entertainment in those days, especially out in the farming districts. Maybe once a year there was a circus in town, ten miles away. I can't even remember a county fair until several years later; so an occasional dance was about all there was for diversion in winter, except visiting in each other's homes.

There were three sisters, and two brothers, older than myself, and one brother younger.[16] With good natured parents who joined in with the young folks in their songs, games, and dances; with lots of music, fun, and food, our place was very popular. But I can't remember anyone but mother doing very much of the work.

At the time none of our family belonged to any church, though we were religious in a way. We never took the name of the Lord in vain, there was no swearing. In fact, I can truthfully say that I never heard my father, or one of my brothers swear in my life. We never worked on Sunday.

Sundays we usually had the house extra clean, and we all put on our clean clothes. Mammy would part her hair in the middle, twist it low down on her neck, and put her white apron on instead of the gingham ones that were worn every day. In winter she usually wore a little three cornered shawl around her shoulders, and on Sunday it was pinned in front with a breast pin, of which there was quite a variety in those days. The cameo type, or the long jet ones, or straight gold clasp.

Anyway, on a Sunday there was a different air prevailing. Mammy would find the only Bible we had, at that time, a little thick volume whose covers were loose. We held it on for several years, and finally discarded it entirely, and just used it without covers.

There was the chapter in Proverbs (?) which has 31 verses in it. By finding the day of the month one was born in, then find that verse which corresponded in number it would tell his fortune.[17] I remember that my father's read something like this: "Not slothful in business, fervent in

---

15. Lelia and "Sadie" were two of Effie's older sisters.

16. The children in Effie's family were Martha Etta (1871–1899), Lelia Jane (1872–1970), James Elmo (1874–1958), Margaret Alzada "Sadie" (1877–1971), John Robert (1880–1982), Effie Lee (1885–1974), and Charles Autie (1891–1932). Lelia married William Henry Ferrell, and "Sadie" married Evert Holt.

17. Effie's family was playfully employing one of many forms of divination using the Bible. See "Bible Divination," *Folk-Lore Journal* 1 (1883): 333, and idem, 1 (1884): 380–81. An extensive discussion of bibliomancy and Bible divination is found in Kevin J. Hayes, *Folklore and Book Culture* (Knoxville: University of Tennessee Press, 1997): 29–30, 33–43.

spirit, serving the Lord." We all agreed that it fit him exactly. Sadie's read: "She shall arise while it is yet dark, and prepare meat for her household."[18]

As a general thing we didn't follow the custom of the farmers around us, of getting up long before daylight whether there was any work to be done or not. We usually sat up late of evenings and slept until daylight, so we pitied Sadie, that fate had decreed that she would get one of those cranks who "arise while it is yet dark." We never doubted but that it would all come true, and we were not a superstitious family either, though many around us were seriously afflicted with it.

One thing my father would not tolerate, was to have anyone tell a spooky story of any kind before his children. If anyone started to tell something of that nature he would raise a finger and very kindly say, "Pardon me, but that is one thing that we never allow before the children." Consequently, I grew up without fear. I had clung to a sort of religion I had, that if we are not afraid, nothing will harm us; while fear of a thing will somehow cause that very thing to gravitate to us. I was past fifty years of age before I found out by an entirely new experience that such was not the case every time, for without any thought of fear, I found myself facing terrible, menacing danger (of which I will give an account later).[19]

Anyway, we grew up with an abiding faith in God, with a deep respect for His Name and His Word. Though sometimes we did giggle a little when we came across funny passages where the Lord threatened to make His people "stink as a dung hill" if they continued in their disobedience. We didn't let our mother know that we giggled. We thought it was funny where Baalam's Ass talked back to him, and where Samson set the foxes' tails afire and turned them loose in the wheat fields.[20]

I hardly think the Lord will hold it against us, for underneath it all we had the most profound respect for His Word.

The little old log house we moved from, when I was about one year old became the home of mama's half brother, Uncle Lawrence Armstrong, after we moved from it. My childhood was so closely interwoven with him and Aunt Fannie that I will have to bring them into the picture to make it complete.[21]

---

18. See Romans 12:11: "Not slothful in business; fervent in spirit; serving the Lord." The last chapter of Proverbs does have 31 verses. Verse 15 says "She riseth also while it is yet night and giveth meat to her household." Sadie was born on December 15, 1877.

19. It is not clear what Effie is referring to here. She may have been making reference to a traumatic experience she had later in life. She did not, however, connect this statement to any subsequent narrative.

20. "Stink as a dung hill" could refer to any of several verses, such as Jeremiah 16:4. See Numbers 22 for the story of Balaam's ass, and Judges 15:4–6 for the foxes tails.

21. Lawrence B. Armstrong (1835–1908) was the half brother of Effie's mother, and his wife, Effie's aunt, was Francis A. "Fannie" Boyd (b. 1834).

Effie's Uncle Lawrence and Aunt Fannie Armstrong.
Courtesy of Hazel Bushman.

At regular and frequent intervals Aunt Fannie would come to spend the day. Their house was across the creek from ours, and it was quite a long road through the cultivated fields to the creek from our place. Some of us usually spied her coming slowly, long before she reached the orchard, and I usually ran to meet her. She always hugged my head against her stomach, and to this day I can recall the nice sweet smell of her clothing. She always kept perfume or a sachet of some sweet smelling herbs in the chest where she kept her clothing.

If it was cold, or muddy, Aunt Fannie always wore overshoes, and I would have to pull them off for her and clean them.

Aunt Fannie had big pockets in her skirts, sewed on the inside, and entered by a perpendicular slit on the outside. Sometimes she would bring me some ginger cake, a piece or two of candy, a pretty empty bottle, or some odd buttons for my charm string.[22] I remember once she brought me a piece of blue checked material for a doll dress.

Aunt Fannie's all day visits called for a good dinner, usually chicken and dumplin's, as she had lost all her teeth from being salivated with

---

22.   Children of the Kentucky backwoods commonly wore strings, bands, beads, or charms to ward off ill-health. See, for example, Gordon Wilson, "Talismans and Magic in Folk Remedies in the Mammoth Cave Region," *Southern Folklore Quarterly* 31 (June 1966): 192–201. Also Daniel Lindsey Thomas and Lucy Blayney Thomas, *Kentucky Superstitions* (Princeton: Princeton University Press, 1920), s.v. "Buttons" and "Charm."

calomel.[23] She always declared that Mammy could cook the best dinners, and wash the whitest clothes of any woman in the neighborhood.

When Aunt Fannie started home she usually wanted one of us to go home with her and stay all night. I was always anxious to go *at the time*, but usually got homesick after I got there. They went to bed by dark, and I would toss around on the hot bed and could not go to sleep for a while. Lots of times I could hear some of them at home singing, as they went to the well for a bucket of cool water, and oh! how I would wish I was with them. Aunt Fannie would be snoring and puffing the wind out between her toothless lips. The frogs in the nearby creek would be croaking, and in summer the whippoorwills would sit right by the doorstep and send out their plaintive call.

In the morning the homesickness would be better. There was always a good breakfast of little brown sourdough biscuits, with butter and clear syrupy pear preserves in a clean shiny cut glass preserve stand, and even if it was not an ideal food for a growing child, it tasted good.

After breakfast there was usually work to do, especially in the spring when the corn and garden was to be planted. Uncle Lawrence usually got some of us to drop the corn for him in the crosses of the furrows he had laid off, while he came behind with a drag (usually a big flat rock) drawn by old Crockett, with which it was covered.

It was my job to go to the spring for water, and as the path lay through the woods it was a pleasant trip in spring and summer. There were always wild flowers, and the slippery elm tree just beyond the spring, with peeled places where bark had been obtained for Aunt Fannie's periodical bilious attacks. I would always leave my bucket by the spring and run and peel off a piece of bark to chew. It grew big and slippery and slimy as I chewed it, but had a pleasant taste.

---

23. Aunt Fannie's loss of teeth was a sign of mercury poisoning from calomel. Today calomel is sometimes used as a laxative or fungicide, but during the nineteenth century, it was used as an aspect of antiphlogistic treatment and ridding or purging the body of excess humors. In what was called the heroic period of medicine, rural practitioners in the South administered large doses of calomel for the treatment of cholera during the epidemics of 1833 and 1873. This was widely practiced in keeping with the teachings of Dr. Benjamin Rush (1746–1813) of Philadelphia. Dr. John Esten Cooke (1783–1853), professor of medicine at Transylvania University Medical School in Lexington, was a major proponent of the administration of calomel in Kentucky. Unfortunately, it may have been a cause of more deaths than the disease it was used to treat. See J. S. Chambers, "The 1833 Epidemic in the Bluegrass," chap. 6 in *The Conquest of Cholera: America's Greatest Scourge* (New York: Macmillan, 1938), 148–79, John Duffy, "Medical Practice in the South," *Journal of Southern History* 25 (February 1959): 53–72, and Frederick Eberson, "A Great Purging—Cholera or Calomel?," *Filson Club History Quarterly* 50 (April 1976): 28–35.

I knew that I must not loiter long, or I would hear Aunt Fannie's voice from the back of the house calling, Eff*ie-e-e*! Then I would dip my bucket down deep in the spring, to be sure the water would be cool, then hurry to the house, and Aunt Fannie would say, "Law me, child, what made you stay so long, I thought maybe you had pitched headfirst into the spring."

Aunt Fannie's face was as round as a biscuit, and she had only a teeny wisp of gray hair left, that was just long enough to come together behind and be tucked up with a little tuckin' comb. She was neatness itself, and took a bath regularly in a big dish pan that was kept for the purpose, and it was also used to rinse clothes in.

It was at Aunt Fannie's that I saw my first roll of toilet paper. Her brother, Tom Boyd, who was a real estate and exchange broker on La Salle Street in Chicago, would send her boxes of things for her birthdays and for Christmas. Handy things that he thought she would appreciate, and, although there was not even an outdoor toilet, there was a rail laid in the low forks of two oak saplings on the brow of the hill just back of the house; they always took the roll with them when they went.

Aunt Fannie gave me one roll, but it was never used for the purpose for which it was intended. It was used as tracing paper, to put over pretty pictures, and trace them. It was placed on the old wall plate of the attic at home with my other treasured possessions, chalk box and trinkets, and was kept for years, a roll of my favorite pictures traced carefully.

Aunt Fannie's house was different from ours. Ours abounded in all kinds of interesting things: the quilt piece box, where I could get cloth for doll clothes; the table drawers with pencils, letters and papers; the school books, slates, and pencils; the upstairs where grandmother's old spinning wheel and flax reel and candle molds, and many other old things from the generation that had passed on before us were still stored. *Hundreds* of interesting things were at home, but Aunt Fannie was one of those immaculate housekeepers who kept everything *but* this year's Almanac and this week's newspaper cleared out and burned.

There was a big old heavy Bible on the lower part of the center table (Uncle Lawrence said it was no good, as it was a Catholic Bible), but we were never allowed to touch it.

Aunt Fannie had saved a smooth white board about 8 x 14 inches, with a hole bored in one corner, and a string run through to hang it up by. This was for us to write on in the absence of a slate. When it was filled she washed it with soap and water, and it was ready to be used again. That, and two Almanacs constituted the sources of entertainment in the house. One Almanac was advertising some kind of patent medicine, and was called the Seven Barks, and had pictures of seven different kinds of dogs on the backs. The other was full of pictures of brownies, greenies, and little pot bellied dwarfs with sharp toed shoes.[24]

There was a homemade carpet on the floor, with straw under it to make it soft, and it was nice to roll on in summer.

There was always the possibility that Aunt Fannie might decide to open her chest, and show me some of the things her brother Tom had sent her, or show us the pretty "shimmy and nightgown" she was saving to be buried in. They were trimmed with Hamburg edging, and were made very nice.[25]

Uncle Lawrence would laugh at her about those things, and she would get the broom after him. He would dodge with his arm above his bald head and say, "Now you'd better be careful old lady, or I'll bust a limb under your big belly." But it was all in fun. He liked to tease her, and would tell her she was a freak anyway. She had two thumbs on one hand, the second one grew out at the big joint of her normal thumb, a little crooked dwarfed one. She wore a little gold ring on it. She never had any children. They were good to us, and we were always sure of a welcome anytime we wanted to go to their place.

These following things are all stamped indelibly on my memory, as a very pleasant part of my childhood. The smell of the Balm of Gilead tree by the kitchen window, and the salve Aunt Fannie made from its buds.[26] The bed of dwarf striped roses, the little cedar tree that was by the path that led out to the orchard that was always kept trimmed as round as a ball. The long sloping lawn with flat rocks imbedded on either side of the path that led down to the front gate. The storm house in the northwest corner of the yard. The steep hill just back of the kitchen that led down to the spring branch where all the rubbish from the place was thrown.

I remember one time, when I was a very small child, (I think it was when I was seven), I had been at Uncle Lawrence's for several days, had been dropping corn for him, and pulling weeds for Aunt Fannie, and was getting quite homesick. Uncle Lawrence gave me four dimes, and I felt almost rich. I kept them squeezed tight in my sweaty hand. It was early spring, and flowers were in bloom along the creek banks, but I didn't

---

24. The *Seven Barks Almanac* was published annually in New York by Lyman Brown. Extant issues are dated between 1883 and 1919. The second almanac cannot be identified based on Effie's description.

25. Hamburg edging is a kind of machine-embroidered edging, usually on cambric or muslin.

26. The flower of the Balm of Gilead tree (*Abies balsamea, Abies balsamifera, Mich.*, and *Pinus balsamea, Willd.*) or American silver fir was commonly used in the South as an external application to wounds. See Porcher, *Resources of the Southern Fields and Forests*, 506.

stop to pick any, as I was afraid I would lose my money, and I was in too big a hurry to get home.

I had crossed the creek, and came out into our field where I could see the house and orchards and I could see the peach trees in bloom. At first I didn't know what it was; I thought they had painted the hen house rosecolored.

I ran nearly all the way home, pausing a few minutes as I passed the sour apple tree, under which I had my little graveyard. Where the dead chickens, and the bird that fell out of the nest, etc., were buried (with genuine grief at each funeral, and plenty of tears). I remember that the flowers had dried and withered, and it looked very neglected. I also remember that I thought home was the most beautiful place in the world.

They had plowed and harrowed the orchard. They had raked and swept the yard clean. Autie, my baby brother, who was just learning to walk had had his first haircut, and had his first pair of pants on.

Standing bashfully at the corner of the house was a little Negro boy with one bare foot crossed over the other. They had found him on the way from town, and not being able to find his folks had just brought him home with them. The joy of that homecoming is still a hallowed memory. Springtime was always a happy time; of course there was work, endless work, to be done, but Mammy always found time to give the old place a thorough going over to get the grime and smoke of winter cleared away.

They always bought a barrel of lime, and everything on the place was whitewashed, including the hen house and chicken coops. It is miraculous what a barrel of lime can do towards changing the looks of an old place, for a while at least. Sadie was an artist at making an old log house attractive, and a wizard at turning out work.

Etta, my oldest sister, was a cripple, caused by infantile paralysis when she was a baby, so there were lots of things she could not do.[27] By the time the first blue bird appeared I would begin to tease her to go fishing with me, and it was never very hard to persuade her. Oh! the fun of getting ready, digging bait, getting hooks and lines rigged up, and selecting the proper fishing poles. There was usually a good supply of fishing tackle that the boys used, and they didn't mind us using them if we would put them back. There was always a surplus of fishing canes, as the canebrake was only a mile or so down the creek from our place.[28]

---

27. Infantile paralysis, poliomyelitis, or polio, is an infectious viral disease that occurs most often in children and in its acute form attacks the central nervous system and produces paralysis, muscular atrophy, and often death.

28. A canebrake is a dense thicket of cane.

The fish were not very large, six or eight inches was usually the limit in length, but it was fun just to be on the creek bank and watch the little red cork bob up and down when I got a nibble; listen to the myriad of songbirds, and hunt for wildflowers. Later, when the spring went dry, we moved the big wash kettle, and the tubs to the creek, and did the washing there.

Then too, there was the task of making soap in the springtime. Mama would save all the trimmings and scraps of fat all winter, she saved the ashes from the hickory wood, and put it in the ash hopper. It was my task to carry water from the spring to run down the lye. The ashes were dampened when they were put in the hopper, just enough to rot them, and then were kept covered, to keep the rain from washing the lye out of them. It seemed to me that it took hundreds of buckets of water before the lye started dripping from the little trough at the bottom.

Mammy would test it with a feather to see if it was strong enough to eat the fringe of the feather off, if it was not, she boiled it down till it *was* strong enough; then she added the grease she had saved and boiled them together till it was soft soap. There was quite an art in soap making, and mammy had the reputation for being a number one soap maker.[29]

I have an idea there was lots of satisfaction in getting a barrel of good soft soap made, for plenty of soap was needed for the domestic shirts and drawers the men wore to work in. The chemise, nightgowns, pantalets, and other everyday underwear for the girls and women were made of unbleached muslin also. Of course the corset covers and the petticoats worn for Sunday were made of bleached domestic,[30] usually with homemade crochet edging, and plenty of tucks, and often embroidered.

I was the sixth of seven children, and up until the time I was five or six years old my mother had sewed for her entire family on her fingers.[31] At that time none of the clothing except the men's coats and pants were bought ready-made, although many of the boys' pants were made at home.

Mammy also carded the wool and spun the yarn and knit our winter stockings and gloves. Our parents were of the firm belief that we would

---

29. The following description of soft soap making appears in Porcher, *Resources of the Southern Fields and Forests*, 135: "To make soft soap—Take ten pounds potash well pulverized, fifteen pounds grease, and three buckets boiling water. Mix, and stir potash and water together until dissolved. Then add the grease, stirring well; put all into a barrel, and every morning add two buckets cold water, stirring it well each time, until the barrel is nearly full, or mixed to the consistency of soft soap." For a description of how to mix lye in hickory potash as part of the soap-making process, see pp. 327–32. See also Andrea Burrell, "Soapmaking," in *The Foxfire Book*, edited by Eliot Wigginton (Garden City: Doubleday, 1972), 151–58.

30. Domestic is a common cotton cloth such as sheeting.

31. By hand.

have died of consumption if we had dared wear cotton stockings in the winter, and they were never discarded till the first day of May.

She usually carried her knitting with her, and every spare minute the needles were flying. It was not necessary for her to look while she knit, and the conversation was never hindered in the least.

We never bought blankets. Homemade quilts were used entirely. Mammy said that one or two new quilts, made each year, would just about replace the wear and tear of the old ones. (Etta pieced quilts) [32]

Since I have had a family of my own I have wondered how Mammy ever did all that she had to do. I have never knit socks or stockings, and have never had to make soap. I have bought most of the covers for the beds, and I have always had a sewing machine, yet I didn't seem to have any more leisure time than she did.

I remember one spring when she had the new bolt of domestic laid out on the bed, and was cutting out shirts, underwear, straw bed ticks, etc. to be sewed on her fingers; every seam of which was felled to prevent ripping.[33] She stopped, propped both hands on her hips, and, as she eyed the stack of garments to be sewed she said fervently, "I wish to the Lord I had a sewing machine."

Less than a week later a man came by selling American sewing machines. He was a highpowered salesman, and didn't even ask if he could bring the machine in, he lugged it in uninvited. Mammy argued that he was just wasting his time, that they couldn't afford to pay forty dollars for a sewing machine. Pappy came in, and the man asked him how he was fixed for farming utensils. He said that he was very well supplied.

"I'm sure you are," said the agent, "I'm sure that if you needed a farm implement half as badly as your wife needs this sewing machine you would persuade yourself to buy it, whether you had the money or not."

He also said that with that nice flock of hens he could see out in the orchard she could make the monthly payments with eggs. Papa told Mammy to get it if she wanted to. But she remembered that even with the chickens, eggs, and butter, they had hardly been able to pay the interest on the mortgage the past year. The salesman said that if they would only make a very small down payment he would leave the machine for them to try for a month, and if they could not finish paying for it he would take it back. There was no money for even a small down payment, so he said at

---

32. This and similar parenthetical notations in the autobiography are probably just reminders for a paragraph or two Effie intended to write at a later time. She refers briefly to Etta's piecing again at other points in the autobiography.

33. Double-stitched with the raw edges of fabric turned inside the seam; Effie defines this term at a later point.

last that he was going to leave it anyway. He took me up on his knees and gave me four shiny new copper pennies, told us goodby, and left. (1889)

That was the last we ever heard of the sewing machine salesman. We waited for him to come back for the machine, but no one came, and no one wrote. Finally, my father found where the American Machines were manufactured and wrote a letter telling them of the one that had been left at our place. They answered that they had no agent in our part of the country; so we had a sewing machine.

Our mother's petition was answered, and that quickly, though she didn't expect it to come in the way it did. The joy and luxury of that new sewing machine was unbelievable. There were hemmers of all sizes; rufflers, and tuckers; it was magic.

Sadie sewed everything she could get hold of, and oh! the ruffles! Ruffles around necks and wrists, around the shoulders, knee ruffles, double ruffles on the bottoms of flared skirts. I was too small to be allowed to sew. The sewing went on at a rapid rate. Sadie soon learned to lengthen the stitches and loosen the tension so she could fairly fly up and down those seams.

Those old sewing machines were made ~~good~~ ^well^,[34] and up until a few years ago (this is 1944)[35] when the old house owned by my stepmother was burned, it was still in running condition; although I don't suppose there were very many garments sewed on it in its last years, as my stepmother didn't know how to sew.

My father often said that he once thought, and argued it was right, that you didn't get something for nothing, but that sewing machine was one exception. We got a good machine and four new pennies to boot. (Autie's and Vera's birth before this)[36]

We were a sentimental bunch. I guess everyone was more sentimental, and more romantic in those days, than they are now. We used to all sit out in the old porch, as we called it. There was usually a pallet on the floor, an old soft comfort, where Autie, the baby had played and slept during the day. Mammy would get two long limber twigs, bend them over the pallet, stick the ends in under the sides, and stretch a thin plant-bed canvas over him while he slept, to keep the flies away.

In the evening this pallet was pulled to the edge of the porch, and we would lounge on it and the doorstep. Lelia or Sadie would get the guitar and sing old songs. The sad ones always made me cry—"Oh Yes, I'll Take

---

34. "Well" is written by hand over "~~good~~."
35. Effie was working on later parts of the autobiography well into the 1960s.
36. Vera Alice (1891–1927) was the daughter of Effie's sister, Lelia, and William Henry Ferrell.

You Home Kathleen"—"The Years Roll Slowly By, Lorena"—"Ronald and I"—"The Dying Cowboy."[37]

The boys were good singers. John would add his bass, and Elmo his tenor.[38] Elmo would have been a good radio singer, high and low. Sometimes Pappy would get his old fiddle out and play softly some sweet old harmony.

Some of us would be washing our feet in the washpan out by the doorstep, and drying them on an old meal sack towel. Whippoorwills would be calling. Bats would be diving for insects, and the crickets would be chirping loudly in every corner.

The memory of those peaceful evenings together, after a long hard day's work is very sweet in my mind.

My father was so constituted that anything that worried his mind also made his body sick, and after a few years of crop failures, and the mortgage still hanging, he developed a serious stomach trouble. He grew thin and sad looking, and his shiny auburn hair was dry and lifeless. For months the old fiddle lay in its case untouched.[39]

Lelia was a beautiful girl, good and sweet, and very popular. With a plump little body that looked pretty in most anything. I remember once when there was to be a big moonlight dance somewhere (I was too small to remember now where it was), they had decided to make it a cheesecloth ball. I'll never forget how pretty Lelia looked when she was ready to start. The dress was made with a tight bodice, and a full gathered skirt, made long, and there were plenty of roses for her hair and for a corsage.

There was not a better dancer in the neighborhood than Lelia. There were some pretty gay fops in those days, and one of our neighbors,

---

37. See appendix one for more on these songs.

38. John and Elmo were Effie's older brothers.

39. The falling prices of tobacco between 1898 and 1904 brought serious economic problems to growers of dark-fired tobacco. Overproduction, poor crop quality, and changing consumer demands, forced many farmers to take collective action toward a marketing cooperative.

   On September 24, 1904, over five thousand tobacco farmers gathered at the Guthrie fairgrounds, near the Tennessee border, to organize a formal cooperative called the Planters' Protective Association (PPA). The Association challenged the monopolistic practices of the American Tobacco Company. Devout members of the organization often engaged in pressuring reluctant farmers to join the Association, resulting in violence and destruction in the Black Patch. Hooded Association loyalists who burned the farms of resistant farmers were called "night riders."

   Having experienced these years of turmoil, Effie wrote a fictional novel set during the Black Patch War entitled, "Tobacker." For more on the economic downturns experienced by the tobacco growers, see Rick Gregory, "'Look To Yourselves': Tobacco Growers, Problems of Production, and the Black Patch War," *Essays in Economic and Business History* 11 (1993): 283–94. For more on the PPA, See Waldrep, *Night Riders*, 36–51, and Campbell, *The Politics of Despair*, 30–52.

Walter Owen, was one of the prize winners.[40] He wore fancy vests, tuxe-
dos, stove pipe hats, and toothpick shoes. Walter was always scheming
some new enterprise to get-rich-quick, with the minimum of labor. I can
remember once when he and Carlos Owen[41] came around with a device
for cleaning feather beds; they did it real cheap; but after they left we
found that the remaining feathers had only a temporary fluff to them,
and when they went down there was only about one third of what was
there before cleaning.

Then Walter told us about going out in his father's old worn out
fields that were grown up with dewberry briars, digging them up and selling them for everbearing strawberries.[42] He said he eased his conscience
by thinking that if they cultivated the dewberries right good they just
might do them as much good as the strawberries would have anyway.[43]

The one redeeming feature about Walter Owen was his frankness.
He usually told it worse than it really was. He was smart, likable, and a
marvelous dancer. His whole family had plenty of sense. Mr. Nat, the oldest, was a school teacher of high degree. Miss Lizzie was also a teacher.
She taught our school and boarded with us. The two younger boys had
nicknames, Bunkie and Ernie.[44] I never knew their real names. Bunkie
was always inventing something. One thing I remember was a tobacco set-
ter. Bunkie and Ernie were confirmed comedians. Bunkie was the magi-
cian who could drive a pin in a certain place in his leg clear up to the
head. He could also wiggle his ears up and down.

I remember one time when we were passing their place coming
home from cousin Boone's;[45] Etta was riding a mule on a side saddle, and
I was riding behind her. The boys were out in the barn and scared the
mule (though not intentionally), he jumped, the saddle turned, and we
both fell off, but neither of us were hurt. That's the only time I ever fell
from an animal.

Mr. Nat taught a subscription school, after the free school was out,
about Christmas, there being no High School in the community at that
time. He taught the higher grades as a private school, each pupil paying

40. A fop is a young gentleman who is preoccupied with his appearance, clothes, and manners. Obviously, Walter R. Owen (1870–1930) qualified.

41. Carlos Owen is not listed in the 1880 census.

42. *Rubus trivialis* Michx., low bush dewberry, or creeping blackberry, was sometimes used
as a substitute for more costly foreign wines.

43. Effie repeats this story of Walter's clever scheme on page 197.

44. Nat or Mat G. Owen (b. 1866). Lizzie Owen (b. 1874) was listed in the 1880 census
with her brother Walter. Bunkie and Ernie Owen are not listed in the 1870 or 1880
census returns.

45. Nathan Boone Fuller (1854–1942).

two or three dollars a month tuition. Sadie attended at least one spring session of his school, and I think she boarded at Aunt Fannie's, as it was the rainy season, and by staying there she would not have to cross the creek which was swollen lots of times during that time of year, and hard to cross.

I remember our spring flood that reached a disastrous climax. Cousin Elijah Armstrong was a fruit agent at the time, and was at our place taking orders for fruit trees, grapevines, shrubs, etc.[46] I remember yet how attractive the colored pages of the peaches, apples, grapes, flowers, etc. were to me, and I'm sure I was not over six years old. I think it was in the spring of 1892. Mammy was cooking dinner while the rest of the family looked at the books.

It began to grow dark, and the wind started blowing. As that section of country was often visited by tornadoes and violent windstorms we were a little nervous, but it was more of a downpour than anything else. One that continued steadily for an unusual length of time. Soon there was a small river of muddy water coming right through the yard. Another was roaring down by the little stable where Pappy made axe handles, and another between the yard and the horse lot. There was water everywhere.

After the rain quit falling we went out in the yard barefooted. There were drowned chickens all over the yard. The coops where they had taken refuge were standing in deep puddles with the chickens drowned inside. The results of long hours of patient labor swept away in an hour.

From the direction of the creek there was a roar like a mighty river. When we got out where we could see, the creek was already out of its banks, and was away up in the fields. Papa remembered the flock of sheep that were across the creek in a little meadow, and he knew that by now it would be covered with water.

The table was set, the dinner was ready to be eaten, but Mammy spread a sheet over it and told me to take care of Autie, the baby. This last order about broke my heart. All of them were running excitedly in the direction of the flooded fields, which had reached proportions we had never seen or heard of before, and I wanted to go too. So I set in to get the baby to sleep. Never did he get such soothing, rocking and singing as he got at that time. The rain had cooled the hot air, and it was a good time to sleep, so he was soon snoozing peacefully. I arranged the canvas so a fly couldn't touch him, then flew to the scene of excitement. (1892)

---

46. Probably Elijah H. Armstrong (1863–1954) who was married to Jean Brasher. He should not be confused with Elijah "Lige" Armstrong (1811–1888), his father. See Meacham, *History of Christian County*, 436–37.

The flood was filled with all kinds of floating debris. Sheep were bleating as they were being carried down on the muddy current. The folks were shouting to each other as they strove to rescue animals. It was an awful sight. The best part of our crop was under water, our daddy wasn't well, the sheep all being drowned, and the biggest part of Mammy's chickens were laying stretched out stiff.

I don't believe many people realize how much little children worry over the troubles of their parents, brothers and sisters, or how seriously they think of the problems of life.

The boys had most of their clothing off, and were out in the water trying to rescue what they could. A pet lamb named Dick, who had grown so large and troublesome around the house, butting every stranger who came on the place, had been put with the flock of sheep. When he came floating down, floundering desperately to keep his head above the water, he heard someone call, "Come on Dick, come on." He turned his head towards the water's edge and bent his energy to reach us, and soon came close enough that he was rescued and brought safely to land. If all the others had acted as intelligently as "Dick," many more could have been saved.

After it was all over, the wet mud bedraggled clothes were hung on the fence, and the tired hungry bunch sat down to the cold dinner. Mammy scolded me soundly for leaving the baby, and not minding her.

Everyone recounted their experiences. Mammy told how she had kept hearing the sheep bell tinkling regularly, and at last had found the old bell ewe hanging with her neck in the fork of a grape vine, still chewing as if she was perfectly contented.

All the chickens that had the least signs of life about them, and many that didn't were brought in the house and laid on the warm floor under the cookstove, and on old rags on the stove door. Several of them that had looked like hopeless cases came back to life.

I can't remember now that we suffered any extra want because of the loss of crops and livestock. We were used to financial calamities. Often, when they had worked all year, and made a good crop of tobacco, they got nothing for it when selling time came.[47]

I can remember that every bit of soil was washed away from the fields near the creek, clear down to the hardpan clay. On this hardpan were the prints of wagon wheels and horses' hoofs. I wished it were possible for us to know who made those wagon tracks. It was probably the bed of an old road at one time.

---

47. See Rick Gregory, "'Look To Yourselves,'" 286–87.

Just south of the horse lot, under the brow of a little hill, was the storm house. I have no idea when it was made, probably some of the older children know, but it seemed to me it had always been there. I can't remember of us ever persuading Pappy to go into it, even when the blackest, most threatening storm clouds were coming up. He said that he would be more afraid of snakes and spiders in that old storm house than he would be of a storm outside. We kids enjoyed throwing old coats around us and running and piling in there. I can still remember the damp earthy smell, the piece of old homemade carpet that was on the floor, and the logs above that held up the thick dirt roof.

There were thorn trees growing above and back of the storm house, so that was one place we steered clear of, for fear of sticking thorns in our feet. I remember when John stuck a big thorn through his foot, and it came out on top. That was on the little branch that ran south from the spring.

Just in front of the storm house, in a big depression, was a big flat rock, a natural bridge. It was hollow underneath, with crevices in the rock. This was a favorite place to play, as it was usually shady there, with the plum thicket on the east bank, and elm trees on the west bank. We had a swing under the elms, and spent many happy hours there. The plum thicket was a favorite spot, the branches overlapping above making cool green shade underneath. An *ideal* place for a play house, and a retreat for the chickens in hot weather.

I remember one time when an old mother partridge made her nest in the thick weeds, on the edge of the plum thicket, and hatched out a brood of little partridges. If I would sit real still, I could hear them talking in tiny little languages to each other as they moved about looking for weed seed and bugs, but with the *least* movement there was a warning from the mother, and every little quail flattened himself among the weeds, and you'd never guess there was anything there *but* weeds.

Among the things that have left pleasant memories, there are none any sweeter than the walk in the garden, a hard smooth path, with flowers growing thick on either side. Spice pinks and "love in a mist." Larkspurs, golden flax peonies, and double hollyhocks.[48] The big beds of peonies were in the yard, a bed on either side of the walk that led to the front gate. On the left of the gate, as we went out, was a big clump of privet

---

48.  Spice pinks possibly refer to small yellow or pink flowers of an aromatic shrub called a spice bush (*Lindera benzoin* or *Laurus benzoin*). "Love-in-a-mist" (*Passiflora incarnata*, L. or *Passiflora lutea*, L.) is a passion flower enveloped in finely dissected bracts. Larkspurs (*Delphinium tricorne* Michx.) are showy but irregular flowers of five sepals with spurred calyxes. They have astringent properties and yield blue dyes. Peonies are garden plants of the genus *Paeonea* with large pink, red, or white flowers.

bush,[49] and right by the privet bush was a peach tree, with deep red leaves, and white peaches. There was a flowering rose vine by the front room window, and other rose bushes scattered all over. An American beauty, that belonged to Etta, grew near the porch. It bloomed the year around, all but January and February. Etta often wrapped her apron around it to protect it from frost. Many times we have had roses at Christmastime.

Northeast of the house, and near the path that led across the field towards Mrs. Moore's, was the little old log stable; not used as a stable anymore, but where our dad made axe handles and hammer handles.[50] There were lots of young hickory saplings on the place which were excellent for these necessary articles.

There was usually a supply of timber sitting in the corners of this little old stable, and on rainy days, when it was impossible to work in the fields, Papa would spend his time blocking out handles, or shaping them down with the drawing knife; then of long evenings in the fall, we would all help polish them down to the finished article. First with wood rasp, then with pieces of broken glass, and last with sandpaper. Papa had the reputation of being an excellent axe handle maker, and he never had any trouble selling them for $3.00 a dozen. The blocking out was a quick and easy task for him, and the polishing up process was fun for us around the fire of evenings.[51]

Near this old stable was a big hickory tree that produced an abundance of pig nuts, as we called them, with a hard, thick shell, and small goodies that were sweet as sugar. I can remember distinctly the delicious flavor of them yet, even though it has been at least forty five years since I tasted them.

Back of the garden, which was directly east of the house, was a big persimmon tree.[52] In the spring, its pale yellow bell shaped blossoms made a thick carpet on the ground beneath the tree, and they were heavy with honey. We would suck them while they were fresh, and had just

---

49. A privet bush is a shrub of the genus *Ligustrum* with small dark-green leaves, widely used for hedges.

50. Ailsie (or Allice) Moore (b. 1838) was listed in the 1880 census with her husband Marion (b. 1841).

51. The process of ax handle-making is superbly treated in Tony Whitmire, Cecil Wilburn, et al., "How to Make a Broadax Handle," in *Foxfire 9*, edited by Eliot Wigginton and Margie Bennett (Garden City: Anchor Press/Doubleday, 1986), 428–37. Effie mentions this family activity again on page 101.

52. A tree with hard wood and orange-red, edible fruit, the persimmon tree (*Diospyros Virginiana* L.) was often used as an ". . . astringent and styptic. The inner bark is used in intermittent fever, in diarrhea, and with alum as a gargle in ulcerated sore throat." See Porcher, *Resources of the Southern Fields and Forests*, 385–86.

fallen. In the autumn there was usually a big crop of persimmons, but they were not fit to eat till after it had frosted, and they became soft and mellow. Up to that time they were bitter and puckery.

I remember one time when John and I were playing under the persimmon tree, and old Bruno was chasing a rabbit up north of the house. I said, "Now that rabbit will come right down by the garden fence, and if you will hurry and get there at the corner and surprise him you can catch him." I had no idea it was a true prediction, but John hid by the corner, and just then here came bunny with Bruno right behind. John jumped out and the bunny ran right into his arms.

There is a magic charm in water, especially in early spring, when it begins to rattle and sing as it babbles over the rocks.

There were lots of cowslip along the creek banks, and when they began to bud I felt as if my heart would burst with joy.[53] We always called them bluebells, and the name cowslip will never fit them for me. The little rosepink buds, the soft lavender as the buds grow larger, and the heavenly blue of the fully opened bell, all on the same stem, makes a combination of beauty and color harmony that is not often found on one plant. There they were before me, *acres* of them, and even if I took an armful, you wouldn't even miss them. I felt rich and perfectly happy.

Another thing that was *so* beautiful was a wild crabapple tree. The trees were usually round, and not very large. The buds were in clusters of ten or fifteen, in different shades, from delicate pink, to deep rose. They looked like tiny rosebuds, and I don't believe there is a more exquisite perfume. Often, when going through a woods, when the wind was right, we could find a blossoming tree by the perfume. Wild grape blossoms have a heavenly scent too, almost equal to the crabapple, but do not possess the beauty.[54]

Even though we were poor, as far as money was concerned, and lived in a crude log hut, we were rich in a few things, such as a fervent appreciation for the beauties of nature around us.

We possessed a stretch of stream that was far more entertaining, as a playground, than the most expensive of parks. There were minks, weasels, foxes, ground hogs, squirrels, and even *tales* of bobcats and panthers, though these were seldom seen, except down where cliffs and caves

---

53.  These cowslip to which Effie refers are probably bluebells (*Mertensia virginica*); or bell-shaped flowers of the genus *Campanula*.

54.  The crab apple tree (*Pyrus coronaria*, Linn. or *Pyrus melanocarpa*) was not used medicinally. "The fruit is very acid to the taste, and is often made into preserves. The bark, with that of the white hickory, gives a yellow dye." See Porcher, *Resources of the Southern Fields and Forests*, 149.

afforded hiding places. Oh! the fun of finding a grinning old possum in a persimmon tree in the fall. Then there was the canebrake, with lovely bamboo canes, free for the carrying home.

There was a big hill beyond the creek, the very biggest hill in the community, with all kinds of interesting and lovely things. Wild flowers of every kind, gorgeous ferns, mosses, flowering shrubs. Along the foot of the hill near the creek there were lots of black haws. The *best* things. I was crazy about them.

There were plenty of rocks and holes, that were good refuge for foxes, and Uncle Lawrence's one weakness was a fox chase. He kept several hounds, and lots of times we could hear him out on the hillside of a morning, before daylight, whooping his hounds up. We had one big old black hound we called Ponto. He was wise, and saved himself lots of running. When he would hear Old Rice, and the other hounds start a fox chase, he would sit out and listen till they came around the hill towards our stretch of the creek, and then he would go down and head the fox off before it got to its den.

I remember one time hearing old Ponto and Rattler barking for a long time down by the creek, so Papa came by to see what the excitement was all about. They had something in a hollow log. John was going to take the gun down, so I went along. Papa was chopping a hole in the log when we got there, and I was terribly excited, trying to guess what kind of animal was inside. When a good sized hole was made, suddenly a big groundhog dashed out and flew at the dogs. He was winning the fight when my dad fired a shot into him, then he gave up the ghost. I felt sorry for him. With three men, two dogs, and a gun against him, he didn't have a fair show.

There was a cave away over towards the west side of the hill that they say a horse fell into once, and its skeleton was still in there. Then there was the gar hole, a real *deep* hole in the creek, down towards the canebrake, that they said a big fish, called an alligator gar, was caught out of it once, and several eel had been hooked there, too. The eels were so hard to kill that pieces of them jumped out of the frying pan when it was being cooked.

According to *our* judgment it would have been hard to find a place *anywhere* more full of beautiful and interesting things than our farm was.

There were also the big mulberry trees, that were always loaded with luscious mulberries in the spring. They were so sweet and good (only in locust years we must not eat them, for they might have locust eggs on them, and then they were poisonous), and when the mulberries were ripe, the boys would take their guns and kill the squirrels that came there to eat them, which meant that we would have squirrel for dinner.

Then there was the well with nice cold water, and plenty of it. It had no cover on it, and *often*, there was not even a rope to draw the water up with, if the rope was needed elsewhere. We used a sycamore hook, and let the bucket down with it. It required *real* ingenuity and skill to sink the bucket and bring it up full without losing it off the hook, and it sinking to the bottom of the well. Although the well was a quarter of a mile from the house we took the milk, in long slim coolers, and cooled it in the well in hot weather, and then we really *did* have to be careful, for if the *least* bit of milk was spilled in the water it would ruin it.

Then we had a big grape arbor of green and purple concord grapes. What a luxury! And then there were the big walnut trees, in the woods, up towards the graveyard, north of the house, that usually had oodles of walnuts, with hulls that were good to color yarn for our stockings and gloves. They stained one's hands almost black in hulling season, but it wore off in time.

Then there were the big scaly bark hickory nut (hickernut) trees that bore an abundance of rather soft shelled nuts with big rich goodies in them. The old fields off to the north of us that at one time had been rich, and bore good crops, but now were worn out and grown up in blackberry and dewberry briars, free to anyone who chose to pick them, and where the cows could graze all summer free.

There were also the birds, all kinds of song birds. The purple martins and bluebirds that built their nests yearly in the bird houses we put up for them. The martins were real helpers, as they kept the chicken hawks away from the place.

Last, but not least, there were the good neighbors. To sum it all up, according to our judgment it would have been pretty hard to find a place anywhere with more interesting and beautiful things on it than our old farm. Besides, it had been grandfather Armstrong's home where Mammy was born, and the land had been given to *him* by great grandfather Ben Armstrong, who was Scotch Irish, and had come straight from Old Ireland, when he was a lad of fourteen.[55]

Grandpa Johnnie freighted to the Mississippi River. He hauled tobacco and other produce, and it was taken to New Orleans and traded for sugar, molasses and other things that they raised that we didn't.

One time grandpa said that he had to think up *something* to *do*. He was scheduled to wrestle with a man a *third* taller than he was. A rail splitter whose muscles were strong as iron, who was working on a flat boat taking produce to New Orleans, and bringing back their commodities to trade for it, as *he* was.

Grandma said she knew what he *could* do, take his shirt off and let her grease him all over good, then the other fellow would not be able to

---

55. Benjamin Armstrong (1778–1864) who was married to Jane Brasher (1783–1864).

hold on to him, and wouldn't be able to throw him. Grandpa thought it was a good idea, so she did it, and it worked.

In a book I read about Lincoln it said that he was a champion wrestler, and never failed to throw his opponent but *once*. When he was working on a flatboat on the Mississippi River a fellow named "Jack (nickname for John) Armstrong," who was short and strong, used some *unfair tactics*, and he failed to throw him. (The grease was the unfair tactics.)[56]

I read another book about Lincoln that had this story in it, and a lot of junk was added to try to make it more interesting that was not true.

I was sure that this story would be interesting to some of my grandchildren and great-grandchildren, to know that their grandmother's grandfather had wrestled with Lincoln.[57]

It was during this time, when Lincoln was working on this flatboat, that he saw them auctioning off slaves on a raised platform, and he swore that if he ever had a chance to *hit* this slave trade, he would *hit it hard*, and he *did*.[58]

---

56. Jack Armstrong and his wife, Hannah, were longtime devotees of Abraham Lincoln. Lincoln's famous almanac trial came about in defending their first son, William "Duff" Armstrong, for allegedly murdering James Preston Metzger in 1857. Poet and biographer, Edgar Lee Masters, wrote at length on the Armstrong family of Clary's Grove, Illinois, in his book, *The Sangamon*. According to Masters, Jack Armstrong's son, John, reportedly said, "Now you see my pap, Jack Armstrong, was a powerful man in the arms, and the truth is Linkern never throwed him. It was a tie, and I don't give a damn what anyone says or any history book. It was a tie. My mother [Hannah] told me about it a hundred times before she died." See Edgar Lee Masters, *The Sangamon*, The Rivers of America (New York: Farrar & Rinehart, 1942), 105.

57. While this story makes for a good family legend, Effie's grandfather, John Armstrong (1803–1885) should not be confused with Jack Armstrong (d. 1854) of Clary's Grove, Illinois. The most authoritative treatment of this wrestling match is Douglas S. Wilson, "Wrestling with the Evidence," chap. 1 in *Honor's Voice: The Transformation of Abraham Lincoln* (New York: Alfred A. Knopf, 1998), 19–51. See also Albert Beveridge, *Abraham Lincoln, 1809–1858*, 2 vols. (New York: Houghton Mifflin, 1928), 1:110–13, and Benjamin P. Thomas, *Lincoln's New Salem* (Springfield: The Abraham Lincoln Association, 1934), 44–46.

  These kinds of stories are often transmitted orally and persist in multiple versions. The phenomenon of family oriented stories is discussed in Mody C. Boatright, "The Family Saga as a Form of Folklore," in Mody Boatright, et al., *The Family Saga and Other Phases of American Folklore* (Urbana: University of Illionois Press, 1958), 1–19.

58. Effie is referring to an incident related by William Herndon, Abraham Lincoln's law partner and biographer. According to Herndon, "a vigorous and comely mulatto" girl was receiving a thorough examination at a slave auction in New Orleans. "They pinched her flesh and made her trot up and down the room like a horse, to show how she moved, and in order, as the auctioneer said, that 'bidders might satisfy themselves' whether the article they were offering to buy was sound or not. The whole thing was so revolting that Lincoln moved away from the scene with a deep feeling of inconquerable hate. Bidding his company follow him he said, 'By God boys, let's get away from this. If ever I get a chance to hit that thing [meaning slavery], I'll hit it hard.'" See William H. Herndon and Jesse W. Weik, *Herndon's Life of Lincoln*, edited by Paul M. Angle (Cleveland: Fine Editions Press, 1949), 64.

The Armstrongs were good people, and it was always a source of great satisfaction to me to know that they were noted for being kind to their negro slaves. I am thankful that I can remember seeing one of the Armstrong slaves, Old Gloss, a barber, a tall intelligent looking man with white hair. We were going to grandma Marquess' and papa teased our mother, and said he guessed she would want to stop in Crofton and see her kinfolk (an old slave). We stopped, and I remember the old negro crying when he saw mama, and he called her "Miss John Susan." She asked him about others of the Armstrong slaves that were still living at that time, and he said that Cindy was living down towards Empire. Mammy's mother died when she was three months old, and I guess there was quite a close bond of friendship and love between her and the negroes who took care of her, and did most of her bringing up after the death of her mother.

This trip to grandma Marquess' must have been when I was real small. I can't remember of ever seeing Gloss again, but I remember many other trips to grandma's, they were the mileposts in my young life. It was talked of for days before the happy time arrived. All our clothes were washed, starched, and ironed, and packed in a little yellow trunk. The work must be all caught up with. The fishing tackle inspected to see that it was in trim. A lunch, which was an important part of it all, was made ready. Mammy made luscious layer cakes, with the layers thinner than we have them now, and applesauce or coconut between the layers flavored with nutmeg and spice. There was usually boiled ham, or fried chicken. One thing sure, we always had plenty to eat, probably too much of the heavy greasy type.

If we had not been of the foraging sort, who was always scraping the woods for oak balls in early spring, the succulent stems of the hickory leaves that were peeled and eaten, the tender sprouts of the young sassafras, wild grapes, nuts, haws, huckleberries, etc., we probably would not have fared as well as we did.

If the trip was in the springtime, we would stop in certain old fields, after we reached the top of the Jane Barnes hill, and hunt for wild strawberries that were hidden in the saw briars and broom sage. They were small, but as sweet as sugar.

The short stop at Crofton was always exciting to me, as our trips to town were few and far between. It had to be a special occasion, for we children to all lumber the ten miles to the county seat in the back of a bumpy old two horse wagon.

The thought of getting to go in the stores a few minutes was a real thrill. We usually bought some candy, and I remember one time when Sadie and I bought a fan each, the kind that folds and opens out in little accordion pleats. But *nothing* could equal the joy of just getting to

Effie's grandma Martha Pettypool Marquess (wife of
Robert Elliot Marquess) at age 80. Courtesy of Itha
Carmack.

grandma's. I think our love for each other must have been a little unusual.
It doesn't seem to me that people love each other now as we did then.

When we neared grandma's place, if grandma saw us in time, she
always ran to meet us. She was a thin little woman, with white hair, but as
active as a cricket, even after she was real old.

When we came in sight of the house papa would be looking, to see
if he could see any of them; and I remember one time the first glimpse we
got of any of them, grandma and some of the grandchildren were out in
the garden, and grandma was chasing a butterfly. We had heard that she
was not feeling well, and we all had a laugh. We had expected to find her
in bed, and we had caught her chasing butterflies.

Effie's uncle Lycurgus "Curg" Marquess. Courtesy of
Itha Carmack

Pappy was her oldest child, and as she was left a widow, with several
small children to support, they were drawn very close together. He would
recall how he used to have to hold the candle for her in the evening so
she could see to weave. He would grow sleepy and drop the candle, and
she would say, "Poor Bozie, you're so sleepy, aren't you?"

She always took great delight in showing us all they had done since
we were there last. The blankets she had woven from the best parts of
the worn out wool socks and stockings. Her dried ginseng and angelico,
and her herb and wildflower garden. The flowers on either side of the
walk. The new quilts, the chickens, and there was *always* an exchange of
seeds and plants and quilt patterns, and everyone talked at the same
time.

In the evening there was always music. Papa and Uncle Curg both played the fiddle, and all the girls played the guitar, and Aunt Emma, especially, had a very sweet voice.[59] Her hobby was *making* guitars and violins. We exchanged songs as well as flower seeds, quilt patterns, etc. How we *did* enjoy that and Aunt Emma's and Aunt May's singing.[60]

If it was fishing season, we would all go to Pond river, camp out, fish, take the music and sing.

When the time came for us to go home, we began to dread the thought of saying goodbye, knowing it would be at least a year before we would see them all again.

Once Uncle Curg saddled his horse and rode part of the way to Crofton with us. When he turned to go back I can remember how very sad I felt. Sadie sang:

Look down that lane, that lonesome lane,
Hang down your head and cry,
Last words I heard my true love say
Was goodbye, my darling, goodbye.

That was the tap that opened the fountain and we all blubbered freely.

One glorious winter Uncle Curg built a new house for Uncle Jim Marquess, his half brother, and he slept at our place. He brought his guitar, and oh, how we did enjoy him. He was a good singer, could read notes as easily as most people read English.[61]

We had a motley bunch of old knives and forks, no two alike, and he named them. He said that they all had so much personality that they needed names, and every name he gave them suited them exactly. There was Old Case, and Old Butch, and Stump, and Sideswipe, and Fro. There were funny stories and lots of laughter.

Pappy and Uncle Curg would tell of things that happened when they were younger, when they lived in Trigg County, till [they moved to?] Wallonia, and the names of people they associated with seemed like old friends to me. (Dr. Waller, Drew Standard)

When Mammy and Pappy were first married they moved into a house that a man by the name of Fay Tally had been killed in.

---

59. Lycurgus Marquess (1852–1936) and Georgia Emma Marquess (1868–1958).

60. Myrtle Mayes Marquess (1874–1964).

61. Probably James "Jim" Washington Marquess (1843–1928). In contrast to Uncle Jim, Effie and most of the other musicians she mentions apparently played mostly by ear. When Effie talks about "collecting songs" and writing them down, she apparently means the texts of the songs only; they relied on their memories for the tunes.

Our father and Uncle Curg were playing for the balls at the summer resort at Cerulean Springs, near Willows.[62] Aunt Sue was staying with mother, and one evening, after Papa and Uncle Curg had gone, mother heard someone fumbling at the side door.[63]

There was a latch fastener, with a leather string through a hole in the door, and when someone wanted in they could pull the latch string, and it released the fastener, and they could then open the door.

When mother was left alone she pulled the latch string in so no one could open the door. When she heard the fumbling she thought either Papa or Uncle Curg had forgotten something, and had come back for it, so, as she had the baby on her lap she said, "Just put your hand through that opening and you can raise the latch."

Whoever it was, when he heard other voices, and found that mother was not alone, he ran, and they could hear his feet on the frozen ground till the sound grew dim.

Another time, while they were living at this place, Uncle Curg had to come back for something they had forgotten. He knocked on the door and mother said, "Who's there?" In a hollow voice Uncle Curg said, "Fay Tally."

Mother said, "Sue, hand me that shotgun there in the corner." Immediately Uncle Curg decided to make himself known. The joke was on him. Mama said that she really should have peppered him with a little buckshot. It was bad enough to have to stay alone every night without having the liver scared out of her, to boot.

Little Bud Marquess,[64] son of John Marquess, of Pee Dee, Kentucky, had got into a dispute with Fay Tally over a dance that each claimed he had engaged with the same girl (Alice Proctor—her mother was Sarah Pettypool before she married).[65]

The dispute ended in a vicious fight, and Fay Tally was killed. Later, grandma Marquess' youngest brother, William (Uncle Billy) married the girl the fight was over.

When the officers came to arrest little Bud he had skipped out, and they arrested his brother. He told them that he was not little Bud, but

---

62. Cerulean Springs, some thirty miles from the Hopkinsville area, would have been too far away for a daily commute by horse or buggy. The Cerulean Hotel, near the famous blue ("cerulean") springs for which the town was named, is no longer standing. The hotel was undoubtedly the site of these dances.

63. Aunt Sue was Tabitha Sue Marquess (1850–1884).

64. According to Mary Ann Willis of Princeton, Kentucky, this person was actually Oliver Marquess (b. 1851), son of James Porter Marquess (b. 1830) and Melinda Ryan Marquess, widow of Thomas Marquess.

65. Alice Proctor and Sarah Pettypool could not be identified.

Effie Carmack's "Aunt Sue," Tabitha Sue Marquess,
wife of Edward Pettypool and her son Samuel. Courtesy
of Itha Carmack.

they didn't believe him, and by the time they learned the truth, little Bud
was far away, in the west, and was never found.[66]

---

66.  The accounts of the killing of Fay Talley are sketchy. However, according to Mary Ann
     Willis,
          My grandmother Permilia Ann Boaz Childress and Frank Marquess and
          his entire family were very close due to age and they had the same grand-

These Marquesses were distantly related to us, but we have never found just how. Aunt Emma said that they used to go to Todd County to visit a William Kidd Marquess, a relative, father of Pee Dee Dolan, who was born in one of the cabins at old Fort Nashboro, where Nashville is now.

The first Fort was built by a Marquess in very early days, when there was not another white settlement anywhere near.[67]

A group of men came by from the old Wautauga settlement of East Tennessee, among them a Capt. [Francis] Nash, who married a Marquess girl, and rebuilt the Fort and called it Nashboro.[68]

This William Kidd Marquess, of Todd County, Kentucky, married Carlotty Armstrong, and they had a large family.[69]

Capt. Nash, and his son-in-law, _____ Robinson, were on their way into Kentucky for supplies and were both killed by Indians near where Guthrie, Kentucky is now.

---

mother. My mother d. age 101 yrs. old, know [*sic*] all about the killing of Fay Talley. It was Oliver b. 8 Dec. 1851 d. unknown. He shot and killed Fay Tally at a place called Red Hill, Caldwell Co. Ky. now near the location of Boaz Cemetwry [*sic*]. After the killing he went to my Grandmother's house and told her goodby—He did go West and joined an Indian Tribe. Mother could not remember when he came back to see his Mother but my grandmother received word that he was back and my Mother remembers Mamaw leaving her home about nine P.M. and returning about 5 AM the next morning. It took from 3–4 hours on horseback to get to Pee Dee from Mamaw's house. Mamaw told her children that Oliver had married an Indian girl and that he had brought her home, said she was very pretty and had long braids and they were below her waist. hair very black in color-her dress was long and looked like it was made from some kind of animal skin. (Mary Ann Willis to Noel Carmack, April 16, 1998)

    The reason Oliver killed Fay Talley was over a pretty girl that ditched Oliver (so my Mother said). Oliver took off joined and Indian Tribe therefore since Malinda [Ryan Marquess] was my grandmother's—grandmother was the reason she sent John Frank and my grandmother word when Oliver brought his wife home. (Mary Ann Willis to Noel Carmack, July 12, 1998)

67. See E. C. Lewis, "James Robertson, Nashville's Founder," *American Historical Magazine* 8 (1903): 285–94.

68. It has been confirmed that William Kidd Marquess (1744–1812) was, indeed, born at Nashboro in 1804. Records have yet to be found that Captain Nash married a Marquess. It is believed that he married a Moore (John Wesley Marquess to Noel Carmack, March 10, 1998). For more on the founding of Nashville, see Thomas Perkins Abernethy, *From Frontier to Plantation in Tennessee: A Study in Frontier Democracy* (Chapel Hill: University of North Carolina Press, 1932), 26–32, 194–210.

69. William Kidd Marquess (1804–1890) was grandson of the above named William Kidd (1744–1812). He was married to Charlotte "Lottie" Armstrong (1808–1859). They had eleven children: Sarah Ann Margaret (b. 1828); James Porter (b. 1830); Jacob Holland (b. 1831); (male unknown) died or left home before 1850; Matthew (b. 1834); John Curry (b. 1836); Elizabeth (b. 1842); Mary (b. 1845); Jasper Newton (b. 1849); Joseph R. (b. 1852); and (unknown).

I've tried in vain to find how we are related, so far I have failed. Aunt Emma said that they called William Kidd "Uncle Billy," but that they knew he was not really their Uncle, but a relative.

He and his wife are buried near Elton, and a relative went there and copied the inscription from their gravestones, and it confirmed what old Mr. Marquess, of Princeton, told Edna, - b. 1804 in a cabin of old Fort Nashboro.

Pee Dee, Kentucky, where John and James Marquess lived was not far south of Hopkinsville.[70]

Long years later, after we moved to Arizona, my brother, John, had a store in Joseph City, Arizona, and his name was out in front on a sign board. Another John Marquess (of Phoenix, grandson of our grandfather's oldest brother, Thomas) saw the name and came to our place, next to John's.

Sadie was there, and we had a long interesting visit with him, and found how we were related, and it resulted in several visits, and in a whole new line of Marquess relatives for my Marquess family record.

He had been a contractor, and one time, when he was working in what was to be the basement of a building, a man above him said, "How about a job?"

This distant cousin, John, said that when he looked up at him he knew the moment he saw him that it was little Bud Marquess.

He gave him a job, and they roomed together. There was never any confession of his real name, or where he was from, but he said that they learned to love one another.

Another thing that I think of now is about my mother and the burning roof. On March 1, 1883, when my brother, John Robert (Johnnie Bob), was three days old, and every one had gone away and left my mother and the little ones there alone for a little while, she kept hearing a crackling that sounded like fire. She suddenly realized that the roof next to the chimney was on fire.

She got up, ran to the barn and carried a big old heavy ladder, took the axe from the wood pile, and climbed up on the roof and cut the burning boards out, and succeeded in putting the fire out completely. She knew that everything they possessed depended on it, and she risked her life to put that fire out. She was thankful that she succeeded, and said that there was no bad after effects from it.

She also said that when it was absolutely necessary to do a tremendous job of that kind, that she firmly believed the Lord would protect you

---

70.  Pee Dee is located approximately 14 miles southwest of Hopkinsville. Effie is probably referring to James Porter Marquess (b. 1830) and John Curry Marquess (1836–1916), both of Pee Dee.

in doing it, but if it was *not* necessary, you had better be careful, "We have no promise of protection."

Our mother was a strong, practical woman, that didn't shrink from tackling anything when it was necessary. She was also a woman of sound judgment, and would not be found guilty of doing a rash thoughtless thing when it was not absolutely necessary.

She had, of course, first took her three day old baby, wrapped in a blanket, and laid him safely away from the burning roof, then had the other little ones watch by him till she had the fire all extinguished.

This is one of the family stories that has lived, and has been handed down. I am thankful to be the child of such a brave, practical, courageous mother.

When we would go to grandma's, or they came to our place, we didn't do much sleeping; of course there were never beds enough for all, so feather beds were made down on the floor, and oh! the fun we kids would have rolling and tumbling on them.

Once, when we went to grandma's, there had been a sawmill on the creek, and we children were having a glorious time playing in the sawdust, when suddenly we heard frantic yelps from the house, "Get out of that sawdust this minute." We wondered if there were rattlesnakes or something worse in it. When Mammy and Grandma came out, meeting us with an armful each of tobacco stems, they informed us that a bunch of hogs had roosted there all winter, and that it was alive with fleas.

They stripped us all naked, and then smoked our clothing with the tobacco stems to chase the fleas out, way down at the back of the garden.

A bunch of fleas can make life miserable for everyone in a house, and the lumps that come where they bite keep burning and itching for days, and sometimes weeks.

I remember once when Kate Miller, Maud Morris and I were playing in the gullies.[71] I happened to go up on the bank for something and saw a wagon load of people coming through the big gate up at the big road. With the second look I saw that it was Uncle Curg driving. I was so excited that I didn't go on the path to get to the house, but plowed right through a briar thicket and stuck a big briar in the knuckle of the third finger of my right hand. It broke off in the muscle, and is still there.

One of the horses they had to the wagon was a beautiful bay mare named Dilsie. Uncle Bob was with them with his new wife that we had not seen, and a tiny baby, not a month old. It was too long a trip for such a lit-

---

71. Kate Miller was the daughter of Mary and Juatt Ivison Miller. Maude Morris (1886–1915).

tle one, and she cried all night. They walked the floor with her, made catnip tea and administered all the home remedies, but no one slept very
much. The jolting of the wagon had probably made her sore and miserable. Poor Aunt Bertha, she vowed she would not take her on another
trip till she was old enough to walk alone. That baby girl has grandchildren now.[72]

Uncle Curg had married also. A sweet, quiet girl named Ada White,
and they had a little girl named Lily, a little round faced miss with dark
hair and eyes, very pretty and sweet.[73] She was just learning to talk, was
the center of attraction, and kept things lively.

There is a very dim memory of one of the grandmothers' daughters, Aunt Matilda, who was left a widow with three children: Alva Lee,
William Robert (called Willy Bob), and Sam.[74] They lived with us for a
while after her husband died, when I was very small. I remember that
Sam would sing *awful* old Negro spirituals.

There was another Aunt, on my mother's side, Aunt Ann Armstrong
Martin. She was my mother's half sister, and was also left a widow with two
children; cousin Mary Susan, and cousin Jack.[75] Aunt Ann used to stay at
our place quite a lot when I was small.

Aunt Ann was Uncle Lawrence's own sister, but they were not alike
in any way. I have often wondered what made the big difference in them.
Uncle Lawrence used *perfect* language. He had a western brogue, instead
of southern, he said crick instead of creek, and he never left his g's off, as
most southerners do. He had a good education, and was especially interested in astronomy. He always knew just what star would be the evening
and morning stars, and just when they would change. He knew all the
constellations, and kept up to the minute with all the eclipses, etc.

Aunt Ann was just the opposite. Her grandchildren used to tease
her and say, "I'll bet you can't guess what granny did this morning, she
'*sot* a *hin in a barl.*'" She lived with cousin Mary after she married, and just
worshipped her children. She had a lot of funny old things she would
sing to them as she trotted them on her knee, like: "Jing ety bung—Jing
ety bung." She just about raised cousin Mary's family, especially Otho,
who was sick a lot.[76] I know now that he had adenoids. Aunt Ann watched
him like a hawk, to keep him from getting his feet wet, or anything that

---

72. Robert E. Marquess (1871–1956) and his wife, Bertha Barnett Marquess (b. 1875).

73. Ada White Marquess (b. 1856) was the wife of Lycurgus Marquess.

74. Matilda Jane Marquess (1858–1941).

75. Mary Susan Martin (1858–1940).

76. Otho Fuller (b. 1883) was the son of Mary Susan Martin (1858–1940) and Nathan
    Boone Fuller (1854–1942).

might make him *snore*. She was always warning him, if we played out when it was the least bit cold or damp, "You'll snore for *something* tonight, young man." But she was as good as gold, and we all loved her, and were always glad when she came. She was especially fond of egg bread (made of cornmeal), butter, and strong coffee, and she took a *round* of some kind of purgative regularly, usually epsom salts.

I must have been about three years old when they moved to one of the old Dr. Wood houses.[77] Bert was still wearing dresses then, boys wore dresses much longer then than they do now. I had a nice little red rocking chair at that time, and when we went to cousin Mary's they had made Bert a rocker by removing the front round of an old homemade chair, and put a low seat in the next lower set of rounds, leaving the side pieces as arms. I fell in love with that chair, and wanted it for mine *so* much that I could think of nothing else, so we traded, and both of us were better satisfied. They all thought that I was very foolish to trade my new red rocker for the old homemade one, but I still liked the comfort of the low split bottomed chair, better than the high narrow seated, hard bottomed rocker, even if it *was* painted red.

About this time Papa and the boys tore an old house down somewhere. An old log house with a floor that had cracks in it, through which the children had dropped things. I'll *never* forget how excited I was over the collection of things they brought home that they had found under that old floor; marbles of all sizes, buttons, pennies, china doll heads, arms and legs, tiny toy cups and saucers.

We didn't have the stacks of toys laying around in the way in those days as children do now, and we really appreciated what we did have.

I had no girl playmates when I was a small child. There were three sets of cousins, in which all of the children were boys. Cousin Mary Susan Fuller's, just mentioned. Uncle Jim Marquess' family. Cousin Narcissy Armstrong Cook's family,[78] who lived on the farm adjoining ours, on the west. Clifton and Ben were the ones nearest my age.[79]

Where we only visited the others on rare occasions, the Cook cousins were always near. When school started we walked the mile and a half there and back together, throughout the term of five or six months.

Clifton was one year younger than I was, but he was unusually large for his age. As an example, when he was 10, and I was 11 (our birthdays came at the same time), I weighed 60 lbs. and he weighed 160 lbs. Cousin

---

77.   This probably refers to Dr. Ben S. Wood (b. 1835).

78.   Narcis E. Armstrong Cook (b. 1848) was the wife of Isaac Cook.

79.   Clifton P. Cook (1885–1910). His brother Ben could not be identified.

Narcissy gave us a birthday dinner and weighed us. The great difference in our weight didn't spoil our friendship in the least.

We didn't visit so very often, as we children were not allowed to do very much visiting without our mothers being with us, but we made us a secret post office that was a great pleasure to us, and kept things from getting monotonous. We dug a little cellar, sank an old wooden box with a door cut in the side, made a shutter for it, and covered it over with dirt packed down so the rain could not find an entrance. It was right by the fence that separated their farm from ours. This fence was at the top of the hill just west of the spring where I went for water every day, and it only took a few minutes to run up to the post office to leave a note and to see if there was one for me.

We would exchange thumb cards (they were cards we used to protect our school books from our dirty thumbs), soda cards, and anything we might have that we thought the others would like to use for a day or two. Hickory whistles and pocket knives were two popular articles; popguns and squirtguns were on the list also. Pencils and chalk were passed back and forth, and once or twice we left candy, but the ants found it, so that was out. Dancers made of half a spool, with a sharp spindle in the hole of the spool, was a favorite.

There was a chinquepin acorn tree on their place.[80] The acorns were sweet as sugar, and Clifton would leave little sacks of them for me in the fall, and gooseberries in the spring.

When school started in July, the Cook boys would "*hee hoo*" as quick as they would get to the west corner of our field, and by the time they had gotten to the east corner where the cutoff path crossed the fence we were usually there to go with them.

I still remember every little crook and turn of that road to school. I can remember where every wild grape vine grew, the crabapple tree, the wild plum tree, near the old Hubbard Steward house, across the branch at the foot of the hill just back of cousin P. Armstrong's, where they said the deer used to come to lick salt.[81] I think it was at this salt lick that grandpa Armstrong wounded a big buck, and then had quite a fight with it.

The spring, that supplied the school with water, was in the woods, northwest of the Hubbard house. It was in a cool shady wood, with the friendliest little atmosphere about it. I have lately learned that it was the

---

80. The chinquapin tree (*Castanea purnila,* W.) sometimes attains a height of thirty feet. The fruit is edible, much like the chestnut.

81. Hubbard Stewart (b. 1855). Benjamin Phillip "P." Armstrong (1856–1911).

spring near the house of great aunt Peggy Armstrong Lindley (grandpa Armstrong's sister, who married Jonathon (Jot) Lindley).[82] Their house stood at the upper end of the clearing just back of the Hubbard house. The remains of the old chimney is still there, I guess.

That was the childhood home of cousin Parthenia Lindley Ferrell (who married Alec Ferrell), and cousin Jane Lindley Brasher (who married Larkin T. Brasher, the lawyer—parents of David, Mollie, Carrie, and Minnie, etc.).[83] I think this was on land that great grandfather Ben Armstrong once owned, and divided out among his children, but at that time I knew nothing of it.

Clifton and Ben and I were of the fourth generation from great grandfather Ben.

The fields, where the slaves had worked, were worn so thin they would not produce crops any longer, and were lying idle. Many old homes, where the second and third generations had flourished, were torn down, but a few, our old home included, was still in use.

Clifton's mother, Narcissy, was a granddaughter of the emigrant Ben, and they lived at his old home place, though the original home, the three story log mansion, with the giant fireplaces, that were so famous, was burned before my time. Some of the log cabins, that were the slaves quarters, were still standing, and part of them were used for stables for the cows and horses.

Cousin Ike, Clifton's father, was one of the most prosperous farmers in the community.[84] He had the finest horses, and the best hereford cattle around, and always had money to lend. He had fought in the Civil War, and I think he drew a pension. He drank quite a bit, but the family didn't seem to mind it much. I thought it was terrible, and asked Clifton once if he didn't hate for his father to come home drunk. He said no, he didn't mind, that he was pleasant when he was drunk, and would tell them interesting things that happened during the war, that he wouldn't tell when he was sober.

The old gooseberry bushes, raspberry vines, pie plant, and walnut trees, and the well of cold water on their old place had all survived from pioneer days. Greatgrandpa Ben, and his good wife, Jane (Aunt Helen said they called her Aunt Jean, she was French), had planted them when

---

82.  Margaret "Peggy" Armstrong Lindley (b. ca. 1806) and Jonathan "Jot" Lindley (1807–1884).

83.  Parthenia Lindley Ferrell (1782–1824). Larkin T. Brasher (1840–1912) married Jane Lindley (b. 1846) on December 3, 1864. Their children were: David Romelus (b. 1866), Vic. (dates unknown), Mollie (b. 1868), Carrie (b. 1874), and Minnie Isabel (b. 1876), Omie (dates unknown), and Lark (dates unknown).

84.  Isaac Cook (b. 1841) according to the 1880 census.

their family was young. We often went up on the hill, west of the house, to the graveyard, where these two were buried. Someone had cut giant slabs of rock, and had made a kind of vault for each of their graves. They were buried in a pretty place. The ground was smooth and mossy, with giant oak trees for shade, and lots of wild flowers bloomed there every spring.[85]

They must have been quite an enterprising couple, judging from the things they have told me of them. He burned all the bricks for two giant chimneys himself, he and the slaves. Cousin Filmore Smith, one of Ben's grandchildren, said there was brick enough in either chimney to have built a small brick house.[86] There were fireplaces in each of the three stories, and the ones in the big rooms on the ground floor were wide enough to hold logs six or seven feet long. He owned many slaves, and was noted for being kind to them. Some of his neighbors, who beat their slaves, could never figure why Armstrong could get more work out of his slaves than they could from theirs. Even when he went to town they doubled their efforts just to surprise him when he got home.

I have heard glowing tales of the good times at Thanksgiving and Christmas time, when all of the children and grandchildren on the adjoining farms (that had been given to them from the original tract) were all invited home for dinner. There was a table that reached the entire length of the big old combined dining room and kitchen. Cousin Fil said that there was a pantry as big as a corncrib, where Negro Lize, the cook, stored the good things she prepared for these occasions; boiled hams, salt rising bread,[87] stuffed hens, cornbread, pumpkin pies, puddings, and all kinds of good things.

Cousin Elijah Armstrong,[88] one of the grandchildren who still lives in Hopkinsville, and has served his county seat in many ways (Chief of Police, City Commissioner, and other capacities) was left motherless when a tiny baby, and the Negro mammy, who raised him, let him have milk from one breast, and left her own little picaninny with one. He said that had caused more fights in his life than any other one thing. The boys would tease him, and tell him he was part nigger, because he was raised on nigger milk.

All of this happened at the place where Clifton and Ben lived. They had four older brothers; Ed, Bob, Charlie, and Jim; all of them were

---

85. The Armstrong graveyard, to which Effie refers here, is located: "From Hopkinsville at intersection of 68E and 91 NW go 5 miles turn right, go 2.2 miles turn right and go 1 mile, the cemetary is on the left by the barn." See Meador, *Cemetery Records, Northern Section of Christian County, Kentucky*, 18.

86. J. Filmore Smith (1854–1942).

87. Bread leavened by means of a fermented mixture of milk, salt, flour, sugar, and soda.

88. See above, note 46.

unusually big. Cousin Narcissa was tall, and weighed between three and four hundred pounds. I think Clifton reached the five hundred pound mark before his death, which was caused from taking medicine to make him reduce.

He had numerous offers by circus men, but was not inclined that way. They were all good scholars. Ben became County School Superintendent. Cousin Bob was one of the best teachers I ever had, and he later was our representative in the Legislature.

I remember an incident that happened when he was teaching; it was in the old log school house, with the long plank benches without any backs, and one big desk up in front. The cracks between the logs were chinked and daubed, with boards nailed over the chinking inside. One day a child, who was sitting next to the wall, heard a slight movement behind the board, about even with her head. Through a crack she could see a monstrous snake moving along. She let out a war whoop, and for a while there was wild disorder, till cousin Bob found the stove poker, pulled a board off, and then plunked down on the floor a writhing mass of chicken snake about six feet long. After it was dead he held it up by its tail with his hand out about level with his head, and its other end touched the ground, and he was a very tall man.

Another thing that happened while he was teaching; we were having a game of baseball, the girls against the boys. I was on first base, and someone at the bat knocked a fly. A boy caught it and threw it to me, but threw it too high. I jumped up to catch it just as the runner scooted into the base, knocking my feet from under me. I hit my mouth on a rock, knocking an eye tooth through my upper lip, and knocking me unconscious. When I came to cousin Bob had me laying across his lap, and he was washing the blood away with his handkerchief, and saying, "Now they've just killed my poor little girl." There's a hard lump in my lip yet, after fifty years.

Other games we played were: bull pen, fox and hounds (Sadie, Elmo, and Bunkie Owen were the champion runners), bear, in which we made a circle in the dust with a stick, all of us but one, who was the bear, got in the circle, and the bear on the outside tried to touch us without getting inside the line. A very simple game, but we managed to get a lot out of it. It was a wild, pushy, pully, scramble to all of us to keep on the *other* side of the circle from the bear, who dashed madly around on the outside.[89]

---

89. In the game of Fox and Hounds, one child plays Fox and the rest play the Hounds. The Fox leaves a trail of paper or broken twigs in the woods long enough for the Hounds to know which direction he is going. Once sighted, the fox must return to the den without getting caught. For more details, see "Fox and Hounds," in *The Foxfire Book of Appalachian Toys & Games*, edited by Linda Garland Pace and Hilton Smith (Chapel Hill: University of North Carolina Press, 1993), 15. These games were common among young school children of western Kentucky. See Bernard Bolton, "Folk

"Elija Armstrong, son of 'Uncle Lige' who was brother
of my grandfather Johnnie Armstrong." He was, for a
time, chief of police in Hopkinsville, Kentucky.
Courtesy of Itha Carmack.

Another thing that kept we girls busy at recess periods, especially
before it turned cold, was our playhouses. Some were on the hill above
the school house, and others in the bed of the dry stream that was just
south of the school. In spring, during the rainy season, it was a good sized

Games from Western Kentucky," *Kentucky Folklore Record* 2 (1956): 123–31, and Wilson
Gordon, Sr., "Traditional Aspects of the One-Roomed School-III: Playtime," *Kentucky
Folklore Record* 13 (1967): 62–67.

"Old East School House and Pupils," Larkin, Kentucky, ca. 1897. Back row, left to right: Allan Williams, John Robert Marquess, Marion Walker, Lawson Hamby, Ellis Walker, Evert Holt, Curtis Holt, (unidentified). Second row, left to right: Serena Smith, Ozie Holt, Effie Marquess, Maude Morris, Etta Marquess, Jennie Bell Durham, Eva Holt, Lily Owen, Laura Marquess, Robert Cook (teacher), Alice Hamby, Sadie Marquess, Lalie Grenshaw, (unidentified). Front row, left to right: ____ Underwood, (unidentified), Worthy Smith, (unidentified), Kate Miller, Essie Cook, Nora Renshaw, (unidentified), (unidentified), (unidentified), Inez Armstrong, (unidentified), (unidentified), Ben Cook, (unidentified), Carlos Renshaw. Photo Courtesy of Itha Carmack.

stream, but it seldom rained during the autumn months and it was a clean swept stream bed, with trees on either side.

On the hillside we swept clean paths through the carpet of leaves, put rocks on either side, and made charming roads from one playhouse to another. We made leaf hats with streamers that reached to our heels, and trimmed them with lots of flowers. We made dressers and chairs, of rocks with moss on them.

Then sometimes we had climbing streaks, and for weeks we did nothing but climb trees. We would bend the slim hickories out, and as they were real springy, we would hold to the top and jump. With a good one we could jump ten feet in the air. It was lots of fun, only sometimes we would catch the top and swing out, but it wouldn't bend close enough to the ground for us to turn loose; then what a strain on muscles and nerves, to somehow manage to get back up, to climb down again, the way we went up. Our mother was bitterly opposed to climbing, as we were always tearing our clothes. But it was hard to resist.

There was a long log in the school yard, that we sat on while we ate our lunch. Our school lunch usually was biscuit and bacon or ham sandwiches, with a glass of molasses; or blackberry jam and butter, a bottle of milk each, with gingerbread, or occasionally halfmoon fried pies for dessert. Apples or peaches were put in to eat at recess. The violent exercise gave us good appetites, making the plain food taste good.

We tried to manage to go to the spring for water during "books," so we would have the recess periods to play.[90] Two of us usually went. In the old fields, that we had to go through before we reached the woods the spring was in, there were tiny "catbells" growing in the grass. They were seedpods not quite an inch long, very dry, with seeds that rattled unusually loud. We would leave the path, wade out through the grass and weeds, and hunt catbells.

There were "last rose of summer" blooming in that old field, too. A sturdy plant, with a bunch of pretty pink flowers in an oblong cluster. They seemed to all blossom at the same time, and they came when most other flowers were gone. Just they and the golden rods were usually left.

I can shut my eyes now and just smell the nutty flavor the wind had in its breath, when it came across those old fields. Fields where my ancestors had cleared the land of its virgin timber; plowed, planted, toiled and harvested. Then [they], like the owners, were worn out, and were lying idle, dreaming. *Now*, (1944), those old fields and hillsides have all been reclaimed, the soil built up, and good crops are being raised on them once more. A highway has also been built.

There were myriads of songbirds along this way to school, and we used to try to mimic them, and put into English what they were saying.[91]

Lawrence and Worthy Smith (other great grand-children of Ben Armstrong), went a part of the way with us. Worthy didn't like school, so she thought one specie of bird was always suggesting, "Quit Worthy, Quit Worthy," and that another said, "I wouldn't go Worthy, I wouldn't go." One clearly said, "Pharmaceti, Pharmaceeta, Pharmaceeta." Another called, "Dick Taylor." Still another one said, "Peetab, Peetab, Peetab."

The red bird, with his top-knot, would get in the very top of a tree, and sing in the rain. Two clear notes like we whistle to the dogs, followed by three short ones, "Whuet, Whuet, tew, tew, tew." There is no way of mimicking the song of the blue bird or purple martin, the friendly birds that came in early spring, and liked to build in the bird houses we put up for them.

---

90. See Gordon, "Traditional Aspects," 62.
91. In her senior years, Effie apparently intended to record these bird mimics for her posterity. See appendix two.

The martin was the ardent love maker. He could talk in the sweetest language to his modest little mate. How happy we were when the first ones came to the bird boxes in the spring.

There was a season in spring of forced idleness, when it rained for weeks at a time. The men were anxious to be plowing, and mammy was in a hurry to get something planted in the garden, but nothing could be done while it rained. It was the time of year when it was almost warm enough to not need a fire, and a little too chilly and damp to be without one.

I can remember wrapping mammy's big old soft woolen shawl around me and sitting in the door while it rained. Watching the water dimple and splash, as it dripped from the eaves into the little ditch that the years of rain had made. There was ground ivy that grew right against the house, and covered the rocks that were the foundation.

I must have been somewhat of a dreamer. I can remember sitting in the dusk, on the stair steps, where they turned to go upstairs. There was a door, to shut out the heat, and the cold, from the upstairs rooms. I would close the door, and sit there alone, and just think and wonder about things. I remember thinking of the different names of Deity, and wondering just how many there really were. There was Lord, and God, and Jehovah, and Christ, and Jesus. It was a puzzle to me, but I was not brave enough to ask anyone about it.

I can dimly remember going with Mammy to see Grandpa Armstrong (I guess it was) when he was sick. It was muddy, and she carried me to the door and sat me up in the door while she cleaned her shoes. Grandpa was on a bed to the right of the door, and the window was darkened. I was afraid, and bawled till she got her shoes cleaned and took me.

Aunt Helen Gilliland Marquess, daughter of great aunt Eliza Jane Armstrong Gilliland,[92] said that greatgrandma Jane had a child born when she was sixty years old. She said that she knew it to be the truth. She remembered hearing a relative say that she went to see her when the baby was first born, and grandma Jane said, "Isn't this *something?* Me laying here with a new baby, and my hair as white as snow."

*But,* I have never been able to find the name of the child, or real proof that it was true. I do wish I could. The census records are not much help until 1850 and after. But Aunt Helen says that she *knows* it was true. If it *is* true, I never knew of anyone else having a child born to them at that age.

---

92. Helen Gilliland Marquess possibly refers to Margaret Helen Marquess (1850–1937), wife of James Washington Marquess (1843–1928). Eliza Jane Armstrong Gilliland (1815–1885) was the wife of John Gilliland (1811–1882).

I have wished that I could have known Grandpa Armstrong. Mammy called him Pap. He was a strong, short man. Shorter than most of his brothers, and *they* called him Runt.[93] His father's nickname was Britt.

I can remember Uncle 'Lige (Elijah) Armstrong, Grandpa's brother (he was tall).[94] He is the only one of them that I can remember seeing. We went there once when I was almost a baby. Mammy helped the womenfolks cook dinner, and I played out in the yard where Uncle 'Lige was sitting in the shade of a tree. He took me on his knees and talked to me. He was a kind, gentle man. Their house was on a hill, east of our place, and we could see it from home. A big, nice, lumber house. There was an old log house, just back of it, that was probably the first old home. There was a distinguishing feature about this old place, or rather two of them. There was a big old apricot tree just back of the house, and a spanish dagger just outside the front fence. They called it a century plant, and we were under the impression that it only bloomed once in a hundred years.[95] I have no idea where they got it, but it and the apricot tree were the only ones I ever saw when I was a small child. There was a Passion Flower vine there too, the only one I had ever seen at that time.

Between our place and Uncle 'Lige's, was our nearest neighbor, Marion Moore, and his wife, Ailsie, and one son, Eddie.[96] They had a dark little log house, settled down among some big old gloomy cedar trees, and there wasn't a sprig of grass in the yard. The house itself had a sort of mysterious charm. There was a front room, on the east wing of the house, with the floor a foot lower than the rest of the house, so that they stepped down into it. She had a deep padded carpet on the floor, and kept the blinds pulled down all the time. I don't know why, as the only window was on the north side, so there would have been no danger of the sun fading the carpet. I was never *in* this room more than half a dozen times in all the years that we lived by them. I recall the musty odor that was always there.

---

93. This John "Runt" Armstrong is Effie's grandfather, John Armstrong, who was believed to have wrestled Lincoln. See pages 60–61.

94. Elijah Armstrong (1811–1888), son of Benjamin and Jane (Brasher) Armstrong, owned about 415 acres in the Hamby Precinct. His wife was Cinderella C. Hamby (1825–1864), daughter of Philip Hamby and Jane Croft. He was the brother of Eliza Gilliland, and John and David Armstrong. See William Henry Perrin, ed., *County of Christian, Kentucky: Historical and Biographical* (Chicago: F. A. Battey Publishing Co, 1884), 557, and Meacham, *History of Christian County*, 436–37.

95. A Mexican fleshy-leaved species of the *Agave* genus (*Agave Virginica*, L.) commonly cultivated in North America. It flowers only once and then dies. The thick leaves of this species contain a juice with laxative properties.

96. Eddie Moore (1879–1927).

One thing that charmed me, above all others (in that house) was a life-sized painting of a young girl, which stood on an easel in one corner of this room. It was the first hand painted portrait I had ever seen. It must have been good work, it certainly charmed me, and when I got a chance I gazed in awe and wonder to think that anyone could make a picture look as much like life as that one did. The details are dim in my mind now, but there was the small waist, and bustle, lace and ruffles, and bangs.

There were lots of mysterious things in that room, but we never dared touch a thing. Just to get to go in there and sit awhile was almost too good to be true.

Once I went with my family to a *musical* in this parlor, as my father was one of the main performers. I think Sadie played the guitar, and Pappy the fiddle. The music charmed the cat, that probably had not heard music before, and they could not keep it out of the room. My father told them to let it alone and see what it would do. It climbed up on the back of his chair, then onto his shoulder, and looked right down at the fiddle while he played, causing a lot of uproarious laughter.

Eddie, their son, was about the age of the older children of our family, with a long face like his mother. A face that was a bright red, and one of the sharpest noses I ever saw. But he was a good kind fellow with plenty of sense, and a good education. He was a good singer, and could read music.

It was at this place that I saw my first Sears, Roebuck Catalog. The first ones that came out cost money. I can't remember how much, fifty cents I think, but anyway we didn't have one until they became free. Eddie's last year's catalog, when they got through with it, was one of my prized possessions.

*Miz* Moore saved her seed catalogs and soda cards for me, too. She always bought the big boxes, that had the big cards in them. They came in series; first animals, then flowers, and last birds. I still have some of the bird pictures, but none of the animals or flowers.

Another thing that charmed me was the glass bowl of an old coal oil lamp. The burner had been broken, and she used it to put buttons in. All kinds of buttons. I would have given most anything to have poured them all out in my lap, and looked at all the many different kinds of buttons it contained; but she was rather stern with children, and I never dared to ask her. Remembering that bowl of buttons I have always kept a glass container of some kind with buttons in it. If any child seems interested, I ask them if they wouldn't like for me to pour them out in a pan or a box lid, where they could see all of them. They usually enjoy it.

Not long ago, when I was browsing around in an old curiosity shop in Los Angeles, looking for an old book, I ran across a big old carpet bag with about two gallons of buttons and beads of all descriptions in it. I bought it, and gave it to my grandchildren, who were living there at the time. Violet said they and the neighbors' children amused themselves most of the time, during that winter's evenings, sorting those buttons, and sewing them on cards and classifying them. It has furnished buttons for the family ever since.

And now, to return to Moores, our neighbors. *Every* evening, rain or shine, summer or winter, as soon as they finished their supper, Eddie came whistling across the field to our place. He didn't stay long; exchanged the news of the day, mentioned what he had read in the papers (he was a great reader, and took several papers and magazines), spoke of the trend of politics, or neighborhood gossip, and at dark would suddenly be gone. He became a part of the evening landscape. One evening, as he was sitting with his chair propped back against the wall, I drew a side view sketch of his face. It looked like him, only more homely, maybe, the nose a *little* sharper. It's the only time I can ever remember of him getting mad. I felt real bad, as I certainly didn't intend to hurt his feelings.

While I was still a very small child, a very tragic thing happened. A mad dog came through our neighborhood, and bit one of Mr. Moore's milk cows. At that time there was no remedy for hydrophobia, at least not close enough to be administered to a cow, so all they could do was wait and see what the results would be. In due time she went mad, and then people came for miles to see the mad cow, before she died. She would run till she could hardly stand, and then bawl and bawl till she was exhausted. She would plow her horns into a bank, and paw and snort. She really lived up to the name of a mad cow. I remember how horrified I would be, to wake up in the night and hear her bawling and bawling. If anyone went near the fence, she would run up to it and stand there panting, with her nostrils spread, and the foam running from her mouth. I was awfully sorry for her.

That, and the tree falling on Bruno, our dog, were the two worst tragedies of my early childhood. The men were in the woods cutting timber for something, and Bruno got in the way of a falling tree, and it hit across his hips. We, at the house, saw something peculiar looking coming down the road from the big gate to the house, a funny little bundle of yellow and white toddling slowly along, not the gait of a dog at all. As it came nearer, we saw that it was Bruno, walking on his two front feet, his hind end balanced up in the air, both hind legs dangling loose, and broken all to pieces. We were so sorry for him, and hurried to get a piece of old quilt for him to lay on. Pappy came in a little while, made some nice splints, set the bones the best he could, bandaged it up good, and for weeks Bruno walked on his front feet, till the broken hips and legs were well.

Bruno lived for several years after that. One day he treed a squirrel up in the woods. Cousin Ike Cook had a bunch of young dogs, just about grown; big yellow fellows, two of them were named Chump and Sharp. I can't remember the others, but anyway, they heard Bruno barking, went where he was, and killed him. We were so sad. It was the greatest sorrow that had ever come into my life, at that time. After he was dead I would imagine I heard him scratch at the door, and whine to be let in, and the tears would start afresh.

No other dog could ever fill Bruno's place. We owned several others. Old Rattler, who would fight at the drop of a hat. Ponto, the hound, who would listen to the fox chase, wait till they were coming around the hill southwest of us, and would then go down and head the fox off, before he got to his den. He believed in saving himself. Then there was beautiful Joe, who would go away for a year at a time, and then come back, so proud to see all of us again that he was almost beside himself with joy. But he never stayed long, and we never knew where he went.

Then for one short season we owned a greyhound, but not long enough to get very deeply attached. That constitutes all the dogs that I can remember of us owning.

Bruno stands out above all the others, though the smallest of any, he was the most intelligent. He would go with me in the evenings to find the cows in the big old Dr. Woods fields. I think that these uncultivated fields was land that Dr. Woods had taken as payment for doctor bills, from people who had nothing else to pay with. There were two or three old abandoned homes on the land. These fields furnished pasture for our cows, and they had big patches of blackberry briars, where we picked our berries in summer (there was no one who cared).

It was often hard to locate the cows if they were lying still, in the shade somewhere. The old fields and woods, where they grazed, were wide and lonesome, but I was not afraid if I had Bruno along. In some places the weeds grew high, far over a little dog's head, but he would run and jump up where he could see over the weeds. He would run far ahead of me looking in this little stretch of woods, and then down another way, and would almost always find them.

If there was a horse in the stable, I would ride. Old Felix, a slim sorrel with white feet, was not much of a work animal, and was used for a saddle horse. It was fun to go for the cows when I could ride Felix. He and Bruno enjoyed racing across the smooth level old fields, past the graveyard, that was just in the edge of the woods, on towards the baseball grounds, where the men and boys of the neighborhood played baseball on Saturday afternoons.

If the horses were too far away in the pasture, and I had to walk, I started earlier, and went by the graveyard. It was called the Armstrong graveyard, and was a pretty place at that time. Many of the graves were a solid carpet of myrtle. There were other pretty flowers that had grown wild down in the woods. The myrtle had myriads of blue flowers, and often I have taken a needle and thread and made long wreaths of these blossoms.[97]

The first funeral I can remember was that of Hosea Simpson's wife.[98] The mourners made a terrible impression on my mind. The two daughters were grown young women, Lulu and Lizzie.[99] I have since learned that this mother who died was William Ferrell's sister, daughter of my mother's half sister, Kezia Boyd Ferrell.[100]

But there! I had almost forgotten my cows. I think I was on foot, if I remember right. If they were very far away, and I was very tired when I found them, I would ride old May back. She was a lanky red cow, very gentle. Her back hips made a perfect saddle with my face turned to her tail instead of her head, so that's the way I rode. Her tail was pulled up to have something to hold on to, and to serve as a sort of guide, which I could twist to the right or left. Sometimes one of the cows would give the others a wink, and off they would all go in a full gallop. It was pretty rough riding, but I can't remember ever falling off accidentally.

There was a little wide spreading dogwood tree, down by the milk gap, whose top was one solid mass of grape vines, forming a complete umbrella. After the calves had their supper, and were drug away to the calf pen, I was free to climb trees, or do anything I chose to do. That little old dogwood had been climbed so many times that the limbs were worn slick as a button. The memory of that milking place, the low spreading dogwood with its canopy of grape vines, the walk home with my mother when the milking was done, the clear view of the sunset sky across the old fields, the talks as we walked slowly home in the twilight, has left some very sweet impressions in my mind. [See the painting on p. 35].[101]

<I think I wrote somewhere that Sadie said that she and Lelia and Etta wore linsey dresses in winter. I was not sure about the spelling and looked it up in the encyclopedia, and it said it was called Linsey-Woolsey, because it was woven of half linen and half fine woolen thread, making a nice warm linen and woolen cloth suitable for warm winter dresses for children, and for other purposes.

---

97. See page 90 for another description of this gravesite.

98. According to the 1880 census, Hosea Simpson (b. 1839) was married to Louisa (b. 1834).

99. Luretha "Lulu" (b. 1870) and Lizzie Simpson (b. 1868).

100. This seems highly unlikely considering William Ferrell (1863–1938) was nearly thirty years younger than Louisa Simpson. Kezia Jane Boyd (1830–1879) was married to Obediah Henry Ferrell (1824–1871).

101. Effie repeated the following section in triangular brackets almost verbatim near the conclusion of the autobiography. See epilogue, note 78.

I like for my older sisters to tell me about their childhood, and their first schools, etc. (Mother said that Lelia walked when she was seven months old. ) Lelia says that she started to school when she was five. She didn't want to go, and mother took her part way, and carried Elmo, a big heavy baby.

When mother started back home Lelia jerked her hand away from Etta, who was leading her, and ran after mama, so mother sat Elmo down in the path and took her the rest of the way to the school house (not very far) and set her over the fence and told her to *stay there.*

Lelia said that she was mad at mother for leaving the baby alone. She was afraid that some sheep, that were near, would come and hurt him. She said that she screamed, and told mother that when she got home she was going to make our dad *whip her,* but she stayed, and after that she was willing to go with Etta.

There was another little girl in school who had been born the same day Lelia was. Her name was Annie Stewart.[102]

The school house was a log room with a fireplace and chimney. It had been a blacksmith shop, and it was across the road from cousin P. (Philip) Armstrong's place. They sat on puncheon seats (a log split in half with a broad axe, and holes bored in each end and legs put in the holes — see picture). [*This picture is not included here.*]

Henry Durham (later a doctor) was her first teacher, he was nineteen years old.[103] They studied in a "blue-backed speller" (I have one), and they made them study aloud. It was called a "blab school." There were only two benches, long ones, sitting *slaunch*ways in front of the fireplace. Cousin Pairlee Croft was her next teacher (grandfather Armstrong's first wife was Susan Croft).[104]

Lelia says that grandmother Marquess wove linen cloth, and she has seen some she wove.

Lelia says that our mother didn't have a cookstove till about the time that I was born. She can't remember whether just before or just after (1885). This shows the marvelous changes from my mother's time, and even from my birth, to the present time.

We had little bullet molds, and I have molded lots of bullets, one at a time. I liked to do it. I felt important, and they used them.>

I had a deep and abiding interest in my sister's beaux. I was most too small to remember Lelia's first ones. I know that she and Lewis Hamby were cronies in their school days, and Lawson Causler [Cansler] came reg-

---

102.  "Connie Stewart" in 1973 version.
103.  "Henry Durbane" in 1973 version.
104.  Pairlee Croft (b. 1857).

Lelia Marquess at age two. Courtesy of Itha Carmack.

ularly for a long time.[105] There was talk of a wedding, but Lawson got sick and the doctor ordered a change of climate, so he went west for awhile. While he was gone, William Ferrell, with a pair of shiny boots, a black moustache, a banjo, a wide hat, and a dashing saddle horse, rode right into Dawson's [Lawson's?] warm place, and camped there. Mammy didn't like it, she didn't have anything personal against William, but she said that they were too closely related, and she would never be happy if she married him.

Mammy was a quiet, peaceable soul, usually agreeable with most anything. She put up with poverty and hard work without a murmur, but

---

105. Louis B. Hamby (b. 1872), according to the 1880 census, and possibly John or James Lawson Cansler.

when Lelia told her she and William were going to be married, I saw another side of her that I had never seen before. She cried, begged and pleaded with Lelia to wait a while before she decided. She told her she would rather see her dead and in her coffin than to see her marry him, but it all fell on deaf ears. They were soon married, but they were never suited to each other. Their dispositions were entirely different, and she endured much unhappiness in her life with him. However, they raised a family of fine children, good and intelligent. William loved his children, and he was a good father to them. But he and Lelia clashed continually.

I was a little child of four or five years when they married, and William was my pal. He would make dancers for me of empty spools, and would show me lots of little tricks; how an Indian pinches, how to feed a crow. He would pretend he was cutting my ear off with the back of his knife blade, and make an awful face at the blood. He could knock off tunes on the old banjo, and played with my dad for dances. He was a good dancer, wore pretty shoes, and kept them shining till you could see yourself in them, almost.

William Ferrell was part Indian. I have never found how far back it was, or of what tribe. Probably Cherokee, as they were the ones who lived in that part of the country when the white men came. But, since I have seen the Navajos, I have thought that William surely must have been part Navajo, as I can see distinct resemblances in every movement they make. The way they point, the way they tie a leather knot, or fasten a saddle girt, or walk, or laugh. In *every* move they are so like him.

About a year after they were married Lelia had a baby boy, born prematurely, who lived a little while and then died. The first dead baby that I had ever seen. He was the first one of *our* family to be buried at the Armstrong graveyard. Etta and I carried many a tubful of rich dirt, to put around that little grave, the flowers we planted had to have good soil so they would thrive and grow. We never guessed, while we were working at the little plot, that Mother's and Etta's graves would be the next ones adjoining it.

My conscience has bothered me when I think of how hard Etta worked to keep that little grave clean and pretty, and how sadly neglected her grave has been. We sold the old place, and moved away the year after she was buried, and the graveyard has long been neglected. We have gone back there a few times, at long intervals, and cleaned it, and put a fence around their graves. Each time the bushes and weeds had grown up until we could hardly find where they were buried.[106]

---

106. These family plots were typical in Kentucky rural areas. See Sue Lynn Stone, "Blessed Are They That Mourn," 230. Traditions regarding gravesites in the South and their treatment are discussed in Lynwood Montell, "Cemetery Decoration Customs in the American South," in *The Old Traditional Way of Life*, ed. Robert E. Walls and George H. Shoemaker (Bloomington: Trickster Press, 1989), 111–29.

Family portrait of William Henry Ferrell and Lelia Marquess Ferrell, Effie's sister, probably taken in Jerome, Arizona, ca. 1902. Left to right, standing: John Robert Marquess (Effie's brother), and Vera; sitting: William, Norman, Leone, Lelia. Courtesy of Itha Carmack.

<When grandmother Marquess was living at the Dr. Hendricks place, not so very far from Wallonia, mother and her three little ones (Etta, the oldest, Lelia, next, and Elmo, the baby) were visiting at grandma's.[107] Grandma and mother were expecting our father and Uncle Curg to be home for supper soon, and were busy getting it ready. The table was set and most of the food was on the table.

The children were playing quite a little ways from the house. Grandmother noticed that it was suddenly getting dark, and when she went outside to see where the children were, she saw a black cloud coming, and she could hear the roar of the wind. She ran for the children, and she and Aunt Emma, her oldest girl, hurried them as fast as they could, but by the time they reached the house it was almost as dark as night. The chickens were huddled together frightened. The cows were bawling, and the dog whimpered by the door.

By the time they were all in the house the storm was on them in all its fury. The din and the roar and darkness was terrible. The air was full of

---

107. Dr. Alex A. Hendrix (b. 1830). See Perrin, *County of Christian, Kentucky*, 564–65. This sentence begins a section which is repeated verbatim near the conclusion of the autobiography. See epilogue, note 77.

flying missiles, and the house was shaking as if it would go any minute. The roof of the kitchen was blown off, and the rain and debris was pouring in on the untouched supper. The dishes and the food was scattered, the tablecloth was carried out and to the top of a big tree, where it remained for a long time.

The big living room where they were huddled close together was blown from its foundation, and lamps, vases, mirrors, and other things were crashed to the floor, but the walls remained intact.

Papa and Uncle Curg were on their way home and saw the cyclone writhing and twisting along. As it came nearer the roar of the wind was frightening. They had no doubt but what it was a destructive one. They were out of the track of it, but it seemed to be heading straight for grandmother's place, and they hurried on as fast as possible.

When they came in sight of the house they could see that the big living room was off its foundation, the roof was blown from the kitchen, and the tablecloth was caught in the top of one of the big trees in the yard.

Their supper was demolished, but they were all thankful and happy that no one was hurt. The house could be rebuilt, and more food could be cooked, and all would be O. K. again. They were so thankful that the men had been clear of the track of the tornado, and that it had not touched them.>

I only remember going to grandma Armstrong's one time. I was small, not over three or four years old, but there were a few things that happened that were stamped on my memory to stay. Some of Uncle Jim's folks went with us. Jimmie and I (we were about the same age) were sitting in the back of the wagon, and Mammy kept warning us not to be looking over the side of the wagon bed, as there was danger of getting our mouths mashed. We were sure that we could be careful, and nothing of the kind would happen, but when the team broke into a trot, down a rocky slope, I was bounced over against the edge of the wagon bed and cut a place in my upper lip, knocking some teeth loose. After that I minded my mother, and kept my face away from danger.

It clouded up and started to thunder before we reached the Tradewater river, and as some of the men folks were going to stay at the creek and fish, I began to feel worried, for fear of a storm. By the time we reached the river bottoms, the wind was tossing the tall tree tops about, and a storm was threatening. I was afraid for them to stay.

I had heard them tell of Uncle Jim and Birchfield being on the river once when there came a storm.[108] After it was over, they could see a house

---

108.    Birchfield Marquess (b. 1894).

Pictures of Childhood     91

on the hill. The roof had been blown off. They went up there to see if anyone was hurt, and it seemed that the storm had caught a mother and a new-born baby alone. When she saw the wind was about to demolish the house, she got up on her knees and elbows over her baby to protect it. A heavy timber from the roof, a joist, I think it was, had fallen, and struck her on the head. She lived only a few minutes after they got there. The baby was unhurt, and a family by the name of Stevenson took the baby and raised her. Her name was Emma.[109] They gave her a good education, and she became a school teacher.

This story had left the impression in my mind that the Tradewater river was an especially bad place for tornadoes, and I didn't want Papa and the boys to stay and fish. It was dark and windy, and the thunder was crashing, but they stayed, and I was miserable.

Elmo drove the team for us, on to grandma's place. When we came to a stream we had to ford, which was usually shallow, it had been raining up towards its source, and now it was a rolling muddy torrent. We stopped, and were debating whether to drive into it or not. While we were waiting, we saw a man with two big oxen, and a wagon, coming towards us on the other side of the stream. Elmo decided to wait and see if he made it across all right, and if it wasn't *too* deep, *we* would try it. The oxen didn't want to go down into the water, but the man cracked a long whip, and hollered whoa at them, and they went in with their tongues out, and bawling. They had long horns with brass knobs on the ends of each horn. He came through safely, so we tackled it too.

It was raining, and we put quilts over us, and by the time we got to grandma's it was just pouring down, and the wind was blowing a gale. Grandma put a feather bed on the floor, and we children all lay down and covered our heads. I suppose we thought that would keep the lightning from striking.

No one lived there but grandma Druzilla (Mammy's stepmother) and her nephew, Ned Wooldridge, but it was interesting to us.[110] They had an upstairs in their house, and the floor of it was nearly covered with hazelnuts and walnuts, drying, while we were there.

The next day after it cleared off Ned took us and showed us his coal mine, which was on their farm, near Empire.

We were wondering how our men made it on the creek during the storm. They had a tent and were O. K. We went back to the river the next day and joined the men. Then we all tried our luck at fishing.

---

109.  Possibly Emma Stevenson (b. 1872), according to the 1880 census.
110.  Druzilla (Drewsilla or Druscilla) Wooldridge (b. 1817) was the wife of John Armstrong, Effie's grandfather. Ned Wooldridge was born in 1858.

They usually caught lots of big catfish in this river, and they were good to eat. They had no scales on them like most other fish have. They had to be scalded and scraped to clean them.

They visited the Stevensons who had taken the motherless Emma. I went out in the yard where some other children were, and a little boy, a little larger than myself, came up and pushed me backwards. I fell flat on my back, and bawled. Someone came to see what the trouble was, and the boy, pointing at me said, "I downed the little bitch."

I don't remember anything about the trip home, it must have been uneventful, probably raining.

It's funny how smells get mixed up with memories, as I have mentioned before. When *one* comes back, the other comes with it. We always burned wood. In the fireplace, and in the old iron stepstove in the kitchen. We burned hickory and oak wood in the fireplace, as they made hot fire, and lasted longer, and the ashes were good to make lye for the soap.

The smell of coal smoke became associated with going to town, and consequently I adored the smell of coal burning. It had a charm with it.[111]

One would think that a long jolt over rough roads in an old two horse wagon, usually in the hot summer, would leave unpleasant impressions, but not so. Those trips to town stand out as glorious monuments in my memory. I asked who lived in every house along the way, and our patient father usually told us.

There was the Hiram Moores, the slow, quiet, soft spoken people, whose daughter Melissa, was the most decided blond I ever saw.[112] She had long thick hair that was almost white, and her eyelashes and eyebrows were white as cotton, and I'll bet she never spoke a loud harsh word in her life.

When Walter Owens would be prompting at the square dances he would call out, when he started to swing Melissa, "And I'll now swing the gal with the bean soup hair," but she didn't resent it, for he had something original to say about each girl he swung.[113]

---

111.  Hopkinsville was the center of Kentucky's dark-fired tobacco market and the processing center for the region's coal mining district. It was also the junction for the Louisville & Nashville Railroad and Illinois Central Railroad systems. The smell of coal smoke would have been strong given the climate of industry in this town. For more on Hopkinsville, see Sue M. Wright, "Spotlight on Christian County: Patriarch of the Pennyrile," *Back Home in Kentucky* 8 (July-August 1985): 25–30; Meacham, *History of Christian County*; and William T. Turner, *Gateway From the Past: A History Commemotating 175th Anniversary of Hopkinsville and Christian County, Kentucky* (Hopkinsville, Ky.: Burdine's Print 1974).

112.  Hiram H. Moore (1834–1906) and his wife, Eliza (1835–1915) had a daughter, Melissie F. (b. 1873).

113.  According to Burt Feintuch, callers were a necessity at these dances. "Generally, the caller stood to one side of the dancers, although he himself sometimes danced or moved through them. In instances where several people knew how to call dances, they

Well, things like that were discussed, as we passed Hiram Moore's place. Then next was John Knight's place. He was noted for making good cider, and when something was just right, it was *like John Knight's cider*.[114]

Next was Bill Cotton's place, at the top of Cotton's hill.[115] We always felt sad for poor Mrs. Cotton, a good woman, who had given birth to three idiotic children, one girl and two boys. The girl had fallen into the fire and burned to death; but the boys were both big strapping fellows, Bob and Bert. Bob grew so unmanageable that a special room was built in the back, to lock him in.

Next was Pleasant Green church, on top of the hill, where we could see clear down into Trigg County.

Then came a stretch of Negro cabins, and the Negro church, then Smith's big farm. He had the family of pretty girls, who were nearly all named boys' names: Tommy, Willie, Johnie, and Jimmie. Probably he wanted them to be boys, anyway they were very popular. The oldest girl was named Jennie.

When we came to the fork of the road, we could smell the smoke from the train, and from the coal grates, and could see the Princeton Pike, leading off to the west, and could hear the telephone wires singing (for years I thought that humming noise was the messages being sent along through those wires). Here the country opened up. No more woods, hills, or rocky stretches. To the south, as far as you could see, lay the broad fair acres of South Christian County.

Off to the southwest, a little ways, was John Young's mansion. The top of the house, which was three stories high, had a flat square enclosure, with a banister around it. They said that there was a fishpond with a white swan, etc., or a swimming pool, or *some*thing mysterious up there.

Other imposing homes could be seen in the distance. There were fine Jersey cattle, and thoroughbred horses, and Negroes working in the fields.

The forks of the road was just a mile from town, and about halfway there was the toll gate, where Alec Poindexter was always waiting to raise the long bar and let us through, and collect two cents. There was a tiny little

---

usually took turns. Calling is highly formulaic, and because of this it was apparently easy for some to learn to call through imitation and practice" (Feintuch, "Dancing to the Music," 57–58). See page 197 for more on Walter Owen's dance calling.

114.    Probably John Richard Knight (1872–1935). The making of apple cider in western Kentucky has been a long and cherished tradition among rural families. See Karen Stewart, "Making Apple Cider in Western Kentucky," *Kentucky Folklore Record* 18 (1972): 92–95.

115.    Probably William Cotton (b. 1869) and his wife, Ellen Gilkey (b. 1873?).

square building out on the side, that I suppose he could retreat into if it rained, snowed, or sleeted.

Just after we crossed the river bridge we came to William Owen's grocery, on 7th street, and we usually got out there and waited while Pappy took the wagon and team and disposed of them. He usually hitched them in the lot back of Pink Nolan's saloon.[116]

William Owen's family lived in an apartment over the grocery. They had two beautiful children, Willie and Violet. Violet was my age, and she had a swing in a little storeroom, back of the grocery, and a playhouse, where she kept her toys, dolls, etc. She could draw too, so there was a sort of bond between us. I could draw also, better than any other child in school, and was always called on to make drawings on the blackboard for Thanksgiving, Pioneer celebrations, Christmas, etc. Violet said that someday she was going to an Art school.

Besides the Owen place, there were three other places we always visited. Cousin Larkin Brasher (who married Jane Lindley, daughter of Susan (Peggy) Lindley, my grandfather's sister) for one. He was a lawyer, and had a big family. David, the oldest, who lived on a farm out near us, and a bunch of girls, who were all school teachers. Miss Vic, Miss Carrie, Miss Minnie, and younger one, Omie, a little older than myself, and Lark, the baby.[117]

We usually stopped for a visit with cousin Elijah Armstrong's family, too.

Then in town, we went to Joe P. Pool's Racket store.[118] It was a forerunner of the present dime stores. It had 5 cent counters, 10 cent counters, 25 cent counters, etc. *There* was where we spent our hoarded nickels and dimes. China dolls, toy cap pistols, fans, combs for our hair, toys, ribbons, and all kinds of attractive things. But they were always in too big a hurry to go, before I got to see half of what I wanted to see.

In the evening, going home, one or two of the girls would usually have a sick headache. Probably from the jolting, and the hot sun, or from looking *and* looking at everything, or too much candy, or sour stomach from wrong foods. Anyway, we rarely ever got home without one or two being prostrate with a headache.

I remember one such evening, when *my* head was splitting. Cousin Ike Cook passed us in his nice springy buggy, with its leather top, to keep the sun off, and old Joab, a big gray horse hitched to it. He halted, as he passed our wagon, and asked if some of us would like to ride with him. Mammy said, as *my* head was aching, maybe I had better be the one. I didn't

---

116.   Probably refers to Charles P. Nolan (b. 1849) a saloon keeper in Hopkinsville.
117.   See note 83 above.
118.   Joe P. Pool (b. 1873).

want to ride with him, as I was a little bit timid, and afraid of him. His eyes were red from drinking, and he smelled loud of whiskey, but it certainly was nice to sit on the nice springy cushions of the seat, and bounce along so easy. It seemed a pleasure to old Joab to trot glibly up hill and down

When we got to Hiram Moore's field there was a little country lane that crossed it, that led to the fields, and across to Uncle Lawrence's place, but it didn't look wide enough for a buggy. It was a road that was not used anymore, but he turned off and went that way. I kept telling him that was not the right way, and that he couldn't go that way with the horse and buggy, but he said old Joab could take us anywhere we wanted to go.

After the road turned into the gate at Uncle Lawrence's back field the road played out entirely and there was nothing left but the creek bed. I was scared stiff, but he wouldn't let me out. When he ran the side of the buggy up on a big log, and the other side up on the bank of the creek, with the old horse way below us wading through a deep hole (Ike was busy with the lines) I took advantage, and made a wild leap, landing in a briar thicket. But I didn't care, briars were a welcome change. He called, and begged me to come back and get in. He said that we would soon be to the long lane that led up to Mr. Moore's house, but I didn't listen, I was running as fast as my legs could carry me. I waded the creek, climbed fences, and soon I knew where I was. I was in Mr. Moore's bottom field, the one where the cow stayed, when she went mad. I knew that as soon as I crossed *them* I would be to our fence, and then I could see our house.

I made for the big sweet gum tree, with the two scalybark hickories near it.[119] I was hot from running, the briars had torn my Sunday stockings, and my best shoes were wet and muddy from wading the creek. My head was throbbing, but I was glad to be out of that buggy and in sight of home.

I got home about the same time the folks got there in the wagon. They stared in open mouthed wonder when I came dragging up, all briar scratched and bedraggled.

"Where in the world have you been?" Two or three of them asked me at the same time.

When I told them of my experience Pappy was so mad he could hardly speak. He was going right over to Ike's, and give him the beating he needed, but Mammy wouldn't let him. She said that they should have

119.   The sweet gum tree (*Liquidambar styraciflua*, L.) is of rapid growth and is ornamental. The bark has astringent properties and is sometimes used to tan leather. The scaly-bark hickory or shagbark hickory (*Carya ovata*) is common to the area and is used in making lye, cogs, and millwheels. The bark is often used as an astringent.

had better sense than to let me ride with him when he was drunk, so it was their fault after all.

Mammy was so sorry for me that she treated me like an invalid. She washed my face, fanned me, and rubbed camphor on my aching head. For a little while I was the *hero*.

## CHAPTER TWO

# Ponderous Milestones

*Each change that today seems to pass with a gallop*
*Were ponderous milestones that marked off the way,*
*The slow-growing stocking on Mammie's deft needles*
*And even when only a week was remaining*
*It seemed that the holidays never would come—*
*I can't explain yet why they held so much magic*
*For children as poor as we were in our home.*
        —"Christmas" in *Backward Glances*, 32

At least twice a year the old place got a *genuine* going over. Once in the spring, and again just before Christmas. Of course, there was a weekly cleaning, when the floors had to be *scoured* with soft soap, and the broom. We had no rugs, and linoleum was unheard of. There were some strips of home made carpet once, I think, but they had been used to cover the sweet potatoes and the apples upstairs. Turnips were holed up in the garden, but sweet potatoes were hard to keep, and had to be kept at just the right temperature, or they would dry rot.

The oak floors were kept scrubbed. Any grease spot showed up ugly, and the walnuts we cracked on the hearth were very bad to make greasy spots, but we couldn't afford to quit cracking walnuts, especially of winter evenings. They and corn bread together made a good supper.

Mammy usually did the weekly floor scouring anyway, but when the general housecleaning time came, *every*body worked. Everything was taken out of the house, so the walls could be whitewashed. The lime was boiling in the big old iron kettle outside (it looked like rocks when it was first bought, but when water was poured on it it swelled and blossomed out into snowy lime).

The old straw was emptied out of the *domestic* straw ticks, and we children usually had the job of filling them, after they had been washed, dried, and ironed. Mammy always gave directions as to just what kind of straw to get. We made a hole way into the core of the stack, where it had not been rained on. We shook all the chaff out, then filled the clean ticks as full as we could get them. We would jump on them to smash them down, and then cram in more stuffing, especially into each corner. When it was full the boys would usually carry them to the house on their heads.

Everything in the house was washed and dusted. The bedsteads, and even the slats were washed. The homemade chairs were scrubbed. The cracks in the hearth and around the fireplace were redaubed. In the spring there was a new firescreen made, and covered with all kinds of bright colored pictures, but it had to be recovered real often, as the crickets cut holes in whatever we covered it with.

A fad swept the country about this time of spatter work screens. A cloth was stretched on the screen, then usually green leaves, maple, ferns, or something that would make a pretty design was laid on the cloth, then a brush was dipped in colored water, usually blued with bluing, and spattered around the leaves. Then the leaves were removed, leaving that place white. Somehow we never did catch the spatter fever.

The lace curtains were all washed, starched, and ironed. This in itself was quite a job, as the irons had to be heated at the fireplace, or on the cookstove.

The whitewashing wouldn't have been such a terrible job, with a good brush, but we never thought of buying *any*thing, if we could make anything *else* do. Mammy would use an old wornout broom, or tear corn shucks up fine, and tie them together on a stick, or some other homemade contraption, that would answer the purpose of a brush. Although at that time, I am sure, good brushes could have been bought at a very reasonable price.

The walls were not so hard to do, but the overhead work on the ceilings was pretty different. Mammy always got the whitewash in her eyes, and it almost put them out. In fact, I know one woman who was blind in one eye from getting whitewash in it. Anyway, we lived through it, and when it was done, the walls were all as white as snow. The curtains, starched and snowy and back on the windows. The beds, high with their new strawticks, and the featherbeds on top of that, with white sheets, and big ruffled pillow shams. The picture frames re-varnished. New split bottoms had been put in the chairs that needed it. The floors were all as clean as soap and hot water could make them. There was a feeling of deep satisfaction, and the knowledge that we had done the very best that we could with what we had. It *did* look clean, and it *was* clean.

Etta, who was crippled, couldn't do everything the others could do, as she had no use of her right arm and hand. But she did her part steadily, day after day. She pieced quilts, knit, made the new pin cushions, embroidered, and *hundreds* of little things. In the long run accomplishing more, perhaps, than many who have two good hands. She planted and tended the flowers. Kept the door yard clean with little buckbush brooms. Fed and tended little chickens. Gathered eggs. She even swept floors.

Etta had some pet hens, big old yellow ducklegged biddies, that would not lay anywhere but in the house, usually on a bed. One of them laid abnormally big eggs, with two yellows, and sometimes she laid twice a day. She was a super hen.

I have planned several times to write some little booklets for children. One on Christmas in Kentucky, in the 90's. I did write a stanza or two on it in my little booklet "Backward Glances,"[1] but I would like to go into detail and tell the intimate story of our happy Christmas times, and of the gifts that Santa Claus put in our stockings, and on the Christmas tree (which was always a Cedar, as there were no pine trees near). The Cedar tree brought the Christmas spirit as strong as any stately pine could possibly have done.

We utilized the time, the few days before the happy occasion, by getting the old log house shining upstairs and down. The whitewashing of the walls usually took place before the cold bad weather set in.

---

1. *Backward Glances* was Effie's 63-page book of poetry, a collection of 39 poems based on childhood memories. It was privately printed and gives no publication date on the title page. Some of the poems are "Spring Housecleaning," "Pickin' Geese," "Mammy, Carding and Spinning," and "Our Yearly Visit to Grandma's." The poem titled "Christmas" includes these verses:

    A tree of green cedar with flowers of paper,
    With strings of white popcorn and apples of red,
    Gave thrills that were sweeter than any rich treasure
    Could cause in my heart, since my childhood has fled.
    The scent of a firecracker stirs mellow memories
    Of red striped socks and a new "chiny" doll,
    A home-made spool wagon, a *piece* of an orange,
    bladder to bust, and a home-made yarn ball.
    fresh sagey sausage bound up in tight bunches
    With shucks as a cover, and tied at each end,
    And oh, the red gravy we sopped with hot biscuits—
    There is no food now with such exquisite blend.
    And no cake compares with the tall ones in layers,
    With apples, all flavored with nutmeg, between;
    For nutmegs were cheap—we bought five for a nickel
    In cute little nuts that looked powdered and clean.
    A fresh ham or pork that was boiled in the wash-pot
    Was part of our Christmas—'twas peeled and then browned
    And spotted all over with spots of black pepper,
    Our Dad did the slicing and passed it around.
    We knew to prepare for a crowd to come Christmas,
    For music and laughter and dancing and fun,
    Though looked on as sin by the church folks and preachers
    Drew life, like the light and the warmth of the sun.

The autumns in our part of Kentucky were, in one way, the best time of year. There were long golden days when everyone was busy from morning till night getting tobacco cut and cured, (I can just smell the smoke from the tobacco barn when that time of year rolls around), getting the potatoes dug, the beans picked and shelled, the corn gathered and the fodder shocked.[2]

The hickory nuts had to be gathered, and the black walnuts hulled and stored in the old abandoned corncrib.

The popcorn had to be gathered, and the broom corn cut and stored. We had to *break* it so the broom heads would hang *down* and the straws would remain straight and nice for the brooms.[3]

The turnips were put in a hole in the garden, covered with cornstalks and then with dirt to prevent freezing.

The apples and sweet potatoes were stored upstairs. Sometimes the wheat was stored for a while in an improvised bin in a corner of the upstairs room.

By the time Christmas arrived everything was stored away, safe from freezing. Usually the hog killing was over, the sausage was ground and hanging in the smokehouse in little long sacks. There were usually several little packages in cornshucks, tied at either end, and kept hanging in the kitchen. We thought it tasted better stored in the shucks. Sometimes it was fried in patties, packed in a stone jar and the hot grease poured over it, and the jar was turned upside down. When we wanted sausage quick we could just open a jar, and it was ready. There is no meat that I can think of that can beat it for flavor, when it is browned, seasoned with lots of sage,

---

2. Effie later wrote that

> All of this work fell to the women and children, as the men were kept busy in the tobacco. It was getting ripe, and the leaves were thick and tinged with yellow. It must be cut at the proper time or it would begin to lose weight. The men of the neighborhood swapped work, the ripest crops being cut first. Jugs of cider at the ends of the rows helped to break the monotony. The stalks were split down the center with a sharp knife and cut off at the ground. It was then turned over and stood on its head until it wilted. When it had stood in the sun until it was sufficiently softened that it would not break, it was straddled close together on tobacco sticks that had been split from strait-grained oak and were about three feet long. It was then loaded on the wagon in two large stacks called coops and hauled to the barn, where the sticks were hoisted and handed from one to another until the top of the barn was full. It was then hung, a tier at a time, until the entire barn was filled within six or eight feet of the grownd. Here it hung until it was yellow, and then was fired.

> See Carmack, "Tobacker," 108.

3. For more on the process of making brooms, see Karen Stewart, "Broommaking in Western Kentucky," *Kentucky Folklore Record* 18 (1972): 46–48, and Annelen Archbold, "Broommaking in Kentucky," *Back Home in Kentucky* 3 (September-October 1980): 38–39.

and eaten with hot buttermilk biscuits, and with the luscious red gravy it was cooked in.

To make red gravy the main part of the grease is poured off, then water poured in the skillet where the sausage giblets and small particles had browned.

Back bones, spareribs, and boiled hams were a part of Christmas too. Our mother saw that everyone around us who didn't happen to be as fortunate as we were, and who didn't have any hogs to kill, got a generous portion of fresh pork for Christmas.

The boys sawed and chopped the oak and hickory wood and piled it in the open porch (or hallway) to protect it from the snow that we always hoped would fall for Christmas. We longed and prayed for a white Christmas.

Whether there was snow or not, we strung long strings of popcorn, made paper chains, and paper flowers and stars to deck our tree with.

We usually had new wool stockings (and oh how I hated to wear them, they always scratched my legs, but they *did* help to keep out the cold).

We usually tried to get a load of tobacco stripped and ready to take to market before Christmas. And our dad made axe handles and worked on them during long winter evenings and sold them for three dollars a dozen. He was an expert at it. His handles were shaped perfectly, and were of fine grained seasoned hickory wood, polished as slick as a button. He would get them shaped with the hand axe and drawing knife, then we children would help him scrape them with pieces of broken glass, and then they were finished with (first coarse, then fine) sandpaper. They were a work of art when he got them finished. Three dollars in those days was a lot more money than it is today.[4]

My brother John said that one time when they were going to Tradewater fishing they stopped at Era, John Roger's store, and bought eggs to take with them.[5] They gave twenty-five cents for six dozen eggs. They were five cents a dozen, in one dozen lots, but by taking six dozen they got a dozen extra. *Now*, six dozen fresh eggs cost $3. 60, over twelve times as much as they paid for them then.

Anyway, we never felt poor, as we had a frugal, industrious mother, who did her level best to keep good food and clothing for her children, and to keep good warm, clean beds. She kept a flock of geese, picked them every six weeks, and kept plenty of warm feather beds and pillows for every bed.

---

4. Effie's description of ax handle-making was mentioned earlier on page 57. See Chapter One note 51 for a source on the making of ax handles.
5. Probably John B. Rogers (b. 1847).

Some people think it is cruel to pluck the feathers from the geese, but if they are not picked every six weeks, they shed them, and then there would be feathers scattered everywhere. We were sure that nature planned it that way so we could have the good soft warm feather beds to keep us warm in the winter. *That* was a custom that goes away back into history. We had no manufactured mattresses. There was a straw tick made from brown domestic (unbleached muslin) and filled with clean wheat straw from the *inside* of the straw stack. *That* with a good featherbed on top of it, and plenty of quilts, made a warm bed.

We had no springs when I was a little child. I can remember our first ones, slats, and corded.

We made bedspreads of muslin, and tablecloths too. Made ruffled pillow slips for the bed in the front room, that visitors slept on.

Sometimes there were lace pillow shams that were spread over big pillows that stood upright on the bolster (a long pillow reaching the entire width of the bed).

Our mother made apple layer cakes. The cakes rather thin, and in several layers. Coconut layer cakes also, and solid pound cakes, and fruit pies, and cookies, for Christmas dinners, and almost always a boiled ham, and often a baked goose.

Sometimes mother made salt rising bread, for special occasions. It was good. I've always wanted to make it, but never have. *Most* of the time our bread was buttermilk biscuits, or flitters for breakfast, and often corn-bread for the midday meal and supper.

Mother baked sweet potatoes in the dutch oven on the hearth, and often cooked the cornbread in it too.

When mother rendered the fat for our year's supply of lard she saved the brown cracklin's and would make cracklin' cornbread. It tasted good, but was too greasy to be healthy, so she didn't make it very often. She molded it into little long ^slim^[6] dodgers so there was lots of brown crust.[7]

At long last Christmas Eve would finally arrive. I cannot figure out the pure joy, and the actually hallowed feeling, different from any other time of year, *far* different, that accompanied the Christmas holidays. It was such an *extreme* happiness that I could hardly endure it. I have often wondered if others experienced the same thrill of joy that I did, and I guess they did, from the things that have been said and written and sung about it.

We built a big crackling log fire, with a huge backlog, had the hearth as clean as could be, and the tree waiting in all its popcorn glory. We never

6. "Slim" is written under an unitelligibly stricken word.
7. Bread made of fried or baked corn meal; usually "corn dodger."

had lights on it as we were afraid to have candles, too much danger of fire. The popcorn, paper chains, stars and flowers were enough. If there had been anything more I'm afraid we couldn't have stood it.

The boys made loose wool balls, soaked them with coal oil, set them on fire and threw them high in the air, so the neighbors could see. They would catch them in their naked hands and then throw them again.

We stood big boards up, and then jumped on them as they went down, so that they would make a loud noise. We usually had firecrackers but no one ever saw them till Christmas morning. Old Chris brought them along with our other gifts.

Mother knit yarn socks and mittens for the boys and our father, then made new balls from old worn out socks ravelled out and wound tight. She made warm mufflers for their necks to keep them warm, and made rag dolls if there was no new ones for we girls. Sometimes she would buy doll heads, the china kind, and put bodies to them, and make clothes for them.

I *have* had a bought doll with china hands and feet, and *once*, I remember Sadie and I getting bisque dolls with *hair*, mine was blonde, hers with brown hair.

Elmo made little wagons with wheels made from a round seasoned pole, with sections sawed off, and a hole bored in the center. Sometimes a shoe box was used for the wagon bed, sometimes it was made of wood. He would also make *little* wagons, with wheels made from big sewing thread spools, for my *little* dolls (these really rolled).

Sometimes we got a *limber jim* that danced on a board, and was lots of fun.[8] Sometimes we got a fox and goose board, like a checker board, or a peg board. Cecil made some lately.[9]

Our socks always had an orange, and some stick candy. A bunch of big soft juicy raisins still on the stem. (I never see that kind now.)

Cookies cut like animals and birds, etc. Mrs. Moore cut them in squares.

---

8.  For a description and instructions on making dancing dolls, see Dave Pickett, "Limberjack or Dancing Doll," in *Foxfire 6*, edited by Eliot Wigginton (Garden City: Anchor Press, 1980), 208–13, and Pickett's "Limberjack," in *The Foxfire Book of Appalacian Toys & Games*, edited by Linda Garland Pace and Hilton Smith, 185, 189, 191.

9.  The game is for two players, similar to checkers. One player moves the foxes, the other the geese. The object for the foxes is to capture the geese by jumping them. The geese attempt to hem in the foxes, so they have no where to move. The layout of the board and the details of "moving" and "jumping" are described in Pace and Smith, *The Foxfire Book of Appalacian Toys & Games*, 37–38. Cecil Eugene Carmack (1904–1984) was Effie's oldest child.

We always had plenty of music and dancing, with the fiddle, banjo, and guitar, and also plenty of singing.

When a racoon, ground hog, or certain other animals with tough hides, were killed, our dad and the boys tanned the hides and made banjo heads, shoestrings, hame strings, etc. out of them.[10] It was used to patch shoes too. Our dad put soles and heels on our old shoes when they started wearing out, but I never remember of him using metal shoe brads (tacks) to put them on with. He used a section of seasoned hickory or maple cut in a long wedge shape, and then he split it into little wooden tacks, bored a hole in the sole with an awl, and drove the wooden tack in and hammered it down solid.

Sometimes we got new shoes for Christmas, but I can never remember of feeling sorry for myself if I didn't, or of feeling disappointed over what I got for Christmas. We always agreed that it was the very best Christmas we had ever had.

There were lots of homemade gadgets. Our dad would take a goose quill and tamp it full of dry and damp gun powder (in different layers), then set it on fire and it would go zigzagging all over the floor, first one direction, then another; it would go slow when it came to the damp powder, then fast when it came to the dry powder.

The boys made whirly-gigs, a contraption the Indians, and the early pioneers used to start a fire with.[11]

We had to work so hard all summer and fall that it was a happy relief to have a season of leisure, not *all* leisure of course, as it took lots of wood, to be chopped and hauled, then chopped again into stick length for the cookstove and the two fireplaces. The stock had to be fed and watered. The cows had to be fed *and* milked.

But the long evenings were happy times, with songs and music, games and dancing, storytelling and reading.

There was *never* any idle time for my mother, or my older sisters. They were always knitting, piecing quilts, mending, or sewing.

Since I have grown older, and since my mother died (in 1899), when I was thirteen, I have marveled at the way she had adjusted her life to a new way of living. Her mother died when she was three months old,

---

10.   Hame strings are part of a harness; the traces are fastened to the hame strings.

11.   These "whirly-gigs" were also called "smoke grinders." The point of the toy is placed in a slight depression and a horizontal bar is pumped with two fingers. The twisting motion of the string around the shaft and weight of the wooden disk made the disk spin back and forth in the depression. See "Smoke Grinders," in Eliot Wigginton, ed. *Foxfire 6*, 229, and "Smoke Grinder," in *The Foxfire Book of Appalacian Toys and Games*, 190–91, 193.

and the slaves raised her, and *they* did *all* the work. It would have been the natural thing for her to have been spoiled.

My dad said that grandpa Johnnie didn't have a very fine house like his father had, but he always had plenty of money. He sent my mother to boarding school at Castleberry. I have never found who any of her teachers were, and I just know of *one* of her classmates, Margaret Smith (I think that was her maiden name), she married a Martin.

One time, this Margaret Smith Martin and her daughter came to a funeral at the Armstrong graveyard, near our place, and came on down to our house. She and mother hugged each other and cried. They had been chums in school.

How I do wish my mother had kept a diary, or a book of remembrance. I realize now what a priceless thing they can be.

My mother was certainly *not* spoiled. She could make good soap, could knit like lightning, was a good quilter, and a wonderful seamstress, could manage to scratch up a good dinner on short notice, and had to do it often, and she kept alive and happy. She and our dad would teach us dance steps of winter evenings.

When the M.I.A.[12] started teaching some of the old dances, like "The Lancers," "The Cotillion," "The Mazourka," "Schottische," and dozens of old square dance patterns, we children, Sadie, Lelia, and I already knew them, the boys knew them too, of course.

The attic at grandpa Armstrong's old place was full of relics of a past generation; spinning wheels, a flax reel, parts of an old loom, candle moulds, a red corded bedstead, flax hackles, and many other things.[13] I have just *one* thing, grandma's old spinning wheel, and I have Cecil to thank for that.

Cecil had the Agency for certain cars, and one time when he was going to Detroit for a load of cars he ran up to the house the evening before he started and asked me what I wanted him to bring me from the big cities. Canvas, paint, brushes, frames, or whatever?

I told him that if he came back through Kentucky to go to the old Boone Fuller place (he married Aunt Ann's daughter, Mary Susan) and see if the old spinning wheel was still in the smokehouse there.[14] It was,

---

12.  Mutual Improvement Association, a social and educational auxiliary of the Mormon Church open to those age twelve and older. The M.I.A. of earlier decades had more adult participation; today a young person usually "graduates" from the current youth organization at age eighteen.

13.  A flax hackle, also called a hatchel, is a comb for dressing flax, raw silk, etc.

14.  Nathan Boone Fuller (1854–1942) and Mary Susan Fuller (1858–1940).

and the folks who owned the place cared nothing about it, so I have it now, and will pass it on to some of my children or grandchildren.

My mother has spun the wool and made the thread to knit many a pair of socks and stockings, gloves and mittens. She washed the wool and carded it into rolls ready to spin too.

I don't believe she ever sheared the sheep, the men did that. We had a flock of sheep that furnished the wool too.

The farm families of those days were almost self-sustaining. I think that greatgrandmother, Jane Brasher Armstrong, used this same spinning wheel that I have now. I think that it was used before the Civil War, and probably long before *that.*

Sadie and Lelia tell me that mother *did* weave the cloth for their linsey wool dresses that they wore every winter, and of Sundays, or when they wanted to dress up. They put a white apron on over it; I suppose sleeveless and low necked.

We were always closely connected with the school, as the teachers usually boarded at our place, that is the *lady* teachers. Before I was old enough to go Miss Lizzie Owen boarded with us. I think that was the year I was four. When I was five Miss Vie Brasher boarded with us, and I went to school a few days. The older children's school books were always around, and Etta had taught me to read before I was old enough to go to school. The first lesson was, "See Rob (a dog), see Ann, see Rob has Ann's hat."

My first teacher was Mr. Morgan, James Morgan, a good kind man, who never once spoke a cross word to me, and I loved him.[15] It was during Mr. Morgan's term of school that I awoke one morning late, and nothing seemed natural. Mammy was not in the kitchen, as she usually was at that time of morning. A strange old woman hurried through the room, going into the kitchen for something, and I could see the blind was pulled partly down in the front room. I could hear my mother's voice, as if she was in pain, and I was terribly worried, but no one paid any attention to me. I wondered if Mammy was going to die, like Mrs. Simpson had. It was one of the worst days that I can remember. Finally, some of them came, and told me that I had a little baby brother, Autie (named Charles); the baby was a big bouncer, with a long upper lip, and a short lower one.

While he was still a tiny baby, he would cling onto Pappy's forefinger so tight that he could lift him up by them. About two weeks from that time Vera was born (Lelia's baby).[16] Lelia stayed at our place, and I can still remember how Autie and Vera looked. Vera had a kind of down or

15.    Effie may be referring to James W. Morgan (b. 1867) according to the 1880 census.
16.    This is Vera Alice Ferrell (1891–1927), already mentioned.

fuzz on her face, giving her face a soft look, as if it was powdered, and her hair came down in a little point on her forehead. She was just darling.

Lelia was at our place a great deal, and Vera was like our own baby. After she could walk, she stayed with us most of the time, it seems to me. She never said Grandma and Grandpa, they were "Autie's Mammy, and Autie's Pappy." She was about four years old when Norman was born.[17] Lelia would come walking to our place carrying the baby. Vera would be away behind, walking slowly, and humming to herself. Her cheeks were as red as apples.

When Vera and Autie could just walk they had a crazy habit of putting some chairs together in the middle of the floor, and running around them, keeping step and humming a little melody. As soon as Vera would get there she would say, "Ottie, yes, you and I yum a yound," and they would be off again, sort of an endurance test.

Pappy made a jumper for Autie, and he would jump till he would fall asleep. No one had to tend him very much, as he enjoyed the jumper, and entertained himself. He was a good child, and grew fast into a big strong boy, and, as I was a little scrawny girl, small for my age, there was not as much difference in our size as there was in our years. We had lots of fun playing together.

One silly thing I liked to do was keep him from seeing me. The old house was L shaped, with the two big log rooms, the front room and Mammie's room in front, and the dining room and kitchen running back of Mammy's room, so we had quite a bit of territory to hide behind. He was free to throw at me if he could see me, but I wasn't the least afraid of him hitting me. One day we were playing this same game. He had borrowed Pappy's knife, and was trimming a forked stick for a flipper.[18] He had sat down on the jutting bottom rocks of the chimney, whittling and watching for me to come around the south corner. When I surprised him at the north corner it scared him. He started to throw his stick, and in his haste he threw the knife instead. It was sharp pointed, keen as a razor, and he threw it hard. The blade went into the big part of my left leg, clear up to the handle, and stuck there. It didn't hurt hardly at all, and didn't bleed. Autie ran for the orchard, and I went to the porch and sat down. Mammy came and pulled it out. I almost fainted, not from pain, but because it scared me, I guess. It was not so very long in getting well, but while it was healing up seven boils came around it.

---

17. Norman Ferrell (1895–1929).
18. A flipper is a slingshot.

We called and called for Autie, and looked for him, but he didn't show up until nearly dark. He was sure that he had about finished me. They were sorry for him, and didn't even scold him, for they knew that it was an accident.

Sadie and I were alike in some things, but entirely different in others. She was very feminine, afraid of cows, dogs, and mules. She was afraid of any kind of a dog, just so it could bark. Cousin Alec Ferrell had a little old bench legged fiste,[19] not much bigger than a cat, and Sadie would even run from it, and when he could get someone on the run he was supremely happy, and did his part of the chasing. I think it was William who saw her going lickety split down across the field one day with that little fiste doing his best to keep up, till she reached a tall rail fence and took refuge. He teased her unmercifully about it, and said that that rail fence was all that saved her.

Sadie was even afraid of a quiet old milk cow, and would take to the bushes at the sight of one. We had an old mule, named Hunter, that had almost as much sense as some people. He could untie hard knots with his teeth, could let the bars down, and could unlatch most any gate. If he ever failed in opening gates or bars, he always managed to get over the fence somehow. He could jump any fence, even the high one our Dad had built around the horse lot. He couldn't endure to be confined. He would have been in perfect tune with the song "Don't fence me in."

Old Hunter knew that Sadie was afraid of him, and never let a chance slip by to tease her. If he saw her go to the well for a bucket of water, he would travel a mile, and jump several fences to head her off on her way to the house with her water. When she saw him coming she would set her bucket down, fly for the nearest sycamore thicket, and climb a sapling. He would kind of wink, smile, lay back his ears, switch his tail, and graze around the bush where she was perched. He usually drank a little out of her water bucket, and stayed close enough to keep her treed. If she stayed a little too long, when she went for water, we always knew what was the matter. It was a great joke in the family, when we would go out far enough to see her up the bush, and Old Hunter on guard to keep her from coming down. If she started down, he would run up with his ears laid back, threaten to turn his heels, and squeal a little. She hastily retreated back up the sapling, as high as she could.

Old Hunter would never think of chasing anyone else in the family, not even Autie or I. He enjoyed chasing Sadie because he could make her run so easily.

---

19.  Usually spelled "feist'; any small dog of mixed breed.

Although she was afraid of things, when it was necessary she would swallow her fear and come to the rescue. One time, when Dolly had a new calf, and Mama was milking her, Sadie and I came to see the little calf. Old Bruno, the dog, came and stood beside me. Dolly didn't like the dog so near her calf, and she lowered her head, lolled her tongue, and started towards us. Sadie grabbed her by the horns and stopped her.

Years after that Sadie and Lelia were going to town in separate buggies. Lelia was back of Sadie's horse and buggy. The old black mare Lelia was driving became frightened of something and came tearing around Sadie's vehicle. Sadie made a leap and grabbed the runaway by her bridle bits and swung on till she got her stopped. In emergencies her fears seemed to leave her. Lelia sympathized with her in being afraid of things, and it aggravated her because I was *not* afraid. She said, "Some people just don't have sense enough to be afraid."

I was not afraid of anything, only snakes, and I was not afraid enough of a blue racer to run from them. They were like Old Hunter. They would chase you if you'd run, but if you just stood your ground, threw a rock, or got a stick, they would go the other way.

There was one other thing I *was* afraid of, too. It was Jim Williams' bull, because I had heard the folks say how dangerous he was. And this brings to my mind the very first time I ever prayed. I was going to Aunt Fannie's, and was taking a shortcut through some tall weeds, when I heard him bellering, and it sounded like he was between me and Aunt Fannie's. I knelt in the path and asked the Lord to please make him go the other way. I waited for a while, and could hear my heart beating. Then I heard him bawling away up the creek, in the other direction. I knelt again, and thanked God for answering my petition. My faith in prayer, and in the protection of a kind Heavenly Father was made stronger by this incident and my fear of even Williams' bull was softened a little.

Sadie and I were both tomboys, full of energy and interest in life. She was the best runner in school, and she and John walked the fences for miles, even the picket fence around the garden. They made stilts so tall they had to get on them from the top of the big gate.

Sadie and Evert had a mare they called Daisy.[20] Sadie would drive her to town hitched to the buggy. One day, as she started to cross a bridge that had a loose piece of lumber in the floor of it, Daisy got her foot hung, or something happened, that caused her to not want to go across that bridge anymore. *But*, if Sadie would get out and go and knock

---

20. Evert Holt (1882–1956) married Alzada "Sadie" Marquess on December 12, 1900. Sadie was Effie's sister.

around with a hammer, and pretend to fix it, she would cross it O. K. with considerable shying.

One day Evert was with her and she balked when they got to the bridge. Sadie told him that she could manage it, but Evert said that that was foolishness, he was going to *make* her cross it without all that silly poppycock. He whipped her, and she reared, and nearly turned the buggy over. At long last Evert had to let Sadie pretend she fixed the broken plank, and then she had to lead her across. The rough treatment had her nerves on edge.

Sadie also had a rooster and a cat that were great friends. They stayed together all the time, and seemed to talk to each other.

Sadie saved her clabber milk for the chickens and pigs. One day we went away, and when we got within hearing distance of the back yard we could hear her little chickens making distressed cries, *streak, streak,* and when we came to the back gate the cat had heard the chickens too, and was looking over the rim of the big bucket of clabber, and the little chickens were in it, and of course could not get out.

Cats will often eat little chickens, and Sadie said let's wait a minute and see what it would do. It reached its right front paw down, got it under the little chicken and scooped it up and over the edge of the bucket. It continued till it rescued every one of them, and then proceeded to lick the clabber off of them.

Evert had an old dog named Rex, too, that loved one of the horses. I can't remember just what it was that happened to the horse, anyway, it was hurt and died, and old Rex would not leave the carcass after they drug it off, but stayed there for days, and kept the buzzards away from it. Stayed without food or water, till Evert supplied it.

In the early days of our sojourn at grandpa Armstrong's old house we had a pet squirrel too, and it was unusually smart and cute, but it became a little too smart. It was continually sneaking things and taking them up to its nest on the shoulder of the chimney; balls of yarn, thimbles, the unfinished sock, the knitting needles. Whenever anything was missing they could guess where to find it. Sometimes, when it didn't get its way it would bite, and it had sharp teeth, too.

We had a pair of pet doves, also, named Romeo and Juliette, that were *real* interesting, they were gentle and sweet, and we learned why they have been used as a symbol of peace and purity.

So, we became familiar with many of our wild friends, and learned of their ways, and dispositions. We didn't have to tame the partridges. They built their nests in the wood pile, and we looked forward to the little ones hatching out. They do not have a period of helpless infancy, like many young things, but are ready to run around as soon as they are hatched.

The Whip-poor-wills came and sat on the doorstep at night and gave his plaintive call. We found that they turn *around* and *around* while they say *whip-poor-will, whip-poor-will.*

There is another evening bird almost like the Whip-poor-will, but with a different song. We called them Bull bats, an ugly name. They would catch mosquitoes of an evening, and if we threw a stick or a rock up they would dive to the ground after it.

It was about this time that cousin Boone Fuller and his family moved away over on the Princeton road, on another of Dr. Woods' farms. Our visits, of necessity, became fewer, and farther between, but how we did enjoy them when they came.

I remember them coming over once. Bert and Otho stayed a few days, and we were going home with them. As the men were busy with the horses, on the farm, we were going to walk. I don't remember how far it was, probably three or four miles, but to me it seemed a long glorious trip. I didn't mind it one bit. We would take a lunch, walk slow, and rest along the way, as Autie was a little fellow. We made us some pop guns to take along, made from a joint of alder (we called it elder), with a stick of hardwood. There would be plenty of dogwood berries and sassafras berries all along the way to shoot in them.

We children were anxious to get started, but there were many last minute things to be done before Mammy could leave home. Autie, the baby boy, was a great attraction for the boys, and everything that he said was funny to them. We children were all ready to go so we went out to sit on the wood pile while we waited. Autie said to Bert, "I telle what le's do, le's be a strikin' on." The boys laughed till the tears came, and retold this to their parents when we got there. At last our Mammy was ready, and we *struck out.*

The road led down through our fields, across the creek, and up the bottoms to Uncle Lawrence's, up the hill to the lane, that turned south by cousin Filmore's and Mr. Owen's. There we left the highway, and turned southeast by Weavers', then across the woods by Lee Witty's, and then it was not so very far on to cousin Boone's. Their place was in that section called south Christian, where the country ceases to be hilly and rocky, and stretches out into smooth green distances.[21]

We kept our pockets well filled with berries to shoot. Found wild-flowers along the way, discovered new kinds of birds, stopped to rest, and ate our lunch. We took turns carrying Autie on our backs when his baby legs grew tired. The last stretch of road led through a big woods, to a gate,

---

21.  This describes the southern border of the Western Coal Fields region and the beginning of the Western Pennyrile region. See U.S. Dept. of Agriculture, *Soil Survey of Christian County, Kentucky,* 2.

and from there on south as far as we could see it was cleared and level, and the wagon road led down through the fields to cousin Boone's house.

There were many interesting things when we got there. Big straw stacks to play on, and big hay lofts. A giant tobacco barn, with lots of sparrow nests up under the rafters, and a row of big maple trees, from the house to the barn, to climb. Old threshing machines, and other farm implements to climb over. Big old turkey gobblers that gobbled every time we hollered at them. A fiddle and a banjo that the boys could play tunes on. Cousin Boone was a fiddler, and he let the boys practice on his fiddle when they wanted to.

Besides the things mentioned, there was lots of laughter, and kindness. I don't remember of ever hearing cross or angry words from *any* of this family. They were always glad to see us, and there was always plenty of good food, so it's no wonder the memory of it is pleasant.

Aunt Ann fussed around, and watched we children pretty close, for fear we would climb too high, and maybe fall, and break an *armer* leg. "We don't have any of that kind of legs granny," the boys would say, giggling.

There were lots of tree frogs in the maples, just the color of the bark, and when we would happen to step on one accidently, they were cold, even in hot weather.

We would go to the fields, where Leonard and Genie were working, so we could ride the big old mules back to the house.

Bert and Other [Otho] had several little wagons they had made, with wheels they had found on the old worn out farm implements, and we would take turns pulling each other in them. When Other was tired of pulling, he would run up the bank at the side of the road and make us think it was going to turn over. It really would sometimes, but they were so low we didn't have far to fall, and it didn't hurt us.

Once, when we went to visit them, cousin Mary said the boys were all working over in the old Doyle fields. I wanted to know the way, as I was anxious to go where they were. She said to go up to the big gate, and *there* was a road leading due west through another big gate, and another stretch of big woods, and I would find the Doyle fields. So I started out bravely. To the first big gate was easy, as it was in sight of the house. The stretch of big woods to the next gate was lonely, and it was much farther than I thought it would be. After awhile I was afraid I had taken the wrong road, and was lost, as the road led on and on. Then a terrible sound began echoing through the woods, an awful blood curdling sound, a jumble of wails and cries all mixed together. I imagined it sounded like wolves, although I had never heard a wolf. I was scared stiff, and ran with all my might. After a while a clearing showed through the trees, and I could see the boys ploughing. I told them of the awful noise, and Genie got on his mule to go and see if he could find what it was.

The road through the woods was not very far from the highway, and on this highway (the Princeton road) there was a Negro church. A child had died, and what I had heard was the mourners. They must have been doing a real job of mourning, from the noise that was coming through the woods. I had had no idea there was a church in ten miles of me.

We went back to the field, and I had my first experience in plowing that afternoon. I ploughed up some corn, and let the mule tramp on some more, but anyway, I did some ploughing, about my first, and my last.

There was an old negro man and woman who lived on that place, and we went to see if we could get some eggs for cousin Mary. The man was greasing his boots when we got there. He had already greased his face. Aunt Cindy, the negro woman, was doubling her sheets and pillow cases and putting them between her feather bed and straw bed, so it would make them smooth, and she would not have to iron them. She was a big fat woman, with very large breasts and tummy. She told us that a fox had killed a hen that had been setting on some eggs, so she was keeping them warm by carrying them under her breasts. She raised one and showed us, and sure enough there they were, and there didn't seem to be any danger of them falling out either. I have wondered lots of times since then what did she do with them at night, surely she didn't keep them there while she slept.

Cousin Mary thought our religion was being neglected. Religion, according to her idea, consisted of going to church and singing. Ours was a different brand.

One time I stayed a week at cousin Mary's. When Sunday was coming she starched and ironed my dress, made me a new petticoat with lace on the edge, and tucks above the lace. Sunday morning we trudged our way to Brick Church to Sunday School.[22]

Brother Spurlin, an old man with a white beard, who had been pastor there for many years, conducted the exercises.[23] He chewed tobacco, and between every sentence he would spit. It seemed he was not as good a spitter as some tobacco chewers I have seen, who could hit a knot hole ten feet away. His tobacco juice seemed to fly in all directions. He talked a great deal of hell fire and damnation.

When cousin Mary asked me if I liked the Sunday school, I said yes, but really, I was not very much impressed. I did like the singing, though.

Not long after that Etta went to cousin Mary's to stay for awhile, and Brother Whittenbraker was holding a protracted meeting.[24] They attended

---

22. Brick Church is 3.8 miles from Hopkinsville on Princeton Road.
23. James W. Spurlin (1824–1909). For more on Rev. Spurlin, see Meacham, *History of Christian County*, 256.
24. Brother Whittenbraker could not be identified.

regularly, and Etta decided to be baptized. Cousin Mary was happy. They all loved Etta very much, and I guess she thought she had *saved* her. We went to the baptizing, and after Etta waded out in the water I noted she stumbled, and nearly fell down. After the baptism was over, and she was out, she said that a snake wrapped around her legs.

We watched pretty close for a while to see if there was any noticeable change in Etta after she *got religion*. One day she tried to chase the old cat out with the broom, and instead of going out she scooted upstairs, as the stair door was standing open a little. Etta said, "You infernal old huzzy," and we told her if she didn't watch out she'd lose all of her religion. She felt bad, cried a little, and said that we expected her to be perfect. She just thought she ought to be baptized, as the Bible says we ought. We apologized, and told her that we were just joking.

There was one thing we couldn't *side* with Brother Whittenbraker on. He was always talking about what a terrible sin dancing was. Even the fiddle was a wicked instrument, and was of the devil.

*We* were a generation of dancers and fiddlers, and didn't feel like awful sinners either. It was pretty hard to believe that the devil was in the fiddle. We could *agree* with him as to drinking, gambling, and swearing.

After Etta was baptized, the folks began to think more about religion, and to read the Bible more. According to the Baptist belief, that she had embraced, she would go to Heaven, and the rest of us would all go to hell, unless we were baptized by a Baptist minister.

Papa said that the more that he studied the question, and the more that he read the Bible, the more determined he was *not* to join any of the churches around us. He said they didn't teach the same things Jesus taught. If he ever found one that did teach the same religion, that is described in the New Testament, he would accept it, but that so far he had not found it.

Cousin Filmore Smith had been going to Brick Church, and he and Cousin Serena, and their two children, Lawrence and Worthy, would come over quite often, and the topic of conversation became religion.[25] The more they read the scriptures, the more they decided that most of the denominations were far from the way the Savior had taught.

*One* thing was clear. In the Savior's time, He and His disciples had preached free. He told them plainly, on one occasion, that they had received the Gospel free, and to see that they gave it to others free.[26]

Cousin Fil said that it was possible that, this being an entirely different time, maybe it required a different method. But they found a little

---

25. J. Filmore Smith (1854–1942).
26. See, for example, Matthew 10:8.

later on that the Lord had said, "If any man, or even an angel from Heaven, should teach any other Gospel than that which He had taught them, they would be accursed."[27] He also said that His Church was founded on Apostles and Prophets, so if it was to be the same forever it looked like if we ever found the Church we were looking for it would have to have Apostles and Prophets.[28]

Every time we got together, while we stripped tobacco, or on Sundays, or on long winter evenings, the subject of religion was discussed back and forth without ever coming to anything definite, except this *one* thing. *None* of the churches around us were teaching the same Gospel that the Savior taught. *So,* if Etta's baptism had done nothing else, it had started up an epidemic of investigation, and of reading the scriptures.

Although I was a small child at this time, not more than eight or nine years old, I listened to every word of their discussions, and it seems to me that my judgment then was clearer on a lot of things than it is now. I felt like I knew whether anyone was sincere or not. Whether or not they were telling the truth.

Many times after one of their long discussions I would sit in the half darkness of the old stairsteps, with my rag doll in my arms, and Mammy's old soft brown shawl around me, and think over all they had said, and of the scriptures they had read. I recalled again and again a prayer that Brother Whittenbraker had prayed over at cousin Filmore's one Sunday afternoon. A special prayer. We all knelt around our chairs. I kept thinking that it didn't sound genuine, that he was just trying to impress us. I wondered if it was mean of me to think that.

I had not been to church many times, and the occasional chapters that Mammy read to us from the Bible was about the limit of my knowledge of religion. Except, of course, the everyday life that was ground into us unconsciously. We must never say the name of the Lord, and we must never swear, even on the most solemn occasions. If we wanted to convince [*between this page and the next is a drawing by Effie with the caption "The Old Swimming Hole"; see page 176*] anyone of our truthfulness, and they would not believe us, the very last resort was to say, "I'll swear it's the truth," or "I'll swear I will do it." That was convincing, for to *swear* a lie would have been an *un*forgivable sin, and we didn't do it. When we *swore* a thing it could be depended on.

I don't know whether we kept the Sabbath Holy or not, but one thing sure we didn't work. Pappy said that there was never anything

---

27. A paraphrase of Galatians 1:8: "But though we, or an angel from heaven, preach any other gospel unto you than that which we have preached unto you, let him be accursed."

28. See, for example, Luke 11:49.

gained by working on Sunday, that we would probably waste more time through the week than we put in on Sunday, and if we would work real hard the six days, we would be ready to rest when the seventh day came, and would need it.

We were a happy bunch, at least we children were happy, and if our parents were unhappy we certainly never knew of it. I have wondered how our mother could possibly have done all that she had to do, stay cheerful, and not lose her patience.

The times when the water ran so low in the spring that we had to take the washing to the creek, seems like a picnic to me, but it must have been quite a task for her. When she got ready to move the washing to the creek, we started packing things down there. The old iron kettle was turned over someone's head, another would take the old wooden tubs (usually half of a barrel), another would take the clothes, soap, matches, lunch, etc.

We always had horses, mules, and wagons, but I can never remember the washing or tubs and kettle being hauled to the creek in the wagon. Probably the season in which we had to go to the creek to wash was the times when they were using the teams in the fields. The work in the fields was the important thing.

I can remember that I looked forward to washing at the creek with as much joy as I do a vacation now. I hunted for wood to go under the kettle, punched the clothes, dipped water to fill tubs, and was general flunky. Between times, I hunted flowers, sugar haws, black haws, or built little chimneys of the rocks on the creek bank, or fed crumbs to the swarms of little fish that would come waving their little tails up to the bank to eat.

One day I had started gathering buckeyes, a peculiar nutlooking growth, that grew five or six together in a big burr.[29] When it dried, and they fell out, they were as smooth and slick as a button with an eye on one side, making its name very appropriate. There was a buckeye tree growing on the bank just above the wash kettle. It was bent over, and was very easy to climb. I was up in it, filling my apron with the smooth odd shaped nuts. Suddenly I heard Mammy, in a voice a little too calm say, "Effie, sit right still, and don't move for a minute, and don't be scared."

I saw Mammy looking around hurriedly for something on the ground, and wondered what she was doing. I had just picked up most of the loose sticks lying around for wood, so, not being able to find anything else, she reached down by the kettle and got a burning chunk, came over to the tree and whacked a big copper head snake on his pate. It was not

---

29. Buckeyes are the podded seed of any of several shrubs or trees, resembling the horse chestnut, of the genus *Aesculus*, (esp. *Aesculus glabra*).

more than six inches from my bare feet. He fell to the ground with a thud. I spilled my buckeyes, and almost fell out of the tree.

Mammy had just happened to see him going up the tree where I was sitting. I had not seen him, I was too busy with my buckeyes. The rest of the time we were down there, that day, every twig that moved, I jumped, and I didn't wade in the weeds looking for wild flowers that day, any more.

I can remember yet just how good the buttermilk biscuits and bacon, or biscuits, butter and blackberry jam tasted, when we got ready to eat our lunch on washday.

We hung the clothes on bushes inside the field, as there was danger of cows chewing them if hung on the creek bank. We had to put the wooden tubs high up on a bank and fill them with water. Although there was plenty of clean running water, if we left a tub down where the cows could get to it they would leave the creek and drink the tub dry. Then the tubs would be ready to fall to staves, and would not hold water until filled again and soaked up.

No park, even with expensive swimming pools, diving boards, etc. could have been any more pleasure than that deep shady creek. In fact, it was a trifle too shady, and as the *big hill* was on the south side of it, with giant trees all along the south bank, the water was cold, even in the hottest weather.

There was one hole, where the foot log was located, just east of the bars, where they brought the horses and mules through to water them. *That* place was exposed to the sun, as at this point there was a meadow on the south side of the creek. The only cultivated spot on that side anywhere along our stretch of the creek, so that was the favorite swimming hole for we girls.

The boys found the deeper holes farther down the creek more to their liking. What a luxury, after a long hot dusty day of plowing in the fields, to take a plunge in the cool running water, that was always as clear as crystal, with the bottom floored with clean, bright colored pebbles, keeping the water from becoming muddy, even when we played in it for hours. It spoiled me, for when I've seen children go in an old muddy pond, or a ditch of water, or some old stagnant pool where there was danger of cutting their feet on glass or cans, I felt like they were pretty poverty stricken for a swimming pool, as my ideal was a clear running stream with gravel for a floor.

After the Morris folks moved in the house that was located where our country lane joined the public highway, called the Buttermilk Road, that led from Hopkinsville to Dawson Springs, a new and interesting chapter was added to our lives. Before, all I had to play with was boys, as the three families of cousins that were my playmates were *all* boys. Cousin Narcissy Cook's *baby* was a girl, Essie, the only girl they had. Aunt Helen's only girl died when a baby, and cousin Mary Susan had no girls. So, when the Morrises moved near with a large family, *all* girls, it was not very long till some friendships were formed that were to last all through life.

The Morrises were a good family, clean and intelligent, with high ideals, and as luck was on our side, not over zealous in any of the narrow religions of the surrounding neighborhood, that were so prejudiced against music and dancing.

John and Elmo were both good singers and dancers, both could play the guitar, and sing with it. We had a sort of mania for learning every song afloat, so our place grew increasingly popular, as the boys grew to young manhood.

The ball park was not far from our place, and the croquet yard was in a little glade between our place and Mr. Moore's. Every weekend, and especially Sunday afternoons, there was always plenty of company there.

The Morris family had two girls about my age. Maud, a little younger than myself, Leona, a little older. Then there was Laura, Sadie's age, and Fanny and Olive, a little older. There was also a widowed sister, Mary Miller. She and her two children, Kate and Ivis, lived with them, also.[30]

We became fast friends, and the joys and sorrows of each family was shared by the other. We visited often, and Maud and Leona, and Sadie and I, often stayed all night at each other's homes. Our parents were very lenient, allowing us to stay up late and carouse as long as we liked, but Mrs. Morris had some strict laws that were enforced with a vim. One of them was that we had to be in bed before nine o'clock, and if there was any giggling after we were in bed, we certainly had to keep it smothered, or we would hear the voice of authority, "Leony, I don't want to hear any more of that now, shut up and go to sleep." We usually obeyed.

Maud and I always had to wash dishes, and we drew straws to see which one of us would wash and which would dry them. We both wanted to wash them, but took whatever we got.

Mr. Morris kept the Post Office, called *Larkin*, and a little grocery in the same building, so there were never many days passed without our seeing each other.

Their lives and ours became very closely interwoven. Maud and I sat in the same seat at school for seven years. The first year *I* went, she was not old enough to go. Jim Morgan was the teacher. We sat on long planks for seats, without any backs to lean against, with our books lying beside

---

30. The Morris children were Maud (1886–1915); Leona (1883–1970); Laura (1877–1959); Francis (1875–1958); Olive (1872–1953); and Mary (1869–1910). Mary married Juatt Ivison Miller. Kate never married. Ivis married Fred Marquess and had one daughter, Allie Marquess Gilliland Davis.

us. There was one huge desk up in front, four or five feet wide. As I remember it it seems to me that it was ten or twelve feet long, and real high, but maybe it just *seemed* enormous to my small childish mind. The older pupils kept their books and slates, etc., in it, and sat up there when it was necessary to write or *cipher*.

Mr. Morgan taught all of the eight grades. He was a kind teacher. When school was out it was a great grief to me to think that we might not see him anymore. I loved him, and blubbered freely when he told us all goodby. That was my first year of school, but I had learned to read, write, and spell at home before I was six.

There was a spelling match, the last day of school, and I stood up to spell with the others. Etta and I were standing together. The pupils formed a line all around the building against the wall. Of course he gave little easy words to children like myself. When a pupil missed a word they dropped out and took a seat.

At the last I was still standing with the few older champions. Mr. Morgan knew my capacity and gave me words he knew that I could spell, but at last there were only three of us left standing. The two champion spellers of the older group, and I of the little easy words.

The word was *gourd*, a catch word that we had talked of at home, and I had learned to spell it. The two older spellers were not familiar with it. The first one spelled *goard*, the other hesitated, as there was only one trial. At last he spelled it *gord*. They both sat down, and I was left standing alone. Mr. Morgan said, "Effie, do you think you could spell gourd?" I sailed through it triumphantly. A loud cheer went up, and Mr. Morgan came and patted me on the back, held me up and said, "Here is our school's champion speller."

I was scared, didn't enjoy it very much, and hardly knew what it was all about, as that was the first spelling match I had ever taken part in. It was followed by many, many others. We specialized in spelling till I was sure I could spell any word in the English language. We gloried in such words as immateriality, hypochondriacal, and elephantiasis. We knew all the small catch words like mullein, phthisic, gourd, and separate.

Often, when we had spelled all the hardest words in the spelling book the teacher would have us give the definitions, and the synonyms, or would switch to the geography, and give us names of countries, cities, and rivers.

A spelling match was fun when you knew how to spell all the words, but I remember one time when I got rattled, and my brain refused to function. When the teacher gave out the word *once*, I couldn't remember ever hearing it before, it sounded foreign and strange. It was funny to the poor spellers to see one of the champions stumped on a common everyday word of four letters. They giggled and whispered, and the teacher even smiled, but no one gave me a clue. After a painful silence, the teacher insisted that I give it a trial anyway. I made a stab at it and said *w u n t z*. I could never figure out what caused that lapse of memory, but later on in life, when I suffered a serious shock, I had a recurrence of this same thing, only *more* serious.

Now that I am nearing sixty (1944),[31] I am not so sure of my spelling. I often find myself debating whether it is ei or ie, or whether a simple word begins with e or i, or if there are two l's or one.

I don't believe we were as thoroughly drilled on words and their meanings as the generation before us. Lelia studied the dictionary as a regular textbook, and it has stayed with her through life. It is hard today to find a word that she doesn't know the meaning of.

We hear lots said of the "Little Red Schoolhouse," where all eight grades were taught by one teacher, but somehow we managed to absorb a lot of things. I learned as much, or more, from hearing the older ones recite their lessons than I did from my own studies, all but English. I loved the poems, the stories, etc., that were in Sadie's and Lelia's grammar books, but the intricate rules of grammar, and rhetoric just wouldn't *take* on me, and never did.

Sadie specialized in English grammar, and was expert at parsing and diagramming. I managed to get through somehow, by memorizing, to me, senseless things, that didn't stay with me till they got cold. Right now I don't suppose I could name the parts of speech, or tell what an adverb is. I think I *do* know what a noun or pronoun is, but that's about the extent of my grammar.

The secret of my ignorance of grammar was the fact that for a year or two, when I should have been laying a foundation for grammar, there was no one in that class but myself, and the teacher didn't have the time or inclination to have a class for just *one* pupil.

Then, when we got a new teacher she put me in a class that was two or three years ahead of me. I had no idea what they were talking about, and I guess I never did find out.

I really think that in conversation and writing my English was as good or better than many who were far ahead of me in the intricacies of grammar.

We did learn the diacritics, the marks that showed the different sounds of the letters. They have not been taught to my children. A self-pronouncing Bible, or other book, would not be of any advantage to them, as they have no idea what a broad A, or an Italian A means.

---

31. Effie began writing the autobiography about 1943. She would often parenthetically note the year in which she was writing.

Another thing we learned, that my children have not, was the names of the bones and muscles of the body. We could name every bone in the body from temporal in the forehead, straight on down to the bones of the toes, without a bobble.

We studied a little book called, "The House I Live In,"[32] before we got to serious physiology, which taught us the, then, newly discovered knowledge of the harm of tobacco, coffee, tea, and alcoholic drinks to the body. Today, leading doctors are paid fabulous prices to publish statements saying that they have discovered that tobacco, specially cigarettes, are positively not the least injurious to the heart, and many gullible people, who want to, believe it.

Our physiology book said that there was a certain type of heart disease, called tobacco heart, that was caused by the use of tobacco. Of course it was true, and is true, but the tobacco trust, who cares for nothing but money, would rather we would believe a lie, and tear our bodies down.[33] They don't care for the welfare of humanity, only money. Doctors, who also place the love of money above the love of humanity, are hired to publish the lies to deceive the human race, so that more cigarettes will be sold.

In this, and some other things, we have gone backward instead of forward. They are using the increase of knowledge, not for the betterment of mankind, but for selfish purposes that result in the degradation of mankind, not knowing, poor fools, that they also will fall into the pit they have dug for others, while they who do the *smallest* thing for the uplift of others, will themselves be lifted up.

I can remember a few times when I didn't mind my mother, with some disastrous results. She was not very strong on harsh punishment, in fact I can *remember* the few times she spanked me, or the *one* time; and *one* slap is all I can remember from my father.

---

32. Effie is probably referring to Eli F. Brown's, *The House I Live In; Or, an Elementary Physiology for Children in the Public Schools* (Cincinnati: Van Antwerp, Bragg and Co., 1887).

33. This refers to the American Tobacco Company (or Trust) which was commanding the tobacco trade of virtually every major industrialized country. According to a commentary published in the *Century Magazine* of March 1903, "No amount of protestation convinces the tobacconists that the score or more of the new, well-equipped, expensively located stores which, under one name, have sprung up like mushrooms all over New York and many other large cities of the country are not trust stores operated by persons in the employ of the trust and designed solely to carry out the veiled intention of that organization to control the tobacco trade from the planter's field to the smoker's pocket." See George Buchanan Fife, "The So-Called Tobacco Trust," *Century Magazine* 65 (March 1903): 793. See also Rick Gregory, "'The Godless Trust': The Effect of the Growth of Monopoly in the Tobacco Industry on Black Patch Tobacco Farmers, 1890–1914," *Essays in Economic and Business History* 10 (1992): 183–91.

An old log barn for smoking tobacco "still in use in some of the rural districts." From Scherffius "Tobacco" (1907), plate XIII.

Someone had put a ladder up to the low eaves of the big old tobacco barn. The roof near the edge was almost flat, and looked very inviting. John and Elmo ran up the ladder in their play, and were chasing each other freely across the roof. Autie, my little brother (I was taking care of him), wanted to get up there *so bad*. I went and asked Mammy if I could take him up there just a few minutes, but she said firmly, "No sir, you must *not*." He was just learning to crawl, and was very active. I was awfully disappointed.

It's funny how very much children want to do a thing sometimes, when it doesn't seem to amount to anything to older folks.

Autie and I played around in the shade of the apple trees for a while, and then went back to the ladder. I took him up a step or two, and sat with him on my lap. He was delighted to be up so high and clapped his chubby little hands in delight, so I took him up a few more steps. There was the edge of the roof just even with my shoulder. Right then I had no intention of getting up on the roof *with* him, but I thought I would just sit *him* on the edge, stand on the ladder and hold him tight. There couldn't possibly be any harm in *that*. It was no worse than sitting on the ladder. About the time I got him planted on the edge of the roof, Mammy came to the woodpile for some stovewood and spied me. To her it looked like willful disobedience, and I could see by all the outward signs that retribution was going to be swift and terrible.

Mammy stopped on the way long enough to break a switch from a peach tree. If I could have explained that we were just sitting on the ladder, and that I was just going to let him sit on the edge *just a minute*, while I stood on the ladder and held him; but there was no time to explain anything. I had barely reached the ground when the peach tree limb began to descend on my bare legs.

"Can't depend on you to even take care of the baby a few minutes. You'll get his neck broke the next thing. I told you not to put him up there," etc. That was my first lesson on the wages of sin.

The next case of disobedience was at school. The news reached Mammy that we children were see-sawing on top of an old ten rail fence, and she promptly put her foot down on it. She said that a decent see-saw was all right, but with nothing but an old rail as a teeter totter, and *it* placed so high that it was dangerous. There was danger of our breaking an arm or a leg. The other children's mothers didn't know about it, so they went gaily ahead with the see-sawing project. Inez Armstrong went home and got her daddy's axe to cut the small saplings that were in the way, so the small sharp stubs were left sticking up out of the ground where they were cut.[34] At first I didn't do any see-sawing, but just kind of helped out.

Then one day during a noon recess there was a rail and only *one* girl, with no one to sit on the other end to balance her, so I thought just this once wouldn't hurt. Up and down we went, till suddenly, when I was in midair, and the other girl was on the ground, the warpy old rail turned and I hit the ground with a wallop, right on those sharp stubbles. *Several*

---

34.  Inez Armstrong (1888–1917), daughter of Benjamin Phillip Armstrong (1856–1911) and Leona Wilson Gresham (1868–1911).

of them gouged me, but *one* stuck to the bone in my shin, and hurt terribly. I didn't say much about it, and Mammy didn't notice it for a day or two. In fact, it didn't make a very big place, just stuck straight in. It healed over in a little while, but still ached.

One night, later on, when I was staying with Mrs. Moore, I woke in the night, started to straighten my legs out, and could not straighten the right one. In the morning my shin was swollen up in a big round hump, and I had a fever. Charlie Cook came by, stopped, and said maybe he had better carry me home. Mammy was worried when we got there, and I had to tell her the whole see-saw story.

I didn't go to school anymore that term, but had to sit with my foot propped up on a pillow, with poultices and plasters on my shin. A piece of the stubble had stuck in the bone, and caused an infection. It was months getting well.

The following summer, I was taking the clothes to the creek on a little old homemade wheelbarrow, made of new, rough lumber. I was running with them, as fast as I could, when the wheel dropped into a hole, stopping the wheel stock still. I went over the top, hitting my sore shin on a corner of the rough lumber frame, causing another season of inactivity.

This was the only *sickness* I can remember having, besides colds in the winter, and chills in the fall. When I started yawning and stretching in school, and feeling chilly, when the others were sweating, I knew what was coming. The teacher could usually tell when a chill was coming, as a child's lips turned blue, and the face took on a dull sallow look. Sometimes I went home, other times the headaches and fever, which always followed the chilly sensation, was so severe that I stopped at cousin Leona Armstrong's, or at her sister's, cousin Octavia Gilliland, who lived at the old Hubbard house for a year or two.[35]

One thing that I remember about cousin Octavia, was that she spoiled her babies. She carried them in her arms while she did her work. She was always kind to me when I stopped there with a chill.

This one thing stands out in my memory about these chills. After I would get home, Mammy put me to bed with a cloth on my forehead saturated with camphor, and a handkerchief tied tight around over it. I would wake about sundown, after I had sweated the fever off, thankful that my head was better. I would listen to the others as they did the evening chores; milking, feeding pigs and horses, bringing in wood and

---

35. Leona Wilson Gresham (1868–1911) was the wife of Benjamin Phillip Armstrong (1856–1911). Octavia Gilliland (b. 1860).

water for the night, and would hear Mammy say, "Don't make a noise, Effie had another old chill, and her head aches."

It seems to me that John and I were the two who were tormented the most with chills. Elmo had them occasionally, but Elmo's cross was eczema on his face.[36] A terrible thing at times, making the whole family sad to see him have to suffer with it. The doctors didn't seem to do it any good. All he could do was try to find something that would soothe it a little, and keep it from burning and itching so terribly. Cuticura soap and salve, and Hoods Sarsaparilla as a blood purifier were the standbys that he usually went back to, after doctors and their prescriptions failed.[37]

We usually kept a little flock of sheep, to have enough wool for our stockings, gloves, etc. The little lambs in the spring, the sheep shearing time, washing and drying the wool, picking it into small pieces to remove all the trash, cockleburrs, etc. and later the carding of the wool, and spinning it into thread, was all a part of our existence.

To see Mammy take the dirty, matted wool from the sheep's back, and in a short time have it clean and carded into long even white rolls, that she spun into smooth white thread, and knitted into nice warm gloves and socks, was almost a miracle to me.

As the socks and stockings for the whole family depended on the sheep they were guarded carefully. The neighborhood dogs were a constant menace to them. When we would hear the bell on the old bell ewe (we said Yoe) clattering regularly, we knew that she was running with all her might, and we knew the dogs were after them. Usually someone on horseback would hurry to the rescue, but once (when there were no horses in the stable) we heard the telltale clatter and Mammy and I started out afoot. We knew that if we didn't succeed in stopping them the dogs were likely to kill half the flock before they stopped. This time they were not very far from the house, and only one old mother sheep, with two lambs that could not run as fast as the others were caught. Her hips and sides were all torn to pieces by the dogs. She was still living when we found her, and was bleating with every breath for fear harm would come to her babies. I stayed with her while Mammy took the orphan lambs to the house in her apron, and to get some of the men to come and shoot the poor old mother.

---

36. Effie herself was apparently susceptible to eczema, though her affliction took a different form and she may not have labeled it as such.

37. Cuticura soap and other toiletries were manufactured by the Potter Drug & Chemical Co. in Boston. The company was incorporated in 1883 with Warren B. Potter as its first president. Hoods Sarsaparilla was manufactured and bottled by C. I. Hood & Co. in Lowell, Massachusetts.

We always vowed vengence on the worthless dogs, but rarely ever found them. There were several families of Negroes who lived on the Jim Williams place, and over towards Joe Renshaw's. They usually had a number of dogs that were always hungry, and were forced to hunt rabbits for a livelihood. At the sight of a strange dog the sheep would start running with all their might, so it was not strange that the dogs would naturally join in the chase.

Few people realize, in their dealings with children, how deep the impressions are, that they make; or that some trivial thing that doesn't seem to amount to anything, will be indelibly imprinted on a child's mind, and will stay there through life. Some poet expressed it when he said, "The thoughts of youth are long, *long*, thoughts."[38]

The Savior said, "Take heed that ye harm not one of these, my little ones."[39] For the memory of a harsh word will stay in their minds forever, as a witness against you (he could have added).

One of the saddest things that I can think of is for little children to have to grow up without love. There is no substitute for it. Neither is it good for one child to be raised alone, and have entirely too much attention showered on them, and to become selfish and spoiled. It's hard to say which is the worst. It seems to me that the ideal conditions for a child to grow up under is to be one of a big family, with mother and father who loves them, who do not have the time or the means to spoil them, with lots of room to play, with woods and fields and streams as playgrounds.

I have been thankful a thousand times that a kind providence caused my lot to be cast in just such an environment.

After I went to my first funeral, and saw the Simpson mother in her coffin, and her children crying, a fear that our mother might die began to torment me. I cried myself to sleep more than once, and one time I dreamed we were going to cousin Ike's, and I thought I pushed my mother into a deep clear ditch of water by the roadside, and I could see her as she floated down with her face turned up. It worried me. I never told anyone of it, but I never forgot it.[40]

We had no toilet, not even an outdoor one, the different stables in the horse lot were used. My mother kind of secretly smoked a pipe. Pappy

---

38. Effie is recalling Henry Wadsworth Longfellow's "My Lost Youth": "A boy's will is the wind's will, / And the thoughts of youth are long, long thoughts."

39. Matthew 18:6: "But whoso shall offend one of these little ones which believe in me, it were better that a millstone were hanged about his neck, and that he were drowned in the depth of the sea."

40. Such a dream would have constituted an omen or a portent of death. See William Lynwood Montell, "Part I: Omens of Death," in *Ghosts Along the Cumberland*, 13–55.

hated for her to smoke, so she kept it out of sight. Of summer evenings, after the dishes were done, and the milk vessels all cleaned and put away, Mammy would whisper to me to fill her pipe and light it for her, and we'd go *outdoors* before going to bed.[41]

The stables, where the horses and cows were kept, were, of course, heavy with smell, but there are no unpleasant memories of that. In fact, these quiet intimate visits with my mother in the twilight, are like a benediction in my memory. There were big flat rocks in the horse lot, out behind the little old corn crib, where we made our regular pilgrimage, and afterwards we sat on these rocks while she finished her pipe. We talked while the whippoorwills called, and the crickets chirped. She was a sympathetic listener, and talked to me of things that she knew I liked.

There was never much of the "Don't do this or that" kind of talk. She just lived it before us, and expected us to follow. She often told us that she expected us to *be* somebody, that there was nothing to hinder us from being great, if we worked for it, as there was good blood on both sides of our family, and nothing on either side to be ashamed of.

When I thought of her dying, the things that made my heart ache most was thinking of milking time without her, and of her not being there to go *out-of-doors* with me before going to bed.

Planting the garden in the early spring was another thing that I enjoyed to the fullest. When the first bluebirds called, Mammy would get out her box of garden seeds (they had plenty of tobacco mixed in with them to keep the bugs and worms out).

Onion sets could be put out in February, and the English peas, and mustard could brave the frost that we knew would come later. Gourds were planted in February too. They were usually the little handled ones. There were also the long crooknecks, nestegg gourds, and many other kinds. They were planted right by the garden fence where they could run up on it. Sometimes the vines almost covered the little old smokehouse.

The garden was too wet to plow early, so we would find the driest looking places and dig it up with the hoe. I enjoyed helping Mammy, digging up the ground with an old grubbing hoe, then she would break the clods and rake it smooth for the seeds.

There was always plenty of seed for me to have all I needed for my own little garden in the corner. A time or two there were string beans in *my* garden long before there were any in the big one.

---

41. While it would be unusual for a woman of today's society to be found smoking a pipe, the practice was not uncommon in southern tobacco culture. See Lawrence S. Thompson, "Some Notes on the Folklore of Tobacco and Smoking," *Kentucky Folklore Record* 10 (1964): 43–46.

Mammy was never stingy in her praise of her children, when they deserved it. It was always sincere, and was deserved, so we appreciated it. She never had the time, nor the inclination for loose meaningless talk. She was too honest and natural.

Mammy was called on frequently to go and care for the sick, summer and winter, and at all hours. We were often awakened in the middle of the night by a "Hello" at the gate. It was not hard to guess that it was someone wanting Mammy to go and see what she could do for a sick neighbor. I don't remember of her ever refusing to go. Our daddy didn't appreciate it any too much, for home was thrown out of kilter when Mammy left. I remember one night, when I bawled so long, and so loud, because she left, that Etta and Lelia lost all patience with me and threatened to give me a spanking if I didn't shut up. They rocked me for a while, and when that did no good, they soused me down on the bed and said, "Just lay there and bawl if you want to."

Another thing Mammy had to her credit was that she never in all her life ever turned any one from her door hungry. We had lots of tramps, peddlers, and just plain travelers of one kind and another. I can remember several wandering musicians who came by and stopped at our place. One, named McClanahan, could *really* play an old banjo. That was when I was real small, about 1890. Later, when I was older, a man named Foxworthy came along who could play the old organ like nobody's business, and we learned a lot of new songs from him. One, "I Was Born About Four Thousand Years Ago."[42]

Then there was a distant cousin, Buck Cravens, who came at regular intervals and stayed a week at a time.[43] A slim, trim, bachelor who could play the guitar; in fact he could do most anything. Each time he came he brought something interesting. One time it would be an expensive guitar, then a telescope that we could look at the stars with, and once he brought one that we could look across the country to the old Abe Ferrell place, on the hill east of Morrises', where Lelia lived, and see her as plain as if she was right down at the back of the garden. We saw her come out on the back porch, get some water, and give it to some little chickens. It was a wonderful thing to us.

Cousin Buck was always bringing expensive guns, too, and showing us how he could shoot. Once, when he brought a rifle, he asked Pappy if he wanted him to mark the ears of a bunch of hogs that had come up from the woods lot where they had been eating acorns. Pappy told him that he had better let those hogs alone if he didn't want to pay for the

---

42. See appendix one for a list of Effie's song repertoire.
43. Buckner P. Cravens (b. 1862), son of Lycurgus G. Cravens (b. 1827).

ones he shot. Cousin Buck cheerfully assured him he would pay any damages, then he turned the rifle upside down and said, "Here's a hole in that spotted one's left ear." *Crack*, the pig squealed and jumped, and sure enough there was the hole. He went the rounds and shot a hole through the left ear of each one with the rifle bottom side up. Cousin Buck had told so many blowy tales that we hadn't believed him.

Once he brought a fine bicycle, and told us we could ride it all we wanted to. I took it to the top of the slanting field, between the big gullies and the spring woods lot, got on it and started down the hill. I had not calculated on the stop, and as one fork of the gully was across the lower end of the field, me and the bike landed in the bottom of the gully. It was hard to tell which was in the worst condition, me or the bike. I decided I didn't want to learn to ride a bike, not right then anyway.

For several years Cousin Buck was foreman on the Widow Clardy's big farm in south Christian. She had many fine blooded horses, and he would ride a different one each time. How I did enjoy them. I was an ardent lover of horses.

Buck had a collection of old love songs he taught us, too. One was the tragic tale of the Milwaukee Fire. He was gallant, and very chivalrous. He would never let any of we girls carry any water, or bring in any wood. He would go with us to the well, and we would insist on carrying *one* bucket, anyway, but he declared that one on each side was much easier, as they balanced him perfectly.

He had long slim, blue hands, that didn't look like he had ever done any hard manual labor. His feet were slim, with high arches, and he always wore expensive shoes. I think he had a speculative eye on my sister Sadie, or he wouldn't have come so regularly.

There are a number of peddlers that I can recall, most of them were foreigners, who spoke with an accent. One stands out clearer than the others, a handsome young fellow, who came one winter day wearing a suit of shining brown corduroy, and boots. It was snowing, and very cold. The poor boy was new in America, and had not learned the language very ~~good~~ ^well^.[44] He was so homesick that he could hardly live. He told us of his home in Syria, and of how desperately his father had tried to keep him from coming to America. He had even locked him up in hopes he could persuade him not to come. He offered him an allowance that would be far more than he could earn by peddling. The father was a stonecutter, and had taught him the trade.

His name was Haffy Dennis, and when he got to the part of his story where he left his home, and his mother was crying, *he* cried like a child.

---

44. "Well" written by hand over "~~good.~~"

He threw his pack open, with all of its bright shawls, beads, bedspreads, and trinkets, and said that he hated it, to take everything we wanted, that he was not going to be a peddler anymore. He was going back home to his father and mother, and if they were still living he would learn to be a stonecutter and help his father.

Another character, though vastly different from young Haffy, was an old Negro, who had a big family. He could never make a living for them, and would come begging, pretty sure of getting something without working for it. One time he came in the spring when our own supply of corn, meat, etc. was getting rather low. My father told him that he was as able to work as *he* was, and that we had as many mouths to feed as *he* did, and he just didn't have anything to give him. His name was Bill Sudkins, and he was a good beggar. He cried and talked at the same time, and he declared that his little chillun hadn't had anything to eat for two days. Pappy was on to his tactics and didn't weaken. I stood it as long as I could, thinking *surely* he would relent and give him *some*thing. When the old Negro started off, muttering, with his lip a-quivering, and the tears streaming down his cheeks, I started blubbering in earnest. I went and grabbed Pappy by the legs and told him to give the old man something, he mustn't let him go without. I guess I yelled so loud that he called him back in self-defense and gave him a sack of corn and some other things, I can't remember just what. I *do* remember what the old Negro said, "Thanky, thanky, Mr. Marcus, may de good Lawd bless yuh."

The remarkable thing about the Sudkins family was the names they gave their children. I can only remember one of them, a little girl. Her name was Harriet chile-Lizabeth-Rosey-Becky-Black hair-Eda-Margit-Maudy-Tyler, and of course I suppose, Sudkins was added, but it is probably doubtful whether it rightly belonged there or not.

The list of comers and goers would not be complete if I didn't mention De-Bill Owen, a kind of a simpleton, who was madly in love with Lelia. He would come and stay for two or three days at a time. Once he came when the snow was deep, and as he came through the bottom fields, where the sheep were, they thought he had come to feed them, and all started in his direction. He was not familiar with sheep, and he was afraid of them, and started running. They followed, and by the time he reached the fence, not far from the house, he was completely exhausted. How we children laughed when he told us that the sheep got after him. He brought a *big* sack of candy beans, the first ones I ever saw. It seems to me that there was at least a half gallon or more of them.

When some of the family would see De-Bill coming across the fields, from the south west, they would hurry and call Lelia. "Lelia, yonder comes De-Bill." I was always in hopes he would have plenty of candy.

The country down the creek from the direction he came was a mysterious region to me. I guess I thought that all the people in that direction were like De-Bill. He was the only contact we had with the people from downcreek way. I remember hearing Mammy saying that if the geese ever went very far down the creek they always came home picked. Goose feathers were used extensively in those days. Every family had several feather beds, and if they did *not* have they just didn't amount to much. Feathers were high, and it was *some*thing to lose the pickin' from twenty or twenty-five full feathered geese.

When the wind was in that direction, from the southwest, as it often is in summer, the sounds carried easily. We could hear voices from the farms in that direction, and one evening, when we mentioned it, Mammy said yes, she had heard men whipping their slaves in that direction. When she was a child, and could hear the slaves beg for mercy, it was a terrible sound to her, as the Armstrongs rarely ever punished *their* Negroes.

The geese, mentioned above, were picked every six weeks. That was the length of time it took the feathers to get *ripe*, and if they were *not* picked off they would shed them, and the place would be covered with goose feathers.

It was a common thing in the neighborhood that the men hated the geese, and the women hated the hounds. Though the geese furnished the feathers for the warm feather beds, which the men liked to sleep on, and the hounds caught the foxes that were bad to catch the women's geese and chickens, nevertheless, the prejudice continued.

It was almost an impossibility to fence the geese out of a field with a common rail fence, and that was the kind of fences that were used exclusively at that time. It seems to me that I was the one who *should* have hated the geese, as I can't remember anyone but myself ever having to stop up goose holes in the fence. The others *probably* had their turn. I suppose the few times I had to do it became magnified.

We would think that we had every crack filled that was big enough for a goose to get through, but in early spring, when the pretty green sprouts of corn would be peeping through the ground in long even rows, we would, some mornings, spy an old goose in the corn field. She would start down one row, and not just eat it off, but would grabble it down to its roots, so it would never grow out again. Then my dad would swear vengeance on all geese, and that one in particular. Sometimes we had goose for dinner, if the offense was repeated two or three times.

We had guineas, too, and although the guinea hens laid an unusual number of eggs, the roosters were very unpopular. They were terribly noisy, with a harsh raspy voice, and if there was the least disturbance in the night the whole flock would set up a chatter that *no* one could sleep through.

The guinea roosters were always pecking the little chickens, and they would kill them if someone didn't go to the rescue. One day Mammy was standing in the kitchen door when an old guinea rooster lowered his head, stuck his wings up on his back, and made a dive at a little chicken. He was going after it red eyed. Mammy said, "Confound your old soul, I'll knock your head off for that." Reaching down for a stick of stove wood she let it fly right at him. He saw trouble coming and raised his head high just in time to catch the stick right in the neck. The head was severed clear, and flew up in the air. We had a laugh over it, and our Pappy said that Mammy was really a woman of her word. When she threatened to do a thing you'd better look out. We had guinea for supper that time, but they had to be cooked a *long* time as the meat was blue and tough.

The guinea hens stole their nests out, far away from the house, but they had a peculiar cackle when they laid an egg, and we usually found the nest. They were like a partridge. If you put your hand in the nest for the eggs they would quit laying in it and find another place, but if you would rake the eggs out with a stick they would keep laying there. Sometimes several guinea hens would lay in one nest, and we would get a hundred eggs or more before they would quit laying or change places.

Pappy was good at finding partridge nests, also, and would keep bringing their eggs in his hat as he came from work. Their eggs were almost as large as guinea eggs, but white as snow, while the guinea eggs were brown speckled.

Pappy liked to spring pleasant surprises on us, like bringing a hat full of mulberries, or eggs, or the first early bluebells. Sometimes, when they were burning plant beds, when it was still winter, he would find a bunch of dainty white windflowers growing in a warm sunny location that had blossomed before their time.

I think I surely must have had an unnatural love for pretty things, especially flowers, when I recall the joy that the first early flowers gave to me. After a day or two of warm sunshine, in early spring, we would go out some morning and the old fields would be carpeted with tiny bluets in bloom. The joy of seeing them again, after the long cold winter, with its ice and mud and ugliness, was almost more than I could hold.

I guess I was just a lover of color, and as life in winter in an old log house that was pretty well crowded with children could not contain too much of beauty we were hungry for such things when springtime came.

Mammy used to put a strip of red flannel in the coal oil of the lamp. She said that it was to absorb the grit that was in the coal oil, to keep it from lodging in the lamp wick, but I really believe it was to add a touch of color to the mantlepiece. I can't recall ever seeing *black* flannel in a lamp bowl.

My father was school trustee for years and years and the teachers usually came to our place when applying for a position as teacher of our school. I'll never forget one applicant, Irene Hiser, who came to see about getting the school the following fall. She was riding a beautiful bay horse, and she wore a tight riding suit with a long red ribbon tied in a bow on her left arm. Her hat turned up on the left side with a long flowing plume, and as she galloped away with that red ribbon fluttering in the breeze behind her I thought she was just about the most beautiful creature I ever saw.

Outside of baseball for the men and boys, and a croquet set (privately owned by someone), about the only entertainment for the young folks was dancing. The churches opposed dancing, even going so far as to excommunicate their members for breaking this rule. Entertainment was whittled down pretty narrow for the children of the church goers. They argued that if the young folks went to church of Sundays, and to prayer meeting and *singin'* through the week, that was all the recreation they needed. They *did* allow them to have *play* parties in some communities. These parties were nothing but a form of dancing, only there was no music to dance by but the singing of the dancers (though they were careful never to *call* it dancing).[45] The songs they sang to dance by were silly old things, not very elevating. One of the favorites was—

Les all go down to Rousers, to Rousers, to Rousers,
Les all go down to Rousers, and get some lager beer,
Good old lager beer, sweet old lager beer,
Never mind the old folks, so we get the beer,
Old folks, old folks, old folks, old folks,
Never mind the old folks, so we get the beer.[46]

Our father said if there was anything more elevating in that than there was in a nice quadrille to the tune of good music, then he was not a good judge.

Public picnics were very popular, and drew large crowds. Sometimes there was an animal barbecued, and sometimes if you wanted something to eat you had to take it with you. There was usually a stand where gum and candy and lemonade were sold.

---

45. For more on play party games, see Gordon Wilson, "Singing Games or Play-Party Games," *Bulletin of the Kentucky Folklore Society* (1925): 26–30, Adam Jacobs, "American Play Stuff: Party Plays," *Theatre Arts* 15 (March 1931): 247–50, and Frank H. Smith, "Dances and Singing Games," in *The Southern Appalachian Region: A Survey*, ed. Thomas R. Ford (Lexington: University of Kentucky Press, 1962), 271–78.

46. See appendix one.

There was usually a square smoothed off and covered with sawdust, with a high platform on the side for the musicians, and there was dancing. It was interesting to watch the dancers too, and to see the fights that usually took place before it was over.[47]

Although these picnics were not very elevating, many good substantial citizens attended them, just to have a chance to visit with friends they were sure would be there too.[48]

The new tub, with the slices of lemon and chunks of ice floating around in it, and a new tin dipper to drink from, was a refreshing attraction. Ice was rare (in the country) in those days, even the old fashioned ice box was unheard of (in the country) at that time. The loud raucous voice calling, "Right this way ladies and gents, ice cold lemonade, made in the shade, and stirred with a spade," never failed to arouse plenty of interest. The children crowded around the lemonade stand even if they had no nickel with which to buy a drink for themselves.

It was not an uncommon thing to see a mother or father go and draw a daughter to one side and tell her not to dance with so and so, as he was drunk as a fool, and if he offered her any candy, be sure and not take it.

The *Moon*lights were a duplicate of the picnics only they were held after dark, and were far more romantic than the daylight affairs. There were usually paper Japanese lanterns, with candles in them, which shed their soft pale light through the pretty colored paper.[49] If any grand ballroom ever caused a greater thrill in anyone's heart than the sight of rows of these lights and the sound of a fiddle and banjo stirred in me I don't see how they ever lived through it.

Probably to some poor church member, who had never danced, they would not have looked so glamorous, and the dancing would have seemed a wicked something to be shunned, but our sense of wrong didn't run in that direction. Our parents had taught us that graceful dancing, and keeping rhythmic time to good music was a good way to show our

---

47.  Apparently fights were common at Kentucky square dance gatherings. Several examples are mentioned in Jesse Stuart, "Kentucky Hill Dance," *New Republic* 79 (May 16, 1934): 15–16, and in Noel Coppage, "Fights, Fiddles, and Foxhunts," *Kentucky Folklore Record* 7 (1961): 1–14.

48.  These gatherings were an embodiment of community and individual values. Dances provided a time for neighbors and family to establish social boundaries within a community. See Burt Feintuch, "Dancing to the Music: Domestic Square Dances and Community in Southcentral Kentucky (1880–1940)," *Journal of the Folklore Institute* 18 (1981): 49–68.

49.  The term "moonlights" is apparently a local term used by—but not limited to—the people of Effie's community.

appreciations for the beautiful, and the only way dancing was wrong was when we made wrong of it by our own actions.[50]

We went to *Moon*lights with a clear conscience, and we had the assurance that no matter how many good dancers were there, we could dance anything they could. Our father had played for the balls when the big boom was on at Cumberland Gap, and for the summer resort at Cerulean Springs. That was the way he earned his living, and I think he taught dancing in the afternoons. He knew all the steps, from the prim Lancers, to the rollicking heel and toe polka. He and Mammy would teach them to us of winter evenings. Lots of times I have seen him, violin to shoulder, play the tune and dance the steps that went with it all at the same time, to show us how it went. How we enjoyed it. Not alone in dancing did they join with us, but in *any* games that we played.

One thing that we enjoyed more than any other, was for them to tell us of things that happened when they were young. Pappy often told us of the first time he ever saw our mother. He and Uncle Jim were riding horseback to a dance. They had heard that a new girl (just home from school), a girl with a funny name, John Susan Armstrong, was going to be there. Uncle Jim said he was going to take her home. When they got there they hitched their horses and went to the window to look things over before going in. The new girl was singing, I think she was singing:

I am sitting on the stile, Mary
Where we sat side by side
In the sweet long ago, Mary
When you promised to be my bride.

Pappy said that he turned to Uncle Jim and said, "No Jim, *I'm* going to take her home myself," and he did. She was only sixteen, but it was not so very long till they were married. She was born in 1853, and they were married in 1869.

The school she went to was at Castleberry, Kentucky, north of us. She probably stayed with the Wooldridges or Fords, her stepmothers's people, as that was where they lived.

---

50. According to Effie, "there were two classes of moonlights: if the front yard belonged to a church member, it would only be a promenade, where couples strolled around and around until the candles burned out of the paper lanterns. But if the yard belonged to someone who was not a church-goer, the ground was scraped smooth, music was provided, and the young folks danced. At the end of each set the prompter called out in a lusty voice, 'Promenade your partners to the lemonade stand!'" See Carmack, "Tobacker," 101.

They told us of a very careless trick my mother did not long after she met her future husband. She had been eating something and had a particle between her front teeth that bothered her. She pulled a big cockleburr from a bush and was picking her teeth with it. She sneezed, or coughed, or something, anyway she sucked the burr down her windpipe and almost choked to death. Her *beau* beat her on the back, and tried every way he knew to help her. Finally he picked her up and ran to the house with her. She gave a cough and the burr and the blood both flew from her mouth. Pappy said he found out then how very much he thought of her. I think the bond of affection between them was mutual, and remained strong and unbroken as long as she lived (she was only forty-six when she died).

Of winter evenings, around the fireplace, his chair was usually next to hers (if he was not working at something), with his arm across the back of her chair, or his foot in her lap, while she knit, darned or mended.

Lawrence Smith, cousin Filmore's son, said that we didn't need to go away from home for entertainment; that we had a better time there, than anywhere else. They had dances in private homes in winter, as there were no dance halls close enough for us to go to.

When I was about seven they gave a dance at our place. Autie was just learning to walk good. I was highly excited over the preparations and could hardly wait for the activity to begin. The beds and other furniture were removed from the big *front* room, which had a good smooth floor. A row of seats was made all around the wall by laying planks on stovewood blocks and covering them with quilts, so they would be more comfortable. A platform was made in one corner for the musicians. By dark everything was ready and waiting for the crowd.

Eddie Moore had *made it up*, that is, he and some others who volunteered to help him went on horseback and invited all the people they wanted to come, and he charged them that there was *not* to be *any* whiskey brought.[51]

---

51. According to Burt Feintuch,
    the concept of neighborhood is at the core of both the pragmatic and symbolic aspects of domestic dance. Participants learned of the dances through neighborhood channels. Word was passed in the course of visiting during the week, and the inevitable country store which was the commercial focal point of the neighborhood served as a source of information—signs were posted or information was shared by word of mouth. Sometimes people would decide on the time and place for the next dance at the conclusion of an evening of dancing, and all the participants would know in advance of a dance to be held the following weekend.
    See Burt Feintuch, "Dancing to the Music," 55–56.

Eddie was a good singer and had been going to Mt. Zoar to sing with a group there. He invited some of the Mt. Zoar church members to come to the dance, and to bring their songbooks, and they would sing during intermission. The folks were surprised to see the Baptist people come to a dance, it was very unusual.

Before any of the crowd arrived, William and Lelia came, as William was going to help make music. Pappy played the fiddle, and William the banjo. I was almost bursting with excitement when they tuned their instruments up in that big, clean, empty room, with a bright fire crackling. When they swung into the stirring tune of "Eighth of January" it was just about more than I could contain. I had to put my hands over my ears to temper it a little.

Right after dark they began coming, and what a crowd. Norman Tyndall and his beautiful wife came, the new folks who had moved into the old East house at the foot of East Hill, and Mrs. Mullen, also a newcomer, came with them. When someone asked her for a dance she said, "Well, sir, I never danced a lick in my life," with a quick northern accent, that sounded funny to us. Mrs. Tyndall had a good voice, and could sing like a bird.

I was entranced with the dancing, but when there was an intermission, and the singers were invited to take the floor for a while, I was *really* charmed. I don't suppose I had ever heard a group sing together, carrying the four parts before. They sang "I Am Longing For the Coming of That Snowwhite Angels Band," and, "When Jesus Shall Make Up His Jewels," and, "Sweeping Through the Gates." I listened with my mouth wide open, and decided right there that I was going to be singer when I grew up, but the singing didn't last very long.[52]

George Vaughn was in the prime of his dancing glory. He prompted the dancers, and called the changes with all the flourishes and trimmings. Autie stayed wide awake, and took in everything. When everyone was gone, and the big floor empty again, he got out and showed us how George Vaughn danced. He bent over and stuck his hands out behind him and went shuffling around the floor, causing an uproarious laugh. Of course, everything he did was funny to all of us. He was smart, and learned things quickly.

I was so excited over the dancing and singing I could hardly go to sleep. The beginning of a big new chapter in my life had opened up.

---

52. For more on Kentucky dance music, see Carl W. Pullen, "Some More Dance Songs from West Kentucky," *Kentucky Folk-Lore and Poetry Magazine* 3 (1928): 15–18, and Kathryn Blair, "Swing Your Partner!," *Journal of American Folklore* 40 (January-March 1927): 96–99.

Etta and I got a song book and learned to sing those songs right away. After that, when there was a dance in the neighborhood, if Sadie and the boys went, I bawled to go with them. Of course I never had anything but my coarse winter shoes, but they could be *blacked,* and I never let that spoil things. The shoes didn't matter, the lights were never very bright anyway, and a clean calico dress was good enough for a little girl to wear.

Some of the girls flourished gorgeous flounces and ruffles, especially at the summer picnics and moonlights. Thin lawns, organdy, and laces were popular, trimmed with narrow black velvet ribbon. It was very impractical, as the ribbon would not wash, and had to be removed when the dress was washed. But that didn't keep it from being used, it was very effective on sheer pink or yellow organdy.

The question of clothes didn't bother me then, nor very much ever after. I could dance, and I enjoyed demonstrating that fact. On rare occasions I was allowed to go to the winter dances, riding behind Sadie or one of the boys. Although I was a thin, scrawny child, ugly and small for my age, dressed in calico and coarse shoes, I usually got a partner of some kind. *That* didn't matter, just so I was on the floor with the other dancers. Nothing but the square quadrilles was danced at the country dances. Not many of the young folks knew how to do the Waltz, Two Step, Schottische, Glide, etc., but sometimes, between sets, a few couples would get the musicians to play a waltz, and they would glide around awhile. The round dances were unpopular, and were booed by the ones who could not dance them. They would yell for a good old square dance tune.

The church people often got up a moonlight, where there was no dancing allowed. They just promenaded around the grounds in couples. To me it was like playing we were eating, when it was only mud pies.

About the first of July, sometimes a little later, the blackberries began to ripen. There was usually a pretty good crop of them, and taking care of the berry crop was serious business. We usually canned a lot, made some jam, and then we picked to sell, in order to get cloth for school dresses. They usually sold for ten or fifteen cents a gallon. I have sold them many times for seven cents a gallon. A very small sum for a gallon of berries, but cloth was cheap also, so it averaged up very well.

We would make us some good strong gloves of old worn out overalls, to keep briars from tearing our hands so. We'd put on some of the boys' big old shoes, to wade into the middle of a thick briar patch with, an old hat or a bonnet, and then we sallied forth with our numerous buckets clattering. We *really* made a picture, but we got the berries. We had to be careful where we put our full buckets, or we would forget where some of them were.

Pappy was good to take the berries to market for us. There was usually chickens, eggs, butter, and vegetables to be taken to market also. We appreciated the small amount of money we received from our berries, and we had a real reason for hunting bargain counters, as we had to make this money go as far as possible. None of it was ever spent for any foolishness, and how we appreciated the cloth we bought with it, and how we enjoyed making the dresses of it.

I was not allowed to sew on the machine very much yet, but I got plenty of practice making doll dresses on my fingers. I usually had one or two china dolls, and at least one big rag doll.

One summer Sadie picked enough berries to buy her a sidesaddle. Before that time she had borrowed Mrs. Moore's saddle when she wanted to go horseback riding. Mrs. Moore herself never used it. In all the years we lived near her I can never remember seeing her on a horse, but she didn't like to lend it any too well, and Sadie felt duty bound to let Eddie go with her, to even things up, for borrowing the saddle so often. We really felt rich and independent when we got a saddle of our own.

It was pretty easy to hurt a horse's back if the blankets under the saddle were not arranged just right, and we were always worried for fear the blankets were working out of place, and the horse's back would be skinned again. We could usually tell when it hurt, as the horse would flinch.

Lelia was always saying that I was equal to George Simpson in finding the blackberries. He must have been a champion berry picker.

We would be a sorry looking bunch when we drug in of an evening, tired and briar torn. Our hands and faces all stained with berry juice (when we grew thirsty we ate berries) and scratched by briars.

The worst feature of berry picking is that we were usually covered with chiggers, a teeny red parasite, no bigger than the point of a pin. But, Oh! the lump he could raise, and if not removed he would bury himself, and the place would itch and stay sore for weeks. The first thing we did when we got home was to get rid of the chiggers and ticks. Strong salt, or soda water, or coal oil, applied to the lumps would usually kill them, but it didn't keep the place from itching all night (I have a lump on my back now, that has been there for twenty years, where a tick had buried itself, and I failed to find it when I bathed).

Ticks, chiggers, briar scratches and all; including the small price we got for the berries; we never once thought of *not* picking them as long as there was a berry on the briars. That was just a part of the process, and we didn't even *think* of it as a hardship.

# CHAPTER THREE

# Raised In A Patch Of Tobacco

*And now since I've studied the problem profoundly*
*And searched out the sources from which we descend,*
*I see many whys and can guess many wherefores,*
*To show why our lives take some definite trend.*
*Our Marquess forefathers were lovers of music,*
*And lovers of beauty, religion and art.*
*And though we were raised in a patch of tobacco*
*These things in our beings still held a rich part.*
> —"Concerning Our Father And Mother"
> in *Backward Glances*, 31

Life on the farm in Kentucky, especially in the dark tobacco district,[1] was made up of so many different hardships, that we were used to them, and really didn't mind them a great deal. I suppose those things kind of helped to strengthen our character, and also to strengthen muscles.[2]

I am an old woman now, almost sixty (1944) and I find I can still stand a lot of hard labor, and it doesn't hurt me either. We grew tough as

---

1. The "dark tobacco district" refers to the area of western Kentucky in which dark tobacco was grown. This dark prime-leaf, with darker leaves than regular tobacco, is grown and prepared especially for snuff or chewing tobacco rather than for smoking.

2. In 1935, Nora Miller, a home economist, described this lifestyle succinctly by stating that "The very nature of tobacco culture with its long growing seasons, detailed labor requiring many workers, short harvesting period, long hours both day and night for curing, storing, grading by the women, and long trips which the man must make to market the crop, disrupts the family life. The fact that the woman and girls devote a great deal of time to the labor on the farm keeps the family from being as well managed as it might be with a different division of labor." Nora Miller, "The Tobacco Farm Family," chap. 6 in *The Girl in the Rural Family* (Chapel Hill: University of North Carolina Press, 1935), 62.

children, and it seems to stay with us. I suppose the Lord meant some such thing as that when he said to "Count it all joy when you are called upon to suffer diverse tribulations, that the trying of our faith worketh patience, to those who are exercised thereby—"[3] I suppose some folks just balk at hard things, and *are not exercised* by them.

I remember a lesson my mother taught me when I was a very small child. I had gone with her to pick blackberries, and she said she would show me how to be a good berry picker, how I could enjoy it, and my bucket would fill up fast. "Just take one limb at a time, pick every ripe berry on it before touching another, until you have finished that briar. Pick them clean as you go, and you will enjoy it." If I ever started moving about, picking a few berries off of this briar, and a few off of that one, I would soon grow tired, and my bucket would not fill up fast.

One day (one summer) I went to the spring for water, and I ran down the branch to see if the berries were turning yet. There was a patch just at the edge of the woods which usually ripened early. Most of them were still red, but about one in every cluster was black, so I hurried to the house with my water, got a bucket and ran back to the berry patch. Maybe I could find enough for a pie for dinner, and surprise Mammy. By picking every ripe one I could find I got enough for a good sized cobbler. Mammy was extravagant in her praise of surprises like that.

Mammy usually put butter and sugar on top of the crust to make it brown good. She put the cobbler on the table in the pan she had cooked it in, and *did it look good!*

Allen Johnson was working for us that day and would be there for dinner. He was a tall, ungainly fellow, very cross eyed, and his mouth usually hung open, revealing black snaggled teeth, but he was a good worker, and Pappy often hired him.

They all sat down to the table, and I stood to one side, very proud of the pie I was responsible for, and hoping they would all enjoy it, and (of course) hoping that there would be a little of it left for me. There *should* be, as there was a *big* pan full.

Allen looked around the table, spied the pie, and without even tasting any of the good vegetables and other things Mammy had fixed for dinner he pulled that pie up, pushed his plate to one side, and didn't stop till he had eaten every morsel of it; with a *big* spoon. He made lots of noise while he was eating, and John and Elmo said they were sure it was a good pie by the way Allen smacked his mouth as he devoured it.

---

3. Effie is paraphrasing James 1:3–4: "My brethren, count it all joy when ye fall into divers temptations; knowing this, that the trying of your faith worketh patience."

I don't believe I cried, but I felt like it. Not that I wanted it so bad myself, but I wanted the others to have a taste. It made him look so piggish that it made us all feel bad that *any*one could be so rude and ill mannered.

We didn't *go visiting* very often, but one day Pappy came home from someplace and said he had seen cousin John Cannon, and had promised him that we would come to their place and spend the night the following Saturday.[4] Cousin John was no relation to us, only by marriage. His wife, who was Victoria Gilliland, was the daughter of Eliza Jane Armstrong Gilliland, a sister of my mother's father, Johnny Armstrong.

The Cannon family were all good looking people. They were always smiling, not forced, nature just built them that way, the corners of their mouths just naturally turned up. Everyone liked them, and liked to be with them.

I remembered something I had heard my mother tell of cousin Victoria. She was good at dramatic readings, which they all enjoyed very much, excepting one she gave called "The Progress of Madness," it was most too real. Mammy also said that Vic was the only person she ever saw with a fever blister on her lip and it looked pretty.

Victoria had a decided way of her own that was perfectly natural. Many of the mothers watched their children so close (or pretended that they did) that they made them look silly. One day, when cousin Vic came to a quilting without her two boys, Johnnie and Adrian, the women asked in alarm, "Where are your children?" answer, "Well, they're at home where they ought to be, they can't quilt." "Ain't you afraid to leave them there alone, with that old well there by the house?" "No, I'm not, and if they haven't got more sense than to raise that old well top and jump in that well, I say, let 'em go!" The women shut up, shook their heads, and worried with their numerous offspring all afternoon, fighting and getting into things, while Victoria quilted in peace, with her boys at home playing.

There were also two girls in that family (younger than the boys), Lettie and Pearl, unusually pretty girls with nice dispositions. I was a very small child when we went to visit them. I think it was before I started to school. We took the music with us, and after supper there was singing and music. Cousin Victoria insisted that Johnnie and I dance for them. We danced the military Schottische. Cousin Vic asked how long I had been dancing, and cousin John said, "Why them children don't have to learn to dance, they knew how when they was born."

Uncle Jim Marquess, Pappy's half brother, had fought in the Civil War, and was wounded. One leg was a little shorter than the other, and he

---

4. Probably John J. Cannon (b. 1846).

Effie Carmack's "Uncle Jim," James Washington
Marquess, when he enlisted for the Civil War at age
sixteen but "swore he was 18." Courtesy of Itha
Carmack.

was hard of hearing. I think he enlisted when he was sixteen, swore that
he was eighteen. I have a picture of him when he enlisted, and he doesn't
look older than sixteen. The rough life in the army, or him joining so
young, left its impression on him. He liked to play poker, and could swear
like a trooper, but he was a good man, and raised a family of good boys,
and we all love him.

Uncle Jim had a hobby of getting fine fruit trees and cultivating
them. Consequently, they always had enough peaches for everyone in the
neighborhood. When they were ripe he always invited my mother to come
and dry all she wanted, so we would dry enough for ourselves, and them

too. The drying racks reached almost across the yard. We would choose the soft peaches that were freestone, and not too large. We would cut till we had a tub full, and then place them on the racks, cut side up.

As soon as there was a lull in the peach business, Jimmie, and Charlie and I would be off riding calves, horses, or throwing at something. Jimmie was a sure shot with a rock.

Uncle Jim used the windfall apples to make cider, and cider wine, so they always had plenty of company of Sundays. He was a great reader, and liked to read stories, even after he was an old man. If the children were studying around the family lamp of evenings he would get the old coal oil lantern, hold it up in front of his book where the light would shine on it and read that way. I have wondered if so much reading at night by a poor light was not partly responsible for him losing his eyesight in his old age.

He could play the fiddle, and liked to play the bugle calls that were used during the Civil War. I think he could play all of them. They had a big family of boys, and one little girl who died when she was small. It seems to me that some old doctor gave her the wrong medicine, which caused her death.

Aunt Helen was bitten by a black widow spider when I was a small child, and it made her very sick. She's the only one I ever knew personally who was bitten by one of these much talked of spiders. Aunt Helen was a sister of Cousin Victoria Gilliland Cannon. She has told me lots of things about my Armstrong ancestors, that I would not have known if she had not had such a good memory.

Birchfield and Otho were the older boys of that family, about Lelia's and Etta's age. Willie and John were about the ages of Sadie and my brother John. Jimmie and Charlie were nearer my age. We always enjoyed them coming to visit us.

One time, when Willie had been to town, and had taken a little too much to drink, he came back to our place instead of going home. He had bought fifty cents worth of penny lead pencils, and he gave them to me. I felt rich. If I could have had one wish granted me, it would probably have been for all the smooth white paper I wanted, and just such a bunch of pencils.

My pencil wish was granted, and not long after that the paper wish also came true. Pappy went to town and hitched his team in the vacant lot back of the New Era office, where the County paper was published.[5] There in a waste paper box was loads of paper strips, nice and white and smooth, from three to five inches wide, and two or three feet long. My

---

5.  This refers to the *Kentucky New Era*, the newpaper serving Christian County, published in Hopkinsville.

father, being a very understanding man, and knowing our love for paper and pencils, threw a quantity of it in the wagon box. My happiness was just about as nearly perfect then as at any time in my life, that I can remember. For a while I drew and wrote all I wanted to. I made story books, sketch books, all kinds of them.

Sadie was a would be story writer. I think she and Lelia both wrote books at different times. All I can remember of them is that Lelia's characters always *ejaculated*, and that Sadie's hero's name was Ben Stale. That always caused a lot of laughter, if you tried to say the name real fast. There was nothing in mine outstanding enough to even remember.

Sadie's diaries were the things that really captured my interest, but that was one thing she didn't intend for me to see. She had written her very deepest secrets in it, nothing was held back. Where to put it, so that I wouldn't find it, was the puzzle. I had the gift of the *probable places*. Once she had it in the bottom of the quilt piece box, where it was handy to get to when she wanted to write in it, while I was outside playing. But I discovered that hiding place, and she had to change it. Then she had me baffled for quite a while. There didn't seem to be any clue as to its whereabouts.

One day John and I were fighting wasps, an old and favorite pastime. They had several nests in the top of the upstairs. Some of the nests were as big as your two hands, with dozens of wasps in them. We got an old quilt that had been used to cover sweet potatoes, that had a hole in it we could peep out through long enough to poke the nest with fishing poles. When the wasps started swarming down at us we would close the hole till things cleared up a bit. During one of these raids, as I was looking through my port hole, I saw a thick roll of paper tucked behind a rafter right against the boards of the roof.

*There*, that's it! Sadie's diary. Why hadn't I thought to look there before. I ought to have known it would be there, for I had looked *every*-where else. I didn't say anything about it them, but waited till everything was clear, and Sadie was away from home, so I could read in peace, and without any fear of disturbance.

I really found out a lot of things I had wanted to know for a long time. Yes, she really liked Ed Cornelius better than most of the others. I did too, as far as that was concerned. I fell madly in love with most of her beaus, especially the above mentioned Ed.

There was also Herschel Woolsey, Frank Wright, and Will Eades. I wasn't any too fond of John Causler [Cansler], another of Sadie's beaux, but I liked to tease him. He always spoke to my mother in just the same way, "Howty Mis Marcus," in a crisp quick way, cutting his words off short. I think he was an *awful* good boy, and a perfect gentleman. His clothes were faultless, and his shoes were trim and shiny. He had a beautiful, squeaky, shiny buggy. A nice fat horse, and a buggy whip that could cut the hide when he popped me with it, which he persisted in doing only on very *rare* occasions. Just as he and Sadie would be getting real serious I would stick my head around a door facing and say, "Howty Mis Marcus," in just the same tone of voice he used. Then I knew I'd better look out, if the buggy whip was near. He was merciless.

I got another thing on him too. There were big walnut trees along the road in front of Mr. Morris' house, and it was a favorite place for the cows to lie and chew their cuds. One pale moonlight night, when the cows *had* been lying there, but had wandered down the lane to the creek, Sadie and John passed by on horseback. John rode too close under the walnut trees and a limb knocked his hat off. Sadie was sorry, and she wondered if he would be able to find it. He assured her that he saw where it had fallen, hopped off, went straight for a big warm cow pile, and reached right down into it with his hand spread out. Sadie said he quietly slung it off the best he could and finished cleaning it on his nice linen handkerchief, then threw it over by the fence.

The next time he came I waited till the opportune minute, then poked my head in and told him that I had found his handkerchief for him. the one he lost under the walnut trees where the limb knocked his hat off. I *really* had to fly that time, as he was coming right after me with red in his eyes.

When Herschel or Ed came I would slip in with my Arithmetic and slate and pretend I was awful busy working problems. Sadie would cast frowny looks at me, but I was hard to move. I liked to look at Ed. His hair was so curly and he had such a nice low laugh, and his dancing was divine. I had seen him dance, and once, when there was no one else he could get for a partner, he had asked *me* to dance with him.

Tom Vaughn was another of Sadie's flames that I had an awful case on. He was my ideal as to what constituted a perfect gentleman. I liked George, his brother, too, but *he* was a monkey. It was like going to a show, to go to a dance where he was. He could beat any nigger stepdancing, and danced with all his might through every tune. He seemed to never tire, and it was punctuated with lots of appropriate gab, that no one but a professional could have thought of.

Lewis Moore, who was about my age, usually came with George to the dances. He was a sort of a small edition of George. He always danced with me, and I liked to dance with him. He always asked me if he could go home with me too, but I always said no. I knew that Sadie and the others would tease me, as I was too small to have beaus. Besides, I didn't want him to walk home with me, or ride, whichever it happened to be. I liked to dance with him fine, but that was all.

Then Lewis Moore went away, and I didn't see him for about ten years, till after I was married and had several children. Then one day I saw him again. He looked just like he had when he was a little boy, and we used to dance together. He asked me if I remembered what good times we used to have at the dances. Of course I did. Then he said that there was one question he would like to ask me. Why was it that I would never let him go with me. I didn't know what to say. I couldn't just say I didn't want to.

He and George Vaughn used to batch together and do their own cooking. It was said that when they wanted to know if the skillet was hot enough for the hoe cake they would spit in it, and if it fried spit it was hot enough.

When I was very small we went somewhere, I can't remember where, but a little girl had a big rag doll, and I was crazy about it. I must have made a good sized fuss about it, for Mammy borrowed it to cut one by, and I hung onto it so tenaciously that she was afraid I would get it so dirty it would not be fit to take home.

Mammy finally hid that doll in the bottom of the trunk. She searched everywhere, in the quilt piece box, and in the rag bag, and couldn't find a piece of new white muslin, but she did find a piece of pale blue material. Thinking it would make no difference, she made it of that, but I wouldn't touch it, it was not like the other one.

I must have been only a baby, but I remember it. I didn't like the blue doll *at all*. Mammy finally cut up a new pillow case and made me a doll of it.

I don't believe that this streak of contrariness was very serious, as I really do not think I was a very contrary child in the years that followed. If the streak *did* live for a while, I believe it was burned out long ago, through years of work, sacrifice and hardships, for which I am truly thankful.

There was *so* much work, of so many different kinds, to be done on the farm, that even the children didn't escape it. We carried water, went for the cows, churned, fed pigs and chickens, dropped corn in springtime, dropped tobacco plants, pulled weeds, cut sassafras sprouts, shelled beans and peas, and helped shell the corn for the grinding, as we ate lots of cornbread.[6]

---

6.  According to Suzanne M. Hall,
    > Throughout the year as the tobacco grew to maturity, family members also worked at putting up vegetables, drying fruits, hoeing corn, threshing wheat, caring for the farm stock, and attending to the hundreds of chores required to maintain a farm. Men further supplemented the larder with meat from hunting and fish from the streams and rivers. Children fished and gathered wild fruits, nuts, greens, and ginseng. Depending on gender, class, and race, people worked in separate areas on the farm during the day. Men toiled in the fields and barnyard; women labored in the house, yard, chicken coop, kitchen, and garden, and milked cows.

In the wintertime everyone helped strip tobacco. There were *two* tobacco *seasons* that depended on the rain, one was in spring when we waited for a rain before we set the tobacco plants out. The other was after it was cut, in the fall. After the firing was done, and it was *cured*, we had to wait for a rain to soften it, so we could strip it. If we had undertaken to do anything with it when it was dry it would have crumbled and been wasted. When it rained it *came in order*, and was limp like a rag.

Everything connected with raising tobacco is grueling, back breaking labor, and it is nasty also. In summer, when it is green, everything that comes in contact with it is covered with a loathsome, sticky, strong smelling gum, that gets all over the clothing, hands, and everything. When suckering and worming, in which we had to bend down to reach the lower leaves, even our hair would get gummy.[7]

The tobacco flies laid eggs all over the leaves, that hatched out into green worms that grew and thrived remarkably. If we failed to see one, when it was small, and left it till next worming time, it would have a good portion of the plant eaten. Only the stems would be left standing. It was a tedious, back breaking job to look on every leaf for worms, and to pull the suckers out that sprouted at the base of each leaf after the plant was topped. I don't believe that there is any other crop that requires more labor to raise than tobacco.[8] Often the men started burning plant beds in late winter before the crop for the past year was all stripped.

---

See Suzanne M. Hall, "Working the Black Patch: Tobacco Farming Traditions, 1890–1930," *Register of the Kentucky Historical Society* 89 (Summer 1991): 274–75.

7.  Kate Strand, the wife of a Muhlenberg County farmer, once remembered: "I don't suppose the Lord ever permitted a harder, hotter, dirtier, filthier, or more nauseating work than that of worming tobacco. . . . I have seen my husband at the close of the day take off his overalls and stand them alone, so stiff they would be with tobacco juice. Worming tobacco is bad enough for men, but when women and children have to engage in it human torture reaches its climax. My children have toddled along through the tobacco rows at my side crying with pain as their eyes were filled with tobacco juice shot into them by tobacco worms" (Kate Strand interview in *Appeal to Reason*, Oct. 1, 1910, quoted in Campbell, *Politics of Despair*, 16). The lore of tobacco cultivation is wonderfully treated in Charles S. Guthrie, "Tobacco: Cash Crop of the Cumberland Valley," *Kentucky Folklore Record* 14 (April-June 1968): 38–43, and Hall, "Working the Black Patch," 266–86.

8.  In 1922, the Children's Bureau surveyed children in five representative tobacco-growing states—Kentucky, North Carolina, South Carolina, Tennessee, and Virginia—to determine child labor patterns in tobacco harvest operations. Of the 278 child workers studied in Christian County, Kentucky, 186 were boys and 92 were girls. Sixty-seven (36 percent) of the boys aged seven through fifteen reported working more than four months a year in the tobacco fields. Of the 272 children who worked cultivating, 131 (48.2 percent) reported a typical work day of ten hours or more. See Harriet A. Byrne, "Child Labor in Representative Tobacco-Growing Areas," 2–16.

Hauling green tobacco in Kentucky. From Scherffius, "Tobacco," plate XI.

"Cutting Tobacco and Putting it on Sticks," near Hopkinsville, Kentucky. From Sauer, *Geography of the Pennyroyal*, fig. 109.

I don't suppose there is another crop that does the human family so little actual good as does tobacco, in fact it does them more harm than most people realize. When we think of the amount of labor expended for something that there is no good in, but actual harm, it is appalling. We wonder if we are as smart as we ought to be.

The tobacco stripping was done in winter in an old open barn that let the cold wind in. The women and children helped with the stripping, too. There was a fire in the center of the group, but it never warmed the backs of the workers. There was always plenty of dust to be breathed. That, with the cold and other things, resulted in severe colds and coughs. I can remember coughing all night long, night after night. Consumption was a common disease at that time, and if the cause of death had been put on every tombstone it would have registered far in the majority.

We managed to have a good time, even when stripping tobacco in a cold barn. We raced, sang, told stories, and passed the time pleasantly.

At that time, in the early 90's, the farmers *prized* their own tobacco. That is, they packed it down in hogsheads (monstrous barrels) and then *prized* it down with a big jackscrew, and hauled it to town packed and nailed up in the hogsheads. Later the *loose floors* were opened, the buyers didn't buy the crop at the barn, but would bid on it at the *loose floors*.

The tobacco buyers were organized, and the farmers were not.[9] The buyers had squeezed the price down so low that it became almost a form of slavery to raise tobacco. Often the tobacco crop would not bring enough to pay the grocery bill that had gone behind while the crop was being raised. Year after year this same condition continued.

I can remember several cases where, after a year of hard, killing labor, the crop actually did not bring enough to pay for the commercial fertilizer they had bought to put under it. At the same time the big tobacco companies were amassing huge fortunes. Everyone knew it, but knew no way to change it.

The foolish thing was to keep on raising it, when they were not getting anything for it. It would have been far more intelligent to have raised food for the winter months. The farmers said, "But tobacco is our cash *money* crop." They couldn't seem to realize that it had ceased to be a money crop. They had gotten into the habit of raising it, and couldn't quit.[10]

---

9.   Effie is referring to the American Tobacco Company (or Trust) which monopolized the tobacco market in virtually all of the major tobacco-producing states and countries.

10.   The land in northern Christian County is not as easily cultivated as those in the southern half of the county. Due to the sandstone table of this "clifty" coal field region, farmers must take extra measures to develop the smaller, less fertile parcels. Regarding the

It was probably some such silly bunch the ancient prophet was referring to when he said, "The days of this ignorance God winked at."[11]

Pappy was always bringing home some kind of herbs or roots from the creek bottoms or the hillsides. Blackroot and white walnut bark as a purgative. Sarsaparilla root as a blood purifier. Yellow percoon for sore mouths (Golden Seal). May Apple root (called Mandrake), Angelico, and Ginseng, which brought a fabulous price when it was dried. Mullein and hoarhound for coughs and colds. Catnip for the babies.[12]

I guess Pappy got his knowledge of herbs, and his interest in them from his mother. At one time she had an herb garden in a little rich, loamy, valley down near the creek. She had many kinds of wild flowers and wild herbs in it. Mainly Ginseng. It was very interesting.

---

tobacco growers of the Hopkinsville area, a comment made by Carl Ortwin Sauer is applicable here:

> Tobacco makes extraordinary demands on labor, ten acres being sufficient to keep a family busily engaged. Such lesser sections have discovered that tobacco brings to them greater returns than other crops, even though it does not yield so well as in the major districts. . . . Thus the farmer of the sandstone table-lands north of Hopkinsville has forsaken the older economy and is now primarily a producer of dark tobacco which is taken down to the Hopkinsville market. He grows dark tobacco because he has available a dark tobacco market. With his tobacco money he buys corn, hay, perhaps even beans and potatoes, for he is too busy with his tobacco patch to raise much other "truck."

See Carl Ortwin Sauer, *Geography of the Pennyroyal*, 199.

Rick Gregory has concluded that "Few growers had the power to break the bonds of culture and tradition that bound them to the staple. Until the New Deal, most Black Patch farmers would maintain their loyalty to dark-fired tobacco—a loyalty for which they would pay a high cost." See his "'Look To Yourselves,'" 290.

11. Acts 17:30: "And the times of this ignorance God winked at."

12. Blackroot (*Chaenolobus undulatus*) is a perennial plant of the South, having large tuber-like rootstocks, sometimes used medicinally. White bark is any of several American trees having pale or whitish bark, such as the white poplar or white-bark pine. In addition to its narcotic properties, golden seal (*Hydrastis Canadensis*, L.), known for its brilliant yellow color, was used as a die in coloring silks, wool, and linen. May apple or Mandrake (*Podophyllum peltatum*, L.) was used as a cathartic. The root was used as a purge and sometimes as a dressing for ulcers. Angelica, of the genus *Angelica*, was used in spasmodic vomiting, flatulent colics, and nervous headaches. The root was known to possess more aroma than any of southern indigenous plants. Ginseng (*Panax quinquefolium*, L.), an herb with an aromatic root, has long been a valued medicinal plant. It was first used by the Chinese and is of widespread use in North America. Mullein (*Verbascum thapsus*, L.) has corse or woolly leaves and a yellow 5-petaled flower appearing in a long dense terminal spike. Mullein is used medicinally in treating sore throats, rheumatism and headaches. Horehound (*Marrubium vulgare*, L.) is an aromatic mint and is very bitter to the taste. It was used as a stomach tonic and as a remedy for coughs and colds. Catnip (*Nepeta cataria*, L.) is a very well known strong-scented herb used as a domestic remedy in amenorrhea, chlorosis, and flatulent colic of infants.

There was a steep bank to go down just before reaching the garden, and one time as she was going down this bank she slipped, fell, and dislocated her shoulder. She was old, and it was quite serious, and very painful.

When the doctor came he said it would just have to be *pulled* back into place. It was hard to do, and hurt her terribly. Every time the doctor would pull, to get it back in place, Uncle Curg (feeling so sorry for her, and hating so terribly to see him hurting her) would hold the shoulder so they couldn't get it back in place. Finally the doctor winked at Aunt Ada and asked her if they thought one of the neighbors might have some camphor. She thought probably they did, so they sent Uncle Curg for it. As soon as he left the doctor pulled the shoulder back into place without a great deal of trouble.

Uncle Lee was a tiny little fellow when my father and mother married, and he was very fond of *John Susie*, as he called her. It was not long before Etta (Mammy's first baby) was born. She was at Grandma's, and there was other company, I can't remember who. They were all talking, and no one was paying any attention to Lee. He had found the old dutch oven, that they had cooked meat in, and had *sopped* it clean with a piece of bread, then he climbed into it and sat down. One leg was broken off of the old oven, and he was rocking back and forth on its uneven legs, humming to himself and nearly asleep. One of the visitors was telling of someone who was very pretty, and Lee said sleepily, as he rocked back and forth in the greasy old dutch oven, "Well, John Susy's the purtiest thing I ever saw, and she's as fat as my old hin." This incident was told and retold many times, and laughed over by all the members of the family.

One thing we planned on a long ways ahead of time, was for all of us to go gathering hickernuts and grapes. As school usually started in July, this had to be done on a Saturday.

There was lots of work to be done in the fall, that the women and children had to do. Potatoes to dig, beans and peas to pick and shell. Fruit to be canned also. We didn't have many glass fruit jars then, most of them were stone jars with stone lids, and were sealed by melting sealing wax and pouring around the lid.

With all the fall work that had to be done it was hard to find a time when we could go, but Mammy usually found a time before it got *too* cold. How happy we children all were as we started out with sacks and baskets.

The leaves of the hickory trees had all fallen to the ground before the nuts were ripe, and there would be nuts mixed in with the dry leaves. The boys would climb the trees and shake the nuts down with a clatter, while we picked them up. They were always trying to surprise us and shake a limb directly over our heads. The nuts would shower down, popping us on the head and making us run.[13]

There was one big scaly bark tree just east of the house, on the bank of a branch (of the creek) that had a bed of smooth white limestone. It was easy to find the nuts there. We just raked back the leaves, and there they were on the smooth white rocks. There were weeds all under the tree, up on the bank, but there were usually lots of nuts on this big old tree.

There were two small trees farther east, by the big sweetgum tree, near the fence that separated our farm from Mr. Moore's, but they never yielded the abundant crop that the big one on the branch did.[14]

We usually stopped in the dry stream bed and shelled the big outside hull from the hickernuts before going to the house. Then they were stored where the rats could not carry them away, and saved for the long winter nights by the fire.

The walnuts were in another direction, up towards the graveyard. There was a big tree in the woods, and past the graveyard, at an old house place, were two others. It was quite a job to shell the walnuts, as the hulls stained everything that touched them. Our hands would be black after shelling walnuts, till it *wore* off.

I remember one fall when Mammy and I shelled the walnuts alone, hauled them to the house in a wheelbarrow, and stored them in a little old corn crib in the barn lot that was not being used. They were giant nuts, with big rich kernels. Any time I felt the least bit hungry I could go to this little old crib and crack me a pan of walnuts and was soon satisfied. Walnuts and corn bread are especially good together, and make a very satisfying meal.

When the wild geese started flying south in the fall, we would know that there was a cold spell coming. Sometimes we would hear them in the night, honking high up in the dark as they wended their way to the land of summer. Pappy would then make preparations to kill at least one hog for fresh meat. He said it usually took most of the first hog for John Susan to divide among her neighbors.

Hog killing time was not a very pleasant time for the ones who did the work. It was always done when there was a cold spell, so the meat

---

13.  In addition to its edible quality, the hickory nut had a number of uses in the rural south. The oil was often extracted to fuel lamps. The nut, when broken and boiled, could also be used in the manufacture of soap.

14.  The sweetgum tree (*Liquidambar styraciflua*, L.) is a hardwood tree with lobed leaves and corky branches. It is sometimes passed as an imitation mahogany and Circassian walnut.

would not spoil. The hogs were heavy, and hard to handle. It was dirty, greasy, ill smelling work.[15]

Mammy usually had a scaffold outside where the entrails were laid out while she removed the fat from them. We children were always interested in this operation, as we were anxious to get all the bladders. With a section cut from the small end of a fishing cane put into the opening of the bladder, we could then blow them up. We had lots of fun slipping up behind other members of the family and forcing the wind out in their ears, making a disgusting noise, besides the unpleasant odor.

We blew them and worked them till we were sure they could not be blown any bigger, then we put beans in them, tied them tight, and hung them up on an attic joist in a row, to save for Christmas. *Then*, on Christmas morning the ones who awoke first could take the bladders down, hold them to the fire till they filled up tight again, lay them on the hearth and jump on them with both feet, making a noise like a shotgun and waking the other members of the family. That was the most interesting part of the hog-killing time for the children.

Later, the grinding of the sausage meat, and stuffing the sacks to be hung up in rows. Often corn shucks were used to pack it in. Then came the rendering of the fat into lard, and straining it into lard cans to be used all winter and spring. The cracklin's from the lard was saved to make cracklin' bread. Later, the heads and feet were cleaned, and cooked and made into *souse* (in some sections called head cheese).

The backbones, spareribs, and liver were used first. The sausage, shoulders, hams, and middlings were smoked with hickory wood in the tight little smoke house, where the barrel of salt, the barrel of soft soap, and the soap grease barrel were kept.

The salt always hardened into a solid mass, almost as hard as a rock. One of my jobs was to go get salt for the kitchen. I would get a big spoon and scrape and scrape till I could dip enough to fill the little brown stone salt jar.

The path from the back kitchen door to the smoke house was kept patted slick from frequent use. We went there many times a day for salt, soap, meat, etc. When Mammy went to the smoke house for meat she usually detoured by the chimley, and gave the knife a few rakes back and forth on one of the sandstones the chimley was built of, to sharpen it.[16]

---

15. For more on this farming practice, see Lynwood Montell, "Hog Killing Time in the Kentucky Hill Country," *Kentucky Folklore Record* 18 (1972): 61–67.
16. As the standard spelling for "chimney" is used elsewhere, this spelling is no doubt intentional.

There were several sharpening places on that old chimley, where many others before my mother had stopped to sharpen their knives.

The old house was burned long ago, with its wealth of old relics in the attic; the flax reel, the old red corded bedstid, the candle moulds; articles that had been used in slave days, long before the Civil War. Stones do not burn easily, or decay, and somewhere I'll bet those old places where the knives were sharpened are still just as they were when I was a child.

I mentioned the old red corded *bedstid.* It is possible that some of my grandchildren, or great grandchildren anyway, would not know what it was. I guess this type of bed was a step forward from the old hard wooden slats. There was a certain manufacturer who put out this special type of bed, and they must have been popular, as every family had at least one, or more.

The posts were round and tall, with a ball on top of each post. The side rails were also round with big iron screws about four inches apart all down the sides, and also across the head board and foot board. A small rope was stretched across both ways and hooked over the ends of the screws that were left sticking up an inch or two. This made a soft springy area for the straw bed to lay on. When the ropes stretched, and the bed became saggy, they were tightened. All of these beds were painted a light orange red. They were comfortable to sleep on.

There was one of these beds in the upstairs room of the old house that had been my grandfather's. I suppose it was there when we moved in, and had been there since slave days, and before. By *my* time these beds were considered old fashioned and clumsy, and a cheaper, much flimsier type had taken its place, with slats and no springs.

I remember the first bed springs we owned. An agent came along selling them. They were in pairs, and were built to hook over the bed slats. They were quite strong, and it seems to me that they stood a foot high. I remember how high the bed looked after we put them on.

Uncle Lawrence and Aunt Fannie knew that we had ordered them, and they said that when we got them they were coming over to stay all night and see how they liked them. In all the years I knew them that is the only time I can remember of them ever sleeping away from home.

We saw them coming up the path by the orchard. Aunt Fannie with two clean sheets over her arm, one to go under them and one over them. Mammie resented *that* a little, she usually had clean sheets, even if we *did* have a big family.

Aunt Fannie *was* quite finicky. She usually washed the dipper in hot water before she drank out of it. That wasn't a bad idea, but we felt a little insulted, as if she thought we were dirty people. Didn't every family in the neighborhood all drink from the same dipper? We wondered if she washed the dippers everyplace she went. Anyway we were glad to see them whenever they came.

Uncle Lawrence was a sweet old soul, jolly and good natured; well up on all the news, as he read his newspapers thoroughly. There was just one little thing that was a fly in the ointment. He was a Republican. He had fought in the Civil War on the Northern side, and my father was a Democrat. Most people were strong in their politics in those days, so that was one question that was left undiscussed when Uncle Lawrence was at our place.[17]

Mammie knew they were coming and had fixed a good supper. Aunt Fannie's teeth were bad from being *salivated* with calomel, so Mammy usually fixed chicken and dumplin's for her, and she liked puddings with sauce to go over them. She usually let it be known what she liked, so it would be forthcoming.

Pappy got the fiddle out and they made some music after supper. Uncle Lawrence kept time with his feet. I often wondered if life wasn't awfully dull for them, with no children and no music, but I suppose they liked it that way.

They were used to going to bed early, so it was not long till they were yawning. They were anxious to try the springs. We had an awful laugh when they were getting into bed. Those springs were really springy, and Uncle Lawrence said that he sank in over his ears. When Aunt Fannie got in he yelled, "Hey, go easy there, I'm about to fall off." He said that if he should have to cough in the night, and started bouncing, it would be disastrous. Aunt Fannie squealed, and said he was right in the middle, and he said, how could he help where he landed, he was at the mercy of them springs.

I think it was in 1896 when Pappy decided he was going to make it a little more convenient around the place by digging a cellar for the milk, canned fruit, etc., and by having a well drilled right by the kitchen door,

---

17. After the Civil War, party politics became a divisive issue in Kentucky. According to Merton Coulter, "Kentuckians fundamentally were conservative," but those with slave interests had attached themselves to the Democratic Party after the breakup of the Radicals and the Whigs. Generally, people of wealth and those with tobacco interests gravitated to the Democratic Party for largely economic reasons. The Republicans became a political force during John M. Harlan's 1871 gubernatorial campaign and after anti-slavery supporters from eastern Kentucky gained a foothold in party politics. Evidently, Lawrence Armstrong held to strong Union sentiments. See E. Merton Coulter, *The Civil War and Readjustment in Kentucky* (Chapel Hill: University of North Carolina Press, 1926), esp. 433–40. See also Lawrence Thompson, "Politics is a Major Sport," chap. 2, in *Kentucky Tradition* (Hamden, Conn.: Shoe String Press, 1956), 9–21.

saving *so many* steps going to and from the old well that was almost to the creek. Somehow both these projects were failures. The cellar filled with water and the well didn't, at least what did raise in it was not fit to drink.

Three boys, viz: Luther Hayes, Will Eades,[18] and Archie Lee were operating the drilling machine. Pappy agreed to pay them one dollar per foot, and give them board and room while they were drilling. It was like a picnic for we children. They were nice boys, all good looking and very pleasant. Sadie was nineteen, and very pretty. I was in the ugly stage of eleven, but I enjoyed them anyway.

Mr. Eades took care of the engine, and I became interested in it, so he taught me how to operate it. I would run it for hours at a time while he went with Sadie to the well for water, or helped her with some of the work, or just sat on the edge of the porch and talked.

Mr. Hayes, the one who operated the drill, was also interested in Sadie, but I could not operate the drill, so he had to stick to his drill, and Eades got in a lot of talk ahead of him. But Mr. Hayes had a horse and a cart, and the horse was a good trotter. *That* made it bad for Eades *after* work hours.

Archie Lee was a slim quiet fellow who had a very interesting and unusual life story. He and his sister were left orphans when the sister was a baby, and when he was a very small child. They were both adopted, and neither of them knew where the other one was. During the year they came to our place he was working in Hopkinsville, where he met the daughter of Mr. Meriwether.[19] They fell in love almost at first sight, and were very happy in each other's company. One day something was said about his folks. He told her that he was left an orphan when very small. She said she was also, and that Dr. Meriwether and wife had adopted her. A little further investigation and they found that they were brother and sister. They were to have been married soon, but decided they had better not.

It is funny how time is magnified in childhood. As I remember it it seems to me that these well drillers were at our place for months, but when I called my sister and asked her how long they stayed she said three weeks. It seems to me it was *much* longer. I imagine it seemed quite a while to my mother, who had to fix three meals for our big family, and for these three men besides.

I can't remember just how deep they sank the well, but I think it was 80 feet at one time. When they had drilled through a layer of blue clay there was a loud smell of oil in each bucket full they brought up. The oil

---

18. Probably William P. Eades (1872–1947).

19. Probably Dr. Charles H. Meriwether, whose vital dates are not found in general county histories or census returns.

spread out on the ground where they emptied the mud. We thought maybe we were going to have an oil well instead of a well of water.

The morning they set the drill up (and when they had the steam up in the engine) Mr. Eades blew the whistle and every old cow on the place curled their tails over their backs and with frightened bellows they disappeared over the hill. For a while it was with great difficulty that we extracted any milk from them. We couldn't get them *near* the house.

Cousin Buck came on one of his periodic visits while the well drillers were there, and it was then that I found out for sure that he was coming to see Sadie. He didn't like the well drillers, especially Mr. Eades and Luther Hayes.

He came into the kitchen where my mother was cooking supper one evening and said, "Cudden John Susan, do you know that you have a *very* attractive daughter." Mammy said that she didn't know there was anything very unusual about her. "Wy she could charm the heart of a wheelbarrow, she has both of those fellows crazy as bessy bugs, and without any effort on her part."

They finally gave the well up as a failure, pulled up stakes and left with their drilling machine. We didn't see much more of Mr. Hayes or Archie Lee, but Mr. Eades continued to come back so steadily that I thought I might have him for a brother-in-law. I wouldn't have objected, he was a very lovable fellow. But finally there was a quarrel that ended it all. I think he drank some, though I never saw him drunk.

Norman was a baby then, and I remember Lelia bringing him over one day with a little blue jersey suit on. I thought he was the sweetest thing I ever saw. Vera was a cute little girl with cheeks as red as apples, always humming a tune, serious and quiet, with her little bonnet on.

About this time I got a wallop I'll never forget. Mammy had made me a new blue sunbonnet with a ruffle around the front, and I was *so* proud of it. Lelia came, and Mammy said that if I would run to the spring and bring a bucket of cool water I could go home with her. Someone had let the clothes line down, and as I was running against the evening sun I failed to see it. I was running with all my might, and the wire was just right to catch me just under the chin. The wire and I didn't stop till the slack was all taken up, and then I was thrown flat on my back on the hard rocky ground. I lay there for a few minutes, stunned, then got up painfully, picked up my new bonnet, and walked slowly to the spring. A raw streak across my throat was stinging terribly, and my head was feeling like my skull might have been fractured. But I was soon all right again, and able to run like the wind again. Children have a marvelous power of recuperation.

I think I must have had an abnormal amount of sympathy. I can remember how very sorry I was for Etta because she was crippled. Her right leg was shorter than the left, and the foot was drawn a little. Her

Vera and Norman Ferrell, Lelia's oldest children.
Courtesy of Itha Carmack.

right arm and hand was small and drawn so that it was useless. When we would go places where there were strangers I made it a point to stand in front of her on that side so no one would notice her little hand.

When she and I started to the creek fishing, or to the mulberry trees, or to the woods lot for toothbrushes, or others of our many jaunts about the place, there was perfect freedom. Etta couldn't run, but she *could* skip, and she could make speed at it too. She would lean on me to keep her steady, and away we would go, me running and she skipping on her good foot.

Sometimes we would take paper and pencils and go to the big flat rocks above the spring and draw pictures of little ferns, and flowers, and pretty leaves. Sometimes we took pieces of keel and wrote on the flat rocks. Sometimes we hunted for pretty colored pebbles, and petrified vertabrae of little living things (and least they had *once* been living), the joints looked like little buttons. Sometimes we hunted for rare specimens of flowers. Anyway, we always had a good time, or at least *I* did. A tiny little girl, and a big crippled girl, but we were genuine pals, and oh how I enjoyed it.

How I appreciated Etta's never ceasing desire to help out with the work all she could. She pieced most of the quilts that we had. She could knit, sweep, and keep things picked up. She could keep the place tidied and dusted, and I guess that in the long run she did more than we who had nothing whatever the matter with us. Etta was also a good singer, and learned all the new songs that came along. We made books of song ballads that we *printed*.[20]

At that time I thought nothing of it, but as I remember it now I'm sure that I have never seen anyone with such shining, golden hair as Etta had. It was a beautiful auburn in the shade, and in the sun it was just like shining gold. I loved to wash her hair and roll it up for her, just to see how it would shine when I took it down and combed it.

Being a cripple Etta had not had many beaus, but she had one that I remember, who used to write to her. I felt very big and important when she let me read his letters. They were from Dan Simpson, a good, gentle, kind fellow.[21] Sometimes, at dances, he would come and sit with her instead of dancing.

Etta tried to stay loyal to her membership in the Baptist church, but it had not meant as much to her as they had thought it might. We went to church occasionally, but their big protracted meetings, and the preachers fervent pleading with the people to "give their hearts to Jesus," and the lurid pictures they painted of our awful fate if death should overtake us in our "unsaved condition" never succeeded in stirring me up very much. It didn't sound too sincere to me, and in the expression of our father, it didn't sound *logical*. I would look at people who belonged to the different churches who, as the preachers expressed it, were "saved," and I couldn't see that they were any better than we were who had not joined any church.

My father said that if he ever found a church that was like the one the Savior set up while He was on the earth he would join it, but so far the teachings of the preachers, and the teachings of the Savior didn't agree. In the first place the Savior told His disciples, when He set them apart and sent them out to preach, "Freely ye have received this, now see that ye freely give it to others,"[22] and one place said, "Beware of them that preach for hire, and divine for money."[23] Paul said, "Ye know that I have

---

20.  Printed out by hand, apparently; she kept such lists all her life. Hazel Carmack Bushman recalls a stapled, typewritten booklet of song texts compiled by her mother, no longer in Hazel Bushman's possession. (Conversation with Karen Davidson, December 4, 1994.)

21.  Daniel R. Simpson (b. 1875), son of George Simpson.

22.  Matthew 10:8: "Freely ye have received, freely give."

23.  A paraphrase of Micah 3:11: "The heads thereof judge for reward, and the priests thereof teach for hire, and the prophets thereof divine for money."

labored with my own hands (he was a tent maker) that I might have the means to support myself, and to give to them that needed."[24]

Paul was a preacher, one of the greatest we have any record of. "But," some of them would say, "this is a different age, and calls for different methods." Then we read in the Bible where the Savior said, "If any man teach any other gospel to you except this which we have taught unto you, let him be accursed," and for fear they didn't understand Him fully He repeated it with a little more force, saying "If any man, *or even an Angel from Heaven* should teach any other gospel he would be accursed."[25]

It was not hard to see that lots of them were teaching things that were contrary to the teachings of the New Testament. It seems that the Savior and His disciples knew that there would be false churches. The Lord said, "Many shall come in My Name saying, Lo, here is Christ, or Lo, there is Christ, and deceive many,"[26] and, "Many false teachers shall arise,"[27] and, "Not everyone that sayeth unto Me *Lord Lord* shall enter the Kingdom of Heaven, but he that doeth the will of my Father which is in Heaven."[28]

What *was* His Father's will? We tried to find out. The Lord said, "By this shall all men know that ye are My Disciples, if ye have love one to another,"[29] and He told His followers to treat others just as they themselves would like to be treated.

Well, there was one thing certain, we loved each other and we loved other people too. Pappy said that he always had to figure on *one* hog at least, being divided among the neighbors. We usually gave every one around a part of it.

Mammy came as near to being the neighborhood nurse as anyone could have, and it was always done freely too. I've often thought what a wealth of treasures she had laid up for herself, though I'm sure she never thought of herself when she was doing it. She did it for humanity's sake.

---

24. In Acts 20:34–35 and 1 Corinthians 4:12 Paul refers to working with his own hands, but Effie's paraphrase sounds more like the words of King Benjamin in the Book of Mormon (Mosiah 2:14): "And even I, myself, have labored with mine own hands that I might serve you."

25. A paraphrase of Galatians 1:9: "If any man preach any other gospel unto you than that ye have received, let him be accursed." See also Galatians 1:8.

26. A paraphrase of Matthew 24:5: "For many shall come in my name, saying, I am Christ; and shall deceive many."

27. Perhaps a reference to II Peter 2:1: "But there were false prophets also among the people, even as there shall be false teachers among you."

28. Matthew 7:21.

29. John 13:35.

So, although not contented with our homespun religion, we read the Bible and waited for a time when maybe the right religion would come along.

One day the family was going to visit some of our relatives, but Sadie and I wanted to go to a picnic that was being held not far away. A neighbor who was taking his family in a wagon had promised to come by and stop for us. We had made elaborate preparations. Sadie had made us a white dress each, trimmed with lace, and stitched with rose colored silk thread. They said that they would be there by ten o'clock, so, long before ten we were sitting prim and curled with our white dresses on, and my leghorn hat with its wreath of little wild roses, and its ribbon streamers.[30]

Ten o'clock came, and no picnickers, ten thirty, and then eleven. By this time we had given them up entirely.

Sadie says, "Well, as we're here alone with nothing to bother us let's clean this place from one end to the other, and change things around." If there was one thing Sadie enjoyed, it was changing the furniture around, so, immediately, we began to shed our picnic finery and get into our work duds. Soon we were busy making things hum. We cleaned that place from top to bottom, upstairs and all. We scrubbed cupboards, made new firescreens, swept the yards, got fresh bouquets, and really made the old place shine. We were racing to get it all finished before the folks got home. When it was all done and we sat down, tired but happy, we both agreed that we had enjoyed ourselves far better than we would have if we had gone to the picnic. We have often since thought of that busy day and the good time we had. We said that it proved the maxim true, that true happiness does not depend on having what we want, but in wanting what we have.

As a small child I had developed a sort of prejudice against all the folks that lived *down the creek*. Maybe from the fact that our geese came home from that direction *picked* several times. I didn't realize that there were lots of *different* folks living in that direction. Negroes, farm hands, and many different classes.

When we grew older, and met the young folks of a family of Wrights who lived in that direction, I was surprised to find them the most charming people I had ever known. Refined, intelligent, fun loving, and witty. Miss Hallie, who had married Dr. Ramsey and was then a widow with two small boys, was one of the most lovable women I had ever seen. Nora, the girl at home, seemed good, and was very pretty. Frank, who went with Sadie for quite a while was just my ideal. I was eleven, I think, when I had

---

30.   A hat made out of soft plaited straw, usually with a broad brim.

the joy of entertaining Frank several times while Sadie got ready to go somewhere with him.

*One* glorious evening when Frank came unexpectedly, and she had *other* company, he gave me his undivided attention. We sang duets, played club fist and slap hand, organized a two piece orchestra with a broom handle and yardstick. I can still remember how cleverly he could mimic a banjo. But, O Dear, our beautiful friendship came to a cruel and tragic end. One day cousin Leona Armstrong, and Leona Morris came to our place when Sadie was not at home.[31] Someone came from the Post Office and brought a letter for Sadie from Frank and they pounced upon it, took it to the teakettle and steamed it till it came unglued easily. It was a nice letter, well written and interesting. There was a blank place at the bottom, below his name, so they added a P. S. and finished filling the page. I can't remember what they wrote, but it was something that made Sadie furious. The bad feature of it was that they had wheedled me into *swearing* that I would not tell her that they had opened it.

When Frank came, and Sadie bawled him out about it, of course it was tacked onto me. I had to just stand there in agony and see my beloved Frank, white with anger, asking me if I didn't know that it was a very serious breach of the law to tamper with the mail, and that people had been put behind bars for doing what I had done. I said that I didn't do it, but no one believed me, and I could not tell who *had* done it, as I had sworn I would not, and when we swore a thing it was *never* broken. And so, our cherished friendship came to an end, and I was sad and hurt, and felt terribly guilty for allowing them to tamper with his nice letter.

I heard of Frank at long intervals after that. He was married, and then one day news came that he had died, and without knowing that it was not I who had tampered with his letter. Well, somewhere, in the place where we go after we leave here, maybe I can see him sometime, and make things right.

When I was a little older, one of Frank's nephews (I guess he was a nephew, anyway a close relative), Claude Wright, and I had a fleeting romance. I remember an evening when a group of us went for a hay ride.

Claude and I were on the back of the wagon with our feet dangling. The moon was shining in a pond of water, with willows around the sides. It was very pretty. We sang silly songs, and at last they all sang a Baptist Hymn:

> Come, oh come to me, said Jesus,
> Come, and I will give you rest,
> I'll take away the burden from your heavy ladened breast,

---

31. Leona Morris (1883–1970) married James Crittenden Marquess.

No matter who the wanderer, Or how long he's been astray,
Whosoever quickly cometh I will comfort him today.

I later heard that Claude and a Poindexter girl were going to be married, but on the wedding night he backed out, and didn't go. Years after
that, when Violet was a baby, Dave Wright, one of Lelia's old flames came
through our neighborhood and someone told him where I lived. He
stopped and visited awhile, talked of old times, and of Lelia. He said that
he had never cared for anyone else like he did Lelia. He asked me if I had
heard of Claude jilting the Poindexter girl. Of course I had. He said that
he went over there that night to see what was the matter with him, and he
was laying across the bed crying. When Dave asked him why he wasn't at
the wedding, he said that it wouldn't be right for him to marry her, when
he thought more of Miss Effie than he did of her. I don't suppose Dave
ever married either, he was still single the last time I heard of him.

Corn planting time and barefoot time came at the same time, about
the first of May. We usually *all* went to the field for the planting. Sadie and
I usually dropped the grains in the crosses, and the men drove the horses
hitched to the drags that covered it.

May was a happy time. During the long, cold winters (and early
spring) with rain, snow, and sleet, and the constant freezing and thawing,
often for weeks at a time we would not even see the sun. So, when the
warm sunshiny weather did arrive, which it usually did about the first of
May, we felt like celebrating, and did it by working from morning till
night, till the crops were all planted.

# CHAPTER FOUR

# A One Horse Religion

*The chronicle so far deals only with childhood*
*The free happy years with my life in its Spring*
*With mammy to feed us and care for and clothe us*
*To bear all the burdens and soften each sting.*

*To teach us a sort of one horse religion*
*Of truthfulness, patience and kindness and love*
*To honor the Sabbath by resting or reading.*
*To never speak lightly of God up above.*
 —"Our Search For Truth"
 in *Backward Glances*, 51

One spring, I think it was 1891 or 1892, when I was six or seven years old, two Mormon Missionaries came to the field where we were planting corn. Pappy was school trustee, and they wanted permission to preach in the schoolhouse. He told them that he had no objections, but they went on and did *not* hold any meetings. When we went to the house at noon, there were two tracts lying on the sewing machine in the porch. Pappy read them aloud, and said that he could find no fault with them.

The only mention of Mormons that I can remember, in the five or six years after that, was a silly story in the old Farmers Almanac (the one that had mottoes by Benjamin Franklin and others, all around the pages on the margins). The story was of two Mormon Missionaries who went to a place and stayed all night. After supper the Missionaries and the man sat out in the door yard and talked while *Hanner* was supposed to be washing the dishes.

They told the man that if he would come to Utah he could see visions in the skies, and that he could have a dozen women if he wanted them, "a heap younger and purtier than Hanner." The man was impressed, but there was one drawback. Hanner had been eavesdropping, and had heard all they said. After the husband went to sleep she tied him to the bed with a *bed cord*, and whipped him till he promised he'd never think of Utah again.

There was a picture of Brigham Young along with it. He was sitting down, each leg was six or seven feet long and reached way out, and on each leg five or six women were sitting. That, and an old song, "Old Brigham Young had forty wives, he might have had some more, etc.," was all I had ever heard of Mormons till I was eleven years old.

I *do* remember Pappy reading about a "Whittling Brigade," whose motto was, "Always whittle away from you, and you'll never get cut." I know now that it was a group of young men of Nauvoo, Illinois,[1] who banded together, after the death of the Prophet,[2] and after their Charter had been taken from them, and their city was being overrun with horse thieves and outlaws. They chose this method and literally *whittled* them out of town.[3]

I think it was in the fall of 1897 when the news came that Mormon preachers were going to preach at Pleasant Green Church. We were all excited and curious to know just how they would look, and what they would preach about. I thought that they would be old men, with long white beards. I don't know why I thought this. I must have seen a picture like that somewhere representing Mormon preachers, but I don't remember it if I had.

---

1. Nauvoo was a city in western Illinois founded by the Mormons in 1838. It served as church headquarters until 1846, when the Mormons were driven out by mob persecution.

2. Joseph Smith, Jr. (1805–1844), founder and first president of the Church of Jesus Christ of Latter-day Saints.

3. The following description of the "whistling and whittling brigade" appeared in Andrew Jenson, ed., *The Historical Record: A Monthly Periodical*, Book I (Salt Lake City: Andrew Jenson, 1889), 806–807:

    Many of the boys of [Nauvoo] had each a large bowie knife made, and when a man came to town who was known to be a villian [*sic*], and was there for evil purposes, a few of them would get together, and go to where the obnoxious person was, and having previously provided themselves with pine shingles, would commence whittling. The presence of a number of boys, each whittling a shingle with a bright, large bowie knife, was not a sight to escape the notice of a stranger. . . The boys would . . . keep up their whistling, as though the chief and only pursuit of their lives was whittling and whistling. . . . There was no law against boys whistling and whittling. The result would be that these people would get out of the city as quickly as possible, for they did not know how soon they might have another visit from the boys.

    See also Thurmon Dean Moody, "Nauvoo's Whistling and Whittling Brigade," *BYU Studies* 15 (summer 1975): 480–90.

Elmo, my oldest brother, was sent to see what it was like, as it was too far for us all to go. We were still up when he got back, expecting to hear some exciting news. But he was very disappointing. He said that they were just ordinary men, young, both good looking, and excellent singers. They preached the Bible, and it sounded sensible.

One day, not very long after that, Mammy was scrubbing the kitchen floor. I was in there with her. I happened to look through the window in Mammy's room up towards the Big road. I saw two men in long frock tailed coats, with derby hats on, each carrying a small grip, coming down the road from the big gate.

Mammy said, "Lordy mercy, I'll bet that's them Mormon preachers, hand me my clean apron right quick." She pulled her dirty apron off, dried her hands on it, and by the time she had the clean one tied on they were knocking. They walked fast.

They wanted to see the husband, they said, as they were told that he was school trustee, and they wanted permission to preach in the school house. Mammy told them where he was, they got his permission, and then invited us to come to services that night.

Our dad hitched the mules to the wagon and we all went. That night marked the beginning of a new life for us. No more groping around in the dark in search of truth. No more trying to fit man made doctrines with the teachings of the Savior.[4]

The school house was small, and of course was poorly lighted. All the lights to be had at that time, in the country, were coal oil lamps, but as I remember the songs, the prayer, and the sermon, our conversation after the meeting, and the buying of a little red backed book, "The Voice of Warning," it seems to me that we all walked in a halo of beautiful light.[5]

They sang, "Oh Ye Mountains High," also, "Praise to the Man Who Communed With Jehovah," and "Truth Reflects Upon Our Senses."[6]

---

4.  In April 1897, the senior elder, Alvin Ipsen, of Bear River City, Utah, reported from Liberty, Kentucky, that 26 people had been baptized and that the missionaries were "hospitably received and entertained." See Journal History of the Church of Jesus Christ of Latter-day Saints, April 22, 1897, p. 4; Alvin Ipsen to Editor, "Returned Missionary," *Deseret Evening News*, December 31, 1898, 15.

5.  *The Voice of Warning* was written by Parley P. Pratt (1807–1857) and has been reprinted by Deseret Book in Salt Lake City as recently as 1978.

6.  "Oh Ye Mountains High" is an indigenous Mormon hymn text still included in *Hymns* (Salt Lake City: Church of Jesus Christ of Latter-day Saints, 1985), #34. "Praise to the Man" is an indigenous hymn text by William W. Phelps, *Hymns,*1985, #27. The text of "Truth Reflects Upon Our Senses" was written by Eliza R. Snow *(Hymns*, 1985, #273) and it has been sung to various hymn tunes other than the one in the 1985 hymnal.

The Senior Elder was Alvin Ipsen, a little Danishman from Bear River City, Box Elder County, Utah.[7] He had a mop of yellow curly hair, was a grand singer, with a wonderful personality, and a power of persuasion that was almost irresistible. I think that the secret of his power for good was in his humility, which gave him an extra portion of the spirit of the Lord, and his intense love and understanding of all kinds of human beings. His companion was a local missionary, Wister G. Wallace, from Center, Metcalf County, Kentucky; a handsome dark haired young fellow, who fitted in perfectly with his companion.[8]

The songs they sang sounded new and unusual. I had never heard anything like them before. No repetitions of "Savior wash me in the Blood," or, "Jesus saves, Jesus saves." During the week of meetings that they held, they sang of "Earth with her ten thousand flowers," and, "High on the mountain top a banner is unfurled," and of a *Beautiful Zion* built above, and to "Our Father who dwells in a high and glorious place."[9] It was hard to tell which thrilled me the most, the songs or the sermons.

The first night we went to hear them Elder Ipsen preached on the scattering of Israel. A rather deep subject for a child of eleven to understand, especially when I had never even heard of the scattering of Israel.

I had no idea what my parents or brothers and sisters were thinking of it, but I was so thrilled that I could hardly contain my feelings. I was sitting about halfway back, with a group of my schoolmates, who kept trying to whisper to me, but I had no time for foolishness that night. Something great and wonderful had come, something we had dreamed of and waited for for years. I'm sure it was the spirit of it, and not the letter, that whispered to my spirit, and filled me with such joy.

"Woe to Ariel, to Ariel the city where David dwelt," the words were like music to my soul, and my happiness was so intense that it was painful.[10]

---

7.  The title "Elder" was—and continues to be—the form of address for Mormon missionaries, many of them very young men. Female missionaries are addressed by the title, "Sister." Alvin Ipsen (1871–1939) of Bear River City, Utah, served as a Mormon missionary in the Southern States Mission in 1896–1898. In 1900, he married Viola Sweeney (1878–1939), of Kentucky, whom he met while in his mission field. Ipsen was ordained one of the seven presidents of the fifth quorum of Seventy in 1901. See Jensen, *LDS Biographical Encyclopedia* 1:398–99.

8.  Wister G. Wallace (1870–1953) was born in Beechville, Metcalf County, Kentucky.

9.  "Earth with Her Ten Thousand Flowers" is a well-known text by Thomas R. Taylor and is still included in *Hymns,* 1985, #87. "High on the Mountain Top" is an indigenous Mormon hymn text by Joel H. Johnson ( *Hymns,* 1985, #5). "Beautiful Zion" is by George Gill (*Hymns,* 1985, #44), and Effie has paraphrased the opening line of Eliza R. Snow's indigenous Mormon text: "O my Father, thou that dwellest / In the high and glorious place." *Hymns,* 1985, #292.

10. See Isaiah 29:1.

"Alvin Ipsen of Bear River City Box Elder Co Utah—
The first missionary we heard preach." Courtesy of
Hazel Bushman

As soon as the meeting was dismissed I hurried up to the front to
see my mother and father, and to see what they thought of it. They were
complimenting the young missionaries, and inviting them to go home
with us. Others were crowding up, wanting tracts and books to read.
*Many* people invited them to go and spend the night with them. It just
seemed perfectly natural that they should go home with *us.*

I can't remember just what month it was, but it was cold enough
that we had a fire in the fireplace, for I remember distinctly that long conversation after we reached home. The eager questions; the logical
answers. The growing wonder that they were teaching *exactly* what we had
always believed, and the complete agreement between their teachings
and that of the Savior in the New Testament.

About one o'clock my mother suddenly remembered that I should
have been in bed hours before, but I could not be shaken till the conversation was ended. I was afraid that I might miss something.

Later in the week a Gilliland family, from the Mt. Zoar neighborhood, attended. They were distant relatives of ours, but I had not seen them before. They had two sons about my age, Forest and Aubrey, who came with them. Also two daughters, Ora, older than I, and Annie, who was younger.[11] They had attended the meetings at Pleasant Green and were interested in the message.

Every night the little schoolhouse was packed, and along towards the last of the week a few of us began to add our voices to the singing. We had been practicing at home, after meetings, of evenings. What a joy to be able to raise my own voice with those of the missionaries in praise to my Heavenly Father, for this beautiful message that had been brought to us. "We Thank Thee Oh God For a Prophet"[12] was full of meaning for me.

Elmo sang a good tenor, and John sang bass. Soon we had quite a choir. The missionaries had a number of small song books containing the words and not the music to the songs. They were soon sold out, and everyone began singing the new hymns.

We would have enjoyed having the missionaries stay with us *every* night, but they had to divide their time with others who wanted them, and of course we must not be selfish.

The hours at home were spent in hunting out the passages of scripture they quoted in their sermons. I went upstairs and lay flat on my stomach by the long low window and searched through the little old dogeared Bible. They were hard to find, and I soon learned to listen when they told where the passages were to be found.

The first time our father went to town he bought a new Bible, and I remember with what pride I stacked our newly acquired bunch of religious books. The new Bible, a copy of the Book of Mormon, The Voice of Warning, several tracts, and the little song books.[13] Not a very expensive set of books, but wonderfully precious to us.

Every day new joys and new wonders unfolded to us as we studied the Gospel Plan. How plain and how easy it was to understand. The wonder to us was why everyone couldn't understand it as we did.

---

11. Forrest Gilliland (1881–1959) and Aubra (Aubrey) Gilliland (1882–1975) were the sons of James Millard Gilliland and Laura Hall. Ora Emma Gilliland (1884–1949) and Annie Pearl Gilliland (1889–1955) were their daughters.

12. *Hymns*, 1985, #19, an indigenous Mormon text, "full of meaning" for Effie probably because the prophet referred to in the hymn is the president of the Church of Jesus Christ of Latter-day Saints, who, for Mormons, always serves as the current (or Latter-day) prophet of God on earth.

13. The Book of Mormon, according to Mormon belief, is a record of God's dealings with a group of Israelites who migrated to the Western Hemisphere about 600 B.C. Joseph Smith was instructed by divine messenger to find and translate this record.

One evening as we sat around the fire, one of the missionaries spied the end of Pappy's violin case sticking out from under the old walnut dresser, and asked who played it. Soon they were tuning the fiddle and guitar together for the first time in a long while, and again the music came streaming from the old violin in sweet harmony. The missionaries were charmed, and kept their feet going in time with the music.

"So you folks are not opposed to violin music?" my father asked, at the end of a lively tune, at which they plainly showed their pleasure.

"No indeed. Music, and dancing also, has given me lots of happy hours in my short life," Elder Ipsen declared.

*There* was another very important thing we agreed on. The preachers of the different denominations around us were bitterly opposed to both violin music and dancing. They often told their congregations that the devil was in the fiddle, though they had never succeeded in making us believe it.

Well, this new found religion had measured up to our every ideal so far, and tonight's discovery was another step in favor of it. A happy people, with a happy religion. One that took care of every phase of life. A time for all things, and everything in order, and in its place.

Through the winter of that year, 1897 or 1898, we studied the Gospel of Jesus Christ thoroughly. When we struck something we did not understand the missionaries were near, and were glad to come and help us to understand it.

It looked as if the entire population of that community would be converted. The Elders were welcomed everywhere, and were constantly in demand to fill appointments to preach.[14]

In February there was talk of them being sent to another field of labor, and my parents were anxious to be baptized before they left. February is often the coldest month of the winter, but this time there

---

14. Mattie Carmack, Effie's mother-in-law, told a similar story of conversion in the Mt. Zoar neighborhood:

> We beleaved that al we need was to give our hand to the preachers and be baptized and we would be saved. We found out that we needed repentance and works to show our faith. Wel beleave me our bibles did not ly in one place long enough to let dust settle on them. Thair wer a bunch of us took our names off from Mount Zore and wer baptized in the Mormon Church, but i love a lot of my old friends in Mount Zore and i think they do me. Wel wee kept the Elders, i wish i had kept name cards id like to no myself, but i am glad that Tom and i made the Elders welcom, for they were doing good, teachen Gods work and trying to get people to be saved.

> See Mattie Olivia Hale Carmack, *My Story: Mattie Olivia Hale Carmack, 1873–1961*, compiled by Donna Bess Carmack Musto (Franklin, NC: Genealogy Publishing Service, 1991), 73–74.

"Effie Lee Marquess. Young lady of 11 or 12." Courtesy of Itha Carmack.

came a few days of nice sunny weather, and a baptismal service was appointed.

I was anxious to be among the first ones to go into the waters of baptism, but my mother said that she didn't know whether they baptized children as young as I was or not.[15] It was a terrible disappointment to me. I retired to my seat in the half darkness of the old stairway and cried till I was exhausted, but everyone was busy getting ready to go to the creek for

---

15. Baptism into the Mormon Church is by immersion. The minimum age for baptism is eight years of age; Effie was in fact old enough at that time to be baptized.

the baptizing, and paid no attention to me. However, when we got to the place where the baptizing was to be held, one of the Elders saw my swollen eyes and asked the reason. When my mother told him he said that they would have another baptizing real soon, and he would see to it that I was baptized if I wanted to be.

The missionaries had told us of the word of wisdom.[16] That we should keep our bodies clean, say our prayers regularly, and keep the Sabbath day holy, so I found some satisfaction in doing those things while I waited. They seemed very small things in comparison to what I would have liked to do to show my appreciation of the Gospel.

I could understand perfectly how the righteous Alma felt when he said he would like to get on top of a mountain, and in a voice of thunder proclaim the Gospel to the Nations of the Earth. But, he said that he knew that he was just an ordinary man, and would have to be content to do what little good he could in the small sphere in which he lived.[17]

I was sure that I could convert all my schoolmates in a very short time, when I had time to explain it to them fully, but to my great disappointment most of them were not interested in it. Some of them giggled, and said I had *got religion*. Well, I certainly had *got* it, almost more than I could contain.

When Mammy said something about being baptized, our dad asked her what she was going to do without her evening smoke, so she retorted by asking him what he was going to do without his *quid*. She looked around till she spied her old brickcolored clay pipe, and going out in the back yard she took it by the stem and threw it away beyond the garden.

The following month, in March, after the first baptizing, in which my parents, my two older sisters, Etta the cripple (who had joined the Baptist Church), Lelia, my married sister, cousin Millard Gilliland, and his wife were all baptized, the Elders announced another baptizing, and my mother said that I could be one of them if I wanted to. She got my clothes all ready. The great day arrived. The sun arose clear and nice, but by the time the services were to be held it had clouded up, and looked dark and stormy, and flakes of snow were beginning to fall. But there was

---

16. Word of Wisdom, usually capitalized, refers to the dietary teachings in Section 89 of the *Doctrine and Covenants*. It is interpreted as a total prohibition against tobacco, alcohol, coffee, and tea, and advocates the eating of grain and "every fruit in the season thereof." Even members of a tobacco-growing community would have been expected to give up the use of tobacco upon becoming a Mormon.

17. A reference to an important Book of Mormon figure, Alma, who proclaimed: "O that I were an angel, and could have the wish of mine heart; that I might go forth and speak with the trump of God, with a voice to shake the earth, and cry repentance unto every people!" (Alma 29:1–2)

*The Old Swimming Hole ~ in Winter*

*The Old Swimming Hole in Winter*, drawing by Effie Carmack. "The old swimming hole where we watered the horses was just the right depth for baptizing, it seemed"; quotation from *Backward Glances*, p. 58. Drawing courtesy of Itha Carmack.

no thought of changing the date. The Elders said they had never heard of anyone suffering any sickness from being baptized. They sang:

Lo, on the water's brink we stand
To do the Father's will,
To be baptized by His command
And thus the Word fulfill.[18]

My happiness seemed complete as the song echoed up and down the creek banks. It seemed that the very trees were happy.

By the time the baptizing was over the snow was falling fast. Just as the last one came out of the water cousin Buck Cravens dashed up on one of the Widow Clardy's thoroughbreds and ordered someone to put me up behind him. We cantered away, and in a few minutes we were at home.

Mammy had made me a pretty new dress for the occasion. It was of a soft shiny material, pale blue, with a little white pattern in it. It had a round collars with a ruffle on it, and a pleat down the front with a ruffle on each side of it. The cuffs also had a narrow ruffle.

As I sat in the chair to be confirmed a member of the Church of Jesus Christ, and as I thought with gratitude that through baptism my sins had been forgiven, I think I felt something like a Saint. When the Elder who confirmed me said: "Receive Ye the Holy Ghost" I wondered if I could stand very much more pure joy.[19]

That summer Mr. Morris offered his big cool, clean new barn for Sunday School to be held in, as it was near the center of the community.

Eddie Moore, our neighbor, had been baptized, and came every evening to sing with us. He could read music very easily, and had a good voice, so he could help us with the different parts. Our singing improved. Athel Hulsey, who worked at Moore's, came with him and joined in the singing a great deal.

We all enjoyed the Sunday School. Pappy was made superintendent, and Lelia was appointed secretary. I memorized whole chapters of the Bible that I liked especially well.

That summer, too, the first conference was held in the Larkin branch. There were over fifty Elders in the Kentucky conference at that time, and what a happy reunion they had. Elder Ipsen and Elder Afflick

---

18. *Hymns,* 1948, #97; an anonymous hymn text not included in the 1985 hymnal.

19. Confirmation follows the ceremony of baptism. Authorized Priesthood authorities place their hands upon the head of the new member and bestow the gift of the Holy Ghost.

had labored together during their first year in the Mission field. Elder Ipsen was looking forward to seeing him when he came to Conference.[20]

Ipsen and a number of other Elders were at our place when they spied Afflick and his companion coming down the road from the highway. Ipsen ran to meet him, and they fell on each other's necks and cried like children. Evidently this was a gospel of love, and to obey it meant to love others who obeyed it, and of course love for one another is what makes life worth living.

How we enjoyed doing things for these clean young men who were willing to give two or three of the best years of their lives to help others to understand the Plan of Salvation.[21]

The day before the big conference meeting was to be held there were thirty eight Elders who ate dinner at our place. It must have been hard on my mother, as she was trying to fix something nice to take to the conference with us. It kept her cooking all day and until way into the night.

For once Mammy had a pretty dress and hat to wear to meeting. A black and white striped shirt waist and a black skirt, a pretty little poke bonnet style hat, like the old ladies of that day wore. It had a bunch of pretty feathers in front with little fluffy balls on the ends of each feather.

John Fielding [Fleming] Wakefield was president of the Kentucky Conference at that time, and he had been very sick.[22] When he arrived on the train they brought him to our place and he went right to bed. The next morning the Elders administered to him, and then they all went to the place of meeting, which was under a huge bowery above Morrises' place, at the old Villa Long place. It was a pretty, level spot, in the edge of a big woods.

After we all left the house, Papa and Brother Wakefield got in the buggy and drove down to the well where Papa drew a tub full of cold water, and President Wakefield took a cold bath. He then went to the house, dressed, and came to Conference and took charge of the meetings.

It was a wonderful Conference, but was saddened by the thought that Elder Ipsen, who had taught us the Gospel, would probably be

---

20. See "List of Elders in Kentucky," *Deseret Evening News*, September 18, 1897, 11. A conference is an ecclesiastical unit involving a larger geographical area than an ordinary congregation within the Latter-day Saint mission organization. Districts are sub-units making up a mission conference. David A. Affleck (1873–1953) served in the Southern States Mission in 1897–1899.

21. As defined by Mormon Apostle, Bruce R. McConkie,"The *plan of salvation* comprises all of the laws, ordinances, principles, and doctrines by conformity to which the spirit offspring of God have power to progress to the high state of exaltation enjoyed by the Father." See *Mormon Doctrine* (Salt Lake City: Bookcraft, 1966), 575.

22. John Fleming Wakefield (1872–1964) served in the Southern States Mission in 1895–1898.

released, and would then return to his home in Utah, and we would likely never see him again.

There was a photographer on hand who made a picture of the group. That is the only picture of my mother that I know of, and I do not have a copy of it. A missionary, Elder Partridge, who was at the conference that day, has one of the pictures, and has promised to lend it to me, long enough for me to get a copy made of it.[23]

Somewhere among my old keepsakes is a copy of the minutes of Sunday School held at the home of Johnnie Boyd and his wife Dona. My father was superintendent, and Lelia was secretary. That was the Larkin Sunday School. I will make an exact copy of it and include it here. [*The autobiography does not include these minutes.*]

We held Sunday School in the bowery where we had our first conference, and later on in Mr. Morrises' new barn, but in cold weather it was held in our homes.

It was not long after this that we sold the old home and moved away to the Palestine neighborhood, next to the Holts. I think I have written a chapter of our sojourn at this place, where Elmo married Ivy West and brought her to live with us, of her conversion and getting baptized.[24] Her coming and helping her to understand the Gospel was a welcome change from the dreary loneliness after our mother and Etta left us.

Ivy and I remained staunch and loving friends as long as she lived. She was not blessed with children of her own, but she helped me with my little ones when she was near enough, but much of the time she lived near her mother in the Pond River community.

Before we sold the old home, where Mammy and Etta had died, a young Missionary by the name of Stanley A. Hanks, came from Tooele, Utah, to Kentucky.[25] I think he came to our place first, after arriving in Hopkinsville. He was only nineteen, very blonde and boyish looking, white and tender as a hothouse flower. He had a shock of yellow curly hair, and handsome features.

We had no telephones in those days, and if we had it would probably have made no difference. The missionaries didn't hunt for easy ways to do things, and the new Elders were not spared any hardships.

When Elder Hanks landed in Hopkinsville, he and the Elder who met him walked the seven or eight miles out to our place. Elder Hanks had on new thick soled shoes. It was hot weather, and by the time they

---

23. Raymond Partridge (1875–1952) served in the Southern States Mission in 1896–1899.

24. Ivy West Marquess (1884–1958).

25. Stanley Alonzo Hanks (1878–1924) served in the Southern States Mission in 1898–1900.

reached our place his feet were blistered all over, and he could hardly walk at all. They stayed about a week, till he could get toughened up a bit.

I can remember yet how intensely interested Elder Hanks was in the birds, trees, flowers, insects, and every part of the outdoor life of Kentucky. He said that it was so different from the part of Utah where he lived. I was also interested in those things, and enjoyed answering his many questions, and showing him new specimens.

I remember particularly how curious he was over an old Bessie Bug we found under a log at the woodpile. He was helping me chop stove wood, and asked what each kind of wood it was.

The hickory, that they make wagons, axe handles, and many other things of, and which has nuts on them, was very interesting to him. We ate the little bumps of sugar that the sun drew out of the bark on the hickory logs.

I showed him how many of the women who use snuff (and others who did not) made tooth brushes of this very sweet bark, carving the handles into intricate patterns. Other favorite woods for toothbrushes were black gum and swamp dogwood.

The black gum had dark mottled bark, and the swamp dogwood was a bright red, and very smooth and straight when it was new growth. It grew along streams, and had a nice flavor. Elder Hanks thought these toothbrush woods were interesting, and he sent samples of them to his folks.

Elder Hanks was also interested in the wild flowers that grew along the path that led to the spring that was in the woods just west of the house.

One day when Elder Hanks went with me to the well for water he found a terrapin, with pretty green, brown and ocher designs on his back, in strange geometric patterns.[26] He was *so* curious to see how it looked inside the shell that while I was gone to take the water to the house he cut it open with the axe. I was horrified, and proceeded to give him a good raking for being so heartless and brutal. He defended himself by pointing out the fact that we killed chickens, pigs, and sheep, and thought nothing of it. Why was an old terrapin so terribly important. Anyway, he didn't get very much satisfaction out of it after he did cut it open. He was interested in the heart that kept beating for hours after he had taken the body to pieces.

I told him that it was a fine missionary he would make, killing everything he ran across. He took it very seriously, and at the supper table asked his companion and the others about it. I think the decision was against the

---

26.    A terrapin is any one of several edible turtles of the family *Testudinidae* living in fresh or brackish waters of the gulf coast region.

killing. His companions told him that it was all right to be interested in things, to a certain extent. How would he like for someone to become so interested in *him* that they would take a carving knife and look inside. They had a big laugh at Hanks' expense, but he was in earnest.

The Elders then had to leave and go to work, as the feet were about well. We had doctored them by soaking them in alum water and blue-stone. That was the summer of 1898, after we had been baptized in the spring. They came again in the fall, and how glad we were to see them after an absence of several months. Elder Hanks had changed. He was more like a man instead of a little boy. He was developing into a good speaker, and when we went to the well for water he was more interested in Gospel themes than in terrapins and bugs. We were still finding new wonders about the restored truth we had accepted, and each day we were more thankful to our Father in Heaven for having found it.

Elder Hanks had been finding out a lot of things also. He was study-ing the Gospel daily, in order to be able to explain it to others. As he learned, his faith in it, and his testimony had grown stronger. He was beginning to realize what it meant to be a teacher of the Gospel. He was astonished that a child of my age could have learned so much concerning our religion as I had in the short time since we had first heard it.

I was thirteen that fall. A skinny, scrawny child, but so intensely reli-gious that at times it was almost painful. Just saying my prayers, quitting coffee, controlling my temper, and things like that seemed so small com-pared with what I *wanted* to do. I knew exactly how Alma felt when he said that he would like to stand on the highest mountain and to shout it so that it could be heard the world over.[27] I had to satisfy myself by studying the books the missionaries had left. The Voice of Warning, The Book of Mormon, the tracts with Bible references that I enjoyed looking up and reading. We had a small red song book too, and I soon memorized every song I knew the tune to—"High on the Mountain Top,"—"Oh, Say What is Truth,"—"The Day Dawn is Breaking,"—"Praise to the Man Who Communed With Jehovah."[28]

We had quite a choir in our own home when Eddie Moore and Athie Halsey would come of an evening. John and Athie sang bass, Elmo sang tenor, and Eddie could sing most any of the parts.

---

27. Another reference to Alma 29:1–2 in the Book of Mormon.
28. "High on the Mountain Top" is an indigenous text by Joel H. Johnson (*Hymns*, 1985, #5) and the text of "Oh Say What is Truth" is by John Jaques (*Hymns*, 1985, #272). The indigenous text of "The Day Dawn is Breaking" is by Joseph L. Townsend (*Hymns*, 1985, #52). "Praise to the Man" is an indigenous text by William W. Phelps which refers to Joseph Smith (*Hymns*, 1985, #27).

I said that almost every one seemed interested in the Gospel, but there were a few exceptions. Uncle Lawrence and Aunt Fannie had become very cool, and didn't come to visit us anymore. Mr. and Mrs. Moore, Eddie's parents, didn't share their son's interest, and didn't like the idea of him being baptized. Cousin Boone Fuller and cousin Mary became cool towards us.

Not one of my father's or mother's people accepted the Gospel, but they themselves, but they had the joy of seeing every one of their children baptized that first spring, and every one of them have stayed true to it.

Elder Ipsen had told us that often the first year in the Church was the hardest, that the devil would try our faith in many ways. When our own folks turned against us he quoted the words of the Savior, "I am not come to bring peace, but a sword . . . and a man's foes will be those of his own household."[29]

After we were all baptized and my father had quit using coffee and tobacco, his stomach trouble left him. He gained weight and his hair became soft and shiny again. We were a happy family, and all went well until just before Christmas of 1898.

Ernest Gilliland came home from some job, where he had been working, with a strange illness. The doctor said that it was La Grippe, or influenza. There was an itching rash with it that was terrible. Ernest took a notion he wanted Etta to take care of him. They came for her and she stayed with him till he died.[30]

---

29. See Matthew 10:34–36.

30. As early as February 1897, the Southern States Mission had experienced a horrible outbreak of yellow fever. "Many of the Elders were somewhat hindered in their work by the great amount of sickness existing throughout the mission. In many sections scarcely a family could be found free from sickness. The angel of death seemed extraordinarily busy." See "History of the Southern States Mission," *Latter Day Saints Southern Star* 2 (May 19, 1900): 197. On January 10, 1899, Elder W. H. Petty sent the following obituary to the editors of the *Southern Star*:

Brother Earnest Gilliland, son of Brother and Sister J. M. Gilliland of Larkin, Ky., died the 8th inst. at 6:15 A.M. after the illness of ten or twelve days. The cause of death was said to be typhoid fever. He was a promising young man, twenty years of age, and well respected by all his acquaintants.

He was baptized Aug. 21st, 1898, by Elder Alivin Ipsen, during our last August conference, and has been a faithful Sunday school worker since. The Elders will well remember the pleasant time all had at the confirmation meeting, which was held at his late home, at night on the lawn and under the trees; after which we had songs and recitations and finally bid the Elders, who were to return home, a good bye.

Funeral services were held on Monday at Mt Zoar (Baptist church) which was obtained for the occasion. The meeting was called to order promptly at 12 o'clock by Elder W. H. Petty, presiding. The building was filled by relatives and friends who sympathized with the bereaved family.

A day or two after Etta came home from there she took a violent chill, followed by burning fever. My mother took care of her and she was the next to come down, then Sadie, next John, and my father was also stricken. Lelia came to help me take care of them, and soon she came down with it also.

Elmo and I were the only ones able to do anything. It was so cold that all Elmo could do was chop and bring in wood, keep fires going, and feed the stock. The log heaps he built seemed to melt and do no good. In all the years that I lived in Kentucky I have never seen such terrible weather. The sleet poured down in torrents and froze to the trees as it fell. The thunder roared and crashed till it seemed that it would split the earth. We usually never have thunder there, only in the spring and summer. Everything seemed strange and unnatural. The thermometer registered 32 degrees below zero.

At that time there were four of the family unconscious. My mother, Etta, Sadie, and John. Lelia and my father were not much better. My father said that he was not going to bed. He sat by the fire and held one of the sick children all the time.

Dr. Moore and Dr. Lovan came, but everything they did seemed to do no good.[31] One of them made a mistake and gave Sadie a dose of horse medicine. For nine days she never closed her eyes.

---

The Larkin Sabbath school choir furnished the singing and Elder M. P. Brown occupied the time preaching the funeral sermon and comforting the hearts of those who had cause to mourn, after which the remains were taken to the Boyd's cemetery, where they were laid to rest. Dedicatory prayer was offered by Elder W. H. Perry.

The weather was fairly good and a large crowd assembled at the grave to pay their last tribute of respect to the deceased.

We were called to administer to Brother Earnest several times during his illness, but it seemed only to quiet him for the time. He suffered by very little apparently during his sickness and passed away peacefully, and in good faith in the gospel.

During his illness, his younger brother, Garnett, was taken very sick with a fever also; we were called to administer to him and he was immediately healed.

The family remain faithful and acknowledge the hand of the Lord in their bereavement.

Brother Earnest leaves a father and mother, six brothers and two sisters, and a sweet heart, to mourn his loss. May the choicest blessings of heaven rest upon the bereaved family, who will miss Brother Earnest, is the prayer of your Bretheren in the cause of truth.

See "Death of Brother Gilliland," *Latter Day Saints Southern Star* 1 (January 21, 1899): 62.

31.  Dr. J. R. Moore (b. 1849) and Dr. G. W. Lovan (1868–1932).

I was kept busy heating irons, and filling jugs with hot water to try to keep the feet of the sick ones warm. One night I forgot to refill the jug of water at Sadie's feet, and when I thought of it in the morning, with a guilty start, I hurried to take it out of the bed. The water in it had frozen, the jug was broken, and her feet were still to it. It's a miracle that *any* of them lived through it.

One evening about dark, when the snow and sleet were pouring down, and the thunder shook the earth, we heard a noise out in front, and there was cousin Leona Armstrong and Mary Miller. They had come on horseback to help us out. They looked like angels to me. It was so cold that it was actually dangerous to try to travel.

That night the doctor left some calomel for us to give to my mother. Lelia didn't want to give it. She said that mother was entirely too weak to take anything so strong. But some of them gave her part of it.[32] During the night she motioned for water. Her tongue was so fever parched, and so dry, that she could not talk. She kept trying to say something. After holding a piece of wet cotton to her tongue for a while, softening it, she finally said for us to take care of Autie, and not let him go over to cousin P. Armstrong's and ride those old wild mules, and for Sadie and me to be good girls. She asked them to take the pillow from under her head, then she lay her head down, closed her eyes, and went quietly to sleep. That was the 9th of February. What a *terrible* February. When they dug mother's grave the ground was frozen hard and solid as deep as they dug.[33]

---

32. This is another instance in which calomel was used as an cathartic treatment. See chapter one, note 23.

33. See "Mrs. Marquess Dead," *Hopkinsville Kentuckian*, February 16, 1899, 8. After John Susan's death, the *Southern Star* reported that she lived

> a true Latter-day Saint and proved herself a faithful worker in the Sabbath School and teacher's meeting, and never shirked any obligation that was placed upon her. She was a faithful mother and affectionate wife, and leaves a husband and seven loving children to mourn her loss, three of whom were bedfast with the same dreaded disease that caused the death of their cherished mother.

> Elders Martin P. Brown and Stanley A. Hanks were present at the time of her death and did all they could to comfort the hearts of the bereaved family. On account of the serious illness of the three sick children and the extreme cold weather they were unable to hold funeral services.

> Sister Marquess will long be remembered by the Elders of the Kentucky Conference, for her deeds of kindness shown to them while on their mission preaching the Gospel.

> Brother Marquess and family acknowledge the hand of the Lord in their loss and are still firm in the faith.

See "Death of Sister Marquess," *Latter day Saints Southern Star* 1 (February 25, 1899): 9.

We didn't tell Sadie or Etta or John. The next morning, when Mrs. Miller came into the room where John was, to get clean pillow slips out of a trunk, he was suddenly conscious, and said, "What are they doing, is my Mammy dead?" Then he sat up in bed with a terrified look in his bony face. I can remember how thin his nose looked, and his hair, which was naturally curly, was flat on the sides and stuck way up on top in a tangled mass. No one had time to comb it, or do any of the comforting things that sick people need.

Mammy had always said that she hoped she would die before any of her children. And I've heard her say many times that when she died she didn't want an expensive funeral. As far as she was concerned she would just as soon that some one would wrap a *tow* sack around her and put her in one of the big gullies. *Someone* brought an expensive black shroud and dressed her in it. I had never seen her wear black, and certainly not black satin. *That* and the unnatural yellow of her face after she died made it all more strange than ever. The black satin was in sad contrast with her hard worked hands.[34]

A tall black hearse, drawn by two big black horses, traveled the treacherous, slippery road from Hopkinsville to take her to the graveyard. How inconsistent it all was, not at all in keeping with the rest of our lives.

The cost too was outlandish. I guess that black shroud cost more than all the clothing she had bought for five years. But people had a way of saying, "It's the last thing I can do for her, and I'm going to see that she has a decent burial, and the best is none too good."[35]

It was too cold for people to leave their fires for a funeral, so only two or three went with her poor body to the graveyard. Good old David Brasher and Eddie Moore, who had helped out faithfully throughout our sickness, were both there. I can't even remember now who dug her grave. My mind was so confused, and so filled with things that *had* to be done day and night that there was no time left for sitting down and mourning.

---

34. These funeral practices would have been consistent with death and burial practices of the region. See Thomas F. Garrity and J. Wyss, "Death, Funeral, and Bereavement Practices in Appalachian and Non-Appalachian Kentucky," in *Death and Dying: Views from Many Cultures*, Perspectives on Death in Human Experience Series, no. 1, edited by Richard A. Kalish (Farmingdale, NY: Baywood Publishing Co., 1980), 99–118; Sue Lynn Stone, "Blessed Are They That Mourn: Expressions of Grief in South Central Kentucky, 1870–1910," *Register of the Kentucky Historical Society* 85 (Summer 1987): 213–36.

35. Sue Lynn Stone states: "Before the turn of the century, many individuals chose white, black cloth-draped, 'plush,' or metal-lined caskets. The importance placed on these types of caskets plainly indicates the growing concern for the preservation of the body and the beautification of the receptacle in which the loved one would be interred." See "Blessed Are They That Mourn," 217–18.

Besides the awful anxiety over the sick ones, trying to keep them warm, and trying to fix something for the ones to eat who *could* eat anything, was the fact that all of the canned fruit, potatoes, and apples that always before had kept perfectly in the upstairs over the fireplace, were frozen stiff, and the jars all broken. I used it anyway, thawing the glass and crockery away from the fruit, and then scraping the frozen lump to remove any particles of glass that might have stuck to it.

I was not used to cooking, and Elmo was kept so busy he had very little time to help me. The winter's woodpile soon vanished and he would cut a tree from the woods lot and drag it to the house with one of the horses, then chop it up and pile the logs on the fire in a vain effort to keep the place warm.

I didn't even have time to pray, it seemed that the Lord, whom we had come to know and trust so intimately in the past year had suddenly gone away and left us to the buffetings of Satan. It all seemed like a horrible nightmare, *nothing* seemed real. We had experienced the greatest joy we had ever known in the year that was past. The pendulum swung quickly back into the dark as far as it had swung into the light, and we tasted a bitterness of sorrow and suffering that was far beyond anything I had ever experienced. [*From this point, Effie digresses to repeat much of the same information on Marquess and Armstrong ancestry mentioned earlier. The fact that she makes the digression at this point in the narrative reiterates her high regard for her ancestors. She also seems to be saying that her families' virtuous qualities originated with honorable progenitors. Effie resumes the tragic narrative on page 200 herein.*]

There is a family tradition (given to me by Frank Marquess, of Princeton, Kentucky) that our emigrant ancestor was Capt. Wm. Marquess, who married a sister of Capt. Wm. Kidd. That he was a very wealthy man, and that he brought a fleet of thirty seven vessels (all his own), and a colony of men (400 strong), besides the women and children and slaves. That he brought a barrel of gold, and a barrel of silver (probably kegs), and was by far the richest man who had ever come to America at that time.

He said that he believed that it was around 1740 that he came here. He pushed out into the wilderness and made the first settlement where Cincinnati now stands. The Indians were troublesome, and they built boats and went down the river to where Nashville now stands, when there was not another white settlement for many, many miles (he said hundreds).

Capt. Wm. and a slave went outside the fort to cut staves for barrels and were attacked by Indians. He was killed, but the slave (too scared to throw down his load of staves) made it safely into the fort.

Later, some men came by from the old Pequon (Opequon) settlement of east Tennessee, under the leadership of Capt. Nash, who stayed and later married a Marquess girl, and rebuilt the old Fort and called it Nashboro.

Frank Marquess, who told me this, said that his grandfather, Wm. Kidd Marquess (who married Carlotty Armstrong) was born in one of the cabins of old Fort Nashboro, 1804. I had never heard of a Kidd ancestor, and I didn't know whether to believe all this or not, but later, when I found my own great-great-grandfather in Frederick County, Maryland, his name was Wm. Kidd Marquess.

I was writing to a Marquess relative of St. Louis, Mo., and he said that he and his wife were going back to Kentucky, and if I wanted them to look up anything for me they would be glad to do it.

I asked them to go to the old cemetery, in Todd County, Kentucky, where Frank said that his grandfather, Wm. Kidd and wife, were buried, and see if there were gravestones on their graves. They did, and found that it was just as Frank had said. Born 1804, in a cabin of old Fort Nashboro, wife, Carlotty Armstrong Marquess buried beside him.

Everything I have ever had a chance to prove has been exactly as he said, so I am beginning to believe all of it.

I said *Frank told me.* He *wrote* me, but he was so old, and couldn't see good, that it was hard for me to decipher his writing, so I got my cousin Edna Marquess Clark, of Hopkinsville, Kentucky, to go to Princeton and copy down all he had to tell. I could tell by his letter that he had a lot of memories stored away.

I also wrote to Nashville to see what early history I could get there, and there were about three generations that had come and gone before their record started. They said that a Felix Robinson [Robertson] was the first white child born in Nashville, and as a matter of fact, he was a grandson of Capt. Nash and the Marquess girl.[36]

I have tried for years to connect with the first Capt. Wm. Marquess, but so far I have not gone beyond my greatgreatgrandfather, Wm. Kidd, and his wife, Eleanor Magruder. He *could* be the son of Capt. Wm. and his *Kidd* wife, but I have not been able to prove it.

Grandmother Marquess was Martha Pettypool, and her mother was Matilda Faulkner, daughter of Benjamin Faulkner, of Halifax County, Virginia, and his wife, Susanna Blain [*sic*], daughter of Ephraim Blaine, who was with George Washington at Valley Forge.[37] *He* had the

---

36. Felix Robertson (1781–1865) was the son of Nashville's founder, James Robertson (1742–1814). Felix Robertson was mayor of Nashville in 1818 and from 1827 to 1828. See Anita Shafer Goodstein, *Nashville, 1780–1860: From Frontier to City* (Gainsville: University of Florida Press, 1989), 23, 102, 114.

37. Col. Ephraim Blaine (1741–1804) was commissary-general of the northern department of the revolutionary army from 1778 to 1783. He was with the American army at Valley Forge, Pennsylvania during the winter of 1777–1778. See John Ewing Blaine, *The Blaine Family: James Blaine, Emigrant, and His Children, Ephraim, Alexander, William, Eleanor* (Cincinnati: Ebbert and Richardson, 1920), 7–43.

responsibility of furnishing supplies to the soldiers of Valley Forge, through the awful winter when they almost starved and froze to death. He was a wealthy man, and he gave nearly all he had trying to keep food and clothing for the men in the Army. Washington said that he was one of the best, and most unselfish men he ever knew.

After the war, when the Governor of Pennsylvania heard of all that he had done for the soldiers, and nearly froze himself to death trying get supplies to the men, it is said that this Governor gave Ephraim Blaine a million dollars. Ephraim's father was Jimmie Blaine of Ireland.

My grandfather John Armstrong's father was Benjamin Armstrong of Ireland, of Scotch ancestry, and his wife, Jane Brasher, of a prominent family of France—Brassieur.

My mother's mother was a widow, Martha Boyd, widow of Beverly Boyd. She was a Boyd before she married Beverly, and I have tried for years to find her parents, and have not yet succeeded.[38]

If my mother inherited her qualities from her Boyd ancestors they must have been strong characters. There is no danger of my exaggerating, or overrating my mother's sterling qualities; her unselfishness and kindness to neighbors and relatives. Her patience in making the best of everything, when often it wasn't too good.

Mother sewed for a big family on her fingers. I can remember when she got her first sewing machine, and that meant a long time sewing on her fingers. She was a neat and careful seamstress. Every seam was *felled*, making two rows of stitching on each seam. Mother was also a good cook, and she cooked on the fireplace, and in a dutch oven, till about the time I was born.

Mother was also an excellent gardener, and knew how to make a scientific hotbed. She must also have been a good nurse, judging by the amount of it that she did.

She was good at making quilts, and was a fast and even quilter. We never bought blankets, but there were warm quilts, and deep featherbeds and pillows on every bed. She raised the geese, and picked them for the feathers that made the beds and pillows, too. She was a natural knitter, made it close and even. She never had to look at it while she knitted, and the needles just flew.

She was a good breadmaker, and made salt rising bread, which is difficult to make. She was a good soapmaker. She *ran down* the lye that she made it with (the ash hopper).

---

38.  Martha Boyd (b. 1813) was the wife of Beverly Boyd (b. 1809 or 1811).

But best of all she made a happy home, and was not too sedate to play games with us. She and our father would teach us intricate dances. The lancers, the minuet, quadrilles, schottische, mazurka, polkas, waltzes. Mother had a good voice, and she sang scads of old songs for us.

She also scrubbed on the washboard for the whole family. I dipped up water when we washed at the creek, and kept the fire going under the kettle, and punched the clothes, and sometimes I tromped the tobacco gummy clothes in some strong suds to loosen the black sticky gum.

All winter we heated the irons in front of the fireplace to iron. In summer we used the *stepstove.* (see picture) [*The autobiography does not include this picture.*]

I have often said that if ever a human deserved a crown of glory it would be a mother who patiently raised a big family of men and women under just such circumstances as those my mother had to cope with, and she never felt like she was doing anything the least *great*. She was just doing what she *had* to do, and did it the best she could.

We didn't belong to any church, and didn't count ourselves as being religious, but I never heard my father, or one of my brothers, swear in my life. We never worked on Sundays, and we never speak the name of the Lord disrespectfully. Sunday was sort of a hallowed day. Everything seemed different of Sundays. We cleaned up, and mother usually cooked a good dinner, and put on a clean wrapper.

Our parents never told us not to quarrel, and they didn't make a big fuss of teaching us good manners, but we would never take the last of anything from a dish at the table, or the last biscuit, or the last piece of bread from the plate. That would have been rude, and look selfish and greedy.

We *didn't* quarrel. Folks say, "You've just forgotten," but I *know* that we *didn't.* There never seemed to be anything to quarrel about.

I don't know how our parents managed it, but they were gentle people themselves, refined, but certainly not sophisticated.

"Having been born of goodly parents."[39] I am humbly grateful to them for the examples that they set before us, and the love and kindness they showed to us.

After I started doing research on my father's line, I found why he and his mother knew so much about herbs and simple remedies. I found lots of doctors, botanists, herbalist, etc., on the Pettypool line (my grandmother's father), and on the Faulkner line also (my grandmother's mother).

---

39. See chapter one, note 1.

The pioneer doctors used herbs and simple remedies almost entirely. Many of them learned from the Indians.[40]

Grandmother Martha Pettypool Marquess had an herb garden down by a little creek near their place. The only things I can remember now is ginseng, angelico, foxglove, mayapple, yellow percoon, black-root, and a little short plant with a blue flower, can't remember the name.

> Some of our simple remedies—probably repeated.
> Tobacco—for bruises, stings, and bites, and for sick cattle.[41]
> Camphor and peppermint—for sick stomach.
> Turpentine—for worms, bellyache, as a disinfectant, (used
>     sparingly, 3 drops, for worms).[42]
> Slippery elm bark—for upset stomach
> Colt's foot tea—for asthma and T. B.
> Camphor—one drop in a teaspoon of sweet milk, for sore eyes (will
>     *cure* trachoma).
> Oil of eucalyptus—tincture of benzoin—spirits of camphor—
>     (small amount of each in basin of hot water, breathe the
>     fumes for a cough)
>     (this can also be put in three ounces of pure whiskey and
>     inhaled easier, and always ready. Keep tightly closed)
> Yellow percoon (golden seal)—for sore mouth, *any* sores, and
>     many, many other things.

My father was grandmother's oldest child, and she depended on him a great deal. His father died early. Grandfather was older than grandmother. He had been married, and had a family before he married her.

My father didn't go to school very much, but his mother taught him at home. Part of the teaching was done while he held the candle for her to weave by of evenings. He was named by his Aunt Eliza Marquess Roberts. Her husband was Dr. Boanerges Roberts, and they had a son by the same name who died in his youth, so when my father was born she

---

40. On the development of medicine in frontier Kentucky, see Medical Historical Research Project, *Medicine and Its Development in Kentucky* (Louisville: The Standard Printing Company, 1940); Madge E. Pickard and R. Carlyle Buley, *The Midwest Pioneer: His Ills, Cures, & Doctors* (New York: Henry Schuman, 1946), 258–60; and John Ellis, *Medicine in Kentucky* (Lexington: University Press of Kentucky, 1977).

41. This remedy is comparable to one found in Lynwood Montell, ed., *Folk Medicine of the Mammoth Cave Area* (Tompkinsville, KY: Mammoth Cave Folklore Project, 1976), entry #16, "Bites and Insects."

42. Ibid, entry #24, "Worms."

wanted him named Boanerges Roberts, and her wish was granted. Of course he was called *"Bo."*[43]

Pappy often said, "Don't add the Roberts to it, the first is bad enough." He received letters with all sorts of variations. Some of them spelled it "Beau," and from this others got the "u" mixed with an "n," and it became "Bean." We children got a kick out of it, and we laughingly called him "Beany" for a while.

Anyway, because of his music, and his gentle, lovable disposition, and his happy ways, *"Bo"* Marquess became a beloved appellation. I thought it was a beautiful name, and my mother had an unusual name for a girl too. Mother was named for her father and his first wife, Susan Croft, and everyone called her by the full name, "John Susan." It was cousin John Susan, and Aunt John Susan, etc., and I liked it. I thought it was a beloved name.[44]

I mentioned the fact that our father had very little formal education, *in a school room*, but he was a well educated man. We could ask him any question on geography, history, or arithmetic, or anything, and he could always give us a ready answer. He could add a long column of figures quicker than anyone I ever knew. He loved learning, and he said that one advantage of his education was that he chose only just what he wanted to learn, and didn't waste precious time on stuff that he would never use.

Pappy's mother used perfect English, and it was natural with him. All of her children called her mother, in a community that usually called their parents *Maw* and *Paw*. I could hardly stand the sound of it. It sounded coarse and ugly to me, but of course it was O.K. to the ones who were accustomed to it.

Having been raised mostly by this gentle mother, even the men of her family were gentle as women, and when they had not seen each other for a long time, after they were married and separated from each other, when they met they embraced and kissed each other.

They were all musicians. Uncle Curg (Lycurgus) played the violin, guitar, and accordion. He and my father played together for the balls at Cerulean Springs, the pleasure resort. My father was janitor for the ballroom, and taught dancing in the afternoons.

Uncle Curg taught "singing schools" for years. He is the only person I know of who could take one of our L.D.S. song books, which he had never seen before, with some difficult tunes, and sing the songs, perfect, without a bobble. *Most* people have to pick the notes out first on the piano or organ, but not Uncle Curg.

---

43. Boanerges Robert Marquess (1848–1903) was the son of Robert Elliot Marquess (1809–1889) and Martha Pettypool (1829–1919).

44. Effie's mother, Susan John Armstrong (1857–1899), was the daughter of John Armstrong (1803–1885) and his second wife, Martha "Patsy" Boyd (1813–1853).

Uncle Curg *made* beautiful violins, with wonderful tones. I remember that his own fine violin, that he played, had a date inside, it was 17__ something. I can't remember the last two numbers. I was just wondering where it is now, and where the several violins are that he made. I am going to write and see if I can locate any of them. I would like for some of my children or grandchildren to have one of them.

My father's violin went to pieces while we were in Southern Arizona, in the hot dry desert country. After his death, Bert Fuller, took it to Gus Bouy (Booey) to have him fix it.[45] He died, and his possessions were taken away by relatives and we lost it.

When the great boom was on at Cumberland Gap, when coal was discovered there, my father and Uncle Curg played with the orchestra that furnished music for the balls. They brought us lots of old songs that they learned from the old settlers around there. My older sisters remember it, but I was too young, but I *did* inherit the old songs. I don't know why we collected those old songs so religiously then, there was no demand for them at that time, but we got a big old school tablet, over an inch thick, and kept a copy of all the old songs we could find. We kept them numbered. "Now, we have 175," and, "Now, that makes 180, etc." *Now* we really *do* have a collection.

(1968) I am almost 83, Sadie is 90, and Lelia is 95, and we are still called on to sing Folk Songs, and play the guitar with them. Our voices are not very melodious any more, but we can still sing them (after a fashion), and folks seem to like it, anyway, they keep asking for more.

A few years ago Dr. Austin Fife, who teaches Folklore at the Occidental College (did then) came up here [to Atascadero] to see if he could make recordings of some of our old songs, which he did, and sent some of them to the Smithsonian Institute.[46] Later, I was invited to the

---

45. L. Bert Fuller (1885–1942) married Carrie Bartlie Carmack (b. 1893), the daughter of Thomas Green Carmack and Mattie Olivia Hale. Gus Bouy is probably Gustavious A. Buie (b. 1851), according to the 1880 census.

46. Dr. Austin Edwin Fife (1909–1986) held advanced degrees in French language and literature. After serving in the Air Force during World War II, he taught French literature at Occidental College in California from 1945 to 1960. He then began teaching French language and literature at Utah State University in 1960. Fife did not actually begin teaching folklore until 1971, only a few years before his retirement. He and his wife, Alta Stevens (1912–1996), were well-known for their work collecting and documenting folklore and material culture in the United States. The recordings Effie mentions here were conducted by Dr. Austin Fife on December 26 and 27, 1948, July 8, 1949, September 5, 1949, and March 26, 1951. The original discs made on a Wilcox-Gay recordio are now housed in the Fife Folklore Archives at Utah State University, Logan, Utah. Copies of the discs were actually sent to the Library of American Folksong at Library of Congress.

"Mrs. Effie Marques Carmack of Atascadero sings ballad of 'Barbara Allen' as Dr. Austin E. Fife of Oxidental College records it for Library of Congress files. Woman's costume is authentic of early Mormon period"; *Los Angeles Times* [San Gabriel Valley Edition], October 9, 1949, I9. Photo courtesy of Special Collections, Sutherland Library, Occidental College, Los Angeles, California.

college to sing for his Folklore class. I thought maybe I would be on a program along with others to sing a song or two, but, I was *it*, and I sang thirty two songs without a letup, for the morning program, with another session in the afternoon, and one in the evening, with all the faculty of the college in attendance.

There was a big dinner in the evening, and we sat at the table for hours and exchanged old songs. "Do you know this one, etc.," and, "Have you ever heard an old song that went like this . . . , etc."[47]

We had a happy time, but I was ready to lay my body down when it was all over, as I had not slept at all the night before, because, on the bus, a drunk got on and sat down beside me and talked all night.

47.  For Effie's full repertoire, see appendix one.

Later, Dr. Fife went to Paris to teach Folklore there, and I received a letter from him saying that he was going to broadcast several of my songs over "The Voice of America," and gave me the date and the hour, but it made it come on here about four in the morning, and I didn't bother to get up. The only ones who did bother to get up was some Eskimo boys who had been taking painting lessons from me, and they said that it was not very clear at their place.

And now I'm off the track. This part was going to be about my father. We were talking one day about someone who had lost his temper, and of how very ugly anger is. We are just not ourselves when we are under the spell of an uncontrolled temper. Our father asked us if we thought that he had a very bad temper. I could say, for one, that I never saw him angry in my life. He said that at one time he had a red headed temper, but he had seen in others what it could lead to, and had determined to control it. He felt that he had, to a certain extent. He said that of course he got angry sometimes, we wouldn't be normal human beings if we didn't, but he remembered the words of the Savior, "Be ye angry, but sin not."[48] In other words, control it, if you don't it will control you, and later you may be sorry.

I never saw anyone more interested in life than my father was, in all phases of it. He would bring me the first early spring wildflowers (anemones) before I knew that they were in bloom, and the first mulberries in a little basket of big leaves pinned together with thorns.

Sometimes he would find a partridge nest, and bring a hatfull of eggs home. They had a habit of several of them laying in the same nest, and if he would rake them out with a stick they would continue to lay (but don't put your hand in the nest). He said that it was no more harm to use *them* than it was to use hen's eggs, and they didn't seem to mind laying more. They were almost as large as a guinea egg, and we liked them boiled.

I would go with father, sometimes, to the big hill to work. A walk with him along the creek bank was a rich experience. He would show me the mayapple plant (mandrake), and tell me what it was good for, and the plant and blossoms of the blackroot, that the Indians used as a laxative. He would show me the leaves of the Golden Seal, and would pull some of it up and show me the deep yellow root, not quite as large as a pencil, and said that the old fashioned name for it was Yellow Percoon, and that it was a wonderful healing plant, good for many things, sore mouths, for one thing, and to just put on any kind of a sore it was a magic healer.

I just worshipped the bluebells, which had three different colors in their blossoms at the same time. Pink, lavender, and blue. The harmony

---

48.  Ephesians 4:26: "Be ye angry, and sin not."

"My beloved father with blue eyes and auburn hair."
Boanerges "Bo" Robert Marquess, age 49, son of
Martha Pettypool and Robert Elliot Marquess.
Courtesy of Hazel Bushman.

of color was just thrilling. I think he said that the real name for them was cowslip. They had big tender succulent stems.

There was one white walnut tree on our creek. Father said that the Indians used the bark of it for medicine, and he said that our first doctors used these herbs, barks, and leaves and flowers as their medicine, and they were just as effective as the chemicals the doctors use today, and are much less harmful, with no bad after effects.

Sometimes father would point out pictures in the cloud formations. A long level cloud, with one upright, made a perfect ship at sea, and, if you were going to paint those thunderheads, over there, you would need to put the halo of white light on the side next to the sun, with a soft gray on the shadow side.

I said, "Did you ever paint, pappy?" (I liked to call him pappy, it seemed like a sort of a pet name.) "No, but your Uncle Curg has, and we've talked about it lots of times. I've never had the time. Your mother could paint, if she ever had the time. She should have been spoiled and lazy, as she had slaves to do all the work when she was first growing up, and she had all the money she needed, but it didn't spoil her did it? She isn't afraid of any kind of work, and does it well, too. And she doesn't grumble if she has to do without anything she needs. She deserves the best."

A girl, who was at our place once, was looking at some pictures, and among them was one of my father (he had a moustache), and she said, "Who is that old codger with a brush heap on his upper lip?" I said, "That is my beloved father." It didn't squelch her much, and after she was gone I thought, "Maybe my love for my parents sort of glorifies them, and kept me from seeing their ugliness, and their defects," but he had some redeeming features. He had kind blue eyes, and the most beautiful auburn hair. It was *not* red. It was a rich brown, and waved as if he had just had a marcel (waves made with a curling iron).

Not one of us children had hair like his. Etta's was the same color, but was straight. The boys had wavy hair when they were young, but were not the same color.

One of my grandsons, Noel's oldest, Wayne, has hair like my father's, and he is the only one in all my father's descendants.[49]

I suppose our love for people keeps us from seeing their failings, but I know our family was a little unusual. We didn't think of it then, but since we are older and can compare, we all know that our parents were unusual, and I think we were an unusually happy family.

Now for something about my brothers and sisters. Etta was my oldest sister, mother's first child. She had infantile paralysis when she was about seven months old. She had not been very sick, but started using her left hand, and would not use her right hand at all. Mother didn't want her to be left handed if she would help it, and put a little mitten on her left hand, but she still would not use the right one.

Mother then found that it was helpless, and knew that Etta was paralyzed on the right side. That little arm and hand didn't grow and develop normally, and her right leg was shorter than the left, and her right foot

---

49.   Effie is referring to Noel Wayne Carmack (b. 1938), the oldest son of Noel Evans
      Carmack (1911–1980), Effie's second son.

was small. What a shock that would be to a young mother with her first little one.

But Etta, when she was grown, was energetic, and did as much work as any of the other girls. She mended clothes, and pieced quilts, swept floors. She died in the winter of 1899, the same time our family all had flu. Mother died in February, Etta in March.

Lelia, mother's second child, was born December 1872, and was an active little one, and walked when she was seven months old. She was a beautiful child, and grew up to be a beautiful girl (see pictures). [*The autobiography does not include these pictures; a photograph of Lelia is included in this edition on page 87, however.*] I remember one time she was going to a moonlight, where they dance outdoors, and have Japanese lanterns with candles in them for lights. It was a cheesecloth ball, and Lelia's dress was made with a tight bodice and a full skirt. She had roses in her hair and at her waist. I thought that she was the prettiest soul I ever saw (and others thought so too).

Lelia was very popular, and had lots of suitors. Walter Owen, the dandy of the neighborhood. He wore stovepipe hats, and real pointed shoes, and fancy velvet vests. He was also a wonderful dancer. He and Lelia always danced together.

Walter Owen was always going into some kind of business. One time he went out into the fields and got a lot of wild dewberry slips and sold them for "everbearing strawberries." He said that one thing that eased his conscience was the fact that if they cultivated them they would be as good or better than the strawberries.[50]

Walter liked to call for the quadrille at the dances, and was very original. One girl, Melissa Moore, had a wealth of the most beautiful flaxen hair I have ever seen, and never, since then, have I ever seen a girl with hair like hers. It was almost white, it was so blonde, and it was real shiny, and it was long and thick. Walter, when he was going to swing her, would call out, "I'll now swing the girl with the beansoup hair." No one was ever offended at anything he said, that was just Walter Owen. There was another girl named Sable McGinnis, and he called her "Sable my Goddess."

Lelia wouldn't have thought of going with him *steady* (as the kids say now) but she did enjoy dancing with him, and it was fun to just watch him dance. He was thin, and got around the floor light as a feather. He was a regular clown, although he was also calm and sedate. His older brother, Mr. Nat, was the Professor. He taught the only High School in the community, and Sadie was one of his pupils.

---

50.  Effie has already told this story, on page 53.

Another of Walter's brothers, younger than him, had a super mind. He was an inventor, and invented lots of things, though he never tried to get patents on them. I don't know what his real name was, but he went by the name of Bunky, a nickname. He and his brother, Ernie, were real comedians.

Now, back to my family. I am not sure just which of the old Armstrong homes Etta, Lelia, and Sadie were born in. Elmo was born in Wallonia, Trigg County, Kentucky. John and I were both born at the Uncle Lawrence Armstrong place (see picture) [*The autobiography does not include this picture*], and my brother, Autie, our youngest brother and mother's last child, was born where my mother was born.

Autie was a choice soul, and one of the last things my mother said, when she was dying, was to take good care of Autie, and not let him go to cousin P. Armstrong's and ride those old wild mules. She was afraid that he would get hurt.

Our father was sick for quite a while after our mother's death. The older boys, John and Elmo, worked away from home, and Autie did a man's work, and didn't seem to mind it. He was as dependable as a man. After my father died Autie went to Sadie's and helped Evert work. Evert said that he had never seen a more dependable boy in his life, and he was jolly and lovable too.

Elmo, my oldest brother, had a beautiful tenor voice, and could play the guitar and sing with it. He could yodel too, and of an evening, after work, when he would go to the creek to water the horses, I remember yet how his voice would echo against the big hill and sound down the creek. He was a good brother, and he sort of spoiled me.

John was the athlete, and ballplayer, and later the scientific dancer. He was very popular, and was quite a lady's man, but he was also a worker. He could make tobacco hills faster, and set out tobacco faster, and do most anything faster than any of the others. He also won the prizes for the best waltz at the big dances.

Elmo had a drawback that spoiled lots of good times for him, and caused him lots of suffering. He had eczema on his face, and they could not find anything to cure it. It would get well for a while, and then get bad again. We were all so sorry for him, but in later years it left him. Elmo married Ivy West (about my age) and we were real sisters, and loved each other.

John married one of my beloved chums too, Ozie Holt (I have mentioned her in other places).[51] John was quite an athlete, but Elmo could

---

51. Ozella Holt (1887–1943) was the daughter of Thomas Warren Holt and Mildred Virginia Martin. Ozella married John Robert Marquess, Effie's brother.

Effie Carmack's brother John Marquess is shown here turning soil behind a gopher plow; Larkin, Kentucky, ca. 1915. Courtesy of Hazel Bushman.

outrun him. Sadie was a runner too. I hated to acknowledge that she could beat me running, my only alibi was that her legs were a little longer.

Autie married Violet Allington, a girl of Salt Lake Valley, Utah.[52] She had a sweet voice, and she and Autie sang together lots. They had a family of sweet children. One choice one, Lois, who married a Wooldridge, has just died (1968).[53] They lived near Oakland. I didn't get to be with his children much, only at short intervals. They lived in the west most of the time, and we lived in the east.

I think we must have loved one another more than the average family. I don't know why, but I can remember when Elmo hired out to David Brasher and stayed all week, only coming home of Saturday nights. I thought the week would *never* pass, and could hardly wait till time for him to come home. I would usually be up by the big gate waiting for him, and he'd carry me to the house on his shoulder.

---

52.   Violet Loise Allington (1894–1947).
53.   Lois Bula Marquess (1917–1968).

Once, Sadie went to cousin Billie Faughn's and stayed a month, because one of their girls had died and we were sorry for them, and thought maybe Sadie might cheer them up a little.

That was the *longest* month that I can ever remember. It seemed she would *never* come home. When she did come, she had gained weight, and I thought that she was just the most wonderful person that ever lived. I followed her around and held her hand and it was a joy just to get to sit by her and look at her.

Lately, I heard a girl talking of her sister coming home from school where she had been for three months. They had not seen her once during that time. She said that the day her sister came home they had had a fight. They were a good Christian family too. Just different from us.

My brother John, who was just older than I, and Autie, my younger brother, would have been the two that I would have quarreled with, or had fights with, but I cannot recall *one* quarrel. The nearest approach to a quarrel was one day when John was beating out a piece of lead to make me a sinker to go on a fishing line. I was in a hurry for the sinker, and kept grabbing in to get it, every time there was a pause, thinking that he was through. He grabbed my wrist and pushed it back, pinching it with his thumb nail, and telling me that I was going to get my fingers mashed with the hammer. It was very unusual for him to pinch me, and I started to cry, and went in to tell Mammy, and for fear the place would not stay clear enough for her to see it when I got in the house I had held my thumb nail on the spot and made it look worse than it did in the beginning.

It just happened that Pappy was in there too, and when they saw the place they called John in and showed him where he had pinched me. He was sitting down, and they were standing up. I will never forget how he looked up at them when they were scolding him and said, "Well, Mammy, honestly, if I pinched her hard enough to make a place like that, I didn't intend to." I felt so sorry for him, and so mean, but was not brave enough to admit that I held my thumb nail on the place to make it look worse.

It is a sad thing that those who love the most, have to suffer greater also. (Now these things are just memories.)

*Now,* back to that awful winter of sickness and death. The weather gradually loosened its icy grip, and one or two of the sick ones were slowly improving. Sadie's mind was blank in spots. She couldn't think what a pillow was called, and she called a backstick, that goes on the fire, a blackboard.[54] Then she studied a long time and said, "That isn't right, is it?" but she couldn't think of the right word.

---

54.  A backstick or a backlog is a large log of wood forming the back of a fire on the hearth.

Etta lay, patient and pitiful, taking no food but buttermilk. One day, during a violent spell of coughing, a stream of bright red blood gushed from her mouth and ran the full length of the floor.

By the first week in March Pappy was able to go to town for some things that were sadly needed. Before he started he came in and asked Etta what she wanted him to bring her. "Oh, a new dress, I suppose," she smiled, but before he returned in the evening she had passed away. That was the fourth of March.[55]

One day, before Etta died, Dr. Lovan had come, and John asked him if he could have something to eat, he said he was hungry. "Not yet," he told him, "In a little while, maybe." John said that he would like to have some tomatoes, but the doctor told him if he should eat even a spoonful of those canned tomatoes he'd probably be sleeping in an earthen bed before long.

The next day I was cooking dinner, and had made a platter of blackberry shortcake, by cutting cold biscuits open and making a layer of biscuits and a layer of blackberries. I was taking it to the table, and passed where John could see me from the other room where he was lying. He motioned to me and said, "Come here a minute." I went, with the platter in my hands. When I got near enough for him to reach it, he took the platter and said, "Now don't tell a soul, but I'm going to eat what I want of this, even if it kills me. I might as well die with a full belly, as to starve to death." I was scared stiff, and begged him not to eat it. I tried to get it away from him, but he hung onto it, and ate *every bit* of it. Plenty for two or three well people, and he had not eaten a bite of solid food for days and days.

I watched for him to grow suddenly worse, but nothing happened, and the following day, when Dr. Lovan came, he said, "Well, well, this fellow will soon be up from here. He's 100% better today. Now you see son, if I had let you eat those tomatoes when you wanted to you would probably have been a very sick boy today." John put his hand over his mouth to smother a grin, as he winked at me, and I scooted into the kitchen. It was *really* a miracle that all that berry pie on an empty, weak stomach, *didn't* kill him. That was a lesson that I never forgot, and several times since

---

55.  Following her death, the *Star* reported that Etta was an "efficient worker in the Larkin Sunday School and other duties connected with the Larkin branch of the Church. The deceased was taken with typhoid fever soon after her mother's death and succumed to the dreaded disease on March 4th, 1899. Owing to the inclement weather it was deemed advisable to defer public services. The Star deeply sympathises with the family in this, their second bereavement." See "Among the Elders," *Latter Day Saints Southern Star* 1 (March 25, 1899): 136.

then I feel sure that I have seen people die of starvation, instead of disease, especially in cases of typhoid fever.

It took quite a while for strength to return. Sadie had a lame hip, and had to use a crutch for a season, while she groped for words to express the simplest thoughts. Gradually, strength of both mind and body returned, and she was soon well and strong again.

John was impatient to be out, and hobbled out into the yard while he was still so weak he wobbled. Getting *down* the doorstep was not easy, but when he tried to climb *up* them, back into the house, he couldn't make it. Finally, mustering every ounce of strength he possessed, he got on his hands and knees and crawled up them, then he lay down on the floor exhausted.

Home was not the same anymore, and as soon as John was able he went to the coal mines and found work. That was the first time he had ever been away from home, and our father was worried and anxious about him. I have a letter yet, that he wrote to him, warning him of the evils he would come in contact with, working among the rough element that is always found about the mines.

That spring was not a happy one, like all the others that I had known. The daffodils and narcissus didn't wake the same thrill of joy they had always done before.[56] When the plum thicket burst into bloom, and the dogwoods and red buds flaunted their challenge from the hillside, they made my eyes fill with tears. *Last* spring, when the first ones had suddenly appeared, Etta and I had raced and skipped to get an armful to decorate the newly whitewashed front room with. I was constantly under the impression that I could hear Mammy's quick step in the kitchen.

I would go out and sit in the fragrant plum thicket and try to forget for a few minutes all the things that had happened since they had bloomed before, and I would think that I heard my mother call me, as she often did when she wanted me to bring some wood, or water, or to do some other task about the place.

I didn't stay in the house any more than was necessary. I milked the cows, brought water, helped Papa with the chores, and in the field when he needed me.

Poor Sadie wrestled with the cooking, and the milk vessels. Nothing seemed to go right. It was a far greater task than any of us had ever guessed. Mammy had seemed to do the work so easily. The hotcakes (flitters) were always just right, light and bubbly brown. The biscuits were always good.

---

56. Narcissus is a popular plant having grasslike leaves and white or yellow flowers with a cup-shaped crown.

The cornbread was light and fluffy. The beans were always done just right, and the one egg *puddin'*, with the nutmeg dip was never a failure.

The cornbread just would *not* turn out right for us, it looked crackled and moon baked, and we often forgot to put salt in it. We invariably let the beans boil dry and scorch. The *flitters* would not rise light and bubbly like hers had always done. The churning would *foam*, and the butter would not come. Then we would put a little hot water in it and the butter would be white and spongy. Try as we would, things would not turn out right, and run smoothly like they had done for Mammy.

One miserable, rainy evening, we felt especially blue, and had finally given away to our feelings and cried copiously, till I had a splitting headache. I was laying across the bed wishing that I could go to sleep and forget the headache, when there was a "Hello!" at the gate. There was Aubrey and Ora Gilliland hitching their horses. They had known that we would be blue and lonely, and had come to spend the night. There was certainly plenty of bedrooms, as *most* of our family was gone. How glad we were to see them. It was not long till my headache was completely well. It was not an imaginary headache, either.

Aubrey came often, and he was my first sweetheart. He came every Sunday evening for a year. He had a nice horse and buggy, and in the year that he went with me, he never kissed me or told me that he loved me.

Mrs. Moore and Aunt Fannie visited us once more. One day, after Sadie had regained her strength, we saw Aunt Fannie and Mrs. Moore coming. That was something unusual, both of them coming at the same time. They usually came separately, and each of them often said unkind things about the other, and *neither* of them had frequented our place since we had been baptized, so we wondered what important mission had united them.

Aunt Fannie greeted us tearfully, and called us poor orphans. They asked about our health, and how we were getting along with the work. Then they looked at each other, as if that was the time to launch their attack. Aunt Fannie was spokesman. She said, "Sadie, you and Effie are nice smart girls, and could go in the best of society if you wanted to. Now that your mother is gone we feel it is our duty to try to advise you the best we can. If I were you I wouldn't have anything to do with them Mormon preachers. People will talk about you if they keep coming here, now that your Mammy is not here."

Unconsciously Sadie and I had both risen and were standing together, facing them, with our backs to the wall. Sadie found my hand which was behind me and held it tight.

"If you want to belong to a church there's lots of nice preachers who don't go a-traipsing around the country afoot." "Now there's the Baptist church, and Brother Whittenbraker is a good preacher."

We grew madder every minute. The very idea of those two old gossips, who cared no more for *any* kind of religion than a goose did, warning us against the Elders. Those humble, good boys, giving their time, and the best years of their lives for humanity. It took us a minute to realize what they were up to, but when we did find words they came in a rush, both of us trying to talk at the same time.

If we were never harmed till a Mormon Elder harmed us we would be safe the rest of our lives, and as far as tramping through the country, the Savior and His disciples did the same thing and were found fault with by the sinners and hypocrites just as the Mormon missionaries are now. The Savior said for His messengers to go two by two, and to take no purse on their journey, and to preach the Gospel free.[57] The reason they thought they were bad was because they knew nothing about them, and Solomon, the wise man said, "He that judgeth a matter without knowing of it makes himself look unwise."[58]

They ventured another rather feeble protest, telling us we were both pretty girls, and could be real popular if we wanted to. That they would help us fix up our clothes, etc., but we were wound up, and let forth such a volley of the Gospel at them that it wasn't long till they were glad to escape.

We told them not to hurry off, but they were already tying their bonnets and pinning their shawls.

After they were gone we looked at each other for a minute in righteous anger, and then as we realized how they had tucked their tails and made their hasty getaway, we saw the funny side of it and started to laugh.

What a joy it was to defend the Gospel, and to tell someone else of the wonderful truths we had learned. Nothing in the world, that I had come in contact with, gave me half the joy that defending my religion gave to me, or of explaining it to someone who would listen.

We found that day that there was still joy to be had in this life, and with our new found faith in the next life, even losing our loved ones for a while was not so terrible, for we knew now that we would see them again, and would know them, and rejoice in their society. We hugged each other, and laughed till the tears came. We could hardly wait for our daddy to come, so that we could tell him of our experience.

It seemed almost unbelievable that life would have changed so completely for a family, as ours had in a little over a year.

---

57. See, for example, Mark 6:7–8, Luke 10: 1–4.
58. Proverbs 18:13: "He that answereth a matter before he heareth it, it is folly and a shame unto him."

First, the Gospel had come and opened up many new vistas. In a short time it changed us from a rather careless existence, to one of intense religious fervor. Studying daily the Word of the Lord, in both the old and the new Testaments, *and* as it had been given to the ancient inhabitants of the American Continent,[59] *also* the revealed Word that had been given in these the Latter Days.

It was a constant joy, and a wonder to us to find how perfectly they agreed, and how each was a witness for the other, proving more surely the plan of life as it was given by the Savior. Then that wonderful first summer as members of the revealed Church of Jesus Christ, the thrill of daily learning new truths, and finding that it would really bear close inspection, for everything that we learned proved to us that it *was* true.

Then there were the new missionaries that we met, with their abundance of life. The new songs that they taught us, the charm of their western ways and speech.

We were even learning to eat different food. Our breakfast changed from hot biscuits and bacon, to oatmeal mush, and we liked it. It was so much easier and quicker, and we were sure that it was healthier too.

One day Dr. Harris, one of our father's friends, came to get father to go hunting with him, as there were lots of rabbits, doves, and quail on our place.[60] Father was not at the house then, but we knew that he would be soon, so he waited. He told us of how he had enjoyed our mother's good buttermilk biscuits and sausage or ham with *red* gravy. Then he said that he had heard we had joined the Mormons. Sadie was busy getting lunch ready, and when he asked what the Mormons believed it was up to me to tell him. I was bubbling over with information. I had not studied for two years for nothing, and it was pure joy to tell it to someone who actually wanted to hear it.

Finally my father came, and Sadie had the lunch (we called the midday meal dinner, and the evening meal supper, so she had the *dinner*) ready. For over an hour he had asked questions and I had answered them.

He asked my father if all the family was as well informed on our new religion as I was. He said that he knew several preachers who didn't know as much about the scriptures as I did, "And she can quote it too, and then explain it. I never heard anything to equal it, and for a kid her size it is astonishing."

I'll never forget the thrill of being able to explain the Gospel to an intelligent and appreciative listener. I don't know whether he ever accepted it or not, but he certainly had a good introduction to it.

---

59.  Effie means the Book of Mormon.
60.  Dr. Lucian J. Harris (1844–1913) was married to Augusta Ann Boyd (1843–1912).

We had made many new friends, drawn together by our new found faith: Gillilands and Carmacks, in our own county; Wallaces, in Metcalf county; Viola Sweeny and Rose in another county.[61]

Life had become full and very satisfying. We could understand perfectly what the Savior meant when He told the woman at the well that He could give her living water, that when she drank of it she would never thirst again.

Our home was a regular stopping place for all of the Elders who passed through, and I enjoyed washing their handkerchiefs and socks, and doing anything that I could for them. I made a collection of their cards, with the Articles of our Faith on the backs of them.[62] How I wish I had them now.

Then followed that terrible winter, and the loss of our Mother and Etta and the boys leaving home, so that only the few of us who were forced to stay remained of the family. The mortgage on the old farm was not paid off, and the big doctor bills and funeral expenses were added to it. There just seemed no way out but to sell the old place.

The news soon leaked out that it was for sale and soon we had buyers. The old place was sold to Charlie Fowler.[63] We packed up and bade farewell to the old farm with its wealth of precious memories. The flax reels and spinning wheels in the attic. The old red corded bedstead, candle molds, and many other old things that reached back to Civil War days, and even beyond it to the slave period.

Aunt Ann Martin, mother's half sister, borrowed one spinning wheel before we moved, so it escaped the fire that soon left the old house and all of its treasures in ashes.

We moved to a little house on the Birchfield Marquess' place and began a new life. Changes continued to come in quick succession. Elmo, my older brother, married a sweet girl only a little older than myself, Ivy West. The pleasant times we had together in the year that followed has left a memory like the fragrance of flowers in my mind.

Ivy and I rode horse back, went swimming, and also helped the boys work in the fields. When there was no work to be done we had a giant grape vine that we cut off, at the foot of a big oak tree, that grew on the high bank of a creek branch. It was matted firmly into the top branches of the tree, and by going up on the hillside and running to the brow of

---

61. Viola Sweeny later married Alvin Ipsen, the first Momon missionary to proselytize the Marquess family.

62. These were printed on personalized calling cards and distributed by Mormon missionaries in the same way they are today.

63. Charles Fowler (b. 1871), son of J. W. Fowler (b. 1844), according to the 1880 census.

the hill we could swing away out over the stream and back again on the other side of the tree.

One day one of us dared the other one to turn loose and drop down on the opposite bank of the stream from midair. Soon it was a regular thing. The fame of our grapevine swing grew, and we proudly displayed our acrobatic stunt of sailing through the air like flying squirrels and landing on the soft loamy bank on the opposite side of the stream. The first time Elmo saw it he set his foot down on any further operations. He predicted that there would be a broken leg, back or neck if it was not stopped.

As a compromise Elmo built us a good swing, down by the spring, in front of the house. The grapevine was in the woods at the back. He made the swing of long slim hickory poles about twenty feet long, fastened with a chain to a big strong limb, with a board seat in it. Two of us would stand in it at once and *pump*, and we could send it to the tree tops.

I guess I was quite a tomboy, as I think back of the things we did. Elmo had a gray pony that Ivy and I rode a great deal. We got so we could stand on his back while he did a lively gallop.

We didn't play all the time, by any means. We helped to clear a three acre plot of new ground, and anyone who ever did that will know what it means. Later we made tobacco hills in this cleared three acres. The roots were so thickly matted in the ground, and it was so rocky, that we often had to find another spot and borrow dirt enough for a tobacco hill.[64]

After my mother's death, and with Etta gone too, I felt like I would really have to live my religion, if I stayed a good girl, the kind that I wanted to be. I studied my religion, to try to find what the real keynote of it was, so that I could use it in my life, to help me keep my faith strong and alive. The more I studied it, the more I became convinced that Charity, in its true sense, is the essence of righteousness. *Now*, after forty five years of study, I am still of the same opinion (1945).

Another thing that I observed was daily prayers, all through that summer. There was a dry stream bed, washed hard and clean by winter rains, with bushes growing thick on either side, and meeting overhead. It was beyond the new ground where we worked, and far enough away that there was never a disturbance. To this shaded spot I went and poured out my soul to the Father in Heaven each day. I asked Him to help me make

---

64. This describes well the state of virgin land in northern Christian County. According to the 1909 farmers' bulletin, "In the dark-tobacco district, virgin soil on beech, maple, hickory, white oak, red oak, and black jack clearings produces the finest quality of tobacco and is preferred to old land even though it be in a fine state of cultivation," see Scherffius, et al., "The Cultivation of Tobacco in Kentucky and Tennessee," 13. Frequently, however, the abundance of roots and rocks in the area required a heavy layer of soil and fertilizer or a "hill" of tilth before the tobacco could be planted.

the Gospel plan plain to Ivy, and that she would accept it, and this prayer was answered.

While we lived there two of the missionaries, Elders Carlyle [Carlisle] and Myler, came to our place directly from a hostile community in Muhlenburg [Butler] county, where a mob had beaten them cruelly. They still had on the same clothing that they had on when they were whipped. I cried when I saw them, for the backs of their garments and shirts were covered with blood. Elder Myler had been afflicted with boils from chigger bites, and his back was still tender from them. He declared, in all soberness, that the licks *did not hurt* him, even though they were inflicted with six foot hickories that a big strapping fellow wielded with both hands. He said that he felt a sort of numbness, and not any pain.[65]

---

65. Francis Philip Carlisle (1862–1939) served in the Southern States Mission in 1898–1900. John Elias Myler (1873–1940) served in 1899–1901. The bloody garments Effie refers to are the characteristic undergarment worn by Latter-day Saints who have participated in temple ordinances. According to an account given by Brigham F. Price,

They had just finished canvassing Butler county, Kentucky, and were hold-ing a meeting at Long Branch District, located five miles from Morgantown, the county seat of Butler county, where many friends and some converts were made. . . . Three of the converts requested baptism before the Elders were to leave. Preparation was begun to perform this ordinance on the 8th of November, the day before the Elders expected to leave the county.

The mobbers learned of this action and determined to hinder it before its consummation. The bretheren were stopping with a family of Saints, Johnson by name. All had retired for the night and were peacefully sleeping. About 12 o'clock the household was awakened by voices demanding the "Mormons." Brother Johnson opened the door to learn of the cause of the clamor, when two revolvers and a shotgun were thrust under his nose and he was commanded to throw up his hands.

At that point, Johnson was ushered out into the presence of twenty masked men who demanded to see the "Mormons." Attempting to give the missionaries a chance to escape, Johnson told the men that the elders were staying at his son's home. Unfortunately, the young missionaries were halted while fleeing through the back door. The elders

mildly marched out of the house to the tune of "Hickory switches" into the road, where they were informed what the "sentence of the court" was, as follows (from the leader, a large, husky fellow): "Nos. ten and fifteen, give each of them five lashes," which they did with a vengeance. Their overzealous-ness or ignorance, judge for yourselves, caused them to miscount, for when they "tallied" it was learned that each Elder had received fourteen lashes. "Now, if you'ens don't leave here 'fore sunup in the morn' we'll string you up to a limb," said the court. With exulting cries the "conquering heroes" departed. Next morning the Elders left the county, being followed to the river by the Saints and the applicants, where the bretheren baptized the believers as previously arranged. Brother Johnson took them accross the river in a boat, when they went merrily on rejoicing in the Lord.

See B.F. Price, "Hickory Switches," *Latter Day Saints Southern Star* 1 (November 25, 1899): 413.

Elder Myler was a good singer, and knew lots of songs that were being sung at that time. After Elder Carlyle left Elder Hamilton came to travel with Elder Myler, and I think it was he who baptized Ivy.[66]

Cousin Filmore Smith and his wife, cousin Serena, who used to come to our place before we heard the Elders, and talk religion, and read the scriptures with my parents, were among those who welcomed them to their homes. Cousin Fil read everything that he could get hold of on Mormonism, always hunting for something *deeper*. He especially liked Martin P. Brown from Ogden, Utah, and he often remarked that Brown was one of the deepest men we had.[67] He liked Elder Myler too, and enjoyed telling him funny old yarns to make him laugh. When the Elders slept there the door between the two bedrooms was left open, and there was conversation going until they all fell asleep.

One night Cousin Fil told Myler about some ignorant old female called Suse, who knew nothing whatever of the Bible. One Sunday evening she happened to go to church when they were having a big revival. The preacher came down the aisle preaching and talking as he went. Spying Suse, and wishing to make her feel at home, he put his hand on her shoulder and said, "Oh sister, did you know that Christ died to save sinners?" Poor old Suse looked up at him with a silly grin and said, "No sur, I hadn't heered a word uv it, didn't eben know he was sick." Elder Myler laughed appreciatively at the joke, and later, when everyone thought everyone else was asleep he said, "Poor old Suse."

Cousin Fil never forgot Elder Myler, and how he had laughed about that poor old ignorant gal who hadn't eben heered He was sick. I think Elder Hall was Myler's companion at that time.[68]

The sad part of it all was that cousin Filmore kept trying to find something deeper before he accepted it, and finally never did get baptized. His wife was baptized about June of 1898. She also had the flu, or whatever it was that my mother and Etta died with, and was unconscious all through the month of February, and until after Etta died in March.

Elder Brigham F. Price, of Mill Creek, Utah, had been to our place before we left the old home.[69] Now he and his companions came to visit

---

66. Either John F. Hamilton or John W. Hamilton. Both served in the Southern States Mission in 1899–1901.

67. Martin P. Brown (1873–1943) served in the Southern States Mission in 1897–1899.

68. Probably William Brooks Hall (1867–1936) who served in the Southern States Mission in 1897–1899.

69. Brigham Francis Price (1866–1914) served in the Southern States Mission in 1898–1900. He was made president of the Kentucky Conference on November 16, 1899.

us again. He was President of the Kentucky conference, and one of the best men I ever knew. Sometimes when he was speaking earnestly his face actually seemed to have a light around it.

My father was already making plans to move west, and President Price suggested that, as my father was coming, that I should go home with him when he went so that I could start school at the beginning of the term. My father seemed to think favorably of the plan, and I lived in the thought of getting to go. But at the last minute, when President Price came and said that he was soon to be released and would be going home before long, my father was afraid something would happen to me so far away, and couldn't make up his mind to let me go. I was so terribly disappointed, though I did hate the thought of leaving them.

## CHAPTER FIVE

# Dear Home, Sweet Home

*Dear Home, sweet home with my brothers and sisters,*
*Guided by parents with wisdom and skill,*
*Planting deep truths that would long be remembered*
*After their voices were silent and still.*
*Let me redeem it from things long forgotten.*
*Let me be the savior to pluck from oblivion*
*All of my kindred from first to the last.*
—*"Some Reasons Why"*
in *Backward Glances*, 50

Frank Long and his wife Josie, were another couple who were interested in the new religion.[1] Frank had a sister, an old maid school teacher, who came to visit them quite often. She was also interested in the message of the missionaries. She was a quiet, gentle sort of person, good looking, with an abundance of long black hair. She was tall and slim, and had pretty soft white hands.

Cousin Millard Gilliland, and his wife Laura, thought it would be a fine thing for my father if he and this old maid school teacher would get married, so they bent their efforts in that direction. Her brothers and sister had started calling her Sis, and most everyone else did the same, but as she was a school teacher they followed the custom of the country and called her Miss Sis.

Second marriages are usually quick affairs, and this one was no exception. I don't believe children, as a general thing, like for their father or mother to marry a second time. I know that I didn't feel very

---

1.  Probably Frank Long (b. 1851); his wife is unidentified.

happy over their marrying. I soon grew better acquainted with her, and learned to like her, but somehow she never liked me, though she was very kind to Autie, my little brother, for which I was thankful.

I had heard so much about stepmothers and stepchildren who did not get along with one another that I was determined that this would be *one* case where there would at least not be any quarrels, as it would take two to make a quarrel. I for one could keep from doing that, and I think I kept my resolve pretty well.

Miss Serena (Sis) was handicapped by not having learned how to cook, or how to do housework, or any of the chores about the place.[2] She was a teacher, not a housekeeper, and besides she was not very strong, so we grew to not expect her to do any part of the work.

After Sadie married I was cook, housekeeper, dishwasher, milkmaid, washerwoman, gardener, and all, combined. Of course, I was not used to doing all this alone, and didn't do too good a job of it. Papa sympathized with me silently. Miss Serena sensed it (or as she would say, she detected it), and I think was jealous of me. She would never praise me for anything I did, no matter how well I did it, and was very quick to blame me when things were not done just right. I wouldn't have minded hearing it once, but she had a habit of repeating the same things day after day. Nevertheless, I think I can truly say that I loved her. The reason I did was because I had to do so many things for her. Everytime she went anyplace, and had to dress up, I fastened her collar pin and her belt for her. I don't believe she ever trimmed her own fingernails, or toenails, in the years we lived together. She said it gave her the *shivers*, so I did it for her. I thought that if I kept doing things for her she would *have* to learn to like me, but it really resulted in making *me* like *her*.

Miss Serena was a like a child to me, who it was my duty to take care of. She had raised her niece, Lena Long, her brother's child, whose mother died when she was a baby.[3]

Lena would come to our place and stay for long periods, and we had many happy times together. She was intelligent, and good, and was especially gifted in composition and writing. Her letters were charming. Lena didn't have half the patience with her "Aunt Sis" that I had. Lena had never learned to work, and in *that* lay the difference. She had not learned to love her Aunt through doing things for her as I had done. *She* depended on her Aunt Sis, and they were two broken sticks together. It

---

2.  Serena Allifair Long (1859–1939) was the daughter of Redding (b. 1824) and Elizabeth Long (b. 1828).

3.  Lena might be Lenora Long (b. 1878), and Serena's brother could be W. R. Long (b. 1840) and his wife Margaret.

was not a good combination at all. Lena was not lazy in the least, she had just never been taught to do anything.

I learned a valuable lesson of life, in the years that Miss Serena and I lived together. It is this: If there is someone that you dislike very much, and would like it to be different, just begin doing nice things for them, and it will not be very long until your dislike will vanish, and you will soon learn to like them. If someone dislikes you, and there is *any* way that you can get them to do something nice for you, then you praise them for it, and never forget to be thankful to them for their services, you will win their friendship. I have been very thankful for this truth I learned through experience, which is the very best way of learning anything.

One of the *true isms* of the Church of Jesus Christ is that we cannot be saved in ignorance. We are saved no faster than we gain knowledge.[4] That knowledge is not only the acquiring of information through study, but the actual application, and the putting into practice the principles of Truth and Light. After all, that is the only way that we can *really* learn anything.[5]

Not long after my father married again there was a series of Old Fiddlers Contests, and they became very popular. Lots of business men, doctors, lawyers, and just plain old farmers who had played the fiddle in their younger years got out their old violins and brushed the dust off of them and started practicing for the next contest. My father had not had the old violin out of its case since before mother died, but he also became interested, after he received an urgent invitation to come and join in the fun of contesting with the many, many others who were going to enter this musical festival.[6]

---

4. Doctrine and Covenants 131:6: "It is impossible for a man to be saved in ignorance." See Joseph Smith, Jr., *Teachings of the Prophet Joseph Smith*, compiled by Joseph Fielding Smith (Salt Lake City: Deseret Book, 1979), 217.

5. This probably is a paraphrase of Doctrine and Covenants 93:28: "He that keepeth his commandments receiveth truth and light, until he is glorified in truth and knoweth all things."

6. These fiddler's contests or conventions were popular and are still held throughout the South. A description of a fiddler's convention in western North Carolina provides a glimpse into the atmosphere of these contests: "The convention is essentially an affair of the people, and is usually held in a stuffy little schoolhouse, lighted by one or two evil-smelling lamps, and provided with a rude, temporary stage. On this the fifteen fiddlers and the 'follerers of banjo pickin' sit, their coats and hats hung conveniently on pegs above their heads, their faces inscrutable. To all appearances they do not care to whom the prize is awarded, for the winner will undoubtedly treat. Also, they are not bothered by the notetaking of zealous judges, as these gentlemen are not appointed until after each contestant has finished his alloted 'three pieces'." See Louis Rand Bascom, "Ballads and Songs of Western North Carolina," *Journal of American Folklore* 22 (January–March 1909): 238. On the sense of fellowship the participants experience in these events, see Burt Feintuch, "Examining Musical Motivation: Why does Sammie Play the Fiddle?," *Western Folklore* 42 (July 1983): 208–14.

A widow, near Gracy, and one of her sons had been bitten by a mad dog. The dog's head had been sent to the experts, and they found that he had rabies, so to help raise the necessary funds to have them treated, it was decided to have a Fiddlers Contest. My father and I were invited, and urged to attend. They sent a list of some of the ones who would be playing, and my father, having played all his life knew most of them. He showed me the letter and said, "Shall we go and try our luck?" He asked my stepmother if she wouldn't like to go, but she said that she had never liked to hear a squeaky old fiddle. Well, my father and I both really enjoyed the squeaks that a violin made, especially in the hands of an expert, so we planned to go.

It was about fifteen or twenty miles to Gracey, and we would have to stay overnight. I hated to leave Autie at home, but he said that he would stay with Miss Serena (as we called her). I made me a pretty new dress for the occasion, and was all excited over the prospects of a happy time. The contest was held in a big new building that had never been used, and was not finished, just a shell. There was a big raised platform for the musicians, and I was astonished at the number of fiddlers, and also many that played guitars, banjos, accordions, and mandolins as accompanists to the violins. I had a beautiful guitar of curly maple, with a nice loud tone.

Before time for the program to start, and while they were tuning up and getting ready, we got acquainted with many of the musicians. There were three young men with instruments, two with guitars, and one with a banjo. They were sons of a man who had a nursery, and were all good in their fields. The boy with the banjo played tunes, most of the guitar players played chords.

Later there were others kept arriving, other guitar players, mandolins, banjos, and one girl who played the violin. Her name was Sadie Satterfield. She asked me if I would play with her, and we retired to a corner to see that we were tuned together, and to practice a little together. She played *real* fast, and one of the nursery boys (I have forgotten their names, which is no wonder, after over fifty years). Anyway he said, "If you keep up with Sadie you're going to have to git up and hustle," and I did, and she kept getting faster, but she could really play, never missed a note.

We had several numbers with just the guitars. I played several tunes and they played chords with me. We had time to practice a little before the program started. Several of the men asked me to play with them, and there was a hectic tuning period. Many of them had not been playing for years, and their violins were not in tune. Some had to put on new strings. The nursery boys were kept busy helping some of the older men get their instruments ready for the fray.

The building kept filling, and new ones kept arriving. The man who had charge of it was happy to see so many. He had gone to a great deal of trouble advertising, sending invitations, getting seats made, and the platform ready. It was for a good cause, and the community really did respond. Finally it was starting time, and the music began. There were trios, quartets, and many with just the violin and guitar.

I was asked to play with so many different ones, that before the program was half over there were big blisters on the fingers of my left hand that I noted the strings with. One of the nursery boys and I went to a drugstore and got something to toughen them with. Alum and turpentine and something else. The turpentine was best, but I couldn't let that bother me.

There was no hope of having the entire group play one number together, so they decided to have a contest on the tune of Dixie. All of them could play it. The judges felt very important, and sat at their table and were busy taking down names, and judging by certain points, and taking notes. My father and I got first place on Dixie. There were prizes offered on several other tunes. Finally it was announced that there would be a contest on dancing. Certain jigs, clogs, and the Highland Fling.

An old fellow insisted that he and I dance the Highland Fling, but it was not one of my specials. If it had been a certain jig step, or a negro double shuffle, I would have tackled it, but not the Highland Fling, so he danced it alone. Next was a schottische, and a young fellow who played a banjo asked if I would dance it with him. I said that I would if my father would play for us, so he and one of the nursery boys played, and another couple joined us and we really did the schottische with all the flourish. My partner and I got first on it, as we did some fancy shuffle steps along with it. (We had slipped in a back room and had practiced a few minutes.) We really enjoyed it, and the crowd cheered and screamed and clapped.

After it was all over everyone agreed that it had been a wonderful evening, and the manager announced how much he had taken in from tickets. Plenty to pay for the treatment of the widow and her son (I wish that I could remember how much).

Several of us went to an eating place and had supper together, and we all decided to be in attendance at the next Fiddlers Contest. It became a regular thing, and some firm friendships were formed that are pleasant to remember to this day.

I must not forget to add that I received, as a prize, my choice of any hat in a certain big Millinery store or shop. I chose a beautiful one that just suited one of my dresses. It was one of the prettiest hats that I ever owned. Another prize I won was a big bottle of fine perfume. The kind they sell little ounce bottles from. It was so potent that it lingered on my underwear after two or three washings. I gave perfume to all the girls in the community.

My father and I stayed all night at a nice hotel, and many other of the musicians did too. We had a happy session in the big waiting room where some of the party played the piano, and we had a sing.

My father won several prizes, I can't remember just what. One was a fine razor, with all kinds of shaving stuff along with it, a set of collar and cuff buttons, and other things I can't remember. We had the old buggy pretty well filled with prizes. Besides the hat and perfume I got a silk parasol, and a water set; pitcher and eight glasses, that I used till after Cecil was born.

We attended many other Fiddlers contests after that, but this one is a fair sample of what the others were like. Some of the contest tunes were old standbies like: Money—Fishers Hornpipe—Sally Goodin—The Girl I Left Behind Me—Eighth of January—Devil's Dream—Cotton Eyed Joe—Dixie.

As I read this over it sounds like *I* and *We* did all the winning, but as a matter of fact I only remember the numbers we won. There were a lot that really played well, and many won first place on certain tunes, and there were also prizes for second place.

These contests were highlights in our lives during the period following our mother's and my oldest sister's death, and the breaking up of our family home life with all we children together. A rather gloomy period for my father, and the pleasant contacts with other musicians and reviving his love for his violin was good for him.

The little house we moved to, after we sold our old home, was surely a sorry place for so large a family, especially after Elmo married. There was one big log room, with a fireplace. There was an upstairs room, reached by a ladder, that was pushed into service as bedroom, In the back was the usual open hallway that led to a tiny log room that Sadie and I used for a parlor. I can't remember whether we papered or whitewashed it, anyway it was cozy, and even pretty.[7]

Sadie had the knack of making any place look homey and inviting, with bright pictures, and *always* vases of flowers, real ones in summer, and artificial ones in winter. There were always books and magazines where she stayed, and plenty of pencils and paper. There were bright dashes of color, such as chair cushions, pillows, etc. Sadie was an ardent lover of beauty, and *had* to have it around her in some form. There was always music, an old guitar or two, banjos, harmonicas, etc. Every new song was captured and sung ragged.

Outside the house a few feet was a big old smokehouse, or at least it was a log room with a roof over it. This was pushed into service as a kitchen. As a family we had *one* redeeming quality. No matter *what* we had to put up with we made the best of it, and never grumbled about it.

---

7.  Although it is difficult to determine conclusively from the text, this seems to describe the single-pen house type with an addition. See Montell and Morse, *Kentucky Folk Architecture*, 17, 22–23.

Sadie at about age twenty. Courtesy of
Itha Carmack

It was while we lived at this place that Evert Holt, the son of our
nearest neighbor, became interested in Sadie. Sadie had gone with lots of
fellows, and had been engaged several times. There was John Causler
[Cansler], Marion Walker, Luther Hays, Will Eades, Will Murphy, Frank
Wright, Ed Cornelius, George and Tom Vaughn, Herschel Woosley,
Theodore Morris; all of them had been rather serious, but she had about
decided she would never marry. Maybe she would be an old maid school
teacher.

    Sadie had an almost uncanny faculty for making children learn. She
had the habit of finding the short cut to everything, and teaching was no
exception. She really had a way of making children learn abnormally fast.
She made the lessons interesting and exciting, and presented them in
new and attractive ways. When Evert came along all previous plans were
quickly upset. Teaching lost its charm, and her disinterest in the opposite
sex suffered a sudden change.

Evert played the banjo with all his might, and with most of his muscles. He didn't sing with it often, but every note was emphasized with a different twitch of his mouth. He was steady and serious, honest as the hills, a hard worker, and a deep thinker. He was always by far the best mathematician in school, with a disposition that won everyone's admiration and respect. There was just one bad drawback to their courtship. Evert was a boy in his teens, and Sadie was past twenty. She had always been younger than her years, and Evert was grown and settled at the age of fifteen. Those two differences helped to even things up, and they still hold good to this day, almost fifty years later. (1945?) [*Effie seems to have estimated this date at a later writing.*]

Sadie took charge of things around the house. Ivy and I, at that time, were still children, and a little irresponsible. I didn't realize then that in so short a time I would have to carry the entire burden of the household, things I had never been used to doing before; such as planning meals, cooking, washing and ironing, as well as milking cows, feeding chickens, planting garden and keeping it hoed and free from weeds all through the summer, and also doing all the canning.

Ivy was certainly far from lazy, she would tackle any task, and stick to it till it was finished. You just naturally have to respect anyone who is so willing to help carry their end of the load, and she usually did more than her part. Her interest in the Gospel was very satisfying to me. When we rested awhile from our work, that was usually the topic of our conversation; she asking questions, and I trying to answer. I didn't know too much about it, and often we would hit for the house to find some book in which we could find our answers. How happy I was when she said that she was ready to be baptized.

Evert Holt and Ellis Walker came to the meetings when the Elders were there, but I'm afraid their interest in religion was not as deep as it could have been. They were not against it, and that was encouraging to Sadie.[8] Ellis and I were not at all serious, he just came along with Evert. I was still a child, and didn't feel very deeply interested in Ellis anyway.

I had already had one love affair though. Aubrey Gilliland had been my steady for a year. We had lots of fun riding horseback, and going for buggy rides. It would sound queer to the girls of that age now, if I told them that he went with me for a whole year; every Wednesday night, every

---

8. Sadie, by all accounts, was firm in her commitment to the LDS Church. In 1908, she wrote the following to the editors of the *Liahona:* "I am glad to bear my testimony to the truth of the gospel. If our Father did not let us know for a surety this is the truth we could not stand the persecutions that are placed upon us. Help us with your faith and prayers." See "Kentucky," in *Liahona, The Elders' Journal* 6 (July 4, 1908): 72.

Sunday afternoon, often of Saturday nights, and other times if there was a party or a meeting or something to go to, he would come for me with his horse and buggy. All during that year he never kissed me, and never once put his arm around me. In those days things like that were reserved for the time after a couple was engaged. But we got an enormous thrill out of holding hands, and I felt that we were rather soft and silly to do that.

I remember one time when Fannie Wallace, of Metcalf County, wrote that she was coming to visit us. Someone was going to meet her at the depot, which was ten miles from our place. A group of us decided to go along on horseback. The train would be there about nine o'clock. We had lots of fun clattering along the pike, racing and hitting each other's horses with our switches. It would have been a tiresome trip to someone not used to riding horseback, but we were tough from constant exercise and from riding horses every day.

I remember another evening when a group of us went to town in a two horse wagon. Elmo was driving. As we were coming home something went wrong with the harness, and Elmo said, "Woop! hold everything. Old Beck's alosin' 'er breeches." *Every*thing is funny when you're young and happy, and in pleasant company. Aubrey was about the *pleasantest* company I could think of about then.

I guess we must have sold our cows, horses, and everything when we sold the old place, for Papa bought a new cow after we moved to the Birchfield place. A man named John Stewart said that he had a good cow that he would sell for twenty dollars. Papa said, of course she wouldn't be any good at that price, but he went to see about buying her. The man said that he owed a debt that had to be paid immediately, as the only reason he was selling her, and he put the price low so that he could make a quick sale. The cow was a gentle little Jersey that looked like a good milker, so papa bought her. When he was ready to take her the mother and several small children came out to say goodbye to her. The mother shed a few silent tears and said she didn't know how they would manage without any milk for the children.

Papa brought the cow home, and after a few days we found that she gave an abundance of good rich milk. He kept thinking of that bunch of little children without any milk, and the very small sum he had paid for the cow. Finally, to ease his conscience, he got on his horse and rode back over there to tell him that he could have his cow back if he wanted her. When the man refused, papa paid him enough extra to ease his mind on the subject.

Those people were *amazed*. They had never heard of a man who would ride several miles to pay more for a cow than the owner had asked for it. I am glad to remember my father as being that kind of man. I also never heard him mention this deal to anyone.

While we were living at this place Birchfield gave a *moonlight.* They had a big level yard, with a row of giant Maples all around the back half of it, and down the west side of the front lawn. The front was sloping, so the level back section was chosen for the dance. There were lots of Japanese lanterns, good music, and lemonade. There was a carnival going on at Hoptown [Hopkinsville] at that time, and a bunch of boys came from the carnival to the moonlight.[9] When they came they kept calling, "Hurry, Hurry, Hurry, or you won't see George."

There was a young fellow there from Mt. Carmel. I danced with him a great deal, and when it was over he walked home with me. We stopped at the swing for a while. The moonlight was filtering down through the leaves, the water was babbling, and the smell of flowers filled the air. It was very romantic, and I dreamed of him after I went to sleep that night.

The following Sunday there was a crowd at the croquet yard at Mr. Morris's, and I went. As soon as I arrived Maude and Leona came giggling, and said, "Say, that fellow you caught at the moonlight surely means business, he's here, and has been asking about you." A few minutes later I saw him coming, and in broad daylight the glamour faded. The soft dark laugh was the same, but his face was covered with pimples and blackheads. They had not shown up by the Japanese lantern light. Some of my defects probably glared in the sunlight too. Anyway we didn't hit it off nearly so smoothly as we did on the moonlight night.

We gave a party at our place one night, and after the crowd was all there it started to rain. It just *poured,* and several of the girls, who had walked, stayed all night. There was a strange girl there that we had not seen before, Mamie somebody. A pretty girl. She was one of the group who stayed all night, and she slept with Sadie. The next day someone took them all home.

A week or two after that Sadie kept saying she believed that she had dandruff, that her head kept itching all the time. She got me to comb her hair. I found something *crawling.* She had lice in her hair, the first we had ever seen. We were *horrified.* We soaked her head in coal oil, washed it with lye soap, and had about all the hide off of her scalp. That was our first and last experience with lice.

---

9. "Hoptown" was the colloquial name for Hopkinsville. According to William Turner, "Back in the 1890s, Hopkinsville and Christian Co. were the only legally voted wet city and county on the L&N Railroad between Evansville and Nashville. Tradition has it that as the railway coaches would approach Hopkinsville the passengers would encounter [*sic*] of the conductor 'How soon would we be to Hopkinsville? I want to hop off and get a drink.'" See Robert M. Rennick, *Kentucky Place Names* (Lexington: University Press of Kentucky, 1984), 144.

We made some lasting friends the short time that we lived in that little house. Holts, of course, who became closely mixed up with our family. Sadie married Evert. John, later, married Ozie, Evert's sister.

The Hamby family was another family we learned to love. Verdie and Alice, who were grown and married. Bertha, Maude, Ida, and Lillian, who at that time were all single.[10] Bertha and Maude were grown girls. Ida and Lillian younger. They were all blessed with an unusual portion of good looks. A beauty that has not faded with the years. They also possessed an inner beauty, of goodness and friendliness. With merry dispositions, and laughter that bubbled over easily. We all had happy times together, and the summer passed by quickly.

Ivy and I worked hard that summer, but there was always swimming, or horseback riding, or something pleasant to look forward to as soon as the work was finished.

The missionaries came quite often, and we enjoyed their visits. We learned a lot of new songs from them. "Don't make me go to bed and I'll be good," from Myler. I think we learned "Two Little Children" from him also. Elder Hamilton was a good missionary too, and to him goes the credit for converting Ivy.

Ivy and I had lots of foolishness going most of the time, and as I think of it now, I'm sure we were a worry to my father, and probably to Sadie too. We were always stealing cream. We argued that since *we* milked the cows it was partly *ours*, and that we would rather have the cream than the butter *any*way. Our argument didn't seem very convincing to Sadie.

Sometimes Ivy and I played while we worked. I remember once when we just about disgraced ourselves. President Price and another Missionary were there eating dinner. Ivy and I were making more biscuits in the little kitchen (Ivy was the champion biscuit maker). She sifted the flour, and I poured the buttermilk in. As I passed her I took a big fingerful of thick buttermilk from the mouth of the empty pitcher and rubbed it in her mouth. She took a piece of the dough she was making up and zipped it at me with her left hand. I dodged, and it flew past me right out through the open door, barely missing President Price's head, and hung on a door knob just back of him. There was no place for us to run, only right out *by* them, and we didn't dare, so we just stood our ground. Ivy swore she was making biscuits with such *vim* that part of it just naturally got away.

In the fall, when the crops were in, there was a general change. Elmo and Ivy moved to Pond River, where her folks lived, and we moved

---

10. This refers to Verdie Hamby (1881–1963); Alice Hamby (b. ca. 1891); Bertha Hamby (b. 1883); Maude Hamby (b. 1885); and Lillian Hamby (1890–1974). Ida is unidentified.

to the Louis Hamby house up on the Buttermilk road.[11] Papa and Miss Serena got married, and Sadie was getting ready for a wedding. Life was certainly going through some whirlwind changes for all of us.

Things were not nearly so funny since Ivy was not with me. Sadie was seriously busy with wedding clothes, and getting things ready to go to housekeeping. Miss Serena didn't believe in fun. Life was really a serious business to her, though she didn't take any active part in it. She was specially blessed as a director.

After Sadie and Evert married we began making preparations to go west. Papa had finally decided to go to southern Arizona. Gillilands' folks had gone there, and John was there too. I wanted to go to Utah, but of course my judgment wasn't very weighty.

Evert and Sadie had set up housekeeping at the old Sol Smith place.[12] I didn't get to go and visit them very often either, as there was plenty of work to do. My days of carefree childhood were in the past. I longed every day to be with Sadie, for we would soon be gone, and then it might be a long, long time before I would see her again.

Finally everything was sold that we could not take with us. Everything was packed that we wanted to take. Our clothing was ready, and we would soon be on our way.

I went for a last visit with Sadie. She had wanted to go west too, but now that was out of the question, and I was sorry for her. I knew she would be awfully lonesome when we were gone. I wouldn't be there to rub her head for her when it ached.

Once, when they were children, she was hiding in the ash-hopper, and Elmo was throwing rocks at her (it was a game). Sadie was a good dodger, and was not afraid of being hit, but after a long wait she thought he had quit the game and raised up just as he let a big rock fly. It hit her in the left side of the temple, and knocked a hole. It didn't give her a great deal of trouble till she was in her teens, and then at certain periods a knot half the size of an egg would protrude there, causing her great pain. At other times there was a dent there. The doctor was baffled, and said he could see no good reason for that knot coming out there at those certain periods, and he knew nothing to do for it. I hated to leave her because of that, I was afraid it might give her serious trouble.

*Now* a trip across the country doesn't seem very serious. We go and come so easily we think nothing of it. *That* was our first one, and Arizona seemed a *long, long* way off.

---

11. Probably the house of Lewis M. Hamby (1834–1891).
12. Belonging to Solomon Smith (1833–1915) and his wife Elizabeth Gunn (1835–1922).

Our goodbye was sad and tragic. Sadie said that after I left she rolled in the grass and kicked and bawled like she did when she was a child.

The train we were going on was due to leave Hopkinsville at eleven in the evening. I can't remember now who took us to the depot, but I do remember passing old Uncle Henry Howard, a negro who had joined the Church. He waved his hat, and said, "Goodbye, *Mistah Makkus.*"

My head was aching from crying, and the waiting at the depot was not too pleasant. Lawrence Smith was going with us, and he and Autie kept up a string of foolishness.

That was my first ride on a train, and it was quite exciting when the engine pulled up with a terrible clang and clatter. We were soon all clambering up the steps with our bags and boxes. We found seats close together. Someone was calling, "All Aboard," and we began moving slowly away from everything that was familiar to me.

It is not very interesting traveling by train at night, and it was not long till I was asleep. When I awoke I felt as if I was in a storybook or fairyland. A full moon was shining bright, and we were in the swamplands of the south. Pine trees and cypress trees were standing in water, and moss was trailing in long pointed fronds from the limbs. A big white bird flew up from the water and alighted on a branch of a tree.

The railroad track was built up on a trestle, like a bridge. I didn't go to sleep any more that night. When daylight came the wonderland still held me charmed. The swamps, the palms, the flowers, the vines, and the water *every*where. It was not a country I would have liked to live in, but it was certainly very interesting to pass through on the train.

When we got to New Orleans, the depot where the train stopped was a long way from the wharf where we were to get on the boat to take us across the delta of the Mississippi River. To get to the wharf we then traveled in a horsedrawn vehicle, and it gave us a chance to see much of the historic old city. We went down Canal street where an army had marched, one rainy day, and the band played a tune that was ever afterward known as "The Eighth of January."

Our father, whose knowledge of everything made the trip much more interesting, said that those big flat stones Canal Street was paved with were not native to this part of the country. They had been brought from Europe in the hold of ships as ballast, when loads of produce were taken over, and the empty ship returned. The street was rather bumpy.

Papa told us of a battle that was fought here, after peace was declared, showing how very slowly news traveled at that time.

We saw wide rice fields, and fields of sugar cane. Once we saw a man cutting hay with a mowing machine. The entire hayfield was growing on the surface of a lake or lagoon. We could plainly see a *wave following* the man and his mowing machine.

At San Antonio we saw our first Mexicans. When we arrived in El Paso there was a general commotion. Word had been received that a band of Mexican rebels were headed that way, under Pancho Villa, and the State Militia was on its way to head them off.

We had to stay all night in El Paso, and there was a dance across the street from the hotel where we stayed. About midnite there was another disturbance. The hotel keeper's daughter was missing. She had gone to the dance, and when they went to look for her she was not there. The police were notified, and when one arrived Miss Serena found that he was a relative, one of Fidella Long's boys.[13] Miss Serena had been talking about that family having moved to Texas, and wondered if she would see any of them as we passed through. Lawrence and Autie had a lot of fun over her expecting to see some of them. The funny part of it was that she *really did*, and had a long conversation with him. He was Chief of Police in El Paso.

The Mexican rebels had not made their appearance when we left, but the Militia *had* arrived, and they found that the hotel keeper's daughter had gone off with a married man. Miss Serena was happy over finding her kinsman, and of the pleasant visit she had had with him.

The nearer we got to southern Arizona the more worried our father became. "If Franklin and Duncan country looks like this I don't like it," he kept saying.

We got to Lordsburg, New Mexico, and had to lay over all night there. The only rooming house there was was in a turmoil. The man and woman who were running it had decided to disagree, and were not in any mood to welcome traveling Kentuckians, and would not rent us a room. The only thing to do was stay in the depot, a little place that was so small that we could hardly all get in it with our baggage. It was snowing outside, but inside it was so hot we could hardly breathe. I kept walking up to the edge of a platform for a bit of fresh air, and then I would try it in the stuffy little room till I was almost smothered, then out again.

The memory of Lordsburg is not very pleasant in my mind. The picture of that old man and woman at the rooming house shouting ugly things at each other, and being cross with my daddy, and the remainder of the night in that bleak little room with the red hot stove, and the snow outside.

The next day we arrived in Duncan. It is on the Gila River, and the big cottonwoods looked inviting after seeing so much barren country.[14]

---

13. This refers to Lindsey Fidela Long (b. 1827), son of Thomas Long. Lindsey Fidela Long was married to Barbara Ann Cauthorn.

14. Duncan, a Mormon settlement on the Gila river, was founded in 1883 for ranching, farming and mining prospects. See Robin Billingsley, comp., *Duncan: Fountain of the Gila River, 1883–1983* (Duncan: Historic Booklet Committee, 1983).

We had a short wait at the depot at Duncan, then we saw a fellow in a wide hat, with long hair, driving a pair of spirited horses hitched to a two horse wagon. He was standing, and the Arizona wind was blowing his hair out behind, making him look rather wild and wooly. When he came closer we saw that it was my brother John coming to meet us. He had allowed his hair to grow so he would look like a *real* westerner of the *mountain man* type, and he had done a very good job of it.

The memory of our stay in southern Arizona is pleasant to me. We stayed on a farm belonging to Joe Wilkins.[15] We had a garden, alfalfa, and chickens. Joe taught me how to irrigate the garden, and he let Autie and me ride his horses, which we took advantage of quite often. Brother and Sister Dallas, an old couple who had moved there from Illinois, lived just around the foot of the hill from us. They had a son, Chester, a little older than Autie. Mr. Dallas had been quite a farmer and stock raiser back in Illinois and had brought a lot of thoroughbred horses and cattle to Arizona with him when he came, but Arizona didn't seem to agree with his stock. They started dying as soon as he arrived. Big, big, fat, fine looking horses just laid down and died and he drug them off. There was always the smell of a dead horse or cow when the wind came from the direction of certain canyons.

I was sorry for Mr. and Mrs. Dallas, they had once had plenty. Now their children were married and gone, and everything they had accumulated was slipping away from them. They were good to me. Mrs. Dallas let me play on her organ. Once, while she was gone to her son's, I went and cooked Brother Dallas's meals, and cleaned the house for him for a week or two.

The first dress I ever made for myself I made on Mrs. Dallas' sewing machine while she was away. I didn't have a pattern, but I spread the cloth on the carpet and cut and sewed till I finally got it like I wanted it. The first set of sleeves I made I couldn't get my arms in them, but there was cloth enough to cut another set. I still remember how it was made. The cloth was light pink, with little deep pink roses, of some soft cotton material. It was made with a narrow double ruffle around the shoulders, wrists, and at the top of a ruffle on the skirt. I felt very proud of it when it was finished, and it really was a very good job, for a first attempt, but I took out and resewed many seams before I had it ready to wear. I bought me a red straw sailor hat to wear with it, and really felt dressed up.

I enjoyed the meetings and Sunday School very much. Brother Losee was my Sunday School teacher, and he was a good one. His wife was

---

15.   Joseph Wilkins (1865–1937) was married to Ivy Jean Rogers (1896–1990).

blind, and he had a daughter, Christine, who I learned to think a great deal of. I liked to go to their place. I helped her to milk the cow, and change her to new grazing places. We would eat bread and butter and onions with a glass of cold milk.

Papa played the fiddle for their dances, and I played the guitar, and May Gale played the organ. May's mother was my teacher in some class that I attended, and she drilled a group of girls for a May Day festival. It was quite an event in my life, as I had never had the opportunity to take part in any Church activities of that kind before. She taught us a number of pretty songs, and we braided the Maypole. I made me a white dress for this occasion, as we were all supposed to wear white.

There was a big swing on a giant cottonwood down towards the river, where the young folks went of Sunday afternoons in the summer. Laura Ellidge, Mary Magrath, Ursula Wilkins, Ella Clouse, May Gale, Janie and Anna Nations (sisters), and Barbara Packer (who lived across the river), are some of the girls that I remember. Of course Ora and Annie Gilliland helped at first.[16]

Some of the boys I remember were the Wilkins boys—Joe, Arvill, and Will. The Gale boys—Jay, Rube, and John. The Hendricks boys— Bayler and Charlie (?). Frank McGrath. The Packer boys—Ed and _____. The Merrill boys—Penrod. [*The second version of the autobiography has a blank in place of the name "Penrod"; Effie may have decided she was not certain of the name.*]

I remember one night when a group of these young folks came by in a White Top to take me to a dance at Packers', who lived across the river. We had a happy time. It rained, and the Gila river was swollen until it was not safe for us to cross it in our White Top, so we danced all night, and returned home next morning when the water had gone down.

Lelia and the children stayed at our place until William and John could find work and send for them. They made it pleasanter for us as Miss Serena was sick a great deal of the time while we lived at the Wilkins place. She lost a baby boy, which was a great grief to her.

Lelia and I made regular trips to the Post Office at Duncan, looking for letters from John and William. It was a short mile down the railroad tracks. There was lots of water down near Duncan, and there were wild greens growing on either side of the tracks. We would take our shopping bags and gather it on our way home, and then cook it to eat.

We cooked with cedar wood, the first time that I had ever used it. We usually had Postum to drink. The west wind brought the strong pungent

---

16.  Those who can be identified are Mary Agnes McGrath (1886–1975) and Annie Pearl Gilliland (1889–1955) who married Owen Garvin O'dell.

Effie Marquess at age sixteen. Courtesy
of Itha Carmack.

odor of greasewood which grew on the hillside near. This mixture of
smells, cedar smoke, greasewood, and sour dock greens, and Postum
became so intermingled with the memories of Duncan and Franklin that
to this day, forty five years later, any one of these smells brings back a rush
of memories of faces and people, of places and happenings, that means
southern Arizona when I was sixteen years old.

One interesting thing that I could never figure out was a phantom
train that appeared on the track about the time of morning that we would
be going for the mail. At first it would be far away, and appeared to be
coming towards us from the south. The first time I saw it I thought it was
a real train, and got out of the way for it to pass, but it didn't pass, though
it came quite near. Close enough to see the white steam shooting out on
either side of the engine. The only thing lacking was the noise. The folks
who lived there said it was just a mirage, and thought nothing of it, but it
still remains a mystery to me.

At last the long looked for letter came. Lelia and the children left us
and went to Jerome, where William and John had found work. How I
hated to see them leave, and how lonesome I was after they were gone.

After the work was done Autie and I would explore the hills
around the place where we lived. There were lots of birds. Funny old

roadrunners that we tried to catch. They always stayed a little ahead of us, jumping bushes with their necks stretched out, and their scraggly old tails bobbing around as they trotted, as if it was not fastened on very good.

One day, when we were out in the hills, the wind brought the most delicious smell, a little like crabapple blossoms, or wild grape blooms. We began a search to see what it could be on that barren rocky hill top that could smell so sweet. We soon discovered a tiny blue flower, like an iris, with the sweetest perfume I had ever smelled. After that we always knew when we caught a breath of that heavenly odor that a tiny blue iris was near, struggling up between hot dry rocks, to gladden the desert.

We hunted for smooth round rocks, and played Jacks with them. Autie had a 22 rifle that we had lots of fun with, and there was one old white range cow that had learned how to get through the fence into the field, and after driving her out a dozen or two times Joe Wilkins suggested using the 22 rifle on her. Autie cracked down on her, she fell flat on her side as if he had killed her, but the next second she was up and running. During the remainder of the summer I guess he shot her twenty five times. She always fell flat, but was always up again like a cat.

There was a mountain west of us with a formation on top of it that looked, from our place, about like a barrel. We wanted to see it at closer range, but it was too far to hike. One day, when the horses had nothing else to do, we decided to go and have a look at that mountain. At that time I was totally ignorant of the fact that there were droves of range cattle around us with dangerous bulls among them, as well as range horses, that made it unsafe for children to be out on an old work mare, and an almost unbroken colt. I was not the least bit afraid of cows, or horses either. The ones I had seen were nothing to be afraid of.

Chester Dallas was going with us, and we started early. We passed the first line of low hills, and in a small valley ahead of us was a bunch of cattle, several cows with young calves. They started milling around and bellowing. My horse shied around causing my wide brimmed hat to fall off. Without the least thought of fear I hopped off and got it, as the sun would have blistered me without a hat. It's a wonder I was not killed, but maybe the Lord pitied my ignorance and fearlessness a little.

We finally reached the foot of the barrel mountain, rode our horses up as far as we could, and then tied them to a bush, and started climbing. It was steep and rough, and I ruined my best shoes, and shoes were not too easy for me to get at that time.

When we reached the barrel we saw that it was a huge rock, the sides almost perpendicular. We were *determined* to get to the top somehow, I don't know why. We could see a train going through the valley near where we lived. It looked like a tiny black string moving along.

1901–1902[17]

About the time we had reached the top we saw several range horses galloping directly towards where we had our animals tied. Chester had sense enough to know that we were likely to be left afoot fifteen or twenty miles from home if we didn't succeed in getting down there before they did.

The climbing down was much more difficult than going up had been, but we made it, and started on our way home.

When we got home I found that somewhere in the last mile of the trip home I had lost a beautiful comb from my hair. I thought I knew where I had lost it, so in the late afternoon, after I had rested, I walked out in the direction we had come, to see if I could find it. There was a lone cow grazing around off to the south of me. I had never been afraid of an old cow, and paid no attention to her. She kept raising her head and trotting around, but I went on looking for my comb. I found where I thought I had lost it, and as I came back past the cow she resumed her trotting exercises, emphasized by an occasional snort. Suddenly she lowered her head and bellowed, with her tongue out, and charged straight towards me. I knew then that she meant business, so I fairly flew. I was a good runner, but she was gaining on me. By a tight squeeze I reached the wire fence and rolled under it just before she ran against it, making the wires squeak through the staples. I was tired, but I didn't lay there. I had found that even fearlessness was no defense against a lone range cow. After that I was a little more careful of taking long hikes away from the house, especially if there were stray cows around.

Later Mrs. Dallas told me of a bull that started chasing a child that was walking home from Duncan. The bull was not very close to him, so he ran up a canyon and dodged it. But it followed him for a mile or two, catching an occasional glimpse of his red sweater, till he came into their lot, scared and exhausted from running. The bull appeared on a nearby hilltop, still looking for him.

Autie and I marked a place up on the side of the mesa where sounds were very clear. There was a watering place away out in the flat, southwest of us, towards the foothills, where there were often lots of range cattle. We would climb slowly up the side of the mesa. We could not hear a sound until we had reached that one spot. There we could hear the cows bawling distinctly.

Then there were certain places in the flat below where there was a mirage. We would watch the moving line of cattle till they reached that

---

17. These dates are written by hand at the top of the page.

strip, then their legs suddenly seemed to be about twenty feet long, and they looked like they were walking on stilts.

These things were all new and strange and interesting to us. We never tired of rambling over the hills, or playing in the big wash. There had been a flood since Dallases had bought their place, and such a mighty stream came down from the mountains that it cut a wash twenty or thirty feet deep right through their farm. There was one thing that surprised me, it showed how very deep the roots of alfalfa will go. After a big rain that caused another section of dirt to fall in, taking off a strip of the lucerne patch, we found one root that was twenty six feet long.

One day when Papa was working out in the field, he caught old Blue, the horse that was staked out there, and got on him without a bridle, to ride him home. Blue decided to have a little fun. He started running as fast as he could, coming straight across the fields, jumping ditches and muddy spots where they were watering. Papa yelled, "Yip, pee," and just as we looked, his hat flew off. They dashed up, and the horse stopped suddenly at the corral gate, looking very pleased with himself. We laughed at papa for getting so wild and reckless out here in Arizona. He said he hadn't wanted the dinner to get cold before he got there to eat it.

My first experience in working away from home came when Christine Losee, who was working for Mrs. Billingsley, got sick and sent for me to work in her place till she was able to go to work again.[18] The work was not hard, and Mrs. Billingsley was real nice to work for, but I didn't like being away from home. While I was at Billingsleys, I met Annie Caid, a young widow who was running a restaurant. I promised to work for her as soon as Christine was able to come back to work again. I enjoyed working for Mrs. Caid. I stayed with her till she sold the restaurant, and then went with her to her ranch, a few miles north of Duncan.

Mrs. Caid's ranch was a funny rambly old place, built right out in the mesquite and greasewood, among some washes. The main part of the house was up on level ground, but the kitchen and dining room was in an old wash, several steps lower. The sides of the wash formed the walls, and there was a brush bowery in front protecting it from the hot sun. It was cool and pleasant down there, the roof rising just high enough from the level ground to have windows on either side for light and breezes to come in.

The cool kitchen, with Annie's good cooking, (which means a lot in the life of a growing child) all made very pleasant memories. There were two boys, a little younger than myself, who kept things lively around the

---

18. This Mrs. Billingsley is probably the wife of Benjamin Franklin Billingsley who ran a general merchandise store in Duncan.

place. Sometimes they would help me with the dishes, especially if there was something they wanted me to do when the dishes were finished.

The river was near, and when there was any water in it we would pull off our shoes and wade, or run races in the sand.

Sometimes these boys were not so nice. One day when Annie's boyfriend came, they insisted that I go up and meet him. I didn't want to, but they kept insisting. "Who's afraid of Jack Wisecarver?" they asked. I told them I wasn't afraid of him, but I didn't intend to go up there, as he hadn't come to see me, he came only to see Annie.

Art, Annie's brother, got a menacing look on, "Don't ever tell me you won't do things. I make little girls like you mind me." I was no weakling, but there were two of them, and they were both big and strong for their ages, so, after a two hour scramble they succeeded in tying my hands and feet together. Then they decided to put boy's pants on me before taking me up to meet Jack. They finally accomplished that part, got my feet tied together again and succeeded in dragging me up there. We were a sorry looking trio. Art's nose was bleeding, and we were peeled all over. My wrists were skinned with the rope, and I was bawling. Annie was real mad at them and threatened to take a board to them if they didn't untie me that minute, but they were not very badly scared.

While I was working for Mrs. Caid I got acquainted with a young fellow named Dick Day; he was very pleasant and I liked him, but he smelled of whiskey sometimes, and I didn't like that. His face would be red then, but he kept it from being monotonous at the ranch, and we were usually glad when he came.

One time while Annie's friend, Jack Wisecarver, was there, Dick brought a whitetop buggy and the four of us went to an open air dance and picnic that was held up the river towards Verdin. There was a floor and good music, and we had a very pleasant time. Before we were ready to start for home, Dick's face had grown very red again, and he looked sleepy. I knew then that our little friendship was going to be a very temporary affair.

This time at the ranch was the first time I had ever stayed away from home for more than a week, and I was getting terribly homesick. It finally got so bad that I decided to walk home. Art said he had a bronco I could ride, but that he was locoed, and had fits every time anyone got on him, and every time you stopped him, too. But I wasn't very much afraid. I had been on every old horse and mule that had ever been on our place, and I had never fallen off, or been thrown from one. I was always afraid for other children to ride when they were not used to it, but I was not the least bit afraid to ride any of them myself, and I didn't care how fast they went—the faster the better. So, I told Art that if he would bring his locoed animal home, that I would give it a trial. I felt that if he could ride him, I could, too. In a day or two I heard the boys' "Ye Hoo" out in front, and when I went out they were holding a scrawny looking little mustang that showed the whites of its eyes every time there was an unusual movement around. The saddle and bridle looked too heavy and strong for the horse, as if they alone were all he needed to carry, without anyone getting in the saddle. I went in the house to get ready to go home, but Annie protested. She was afraid I would get hurt on the horse. She kept asking me if I had ever ridden horses, and wasn't I afraid of that crazy locoed thing, but my desire to go home was much stronger than my fear.

Art said he would make a pass at getting on him and let him get his first bucking spree over with, and then maybe he would go along all right—just so I didn't let him stop. If he stopped, he would start bucking again when I started him. Art put his foot in the stirrup, leaned his weight on the saddle, and the action began. Up in the air, then down; up and down, with his head between his forelegs. The boy held onto the reins and let him buck himself down.

As soon as he slowed up, Art said, "Now, it's your time, Skeezicks, come and get on, and make him go like the wind and he'll be too tired to do very much bucking." I got on and away we went. My red sailor hat was fastened securely with elastic under my chin, and pins to hold it in place. The horse seemed to enjoy running, and it just suited me too. They had warned me to keep the reins tight and not let him get his head down. This I tried to remember as we streaked along—out through the grease-wood and mesquite, across the wash, up the hill, then over the level stretch to Duncan.

All went well till we got into town, and my steed wanted to go to the Post Office where he was in the habit of going. I pulled on the left rein till his head was yanked sideways, but he kept galloping to the right till he pulled up at the Post Office and stopped with a thud, and wouldn't move. There were several old men sitting out in front who seemed to enjoy the little show. When he did move, he started bucking, just as Art had predicted. Around and around we went, and up and down. I was so busy holding onto the bucking straps that I couldn't hold his head up. Finally I got the quirt and started laying it on as hard as I could. Those old men laughing had made me mad. He wanted to go back to the ranch, but I finally got him headed south towards Franklin. I plied the whip, and he really did stretch out.

The folks had moved over close to Prather's Windmill, just north of the church, so I had a long level stretch right down the railroad tracks. Papa was working out in the field and saw me coming. He said he wondered if anyone else had a red sailor hat like that. By the time I got to the big gate, he was there to meet me. "I said that was you when that red sailor was only a speck, but what in the world is all the rush about?" I told him I was in a hurry to get home. "Well, you were certainly not wasting any time."

How glad I was to see him! He looked thin and sick. He was homesick, too. He said that if he could ever get away from that glaring desert sun to where there was soft grass under shade trees, and birds that nested in them, and water that was not full of alkali, he would never leave it again. I knew right then that our stay in Arizona was limited. I didn't want to go back to Kentucky, but I was sure that that was what we were going to do. Papa was of a disposition that when his mind was upset his body became ill, and I knew he had never liked Arizona, try as he would.

I was not a very good cook, as I had not had very much experience. I was not used to making "light bread." We usually had cornbread or biscuits, made with buttermilk, in Kentucky. We had no cow, so Lelia had taught me how to make light bread.

We drank Postum for breakfast, and even today as I write, the smell of cedar smoke and a plastered dobie wall brings back memories of Postum and sour tasting bread and the odor of greasewood, and a number of other things that went to make up our life in Franklin.

Other memories are of Mrs. Dallas jumping up and flirting her apron as she hollered "shew!" at the hawks that kept bothering her chickens, of playing in the deep washes that had ruined the Dallas farm, of long explorations into the hills with Autie, or up the river towards Virden.

One dark night I will never forget. Ora Gilliland and I decided to come straight across the fields from the church to our place. We got lost and came onto the railroad tracks, got into a field that had been irrigated and floundered around in the mud and ruined our best shoes. We spent the biggest part of the night getting home. The tracks were away to the south of Franklin, so we were far out of our way, and got our biggest scare when we nearly ran into a camp of Mexican men down by the railroad. To two young girls, this was really an experience.

Before the crop was harvested, papa sold it and began packing to start for Kentucky. Our boxes and trunks were all ready to go, and we were ready to start on the morrow. That evening Dick Day came for me to go with a group of young folks to a dance in Duncan. Papa didn't want me to go, but as it was the last night I would be there, of course I wanted to go very much.

Papa didn't usually object to my going places unless there was a good reason, and when he said he would rather I wouldn't, that was the final word. But this time the boys and girls begged him so to let me go till he finally said if I would promise to be home by eleven o'clock, I could go. I meant it when I promised, but when eleven o'clock came, they would not bring me home, and at one o'clock I said I was going to walk home alone, so they finally took me. I think that was the only time I ever really disobeyed my father. On the way home Dick asked me to stay in Arizona with him. He begged and pleaded, said he would never drink another drop if I would, but I didn't even remotely consider it. He gave me a beautiful white feather fan that probably cost more than everything I had on. Papa was awake when I went in, and I just told him the truth, but he didn't scold me.

We had a pleasant trip back to Kentucky, crossed the Mississippi at Memphis. We were going down some wide steps from the waiting room, down into a shady yard where hundreds of people were sitting or milling around; about halfway down the steps my petticoat lost its button and dropped down around my feet, almost tripping me. I just stepped out of it, rolled it up and put it in a satchel I was carrying. I didn't feel so terribly embarrassed, since there was not a soul among the crowd that was looking at me that I knew of, and I would probably never see them again anyway. I was thankful that I didn't fall down the steps. Papa said I picked it up as casually as if it had been a handkerchief I had dropped.

Back in Kentucky papa was happy again; to hear the birds sing, the babble of water over rocks, the soft grass under the shade trees, and the mellow sunshine that filtered through the leaves was all he needed, but not me—I was lonesome for the west.

We rented a little house on the hillside, below Mr. Holt's place. Ozie, Evert's sister, and I became fast friends. Evert and Sadie lived at the old Sol Smith place, just across the creek to the East of us. Ozie and I both enjoyed going to their place. We had many happy times together that fall and winter. I remember one time especially, when I was up there, and Ozie and I were planning something, as usual. I can truthfully say that we never planned anything that was undesirable, usually to embroider something, make a basket of crepe paper flowers, or remodel some of our clothing, write letters, or practice some new song we had learned. About the only harm there could possibly have been was the fact that we would stay awake longer than was good for us, for both of us had to be up early to help with the work around the place.

Anyway, this special evening we begged Mrs. Holt to let Ozie go home with me for just a minute, we wouldn't be gone long. She would not give her consent, so we went out, very dejected. Of course Ozie walked part way home with me. When we reached the barn, there was the house in sight, so I said we could run right quick and see those patterns she wanted to look over, and be back before Mrs. Holt missed her. We took hands and ran as fast as we could, hunted up the box of patterns, found what we wanted, and started back feeling a little guilty. When we neared the big barn, at the top of the hill, there stood Mrs. Holt, almost filling the road, for all the world like a big thunder storm, with a long switch in her hand.

"Ozellie, I'm agonta give both of you a good whipping for not minding me. I told you both plainly that you couldn't go." We swore that we had not meant to go when we left the house, and explained humbly about the patterns, and how we thought we could run and get them and be back before she missed us. She finally hit Ozie a little tap or two, and told us she ought to raise welts on both of us, and that she would do it the next time we disobeyed her. I know she must have been disgusted with us lots of times. When Ozie was learning to play the guitar, we practiced over and over again the 1, 2, 3, 4. —1, 2, 3, 4. Mrs. Holt said it seemed to say, "Jack's a poopin', Jack's a poopin'." I suppose she grew pretty tired of hearing it so much, but not so with us.

Mr. Holt bought Ozie a lovely sweet-toned guitar with twelve strings, and our happiness was about complete.

Eugene Fuller was Ozie's boy friend, and Garvie was mine.[19] They would come together to see us, sometimes at my place, but more often at Ozie's, as she had a front room, and in the summer there were lots of roses, jonquils, and honeysuckle. One special rosebush, which had tiny pink roses in clusters, was our favorite, and their perfume was heavenly.

Garvie prided himself on his fast buggy horses, and he really had one that could get over the ground, named Damon. He was not a trotter, but he paced, and no one could ever pass us when he had old Damon to the buggy. He had another scrubby old nag he called Dude, that was not much for looks, but he had the speed. Garvie would spread his tail out over the dashboard, then tell him he was three quarters to the breeze now, so just take off. It didn't take much encouragement. I was always afraid he would fall down and kill himself and us, but he seemed to be pretty surefooted.

Papa bought a crop of tobacco that had already been set out, and we finished working it. I can remember going to work with him early of a morning when the dew would be white all over the fuzzy leaves of tobacco, and in thirty minutes we would be dripping wet. The mornings were chilly, too, until the sun was high enough to dry the dew. Sometimes it was foggy, and the sun would not come out till nearly noon.

Worming and suckering tobacco was a terrible, backbreaking job, and the gum from the sticky green leaves would soon be all over our hands and clothing, so thick that when a garment became folded and stuck, it was hard to pull it apart again. The sickening smell of the hot sun on the green tobacco usually gave me a headache.

I have already mentioned keeping company with Garvie, but now I want to go back to the first part again:

---

19. Eugene Fuller (b. 1880), son of Boone Fuller, and Owen Garvin O'dell (1881–1968).

There were lots of apples on some big old apple trees on the hillside below the stables. One afternoon while I was picking up apples to dry, I heard someone call me. Coming up through the field was Garvie Odell, who had been ploughing in a field across the creek. He asked me if I needed help, and said that he was working for Ellis Walker, who had married his sister Alice. We sat in the shade and visited while his horses had a good long rest.

When I was younger, Garvie used to come home with John, to sleep sometimes (at least once that I remember of), as they were going with two of the Smith girls. I was still a child at that time, but I thought he was about the handsomest, most romantic looking young fellow I ever saw. He wore gorgeous ties, and fastened ribbon streamers on his buggy whip, and they fluttered in the breeze as his horse cantered along.

Now that I was older, and he was showing an interest in me, my dream of the perfect prince charming was almost a reality.

Long after all the apples had been picked up, and the sun was getting low, he said he must be going, and asked me if he could come and take me for a ride the following Sunday. I almost walked in a trance the rest of the week. Everything went smooth and lovely till later, when we had bought the old Ferrell place, on the hill east of the Morris place. Garvie came one evening when two of the missionaries were there: Elders Hand and Petersen.[20] Papa played the violin, and Garvie played the guitar, and Elder Hand and I danced a little. That made Garvie furious. He said, "You can't tell me, that doggoned scrappah's stuck on you." That was the first fly in the lovely ointment. We continued to chew the rag. He tried to make me promise that I wouldn't dance with him any more, but I was stubborn and wouldn't promise.

Finally one Sunday evening, when President Kimball and his companions were there, Garvie and I were sitting in the back of the room and he said, "What is there about that doggone Mormonism that you're so crazy about, anyway?"[21] I proceeded to tell him, and it took quite a while. He was not very favorably impressed, and went home sullen.

The next time he came he proceeded to tell me how dear his mother was to him; how he had always obeyed her in everything. At last he said she

---

20. Possibly refers to a David A. Hand (1882–1963) who served in 1901–1902 in Mississippi and Ohio but was unrecorded in the Kentucky Conference. Elder Peterson probably refers to Niels Alma Peterson (1878–1964) who served in the Southern States Mission in 1897–1900.

21. Thatcher Kimball (1883–1956), son of David Patten Kimball. He should not be confused with Spencer W. Kimball (1895–1985), the twelfth president of the LDS Church who served in 1973–1985. Thatcher Kimball was at that time president of the Kentucky Conference in the Southern States Mission.

told him she wanted him to marry someone he loved, and that she had just one request, that he would not marry a Mormon. I told him that I thought it would be a fine thing if he would obey her, and that I had made a resolution that I would not marry anyone who was not a Mormon.

I don't think he was expecting that kind of an answer. He knew I liked him very much, and he couldn't imagine anyone choosing a funny old religion in preference to him. We wept a little and said a sad goodnight.

The next Friday, Elmo and Ivan Cooksie [Cooksey] came and stayed all night, and on Saturday the Elders were there again. Garvie had not said he was coming back Sunday (neither had he said he would not), so when Elmo asked me to go home with him, I decided I would. I didn't leave any word for Garvie. Miss Serena said when he came Sunday and found I was gone, he was furious. I hated to leave the missionaries, they looked so forlorn when I said I was going.

Miss Serena said Elder Hand cried after we left, and had to leave the room. He said, as he left, "Brother Marquess, you have an awful good girl, and I sure like her."

I spent six miserable weeks at Elmo's. I kicked around and passed the days off very well. Cy, Ethel, Pearl, and Ivan Cooksie [Cooksey] were often there, or I was with them at their place. But when night came, and we went to bed, I cried myself to sleep lots of times.

Still, the memory of Garvie's mother's request, and him thinking he should obey her, was enough to make me determined to stay away long enough that it would all be over when I went back. The funny thing about that affair was that Garvie finally married a Mormon girl and became a staunch Mormon himself, while I married a fellow who was not a Mormon, and had a difficult time converting him.

CHAPTER SIX

# Bitterness and Sorrow Helped Me Find the Sweet

> *One in tender mercy, heard my fervent prayer;*
> *Days of anguish over, calm instead of care.*
> *Peace and joy like heaven, gratitude complete;*
> *Bitterness and sorrow helped me find the sweet.*
> —"One of Earth's Lessons," Carmack,
> Miscellaneous poems

One day, in the fall, Edgar Carmack was hauling corn for my dad, and I climbed up on the load with him.[1] We were jogging along, when in the distance we saw Garvie and Annie coming in the buggy. He had it all dolled up with ribbons on the sides of the horse's head and on his whip, with a flashy robe over their laps to keep the dust off. We hurriedly pulled our shoes off, put them behind us, and hung our bare feet off on the side next to them so we would look like real hillbillies.

Lena, Miss Serena's niece, came and stayed most of that winter with us, and we had pleasant times together. Eddie East went with her, and the Missionaries were there a lot. We always enjoyed them.

That winter, while stripping tobacco, my father began tasting it. I knew it the first day he put it in his mouth, and asked him if he had been chewing tobacco. He looked astonished, and asked me how in the world I knew he had tampered with it, as he had only put a tiny little piece in his mouth to see if it had a nice flavor. He continued to taste it, and soon his old stomach trouble came back. I begged and pleaded with him to leave it

---

1. Henry Edgar Carmack (1883–1952) was the son of Thomas Green Carmack (1864–1946) and Parlee Gunn (1870–1887). See appendix three.

alone. I think he did quit several times, but always tasted it again. One time, when there was a Conference being held at our place, President Kimball prophesied that if he did not obey the Word of Wisdom that he would die before the year was out. After the meeting he went to my father, put his arm around him and with tears streaming down his cheeks he told him that he loved him, and please not to feel that he wanted his prediction to come true, that he had only spoken as the spirit of the Lord had directed him. Papa grew thinner, and nothing he ate agreed with him. At last I quit school to take care of him and do the work around the place. Autie did most of the work on the farm. I helped him when I could. We had a nice garden, and I canned tomatoes and apples for winter.

I made soups and gruels, and everything I could think of for papa to eat to keep his stomach from hurting, but nothing relieved it. The medicine the doctor gave him did no good. Finally he became so weak that he lay on the bed most of the time.

One morning when I came in his lips were blue, and there was a glaze over his tired blue eyes. He said, "Well, daughter, it's here at last. Now that I've waited too long, I wish we had sent for Lelia and John to come home. It may be a long time before I see them again." I answered, "Let's send a telegram and tell them to come right home. I'll keep you alive till they get here." He asked me how I thought I could keep him alive. I told him I would keep the blood circulating by rubbing him all the time. I succeeded in convincing him that I could do it. Elmo was sent to Hopkinsville as fast as he could go, to send the telegram. He had to wait about two hours for someone to go to the field where John and William were working before they could send word back as to just when they would start. Finally the answer came back, "We will start for home Thursday morning."

As soon as I had written the message for Elmo to take to town, I had started my task of rubbing. I rubbed him all over continually, with my hands next to his flesh. I begged the Lord to let it be effective, and to let him live till they got here. All day and all night I rubbed. When I would start to doze and slow up papa would say, "Keep it up, daughter, if you possibly can. This old clock is about to stop again."

I'll never forget how thankful I was when I saw Sadie getting off a horse at the stile block out in front. Together we kept the rubbing up till they arrived Sunday morning. It had been told around that Mr. Marquess was dying, and that we had sent for the children to come home from Utah. By Sunday morning the yard was full of people, also the lot in front of the yard. We kept most of them out of the house, as it worried him.

He said, "What in the world do all those people want to come for? I guess they want to see how a Mormon will die."

I will never forget those long nights when I sat on a footstool by his bed and rubbed to keep life in him. There was a moon, and a mocking-bird sang all night those three nights that we battled with death. One of the nights a little dog, who must have been lost, started howling in front. It was a strange dog, as we didn't possess one. Someone went out and started throwing rocks at it to drive it away. Papa heard them and said not to hurt it; it sounded lonesome enough without having rocks thrown at it.

I think it was about ten o'clock that Sunday morning when I heard arguing by the front door. Someone was trying to keep John from coming in too abruptly, as papa was dozing, and all were afraid that it would be too much of a shock for him. Lelia's folks had hired a rig from the livery stable, but John had been in too much of a hurry to go around the road, and had cut across the field afoot, and had got there ahead of the carriage. Suddenly Papa opened his eyes and said, "John's here, isn't he?" Johnnie tried to control his feelings, but it was impossible, and he cried until he was exhausted. The others soon arrived, and Lelia didn't shed a tear, but set to work trying to devise some way to help him regain his health.

Papa was happy, and seemed to feel better for a while. They were so sorry we had not sent for them sooner. He lived a few days more, and about noon he said he wanted all of us near, as he guessed he would have to leave us. It was getting hard for him to breathe, and there seemed to be a mist before his eyes. He wanted to make sure we were all there, calling us each by name, and groping with his hands to find us. He told us just how death seemed. He said his breath was getting shorter, "About two more breaths and I'll see what's on the other side." He asked where Autie was, and praised him for his faithfulness in doing all the hard work since he had been sick. He told him he could have old Bob (the horse), and the saddle and bridle for his own. He told us to be good to Sis (Miss Serena), as she had been a faithful old soul to him. Suddenly he looked up with a surprised and happy look and said, "*Etta!*" Then, after a short pause, he said, "My, what beautiful flowers," then his head dropped forward, and he was gone.[2]

I hurried out, and down past the stables, to a place where I had often gone to say my prayers. For a while I could hardly get my breath. It seemed to work on a valve that would only work one way. I wondered if I was going to die too, but after lying on the ground for a while, I began to feel better and went back to the house.

What a comfort it was to have Lelia and the children and John with us!

---

2. Boanerges Robert Marquess died on October 7, 1903. See "'Bo' Marquess Dead," *Hopkinsville Kentuckian*, October 9, 1903, 1.

After the funeral Miss Serena began to prepare for a sale. She and her brother, Frank Long, were strong on people's rights by law, and reminded me a number of times that I had no right to even touch a wind-fall apple, if they were a mind to go strictly by law. They thought we were a peculiar bunch of children, to not want anything on the poor old place. I did keep the guitar papa had bought for me, though she said by rights she could have sold it if she had wanted to.

It made us sad to even think of squabbling over the few things papa had accumulated, and were determined that we would never stoop to such a thing. I'm sure Miss Serena was a little disappointed, as she was anxious to show her knowledge of legal proceedings.

I want none of my children, or grandchildren to think that there was discord and squabbling between me and my stepmother, for there was not.

I did all the washing (scrubbed on a washboard) and the ironing, milked the cows, did the cooking and dishwashing, and although Autie teased her continually and laughed at her one time (she hummed, and he would hum it after her), she thought a great deal more of him than she ever did of me.

After the sale, Miss Serena went to her brother's, Frank Long, and I went to Sadie's. Here at Sadie's, Ozie, Evert's sister, and I renewed the friendship that had existed between us since childhood.

Edgar (Carmack) went to work for Evert, and we were soon married, and moved to the old Birchfield Marquess place.

William, Lelia's husband, came home after he had disposed of their crop in Utah, and they moved to the old Hubbard Stewart house (which was near the old homestead of Jot Lindley, who married my grandfather's youngest sister, "Peggy" Armstrong Lindley—see special mention of her in my great-grandfather Ben Armstrong's will). [*The will is not included in this edition.*]

In the spring Edgar rented my father's old place from Miss Serena, and we moved back to the old house, where Cecil, my first child, was born. I helped Edgar all spring, anxious to get a big crop planted so we could have extra for the little one that was coming. If I had been wiser I would have kept a little more quiet, as I was in constant pain, but this was my first, and I thought that was only natural, and worked in the fields in spite of it.

One day, as I was going to the house, a shower came up. I was running to keep from getting wet. Between the well and the house, along the row of fruit trees, the path was very slippery. Suddenly my feet flew from under me, and I fell flat on my side. We laughed, and went on to the house, fixed lunch, and did the usual chores around the place.

I went to bed that night not feeling any worse than usual. I remember thinking, before I went to sleep, that I must get some material for

The family of Thomas Green Carmack and Mattie Olivia Hale Carmack, ca. 1901. Left to right, rear: Vivian, Edgar, Carrie; front: Lewis, Thomas, Lizzie, Mattie Olivia, baby Ernest, Myrtle. Courtesy of Itha Carmack.

some little clothes and get them made soon; there was no particular hurry, though, as I had about three months in which to get them made.

About one o'clock I awoke with a severe colic. I endured it till almost daylight, before waking Edgar. When it was light he went for Mrs. Carmack, his stepmother, who was a pretty good nurse.[3] When all of her colic remedies failed to do any good, and the pain grew worse, they sent for cousin Sis Causler [Cansler], the granny woman.[4] About one o'clock after noon, a tiny little son was born, weighing about two pounds. None of them expected him to live, but I did. I was sure he would.

Poor little thing, not one garment to put on him. Mrs. Carmack brought some of Ernest's old leftovers and put them on him till we could get some clothes made. They were so big he was lost in them, but they kept him warm. The baby slept continually, and would not stay awake long enough to eat. About one swallow and he was sound asleep again, but I made him swallow so often that he survived. The baby was born on a Sunday. The following Sunday morning there was no one there but myself and the baby. I needed some warm water to wash him with, and I

3.  Mattie Olivia Hale Carmack (1873–1961) was the daughter of John Wayland Hale and Elizabeth Shepherd.

4.  Sis Cansler, a midwife, was the daughter of James Curtis Cansler and Sylvia Adams Cansler.

went to the kitchen after it. I tilted the big old iron teakettle over to pour the water, and something happened. I turned blind and sick, and a terrible pain seized me. I groped back to bed, and the rest of the day I was in such terrible agony that my tongue even refused to function. I was conscious, but could hardly speak.

Edgar sent for Mrs. Causler again, and Sadie and Lelia came. For several days I was turned over only in a sheet. My one worry was that maybe my milk would not be good for the baby, with me sick, and that they were not feeding him often enough, but after another week I was able to take care of him myself.

When he was two months old I went to Lelia's and cousin Leona Armstrong weighed him, and he weighed four pounds and four ounces. I cried, as I had expected him to weigh much more than that.

There was not much more outside work for me that summer. It is wonderful how a mother can love a baby, even when he is a tiny little thing. My whole soul was wrapped up in him. My heart just sang with happiness and thankfulness for him. After he once got started to growing, he fattened like a little pig, and became a perfect roly poly of a baby.

There were two houses on the old place, and we moved to the one down on the Buttermilk road. Edgar made cross-ties that winter for spending money. We got a bunch of chickens, and I was interested in taking care of them. I sold eggs for seven cents a dozen. Wayland Hale worked for us, and there was a great deal of snow. The men killed rabbits, and we had fried rabbit, rabbit pie, rabbit dumplings, and every way I could fix them so we would not get too tired of them. I baked sweet potatoes in the dutch oven, too. It was very cold in the kitchen. The walls were thin, and it was on the north side of the house. I had lots of dried peaches, too. When I remember that winter, part of the memory is of fried peach pies, rabbit dumplings and good cornbread with butter and sweet milk, and my baby growing fat and round and learning the cute little things like first words, and playing with his toys (which consisted of a soft ball I made for him, and a string of spools).

Edgar was able to chop out about ten cross ties a day with the broad axe, getting ten cents a tie for them. Mr. Carmack let us milk a little black heifer who had her first calf, and I sold buttermilk to the sawmill crew who had a camp not far away.[5]

It was at this place that I first met Mr. and Mrs. Galloway, who later became our very dear friends.[6] When they moved the sawmill camp over

---

5. "Mr. Carmack" refers to Thomas Green Carmack, Effie's father-in-law.
6. Robert and Hazel Galloway. Effie's daughter, Hazel, was named after Mrs. Galloway.

to the Jim Williams hollow, Edgar hired out to them and we moved with them. They built new lumber cabins for the mill hands. Galloways' and ours were very near to each other.

Cecil was exposed to whooping cough just after we moved there, and Mrs. Galloway said that since we were so close, we would not try to keep the children apart. I regretted that decision many times, as her little girl, Jewel, took whooping cough and died. Cecil grew pale and thin himself before he was finished with it.

Edgar and Hol Boyd worked together hauling logs for the mill, and he stayed at our place part of the time. He became very fond of Cecil, and seemed to think as much of him as Edgar did. Adrian Cannon was there a lot, too, and if Cecil could have been spoiled, they would have spoiled him.[7] Adrian called him Stud, and Galloways called him "Sat Boy." Their baby Hazel and Cecil, were nearly the same age, so on her washdays I would keep her baby, and on my washdays she kept mine. She even let them both nurse her breast when they were hungry, I did the same when I kept the two of them. We grew to love each other very much, and our men were good friends. She had a good bunch of children: Shelby, Guy, Mary, Marvin, Jewel, and baby Hazel.

I must not forget Rick Worthington, the manager of the mill. He was a good man, and very intelligent.[8]

The friendships that were formed during the two years we worked with this group have lasted through life, and I am sure will continue on into the next life.

I often grew homesick for my own folks. I can remember the thrill I experienced one day when I saw Vera and Norman, Lelia's children, coming in the distance. They had walked a long way alone. Vera had brought some cloth for me to make her a dress, and I was so anxious to make it very pretty that I made it so fancy that I don't believe she ever wore it. I was very remorseful about it. We didn't have too many nice new dresses, though always enough to be neat.

The next move the sawyers made was to a place they called Happy Hollow, eight or ten miles north west of Crofton, away out in the hills where there was lots of good oak timber.

Mrs. Galloway said that if they would let us live close to each other, she would go; if not, she would not move away off down there alone. We first moved into an old schoolhouse and lived together while they were building our houses. The new places were built near each other, both

---

7.   Adrian Cannon (b. 1876).

8.   Effie may be referring to R. L. Worthington (1870–1925).

close to a spring of clear cold water. In winter, when it rained a lot, we caught wash water in barrels. In summer we washed at the spring.

We built chicken houses of poles and sawmill slabs and raised chickens, enough to have what we needed for meat and eggs. We set some eggs in the spring, and raised little chickens. One day we heard an old hen scolding and flogging and making an awful noise. When we went to find the cause we saw a rattlesnake, whose tail end was still in a hole beneath a big tree. He was in the act of swallowing one of the chickens, which was nearly big enough to fry. A boy was passing, so we called him, and he took a stick and drug him out of the hole; got him by the tail and popped his head against a tree, and slung him off in a brush pile. It was over three feet long. There were lots of rattlers down there. One day Mr. Campbell, the woods boss, killed a big one, about five feet long. He was interested in its rattles. He pried its mouth open to see its fangs at close range. It was not entirely dead, and blew its poison breath in his face (or sumpin'), anyway he grew deathly sick, and was barely able to get to Gambles' place, which was near, where he stayed in bed all day.

Cecil had grown plump and well again. He had yellow curls, and was a beautiful child. There was no school for the Galloway children to go to, so they took care of Cecil most of the time. One cold rainy day they came over and asked if they could take him to their place for a while. I paid no attention, knowing that Mrs. Galloway would take as good care of him as I would. About an hour later I started over there to bring him home, and to my horror I saw that they had not taken him in the house, but had him out on a seesaw where they were playing. He was wet, and his feet and legs were as cold as ice. I hurried home, gave him a warm bath and a glass of warm milk and put him to bed. He went right to sleep, slept too long, and when he awoke he was hot, and breathing with a catch in his breath. He was hot all that night.

The next morning I sent for the doctor, who came and said he had pneumonia. I hardly ate or slept till the first danger was over. Just when I was thinking he would soon be well, he had a relapse, and the other lung was affected. I can't remember just how long it lasted, but too long. The doctor said he was going to be awfully weak when the fever had run its course.

Then one day he said there was no use in him coming back any more, that he wasn't doing any good, and was only making a big doctor bill (that was Dr. Eugene Croft). I didn't realize that he was giving him up as a hopeless case, and insisted that he come back. He said that if I wanted him to he would send his brother Charlie, who he considered a better child doctor than himself.[9] The next day doctor Charlie came, in

---

9.   Dr. Marion Eugene Croft (1875–1956), and Dr. Charles C. Croft (1877–1948) sons of
      Larkin C. Croft and Francis Victoria Armstrong.

the afternoon. He sat and looked at the baby for a while, felt his pulse, and listened with his stethoscope, and then asked me where my garbage can was. I told him it was just outside the window, on the downhill side of the house. He raised the window and took all the bottles of medicine we had been using and dropped them into it. He then said, "He'll not be needing these anymore." I asked him if he was going to change the medicine. He said, "My dear, he'll never need any more medicine, he's gone." I couldn't believe it, and told him so. He said that the baby had not breathed, nor had his heart beaten for twenty minutes.

I told him that I thought the baby was just so weak from the fever leaving that he couldn't hear the heart beat. He made me listen with his stethoscope to convince me, and he took a small mirror from his left hip pocket and held it near his mouth. He told me that if he was breathing, the least bit it would fog the mirror. He said that the baby had put up a brave fight, but the fever had just lasted too long, and he was too weak to stand it. He also said that lots of mothers had been forced to give up their children, and he told me of several children who had died of pneumonia that winter. He said that if I would fix a place, that he would straighten him out on the bed. I told him that I'd rather he would leave him in the crib so I could keep it near the stove, as I meant to see if I couldn't get him warm again. He assured me he would never be warm again, for according to all he knew he was dead. I had depended on their judgment, and had done everything just as they had decided, but when I saw that the doctors had given up, I wanted to try my hand.

I was glad for him to go so I could get to work. As he went out through the kitchen he met Mrs. Galloway coming in. I could see them in the mirror of the dresser, saw her ask him how the baby was. He shook his head, and held his hands out. I could see that he was telling her he was gone.

I poured some rubbing alcohol into a pan of hot water, and prepared to start rubbing him. I closed the window that the doctor had advised me to keep open, made a hot fire, and put the baby on a pillow as near to it as I dared, then started rubbing him with my hot wet hands. It was now about sundown, of a short winter day in February. I remember Edgar coming in, and of me asking him if he would join with me in a prayer that the baby would live. He said that if it was best for him to get well he would, and if it was his time to die we would just have to give him up. I told him that the Lord had said, "Ask and it shall be given you," but He didn't promise anything to the ones who didn't ask.[10]

---

10.   Matthew 7:7.

I can't remember much else that happened around me. My interest was centered in getting that little body warm again, and starting up the circulation once more.

There were none of the Elders where I could reach them. Edgar had not been baptized, and was not very much interested in religion, or prayer. Mrs. Galloway went home to get her little ones fed and in bed. Edgar had worked hard all day, and went to sleep. I never halted in my rubbing. I was so near to the hot stove that I was sweating, but Cecil's little body was still as cold as ice all over. I longed for someone with the authority to administer to him. Not wanting to leave a thing undone that might help, I got a small bottle of olive oil, asked the Lord to bless and purify it, and to recognize a mother's anointing and blessing on her child, and to bring him back to life.[11] I promised Him solemnly that if He would do this, that I would dedicate the rest of my life to teaching the Gospel to everyone that I could get to listen to me. I also promised that I would raise this precious child the very best that I could if He would only give him back to me. I promised that any other children I might have, I would raise as nearly right as I could. I'm sure the Lord knew I meant every word of that promise.

I don't remember even considering giving up. I don't remember weeping. I was too busy and too desperate to weep. My whole body and soul was a living, working prayer. Occasionally I put a few drops of stimulant in a spoon of warm milk and poured it in his mouth, and then

---

11. By "someone with authority to administer to him" Effie means someone who holds the Mormon priesthood and thus has authority to anoint her child with consecrated oil and pronounce a special blessing. Current Mormon policy expressly states that "Only Melchizedek Priesthood holders may administer to the sick." See *Melchizedek Priesthood Leadership Handbook*, 13. Effie had tried to summon the Elders to perform this ordinance, since she, as a woman, did not have this authority. When she could not find the Elders or any other member of the priesthood, she went ahead to perform a "mother's anointing" on her own initiative.

While Mormon women are prohibited from performing such an ordinance *by the authority of the priesthood*, it was doctrinally acceptable for a female to administer to the sick *by the power of faith*. Interestingly, on April 28, 1842, Joseph Smith approved of females performing this ordinance: "Respecting females administering for the healing of the sick, he further remarked, there could be no evil in it, if God gave sanction by healing; that there could be no more sin in any female laying hands on and praying for the sick, than in wetting the face with water; it is no sin for anybody to administer that has faith, or if the sick have faith to be healed by their administration." See Joseph Smith, *Teachings of the Prophet Joseph Smith*, compiled by Joseph Fielding Smith (Salt Lake City: Deseret Book, 1979), 224–25. For more on Latter-day Saint women administering to the sick, see Linda King Newell, "The Historical Relationship of Mormon Women and Priesthood," in *Women and Authority: Re-emerging Mormon Feminism*, edited by Maxine Hanks (Salt Lake City: Signature Books, 1992), 23–48. Also. Claudia L. Bushman, "Mystics and Healers," in *Mormon Sisters: Women in Early Utah*, edited by Claudia L. Bushman (Logan: Utah State University Press, 1997), 1–23.

stroked his throat to help him swallow. Hour after hour I rubbed him with the hot water and alcohol. About twelve o'clock it seemed to me that his sides and back felt a little warmer, as if there was life. Mrs. Galloway was sitting loyally and silently by. At twenty minutes after twelve I asked her to listen and see if she could hear heartbeats. She listened intently a minute, and then all excited, she started crying, and said, "Upon my word, that child's heart is actually beating again."

She hurried out and across the road and woke her husband, Robert. He came back with her, sleepy and shivering, knelt down and listened, and with tears running down his cheeks, he said, "Our Sat Boy's a'goin' to live again." I continued rubbing and administering the stimulant till he was breathing regularly. I was afraid to stop for fear his heartbeats might stop again. About dawn, little Mary Galloway came in with some bread and butter in her hands. Cecil opened his eyes, reached out his hand and said, "Bite." That was the first time he had paid any attention to anything in days. It was no trouble for me to cry then, my heart was melting with thanksgiving.[12]

The news had been all over Crofton that Cecil was dead. A few days later Charlie Croft, the doctor who was there when Cecil "died," rode several miles out of his way to come by and see for himself that he was really alive. He was a good man, and was ashamed that he had tried to kill my faith. He said, "The fact that that child is alive is proof that there are still miracles on earth."[13] He quit practicing doctoring shortly after that, and

---

12. In an undated poem entitled "One of Earth's Lessons," in *Poetry Broadcast*, 56, Effie offers her thanks for preserving Cecil from death:

> Peevish cross and fretful, everything gone wrong;
> Tired and impatient, had to work too long;
> Supper dishes over, children tucked in bed;
> Found one precious darling with hot and throbbing head
> Breathing short and catchy, hurting in his chest,
> Held him until daylight, close against my breast.
> Doctor looking serious, "Very stubborn case,"
> Not one ray of hopefulness in his worried face;
> Long dread hours of watching—; heart will surely break;
> "Oh dear Lord in Heaven, save him for my sake."
> One in tender mercy, heard my fervent prayer;
> Days of anguish over, calm instead of care.
> Peace and joy like Heaven, gratitude complete,
> Bitterness and sorrow helped me find the sweet.

13. Many years later, Effie affirmed her own belief in modern-day miracles saying, "One time when Sadie and I were together, one of our neighbors came in and the neighbor says, 'Why don't we have miracles now like they had in the days of the Savior, recorded in the New Testament?' And Sadie looked at me and she says 'Effie, if you and I should put down every miracle that we have experienced with our children, it would be *three* times as many as there is recorded in the New Testament'—and it was true too" (undated recording, ca. 1970. Tape in Noel Carmack's possession).

never took it up again, though I think he was a much better doctor than his brother Eugene. He worked in a drugstore in Crofton for years.

I had tried to teach the Gospel to the Galloway family, and to Hol Boyd, and Rick Worthington, the mill foreman, without a great deal of success. After Cecil's miraculous recovery, however, they showed more interest, and it became a regular thing for us to gather once or twice a week and discuss religion.

Often, after supper, Worthington would come to our place, and when Galloways knew he was there they would come also. Mr. Galloway would poke his head in at the door and say, "What's going on over here, we don't want to miss out on anything." Rick had me order a Bible and a Book of Mormon for him, but the thing he gloried in most was a little reference book. He called it his shotgun, and carried it in his pocket all the time. He delighted in an argument, and usually came out the winner.

Mr. Galloway carried his scriptures more in his head, and was gentle and persuasive. The boys at the mill, who nicknamed everyone, called him "preacher."

Ethell Bagget, the boy who drove Galloway's teams, was an expert on the guitar, and enjoyed playing for our songs. He said he never did "go much on religion," though. They said in McLean county, where he came from, that one Sunday when he was lit up he rode his horse up inside the meeting house, around in front of the pulpit and yelled "glory hallelujah." But we all liked him, and he was always a welcome addition to our little get-togethers.

Hol Boyd was of a devout Baptist family, a good gentle man, rugged and kind, the Abe Lincoln type. I'm sure he believed the Gospel. He was certainly exposed to it a-plenty, whether it took or not.

Speaking of Hol Boyd—he and Bagget wrangled the oxen. They used them to snake the big logs from the steep hillsides. The oxen were slower and more patient than the horses, and would go into all kinds of places. I became quite well acquainted with them, and learned to respect their strength and their dependability (the oxen). One big old fellow, they called him Blue, was a lovable ox, with plenty of sense. One day someone carelessly left an axe lying in the woods, and Blue stepped on it, cutting his right forefoot between the split hoof. It was not a bad cut, but it got infected, and for days he lay in the yard of the ox sheds. He would moan with pain day and night. We could hear him distinctly from the house. When I had time I would take out a bucket of warm salt water, sit by him and bathe it. As soon as he would see Cecil and I coming, he would stop moaning. He would lean his head against me, and be perfectly quiet while we were there. Cecil would rub him, and he seemed to enjoy it. One evening Edgar and Hol didn't come to supper at the regular time. The food was getting cold, when at last they came, walking rather slow. They sat out on some big rocks and didn't talk much. I could hear them blowing their noses, and I knew that poor old Blue had passed away, and they had been dragging him off. They said when working in the timber with him that he had sense, almost like a human. He had good judgment about dragging the logs, or anything he did. Hol said that it was a dirty shame that it couldn't have been old Baldy who had stepped on that axe. *He* was stubborn and mean and always did just the opposite from what they wanted him to do. There were ten or twelve of the oxen, each with dispositions as different as people.

Not long after this they moved the sawmill to a wild, remote canyon, where it looked as if man had never penetrated. Mrs. Galloway and the children went to visit her people, in McLean County, while the mill was being moved. They got our cabin almost finished, and we moved into it before they put the windows in. There was no other building near it yet, and it was lonely, when only Cecil and I were there alone. But the woods were beautiful, and there were long ferns all around the spring, and wild flowers everywhere. The men were hauling hay from somewhere a long way off, and didn't get home till after midnight. There were tales of wild animals in the woods here, and once I heard a noise at the window, and there was a big old dog with his forefeet and head sticking up in the window, looking in at me. I then tacked a blanket over the window, but it would have been poor protection in an emergency. Another night I heard something under the floor, rubbing its back against the boards as it moved around, purring like a giant cat, which I guessed it was, for I heard later that there were plenty of wildcats in that part of the woods.

We had a letter from Sadie saying that they and Mr. and Mrs. Holt were going to Imperial Valley, California, where Mr. Holt's brother, Uncle Judge, was living, so we moved to their place and stayed till they came home about a year later. This was the old Solomon Smith home. Before he owned it, it had belonged to Edgar's mother, who had inherited it. She and Edgar's father were married at this place, and so were we. It was a big old rambling two story house, with an L shaped kitchen and back porch, and a cistern in the back yard. There was a loom room, out in the horse lot, with a big old loom in it in perfect condition, with all the attachments. Elmo's wife, Ivy, was a scientific weaver. She said she would teach me if I wanted her to.

One day, when we were at Edgar's father's house, his old grandmother, Mary Ann Thomason (called Polly Ann, or more often, "Aunt Pop"), was there.[14] I told her of the loom at the old Smith place. I said that if I could get enough rags I would weave a rag carpet. She then said, "Well, you have no excuse, I have a whole barrel of carpet strings, all tacked, colored, and rolled into balls, ready to weave." We took them

---

14. Mary Ann Thomason (b. 1836).

home with us, and Ivy got the loom into working order. I bought the warp, and Ivy helped me to get it all set up, ready to start weaving.

Aunt Pop predicted that I would never get enough woven for a carpet. She said, "Maybe a rug or two." I told her that if there were strings enough, I would weave a carpet. She wanted me to shake hands on it, so I did. So, I was in for a long tedious job, but I learned to enjoy weaving. I was not very swift at first, but I gained speed, with practice, and before Violet was born in 1908, I had it all finished, sewed together, and on the floor. That was the only loom I knew of that had been taken care of, and all its parts intact. I'm so thankful that I had the grit and stick-to-it-iveness to finish it.

Lots of interesting things happened while we lived at the Smith place. Weaving the carpet was the big job, but during the winter months we took two of Sister Dona Boyd's children and kept them for her. She lived in Hopkinsville, and it was hard for her to make ends meet. We had plenty of milk, meat, beans and flour meal.

There was a little sharecropper's cabin near the Smith house. There were several families around who had children. My sister Lelia, the Simmons family, and the Boyd children I was keeping. We decided to have a little Sunday School in the sharecropper's cabin. We met, organized, and appointed officers. Certain ones to get wood for a little heater, others to act as janitors, others to help clean and paper the room. We hunted up all the religious pictures we could find and put them on the walls.[15]

The first Sunday was a happy occasion. All had helped in getting it ready, and we had a happy time together. I'm sure every one who attended still remembers our little meeting house with loving memories. Later, the parents came, and we had an adult class, and ordered Sunday School literature for our lessons. That was the beginning of the Woodland Branch. In all the years that I have attended Sunday school, in the different branches and wards of the church, that little Sunday school, in that dilapidated little old cabin, ranks high in my memory for happiness in worship and for an outpouring from the Spirit of the Lord.[16] We soon organized a branch officially, and Elder Orville [Arvel] Udy from Utah and Elmer E. Brundage from Mesa, Arizona, were sent by President

---

15. According to an entry in the *Liahona*, "Elders J. P. Leseuer and L. R. Abbott baptized three converts at Larkin, in Christian county. Arrangements are being made to organize a Sunday school at that place." See "Kentucky," *Liahona, The Elders' Journal* 5 (April 11, 1908): 1151.

16. In April, 1911, an entry in the *Liahona* stated that "Elders J. L. Molen and J. Robins report one baptism and eight meetings for the week. They also organized a Sunday School at Lark[in], Chester county [Christian county], with Brother J[ohn]. R[obert]. Marquess, superintendent, and Sister Ozie Marquess, secretary and treasurer." "Kentucky," *Liahona, The Elders' Journal* 8 (April 11, 1911): 682.

"This old house had a big playroom upstairs (left)." Old Holt place near Larkin, Kentucky, where the Carmack family lived from about 1921 to 1924. Courtesy of Itha Carmack.

Charles E. Callis to help build a meeting house, which served us for many years, till most of the members moved away.[17]

---

17.    Arvel Ray Udy (1891–1981) served in the Southern States Mission in 1912–1914. Erven Elmer Brundage (1890–1974) served in the Mission in 1912–1914. Charles A. Callis (1865–1947) served as president of the Southern States Mission in 1908–1934. He served as an LDS apostle in 1933–1947. See Jensen, *LDS Biographical Encyclopedia,* 4:380. Mattie Hale Carmack remembered how her husband helped in the effort to build a meetinghouse: "We stayed at our place several years. Finly Tom sold out, but before he sold, he had a lot of nice timber he gave to build a church, so the members helped. The President Calas sent 2 Elders to build the Church." See Mattie Carmack, *My Story,* 76.

The Woodland Branch building was dedicated on April 25, 1915 during the meetings of the Kentucky Conference. "President Callis and Elder Ernest Marti[n?], from Chattanooga, were in attendance. About two hundred saints and friends attended the spirited meetings that were held. Pres. Callis delivered some very powerful sermons. He urged the saints to live their religion and impressed upon them the necessity of keeping the word of wisdom. He told of the broadness of the belief of the Latter-day Saints, wherein those who are called away from this earth without a knowledge or without even hearing the Gospel, would have a chance in the spirit world of accepting it.

All the elders present bore testimony of the divinity of the work in which they are engaged. Many friends were made. On Sunday, the 25th, the new church at Larkin was dedicated by Pres. Callis. After the morning services lunch was served by the kind saints and friends of Larkin. Their kindness will never be forgotten." See "Kentucky," *Liahona, The Elders' Journal* 12 (June 1, 1915): 783.

We moved from the Sol Smith place to Mr. Holt's old home, as they were still in California, and Sadie and Evert were coming back to occupy the Sol Smith home. I remember the day they came; we were still living at the Smith place yet. Cecil had a sore knee, I can't remember now just what was the matter, but he was bashful, and went back in the kitchen and didn't come out to greet them till they kept asking about him, and we hunted him up.

We moved to the Holt place right after that. When I was cleaning out some old newspapers that had been stored on a shelf over the door of the hall, I found an old "Globe Democrat" published in Louisville. I wish I knew the date it was published. In that old newspaper I found an article titled: "An aged man confesses to taking part in the mobbing when Joseph Smith, the Mormon Prophet, and his brother Hyrum were murdered."[18] He said that he was glad that he could say that he didn't fire a shot that entered either of their bodies, but it had tormented him all his life, anyway. He said that the one man called Joseph fell from a window. They propped his body up against a well curb and were going to use it as a target to shoot at, but when he was dying a shaft of bright light came around his face and extended for several feet around him. Members of the mob afterwards said that it was lightning, but all of them knew it was not lightning. They all ran in fright, falling over each other in their haste to get away, "like the guilty criminals we were." He said that all his life he had felt sure that the man they had killed was what he claimed he was—a prophet of God. I do wish I had kept the article, I did keep it for years.[19]

One day, not long after we moved to this old house, I was sewing, making little overalls for Cecil, when Elder Richins asked me to guess who they had just baptized. I had no idea, as I didn't know where they had been laboring. He said that they had just come from Crofton, but I still couldn't guess.[20] Then he told me that the entire Galloway family was baptized, except the little one, who was not old enough. I was so happy that I couldn't keep back the tears. I had not known they had moved back

---

18. Joseph and Hyrum Smith were shot and killed by a mob on June 27, 1844, in Carthage, Illinois.

19. This is the incredible account of the murders of Joseph and Hyrum Smith as told by William M. Daniels and others and has persisted in unofficial Mormon Church publications. See William M. Daniels, *Correct Account of the Murder of Generals Joseph and Hyrum Smith at Carthage on the 27th Day of June 1844* (Nauvoo: John Taylor, 1845), and N. B. Lundwall, comp., *The Fate of the Persecutors of the Prophet Joseph Smith* (Salt Lake City: Bookcraft, 1952), 226–33.

20. Wellington B. Richins (1887–1967) served in the Southern States Mission in 1906–1909. Interestingly, the *Liahona* reported that Richins and N. M. Stewart "made many new friends in Christian County" during the month of February 1909. "Kentucky," *Liahona, The Elders' Journal* 6 (March 20, 1909): 977.

to Crofton. I knew they would be good Latter-day Saints, since they were already good people without it. The years since have proved their genuineness. I heard much later that Guy, one of the boys, grown and now married, was Superintendent of Sunday School in Madisonville, the county seat just north of us in Hopkins County. Mary, the oldest girl, had married Welby Ray, who accepted her religion and had been made District President of the Western Kentucky Conference, an important position.[21] This all made me very happy, to know the family had stayed active in Church work. Once, when I visited Hopkinsville, where Lelia and her children lived, when our Church was having Conference there, Mary and Welby came. I was so glad to see them, and to know of their good work in the Church.[22]

When Holts were coming home from California, we moved to the little house on the hillside between Mr. Holt's big barn and the red house. I was expecting my second child. Cecil was four years old. I stayed busy trying to get several things accomplished before time for the baby to arrive. I canned and dried apples, sewed the long strips of carpet together to fit the living room of the little house, and put it down. It was cozy and pretty, made of bright colors. I looked forward to telling Sadie "I wove a carpet."

I had decided to be old fashioned in another line. I raised ducks, so I could have feathers enough to make all the pillows I needed. I had very good luck with the duck eggs hatching, and I raised thirty-six. They were all full feathered and just about ready to pick, when one morning about daylight, I kept hearing a strange noise and got up to see what it was. Mr. Shelton's hogs were out of their pen, and were running at large, and were eating my ducks. The hogs were just grabbing and gobbling right and left, with ducks legs and heads hanging out of the sides of their mouths; soon not even the legs and heads were left. Only one duck escaped. I gave that one to Mrs. Shelton, the owner of the hogs, as she kept ducks, too.[23]

When Violet was born I was happy that she was a little girl. It was in September, and getting cool, and the new carpet gave warmth to the room.

---

21. Welby Ray is unrecorded in mission manuscript sources. He possibly served in the Southern States Mission in 1906.

22. Evidently, Hopkinsville, because of its centralized location, was headquarters of the Kentucky Conference. For example, in 1907, the *Liahona* reported "A well attended conference was held at Hopkinsville, Christian county. Three public meetings were held and the Gospel plan explained to the people. Much good, we hope will result from this conference. The people who attended expressed themselves as being well pleased and the elders returned to their fields of labor with renewed determination to press on in the Lord's work. They are all in good health." See "Kentucky," *Liahona, The Elders' Journal* 5 (August 24, 1907): 279.

23. These hogs were probably owned by George S. Shelton (1857–1936) and his wife Lula E. (1872–1961).

There was a good fireplace in the room also, and I enjoyed it. I had had a class of girls through the summer that needed to brush up on some of their schoolwork—Bernice Pollard, Vera (my niece), Carrie, Edgar's sister, and Lilian Hamby.[24] We had a pleasant time, and I learned as much as they did.

Mr. Holt's folks had moved back to their old place, and Ozie came and helped me out when Violet was tiny. She was a beautiful auburn haired baby, good, healthy, and never any trouble. I had an abundance of milk for her, and she thrived. At first I kept her wrapped too much, and nearly smothered her till Lelia came and made me take some of the blankets off. I was proud of my two sweet children. Cecil, now four years old, had a perfect little body, and was an ideal child, well behaved and obedient. He was like a little man, very proud of the baby when she came, and wanted to help take care of her. He was my little helper, anxious to do anything he could.

Cecil had one quality that worried me a little, though. He was not the least afraid of snakes or worms, or anything else much. I had a garden down by an old barn in the meadow, and one day when I went for some vegetables and Cecil was with me, (he was about three), I noticed him squatted at one corner of the barn very interested in something. In a few minutes he came over to me carrying a little snake about a foot long, on a real short stick which was only about three inches long. The snake was wrapped around it once, with its head sticking up, and its tail hanging down. Cecil said, "Look, mama, isn't this a cute little bull snake?" I was horrified. It looked like a poison snake to me, thick and short, but I didn't take time to examine it to see what kind it was, I knocked it as far as I could send it. He was sorry for me to be so brutal with his little snake. He said that it wouldn't hurt anybody. I gave him a good serious lecture: How even a little rattlesnake or a copperhead could bite you and it might kill you, that snakes were not good things to play with, and he must never touch them. I wonder if Cecil still remembers that. At this writing, 1968, it has been sixty years ago.

When Violet was six or seven months old, she developed a habit of vomiting her milk up a little while after she took it. She didn't seem sick, it just came back up.

## 1909[25]

I remember that she weighed seventeen pounds, a normal weight for a baby her age. Several older mothers said that I needn't be worried about it, that lots of babies did that, but it continued, and she didn't gain weight. I tried all the simple remedies that were recommended, but she

---

24. Bernice Rena Pollard (b. 1894) married Clarence Vernon Walker (b. 1890) in 1916.
25. This date is written by hand at the top of the page.

continued to throw up her milk. About this time we moved to a place near Mt. Zoar, next to the Joel Boyd place. The missionaries came to our place quite often here. President Thomas E. Secrist and Elder Alvin Thorup were the two that I remember best.[26] Elder Thorup was one of the handsomest men I ever saw, very blond, with red cheeks and curly hair, and perfect features.

President Secrist said that Violet (now about 8 months old) was the smartest child of her age that he ever saw, and he had three of his own. He was there one day when I went to the garden for something, and she awoke and wanted to go with me. She didn't cry, and she didn't fall out at the front door, she turned around and climbed carefully down the steps and started crawling across the old rough yard. There was a maple tree in the yard, and the roots protruded. Violet's little apron hung up on one of the roots as she crawled by. President Secrist said that she didn't cry and pull, as most babies would do, she just backed up, unhooked her apron from the root, and continued on her journey with the rough rocky ground scratching her tender little knees. She really was a choice spirit, and the after years have proved it.

Though Violet didn't gain weight at this time, she seemed well, and her mind developed. Finally, after she was over a year old and still weighed only seventeen pounds, I tried browning some buttermilk biscuits real brown, and soaking them in postum, with a little milk and honey in it and fed it to her. She was able to hold this down, and began to gain weight. After that, most anything agreed with her. Violet helped me to raise the other children who were born in the years following. She and Cecil both were a joy to me, and a help and a mainstay during a busy and hectic life.

When Violet was three years old, Noel was born.[27] I chose Noel for a name because I was expecting him at Christmas time, but he delayed his coming till January 11th. He was as big as a calf, and was born during a terrible siege of weather. The rain, sleet and snow froze on the trees and broke them down. There was no way to get to town. Telephone lines were down, and the roads were filled with broken trees. I had meant to have old Dr. Moore, who lived not far from us, but he had pneumonia, so Lelia and Sadie had to be doctors, nurses and midwives. It was a prolonged labor, from Saturday to Monday about 1 P.M. Sunday night and Monday morning was a horrible nightmare, but I was finally rewarded by a big

26. Thomas Edwin Secrist (1872–1942) served in the Southern States Mission in 1908. He was appointed president of the Kentucky Conference on July 3, 1908. Alvin Theobald Thorup (1888–1956) served in the Mission in 1908–1910. He was appointed president of the Kentucky Conference on September 5, 1909.

27. Noel Evans Carmack (1911–1980) was Effie's second son.

fine healthy baby. I was so thankful that he was all right, but the long siege had been hard on him too. His head was out of shape, and his face was swollen. Lelia said that he looked like Sitting Bull, but I thought he was beautiful, and didn't appreciate her verdict.

Noel had a close call when he was still very young. There came a clear morning after a stormy spell, so I hung some blankets out in the sun. In the afternoon it clouded up and looked like it might rain. Noel was asleep on the bed. One of Edgar's little sisters brought the blankets in and threw them on the bed, right on top of him, then ran back for the rest of the things from the clothes line. When I came in and saw that pile of blankets on my baby I grabbed them off. He was nearly smothered to death. He was white and wet with sweat. I rocked him and cried, and thanked the Lord that I had come in the house in time.

We were getting ready to go to Utah while waiting for Noel's arrival. We knew that it would be colder in the Salt Lake Valley than in Kentucky, so we had to get warm coats, etc. Now I had three beautiful children, and enjoyed making pretty clothes for them. At that time little girls were wearing long-waisted dresses, and I made new ones for Violet. I embroidered a linen one, and put tucks and lace on the front of a white one.

At last we were ready to start for Utah. I hated to leave the little Woodland Branch, my folks, and the Simmons family, who we had learned to love like our own.

Someone suggested that I get a bottle of Paregoric, or Mrs. "Somebody's" soothing syrup for the baby, while we would be riding on the train. I didn't want to do it, but others argued that three days of medicine wouldn't hurt him, and would make it so much better on the train, as other passengers resented a crying baby when they wanted to sleep. I can't remember what I did get, but it was something to quiet the baby's nerves, and it worked. At home I was used to making catnip tea, but it would have been awkward on the train. I never gave him any more after we landed, and I never gave it to any of my other children, either. That was only for an emergency.

We had had several Missionaries from Holladay, Utah, in Kentucky on missions. Elder John Wayman, who was sick at our place for quite a while, and Elder Sorensen.[28]

Elder Hand lived in Salt Lake, also Elder Alvin Thorup; President Price, from East Mill Creek, and others we knew. Elder Wayman had written us to come to his place and stay till we could get located, and we

---

28.  John Henry Wayman (1867–1959) entered the Southern States Mission on April 25, 1910 but had to return home on November 1, due to illness. Alden Conrad Sorensen (b. 1896) served in the Mission in 1919–1921.

Effie holding Violet and infant Noel, ca. 1912,
probably taken at the same time as the photo of the
children with Aunt Ivy mentioned in the text.
Courtesy of Itha Carmack.

did. They had a nice family. Sister Wayman was a good wife and mother,
and was kind to me and made us welcome. We were not long in finding
a place to live, however, and Edgar found work. Autie was with us, and
Elmo and Ivy came later, and it was good to have them.

Aunt Ivy, Elmo's wife, wanted a picture of Violet and Noel taken
with her. The photographer thought Noel had such a perfect body he
would take a nice picture without his clothes on. This nice photograph of
the three of them was made after we landed in Utah.[29]

We got milk from Brother Wagstaff, who lived at the end of the
driveway that led to the highway.[30]

---

29. This picture is extant but not included in this edition. However, the photo on page 259
of Effie and the two children was probably taken at the same sitting.
30. Probably William or Arthur Wagstaff of Holladay.

We did our trading at the Goodwill Store in Murray (later Penney's), and went to the Happy Hour Theatre. We also traded at Neilson's Grocery, near us. Their son, Ernest, who had just returned from a mission, delivered the groceries.[31] I enjoyed talking to him. Sometimes we went to Sugarhouse to do some of our trading. I could go to Salt Lake on the street car, but it always made Violet car sick. It was a great disappointment to both of us; she wanted so much to go with me, and I wanted her to go, too. The driver would take her up in front and let her look down the highway, thinking maybe that would keep her from being sick. She tried to use Christian Science, and would declare that she wasn't sick this time, till she would be as white as a sheet—so we just finally had to give it up. Mable Johnson would keep the children, and I would go alone.

I remember the first big Conference we went to in the Tabernacle.[32] I guess Mable kept Violet and Noel, and I don't believe Edgar was with us, either. I think he was away at work. Cecil and I sat in the balcony. We had a good place where we could see and hear real well. It was a thrill to us to see the Twelve Apostles sitting up in front, and we could pick out the leaders that we knew from their pictures: B. H. Roberts, Reed Smoot, President Joseph Fielding Smith, Anthon H. Lund, John R. Winder, and many others.[33]

The great organ started playing, and it was almost more than Cecil and I could stand. It moved us both to tears. Cecil said, "Mama, your cheeks are wet." Then he put his hands to his face and said, "Mine are, too." It was a wonderful day for us, a dream come true. I can't remember the speakers now, but I do remember the spirit of the meetings.

A funny thing happened the first Sunday I took Violet to Sunday School in the Holladay Ward. When they passed the sacrament bread, Violet said, out loud, "I want mine buttered."[34] I whispered, "No, we don't have butter on this bread." She pointed up to the bookcase and

---

31. Ernest James Neilson (1885–1948), son of James and Camilla Neilson.

32. The historic meeting hall built by the pioneers in Salt Lake City, formally dedicated in 1875.

33. Under the First Presidency, the Twelve Apostles are the governing body of the Mormon Church. Among the leaders Effie could identify were Brigham Henry Roberts (1857–1933), a well known LDS author and editor. He was elected to House of Representatives in 1898 but did not serve his term; Reed Smoot (1862–1941) served as an LDS apostle in 1900–1941. He also served as a United States senator in 1903–1932; Joseph Fielding Smith (1876–1972) was tenth president of the LDS Church, serving in 1970–1972; Anthon H. Lund (1844–1918) served as an LDS apostle in 1889–1901; and John R. Winder (1821–1910), who served as first counselor to the president of the LDS Church in 1901–1910.

34. Mormons take broken bread as a weekly communion (or "sacrament") observance.

Carmack family portrait taken in Utah, 1912. Clockwise from left: Effie, Cecil, Edgar, Noel on his father's lap, Violet. Courtesy of Itha Carmack.

said, "There's the cupboard." One would think she had never had the sacrament, but she had, as we had gone to Sunday school regularly in the Woodland Branch. However, I had missed many Sundays, just before Noel was born, and afterward, too. Her remarks created a laugh that spoiled the quietness of the sacrament, but they were good children in Church, and I had no trouble with them.

We moved to a fruit farm belonging to a Brother McDonald.[35] His son, Howard, then about seventeen, was later President of the Brigham Young University, and I think he is now President of the Salt Lake Temple.[36] Anyway, Howard and I picked black currants together, and irrigated the garden, and were good friends.

One day, while we were at work in the garden, I missed Violet. I called and called and looked for her. They had just turned a lot of water into the irrigation ditch, and my heart just stopped when I thought that she might have fallen into it. There was a storeroom back of the house, and I noticed the door was open a tiny bit. I looked in, and Violet was sitting with a crock of raw oatmeal (her favorite food) between her knees, eating it in spite of the fact that it was filled with worms. I was so glad to find her that I didn't even mind the worms.

Elmo and Ivy stayed with us at McDonald's place for a while, and Ivy worked for a gardener, picking beans. In the evening, when it was time to quit work, Violet would say, "It's time o'clock, Aunt Ivy is coming," and would walk down the driveway to meet her.

We lived at the foot of Twin Peaks, in the Holladay Ward, at the end of the street car line. Brother Larsen was Bishop of the Ward at that time.[37] It was over a mile to the Meeting House, but I walked it, and carried Noel, and took Cecil and Violet to Sunday School every Sunday. Noel was a load too, but I was young and strong, and I didn't mind.

We lived near the Fred Allingtons and their two daughters, Violet and Bernice.[38] They came to our place often. Also the Johnsons (Mrs. Johnson was Mrs. Allington's sister) lived near us. The Johnson girls, Mable and Esther, took care of my children when it was necessary.

Johnsons' kitchen was much lower than the dining room. They said that it was built in the dry canal that was used to float granite blocks from the quarry in Little Cottonwood Canyon to the Temple block, when the Temple was being built. The granite mountain is the same one where the Genealogical Vault now is located.[39]

---

35. Francis McDonald (1851–1920) was an established farmer in Holladay. His wife was Rozella Stevenson.

36. Edward Howard Stevenson McDonald (1894–1986) served as President of Brigham Young University in 1945–1949.

37. Joseph Y. Larsen (1865–1955) was first Bishop of the Holladay Ward, serving in 1911–1921.

38. Frederick Mosedale Allington (1869–1953) was married to Emma Johanna Swaner (1872–1943). Their daughters were Violet Louise Allington (1894–1947) and Bernice Rebecca Allington (1896–1975). Violet married Charles Autie Marquess, Effie's youngest brother.

39. Construction on the Granite Mountain Records Vault, located in Cottonwood Canyon, Utah, was begun in 1960 and completed in 1964. It is used as a perpetual microfilm storage facility for LDS genealogical records.

Someone gave Violet a bright little collar pin fashioned like a but-terfly. One of the Allington girls asked her what it was, and [she] said it was a "gallinipper." I think that is another name for a dragonfly that was common in Kentucky.[40] The girls got a great kick out of it, and never for-got it.

My brother Autie, who lived with us, and Violet Allington later mar-ried and had a family of girls. Their first baby—named Lorenzo, was a boy, but did not live.

Autie and a young returned missionary (Floyd something or other) sang together for many programs. I remember them singing "Alexander's Ragtime Band." It was new then, and they made a hit with it—both of them were good singers. Mr. and Mrs. Allington went to the World's Fair in Seattle and brought back some new songs. All of the Allingtons were good singers, and first time I heard "Aloha," Autie and Violet sang it.

Edgar was working for Brother Joseph Andrus at Park City, where he owned land and raised hay.[41] He and his wife, Rett, went with them, and she cooked for the men. (They afterward became our beloved friends.) Later we moved to an old dobie house that had been built in the early days.[42]

Edgar helped the Andrus men dig a ditch to bring water from a stream in a canyon. It took longer to dig it than they had calculated, and the last week or two they were up there, all the food they had left was white bread, bacon and some potatoes.

When they had finished and started home, (the men were all stand-ing in the back of a pickup) it started to rain, and a cold wind was blow-ing. The men were wet and cold, and not long after they got home, Edgar took inflammatory rheumatism.

The doctor from Murray gave him a lot of tablets to sweat the rheumatism out of him (probably aspirin). At that time I had very little knowledge or judgment of my own about drugs, and I had confidence in the doctor's judgment, so I poured the sweating tablets to him according to directions, and it probably ruined his heart.

That winter, I think it was the winter of 1911–1912, has some unpleasant memories (with pleasant ones mixed in). Edgar got sick the first of October, and outside of about a week in January, when he got up and then had a relapse, he didn't walk any at all till March, about six months, and he didn't want anyone to do anything for him but me,

---

40. Standard dictionaries list "gallinipper" as a word of unknown origin meaning a large insect, especially a stinging insect.
41. Joseph Andrus (b. 1868?).
42. "Dobie" is the common useage of the word adobe.

although there were many who offered. Joseph Andrus came daily and would help me with the work, or anything he could do.

Towards the last of that winter it was getting time to wean Noel. I was still giving an unusual amount of milk, and when I weaned him, the milk would not dry up. I had breast pumps, and did all the usual things, but finally my breasts were both caked, and causing me terrible pain. I had a hot fever, and for one whole day I didn't know a thing. Friends sent for a doctor, and he said that he would either have to lance my breasts in several places or put plasters on them that would ruin my milk supply.[43] The plasters were chosen over the lancing, and as a result I didn't have milk for any of my last five children.

There was a small irrigation ditch just south of the house. One day when I was busy (this was in the fall while Noel was still crawling), Noel crawled out the back door (there was snow and ice on the ground) and fell into a hole I had just chopped in the ditch to get wash water from. As soon as I missed him I ran out, and he was just coming to the top of the water, after having sunk to the bottom. Of course I stripped him of his wet clothes and wrapped him in a warm blanket, and he suffered no ill effects from it.

Another very unpleasant thing happened about this time. Cecil was walking to school, and there were several boys larger than he was, who just made his life miserable on the way home from school. They would hit him in the face with pine limbs, and kicked him in the seat till it was black and blue. Joseph Andrus advised me not to raise a row about it, that I would only get the reputation of being a busybody. I didn't care what anyone thought—he was only a little boy and they were great big, and he was very outnumbered—so I went up to the road and waited till they came along. I think I succeeded in making them a little afraid to bother Cecil any more. I have often wondered what kind of men they grew up to be.

Finally that long snowy winter passed. The snow stayed on the ground all winter long, Edgar recuperated, except now his heart was damaged, and the doctor said that we would have to go where the altitude was lower, or he would not live long. We moved away for the summer to a fruit farm belonging to a Mrs. Burnett, near Elizabeth Allington, whose husband was in England on a mission. Elizabeth worked hard trying to earn money to send to him and still have enough for her family. It seemed to me that she had to work too hard, but she was independent and would not accept help.

Mrs. Burnett had a piano, and gave me permission to practice on it, which I did. I had such a desire to play that it was painful. I got along very well, but when we left there I had no piano to continue my practice.

---

43.   Plasters are pastelike mixtures applied to a part of the body for healing purposes.

I remember one hallowed evening when we lived at this place. Edgar, Cecil, and Noel didn't go to Sacrament Meeting in the evening that special Sunday, and Violet and I walked and went. As we came home we took our time, walked slowly and talked. She was about four, but could understand big things. I can't remember our conversation, but I remember the sweet feeling of togetherness, and how we both enjoyed our walk. We had not had many quiet talks together for some time. I had been working hard picking and packing fruit, and at night the housework was to be done, and I was tired at bedtime. I'm sure that most of us fail to take the time to have quiet, serious talks with our children—talks they can enjoy, and will remember.

I hated terribly to leave Utah, but at the end of that summer we went back to Kentucky. The thought of seeing our loved ones again was pleasant to look forward to, but the change was even worse than I had pictured it to be. I was used to eating lots of fruit and vegetables, and not very much meat. When we got to Kentucky they were just killing their first hogs for the winter, and fresh greasy pork made up a great part of our food. I scratched around among the leaves in the orchard, under the apple trees, hoping to find some stray apples, but they were all gone.

I soon got sick. First I had a terrible cold which would not clear up. I remember doing the family washing and hanging the clothes around the fireplace to dry, and I had such a fever and headache that my brain was not clear. I finally had to go to bed, and Edgar's little sister, Myrtle, came to help him with the housework and take care of the children.[44] Noel was still almost a baby, just starting to wear little pants and rompers. It was a cold winter, and there was snow on the ground.

Ozie came and asked me where Noel was. I didn't know. Myrtle had let him go to the toilet outside, and soon he came plowing through the snow. He had fallen down, and the back of his panties were hanging down, and were full of snow, but he wasn't crying—just making the best of it. Ozie asked him, "What were you doing out there in that snow?" He answered, "I feezin' out there." She never forgot it.

I had a cover on the mantel with geese on it. Noel had never seen geese, but there had been pigeons at Burnetts' place in Utah. When he first saw the geese, he said, "Well, a pigeon," with a funny drawn out accent. Ozie could mimic it exactly; she was a child lover, and was a great help to me while I was not feeling well.

Cecil was past eight now, and big enough to help me a lot. No one realized how sick I was, and that was one time I almost felt sorry for

---

44. Myrtle Ilene Carmack (1899–1960) was Edgar's fourth half sister, born to Thomas Green Carmack (1864–1946) and his second wife, Mattie Olivia Hale (1873–1961).

myself, which is not a good thing. (I can't remember Lelia or Sadie coming at all.) Edgar would eat and go to work and not even come in to see how I felt. I had always been so independent that they all thought that I could take care of myself, I guess, under any circumstances.

## 1913

Grace was born the first of March, and at that time I had not realized that my milk supply had been ruined for good, so kept trying to nurse her.[45] But my milk only made her sick, so that she cried all the time.

Bernice Pollard came to help me, and was a comfort. Finally one day Lelia came and said that she was sure Grace was crying because she was hungry. She got a bottle and fixed some warm milk, and that solved the problem.

While Grace was tiny, my stepmother, Miss Serena came and stayed for two weeks—the first time I had seen her since my father died. She held Grace on her knee and looked at her a while and then said, "Effie, this little thing looks like she has had years of experience." She did have a wise little face, and she had had some sad experiences, too.

My stepmother said that she had a confession to make to me, that in all her years she had never had anyone who did as much for her as I did, not even her niece she had raised, or any of her sisters, and she knew that sometimes she didn't seem to appreciate it. I think it was good for her to confess that, as it was the truth, and I was glad to hear her acknowledge it.

When Grace was a little over a year old Hazel was born, an easy birth, as Grace's had been.[46] I was alone, as Edgar had gone to call Sadie. Hazel didn't look at all like Grace, they were both pretty babies, but different. Again I tried to nurse Hazel, with the same results, only she suffered in silence, and didn't cry. Elmo came one day, and as soon as he entered the door he said, "Effie, that baby looks hungry." So, again we tried the bottle, and things were better. But I didn't want to have two babies on the bottle at the same time, so I weaned Grace from hers. It makes me feel so sad, even today, when I think of how she missed it. When I would fix a bottle for Hazel, Grace knew that she wasn't supposed to take it, but she would put her cheek against it lovingly. I still wish that I had let her keep her bottle.

---

45. Grace Carmack (1913–1984) was Effie's fourth child. She married Manson John Bushman on June 21, 1933.

46. Hazel Marguerite Carmack (b. 1914) is Effie's fifth child. She married Donald William Bruchman (1915–1962) on September 23, 1938. She had twins (Dona and Linda) from this marriage. She is now married to Manson John Bushman (b. 1912), Grace's widowed husband.

When Hazel came, Violet said, "Mama, can I have Grace now?" I said, "You surely can." Violet just about took over, too, even if she was only about six.

I was still not very strong, and had a cough. The washings were almost more than I could do. Now there were five children, and it took a lot of clothes. In the summertime it was not so bad. I made little one-piece garments for Grace and Hazel, after they were big enough to walk. At night I would give them a bath and put on a clean garment to sleep in, and then in the morning I would put a clean apron on over it. They lapped over in the back, so there was no necessity for buttoning and unbuttoning. I had to learn to save time and labor. One day Dr. Lovan was passing our place, had car trouble, and came in for something. He saw that I was not well, and told Edgar that he had better get someone to do the work, as he was sure that I wasn't able to do it. He also asked Edgar what there was that I could do that did not require manual labor, something I would enjoy doing. Edgar said that he guessed there were lots of things that I would like to do if I had time, like writing, or painting. Dr. Lovan told him that he had better let me do it, as it would be far better to have a mother doing easy things I enjoyed than not to have any mother at all.

Edgar told the Doctor that he could do the washings easy, but after just one attempt, he hired a negro woman to come and do it, and she did a good job of it.[47] Then he got Lola Jones to come and stay and help with the housework.[48] Lola was a great help and did the work well. I enjoyed making her some pretty dresses, which she appreciated very much. Her younger sister Gertrude (Gertie) stayed with Sadie, and their older sister Annie (a beautiful girl) married Fred Daniel.

While Lola was with us I first started painting. Oh, I had done lots of little things. I knew that I could paint, if only I had the time and the material. Bernice still came occasionally to help me, and we dabbled with water colors, and enjoyed it. She had taken art in High School, and gave me some pointers, and Bernice Allington, in Utah, had also given me a tip or two.

---

47. Edgar's course of action is not surprising since the housework on a tobacco farm was seldom a man's chosen duty. Nora Miller explained that "The woman does the housework with the help of the girls, cares for the children, feeds the chickens, milks and feeds the cow, hoes the garden, and helps with the field work. She begins the day at daybreak during the summer and about five-thirty in the morning during the winter months. Her work day ends at about eight o'clock at night and she has little rest between the beginning and the end." See Nora Miller, "The Tobacco Farm Family," chap. 6 in *The Girl in the Rural Family,* 59.

48. Probably Lula Jones (b. 1896).

I awoke one night strangling, and when I coughed it up, it was hard clots of cold blood, a lot of them. Edgar heard me coughing, and came in and saw it, nearly fainted, and had to lie down. After that I continued to spit up blood when I would cough. I didn't feel so very bad, even though I was thin and weak. I would get the children ready for Sunday school on Sunday mornings, and Edgar would take them in the buggy. I would stay and straighten up the house, and then walk to Sunday School. I can remember the effort of walking up the hill from the red house. I would spit red blood all along the path. I was sorry when I got so I couldn't sing.

After Bernice was born, when Hazel was a little over a year old, I began to get better.[49] I was interested in painting, and enjoyed it, and was surprised that it was so easy for me, and I tackled hard subjects. I painted a picture of Hazel asleep on a window seat and one of Grace sitting in a little rocker with Ducker, a little white dog in her lap. It was easy to recognize who they were. I wish that I had kept them. Years later, after we had been in Arizona a long time, I went back to Kentucky, and I was astonished to see many of the water colors that I had done in the homes of friends and kinfolks. They were about as good as the oil colors that I did later.

Cecil was old enough now to work, and I felt real sad for him to stay out of school to help in the fields, but he managed to keep up with his classes. He was a good student, and his teachers were good to help him.

It was about this time that Cecil was harrowing some ground with a mean old mare that we called Wild Sal, hitched to the harrow. I heard a noise and ran out into the yard where I could see him. That crazy old horse was running with the harrow, and it struck a big root in the ground and stopped them short. Cecil fell flat on his back. I could see them clearly from where I stood. Sadie was in the house and could see me. The old mare reared up on her hind feet and came straight towards Cecil as he fell, and her two front feet hit directly on his chest. Sadie said that I knelt down with my hands clasped over my head and cried, "Oh, Lord, save him, I know you can do it," and He did: the print of the horse's feet were on his chest, but he was not hurt at all, and never suffered any bad after effects from it. I was humbly grateful, and made some serious promises for the goodness of the Lord to us.

Noel was getting almost old enough to go to school, and I taught him to read before he started. We had a good time learning the phonics, which had been discontinued in the schools, but I had some of Cecil's first books. We learned the sounds of the letters, and laid a good foundation for his learning. Noel has always had a good memory, and did not forget things once he had learned them.

---

49.  Lenora Bernice Carmack (1915–1950) was Effie's sixth child.

Grace, Hazel, and Bernice were all born at the red bungalow, and were all babies at the same time, only a little over a year apart. When Hazel was big enough to sit up in the high chair, and Grace was not yet two years old, she was sitting in the high chair in front of the fireplace one day, and Grace climbed up on the front of the chair to give her a toy, and the chair turned over right into the fire. Although Grace was just a baby herself, she pulled the chair back, and put the fire out where Hazel's clothing had caught, and was starting to burn. Grace burned her little hands so that there were blisters all over them later, but she didn't cry. She stood with her hands hidden behind her and didn't even whimper. When I found how badly they were burned, I was so sorry for her, and held them in cold water and rocked her. She was such a good sweet child. It was a miracle that Hazel was not burned badly. I could never figure out how she escaped it, as she had fallen right into the fireplace.

About this time Santa brought Grace a bisque headed doll. She was so proud of it, but before the day was over she dropped it on the hearth and broke it. She was just grief stricken, and went and stood looking out the window, and in a choked voice she said, "Santa Claus ought to be ashamed of hisself to bring a little girl like me a break doll." I promised her that I would get her another one the next time I went to town.

Our children did not have toys all through the year like the children have now, and the Christmas doll meant a lot to her. Nowadays, Christmas isn't very different from other days, but at that time it was really a red letter day.

I don't believe there were ever three babies who were less trouble than Grace, Hazel and Bernice. Grace cried the first two weeks after she was born because she was hungry, and I didn't realize it, but she hardly ever cried at all after we began to feed her. Hazel was not a crybaby, and although Bernice didn't walk or talk till she was nearly four, she was a good baby, really too good. I had been sick all the year before poor little Bernice was born, and she was born with a weak constitution. The day she was born she nearly strangled to death, and had a hard time getting started. When she was two or three years old she would just sit patiently in her high chair. I think my brother Autie's wife helped her learn to walk. They came to visit us, and she walked her daily all over the place, and didn't give up. I got her a walker that helped after Aunt Violet had to leave.

David was born, and was walking and talking before Bernice ever did.[50] He was a sturdy, healthy baby. I seemed to have regained my health,

---

50. David Edgar Carmack (1917–1952), Effie's seventh child, married Sybil Lee on June 30, 1938.

and from then on seemed free from any lung trouble. I had hunted religiously for everything I could find that was recommended for my ailment. I took cod liver oil, and olive oil, tried to eat what I should, and tried to prevent colds. I started working again, hard work. Lola Jones, the girl who had helped me, married and left.

David, poor little darling, never had a chance to be spoiled: Bernice was still like a baby.

Mr. Buck, Mrs. Simmons' father, who lived with the Simmonses, would come by our place on his way to the mailbox, and would make rhymes about the children:

"Old Sadie Grace forgot to wash her face."
"Hazel Marguerite, gentle, good and sweet."
To Bernice, he would always say, "Hello there, best child in the
    world."

Later, when David was big enough to go with the boys to work, he was riding on a load of hay, and it fell off, and he was under it. Mr. Buck said, "What did you do when you found that you had a load of hay on top of you, David?" Dave answered, "I just come a crawlin' out from under the hays." Mr. Buck thought that was awfully funny, and repeated it often.

All three of my little girls were born when I was not very strong. I was alone when Grace arrived. Edgar had gone for Sadie. I came very near to being alone when Hazel was born, but Ivy came in the door just at the right moment. Grace and Hazel were both quick and easy births. Bernice's was not so easy. It was partly my attitude, I guess. I was dreading it and was afraid, something I had never felt before. By the time Dave was born my health was better, and we were happy over a big healthy boy after three little girls. David was a lively one. He would throw his bottle off the bed when he had finished his milk. He broke so many bottles that I finally put a thick blanket by his bed to save them.

It was quite a job keeping fresh milk for just one baby. I had no ice box, not even a cooler, and of course no ice out in the country. Many people did put up ice in the winter, made crude ice boxes and kept ice nearly all summer, but we didn't.

All three little girls were born in the springtime, so early in the morning, as soon as the cows were milked, I fixed bottles enough to last all day. I then put them in a bucket and let them down into the well. When it came feeding time I would draw the bucket up, take out a bottle of milk and return the others to the well to keep cool. In this way I kept their milk cool and sweet all day.

However, I did let them have pacifiers, and when there was not a pacifier handy, an old discarded nipple was scrubbed, and it answered the same purpose. They had to have them to go to sleep on. I have gone out into the yard at night with a lantern, searching for a nipple for a baby to go sleep with. I have said, when I had three or four babies at the same time, that if I had one wish, it would be for a barrel of good clean nipples. Some finicky people were always telling me that I should not let them have a nipple or a pacifier, that it was not very healthy. I told them that it wasn't very healthy for a mother to try to get along without them, either. I tried to keep my children healthy, and tried hard to have the food they needed. I have never noticed any bad effects from a pacifier. No teeth out of shape; now, 1968, (they are all middle-aged women) there has never been any trouble with any of them that I could lay to a pacifier.

Oh, the comfort, when a little one was cross, and didn't want to go to sleep. A pacifier was just what the name implies: they made life smoother for everybody concerned. For over seven years I was not without a baby on a bottle.

They were all good children, and I enjoyed teaching them. We have official "home night" now, but then we had a home night more than once a week.[51] Edgar worked away from home most of the time, and left the farm work for the children to do. It was too big a job for children, and they would beg me to go help them, and then they would help me at home. Instead of taking the long rows of tobacco to hoe the weeds out of, or to find the worms and pull the green suckers off, we would mark off little squares and work it, with short rows, and we would sing while we worked.

Noel could never work in the green tobacco, it made him sick. He was not the least bit lazy, and did a man's work when he was only eight years old, wrestling a big old plow, with two contrary old mules to it. It was entirely too big a task for an eight year old boy.

We were great movers, and moved again to the little house below the Holt place, near an old maid, Miss Betty Daniel.[52] She lived out in the woods not far from us.

Mrs. Simmons (whose children were main characters in our little Sunday school in the cabin) proceeded to give me some good advice when we moved. She said, "You are always trying to convert your neighbors, but I would advise you not to waste your precious time on Miss Betty. She's set in her ways, and you couldn't convert her in a thousand years."

The Simmons family and her two other children by a previous marriage had all been converted, all but Mr. Simmons. He liked it at first, but

---

51. Among Mormons, "Family Home Evening" is officially designated as Monday evening at the present time; the First Presidency had urged a weekly "Family Night" as early as 1915. See Ludlow, ed., *Encyclopedia of Mormonism* (New York: Macmillan Publishing Company: 1992), s.v. "Family Home Evening."

52. Probably Betty Daniel (b. 1857).

when the rest of the family became interested, he turned the other way, and caused them lots of trouble. Mrs. Simmons and I were bosom friends, and spent many happy hours together. It was a joy to us when she and her children were all baptized. They helped with building the new church, and were staunch members of the Branch when it was organized. She warned me solemnly against wasting any time with Miss Betty. She told us that Miss Betty had said, "The old Mormons can build their old meeting house in my door yard, but I'll never set foot in it as long as I live." I told the children that the best way to win most people is to get them to do something for you, so we would try to think of something we could get Miss Betty to help us do.

Thelma, Mrs. Simmons' little girl about the same age as my Violet, came to our place, and the two of them wanted to go and visit Miss Betty.

I told them to ask Miss Betty if she knew how to make molasses candy, and if she did, to ask her if they could have a candy pulling at her place. They were thrilled with the prospect. Off they went, and when they asked her if she knew how to make molasses candy, she said, "Wy, yes. I've made it all my life. I ought to know." Then they asked her if she would have a candy pulling in her front yard, that they would help her to clear a place, and fix the rack for the pot to boil the molasses in. Miss Betty was all excited. She had stayed there all alone for years and years, no one ever visited her. The girls told her that they would bring the molasses—Mrs. Shelton was making molasses at that time—then they set the date for it. Violet and Thel helped her to clean the yard, and fixed the rack for the pot. They had the candy pull, all thanked Miss Betty profusely for making the candy, and told her what a wonderful time they had all had.[53]

One day in Sunday school someone was being praised for a good deed done. Evert Holt said that he wished that just once he could find something worth while to do for someone and receive honest praise like that. I told him that I knew of just such a deed that he could do. There were lots of treetops on Miss Betty's land where logs and crossties had been cut, and if he and the boys would go and saw up a load of firewood for Miss Betty, it would be a noble deed. She had to go out and cut down small trees with a dull old axe; had to cut it up herself for her fireplace, and she was getting old, and it was a big job for an old woman—almost more than she could possibly do. He said that he would do it, and did. Miss Betty was almost overcome with gratitude, and couldn't express it. Later, some of the children found out the date of her birthday, though

---

53. This candy was probably made from sorghum cane molasses. See William E. Lightfoot, "'I Hardly Ever Miss a Meal Without Eating Just a Little': Traditional Sorghum-Making in Western Kentucky," *Mid-South Folklore* 1 (spring 1973): 7–17.

she would not tell how old she was. They told her that they were going to give her a birthday party at the Church, and she agreed to come.

We sent word to the Baptist group that she belonged to, and told them to be sure and come and bring presents. We had her on the program to give a sketch of her life, and to tell of her several brothers who were school teachers, and of her mother having cancer, and how she had had to stay home to take care of her till she got so far behind in her classes that she was ashamed to go to school any more.

The party was a howling success. One whole corner of the Church was filled with presents, all kinds of things. I told her that my present would be a new dress. I made her a pretty dress and got her a pair of shoes that fit her. I also washed and curled her hair, and she was a different person. After we had moved away I had a letter from Mrs. Simmons saying that there had just been something happen that had proven her judgment wrong: they had a big dinner at the Baptist Church at Palestine, where Miss Betty belonged. During the dinner the preacher said that if anyone had anything they wanted to say, he would give them time.

Miss Betty stood up and said that she had been a member of that church for twenty five years, and through sickness and sorrow and death, not one of the members had ever called on her nor offered help or sympathy. She said, "It remained for me to find pure religion among the old Mormons," and proceeded to tell them all that they had done for her. Mrs. Simmons acknowledged the wonderful change in Miss Betty. It had not taken any thousand years, either.

This little house where we now lived (1916) was at the foot of the hill from Sadie's, and in the edge of the woods. There was a stream at the lower end of the field on the west that was an interesting place for the children. I had a bird book, and we all decided to take one bird each, and see if we could find its nest. Noel took the cuckoo, and he found its nest not far from the house. Grace took the wren, and soon found its nest in a tow sack hanging on a post. Hazel took the redbird (cardinal), and although we heard one singing daily from the top of a hickory tree north of the house, we never did find the nest. Violet took the scarlet tanager, and found its nest on the lower limb of the big oak tree in the dooryard.

We had several missionaries who came regularly while we lived in this little house: Glen G. Smith, the younger brother of President George Albert Smith, was one of them.[54] He was real tall, and had a collection of beautiful poems. He was a great arguer, and when he asked me for a poem for his collection, I couldn't think of a suitable poem, but I gave

---

54. George Albert Smith (1870–1951) was the eighth president of the LDS Church, serving in 1945–1951.

"The children, all but Cecil, who was rabbit hunting," ca. 1918.
Left to right, rear: Violet, David, Bernice, Noel; front: Hazel,
Grace. Courtesy of Itha Carmack.

him a new saying that I had just acquired, "A fool never loses in an argument." He wasn't very happy over my contribution at the time, but years
later, when I went to a Conference in Salt Lake, and went to his place, he
went upstairs, found his old book of poems, and said that the thing that

had helped him most in his life was the saying I had contributed. He said that it had been a constant reminder for his argumentative nature.

Another missionary we had there was Elder Nelson.[55] He called Noel "Tuffy." The children had whooping cough while we lived there, and Elder Nelson would try to get Noel to whoop for him.

Elder Hunter was another, and I have him to thank for a picture of our children taken there.[56] This picture has all the children in it but Cecil, the oldest, and Harry, the youngest. This was before Harry was born.[57]

Another Elder was Virgil Bushman, who was released while were we living there. His wife Ruth and their three children came out from Arizona for a visit, and all our children had a great time chasing lightning bugs (fireflies) and catching them. They tied them in hollyhock blossoms, making little lanterns. They hunted animal tracks in the sand down by the creek and spied on the rabbits playing in the path not far from the house. All would congregate about dusk, and have a good time together.

Elder Glen Smith liked gingerbread muffins, and when they came, he would call from the path towards the top of the hill, "Halloo, do you have any gingerbread? If not, start mixing it."

The Galloway family visited us at this place, too. Mrs. Galloway had passed away, and it made me sad to see the children without their good mother.

David was born at this little house, so there are lots of memories connected with it. He was a sturdy little fellow. He wouldn't lay in any position but on his back, which made the back of his head flat. When he was older, he hated it, and wondered why I didn't make him turn over on his sides more often.

Once, while we were living here, I was getting ready to give the children baths, and had a big teakettle on the fire heating. Grace was sitting on the hearth pulling off her shoes when the big stick under the kettle broke and let the boiling water run under her. She had on heavy underwear and bloomers (it was cold), and they held the heat of the hot water. I ran to her and she climbed to my shoulders in an effort to get away from the heat. My heart was just torn. I sent Noel to find some Cloverine salve to put on it.[58] Poor Noel, he always had to take the tragic messages.

---

55. Probably Noland James Nelson (1897–1966) who served in the Southern States Mission in 1917–1919.

56. Archie Antone Hunter (b. 1892) served in the Southern States Mission in 1916–1918. See page 274 for family photograph.

57. Harold Grant Carmack (1919–1923) was Effie's eighth child.

58. Cloverine salve was a widely-used ointment for treating cuts and bruises.

There were blisters as big as a teacup hanging down where she was scalded, but Noel ran all the way to Sadie's, and when he returned I plastered the salve on it thick, and prayed fervently for the Lord to help her to endure the pain, and that it would heal quickly. That was on a Saturday, and by the next Saturday it was all healed and peeled off as if it had never been burned. I was so thankful. Grace was a brave sturdy little soul, and she didn't cry over small things.

And now, back to the Church. We had mantle lamps and lanterns that gave good lights, but they were a little troublesome. Later on we progressed to carbide lights, and they were almost as good as electricity. They were installed just before Christmas.

We had cut a tree, and the snow just poured down, and everything was white. It was still snowing hard Christmas Eve, so Edgar fixed a cover for the wagon, and we took the children to the Christmas program in it. We had songs and poems and stories, and a big Christmas tree. A happy spirit prevailed, and everyone had a good time, and the new lights were glorious.

Edgar got the moving fever again, and this time we moved to the old McCord place, up near Lelia's. It was the year of the flu, and we all had it but Edgar. I was expecting my eighth baby. All of the children were sick at the same time, and I was, too. I kept going, though, and taking care of the sick children. I had such a hot fever that I didn't have very much sense. Grace, Violet and Cecil were delirious, and Bernice slept all the time. Hazel was real sick, but knew everything most of the time. Poor Noel and David were not quite so sick as some of the others, and were in a room alone, and didn't get very much attention; I would take them hot lemonade, and get them a drink occasionally. I was kept busy every minute with the others. Cecil stayed sick after the others began to get better. I called the doctor regularly and told him what I was doing, and he said that he could not do any more if he could come, which he couldn't—there were so many sick people that he was kept busy day and night.

Finally one day Cecil said that he wished Uncle John and Uncle Evert would come. My mind was in a stupor, and I had not even thought of having anyone come and administer to them. I called them, they came, and right then I thought of several things to do for him that helped. I got an herb tea and gave to him, and he soon started to mend. It was an awful siege of sickness—almost as bad as the winter my mother and Etta died. One thing I was thankful for though, I didn't lose my expected baby with the flu, as many mothers did. Bernice became so weak that even after she seemed well of the flu, she still couldn't walk. Aunt Violet, Autie's wife, came and stayed a week or two, and again she patiently walked her from one room to another till she gradually was strong enough to walk alone again. As soon as Cecil was able to, he had some one bring him some

Aunt Fannie Armstrong. "Early Water color painted on back side of wallpaper," by Effie Carmack. Courtesy of Hazel Bushman.

pieces of smooth hickory, and he made hammer handles and whip handles to pass the time away while he was gaining the strength to be able to walk again.

Harry (Harold Grant) was born at this place, a fine healthy beautiful baby. I had a woman doctor, Mrs. Frisby, with me for his birth.[59] In the summer Aunt Fannie Armstrong came and stayed quite a while. She liked to hold Harold in her lap. He was a good natured baby, hardly cried at all. Later on, when Mr. Buck visited us with his jokes and nicknames for the children, he called Harry "Harold Bell Wright, Heber J. Grant."[60]

But back to Aunt Fannie—I drew a picture of her watching an old hen and her little chickens out in the yard. She wouldn't have sat still that long if she had known I was getting her picture. I colored it with water

---

59.  Possibly Martha Frisby (b. 1857), daughter of Mathias and Eliza Frisby.
60.  Heber J. Grant (1856–1945) was the seventh president of the LDS Church, serving in 1918–1945.

color, framed it, and took it to the County Fair, where I got a red ribbon on it. I have the old picture yet.[61]

It was quite a distance from this house to the Woodland Church, but as soon as spring came, and as soon as Harry was old enough, we lumbered down there every Sunday in the wagon. Then we moved back to the old Holt place, where we lived till we moved to Arizona.[62]

I was needing more money for children's clothes, shoes, and everything. I raised a big garden, and began to sell vegetables. We had a good buggy and several horses, not one of which was safe for a woman to drive. I used a big old black mare that was fractious, and she ran away with me several times.

I got a chance to buy a jersey cow that had injured her udder wading across sassafras sprouts and bruised her till she gave milk only out of one side, but she gave as much as she did before it was injured. It was rich creamy milk, and made lots of butter, so then I started selling milk and butter and cottage cheese, as well as vegetables.

There was one thing that was disappointing. Violet and I could never go together. She had to stay and tend the children. There was never a more trustworthy dependable child than she was. She would clean house and cook for them, and at night she would help me straighten things after the little ones were in bed.

Cecil got a wide poplar plank eighteen or twenty inches wide and one and a half or two inches thick, and polished it as slick as a button, nailed a cleat on one end of it and hooked it onto the foot of an old iron bed. I put a rug on the foot of the bed, and the children would climb up on the bed and slide down this long board. It was a means of entertainment on many a rainy day in winter, when they had to stay indoors. He made them a rocky horse too, and put it in their playroom. Once, at Christmas time, he made me a sewing cabinet that was a great help to me. It was of two pieces of three ply about a yard square, fastened together with hinges, so it could be folded together when it was not in use. When I was sewing, I would open it in a corner of the room and it took up very little space. It had pockets for thread and bias tape and patterns, and everything a seamstress might need.

---

61. This watercolor is in the possession of Hazel Carmack Bushman, Effie's daughter. See page 277.

62. This house, shown on page 253 was a typical "double-pen" house which is "found throughout Kentucky and the American South but the extant specimens are noticeably old, perhaps signifying the end of a popular folk house type which has no precise American or European antecedents. The double-pen house is most assuredly related to the European idea of an end addition; but it appears to be primarily a product of the American westward movement, finding fruition among the poorer whites and black sharecroppers of the region." See Montell, *Kentucky Folk Architecture*, 18.

He worked on it out in the gear room, getting it ready as a surprise for Christmas, while I was busy making things for him and the other children. Christmas Eve he slipped in, carrying the sewing cabinet. He thought I had gone to bed. I was slipping to his room with my gift for him, and we ran into each other in the dark hall. We both had a quite a laugh.

I want to repeat what I have said many times: I don't believe there were ever more dependable children than mine were at that time:

Noel had certain chores to do, milking and feeding the stock. He never had to be awakened, or told to do his chores, he did them as regularly as a man. By this time Harry was big enough to go with him to the barn in the mornings, if he could wake in time. I would be busy cooking breakfast, most always making hot buttermilk biscuits, and Harry would try to surprise me and scare me. Noel said that Harry would sit on the boards that divided the milk pens and talk to him while he milked. He would suggest that they talk about their girls, and he usually decided that he wanted either Violet, or Thelma, or Erma for his girl; he never could decide which of the three he liked best.

We just about worshipped Harry, he was such a good sweet child. I don't think I ever scolded him. If I did, I don't remember it. He was unreasonably afraid of fire. He would tell the other children to be careful with matches, and how awful it would be if they got their clothes on fire, and no one there to put it out. He seemed to have a premonition.

I don't have many serious regrets of my directing the children. If I could take back every spanking, I would. There were never any better boys than Cecil and Noel, dependable and industrious. Cecil liked to go fishing, and he would work overtime to get his tasks done so he could fish.

Noel loved horses, and finally got himself a horse, not a very big one, but it could run like the wind. There was one drawback, there was some danger of it falling down. Violet wanted so much to ride him, but the boys were afraid she would get hurt. She wasn't afraid, so one day she caught it out in the field and had a ride without bridle or saddle. She said that it was a pretty wild ride, but he didn't fall down, and she didn't fall off.

Noel and Cecil were just as dependable as Violet was. I would go to town to take the produce for sale, and could trust them to do the work in the fields while she took care of the children and the house, and even helped in the field when she was needed.

Violet had a strong desire to have a flower garden, and there didn't seem to be any place for one, but one day, while I was gone, she decided to clean a place between the horse lot and the road. That particular place was grown up thick with briars and buckbushes. She dug them all out by the roots, an awful job, as the buckbushes had lots of roots that went deep. She cleared it out good, dug it up, raked it smooth, and said that she was going to have her flower garden there. When her dad saw it, he

Woodland Branch Sunday School, Christian County, Kentucky, ca. 1915. Along with the Carmacks, the Simmons, Holt, and Rogers families are represented. Effie is sitting in the center of the front row. Grandmammy Mattie Hale Carmack is holding Violet on her lap at the far right. Thomas Green Carmack is standing to the right of Mattie. Courtesy of Hazel Bushman.

said that anyone who wanted a flower garden that bad should have some help, as he knew that the chickens would scratch up everything she planted. So he got chicken wire and fenced it with a tall fence that the chickens couldn't get over, and he made a good gate for it. Violet soon had a nice little garden with her seeds coming up in neat little beds with walks between them. She planted cypress vines around the fence on the outside, and it flourished, and making a thick wall of pretty green vines with a little red star-shaped blossoms. Everyone who passed admired it, and Mrs. Simmons gave her some plants, already started, from her own flower garden. Soon she had flowers blooming, and all of us enjoyed it. It was the beauty spot of the whole place.

I had planted rows of asters and zinnias in the vegetable garden so I would have bouquets to take to Church, but Violet had a variety, and she kept it neat and clear of weeds.

I am sure that flowers are good for children to live with. At one time I had planted a row of French pinks, and the children were anxious each morning to see what new variety had blossomed. There were dozens of different patterns, of many different colors, and sometimes they said they looked as if the paint was hardly dry on them. Flowers and music both have a good influence. I have read of a settlement school of music in a slum district of New York. The sponsors of it kept a record of the ones who took lessons, after they had left the school. They said that in the twenty five years that the school was in operation, that not one of the students had ever been before a juvenile judge. A wonderful, unbelievable record, considering the families they come from.

We had conference in our little Woodland Branch regularly, and they were spiritual feasts. President Charles A. Callis, who was President of the Southern States Mission, with headquarters in Atlanta, came to each Conference, and of course, all the Missionaries of the District would be there. Kentucky was divided into two Districts at that time. We usually knew most of the missionaries of our district, and at conference times there was a happy reunion.[63]

---

63. See chapter four, note 20 for an explanation of "conferences" and "districts." In June 1924, the following summary of a conference at the Woodland branch was reported:

> From far and near the saints and friends came to the conference which was held at Larkin, Saturday and Sunday, June 28 and 29. A cool bowery had been built by the elders and members and in this place the meetings were held. The congregations were large and attentive.
>
> Owing to important mission matters, President Callis was unable to get to Larkin before Monday morning. The following named elders spoke forcefully on the doctrines of the Gospel: Louis A. Schrepel, Vaughn Skinner, Geo. Q. Spencer, Orson M. Allen, A. B. Robinson, Norman J. Holt, Horace E.

President Callis was a dynamic speaker, and we always enjoyed him, but we had lots of good speakers besides him. Elmer E. Brundage and Orvil Udy helped build the Chapel, and were both good speakers. Delbert Stapley and Thatcher Kimball were both good, and I could name lots of others.[64] I have pictures of lots of them.

Not long ago (this was in 1946 as I was writing) Elder Stapley, an Apostle by now, was going to be in Santa Barbara to Conference, we went, and I wondered if he would still recognize me after over forty years. He stood up on the stand, looked over the audience, spied me near the front, and waved a tiny little wave with two fingers. I was surprised and happy, as we change a lot in twenty five or thirty years.

President Callis came to our Ward in Winslow many years later, after he was made an Apostle, and Noel and I took him to the Meteor Crater. Several of us also went to the Hopi Reservation with him. He was touched by an old, old, Hopi grandmother who was grinding corn. I think she was blind, or nearly. She was sweating, and her hair was in her face. He bent down and looked right in her face, and fanned her with a paper he had in his hand. She held her face up and said, "uh - h - h" while she enjoyed the fan. He was so sorry for her, he said that it seemed like all she had left was the knowledge of how to grind corn.

President Callis has also been to California since we have lived here. He said that this stretch of coast, from Cambria to Ventura, or there-abouts, was a blessed stretch, and that if the Latter-day Saints would live their religion, we would be the means of saving it (I don't know what from, I wish I did), possibly earthquakes. Or invasion?

Well, back to the Woodland Branch, and the things that happened there:

I spoke of runaway horses. One experience I had with a runaway, not long before Harry was born, (David was still a baby, about eighteen or twenty months old) was this: Jessie Simmons and David and I were going from our place up by Lelia's to Sadie's, down by the Church. The mare

---

Thackeray, John H. Rencher, and Harrie E. C. Hunsaker. The Spirit of God was richly manifest.

With characteristic hospitality the members and friends furnished a splendid Southern dinner which was enjoyed by all.

On Monday, Prest. Callis met with the elders in priesthood meeting and gave timely and profitable counsel. He commended them for their dilligence and impressed upon all the necessity of preaching the Gospel by example as well as by precept.

Prest. Schrepel presided at all the meetings of the conference. The saints rejoiced in the instructions they received and in the splendid spirit that prevailed.

See "Kentucky," *Liahona, The Elders' Journal* 22 (July 15 1924): 32.

64.  Delbert L. Stapley (1896–1978) served as an LDS Apostle in1950–1978.

that I was driving was trotting along and the harness up over her hips came unfastened, letting it drop down on her hind legs. She started kicking, and I jumped out to see if I could pull the harness up, but I couldn't stop her. I was taking steps about six feet long, trying to keep up with her, but I saw that she was going to get away from me.

I told Jessie to get out quick, and I reached in with my left hand (holding the lines with my right) and grabbed David by the arm and pitched him out in the weeds by the side of the road. About that time the horse gave a jump and got away from me. She ran like a streak as far as David Payne's place, where a gate to a horse lot was standing open about two and a half or three feet. She dashed through the opening, the buggy turned over, and she left it on the outside of the gate. I went back for David. He was still sitting there with his eyes big and wide and scared stiff, but not crying. It was a miracle that no one was hurt. I was so thankful that I had managed to get David and Jessie out of that buggy before the horse got away from me. Superhuman strength seemed to have been given me, and I had no bad effects from it, either. The buggy was a total wreck. When it turned over, the horse had swerved to one side, and some fence rails rammed clear through the buggy, right in the location where Jessie and David would have been sitting.

I'm sure that when we do our level best the Lord recognizes it and protects us—or maybe it is our guardian angels—anyway, I was sure that some unseen power helped out in that wild and dangerous scramble that day.

I'll tell of one other runaway. I had Old Blackie hitched to the buggy and was on my way to town with a load of produce to sell. There was a big roll of wire near the road that had not been there before. Apparently someone had rolled up a fence and left the bundle there. Blackie got frightened by this, and she dashed to the right of the road and right out into the thick woods. I propped my feet on either side of the dashboard and guided her in and out among the big trees and saplings, and soon got her back onto the highway. She was trembling and skittish the rest of the way to town, as if she had seen an awful monster, and so was I.

I have found that horses are like people, with different personalities; some have lots of sense, while others don't seem to have very much. Some are afraid of every little thing, and others are afraid of nothing.

This reminds me of the sad fate of poor old Blacky: not too long after this runaway, we had an early freeze which froze some corn that had not fully matured, and it moulded next to the cob and formed prussic acid. Blacky ate some of it, and it poisoned her, and as a result she got what they called "blind staggers." One morning, when the boys went out to feed the stock, they found that she had backed through the big gate, and was lying in the road. She had made a big wallow in the mud, throwing her head up and down. Harry saw her and was horrified; he ran into the house to tell me. He said, "Mama, Blackie fell over the fenth and killed sheself." I was sorry that he had seen her—it left an awful impression with him. He talked about it for days. My mother never wanted us to watch the men kill the hogs, for fear it might harden us to such things. When I think of the awful things that our children see on T.V. today! Fights, killings, and violence till it becomes common to them, and they think it is a common thing for one person to kill another. I'm sure that children should not be allowed to see lots of today's programs.

Sadie and I had good times together, even through hard work, sickness, and everything. We lived near each other, so we washed at the creek together during the summer months. I remember one time when we had a big kettle of clothes boiling, and a rock under one side of it broke with the heat, and the kettle of white clothes turned over into the dirt. In hurrying to get to it, one of us upset another tub of clothes which were in the rinse water, ready to wring and hang out, and it also spilled into the dirt and ashes. I can't tell all of it, it's not tellable, but we became almost hysterical, and laughed till we had to sit down. Sadie suggested that we tip the other tub over also, over the bank and down into the creek, and just make a clean sweep of the whole dirty business, but we didn't. We did laugh like crazy idiots. The re-washing was a terrible, backbreaking job— scrubbing the dirty clothes again on a washboard. The trash and ashes that they fell into was as hard to wash off as the dirt had been in the first place. We had to dip up tubs and tubs of clean water, reheat some of it and rinse and rinse the dirt out of the clothes. By being together, it lessened the labor a little, though it didn't shorten the time it took. Our folks at home wondered what was keeping us all afternoon.

At one time, Sadie and I were both invalids, both skinny as rails. I weighed an even hundred, and she a hundred and one. We needed something, one day, from Albert Clark's store, and the only way we had to get it was to walk, so we decided to tackle it.

The road (or the way, there was no road) led across the creek and up a steep hill, across an old field that had lots of passion flowers growing in it—then the Buttermilk Road, and Albert's store, just across the road. We did very well while we were on level ground, but by the time we got to the steep hill we were fagged out, and it was all we could do to climb it. We'd hold to each other and gasp for breath, and laugh like fools, sit down a few minutes and then get up and try it again. This is to illustrate how frail we were, yet we carried on, somehow took care of our big families, and did all the work.

Our children had a wonderful time, and wanted to play together all the time. I remember Sadie sending Paul to my place once in a big hurry for something she wanted to borrow, but he got to playing and forgot he

The Carmack family, Larkin, Kentucky, ca. 1922. Clockwise around back from left front: Grace, Violet, Cecil, Mattie (holding Alden), Henry Edgar, Effie, Noel, Elder Brown (in black suit); four children in front center, clockwise from left: Bernice, Hazel, David (with hand over eyes), Harold (wearing black hat), Courtesy of Itha Carmack.

was in a hurry, till he heard someone calling from the top of the hill, then he ran all the way home. When Sadie wanted to know why he hadn't hurried back as she had told him to, he said, 'Well, they held me." Sadie said, "Yes, I know, they hold me, too."

I must not forget to tell about Vic when he was a baby. There's no telling what he could have accomplished in the musical line if he had tried harder, and cultivated it. When he was only seven or eight months old, before he could say a word, he could hum any tune he would hear, and he only had to hear it once. I remember one night when Sadie gave a farewell party for one of the missionaries who was being released. Elder Catmul [Catmull] was there, and he played and sang a new song, "In the Valley of the Moon, Where I Met You One Night in June."[65] Vic was awake and heard him, and by daylight next morning, he was holding to one of

---

65.  Nathaniel Owen Catmull (1894–1972) served in the Southern States mission in 1917–1919.

the iron bars of his crib, rocking himself, humming the new tune, and keeping time. He never missed a note.

Often, when Sadie or I would sing, he would hum a perfect alto. I never knew of another child who could do that, although we didn't think of it as being so very unusual then.

It was in the spring of 1924 [1923], and Easter was drawing near. The children were looking forward to an egg hunt, especially Harry, my youngest child. He had just had his fourth birthday, and since he was our youngest, was the darling of us all—even my folks: Evert, Sadie's husband; Elmo and Ivy; Leo and Ermal Holt, Sadie's oldest son and wife who lived nearby.[66]

Once, when David, Bernice and I all had the flu, they got well enough to want to get up and play before I was able to sit up. Some of my folks were there helping with the work. There was a cold wind blowing, and I kept telling them not to let David and Bernice go out in the wind, as they were hardly able to be up at all. Finally I heard them out in the yard and told the girls to make them come in. But it was too late and they both took pneumonia and were very sick, and I had to get up and take care of them. Jessie Simmons was a nurse, and she came and said that we must turn David over often, as it was not good for him to lie in one position very long. The doctor came and said that I should let Harry go with some of my folks, who were near, till Dave and Bernice were better.

Both Evert Holt, and Elmo, (my brother), were there, and they both wanted to take him. They finally said that they would let Harry choose which place he would rather go to. When Harry chose to go to Elmo's, Evert cried because he hadn't wanted to go with him.

Bernice's pain was better when I held her on my lap, so I sat by the fire and held her all one night. I was expecting another baby, was four months along, and all that night I had pains and felt pretty miserable. Later I realized that my baby had died that night. When it came time for me to feel life, there was no life. I went to Dr. Sargent, who said that there was no life there.[67] I cried when he told me. He asked me how many children I had, and when I told him that I had eight, he shook his head— "And now, crying over the loss of a ninth. You must be a real mother. You would be surprised how many women (I'll not call them mothers) come to me to find something to help them get rid of their babies."

---

66. Evert Leo Holt (b. 1901) was married to Ermal Adams (1901–1987), the daughter of W. J. Adams and Caroline Reynolds.

67. Dr. Andrew H. Sargent (1858–1942). See Meacham, *A History of Christian County*, 623–24.

This was in October, and my baby was not born till February, four months later. I went to Dr. Sargent once a week all that time, and he assured me that he thought it best to let nature take care of it, and that it might go to its full time; that it would probably take almost all the blood in my body to expel it; that I would not need a doctor because he could only sit and wait. It happened just as he said, there was no inflammation, and the baby was a little girl.

Bernice got better from the pneumonia before David did, and the neighbors brought him toys and nice little things to play with, till he said that he had about the best time he ever had in his life (after the pain left), and he felt O.K., only too weak to walk.

When Easter came, Ermal gave Harry a goose egg for Easter. He was all excited over the big "gooth" egg. He said, "A gooth laid it, too, in a nest under a porch floor."

I had been asked to give a talk on the resurrection for the Easter program at Church that Sunday. After the meeting, our neighbor, Aubrey Majors, said that if he had the faith that I had he would not dread death, and that losing some of his loved ones for a while would not be so bad. We had no idea that I would lose my precious darling Harry before another Sunday had gone by.

Cecil and Noel were plowing in the field just south of the house, and were burning the sawbriars and grass in the fields, as it made the plowing easier.[68] Dave and Harry were playing with stick horses, and they had made a mill on the side of the bank by the road, and were playing that the fine sand was their cornmeal. I had given them some salt sacks to play with, and they were putting their meal in these little sacks and fastening them to their stick horses, like papa did when he went to the mill. One of them suggested that they ride their horses down a steep hill just in front of the house, and through some tall sage grass at the foot of the hill. The tall grass was dry from the year before, and when the wind blew the little blaze where the big boys were plowing, it caught the dry sage grass on fire (it burned like powder) at about the same time Dave and Harry were in the thickest part of it.

Harry had put on a pair of Dave's old shoes so they would make a noise like a horse when he ran, and they hindered him from running fast through the tall grass, which was over their heads. The blaze caught up

---

68. A 1909 farmers' bulletin on the cultivation of tobacco reported the following on the preparation of the seed bed: "The main object in burning the bed, so far as the writers can see, is the destruction of weed seeds which would otherwise produce weeds to interfere with the growth of the young [tobacco] plants. Most of the weed seeds are lodged in the upper 2 inches of the soil, and their vitality is readily destroyed by burning or heating the bed." See Scherffius, Woosley, and Mahan, "The Cultivation of Tobacco in Kentucky and Tennessee," 7.

with them. Dave tried to help Harry, but the fire was roaring, and since Harry was almost as big as David, he left him and ran screaming for Cecil and Noel to hurry and come and help. He apologized a hundred times for going and leaving him, but he hadn't known what else to do. Cecil and Noel heard them, but just thought at first that they were playing. When they realized that the cries were coming from the direction of the fire, they were too late. Harry still had his winter underwear on, and his thick coveralls, and they were burned off.

I didn't hear anything; I was sitting at the sewing machine, setting a quilt top together, but I suddenly felt panicky, ran to the door and saw one of the boys running as fast as he could towards the fire. I knew then that there was something terribly wrong. I ran to the top of the hill and saw Edgar carrying Harry up the hill. He was burned all over, only his poor little eyes still looking.

I ran the other way. Our phone was not working that day, so Noel got a horse and rode across the fields and woods to Grandpa Carmack's to call a doctor. "Grandpappy," as the children called him, was plowing in his field, and heard Noel crying and thought at first that he was singing. But when he saw that he was riding as fast as he could, and leaning down on the horse's neck, he realized something was the matter.

Harry was burned about four o'clock in the afternoon, and lived till about nine. I stayed by him and didn't let myself cry for his sake. He was sorry for me, and kept assuring me that it didn't hurt at all, but he kept saying, "I hath to go to the toilet, mother, I hath to go now." But all that was left of his little penis was a little black stub.

He said, "Just look at my feet, mama, they're not burned at all. I had on Dave's big old shoes. Aren't you glad I had them on, and my feet didn't get burned?" He kept whispering to his dad to keep his hands covered up, so I couldn't see them. He said, "It makes her feel tho bad."

When Cecil had tried to pull the burning coveralls off, the cuffs had pulled the burned flesh, and it was hanging down, and looked awful. Harry was sorry for me and kept telling me, "It doesn't hurt at all now mama, weally it dothent."

His mind was clear till just at the last minute. He held his right hand out with his fist closed the best he could and said, "Take this little clod I hath in my hand Dave." Then, with a frightened look, he said, "Don't ever go back down there David, don't ever go back down there," and in a few minutes it was all over. Long after this time I wrote this:

Wondering

Oh little boy of mine that went away
Who hung so lovingly about my knee,

Is there a place in that dim land where you have gone
Where you can wait and not be sad for me?
I wonder if your heart was torn like mine,
Can love so strong be severed without pain?
Do you look forward, longing for the time
When we shall be together once again?

I shut my eyes and try to see your face—
I have no picture of you in my mind
Only those tortured features scarred by fire
When you went on and I was left behind.
I never dreamed a child of four could be
So brave in death; his patience was sublime—
Apologizing that he caused me grief,
No thought of his own suffering, only mine.
And though my heart was frozen in my breast
And torturing anguish choked my very soul,
No tears relieved me, but he knew full well
The awful suffering underneath control.
But time I know will lay her soothing hand
With gentle touch, and heal my wounds for me,
And I shall see again my little man
Who went so bravely out on death's dark sea.[69]

The doctor had come long before he died, but there was nothing he could do. He was kind, and was hurt, and moved to tears himself. On his way back to town he stopped at Mr. Morris', at the Post Office, and said that he just had to wait a little while and get himself pulled together. He didn't dare drive when he was so shaken and upset.

It was almost more than I could stand. I suffered physical pain as well as mental. I had an awful pain in my eye, and the left side of my chest felt like a rock, and I could hardly get my breath at all. My hands and feet kept cramping and drawing in, and the muscles of my arms and legs drew in knots if I didn't keep them straightened out as straight as I could get them. I could hardly see anything, and next morning, when I went to the door and looked outside, everything looked dark gray and blurred.

---

69. According to Sue Lynn Stone, "Memorial poetry, both copied from literature and composed by area residents, provided another mode of expression. Whether shared with others in gift or in newspapers or kept privately in scrapbooks, these elegies and odes gave the writers and readers opportunities to explore their personal thoughts concerning death." See Sue Lynn Stone, "Blessed Are They That Mourn," 223. See also William Lynwood Montell, *Upper Cumberland Country*, 120–21.

Later, when I went to an eye specialist, he said my eyes would never be any better, and if I wasn't careful, I would lose my eyesight entirely. Much later, I heard that sunflower seeds were miracle food for the eyes and nerves. I started using them, and my eyes improved.

Now, forty years later, they are about as good as they were before Harry was burned, but I was left a wreck. Besides my eyes, I became allergic to the sun and wind, and had to put something heavy over my head every time I went outside. I was also allergic to all dark yellow foods, like sweet potatoes, bananas, strawberries, etc., all were like poison to me, and made my face and eyes swell.[70] I was allergic to laundry soap, too, and that was bad, considering all the washing I had to do. Ivory soap didn't bother me much, so I used that.

Violet had gone home with Lelia's folks the day of Harry's accident. Lelia said that she came in about the time Harry was burned and said that she felt awful. She said she knew that she shouldn't have come home with them. She felt like I needed her for something. Lelia told her to lay down for a while and maybe she would feel better. Violet dozed and awoke crying, and said that she had dreamed of a big brush heap on fire, and that Harry was right in the middle of it.

Just then the phone rang and someone told them that Harry was burned so terribly that he would never live.

Two of the Elders had been with us for several days, and they had only left in the morning before Harry was burned. They were going into a strange new neighborhood, where Mormon Elders were very unpopular. They hated to leave, and when they were leaving they said, "Well, if any of you die before night, send for us and we'll come back. It will take something as drastic as that for us to get permission to return." We certainly had no idea that one of our children would die before bedtime.

Cecil had burned his hands badly trying to put the fire out in Harry's clothing, or trying to do something. Almost hysterical, he tried

---

70.  Effie describes this serious skin problem later in more detail. Marian Brubaker, M.D., whose specialty is dermatology, has kindly offered the following suggestions as to the cause of these symptoms:

   I suspect [Effie] had atopic dermatitis (eczema). This disease has a genetic component. Usually it manifests itself in early infancy or childhood. Many times it disappears in later life, but can manifest itself again, especially under emotional stress. Atopics, as they are referred to in medical terms, may also have other systemic manifestations, such as food allergies, asthma, hay fever. They have very sensitive skin; sun, wind, soaps, extremes in humidity may aggravate their symptoms or cause a rash. Their skin becomes easily infected causing marked weeping, denudation of the skin, along with purulent exudate and 'boils.' I think this would explain her symptoms. (Marion Brubaker to Karen Lynn Davidson, June 26, 1994)

Faded grave marker of Harold Grant Carmack, who was born on February 17, 1919 and died tragically on April 10, 1923, Hamby Cemetery, Christian County, Kentucky. Courtesy of Donna Carmack Musto.

cutting the coveralls off with his pocket knife, but when it didn't work he threw his knife away.

Cecil told me not to even ask God for Harry to get well, but to ask for him to be released from his poor little burned body quickly. He said, "I can hardly stand my hands, they hurt so terribly."

When someone mentioned trying to find the missionaries, Cecil was the one chosen to see if he could locate them, but he could find no trace of them. Driving the car must have been torture on his poor hands, not a thing had been done for them. Later, when he returned maybe, someone tried to do something for them.

I asked someone where Edgar was, and Sadie found him out in the hall on a couch. He said that his head was just bursting. I was suffering so terribly myself that I couldn't think of anything to do for anyone else. It's terrible what a human can suffer and still live. The following weeks were pretty bad, *everything* reminded us of Harry: when I would get breakfast, and when Noel would go to milk the cows. We had been in the habit of making a work program in the morning, and each child was given a task.

When tasks were finished, each would check it with his or her special color of crayon. Harry had always wanted to do lots of things, and enjoyed checking his tasks off by his name. We couldn't stand to make a program after Harry was gone; instead of fun it was grief.

Time is kind to us, and work is a panacea, but I was so plagued with allergies and the pain in my heart that I couldn't do much for a while.[71]

Cecil went to the Western State Hospital to work, and one day, not long after Harry's funeral, my face just started peeling. My entire face was left as raw as a piece of beef—every part of it, even eyelids, ears, nose, every bit. My face was perfectly raw, and a thick yellow liquid oozed from it. I had to keep old sheets or towels around my neck and face to catch this fluid, and it had to be changed often. This continued for several days, and then it started drying up and forming a scab. My entire face was covered with a thick, ugly scab; eyelids, nose, lips, ears. I have never seen or heard of anyone having such an affliction. While it was in this scab stage Cecil came home from the Asylum for a visit. I heard his car stop, and I hated for him to see me, so I covered my head with a towel. The children all ran out to meet him, and I heard him ask them where I was. "She's in the house." "Is she sick?" "Well, she's not very well."

He came in and squatted down by my chair and said, "What's the matter, Mom?" When he saw my face he was horrified. It would be hard for anyone to look much worse than I was looking about then, but it did finally clear up, although I had boils on my face after that, especially on my eyelids. I couldn't expose my face to the sun and wind at all, and my hands and arms to my elbows were the same. I remembered Job, and all that he suffered, and I took a little consolation in the words of the Lord, "Count it all joy when you are called upon to suffer diverse tribulations."[72] Another scripture that consoled me was: "Though He was the Son of God, yet learned He obedience by the things He suffered."[73] I tried to think that there was some wise purpose in everything. I remembered "Whom the Lord loveth He chasteneth."[74]

---

71. Apparently Effie's bereavement resulted in a number of physical ailments. These ailments can be expained by medical case studies which have shown a relationship between bereavement and adverse physical changes. See R. W. Bartrop, L. Lazarus, E. Luckhurst, et al., "Depressed Lymphocyte Function After Bereavement," *Lancet* 1, no. 8016 (April 16, 1977): 834–36; S. J. Schliefer, S. E. Keller, et al., "Suppression of Lymphocyte Stimulation Following Bereavement," *Journal of the American Medical Association* 250 ( July 15, 1983): 374–77.

72. A paraphrase of James 1:2: "Count it all joy when ye fall into divers temptations."

73. Hebrews 5:8: "Though he were a Son, yet learned he obedience by the things which he suffered."

74. Hebrews 12:6.

Sometimes I felt like I was getting more than my share, but I never felt rebellious nor did I blame the Lord for my affliction.

I went to many doctors, but none of them did any good. Dr. Sargent said that there had been many songs and poems written about broken hearts, but *very few* people ever really have broken hearts, but he thought I was one of the few who did.[75] I had a pain in my heart continually, and it didn't get any better till years later when I learned that wheat germ oil was good for the heart.

I quit the doctors and started studying about food and diet as a cure for bodily ailments, and became almost normal again and a much wiser person.[76] Here are some of the precious simple things that I have learned:

Sunflower seed for the eyes.
Pumpkin seed for the body and for worms and to prevent prostate
    trouble.
Brigham tea for the kidneys, with honey.
Wheat germ oil for the heart.
Camphor, benzoin, and eucalyptus combined and fumes inhaled
    for coughs.
Whey for upset stomach.
Lettuce as a sedative.
Brewers yeast for vitamin B.
Green wheat juice for emphysema.
No white bread or white sugar. These are the two foods that cause
    the four major killing diseases.

Later, Violet got married, just as we were preparing to leave for Arizona. Almost everything we possessed had been sold.

I wasn't very sure about the boy she had married—Oscar Pyle.[77] One evening a little brother and sister of his were passing my place, going to visit a relative.[78] It was cold, and I had a fire in the fireplace, so I went

75. Interestingly, studies published in 1981 and 1994 show evidence that increased mortality among the widowed can be a causal effect of bereavement. See M. S. Stroebe, W. Stroebe, et. al., "The Broken Heart: Reality or Myth?," *Omega: Journal of Death and Dying* 12 (1981): 87–106, and Margaret S. Stroebe, "The Broken Heart Phenomenon: An Examination of the Mortality of Bereavement," *Journal of Community and Applied Social Psychology* 4 (February 1994): 47–61.

76. Effie continued her interest in home remedies, vitamins, and health food until her death in March 1974. Her kitchen was well-stocked with bottles of vitamins and herbal remedies (Noel Carmack, personal observations in early 1970s).

77. Oscar Pyle (b. 1905).

78. Lester (b. 1910) and Florence Pyle (b. 1914).

out and invited them to come in and warm themselves (I wanted to ask them about Violet).

I asked them how they like Violet. They said that they just loved her. "She does everything for us. Cooks good meals and washes our clothes and irons them nice. She gives us baths and is just like a mama."

Then Florence said, "But I don't think Oscar likes her, he swears at her, and makes her cry. Our dad told him that if he didn't do better she might go back home," and they didn't want her to do that. Oscar's mother had died, and they had been doing without a cook and a house-keeper, and Violet (still only 14) was doing the big job of keeping house and doing the work for a good sized family.

As soon as the Pyle children left I went out to the horse lot, and the only horse out there was a crazy old thing they called "Lady." I got a bridle and saddle on her, and, although it was late I started for the Pyle resi-dence. Violet was astonished when she saw me hitching that crazy horse to a post. She said, "Mama, what are you coming so late for?" I told her that I just wanted to visit with the folks a little while. I asked one of the boys where his father and Oscar were.[79] He said that they were in the other room playing cards. I told him to go tell them that I wanted to talk to them for a few minutes. Violet looked worried.

They came in, and I told them what Florence and Lester had just told me about Oscar swearing at Violet and making her cry, and that I just wanted to see them and find out if it was true. Mr. Pyle said, "I'm afraid it is, Miss Effie, I've been telling Oscar that if he didn't do better he might lose her." I told them that we were about ready to leave Kentucky, and I came to let Violet know that she didn't *have* to stay, just because she had married Oscar. She could come home and go to Arizona with us if she wanted to.

Mr. Pyle said that he thought it was a serious thing to try to break up a couple after they were married. I replied that I knew it was serious, that the only thing I could think of that was worse, was for a fellow to promise to love and cherish a good girl, and then break his promise and treat her like a dog. I also told Oscar that it would be a month or six weeks before we could leave, and that he would have time to prove whether he could treat her right or not, and that I just wanted Violet to know that we would be glad to have her back if he was not going to be good to her. I told them that I felt sad to have to leave her, even with someone who loved her and was good to her, and that it would be awful to go away feeling that she was being mistreated. Mr. Pyle acknowledged that he could see my side. I then left.

---

79. The father was George Monroe Pyle (1878–1963).

I had no idea whether Violet would come home or stay with Oscar. I could hardly stand the thought of leaving her under those conditions.

Not long after that I felt that I wanted to be all alone for awhile, so I walked all the way to Lelia's. I went through the big woods where there was no road. It was a shorter route. I spent hours in prayer (I think I wrestled with the Lord); I told the Lord all my troubles and perplexities, and begged Him to help me unravel my puzzles. I shed all the tears that were in me, and then I felt somewhat relieved.

Harry's death had been awful, but at least it was a sweet sorrow. This trouble about my girl was a bitter one, and I couldn't think what to do, or how it would end.

Later in the month there came a tobacco season, (that is, it rained and softened the tobacco so it could be handled) and Mr. Pyle and his boys took a load of tobacco to town, and Violet and the children were left at home alone. She caught a horse and came home. She said that Oscar was not being any better, and she felt like she couldn't bear to see us leave and her stay there with him so cranky. The main thing that he was peeved at her about was her religion. His folks were all Baptists, and I guess he wanted her to be a Baptist too, but he couldn't move her on her religion. She didn't eat on Fast Sunday, and that was what he swore at her about, and I think he slapped her.[80]

She wanted Noel to take the wagon and bring her things home before the men returned from town.

It was a hard decision for her to leave him; she was sad, and she cried herself to sleep every night, but the marriage had not been what she thought it would be. She was sadly disillusioned. I was glad of her decision and counted it an answer to my prayers. As soon as they got home and found her gone, Oscar came after her, saying that she had a cold and she should come home and doctor it. I told him that I had taken care of her colds, etc., for *several* years, and I thought I could do so yet. He finally left, and Violet felt bad, but she said that she had thought it over seriously, and had prayed about it before she made up her mind to come home (it was not a hasty decision).

We took the train for Arizona not long after that, the children and I. Edgar stayed to collect money for several things. We had sold the furniture, and the people were wanting it, so we left. Most of the children became train sick, and were pretty miserable. Noel thought he would use psychology, and just not get sick, but before we got to Kansas City he too was getting white around the mouth.

---

80. Mormons customarily go without two meals on the first Sunday of each month and contribute the cost of those meals to church charitable funds.

Cecil had gone ahead of us, and John and Ozie were already living in Joseph City, so we went there.[81] By the time we arrived (Cecil hadn't yet found a house for us to live in) he had fixed a tent, boarded up half way, and with a board floor in it. He had shelves, and a table, and even dishes and food ready for us. (There never was another son like him! It is said that the world is full of two kinds of people, "lifters and leaners." Cecil has certainly always been a "lifter." In fact, I don't believe any of my children are the "leaner" type.) Cecil met us at the depot, and we were astonished at how brown he was. The Arizona sun had already given him a deep tan.

It was a new experience to go to sleep with the spring wind flapping the tent, but we soon got used to it and kind of liked it.

Mother's Day was coming up, and someone had asked me to paint a picture of a mother for a program. I was working on it when I realized that someone was standing in the tent door back of me and watching me. I looked around, and at first I was sure that I knew the fellow, his face looked so familiar. He had on a khaki suit, and stood there waiting for his companion who had gone for some milk (John had a grocery). He told me that he and I should go into business together, that he could do the writing and I could do the illustrating. Just then his companion came and they left. A few minutes later I remembered who he was, it was Zane Gray. (I had seen pictures of him.) They were camped out by Valley Hills, and he was getting material for a book he was writing (I found out later).[82]

Edgar joined us soon and we moved into the old house with a porch around three sides across the street from the meeting house, and while we were living at this place Violet's baby was born. We thought of a lot of names, but every one I mentioned Bernice would make it sound silly. I mentioned Lydia, and she said that it would be called "Liddy, Skillet Liddy." Grace or Hazel said "Let's think of a pretty double-name." Bernice said, "Something like *Fig Newton* or *Self Starter*?" Finally Violet and I thought of *Rebecca*, and I knew at once that that was the name for her. I

---

81.  Originally known as Allen Fort, Joseph City was settled by James S. Brown in 1876 as an LDS mission outpost. It is located on the Little Colorado River in Northern Arizona. See George S. Tanner and J. Morris Richards, *Colonization on the Little Colorado: The Joseph City Region* (Flagstaff: Northland Press, 1977).

82.  Although it is difficult to place Zane Grey in the Joseph City area during the spring of 1924, Grey had been in the Flagstaff area during the fall of 1923, investigating sites for a film adaptation of his novel, *Call of the Canyon*. "Filming of Famous Grey Novels," *Coconino Sun*, September 12, 1923, 1; "Filming of Famous Grey Novels to Carry Fame of Our Scenery Over World," *Coconino Sun*, September 14, 1923, 1. See Candace Kant, *Zane Grey's Arizona* (Flagstaff: Northland Press, 1984), 27, 38, 140–41.

Effie with her granddaughter Rebecca, ca. 1926.
Courtesy of Itha Carmack.

told them we didn't care what any of them said, it ^was^ going to be *Rebecca.*[83] It seemed to just suit her, and always has.[84]

Ethel Randall's little boy, Rich, stopped to see the baby, and he asked what we were going to name her. His mother said that he ran all the way home and burst in and announced that the Carmacks had the ugliest and littlest old baby, and they were going to call it "Roebucker."

Violet wanted to let her nurse the breast, and did so for a while, but found that she was still hungry, so we put her on a bottle. We had a hard time finding a suitable formula. The milk didn't agree with her, and she didn't grow like she should have.

We all just about worshipped her. She seemed to fill the void left by our Harry. She was real smart, and learned things early. She responded to music, and when she heard a tune she liked she had to dance. She danced the Charleston when she could barely walk. One of the popular songs then was "Collegiate, Collegiate, Yes We Are Collegiate," and the very sound of it would start Rebecca to dancing.

[*This entry marks the end of the 1948 version of the autobiography, except for a five-paragraph section titled "About David." The section was included near the end of the 1973 published version of* Down Memory Lane *(see epilogue, note 90) but has been editorially omitted in this edition.*]

---

83.   "Was" is written above the word "going."
84.   Rebecca is the daughter of Oscar Pyle and Violet Carmack, Effie's daughter.

NORTHERN ARIZONA, 1920 - 1940

GLEN CANYON
Colorado River
UTAH
COL

MONUMENT VALLEY

VERMILLION CLIFFS

Colorado River

NAVAJO INDIAN RESERVATION

Keet Seel
Betatakin
Kayenta

NEW MEXICO

GRAND CANYON

Tuba City

Little

HOPI INDIAN RESERVATION

Chinle

Indian Villages

Colorado

Window Rock

Gallup

River

Indian Wells

FLAGSTAFF

Winslow
Joseph City
Holbrook

Jerome

MOGOLLON PLATEAU

Little

Colorado

River

Camp Verde

Snowflake
St. Johns

# The Outskirts of a Desert Town

*I have a little Hobby House that you could never guess,*
*And of all the houses I have owned I think I like it best.*
*The outskirts of a desert town is where my scene is laid*
*Where playgrounds are not thought of, nor parks, nor grass,*
    *nor shade.*

          —"My Hobby House," Carmack,
          Miscellaneous poems

After Becky was born, in Joe City, and we moved to the Westover place, Noel and I milked John Bushman's cows.[1] Noel took the job first, and I knew it was too big a job for him alone, so I helped him, and we agreed we would both take the job of cleaning the schoolhouse, also. It wasn't too much for both of us, and besides, we were both already used to hard work, and didn't mind it.

Then, some of the young folks wanted me to give them art lessons, and my time was limited, so we decided we would have a class after school was out, in the evening. It was handy, we were already there, and the water colors and drawing pads were there also.

Then the teachers wanted the lessons too. I would choose a subject (we took easy landscapes first) and draw it with charcoal on a big sheet of drawing paper fastened on the blackboard with masking tape. First, the horizontal line, then a quick checking: the tallest tree will come to here, our water to here: then put in the sky first, beginning at upper left hand corner; deeper blue at top, gradually growing dimmer till there was no

---

1.   The house was probably owned by John L. Westover (1880–1971). The cows probably belonged to John Lehi Bushman (b. 1883), son of John Bushman (1843–1926) and Mary Ann Petersen.

blue where it joined the land; far off objects dim, closer objects clearer. Near objects bright colors, and before they knew it they had a pretty landscape, and were thrilled.

I gave assignments each week, and then criticized their work. Many of them learned to do good work and have carried on to this day. I had them draw from nature—a small picture of a tree and rocks, or a sunset sky, or whatever they chose to do.

Noel would start cleaning rooms while the art lessons were in progress, and then I would help him finish.

I gave the music teacher, Owen Porter, private lessons at my place, and he gave me music lessons.[2] We both enjoyed it, though it ran into too much time, it was hard to find a stopping place. It wasn't limited, and often lasted till midnight. I timed the lessons at school though, and when our time was up we quit. They learned to work fast.

About this time they had a play at school, and Noel took the part of the Devil. He wore a red suit, with horns and tail. After it was over the boys started calling him Satan, and it continued till there was danger of it becoming permanent. He said that it took six fights to stop it, but after that the nickname stopped. Noel was a very quiet, peaceful lad, but determined.

Noel and David had a dog they called Rex. We burned cedar wood in the kitchen stove, and the boys would go to the cedars for wood occasionally. Old Rex enjoyed going with them. Sometimes he would ride in the old jalopy, and other times he would run alongside the car, and they would check to see just how fast he could run by the speedometer. They had many adventures with the Model T, and Rex, and just being boys. One time out at the "cedars," the dog tangled with a porcupine, another time with a skunk. But one day a horse kicked him in the stomach and almost killed him. He lay like he was dead, only the boys could tell that he was still breathing. For a whole day he lay still, without moving at all. His mouth was slightly open, and flies were all around him. It looked as if the end was near. That night, after the boys went to bed, David got up and took a pan of milk out to see if he could pour a little in his mouth, enough to keep him alive, but there was no response. After Dave went back to the bedroom he suggested that they have prayer, so they both knelt by the bed, and asked the Lord to bless their dog, and help him to get well, he had been such a good dog, taking care of Becky and all. They lay there for quite a while, but could not go to sleep. It was getting late, and they knew that they both had to get up early in the morning. Finally Dave went out to where the dog was, and he was up drinking the milk he had taken out there earlier.

---

2.   Theodore Owen Porter (b. 1904) was married to Mary Fish (b. 1903). He taught at Lamson Business College in Phoenix and later taught music in Mesa, Arizona.

Old Rex was soon well, and running with them to the "Cedars," with no bad after effects from the kick in his stomach, that had almost proved fatal. It was a complete miracle, and the boys both knew it.

Noel's dad had an old Ford milk truck that was hard to start on cold mornings, so while Edgar and Dave bottled milk, and got ready to take it to Winslow, Noel was given the task of starting the old Ford. He said that he would do everything that was ever known to start an old Ford: prop it up, build a fire under it, crank and crank, and would be just about worn out by the time he would get it started.

One time the crank kicked back and hit him just over his left eye, cutting it to the bone, at the upper edge of the eyebrow. The skin fell down over the eye completely, closing it, and it looked horrible, just a big bloody blob. (I thought it had knocked his eye out.) Someone called a doctor, but meanwhile I washed it and raised the eyelid up and put it back in place, cut the eyebrows off, and stuck a piece of tissue paper in it to hold it in place. It dried and stuck there. The doctor said that if it continued to hold, it might not be necessary to sew it back. It stuck, and soon grew back without any stitches. Right now, if there is a bad scar there, I can't remember it.

Noel seemed to take life by the rough handle, and was always having drastic things happen to him.

While we were living there I received a book, "Who's Who in the South and Southwest," by Larkin, Roosevelt, and Larkin, with my name on page 996.[3] I had received a list of questions in the mail, and was asked to answer them and return it. I didn't know what it was for, and had forgotten it.

Later on, when I went to quarterly Conference in Snowflake, where the Stake House was located, I was a little late, and as I passed some of my friends in the hall they said, "I suppose you'll be above speaking to commoners like us from now on."[4] I had no idea what they were talking about. Then afterward someone told me that in the opening exercises of Conference, my name had been listed as one of the six outstanding people in northern Arizona. (I'm sure I don't know what for). I worked hard at half a dozen things:

Noel and I milked brother John Bushman's cows, and we did the janitor work at the school. I taught art in the school after the school was dismissed in the afternoon, so the teachers could all take the lessons. Mrs.

---

3. *Who's Who in the South and Southwest*, vol. 1, 1st ed. (1947), s. v. "Carmack, Effie Marquess."

4. A stake house is a meetinghouse that serves not only local wards but also houses meetings on the more inclusive stake level.

Bertha Reese, who was principal; May Winn; Helen Ash, from Utah; Rilla Solomon. I think Bessie Richards and Ina Peterson were teachers too, but I don't remember them taking art.

I taught a Sunday school class, worked in the Mutual Improvement Association, taught Theology in Relief Society, and exchanged art lessons for music lessons with Owen Porter, the music teacher, in my house.[5]

I taught the Seagull class in Primary, and after Bernice's eyes began to bother her, and the nurse said that she should quit school, I got some big old charts and taught her at home till they were better.[6] I didn't have any idle time, but I think I enjoyed it all, as I had been used to hard work all my life, and didn't mind it at all.

Later, after we moved to Winslow, I bought two sets of books for Bernice, called "The New Human Interest Library," and "Lands and People"—a High School course at home, which she studied through, and enjoyed it.[7] A few years later she went to a boarding school in Tucson, and she enjoyed that also. So, she finally got a pretty good education, and was an avid reader, remembering well what she read.[ . . . ][8]

When we were living at the little gray house where Rebecca was born one day a big car stopped in front and a big kind faced man asked me if my name was Carmack. I said it was, and he asked me if I had any buttermilk. (Edgar had the dairy, and he had inquired, though of course I had no buttermilk there.)

He asked me if I would mind answering a few questions. I told him that I would be glad to. He then asked me if this little town was a Mormon town. I said that it was. Then he asked me if it was possible that it was named for Joseph Smith, the founder of the Mormon Church. I told him that I thought it was.

"Are you a Mormon?" "I am."

He told me that all his life he had wanted to contact a member of our Church. He said that he was from Nova Scotia, and was a Congregation Minister.

He started to ask questions, and I enjoyed answering them. He stayed all afternoon, and at last I found out that his wife was in the car, but he said, "Don't worry, she has a new book."

---

5.  The Relief Society is the adult women's organization of the Mormon Church.
6.  The Primary organization provides weekly lessons and activities for children from eighteen months to twelve years of age. The Seagull class was the name at that time for the class of eleven-year-old girls.
7.  Bernice's books were S. E. Farquhar, *The New Human Interest Library*, 6 vols. (Chicago: Midland Press, 1928), and probably Gladys D. Clewell, ed., *Lands and Peoples; The World in Color*, 7 vols. (New York: The Grollier Society, 1929).
8.  The editors have omitted Effie's subtitle, "Joseph City, Arizona."

He seemed genuinely interested in everything that I told him. It was springtime, and they were on their way to Calif.

By fall we had moved to the big old Westover house at the east end of Joseph City.

One day there was a knock at the door, and it was my minister on his way back to Nova Scotia. He smiled a big wide smile and asked me if I had some of that same brand of buttermilk left. I assured him that there was an unlimited supply left. Then he started asking questions. He had some jotted down.

I gloried in answering his questions, and gave him a Book of Mormon, and a lot of tracts. I feel like he investigated further, as I think he believed all I told him. I also gave him a price list of books that he could order if he wanted to.

He seemed such a sincere, sensible man, interested in the Truth, and our conversation made me very happy.

While we lived in Joseph City they had a teacher training class, and Rulon Porter taught it.[9] It was made up mostly of the young parents and the school teachers, and the young folks who were working in the M.I.A. (Mutual Improvement Association).

I wanted to take the course, as I was teaching a Sunday School class, and was helping in M.I.A., was teaching Theology in Relief Society, and had a class of girls in Primary. I thought it would probably be a help to me.

Everyone else in this class were college graduates. I had not even finished the eighth grade, as my father got sick just before school was out, and I had to quit.

It was a good course of lessons and I enjoyed it. Mr. Porter said that it would not be graded, it would be unjudged.

At the close of the course he gave a long intelligent test, a hard one. When the test was over he said, "Mrs. Carmack, didn't you say that you did not even finish the eight grade?" I said, "That is right, I did not." Then he said, "You folks will be surprised to know that she has more correct answers than anyone else in this class. The reason I am bringing this out is to let you all know that you can continue to learn after you have graduated from college. Mrs. Carmack undoubtedly possesses a healthy hunger for knowledge."

I think the real reason was that the others, the college graduates, had taken courses they were not really interested in, and had been required to read so much that they didn't care for, that they were tired and fed up on reading so much.

---

9. Rulon E. Porter (1882–1972) married Nellie Emily May Knight (1880–1920) in 1913.

I just studied the things I liked, and read the books I enjoyed, and it stayed with me.[ . . . ][10]

Before Cecil was called on a Mission he and I were appointed by the M.I.A. to go to Salt Lake for June Conference.[11]

Grandma Williams, O. C. Williams' mother, of Holbrook, and her two granddaughters went with us. We had a happy trip, outside of a few undesirable happenings.

We stopped at Moab for breakfast at Mr. Hazard's restaurant. We wondered if his first name was *Hap*. Anyway, when referring to it later we called it Hap Hazard's breakfast.

Cecil was hungry, and we had to wait quite a while. Soon we saw a girl coming in our direction with a big platter full of food. Cecil thought it was for us and was looking happy (so Lucy said), but when she passed us up and went on down the line Lucy said that she was sure, for a few minutes, that Cecil was going to burst into tears, from the tragic look on his face. The girls laughed till the tears came. Cecil smiled.

Finally, at long last, we got our breakfast, and all felt better. Then we prepared to be on our way across a desert.

There were many warnings for us to take *extra* water, as we might need it. Cecil said that we had everything full. It would have paid us to have heeded the warning, as there was no paved road across the desert, and in many places the sand had blown over the trail, so you could hardly tell where it had been, and we got stuck.

Others ahead of us had cut scrub cedars and desert growth and put on the stretches of sand, but it did us very little good. The cedars were soon covered deep with sand.

Finally we were stuck so deep we couldn't move. We all got out and dug sand from under the tires and all pushed with all our might, but nothing moved. The motor of the car was boiling hot, and Cecil had put nearly all of our water in the radiator, and we had barely *started* across the expanse of desert, and now we had no water left. We all got out.

Sister Williams said that she was sure everything would be OK, as she had her family records with her, and we would be protected. She started off down a draw alone.

---

10. The editors have omitted Effie's subtitle, "Joseph City, Arizona—Before Cecil was called on his Mission."

11. Mormons, usually young people of twenty or so, are 'called' on missions of approximately two years' time. The call, in the form of a letter from church headquarters, specifies the geographical area in which the missionary will be serving. Here is yet another meaning of the word conference. This refers to a bi-annual general LDS Church meeting held in Salt Lake City, with special sessions for those working in church auxiliaries such as the Mutual Improvement Association.

Cecil started in the other direction with a five gallon can and a tin cup.

It certainly didn't look like there was much hope of finding water anywhere around where we were stuck.

Cecil told me later that he prayed, and asked that if there *was* any water near, that he would be guided to it.

He went up a draw full of tumbleweeds, finally stopped, began cleaning weeds away, then dug down to dirt, and in a few minutes struck some water, not much, but when he dug a hole and waited for a few minutes, it filled with water, enough that he could get his tin cup full.

He was gone quite a long while, then came back with his can full of water. He said that he wondered how he happened to dig in that special place, as he dug in a dozen other places later, but there was no sign of water except in that first place he dug.

The very fact that we were out of water seemed to make us all thirsty. Grandma Williams said that it was because the bacon and eggs we had for breakfast was too salty.

Later, we saw in the distance a strange looking hill, with a hole through the top of it, and not too far from it, on the opposite side was a stream bed, or at least a place where there had been water. There was a dilapidated cabin, with a door hanging sideways. We stopped and probed around. There was a woman's corset, and a baby's worn out shoe.

Cecil said that there is probably a spring somewhere near, so we instituted a search and found it at the bottom of a little hill. It certainly was a stingy little drip that supplied it. There was the remnant of what had been a harrow, so somebody had undertaken to farm the land near the cabin. We wondered why, in a country with so many desirable places to live, why any man would take his wife and children to such a desolate spot as this. It was hard to figure out, but there was the evidence.[12]

We refilled some of our water cans, after so long a time, and finally made it safely across that treacherous stretch of sand and desert. We had learned a lesson.

We came to Bluff, in the bottom of a canyon, with Moab at the foot of the mountain on the opposite side.

We arrived in Salt Lake City without further trouble, had a wonderful time at the meetings. At one meeting, in a gymnasium, two of the authorities had compiled the lessons for the class I was teaching for the following year. He told how they enjoyed writing the lessons, saying, "We were as enthusiastic as . . . "—he looked up and down the line of

---

12.   Effie's comments are worth noting since the unusual arch formations in this red rock country would have appeared foreign to someone from the hills of western Kentucky.

teachers—"as Genealogical workers." Evidently there were several in the group, as they pointed to one another and there was a general laugh.[13]

One woman said, "You must have enjoyed it very much, and so probably we will enjoy teaching them also."

Sister Williams and the girls didn't go back with us, and we went across Monument Valley. I was really struck dumb. I had never even heard of Monument Valley, and had never seen anything anyways near like it. Since then I have become well acquainted with it, and have a dozen paintings of it.

We arrived home safely and reported the valuable information we obtained at the Conference, and were thankful that we had been asked to go, but were glad to get home again.[ . . . ][14]

All his life we had planned and hoped that when Cecil was old enough he would go on a Mission. While we were living at the Westover place, his call came.

I think I mentioned elsewhere that Vera's family was at our place, and were living in the little building down near the highway, and of Cecil teaching Nelson and Rebecca to walk just before he left.[15] He also baptized David and Clay.[16] I think it was the spring of 1925.

He was called to the Southern States Mission, and after their two weeks' training in Salt Lake City, they were all given several shots for different diseases. Then they insisted on Cecil having his tonsils out. Cecil assured the doctor that he was not having any trouble with his tonsils, but the doctor insisted, so it was done. They bled profusely, and would not stop, and he had to stop along the way for treatment, while the other missionaries went on ahead of him. He also stopped over (with permission) in Kentucky and visited our folks there.

Oh, how we did enjoy his letters, and watched the mailbox for them.

When vacation time came, Noel went to the Navajo Reservation to work for a man who had an Indian Trading Post out there, a Mr. Bush. He lived near a little spring, and the Navajos called him To-hul-chinty (Little

13. Because vicarious ordinances are performed in Mormon Temples for deceased family members, genealogy is an important responsibility among Mormons. Consequently, the LDS Church has an extensive system of genealogical libraries. These libraries (the largest in Salt Lake City), serve some of the most tenacious and enthusiastic genealogists in the world.

14. The editors have omitted Effie's subtitle, "Winslow, Arizona—Cecil's Mission and Marriage."

15. Nelson East was the son of Leslie East and Vera Ferrell.

16. Clay Marquess was the adopted son of John Robert Marquess and Ozella Holt. A Mormon man as young as sixteen may perform baptisms, as long as he has been ordained and given the proper level of Priesthood authority.

Water), and they called Noel To-hul-chinty-begay, Little Water's boy. Noel helped Mr. Bush around the trading post at Dilcon, and took care of a flock of goats. He got acquainted with Indian boys and learned to speak the Navajo language. Now, about forty years later, I think he could still carry on a conversation in Navajo.

Those Navajos knew where we lived, and never forgot Noel. When they would pass our place, usually the mother driving the team to the wagon, and the man riding horseback ahead, I would hear the woman call to her husband, "Hey, hey!" When she got his attention she would point to the horse lot, or wherever she saw Noel, and say, "To-hul-chinty-begay!"

While Cecil was gone, we moved to Winslow [*a non-Mormon community twenty-three miles west of Joseph City*], and I'll never forget the day he arrived home.

It is a hard time for a missionary when he just returns from his mission. He has been spending all his time meeting new people, studying the Gospel and explaining it to others, and for a while he is still homesick for the missionary work. Cecil was so restless for a while that he even packed his grip and walked to Joseph City to satisfy the urge to do missionary work.

The young folks he knew when he left were not the same. Many of them had married, and they almost felt like strangers for awhile, but it didn't take too long to get back into the swing of things.

Cecil was interested in music. He played the violin, the saxophone, and the banjo, and enjoyed helping play for dances. It was not long till he found work, and a girl, and was soon accustomed to life at home once more. Then it was not too long till he was engaged, and planning to be married, to Gladys Bushman, our friend John's daughter.[ . . . ][17]

About the time we moved to the Campbell place Grace and Hazel were having difficulties in school. Several of the teachers made disrespectful remarks about the Mormons, nearly every day.

I guess Grace and Hazel were among the first Mormon children to go to High School in Winslow.

Grace would come in pulling off her sweater and go straight to the piano and play as hard as she could for about half an hour. Then she said that she felt some better.

The girls threatened to quit school, but I told them to wait, and maybe I could help a little. "Now don't go over there and talk to them about it, that would not do any good."

---

17. Gladys Bushman (1910–1983) was the third child of John Lehi Bushman (1883–1967) and Etna Novella Cooper (1886–1960). Editorially omitted material discusses Cecil's marriage and family. The editors have also omitted Effie's subtitle, "Dinner for School Teachers around 1930" (the last two words are in Effie's hand).

I told them that I wouldn't do that, but I did send each one of their women teachers an invitation to come to my place for an old fashioned southern *supper.*

I went to a great deal of trouble; I rearranged the paintings, and cleaned the old place till it was shining. Then I bought an expensive linen tablecloth, and painted some little southern landscapes for place cards, with little frames on them (see picture). [*This picture does not appear in the autobiography.*] I have kept one as a souvenir of an occasion that cleared up a very disagreeable situation for the girls.

I made buttermilk biscuits, and good cornbread with lots of eggs in it. I made a big cobbler pie with butter and brown sugar on top.

I had an old fashioned preserve stand and had peach preserves in it. I bought two pounds of butter and remolded it, and made designs on it like my mother used to make.

There was a turkey platter full of fried chicken, browned just right, and plenty of chicken gravy and mashed potatoes.

I had string beans and turnip salad, and an apple layer cake like my mother used to make. It was a real feast, and it was a typical Kentucky supper, and it was pretty, and filling.

The teachers arrived on time. Grace and Hazel were dolled up pretty with frilly aprons and waited on the table, and kept hot biscuits, poured their coffee, etc.

I had carefully planned a few things to tell in our table conversation. A few of the accomplishments of our Church, and what prominent people had said of us, and of the many scientists our Church had produced. Also of Utah's educational standards, and of how our Church ranks in the number of illegitimate children.

I said that of course there are many ignorant people who are not keeping up to date on things like that, who still believe there is a high wall around Salt Lake City, and that the men make slaves of the women, but of course intelligent people, who are well informed would know better.

After supper the girls took the dishes to the kitchen, but left the food for the men and boys who would come later. Then Grace played the piano, and we all sang community songs (singing has a way of smoothing ruffled dispositions).

I even played the guitar and sang an old, old song or two. It was a typical Kentucky evening.[18]

---

18.  This suggests that Effie placed significance on these family oriented activities and ascribed symbolic meaning to those events that reminded her of her Kentucky childhood. See Barbara Allen, "Family Traditions and Personal Identity," *Kentucky Folklore Record* 28 (January–June 1982): 1–5.

I asked them several questions on different subjects, that gave them a chance to air their learning, and I praised them for it sincerely.

When it was time to go they each one said that it had been a happy evening, and they thanked me profusely for the supper, and the *good* time they had had.

The girls had no more trouble with insulting remarks about the Mormons, and they said, "Mama, why didn't you do that a *long time* ago, it would have saved us a lot of humiliating experiences, and from the unpleasant feeling of having to stay angry half the time."

Grace and Hazel were the two youngest pupils in school to graduate, when graduation time came. Since then several of the Mormon pupils have been a recommend to our Church.

It was not long till there was a thriving Ward in Winslow. A nice Chapel was built, and a big recreation hall that furnished the recreation for all the High School kids.

Several mothers told me that it was the only place that they felt safe in letting their children go to, since they *knew* there would be *nothing* but clean supervised recreation.[ . . . ][19]

Noel was eighteen in January, and was called on a Mission 2 May, 1929.

Brother John Hatch, our Patriarch, was coming to Winslow, and he usually came to my place, and I took down the blessings as he gave them.[20] I used a sort of *pidgin* shorthand that no one but myself could read, but I would copy it before it got cold.

Noel wanted a blessing before he left, and made an appointment for it with Brother Hatch, but he had promised Ben Gibbons Sr. that he would overhaul his car when he was ready for him to, and he was ready at the time he was to have had his blessing.

Violet also wanted a blessing, but all the Patriarch's time was taken up. She came to my place to help me at the time of Noel's appointment, which he couldn't keep, so she took his place, and he gave her a wonderful blessing.

---

19. The editors have omitted Effie's subtitle, "Winslow, Arizona—Noel called on a Mission later 1929" (the last two words are in Effie's hand).

20. Patriarch John Hatch (1860–1946) was the son of Lorenzo Hill Hatch. John married Mary Jane Standifird (1867–1947). They resided in Taylor, Arizona. Each stake has at least one man designated as a patriarch, and his calling is to give patriarchal blessings to members of the church who request the special blessing. It is always transcribed and becomes part of church archives; the recipient also keeps a copy. Usually the patriarch declares the lineage of the person receiving the blessing, and also includes specific admonitions, promises, and encouragement.

Carmack family photo, ca. 1928. Left to right, back row: Cecil, Gladys Bushman (Cecil's wife), Edgar, Grace, Noel; middle: Effie, Hazel, Bernice, David, Violet, Arnold Mattice (Violet's husband); front: Rebecca, Wayne (Violet and Arnold's children). Courtesy of Hazel Bushman.

Later, after Noel got to Salt Lake City, a Brother Kennedy [Keddington], a Patriarch, gave him his blessing. He was called to Mississippi for his Mission, the same *field* of labor where Cecil had been called. How we did look forward to letters from *both*.

While Noel was in Mississippi a sister, (can't remember her name), who made necklaces of little shells, gave Noel one to send to me for my birthday. I wore it a lot, and liked it, but it got broken, and restringing the shells was such a complicated job that I couldn't restring it. I still have the shells.

Noel and Don Brinkerhoff were both called to Mississippi from northern Arizona, and they were both released at the same time, and returned home by car.[21]

A Church Mission is a wonderful experience for a young man or a young woman.

Cecil and Noel both stayed two weeks at the Mission Home in Salt Lake City. I think both of them had President David O. McKay as a teacher while there.[22] He was an Apostle at that time, and they both said that he was a wonderful teacher.

President Grant and Evan Stephens were also their instructors.[23]

I had planned to go to Salt Lake City with Noel. All of our old friends, that we had made at the time we had lived there, would welcome me.[24]

I wanted to make Noel's last week at home pleasant, so I fixed food that he liked, especially sweet potato pies, and baked potatoes.

I had not realized then that I was allergic to sweet potatoes, and I ate freely of them. Consequently my face became swollen, my eyes, especially, were swollen together. Mouth, ears, even my neck, was so swollen I could not lay down without smothering, so I sat up by the stove.

I had not slept much, and the second or third night, by the stove, at about two o'clock in the morning, the coal and wood we used in the stove gave out (it was cold).

I didn't want to awaken anyone to go and get more, so I put a robe over my head (the cold wind on my face made it ache) and started out for fuel.

---

21. Don Brinkerhoff and his wife, Thelma, currently reside in Snowflake, Arizona.
22. David O. McKay (1873–1970) was the ninth president of the LDS Church, serving in 1951–1970. At this time, the missionary force was relatively small, and outgoing missionaries could receive more intimate first-hand instruction from church authorities.
23. Heber J. Grant (1856–1945) was the seventh president of the LDS Church, serving in 1918–1945. Evan Stephens (1854–1930) was a popular Mormon musician and hymn composer.
24. Newly called missionaries report to the Mission Home in Salt Lake City for a short period of training before departing for their assignments.

Noel was sleeping in the back room that Lelia's husband, William Ferrell, had built on for us back of the kitchen. When I got about even with Noel's bed, I knew that I was about to keel over. The last I remember was trying to call him, just as I was going down. The next thing I remember I was on the couch in the front room, and Noel was fanning me and rubbing my face. He didn't dare put water on it, as it was all broken out.

Well, of course he went for the wood and coal. I got propped up with pillows so I could be half laying down in the hope that I could sleep some.

All thoughts of going to Salt Lake with him were out, and I could not even help him get his things ready to leave.

I had not had a doctor, as I had given them up long before that.

Noel left, and was going down to Cecil's shop, and would leave from there later. I remember how miserable I was after he left, and I knew he was still down there.

A few days after that Arnold came.[25] I can't remember where he and Violet were living then, but not in Winslow. He was horrified at the way I looked, and asked me what we had done for it. I told him that we had not done anything.

Arnold left, and in a little while he came back with a whole bunch of remedies. Zinc Oxide, a salve to cover my face, as the wind or air made it ache and hurt. A sedative to ease the pain and make me sleep. Two or three other things that the druggist recommended (I can't remember what now), and they really helped, and I *did* appreciate it a lot.

Arnold's sympathy, and his desire to *do* something made me feel better.

Noel got home from his Mission on a Sunday evening, and we were in Church. He took a bath and got cleaned up and came down just as Church was being dismissed.

Grace started out at the front door and saw Noel standing down by the steps. She was so glad to see him that she didn't take the time to go *down* the steps, the front way, she jumped off of the side, and almost knocked him over.

There were two strange women to Church that evening. I never did learn their names, but later I saw one of them on the street and she said, "You are the mother of the boy who had been away somewhere and came home the evening we were at your Church." She said that seeing people who loved each other as we did, made them happy, and made them know that we were good people. She also said, "I'll never forget that sweet boy of yours. You could tell he was a good fellow by just looking at him."

---

25.   Loren Arnold Mattice (1904–1976). Arnold married Violet Carmack on June 11, 1926.

While he was in Mississippi he met a family of Kennedys that he liked. I had sent him a diary of a hunting trip Cecil and Mr. Hart and I took to the Kaibab Forest, and he had it in his suitcase. He left the suitcase at the Kennedys, and they looked into it to see if he had any clothes that needed washing, and they found the hunting story. They read it and were charmed with it, and said that I should have it published. The Christmas after that he sent them a little Christmas card.

Lately, one of the Kennedy granddaughters, living at Princeton, Kentucky, heard of me through a relative, Fanny Newson, who was helping me with my family research, and the Kennedy girl wrote me a note and sent the little Christmas card that Noel had sent to her grandmother in Mississippi in 1927, forty years ago.[ . . . ][26]

I was a busy woman while we lived at the house we bought from Arch Campbell in Winslow. There were two houses on the same lot, and Cecil and Gladys lived in the other house awhile. Then Virgil and Ruth Bushman's family moved there. They had a bunch of boys.[27] David and Bernice and these boys were around the same age. They did all sorts of things together.

They went to all the junkyards in the community and found old wheels of different kinds and made several little wagons. They got willows and made bows, and robbed our dish towel drawers and got big dish towels for wagon covers.

We were living almost on the edge of the desert on the north side of Winslow, and they cleared a road away out onto the uninhabited land and made a camp. I didn't realize for a while that they were going to be pioneers. They stripped our cupboards of all the food that was in them, and they had their covered wagons loaded. It was really an impressive sight as they wended their way along their new trail, away out to their first camping place. They arrived at camp about sundown one evening, and we could see their smoke rising while they were cooking their evening meal. They had taken old blankets and some cushions for pillows, and when it was good and dark they made their beds and went to sleep, but some of them woke in the middle of the night and woke the others, saying they believed it was getting daylight, when it was really only the late moon rising.

---

26. The editors have omitted Effie's subtitle, "Winslow, Arizona—David and the Bushman boys, about 1934."

27. Jacob Virgil Bushman (1889–1969) and Ruth Campkin Fuller (1891–1969) were married in 1909. They had seven sons: Virgil Fuller (b. 1910); Manson John (b. 1912); Vaughn Jason (b. 1914); Burton Delbert (b. 1919); Preston Wilbert (b. 1921); Grant Moroni (b. 1923); and Burl Jesse (b. 1927).

They cooked their breakfast and sat and waited, and waited. Some of them finally went back to sleep. It was quite an experience.

They had meant to travel farther, maybe to Tucker's Flat, where there was a big spring of clear water in the top of a hill, but the person who owned the land shattered their pioneer dream. He told them that there was danger of them starting a grass fire, and ordered the camp broken up.

The children were very enterprising, and soon they became busy hauling old milk crates from the milk bottling station till they had a monstrous pile in the back yard, and then proceeded to build a ship, with cabins and everything. The old aviation field out east of our house was the ocean. They had a lookout, high up, and some old field glasses, with which they could see any enemy vessels that hove into sight. They rummaged the place for toilet articles for the cabins: old face cream bottles, old hair brushes and combs, powder and perfume, till the girls raised a kick.

One evening a good movie was on, and Edgar and I, and Ruth and Virgil went to see it. The girls were away. So the boys decided to have a carnival. They built a ferris wheel, a tall one with seats made from old milk crates or egg crates, a merry-go-round, and a tall tower with a seat at the top—I can't remember what it represented. There was a calf shed in the back yard, and they had established a restaurant there. When we got home, the carnival was really going full swing. The ferris wheel was turning with passengers really occupying the seats.

There was someone in the little trap at the top of the tower, and the merry-go-round was really in operation. They had even cut into the main line and put up wires and had lights everywhere, so there were no light bulbs left in the houses.

The old calf shed with its lunch counter emitted a smell of something scorching.

Burl, Bushman's youngest boy, was dressed and painted up, and on the door to his stall someone had tried to print "Trick Dancing," but the sign painter had made a mistake, and it was "Frick" instead of "trick." Still it didn't alter Burl's performance as a Trick Dancer. When Ruth saw her baby boy and his makeup and his sign on the door, she was already laughing till she had lost control of herself. Burl's trick dancing made her almost hysterical.

It was a wonder some of them didn't get hurt. You could easily have shaken the tower down. It was taller than the house. The ferris wheel was a shaky contraption too, but someone was making it go around, and the passengers were enjoying it, without any worries.

They had torn their ship down and used the material for the carnival. It really showed lots of work and ingenuity.

Another day they were playing pirates and were hunting for treasure. Preston was raking in a rubbish pile and found a perfectly good dollar bill.

There was a loud whoop and they quickly shed their pirate masks and hit for town. The dollar bill didn't last long.

Ruth and Virgil operated a root beer stand on Third Street, and lots of evenings while they were still working, we had programs at our place. They even wrote their own plays and staged them. Their inventiveness and originality was a big part of it all. We had a colonnade in the front room, and it was easy to put up a sheet for a curtain to have shadow plays and programs. The Bushman boys were almost like my own, and have been ever since.

Grace finally married Manson, their oldest living son, and then he really did become one of my family, and fits in perfectly. I don't know how we could have done without him. They have not been blessed with any children, but they adopted a baby, Judith Ann.[28] We just about worshipped her. Edgar couldn't stand to be away from her. She was real smart, affectionate and gay, and could sing like a bird. She grew almost too quickly, and was like a woman when she was in her early teens. She was a beautiful child, with pretty brown curly hair, and was talented. Now she is a mama, and I have just received a Mother's Day card from her and her little daughter, Leanne. Leanne's father went to Thiele [Thule] in North Greenland, and has not returned at this writing.

During this era I had been painting, and a man from the Southwest Museum came to Winslow and saw some of my pictures at the Bruchman Curio store, and he got my address and came up to the house.[29] He said that he was sure that Mr. Harrington, the man in charge of the Southwest Museum in Los Angeles would like to exhibit some of my paintings of Indian life.[30] I soon received a letter asking me if I could have about twenty five paintings of Indian life there by the first of May. I already had several, and I set to work in earnest to get the twenty five done.

I did a big one of a Navajo woman weaving a rug, another carding, one spinning, one dyeing wool, and in the distance two women were shearing sheep. I called it "The Evolution of a Navajo Rug." I had them about ready to send—just needed to do two more when Hazel asked me if I had done any Hopi pottery. I had not. She said that it would not be representative of our Indians without some Hopi pottery, because that is what they are noted for producing.

---

28. Judith "Judy" Ann Bushman (b. 1945) was born in Gallup, New Mexico.

29. This trading post in Winslow was owned by Otto Richard "Max" Bruchman (1880–1986).

30. Effie does not specify the year of this exhibit at the Southwest Museum, but her vitae in *Who's Who in the South and Southwest* (1947) indicates the year was 1942.

"At an Art Exhibit in the Park, Atascadero California & two of my pictures I painted [in] Taos." Courtesy of Itha Carmack.

The Hopi Reservation is just north of Winslow, so I got busy and did a still life of pottery. The first of many I have done since then. It was one of the best small paintings I sent.

The exhibit stayed through May, then I had a letter asking me if they could keep them through June also, as some people from the east who ran an article about them in an art magazine wanted to see them and could not come out till June.

My good friend, Bernice Pollard Walker (who was our dear neighbor in Kentucky) went to the Museum to see the pictures while they were there. She didn't let Mr. Harrington know that she knew me, wanting to know what he thought of them. So she asked him for his opinion of the collection. Mr. Harrington said that it was the best coloring of Indian life he had ever had in his museum.[31] There was just one thing against them—the frames. I couldn't get them framed properly in Winslow. There was no one there who did good framing. But I was happy to hear his estimate of them, and it encouraged me.

---

31. A thorough search of the official Southwest Museum publication, *The Masterkey*, did not disclose any references to Effie's exhibition.

*Tzin Tzun Tzan*, by Effie Carmack. Oil on canvas panel, n.d., 31 3/4" x 19 1/2". Original in the possession of John K. Carmack.

*Emery Falls, Lake Mead,* by Effie Carmack. Oil on canvas, n.d. 47 1/2" x 30 3/4". Original in the possession of John K. Carmack.

About this time I received an invitation to display some paintings in the Hobby Division of the New York World's Fair. I had a small painting of a place called "Tzin-Tzun-Tzan," in the State of Patscuaro [Pátzcuaro] in old Mexico. That is where the Tarascan Indians live. They were at one time very expert in feather work, and they are the ones who fish with the butterfly nets. They are a colorful tribe of Indians, and are very interesting. Well, my picture was of an old gateway that leads into an old church-yard, dating back to the days of Cortez. I thought it would be quite an honor if I could get a painting hung in one of the divisions of the World's Fair, so I almost fainted when I received notice that I had won second place in the exhibit.[32] From that I had orders for two more pictures.

When my pictures were ready to be sent home from the Museum, I realized that I didn't have any place to put them. I went out into the back yard and surveyed the premises. I could see a place where a sort of gallery could be built. There was a long garage, and at the end of the garage nearest the house there was a coal shed jutting out about twelve feet. I saw that it would not take very much lumber to make a good sized room, the garage furnishing the back, the coal shed would be the east wall; so the west wall and the roof was the main thing.

An old drug store had been torn down in town, and they had given Edgar about six or eight big long glass doors, if he would haul some other stuff away for them. The glass doors were stacked in the back of the garage, and no one cared anything about them. So there was the north wall of my studio, and would furnish the good north light I needed to paint by.

As I thought and planned how to build it, I suddenly thought of a fireplace in the west end. I mentioned it to David and he said that he would haul the rocks for me and help me to build the chimney. So, I set to work. There was a pile of old lumber out in back of our place that was all knotty and full of big nails, but I knew that I would have to make it of whatever I could get hold of. David hauled some old railroad ties for me, and I used them for sleepers to nail my floor to. I used an ice box pan as a level and got the ground leveled and the ties in place.

The boards for the floor was all the lumber I bought. It had knot holes in it, but I patched them with pieces of tin. It took quite a while to get the big nail[s] out of the knotty two-by-fours, but I finally got them out, and got the framework of my building up. I got a motley array of stuff as sheeting for the roof. I found a big old piece of lumber just long enough to make the foundation for my glass windows along the north side. I had to have help to get it moved into place, it was so big and heavy. Then I put the floor down, and proceeded to put most of the roof up.

---

32. Correspondence in the files of the Department of Contemporary Art, New York World's Fair, did not disclose the outcome of Effie's entry. E[ffie]. Marquess Carmack to "Mr. Cahill," New York World's Fair Commission, ca. May 23, 1938; and (unsigned) Assistant to the Director, Department of Contemporary Art, to E. Marquess Carmack, June 2, 1938, Box #53, New York World's Fair Collection, 1939–1940, Manuscripts and Archives Division, New York Public Library; photocopies in the possession of Noel Carmack. For other division award winners, see "New York World's Fair, 1939," *Magazine of Art* 32 (May 1939), and "N. Y. World's Fair Special Number," *Art Digest* 13 (June 1, 1939).

I got tired of waiting for David to get time to help me with the chimney, so I went to work on it myself. I remembered how the chimneys in our old log house in Kentucky were built, and I knew the pattern they would have to be made on to keep them from smoking when a fire was built in the fireplace. A big hole just above the fireplace, and then a smaller opening the length of the chimney to the top, just the same width all the way up. I got it built to within about three feet of the top when Dave came and ordered me down, saying that he would finish it, but when he was through, I saw that he had tapered it (smaller at the top). After he left I built a fire in the fireplace and saw that it didn't draw, but let the smoke come out into the room.

I climbed up with a sledge hammer and knocked the tapering part off and rebuilt it straight up, and then it drew perfectly. But first, getting the arch rock just about the fireplace was almost an impossibility, but Bernice helped me. We pried it up a little at a time, and propped it till we got one end up, then after resting a while we finally got the other end up. Then I could start building the chimney proper.

After it was all done, the inside of the fireplace was all rough and ugly. There were some big flat smooth rocks out in the pile Dave had hauled, and Bernice and I proceeded to see if we could line the fireplace with them and make it look better. We got the sides up, and had the big piece for the back in on the hearth, but it was awful heavy and hard to handle. In getting it dropped into place, Bernice got her thumb caught and took the entire nail off, root and all. I felt so bad, and did all I could to ease the pain. I made her lie down, and I rubbed her head till she went to sleep. A peculiar thing happened, the nail on her other hand came off, every bit of it, and she had two thumbs without nails, and they both grew back at the same time, both perfect nails, without a ridge or a thing to show they had come off.

Well, we got the fireplace lined with smooth rocks, the chimney next to it would draw, it had a nice smooth hearth, and the floor was down. The roof was next. It was no trouble to nail the roofing on when once I got the sheeting ready, then all I lacked was the windows and the door, which was comparatively easy.

Manson was assistant manager at Penney's, and they were putting a new carpet on the mezzanine floor. Manson picked out enough good carpeting to cover my studio floor. It was a beautiful expensive rug, and made my studio look cozy. I then made a window seat, the entire length of the north side, under the windows, covered it with black oilcloth, with a bright ruffle around it. Got the fireplace whitewashed, and a pretty mantel fixed. Papered the rough ugly walls and ceiling with a soft gray building paper. I got the garbage man to bring me all the big pieces of cardboard he could find, and he found plenty, some that came around furniture and other big things. I put a layer of cardboard on the sheeting of the roof, before I put the roofing on, as it was very uneven, also a layer over the boards of the floor. I ceiled [sealed?] the walls with it, and the ceiling overhead before putting up the building paper, and before laying the carpet Manson brought me. When it was all finished it was actually a beautiful room, and became very popular as a meeting place.

Edgar even said that he had no idea that I would be able to make such a pretty room with the old junk that I had had to work with.

Mr. Shipley had built Dell, his wife and my artist friend, a nice studio, but she declared she liked mine much better, and it did look cozy and homey.[33]

One of the bad things was mixing the mud and cement to go between the rocks when I was building the chimney, and then carrying it in a coal scuttle, and hauling it up to where I was working. Grace came one day while I was working, and she said that she would mix the "dobbin" to go between the rocks, she could at least do that, but by the time she had mixed one batch she had a splitting headache, and had to quit.

It was hot weather and hard work, and I was supposed to have a weak heart, but it didn't seem to hurt me at all. I would be dog tired at night, but was rested by morning, and ready to go at it again. I found that the hard life I had led had made me tough, and I could stand much harder work than my girls (excepting Violet, she would tackle most anything). My motto was from Caesar: "If you want a thing done, do it yourself." I've found it a good and true saying.

I built a long low table to work on, and put a plain colored oilcloth on it to match the gray building paper on the walls and ceiling. The gray made a nice background for my pictures, and when I got them hung it really looked like an art studio. I found out later that there had been a cow pen where I built it, and in rainy weather it was a little evident, so Mrs. Shipley suggested that I name it for the sacred cow "Hathor."[34] I had a big old tin sign, about two by three feet, with a beautiful elaborate edge around it. It was an easy task to paint out the lettering and make a sign for my studio, to put where it could be seen from the road: Art Shanty "Hathor." I planted a row of little Chinese elms along our driveway leading to my Shanty, and they grew like magic, and helped the look of things.[35]

33. Dell was the wife of Leo M. Shipley.
34. Hathor is an Egyptian goddess often represented by the head of a cow.
35. After the studio was completed, Effie wrote a poem entitled "My Hobby House" from which the epilogue's title is taken.

I had been appointed a Stake Missionary, and I held cottage meetings in the studio with different groups.[36] Brother Dargie brought a Navajo man, Charlie, who had taken the part of Chief in an Indian Pageant that was put on at the Mesa Verde ruins in Colorado for at least one season, maybe more. He was a handsome intelligent fellow. He asked me if he could bring some Indian men and their wives, men who were working under Mr. Dargie on the railroad section. I told him he could. They came on a Thursday evening. It was getting cool enough now to have a fire. Some of the Indian women had their babies with them. We popped corn and had nuts. We sang, and I played the old guitar. They asked if they could come back the next Thursday, so for a long time we had a weekly meeting.

I told them of the Gospel, and of their history, called the Book of Mormon.[37] They liked it. It was good missionary work. The Indians are very artistic, and enjoyed the paintings of Indian life.

I was teaching a Sunday School class at Church, and when we didn't have time to finish our lesson before closing time, we would adjourn to my studio and we would finish the lesson there. Several of the class who were not members of our Church were later baptized.

I had organized a Primary at the recreation hall of a housing unit called "Sunset Vista" on the west side of town, and occasionally I would invite the members to my Shanty for a Primary party. One time when I got to the housing unit hall, two of the boys came running and said, "Mrs. Carmack, old Butch and Chicago (two bigger boys) are coming to this meeting, and they say that they are going to break it up." I did some quick mental calculating and decided to change the lesson. Manson was by then flying instructor at the Thunderbird Airfield in Phoenix, and through him I had learned some interesting things about airplanes, so we had a lesson on airplanes. Sure enough, the two big boys came. I made them welcome, and told them that I was glad to have them, as they might help us out with one lesson on airplanes. Those two boys behaved, and felt very important to be asked to help out with the lesson.

I asked the boy they called Chicago if he was really from there, and he said that he was. I said that we could usually tell what kind of people a person had been living around, as they would be somewhat like them. I quoted from one of the teachers in grade school who had said that she

---

36. Stake missionaries work part time in local areas, as opposed to full-time elders who have figured so importantly in this autobiography. Cottage meetings are small gatherings, usually in the home of a member of the Mormon Church, for the purpose of inviting missionaries to discuss the church with interested non-Mormons.

37. The Book of Mormon gives the history of the Lamanite people, from whom the modern-day Indians on the American continent are believed to be descended.

could tell what kind of mothers the children had without ever seeing the parents. I said that I knew that most of those present had nice mothers who had taught them good manners; and so we had an ideal class, and I invited them to come again. The next Thursday, when my regular little class members came, they said, "Boy, you really knew how to manage old Chicago and Butch last Thursday. They didn't even act like themselves." I told them that we have to use strategy in handling people, and then we had a short discussion of the meaning of the word strategy, and they liked it.

A little later I organized another Primary at the Sunrise Vista housing unit on the east side of town. Of course, I first asked permission of the one in charge, to hold the meetings. Then I appointed two girls with bicycles to take a written notice to each house where there were children, announcing a Primary class after school at the Recreation Center.

The first evening there were eighty seven children there, and I had come alone. I knew then that I was going to have to have two classes—one for the little ones who got out of school early, and one for the larger ones who got out at four.

That worked better, and I got along fine with them, by planning my meetings ahead of time, and being prepared. I wish I could have a reunion of the members of those two Primaries now, thirty seven years later. They would be middle-aged men and women, most of them with families.

My studio became almost too popular with a group of children living not too far from me, and it began to be sort of a public playground around our place. One day I invited them into my studio and told them that I was too busy to have visitors every day, but if they would choose just one evening, after school, and all of them come just that one evening, and not any other day of the week, we would have a party with a program and refreshments. I asked them what kind of a party they would like, and they said, "A Cowboy Party," so I agreed. I told them to wear cowboy costumes if they had them, but it wasn't necessary, and to come anyway. It is surprising how many good cowboy stories you can find. I took Joseph, whose brothers were cowboys, and told them how he went to take food to them, and the whole tragic story, even of the famine, and Jacob's family coming down into Egypt, where they had food stored up.

One of the main things was regular reviews, to see how much they remembered.

One family of children who came had a mother who neglected them, and was gone most of the time, and didn't pay any attention to their clothing or their meals, and much of the time they were without food. I was chairman of the physically handicapped children of the state at that time, and it finally grew so bad that I reported it to the officers, and they suggested that they be sent to their grandmother's, which was done.

The oldest of these children was a beautiful little girl about eight years old. She had the care of her two smaller brothers, and did the best she could.

Not long ago I received a letter from her, she had joined our Church, had married and converted her husband, and they had a little child. She sent me their pictures. It made me very happy. Her husband was a Branch President where they were living.[38] Her married name was Fames.[ . . . ][39]

Hazel was called on a mission to the East Central States in April, 1934. She was the third one of our children to be called on a Mission, and we were very happy about it.

We knew that she would make a good missionary. She was good at anything she undertook. She had majored in Spanish, and could speak it well, but we didn't make that known when she was called, or she would probably have been sent to old Mexico, or to a Spanish American Mission.

Cecil and Noel had both filled missions in the Southern States. It is pure joy to have a son or a daughter on a mission, and how we did look forward to their letters.

At first Hazel was assigned to the Mission office in Louisville, Kentucky. Sitting at the typewriter all day, without much exercise caused her to gain weight. She said that she would fatten on a glass of tomato juice, while the others ate all they could hold and didn't gain an ounce. She and her companion went out one evening a week to help the Elders hold street meetings. Our cousin, Cleatis Overton, who was singing over the radio station in Hopkinsville, would visit his Uncle Ben Marquess in Louisville occasionally, and would join them with his big concert guitar, and help with their singing. He had a good strong voice, and with his guitar helped attract attention.[40]

Hazel and her companion, Florence Anderson, originated a little scheme on "how to win friends and influence people" (before Dale Carnegie).[41] It was a secret little club of two, and it worked. One day a fellow came along with gold wire and pliers, making pins to wear—usually saying "Mother," or any name you wanted to have made to wear. They had him make one each for their little club. It consisted of these letters, B. I. D. The other missionaries racked their brains trying to guess what b. i. d. could possibly stand for. It was the abbreviation for "Being intelligently

38. A unit smaller than a ward is termed a *branch*, with a president rather than a bishop.

39. The editors have omitted four asterisks centered on the page followed by the subtitle, "Winslow, Arizona—Hazel's Mission—The Art Tour."

40. George Cleatis Overton (1911–1999) was the son of Georgia Emma Marquess (1868–1958) and John Henry Overton (1864–1929).

41. Florence J. Anderson of Otto, Wyoming served in the East Central States Mission in 1934–1935.

dumb." They would find out ahead of time what the people they were going to visit were most interested in, and then would pretend that they didn't know a thing about it, and act interested, and ask questions. Anyone likes to find someone who is interested in them, and in this way the girls made many new friends. It will usually work with most anyone, anytime. There's a psychological truth there, and they had lots of fun keeping the other missionaries guessing.

Brother James N. Kirkham was president of the East Central States Mission then, and Hazel liked him very much; he was kind, helpful and understanding with the missionaries.[42] One day he came home with an armload of candles, and Sister Kirkham asked him what in the world he wanted with all those candles. He said he had got them real cheap, and they could come in real handy sometime. She said that she wouldn't be at all surprised if he should come home some day with an armful of wooden legs, if he could get them real cheap. But it wasn't long till something went wrong with the lights, or there was a storm and the electricity was off; then Brother Kirkham's candles were a real blessing.

At another time, President Kirkham suddenly decided to change locations, and leave the old mission home, where the church office had been for years. He found a building on much higher ground. They couldn't figure out why he was going to spend precious time moving, when they were all so busy. That was in 1936, and in 1937 came the big flood on the Ohio River. The building they had moved from was flooded, and if they had not moved, their precious old mission records, their books and many other things would probably have been ruined. It began to look as if President Kirkham had an uncanny sense of premonition.

Hazel said that working in the mission home proved to be a wonderful experience, because there she had the blessing of being in contact with many outstanding people:

Apostle Lyman and his wife,[43] who they found to be delightful people; President George Albert Smith; President Charles A. Callis, who had served as President of the Southern States Mission for about twenty years when we were in the South (and he came to our little Woodland Branch for Conferences about twice a year, stayed in our homes, and ate at our tables); Brother Melvin J. Ballard.[44] It was a blessing just to be in the daily presence of these great men, and they had some lively discussions at the big dinner table.

---

42. James Mercer Kirkham (1872–1957) served as President of the East Central States Mission in 1934–1937. He married Kate Woodhouse (1872–1946) in 1893.

43. Richard R. Lyman (1870–1963) was married to Amy Cassandra Brown (1872–1959). He served as an LDS Apostle in 1918–1943.

44. Melvin J. Ballard (1873–1939) served as an LDS apostle in 1919–1939.

At one time Apostle Lyman and his wife came out to make a tour of the Mission, and President Kirkham gave Hazel a vacation from the typewriter and invited her to go with them on a tour of East Kentucky and West Virginia. It was a happy privilege. As a secretary in the office, she had contacted all the different branches of the mission, and felt half way acquainted with many of them through correspondence with them. It was a rewarding trip, and she even got to visit the Big Smoky country, and was intensely interested in the people, their way of life, their customs. Then when they returned to Louisville she wrote and told me all about their interesting trip, and we enjoyed every bit of it with her.

The latter part of her mission, they let her go out into the country with a companion, Lavinia Wells.[45] They worked around Elkton, Madisonville, and our old home town of Hopkinsville, where many of our relatives were still living.

Then she went to Tennessee with a new companion, Lucille Thomas, from Pinedale, Arizona.[46] Lucille had been blind as a child. I remember two of her little cousins bringing her to our place, when we lived at the Westover house in Joseph City. The little cousins were leading her, and I felt so sorry for her.

Later, Lucille's parents sent her to the Primary Children's Hospital in Salt Lake City, and her sight was restored so that she was able to finish high school, and to fill an honorable mission. She later married a fine man, Roy Palmer, and raised a family of lovely children.[47] She also had a beautiful voice, and was a noted singer.

It was cold weather while Hazel and Lucille worked in Nashville. There was a fireplace in the room they rented, and sometimes there was not either any wood or coal for the fireplace, but there was a pile of old newspapers in a corner, so they would twist them into a hard knot and they would make enough heat to help a little, but didn't last long. They were supposed to study a certain length of time every morning before going out to work, so they usually studied in bed to keep warm.

Then Lucille was transferred, and Hazel's last companion was Camilla Kutch, from Woodruff, Arizona.[48] Some deep and lasting friendships are formed on missions, and missionary reunions in later years are happy occasions.

---

45. Lavinia Wells of Logandale, Nevada served as missionary in the East Central States Mission in 1933–1934.

46. Lucille Thomas (1915–1990) of Pinedale, Arizona served as missionary in the East Central States Mission in 1934–1936.

47. Lucille married Leroy Arthur Palmer.

48. Camilla Kutch of Lakeside, Arizona served as missionary in the East Central States Mission in 1936–1937.

Art tour group at Carthage Jail, Illinois, 1936. Effie is fifth from the left, front row; Geneva and B.F. Larsen are to the right of her. Courtesy of John K. Carmack.

Hazel saw a notice in a Church paper that the Brigham Young University was going to sponsor an Art Tour during the summer of 1936.[49] They would follow the old Mormon Pioneer trail, when it was possible, and paint landmarks along the way, (back to Nauvoo, Illinois, where the Mormons were driven from when they went to Salt Lake Valley). Hazel wrote to the Art Department and told them that her mother painted, and asked if she could go with them on this Art Tour to Nauvoo. Professor B. F. Larsen, head of the Art Department of B.Y.U., said that I could go.[50] Knowing that I never had any money, Hazel began saving out of her monthly allowance that she received from home for her mission expenses. She said that she and companion really enjoyed lots of oatmeal about this time. Then Noel started sending her a monthly donation, and besides saving enough for me to go with the Art group, she saved enough for a year at the Brigham Young University (about $250).

The Art Tour was scheduled to leave Provo about the same time that Hazel was released. I sure hated to leave just as she was coming home,

---

49. Hazel probably read H. R. Merrill, "While Yet The Old Trail Lasts: Artists Plan Trip to Preserve Historic Scenes," *Deseret News* (Church section), February 22, 1936, 1, 8. See Noel A. Carmack, "'The Yellow Ochre Club': B. F. Larsen and the Pioneer Trail Art Tour, 1936," *Utah Historical Quarterly* 65 (Spring 1997): 134–54.

50. Bent Franklin "B. F." Larsen (1882–1970) was professor of art at BYU in 1931–1953. He was head of the Art Department in 1936–1953.

when I had not seen her for nearly two years, but it was one of the most wonderful experiences of my life, and I will be eternally grateful to Hazel for her pure unselfishness and sacrifice that made it possible for me to go—and for Noel, too—he actually furnished the money, while he worked at road building near Benson, Arizona.

Back in Winslow, Edgar had hired a boy to help him, and he was boarding at our place, so Hazel did the cooking for them both, while I was having a glorious time.

I got to Provo on a Sunday afternoon, and spent the night with a beloved old friend of Hopkinsville, a beautiful girl, Mamie Melton, who had married Thatcher Kimball, grandson of the wonderful Heber C. Kimball, one of the stalwarts of the early days of the Church in Nauvoo.[51] Mamie and I talked most of the night, Sunday night, the Art Group was leaving Monday morning.

There were seventeen of us, counting the driver, George Strebel, who was to be official photographer for the trip.[52] We had some difficulty getting started. Someone had failed to service the bus, and it had no gas in it, but that was soon remedied. Later, when we were sailing along and everyone was writing industriously, Professor Larsen had the driver stop the bus, and told us that we were not going on this trip to write diaries, but to sketch and paint along the way, and to be ready to put finishing touches on our sketches in the evening. He said that he would have a reading of all the diaries so far, and then he would choose the best one and have that one keep the diary the rest of the trip, and the others should spend their time on art.

I had written my diary in rhyme, and the committee voted for me to be the one to keep the record of the trip.[53] They suggested that the others give me copies of their snapshots of the trip, and in return I would give each of them a copy of the diary. Professor Larsen had said that there would be a prize for the winner of the diary contest, so he passed a hat around and collected $7.65 with which to buy a prize of my own choosing. I waited until we got to Omaha, then while the others hunted a

51.  Thatcher Kimball (1883–1956), mentioned earlier, was married to Mamie Lee Melton (b. 1885).

52.  The members of this group were: B. F. and Geneva Larsen, Euray Anderson, Wilford Biggs, Effie Carmack, Lorin Covington, Viola Hale Curtis, Ralph Huntsman, Mary Jensen, Georgiana Johnson, Thera Lou Olsen, Alta and Myrtle Peterson, Merla Robinson, Ethel Strauser, George Strebel, and Anna R. Williams.

53.  As Hazel Carmack Bushman remarked in a conversation with Karen Lynn Davidson on December 3, 1994, "My mother liked to jingle everything." All kinds of occasions, from sad ones such as the death of baby Harry to happy ones like the completion of her "Hobby House" in Arizona, called forth rhyming couplets. Only a fraction of her poems were collected in *Backward Glances* (see chapter two, note 1).

paint store for some extra tubes of paint and some brushes, Wilford Biggs, of Phoenix, a three hundred pound (more or less) clown, volunteered to go with me to find my prize.

We went to a second hand store and asked the man if he had a good guitar, reasonable. Biggs told him that he and his wife (me) were stranded in Omaha, and we thought that if we could find an old guitar with a good tone we might collect enough money on the street corner to buy a ticket to our destination in Arkansas. He said that all the money we had was $7.65, and did he have a guitar for that amount.

The man brought out a cheap old thing with a raspy tone, and a neck that didn't note true. We didn't want it, but I saw another one that had been much used, but with a glorious tone. He said that it was twenty five dollars. Biggs told him that we didn't have that amount of money, but that we would give him the $7.65, which was all we had. He said that he couldn't possibly take that for it, so we turned sadly to leave, got to the door, and the man called after us and said, "Come and take it. I paid more than that for it, but I'll let you have it."

It was a good guitar, and we were glad to have it. From then on we sang our way along. We had a theme song as we were leaving the towns. We sang, "Fare thee well, for I must leave you." It is a miracle what an old guitar can do for a group of pretty good singers. Every evening we had a song fest. Most of the group could sing, and enjoyed it.

I would like to tell of all the interesting things that happened along the way. If there was enough space I would include the diary, and some pictures.

We arrived at the edge of the mighty Mississippi River. Professor Larsen had some advice to give us before entering Nauvoo.

A big flat boat called "The Nauvoo" docked, and our big old Pioneer Trail Bus was driven on to it, across the wide expanse of the big river, and to the old, old landing near the Nauvoo House, which was being built for visitors at the time the Prophet Joseph and his brother Hyrum were killed.

We stayed there for two weeks—slept, cooked, and ate in the Nauvoo House which Emma Smith had used for a boarding house.[54] We slept on beds with wooden slats and straw mattresses, the same ones Emma had used. We used the same dishes and long table that her boarders had used.

We all painted every day. Then, in the evening, we exhibited our pictures and Professor Larsen criticized them. I had never used very brilliant colors in my paintings, and they all teased me, and would say, "Here

---

54. Emma Hale (1804–1879) was the wife of Joseph Smith, Jr. After Joseph Smith's death, Emma married Lewis Bidamon of Illinois.

comes Carmack and her pictures that look like an Arizona dust storm had struck them." But I didn't care, I like to reproduce the natural colors as I see them, and I liked the results.

George Rogers and his family were living in the house next door to us in Winslow, and their boys, Lawrence and Pearly, were at my place often.[55] They were good boys, and I liked them. One day, as we were starting out to paint, a letter came from Hazel saying that Lawrence and Pearly had gone out to the ditch to go swimming, and had waded off into an old Santa Fe well that they didn't know was there, and both of them were drowned.[56] It was a terrible shock to me, and I couldn't quit crying. I had planned to paint the home of the Prophet's mother, which he had built for her, but my glasses kept getting blurred till I couldn't see. I went into the house for a drink of water. A nice old couple was living in it, and they saw that I had been crying, and I told them of the sad news from home. The man went and picked a bowl of raspberries for me, and I appreciated it.

It was a warm day, and I asked if I could do an interior of the old house. They said that it was O.K. and showed me grandma Smith's kraut cutter, and her bread board, and a little basket hanging on a rafter that had belonged to her. While they talked, I got a good sketch of both the front room, where she had kept the mummies sitting, after her sons were killed, and one of her kitchen, too.[57] It was a friendly looking little place, with a fireplace and a warming oven on the side of it. There was a big fallen leaf table and other old pieces of furniture they said had belonged to Lucy Mack Smith.[58] These folks were kind enough to keep all of these old things for the benefit of visitors who seemed interested in them.

The day we left Nauvoo was in the first week of July, and was hot as blazes. The bus was ready to travel, and the others were at a grocery, buying food for the trip, all but Georgiana Johnson and I. We found a big old building with big glass windows in front. On a platform back of the

---

55. George Walter Rogers (1900–1940) and Matilda Porter Rogers (b. 1900) had seven children (five boys and two girls).

56. Lawrence Walter Rogers (b. 1924) and Perlie Theodore Rogers (b. 1925) were drowned June 19, 1936.

57. Joseph Smith, Jr., is believed to have translated the *Pearl of Great Price* (part of the LDS canon of scripture) from ancient Egyptian papyri which accompanied mummies that were purchased from Michael Chandler in 1835. After the death of Joseph and Hyrum Smith in 1844, the mummies were displayed in the house of Lucy Mack Smith (1775–1856) and various locations before their disappearance in about 1856. See James R. Clark, *The Story of the Pearl of Great Price* (Salt Lake City: Bookcraft, 1955), 142–53.

58. Lucy Mack Smith (1775–1856) was the mother of Joseph Smith, Jr.

windows was a big piece of yellowed wrapping paper with FOR SALE written on it, so we went in and found that it was a regular museum. There was one big box that the lady said contained articles from Joseph Smith's home, and when we examined the things in it we knew that she told the truth. There were letters addressed to Joseph Smith, and some to Emma Middleton [*Effie probably means Emma Bidamon*]. The old lady said that that was a girl who had lived with Joseph and Emma for a while. There was a velvet and celluloid photograph album with Joseph Smith's name and HIS BOOK written under his name. The first photo in it was of William Wadsworth Longfellow, and following his name was written, "To my good friend Joseph Smith."[59] It was taken when Longfellow was young. Photography was in its infancy at that time, and most of them were tintypes. The old lady said that she would take a dollar for the book. I handed her the dollar, but on second thought she said, "maybe I had better not sell this," and took it back. I was so disappointed. I did buy two fans from the box, though, and then I saw an old split-bottomed hickory chair, and asked her how old it was. She said that it had been her grandmother's, and told me the name of the man who made them, but I didn't remember his name long enough to put it down. She said that her grandmother had had four of the chairs made. Georgiana asked her if Joseph Smith ever came to her grandmother's place. She replied that her mother had told her that he came to her grandmother's house often to get her mother, a little girl of ten or eleven years, to go and wash dishes for Emma, as they always had a lot of visitors.

Then we asked her if she thought Joseph had ever sat in that chair. She said of course he did, as often as he came, it would have been a wonder if he had missed it. She said that while her grandmother combed her mother's hair, and put a clean apron on her, that Joseph talked to her grandfather, and tried to convert him to the Mormon religion. I asked her if she would sell the old chair to me. She said that it was so old that it might fall down, but she had some new chairs at her home, not far away, and she would sell me one of them, if we needed another chair. I told her that I would just as soon have this old one, and she sold it to me for fifty cents. It is one of my precious possessions.

I left the old chair at the B.Y.U., as I was coming home on the bus, and the next summer, 1937, the Art Club came down through the southwest to visit Indian villages, and Professor Larsen brought the chair to me.[60]

---

59. Effie may mean Henry Wadsworth Longfellow. There is no record, however, that Longfellow ever visited Nauvoo.
60. See H. R. Merrill, "B.Y.U. Art Tour Includes Visit to Arizona, New Mexico," *Deseret News* (Church section), March 20, 1937, 1, 4.

He said, "The very fact that I brought this chair to you proves that I am an honest man, because I wanted to keep it." He said that he had sat in it whenever he painted, ever since I left it in Provo.

He is a wonderful man, and the members of the Art Club all loved him.[ . . . ][61]

About the time Grace adopted Judy, I was going to "Indian Town" across the railroad tracks, holding cottage meetings. Annis Jackson, who was teaching in the grade school in Winslow, and Pearl Shelly Davenport agreed to take me to the meetings—Pearl would teach a little Primary class while the two of us held a Relief Society meeting with the mothers.[62]

The Relief Society meetings were usually at Lena Charlie's place.[63] Sometimes Pearl would hold her Primary class at Stella's (who lived near Lena). If Pearl could not go, we had the children sit in with our Relief Society class, and I could slant the lessons partly to the children. We had good meetings, and occasionally had work meetings along with our lessons. We pieced a quilt and quilted it, and they enjoyed it. But sometimes Annis would have a teacher's meeting she had to attend, or some other school function, and when she did, we couldn't keep our appointments. We had no way of letting them know that we couldn't come, as none of the ladies had telephones. Then they would meet and wait for us, and were not very happy when we failed to show up, and although I had a legitimate excuse, it didn't help much, so I began to wonder if it was worth while. Should I quit trying to hold the meetings regularly?

I made [it] a matter of prayer, and I had the most beautiful dream, or vision, about it. I dreamed that I had taken the children on a picnic, and I told them that they could go and play in a grove of little trees while I got the lunch ready. They didn't play, just sat in a little group, and one of the little girls had her mother's baby, and was holding it in her lap. It was near sunset, and the western sky was very beautiful.

I was looking at the peaceful scene, and I saw two objects, between me and the sunset sky. They were far away at first, and were just gray in color. Then I realized that they were coming towards me, and when they were nearer I could see their clothing was thin and beautiful, floating around them like a halo. The sunset colors were reflected in them, and seemed to be a part of their costumes.

---

61. Editorially omitted material consists of two short narratives subtitled, "Going to Violets in L.A. with Chester Lewis about 1941 or 42" and "Picking Grapes in Jack's Canyon in Winslow (about 1940)." The subtitle, "My Vision," has also been omitted.

62. Probably Annis Rebecca Jackson (1876–1953) was the single woman who did missionary work with Effie in Winslow. Pearl Shelley Davenport (b. 1921) was married to James Lawrence Davenport (b. 1918).

63. Lena Charlie was a Hopi woman whom Effie befriended while living in Winslow.

They first went to the group of children, and in my dream I thought they ministered to them. With a soft magic touch they made the baby's face clean and its clothing dry and white. They touched each child, and seemed to make them beautiful. Then they arose and came towards me, and their beauty was beyond description. Both seemed the personification of goodness, beauty, and love. They stood in the air in front of me for a few minutes, and their presence was a blessing and a benediction. They then started moving back, with their sweet faces still turned towards me.

Hazel was coming, and I told her to hurry and look, and she said that she saw only two gray figures with the sunset colors surrounding them.

I awoke, and I was sure that it was a wonderful witness to me of the importance of the work we were doing among those choice, humble people, and especially with the children.

Years later, after we had been away from Winslow for several years, I went to an Indian Sunday school, and many of the teenagers remembered me, and were disappointed that I couldn't recognize them.

I think that most of our Primary children later joined our Church, and were baptized.[ . . . ][64]

After many serious heart attacks in Winslow the doctor told Edgar that he should go where the altitude was lower. He had been in the hospital a long time, and it cost a lot of money. Our savings were about exhausted, so when he had the last attack and it was necessary for him to go to the hospital, they required the money before they would admit him. Mr. Bruchman volunteered the $1500.00 required, and there was not much hope of him getting it back soon.[65] It was a very unselfish thing for him to do.

When the doctor advised a move, we thought of California, as Cecil and Noel were both out here then. We made several trips back and forth looking for a suitable place to buy. We had a buyer for our home in Winslow. I hated to sell the place: my shanty with its fireplace where I painted, and the wall of petrified wood around the front lawn, and my row of little elm trees that were just getting started good, but it had to be.

We finally got located in the summer of 1946, not long before Edgar's birthday, July 17th. The children came and brought a birthday dinner. It was hot as blazes, and someone suggested we go to the beach to eat our lunch. The young folks took their bathing suits and we put some blankets in the back of Arnold's pickup and away we went.

---

64. Editorially omitted material consists of a short narrative subtitled, "Winslow, Arizona—Negro Soldier." The subtitle which follows, "Moving to California," has also been omitted.

65. This refers to Hazel's father-in-law, Otto Richard "Max" Bruchman (1880–1986), the father of Donald William Bruchman (1915–1962). Otto Bruchman owned a well-established curio store in Winslow, Arizona, mentioned above.

When we got to Morro Bay, it was real foggy, and cold as the dickens. There was no swimming or even wading. We hunted up some wood and made a big fire and got the blankets out of the pickup and tried to keep warm. We didn't stay too long, as the children had to disperse to their respective homes.

I was determined to pay Mr. Bruchman back the $1500.00 he had given the hospital for Edgar's last heart attack. He had gone back to Winslow after we moved to help Mrs. Marley get started in her new market, and had another heart attack there, with another stay in the hospital.[66] Grace stayed here at our place while I went back to Arizona to take care of Edgar at Sadie's, after he was able to leave the hospital.

I asked Mr. Bruchman then if he thought that he could sell paintings of Indian life in his curio store. He said that he could try it and see. So as soon as we got settled at home in California again, I started painting pictures of Indian life and sending them to him, and they sold.[67] I can't remember just how long it was before I had the $1500 paid off, but it was a happy day when I got a notice saying, "Paid in full."

After that last attack, Edgar was left an invalid. He had lost the sight of one of his eyes, too.[ . . . ][68] After we moved to [Atascadero] California and I realized I would have to be the breadwinner (the doctor in Winslow assured me Edgar would never be able to do hard work any more) I first tried having an art class. I had several pupils, but not a very suitable place for painting.[69] Bernice Walker came up from L.A. and said she thought I might get a job at Knott's Berry Farm. So I went down there and told him I had a collection of Folk songs and a trunk full of authentic old dresses— many of the 90's in good condition. Mr. Knott had me play the guitar with an old lady from the Ozarks who played a dulcimer in front of her log cabin; it had been moved from the Ozarks and fully furnished with old pieces of furniture suitable for the cabin.[70] We got along fine, as I was able to play a chord to her tunes. He also had me play with "Bob," the

---

66. Probably the wife of Joseph W. "Pop" Marley of Winslow. See Stella Hughes, *Hashknife Cowboy* (Tucson: University of Arizona Press, 1984), 12–14.

67. In appendix two, the reader will note Effie's statement: "Paint pictures I have promised—And for Hazels curio store + for Mr Bruchman."

68. Editorially omitted material consists of several redundant sentences and a narrative under the subtitle, "Atascadero—Storeroom Burning, etc." The subtitle which follows, "Singing With Ernie Ford, 1947," has also been omitted.

69. Effie and Edgar moved to a home at 7379 Ysabell Ave. in Atascadero, California. The house and garage with art studio are still standing at that address.

70. Walter Knott (1889–1981), was the founder of the Knott's Berry Farm amusement park in Buena Park, California. See Helen Kooiman, *Walter Knott: Keeper of the Flame* (Fullerton: Plycon Press, 1973).

young man who sang for the group around the campfire in the evenings. There was a room with several big old music boxes, one from Germany and one from Switzerland, several others from different places. Mr. Knott said he would give me charge of this room during daytime. I told him my husband was a semi-invalid, not able to do hard work, so he said bring him down with me and he could find him an easy job at something.[71]

I went to Bernice's for a while, and she suggested we call the Giffie Stone program and see if we could get on with them to sing folk songs. Bernice knew a fellow from Paducah, Kentucky, who played the guitar on the program with the "High Nooners."[72] Ernie Ford was one of the main performers.[73] They had a big white dog that barked and they rang a bell. The man from Paducah called us cousins and said they would be glad to have us on the program, so we got ready and started early, in plenty of time to get there by noon, but they had been working on the streets and had them all torn up, and we had to go a long way around so that by the time we got to the big building where the High Nooners broadcast from, we were late, and it took us about 30 minutes to locate the right room in the Huntington Hotel. We finally found it, just as they were closing. They motioned for us to come in, and Ernie Ford said we wouldn't let us being late hinder us from singing together—there was a vacant room next door. So several of us congregated in the vacant room, and for about two hours we had a happy time exchanging old songs. Ernie Ford said, "Where did you say you were from?" Bernice said, "Hopkinsville, in Christian County, Kentucky," and he said, "Why, that's in spittin' distance of where I live in Tennessee. How did you happen to find all those old songs that close to me, and I never heard them?" I told him I guessed we just dug a little deeper; in fact, we had acquired our collection from several different sources: papa and his brothers and sisters had been collectors of old songs all their lives.

Papa and Uncle Curg helped make music for the balls during the boom in Cumberland Gap when the fabulous coalmines were discovered

---

71. During the 1940s, Walter Knott was successfully operating the berry farm and Chicken Dinner Restaurant. Knott had built his historical cyclorama and Ghost Town adjacent to the restaurant. See Kooiman, *Walter Knott*, 99–105.

72. This program refers to Cliffie Stone's "Hometown Jamboree," originating from KXLA in Pasadena in the late 1940s. Ernie Ford was a performer on this radio program in 1948. Cliffie Stone, born Clifford Gilpin Snyder (1917–1998) was a country-western recording artist, songwriter, producer, and radio and television personality.

73. Ernest Jennings "Tennessee Ernie" Ford (1919–1991) was a popular country western musician and entertainer. See Tennessee Ernie Ford, *This is My Story, This is My Song* (Englewood: Prentice Hall, 1964). Ford was a radio personality in the Los Angeles area from 1945 to 1953, just prior to working in television. He regularly performed in Cliffie Stone's "Hometown Jamboree" in 1948.

there, and it was in the heart of the old settled places of Eastern Kentucky, Tennessee and Virginia and West Virginia—in the Cumberland mountains where the people had kept the same customs, costumes, language and songs that they brought with them from the old countries, when the U. S. was young. Papa and Uncle Curg were both quick to pick up the old songs, and they brought many of them home with them. I was too small to remember that, but I did inherit the old songs, and still have many of them.

Ernie especially liked "The Kickin' Mule," "Mishaps of a Minstrel Man," and also some of the sad old love songs—"Thou Wilt Come No More, Gentle Anna" and "We Drifted Apart." He liked the crude one about the tobacco roller, "I'm a goin' down in town," how she hunted up her lover with her dog and her gun, and "Billie Grimes, the Drover." There were two or three crazy old songs we both knew, and we had fun singing them together. One was "Lattie bodie rigdum, a kimeo," though our versions were not exactly the same, but almost.[74]

I've never found anyone that had ever heard the one about the Minstrel Man but Jo Reese, an LDS missionary that I learned it from. And I've never heard anyone but Aunt Ann sing "Gingety Bung," and now I can't remember it, either.

Ernie Ford has a charming personality, and if I am any judge of human nature, I would guess he is a good man, too. They invited us back for another program, but my time was limited—I had left a sick husband at home.

Another time I went down to Los Angeles, and Bernice and I went to an audition, where many people tried out for different programs—night clubs, T.V. programs, everything. It was real interesting, and we enjoyed it. I wore an old green silk dress with a knee ruffle and a ruffle around the shoulders and a velvet hat with a big plume on the turned-up left side. The dress had belonged to Dell Shipley when she was a girl. She played the violin and piano in a Chautauqua, and traveled all over the country.[75] She was a real musician. Most of the old dresses she gave me were ready to drop to pieces, but this special green silk seemed immortal. She was around 80 when she gave it to me, and she had worn it when she was young—this was at least 25 years ago, and the dress is still in good condition—not a break in it; it seems indestructible.

And now back to the audition: I had developed a sore throat from the smog, and when it came my turn to perform, I did a sorry job of the

---

74. For more on Effie's repertoire, see appendix one.
75. The Chautauqua movement originated in New York in the 1870s. "Chautauqua" became a generic name for programs that sent lecturers, dramatic productions, and musical performers throughout the United States, especially to rural areas.

singing. There was a long line of men sitting at a long table, all taking notes as each person performed, and when it was over they contacted the ones they were interested in. A man that operated a night club said he would give me a job singing folk songs in costume; and another fellow who was soon starting a TV program said he would like to have me on it. We went to the Knott's Berry Farm again, and told Mr. Knott of these two offers, and he said he would arrange it so I could be on these two programs once a week and still hold my job at the Berry Farm. But none of it worked out—every time I went to L. A. I got a sore throat from the smog, and by the time I would get out to Mr. Knott's, I couldn't sing a lick. I went and tried it three times and gave it up. I was sorry, I felt like I would have enjoyed it.

Meanwhile I was working on a plan to help Edgar regain his health. I got a program of multiple vitamins called Nutralite for him to take, and got wheat germ oil that two doctors in Canada had found was just wonderful for heart patients. He began to improve, and I can't remember just how long it was after we came to California that he went daily with a group of men to a big chicken ranch near Santa Maria and handled 3,000 chickens a day for months, without any bad effects. Before this he had been working at easy jobs—as a Watkins agent, and a night clerk in the Blackstone Hotel in San Luis Obispo.[76]

But he decided he was well, and didn't need either the vitamins or wheat germ any more; all he needed now was time to get his health back. I tried to persuade him to keep taking the Wheat Germ oil, as he needed it for his heart, but he was stubborn about taking pills. Then one day he had a bad heart attack and fell on the sidewalk, and was an invalid until he died, on February 14, 1952, in the early morning.[ . . . ][77]

As a general thing when we lose one of our children we wish we had done different, and feel remorseful about things; but I had no serious regrets about things like that when we lost Harry. I couldn't even remember scolding him; he didn't need it, and he had never been spanked.

There was one little thing I felt bad about, though. I had a guitar that we had used in our home evenings—we called them story telling time then, but the strings were broken, and it was hanging upstairs

---

76. Watkins agents were door-to-door sales representatives for the J. R. Watkins Co., selling personal care products, cleaning agents, and spices.

77. Editorially omitted material consists of narratives and genealogical material under the subtitles, "The Cyclone" (included in chapter one, pp. 90–91, nearly verbatim, between angle brackets), "Sadie and I Sing Old Songs for Pioneer Day in Costumes (Picture, 1967)," "A Brief sketch of Grandfather Robert Elliot Marquess' brothers and sisters," and "The Blaines." The subtitle which follows, "1921—The old guitar," has also been omitted.

unused. But we were going to have a program and would need it, so I got some new strings and rejuvenated it. When the children came in I played a chord and sang a song the children knew, and Harry's eyes were just shining. He was really thrilled. He said, "Mama! I didn't know you could do that; play it some more." I had not realized that it had been so long since I had played it, and I felt sorry. Children need music and songs and laughter. After that I tried to make up for lost time. We used it in our story telling in the evening, to go with our songs.

Not long ago, I wondered what I could send to my children for Christmas that would kind of surprise them, so I typed all the first little songs and poems they had learned as little children. I put pretty covers on them and painted the covers, and they all liked them. But I would guess if a one of them has kept that little book it will be Violet.

It is good for children to learn little songs and stories when they are small. They have Primary nowadays where the children learn little poems and songs, but when our children were small we didn't have Primary, and so we created our own at home, and I am glad we did. It takes time and patience, but it can be done.

I made programs and gave the children certain parts for our home evenings (our story telling time). Sometimes Harry would tell an original story and the other children got a kick out of it. He was quite a story teller. Once they sang "God Speed the Right" in Sunday School, and in the afternoon the children were having a play Sunday School and Harry was song leader. He stood on a little table and had a stick to beat time with, and he sang, "Tum de dum dum, Tum de dum dum 'Sam beat the Rye'" instead of "God Speed the Right." We all had a good laugh over it.[ . . . ][78]

My dad played the violin and would often teach us dances, and our mother would join with him in demonstrating the steps of the schottische, polka, mazourka, quadrilles, minuets and the lancers.[79] Our dad had been a dancing teacher.

Sometimes we played "William a Tremble Tow" or "Slap Hand," or "Packet." In the game of "William, etc." we each put one finger down in a circle and one was chosen to say the jingle and see who would be "It" for the next time:

---

78. Editorially omitted material consists of narratives subtitled, "Lelia's First School, 1877 and Their Linsey Dresses" (included in chapter one, pp. 86–88, nearly verbatim, between angle brackets, and "John, and Baseball, Games We Played, etc." (discussed in note 79 below).

79. This narrative is taken from the section subtitled, "John, and Baseball, Games We Played, etc." The paragraphs included here are preceded by several paragraphs discussing her brother, John Robert, and his participation in a local baseball team. The paragraph immediately preceding the included material discusses Effie's playtime with her younger brother, Autie.

William a-tremble Toe, he's a good fisherman
Catches hens, put them in pens,
Some lay eggs, some none,
Wire, briar, limberlock, three geese in a flock,
One flew east and one flew West,
And one flew over the cuckoo's nest.
Old dirty dish of kraut spells O-U-T, out.
The first one shows his teeth will get . . .

(and the one that was it decided what punishment to deal out on the one that showed his teeth first, then the next one to show his teeth was punished, and so on till all had showed their teeth and received their punishment—which was something like: "six pinches and a hard slap," or "one kick on the shin," or "his nose pulled," etc.)

"Packet" was a memory test. Some small object is chosen as the packet, and it is passed around the circle of players, each one asking, "What do you have there?" and the passing it says, "A packet," the next time it is passed, it's: "Two turtle doves and a packet," next "three french hens, two turtle doves and a packet," then "four squawking wild geese, three french hens, two turtle doves and a packet"; next time it's "Five lemonoystics, four squawking wild geese, three French hens, two turtle doves and a packet; next," "six bottles of mortifiasco, five lemonoystics, fours quawking wild geese, three French hens, two turtle doves and a packet"; then "seven fine fantastic phandolphin tweezer cases, six bottles mortifiasco, five lemonoystics, four squawking wild geese, three French hens, two turtle doves and a packet"; next, "eight pairs of paragon parachutes, seven fine fantastic phandolphin tweezer cases, six bottles mortifiasco, five lemonoystics, four squawking wild geese, three French hens, two turtle doves and a packet"; and last, "nine pocket knives and a sawmill, eight pairs of paragon parachutes, seven fine fantastic phandolphin tweezer cases, six bottles mortifiasco, five lemonoystics, four squawking wild geese, three French hens, two turtle doves and a packet." Anyone who failed to remember any of the nine has to drop out and pay a fine (some personal belonging), and to redeem it, the leader will have him do something: sing, dance, recite a poem, kiss someone, or anything he chooses to have him do.

We had lots of other games we played of evenings: one favorite was a "guess who" game; we would hang a sheet in a corner and two or three of us get behind it. The sheet would be about two inches above the floor. We would let our feet show and make an imprint with our nose to indicate our height, but we would change shoes and make an imprint with our fist higher or lower than our real nose. The one waiting to guess had to turn around and look at the fireplace till we called "ready," and then he would guess who was who behind the sheet. This sounds silly, but we had lots of fun playing it.

We had shadow plays on a sheet, too.

These games and entertainment made a rich, full life with all our family, along with mother reading aloud to us, mostly from the New Testament. Often Cousin Filmore Smith's family would come, and he and my father enjoyed discussing the scriptures, and why it was that no church they knew of ever taught the complete gospel, founded on Apostles and Prophets, that it was to be taught free, and that it was to be "fitly framed together."[80] Of course this was in the time before the Mormon Missionaries came to us. After that, there followed a happy period of hearing wonderful sermons, and reading "A Voice of Warning," and another little book "Mr. Durant of Salt Lake City."[81] The Elders brought a new way of life; everything we heard and read fit in perfectly with Christ's teachings. We studied and discussed these wonderful new things we were learning every evening of the winter of 1897 and 8. And in February of 1898 the Elders came back, and my parents applied for baptism, as I have already related.[ . . . ][82]

I am so thankful that through the years when my children were small and I had no money, that I managed to keep them decent by making over old clothes and by sewing them neat and making the garments look nice. Not that their father was lazy, he worked hard all the time; but the money he earned never seemed to do the children or I any good, and I know now it was my own fault. If I had demanded more, I'm sure I could have had more. He loved horses, and kept far more all the time than he needed, and feed was high and the soil worn out till it couldn't produce enough feed for all the animals. So he had to buy feed for them, and he liked pretty harnesses and they were expensive. So there was never any money left for the family.[83] He was a kind father and loved the children,

---

80.  See Ephesians 2:20–21: ". . . built upon the foundation of the apostles and prophets, Jesus Christ himself being the chief corner stone; in whom all the buildings fitly framed together groweth unto an holy temple in the Lord."

81.  Ben E. Rich, *Mr. Durant of Salt Lake City:"That Mormon"* (Salt Lake City: George Q. Cannon & Sons Co., 1893).

82.  Editorially omitted material consists of material subtitled, "Edgar's Story" (see appendix three), "The Storm That Took All My Trees—Early Days and Great Grandpa Bens's Slaves," and "A Friend In Time of Need." The subtitle which follows, "Some Things I Am Thankful For," has also been omitted.

83.  The primacy of the male in southern rural culture is probably the reason for Effie's grievance. Nora Miller described the typical routine of living on a southern tobacco farm by saying:

    The family is paternal. The man handles the money, directs the work, play, and religious life of the family. The wife and children ask for money and get it if he thinks they need the amount of money they ask for. The oldest boy will probably have a small share of the crop to sell for his money. The man

especially when they were small. He would take one on each knee and sing "Two Little Children" and he liked to tell them about his grand-mother and the songs she would sing for him and the things she cooked when he would go there. But as I grow older and look back, the thing I am most thankful for is the fact that I didn't neglect to teach them the important things they needed to know. It didn't take money to do that, just precious time and patience. And it has paid off. Every one of my chil-dren have a deep abiding faith in the Gospel of Jesus Christ, and they obey it. And it's possible that if I had had lots of money, they might not have been as strong in character as they are today. And those are the greatest things I could ask for. They are honest, industrious, hard-working men and women; obeying the new commandment of this dispensation.[84] I remember there used to be written around the margins of the mission-aries' handbooks the following: "A new commandment I give unto you. Thou shalt not idle away thy time."[85] That is one thing that can never be held against me. I have worked ever since I was old enough and I didn't mind it. I have enjoyed life, and I tried hard to get the proper food for my children to help them to grow up healthy and strong in body and mind. That was one thing that worried me constantly, was the right kind of bread for my children. I pleaded with Edgar to go to Cates' flour mill and get the fresh ground whole wheat flour, it was not any more expensive then than the dead, white, bleached, patent flour that he usually brought home. But he would forget it or didn't have time to go out to the mill. A few times I asked Sadie's husband, Evert Holt, to get it for me, and he did and didn't seem to mind it even though it was a little out of the way. They all thought I was a food crank; and I guess I was, measured by their stan-dards. But I had studied the food question (I had to to keep alive) and they were not interested in it. And I knew what the children needed, that was *one* thing that was a constant worry to me. I baked my own bread and I did hate to make it of the white, bleached flour, when I could have had the whole wheat almost just as easy. And it is so much better. Hazel said it tasted like it was already buttered. I wanted brown rice, too. I had read of

---

buys the groceries an article at a time as he goes to the store. He also buys his clothes, farm supplies, and tobacco. The woman and children try to provide for his physical comforts when he is at the house. He demands his meals on time and food that suits his appetite. He wants it on the table as soon as he comes in from work. After the meal he sits on the porch or in the living room and smokes his pipe or reads the paper or a farm magazine till time to return to the field or to go to bed.

See Nora Miller, "The Tobacco Farm Family," chap. 6 in *The Girl in the Rural Family*, 58.

84. Mormons consider "this dispensation" to be the latter days.

85. Doctrine and Covenants 60:13.

the Chinese people getting Beri-beri from eating white rice, but I usually had the white. But the children stayed pretty healthy and made good grades in school. Grace and Hazel were the two youngest graduates in high school in Winslow. And one or two of David's teachers said if they were equipped with the necessary facilities for extra bright pupils, there was no telling what David could accomplish. He was especially good in English and Music. He wrote an essay once and brought it home, and Hazel was astonished. She made me read it. It was a masterpiece. He could have been a writer. Hazel asked him what Miss Kerlin said about it. He said she took it to several other rooms and read it to the pupils and told him to bring it home for Hazel and me to read. He said she made a silly fuss about it, but I could see he was pleased.[ . . . ][86]

Bernice was such a good baby, I would say abnormally good, never crying. She was born with a weak little body but grew up to be a happy person, interested in life and an avid reader. She went to a subscription school when she was 6 and won a prize for reading more books than anyone else in school. Sadie taught it—[87]

Hazel was a beautiful child, and real good natured, and stayed that way. She says she remembers going to sleep at the supper table many times. One Sunday night she coaxed to go to "Mutual" with us at the church, and I didn't want her to go because it was way past her bedtime when it let out. But we changed her dress and washed hands and face and combed her hair and let her go. She was asleep before the second song was through, and says she remembers being awakened by the strains of "God Be With You Till We Meet Again," having slept through the whole meeting.

Grace was born in the spring of the year after we had returned to Kentucky from Utah. I spoke earlier of my stepmother saying that Grace (when she was a baby) looking as if she had *had years of experience*.[88] She was a wise little soul, and did several things that displayed judgment beyond her age. I took her to Sunday School when she was less than a year old. I made a soft pad to lay her on at church while she drank her milk from the bottle, with her rattle and other toys beside her to keep her amused. So then she discovered that if she would hold her bottle with her feet it left her hands free to pick up her rattle; ^etc.^[89] and this became a

---

86. Editorially omitted material consists of narratives under the subtitles, "Edna Uncle Jim's Grandaughter, and Hamby Girls," "How I Stopped a Fight (after we moved to Atascadero)," and "The Antique Exhibit Friday Evening, September 7 about 1935." The subtitle, "More About My Children," has also been omitted.
87. Last three words and em dash added by hand.
88. Last four words underlined by hand.
89. "Etc." interlined by hand.

fixed habit, and she held her bottle with her feet regularly so she would have her hands free for other things. I have never seen another child do that since then; this was in the first half of her first year. I have already told of her pulling Hazel from the fireplace where she had fallen, and hiding her blistered hands because she felt she was at fault—this before she was 2 years old. We didn't think too much of these things then (this was the first family I had ever raised), but now I realize several things that happened were very unusual, and I know that I was given a choice group of spirits to care for and to raise. As they have grown older they prove their worth.

Harry was a good judge of human nature when he picked Erma and Violet and Thelma as the "goodest."[90] All three girls were hard to beat. Violet was as dependable as a grownup when she was just a little girl. It was a source of grief to us that she could never go to town with me, she always had to stay at home and take care of the little ones. And she did a good job of it. When I got home from a long hard day of delivering milk, butter, eggs and produced she would have the house clean, and if I was late, would have supper cooked.

When Erma (Lelia's girl) was still in her early teens, she took over the job of washing for the family on the old washboard, with no conveniences. She had to draw hard water from the well, or take the washing to the pond and dip the water up a bucket full at a time. I remember Lelia saying once, after Erma had started washing, that their washing didn't seem to be as big a job as it used to be. But no matter how big a job it was, Erma never grumbled, she just did it patiently.

The only time when I was not able to do my own washing, Edgar had a nice colored woman come and do it, so my girls did not ever have to do the washings, though they did other things that may have been harder. But it wouldn't have hurt them. I think it's good for young folks to do hard things; it helps build strong characters. I am thankful for the hard work and the big responsibilities I had in my teens. It didn't hurt me, and I think it helped me be a strong woman. I am still pretty tough for an 85-year-old (though I am weakening lately). I do hope I can stay active and able to take care of myself as long as I live.

I am also thankful that my children came up the hard way and were not spoiled. They know about life on a worn-out farm in Kentucky, and still know how to appreciate the conveniences we have today. And Thelma, Violet and Erma's pal, was from a home of about the same caliber as ours.

---

90. Erma was the daughter of William Henry Ferrell and Lelia Marquess, Effie's sister.

Effie Carmack in her art studio, ca. 1970. Courtesy of
*Atascadero News.*

It seemed our families were more than just friends—there was a strong
bond of love that still holds good.[ . . . ][91]

Well, here it is February 1973, and I must get this story to the
printer. I hope I have not left out any important thing or person that
should be included. Some things are repeated, some lengthy, and my
grammar and sentence construction is not the best, but here it is, for
what it is worth.

I hope my dear ones and acquaintances will enjoy reading it, because
that is the purpose for which it was written. I wanted to leave something of

---

91.  Editorially omitted material consists of short narratives, family reports, and sketches
subtitled, "Lelia's Family," "More About Lelia's Family," "Mattie Carmack's Story—
(Edgar's Stepmother)," "About David," "Life Story of Betty C. Hendrickson," "John K.
Carmack," "Cecil Ray's Story," "Rollins Story—" [in Effie's hand], "The Simmons
Family," "Violet and Arnold and the Earthquake," "Letter from Sadie's Daisy (Living in
Winslow)," "Mary's Story—John and Ozie's Daughter," "Violet's Family Story," "Ray
Holt's Story—Sadie's Boy," "The M. J. Bushmans—1973," "Cecil and Gladys' Family—
1973," "Noel's Last Report—1973," and "Hazel's Family—1973." The subtitle, "Finale,"
has also been omitted.

value to my children and grandchildren, and great grandchildren—and this seemed better than riches, of which I have none anyway.

I have many more pictures we could have added, but since Violet has sorted them into family groups for me and placed them in albums, you will be able to enjoy looking at them, anyway. I hope you will treasure the old pictures as well as the later ones. They are my precious possessions.

I like this quote by Kingsley: "Thank God every morning when you get up that you have something to do that day which must be done, whether you like it or not. Being forced to work and forced to do your best will breed in you temperance and self-control, diligence and strength of will, cheerfulness and content, and a hundred virtues which the idle never know."[92]

[signed]
Effie Marquess Carmack[93]

---

92. This is slightly misquoted from Charles Kingsley (1819–1875), "Sermon XII. Work," in *Village Sermons, and Town and Country Sermons,* New Edition. (London: Macmillan and Co., 1878), 273.

93. This is followed by a personal essay by Diane Gustafsen Gouff entitled, "My Most Unforgettable Character," which has been editorially omitted.

# Effie Marquess Carmack's Family

| Grandparents<br>*(spouses listed in italics)* | Parents, Aunts, and Uncles<br>*(spouses listed in italics)* | Effie and her<br>brothers and sisters<br>*(spouses listed in italics)* | Children of Effie Carmack<br>*(spouses listed in italics)* |
|---|---|---|---|

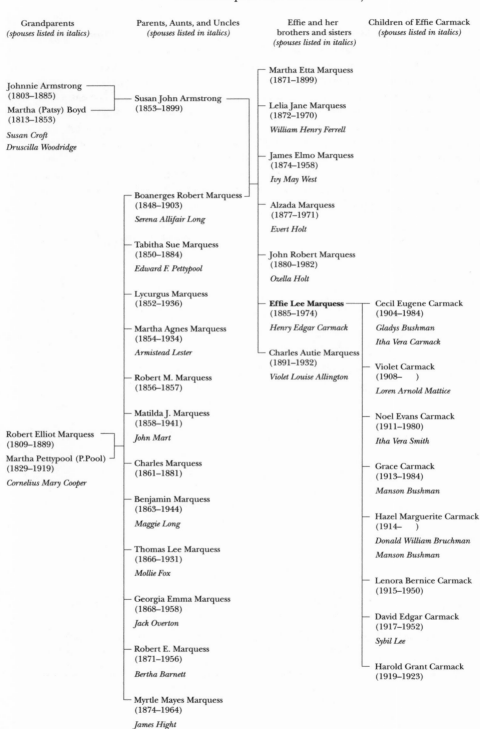

Johnnie Armstrong
(1803–1885)

Martha (Patsy) Boyd
(1813–1853)

*Susan Croft*
*Druscilla Woodridge*

Susan John Armstrong
(1853–1899)

Boanerges Robert Marquess
(1848–1903)
*Serena Allifair Long*

Tabitha Sue Marquess
(1850–1884)
*Edward F. Pettypool*

Lycurgus Marquess
(1852–1936)

Martha Agnes Marquess
(1854–1934)
*Armistead Lester*

Robert M. Marquess
(1856–1857)

Matilda J. Marquess
(1858–1941)
*John Mart*

Robert Elliot Marquess
(1809–1889)

Martha Pettypool (P.Pool)
(1829–1919)

*Cornelius Mary Cooper*

Charles Marquess
(1861–1881)

Benjamin Marquess
(1863–1944)
*Maggie Long*

Thomas Lee Marquess
(1866–1931)
*Mollie Fox*

Georgia Emma Marquess
(1868–1958)
*Jack Overton*

Robert E. Marquess
(1871–1956)
*Bertha Barnett*

Myrtle Mayes Marquess
(1874–1964)
*James Hight*

Martha Etta Marquess
(1871–1899)

Lelia Jane Marquess
(1872–1970)
*William Henry Ferrell*

James Elmo Marquess
(1874–1958)
*Ivy May West*

Alzada Marquess
(1877–1971)
*Evert Holt*

John Robert Marquess
(1880–1982)
*Ozella Holt*

**Effie Lee Marquess**
(1885–1974)
*Henry Edgar Carmack*

Charles Autie Marquess
(1891–1932)
*Violet Louise Allington*

Cecil Eugene Carmack
(1904–1984)
*Gladys Bushman*
*Itha Vera Carmack*

Violet Carmack
(1908–    )
*Loren Arnold Mattice*

Noel Evans Carmack
(1911–1980)
*Itha Vera Smith*

Grace Carmack
(1913–1984)
*Manson Bushman*

Hazel Marguerite Carmack
(1914–    )
*Donald William Bruchman*
*Manson Bushman*

Lenora Bernice Carmack
(1915–1950)

David Edgar Carmack
(1917–1952)
*Sybil Lee*

Harold Grant Carmack
(1919–1923)

# The Song and Rhyme Repertoire of Effie Marquess Carmack

## Introduction

Effie's talents for writing and painting should not overshadow her ability to collect and transmit the musical traditions of western Kentucky. When they were children, Effie and her sisters learned the songs from their father who had played violin at the dance halls in the Cumberland Gap. "I don't know why we collected those old songs so religiously then," she wrote. "There was no demand for them at that time." But by 1947, when Effie began performing at Knotts Berry Farm, she had build her repertoire to over 450 ballads, making her a primary bearer of Kentucky folk songs.

In an effort to complete a comprehensive search of Mormon folk songs, Dr. Austin E. Fife and his wife Alta, began systematically recording songs that were of "Mormon inspiration." "During the Summer of 1946 we spent about two months exploring the field," they wrote. "Our project was sponsored by the Archive of American Folk Song, Library of Congress, which supplied the phonographic discs, and by the Utah Humanities Research Foundation, which underwrote a portion of the travel expenses. Recordings were made with a Wilcox-Gay portable recordio, the property of the collectors."[1] When Fife indexed Effie's portion of the collection, he noted, "The repertoire of this informant is significant for several reasons. Most of her songs were learned in the Kentucky mountains where she was reared. However, as a convert to the Mormon Church she migrated to Utah, subsequently to a Mormon settlement in Arizona, and finally to her present home in Atascadero, California. Her repertoire is amazing in its

---

1.  Austin E. and Alta S. Fife, "Folk Songs of Mormon Inspiration," *Western Folklore Quarterly* 6 (January 1947): 42. See also "Collectors and Collections," *Western Folklore Quarterly* 7 (July 1948): 299–301.

variety and extent." The Fifes concluded by noting that the recorded songs represented "only a sampling of her entire repertoire."[2]

Oddly, the Fifes classified Effie's repertoire, grouping them among those of "Mormon inspiration" rather than of British or Scots Highland origins. In an uncharacteristically critical review of Austin and Alta Fife's classification of the Mormon folksong collection, folklorist Thomas E. Cheney wrote:

> One singer, Effie Cormack [*sic*], furnished the Fifes with many significant folksongs. Mrs. Cormack, a resident of California and a Mormon convert, came from the South. The songs she has in her memory all came out of her own South, and, as one would expect, many of them reflect the traditions of that area with its racial, geographical, and local heritage. Mrs. Cormack's songs have not been sung in Mormon society enough to become Mormon thought or expression. To consider them Mormon folk song would be as ridiculous as calling 'Yankee Doodle' a Russian song because it was sung by a former American who became a Communist.[3]

As an ironic post-script, a photograph of Effie (courtesy of Austin Fife) was used to illustrate the cover of the most recent edition of Cheney's *Mormon Songs From the Rocky Mountains: A Compilation of Mormon Folksong* (Salt Lake City: University of Utah Press, 1981).

The recordings are dated December 26 and 27, 1948; July 8, 1949; September 5, 1949; and March 26, 1951. The songs were recorded primarily at Effie's home in Atascadero, California. A number of them were also recorded in a group setting at the Occidental College in Los Angeles.[4] Dr. Fife read the list onto records at Atascadero, California on December 26, 1948. Copies of the Fife recordings were sent to the Archive of American Folk Song at the Library of Congress for preservation, while subsequent copies of the tapes were sold commercially. The original field recordings are housed in the Fife Folklore Archives at Utah State University, Logan, Utah.

What appears below is an amalgamation of two extant repertoire lists by Effie Marquess Carmack: a list dictated to Austin Fife on

---

2. Austin E. Fife, Fife Mormon Collection (FMC), I:980:2.

3. Thomas E. Cheney, "Mormon Folk Song and the Fife Collection," *BYU Studies* 3 (1960–1961): 62–63. In the next issue, Dr. Fife responded to Cheney's criticisms by writing, "We wonder if you have not been a bit like the miner who came out of the shaft with a beautiful diamond which he threw away because it had not yet been cut and polished?" See *BYU Studies* 3 (1960–1961): 108.

4. This information is based on the text and conversations with Alta Fife on July 26, 1991, and November 14, 1996. See also "Oxy Educator Collects Mormon Folk Material," *Los Angeles Times* [San Gabriel Valley edition], October 9, 1949, I9.

December 26, 1948, and a list now in the possession of Effie's daughter, Hazel Carmack Bushman.

The classification of the songs is Effie's. Additional ballad sources and other editorial notes appear in brackets. Abbreviations are followed by a ballad classification number or the volume and page numbers of published source notes. However, although many of the song texts are recorded and transcribed in the Fife Collection, many are not. Without having access to the texts it is difficult to compare Effie's versions with other versions of similar titles.

For more sources on Kentucky folkmusic, the reader should consult Burt Feintuch's *Kentucky Folkmusic: An Annotated Bibliography* (Lexington: University Press of Kentucky, 1985).

## Key to Abbreviations

Sharp= Sharp, Cecil J. *English Folksongs from the Southern Appalachians*, 2 vols. (London: Oxford University Press, 1932).

Child= Child, Francis James. *The English and Scottish Popular Ballads*, 5 vols. (Boston: Houghton Mifflin and Company, 1882–98).

Combs= Combs, Josiah H. *Folksongs of the Southern United States*, edited by D.K Wilgus, Publications of the American Folklore Society, Bibliographical and Special Series, vol. 19 (Austin: University of Texas Press, 1968).

FMR= Fife Mormon Recordings, Merrill Library, Utah State University.

Henry= Henry, Mellinger Edward, ed. *Folk-Songs from the Southern Highlands* (New York: J.J. Augustin, 1938).

*JAF= Journal of American Folklore*

*KFPM= Kentucky Folk-Lore and Poetry Magazine*

*KFR= Kentucky Folklore Record*

Laws= Laws, G. Malcolm. *American Balladry from British Broadsides* (Philadelphia: American Folklore Society, 1957).

*NAB*= Laws, G. Malcolm. *Native American Balladry: A Descriptive Study and a Bibliographic Syllabus*, Rev. ed. (Philadelphia: American Folklore Society, 1964).

*WF= Western Folklore*

## Key to Symbols

\* asterisk= item was recorded by Austin and Alta Fife but was not listed in Effie's dictated repertoire.

† dagger= item only appears in the repertoire which is in the possession of Hazel Carmack Bushman.

superscript[a] = classified as "Old Song Ballads"

superscript[b] = classified as "Old Silly Songs"

superscript[c] = classified as "Songs of the Gay Nineties"
superscript[d] = classified as "Indian Songs"
superscript[e] = classified as "Old Religious Songs"
superscript[f] = classified as "Old Negro Songs"
superscript[g] = classified as "Children's Songs and Recitations"
superscript[h] = classified as "My Children's First Poems"
superscript[i] = classified as "Old Love Songs"
superscript[j] = classified as "Sad Ones"


ABC Song* [FMR 318-A-1]
"Aloha," She Sang, "Aloha"[c]
'Mid the Green Fields of Virginia[c, i]
'Til We Meet Again[c]
'Twould Have Been Better for Us Both[j, †]
Abdullah Bulbul[b, †]
After the Ball[c]
Alabama Lullaby[c, f]
Alexander's Ragtime Band[f]
All Around the Water Tank[c]
Always Me[c, j]
Amazing Grace[e]
An Indiana Murder (or Pearl Bryan)* [FMR 402-A-2]
An Old Fashioned Couple were Seated[c, i]
An Old Crow Sat Way Up in a Tree[h]
And So I've Come Back to You, Mother[j, †]
And So You Have Come Back To Me[a, i, j]
Animal Fair[b, †]
Annie Laurie[a]
At The Foot of Yon Mountain (Red River Shore)[i] [FMR 209-B-4 and 207-B-2]
Baby Left the Cradle[a]
Baby Was Sleeping, The[a, i]
Back Home in Indiana[c]
Barbara Allen (two versions)[a, j] [Child 84; Combs 24; FMR 208-A-3, 208-B-1, 310-B-2, and 311-A-1; Henry 15; Sharp 24]
Battle of Fredricksburg[a, j] [FMR 404-A and 404-B-2; Henry 130]
Battleship Maine, The[c, j] [FMR 407-B]
Beautiful Garden of Roses[c]
Beautiful Ohio[c]
Before the Battle[a]
Ben Bolt[a, i]
Bessie, the Drunkard's Lone Child[a, j] [FMR 214-B-5; Henry 141]
Beware[c, i]

Bill Bailey (Won't You Please Come Home Bill Bailey?)[b, c, f]
Billy Snipes[i, †]
Billy Boy[b, †] [Henry 142; Sharp 89]
Billy Grimes, the Drover[a] [FMR 207-A-1; Sharp 176]
Bingen on the Rhine[i, †]
Bird in a Gilded Cage[c]
Birdie, I Am Tired Now[a]
Birmingham Jail[i, †]
Blind Boy's Cry, The[a, j] [FMR 215-B-1]
Blind Child, The* [FMR 210-A-3; Henry 136]
Blue Feather[d] [FMR 402-B-1]
Bonnie Doone[a, i]
Brave Little Blue Aster[g]
Broken Heart I[j, †]
Broken Heart II[j, †]
Brooklyn Theater Fire, The* [*NAB* G 27; FMR 401-A-2 and B-1; *WF*
    17:240]
Brother Slocum[f]
Brown Girl, The (same as Fair Ellender Green)[a, j] [Child 73; Combs 18;
    FMR 208-B-2; Henry 11 A-B; Laws O 2; Sharp 44]
Buffalo Gal[b, †] [Combs 310]
Bury Me Beneath the Willow[a, j] [FMR 213-A-3]
Bury Me Not on the Lone Prairie (same as Dying Cowboy)[a, j] [Combs 49
    and 50; *NAB* B 2; FMR 504-B-4; Henry 127; Sharp 169]
Call Me Back (parody)[b, †]
Call Me Back Again[a, i]
Camp Meeting in Georgia[c]
Camptown Races[b, †]
Captive Jews[j, †]
Careless Love* [FMR 401-B-2]
Cherished an My Memory Like a Happy Dream[a, j]
Clementine[b, †]
Clickety Clack, Kurlunk Alunk[g]
Climbing Up Those Golden Stairs[b, †]
Clocks are Striking and the Hour is Late, The (or Together We Will)[i, *]
    [FMR 317-B-2]
Clover Blossoms[c, i]
Club Had a Meeting, The[b, †]
Cobbler, The* [FMR 213-B-5]
Cold Drops of Rain[a]
Come Biddie, Come Speckle[g] [FMR 306-B-2]
Come Dearest, the Daylight, the Daylight is Gone [Come?][a, i]
Come Little Sister and Go with Me (A Dream)* [FMR 312-A-2]

Come Sit by My Side, Little Darling[a, i] [FMR 317-A-2]

Courtship, The[a]

Crawfish Pond[b]

Cruel Sister (or Two Sisters)[j, ]* [Child 10; FMR 207-B-1; Henry 4 A-C; Sharp 5]

Curfew Shall Not Ring[j, ] †

Dan McGinty[b, ] †

Darling Black Mustache, That[b] [Combs 154; Henry 96 A-C]

Dauntless Little Peter[h]

Dear Little Blossom[g]

Dendermere by the Sea[c]

Dermont, You Look So Healthy Now[a]

Devilish Mary[b] [Laws Q 4; FMR 209-B-3; Sharp 149]

Do They Miss Me at Home?[j, ] †

Do They Think of Me at Home?[a, j]

Dolly Gray (same as Nellie Gray?)[j]

Don't Wear Your Heart on Your Sleeve[c]

Down on the Farm[c]

Downtown Strutters Ball[f]

A Dream, Just a Dream, it Could Never Be[e]

Dreamy Eyes that Haunt Me Still[c, i]

Drifting Apart (same as We Drifted Apart?)[a, i]

Drunkard's Dream, The[a, j] [Henry 140 A-C]

Dying Californian, The[a, j] [FMR 211-B-1 and 311-A-2]

Dying Child, The[a]

Dying Cowboy (same as Bury Me Not on the Lone Prairie)[a, j] [Combs 49 and 50; *NAB* B 2; FMR 504-B-4; Henry 127; Sharp 169]

Dying Girl's Message, The[a, j] [FMR 212-A-2 and 405-B-2]

Ella Bell[a]

Ellaree (Sweet Ella Rhee)[f]

Ellen (fragment)* [FMR 311-B-2]

Ellen Taylor (fragment)[b, ]* [FMR 207-A-4 and 207-A-5]

Evening Bright Stars they Were Showing, The[c]

Fair Hawaii[c]

Fair Ellender Green (same as The Brown Girl and Lord Thomas and Fair Ellender Green)[a, j] [Child 73; Combs 18; FMR 208-B-2; Henry 11 A-B; Laws O 2; Sharp 44]

Fallen Leaf[a, d] [FMR 403-B-1]

Far Away in Memory's Valley[a, j]

Far From Home I Have Strayed* [FMR 215-B-2]

Fare Thee Well[b, ] †

Fatal Wedding, The[c, j]

Father, Come Tell Me, is it True?[a, j]

Father, Dear Father Come Home[a, j] [FMR 308-B-5 and 309-A-1]

Father, Dear Father Come Home (Parody)* [FMR 215-A-1]

Father Noah[b,] * [FMR 212-B-2]

Father, We Thank Thee[g]

Fellow that Looked Like Me, The[b] [*NAB* H 21; FMR 213-A-2]

Fiddlin' Soldier, The (The Nightingale or While The Nightingale
    Sings)* [FMR 407-A-2;    Sharp 145]

Floella[a, j] (The Jealous Lover) [Combs 63; Henry 63 B, D; *NAB* F 1 A]

Follow Me[d]

For I Love You, Darling I Love You[i,] †

Forever and Ever[j,] †

Four Thousand Years Ago (I Was Born About Four Thousand Years
    Ago)[b] [FMR 212-B-1 and 317-B-1]

Fox Hunt, The[b,] †

Frankie and Johnny*[Combs 83; Henry 122 D; *JAF* 45:142 and 63:271;
    *NAB* I 3; FMR 317-A-1]

Frisky Jim[b]

Frog Came Out of the Pond One Day, The[g]

Froggie Went Courtin'[b] [FMR 209-B-1; Henry 144 A-E; *KFPM* 3:12–13;
    Sharp 220]

Gal I Left Behind Me, The[a, b] [Combs 111; Henry 145 C; Laws P 1 A, B]

Gallows Tree, The (same as Maid Freed From the Gallows or The
    Rambling Man)* [Child 95; Combs 28; FMR 314-A-2; Henry 13;
    Sharp 28]

Garden by the Sea[c]

Gay Paree* [FMR 213-A-1]

Gentle Anna* [FMR 216-A-1, 309-A-4, and 309-B-1]

Go Dig My Grave Both Wide and Deep[a]

Go in and Out the Window (fragment)* [Combs 307; FMR 308-B-4]

Go, Love, Go and Ask Your Father[i,]†

Go Round and Round the Levee* [FMR 308-A-1]

Go Tell Aunt Dinah (fragment)[b,]* [FMR 315-B-2]

Goat Under the Bamboo Tree, The[b,] †

Golden Slippers[a, f]

Good Morning Merry Sunshine[g]

Goodbye Dear Old Step Stone[j,] * [FMR 316-B-1]

Goodnight, Goodnight[g]

Googoo Eyes [c, b, f]

Got a Little Home[b,] †

Ground was All Covered With Snow One Day, The[g]

Gypsy's Warning, The[a, j] [Combs 152]

Hawaiian Butterfly[c]

Hawaiian Hoola[c]

He Turned Around and Started Back[a, i]
Hello Central, Give Me Heaven[c, j]
Her Little Boy in Blue[c, j]
Here is Your Ring, Dear Charlie[a]
Here Rattler[b, †]
Honey, Does You Love Your Man* [FMR 214-B-3]
Hop Along, Peter[f]
Hopi Song* [FMR 403-A-1]
How She Hunted Up Her Lovers (same as She Hunted Up Her Lover)[i, †]
I Am Longing for the Coming of that Snow White[e]
I Don't Want You To Grieve[j, †]
I Got Mine[b, †]
I Have a True Love in the Army[a, i]
I Have an Aged Mother* [FMR 307-A-1]
I Have No Mother Now[a] [FMR 312-A-3]
I Hear Dem Owls a Whoo-Whoo-Whoo!* [FMR 403-B-2]
I Hear the Soft Wind Sighing* [FMR 214-A-1]
I Know a Little Man in the Forest Green[g]
I Know That You Will Call Me Back Again[a, i]
I Love My Susie* [FMR 308-A-2]
I Passed Through the Garden[e, j] [FMR 214-A-2]
I Remember[a, j] [FMR 216-A-4]
I Saved My Cake for Santa[h]
I Wandered Today in the Hills, Maggie[a, i]
I Want to be Sombody's Darling[a, i]
I Was Born About Four Thousand Years Ago (Four Thousand Years
      Ago)[b] [FMR 212-B-1 and 317-B-1]
I Will Arise and Go to Jesus[e] [FMR 402-A-3]
I Will be Home Love, Tonight[a, c, i]
I Wish I Was a Little Sparrow[i, *] [FMR 210-A-2]
I Wish I Was Single Again[b]
I'll Build Me a Castle[a, *] [FMR 211-A-2]
I'll Remember You, Love, In My Prayers[a, i]
I'll be All Smiles Tonight[j, *] [FMR 315-B-3]
I'll be Strolling By the Bay Away in Sunny Hawaii[c]
I'll Sing and I'll Dance[j, †]
I'm Not Particular[b, †]
I'm A-going Down in Town[b, †]
I'm Sitting on the Stile, Mary[a, i] [FMR 214-B-1]
I'm Lonesome and Sorry[c, j]
I'm Free Again (I'm Free, I'm Free Again)[a, i]
I's a Going From the Cotton Fields[f]
Ida Red[a, i] [Combs 228; *NAB* dI 23; FMR 403-A-3]

If You Love Me Tell Me So[a, c]
In the Gloaming[a, i]
In the Shadow of the Pines[c, j]
In 1861 (fragment)* [FMR 312-A-4]
An Indiana Murder (Pearl Bryan)* [*NAB* dF 51; FMR 402-A-2; Ann B.
    Cohen, *Poor Pearl, Poor Girl!* (Austin: American Folklore Society;
    University of Texas Press, 1978); *KFR* 12:1–3; *KFR* 21:119–20]
Into a Ward of a Whitewashed Hall[j, †]
Iroquois Lullaby* [FMR 403-A-2]
I Shall Have a Pretty White Horse to Ride, to See[g]
It's a Rainin'[c, i] [FMR 216-A-2]
Jealous Lover, The (Floella)[a, j] [Combs 63; *NAB* F 1A]
Jeff Walker* [FMR 209-A-1]
Jesus Had to Walk that Lonesome Valley* [FMR 213-B-2]
Jippy Bo Jay[c]
John Henry (fragment)[b, *] [Combs 81; Henry 179; *NAB* I 1; FMR 216-B-
    2; *WF* 24:155–163]
Julie Jenkins* [FMR 406-B-1]
Jungle Joe[b, c]
Just as it Happened[a]
Just as the Sun Went Down[c, i]
Just Before the Battle, Mother[c]
Just Break the News to Mother[j, †]
Just One Girl[c, i]
Just One Kiss of Love My Darling[i, †]
Just Tell Them that You Saw Me[c]
Kathleen[c, j]
Keep the Pig in the Parlor (fragment)* [FMR 308-B-1]
Keyhole in the Door[b, †]
Kicking Mule, The[b] [Combs 175; FMR 209-A-3; undated recording, ca.
    1970. Tape in Noel Carmack's possession]
King William was King James' Son* [Combs 286; FMR 308-B-2]
Kingdom is Coming, Oh Tell Me the Story, The[a, e]
Kitty Wells[f] [FMR 213-B-1 and 405-B-1; Henry 156]
Lady Awake (Midnight Serenade)* [FMR 315-A-1]
Lady Spring has Come to Town[g]
Lassie Mohee* [Combs 80; *JAF* 35:408 and 52:65; *NAB* H 8; FMR 316-A-1
    and 316-A-2; Henry 94]
Last Night was the End of the World[c, i]
Last Rose of Summer[i, †]
Leave Me with a Smile[c]
Left Me with a Smile (parody)* [FMR 312-A-1]
Leona[c, i]

Let Me Call You Sweetheart<sup>c</sup>

Let the Rest of the World Go By<sup>c</sup>

Let's All Go Down to Rowsers* [FMR 308-A-3]

Letter Edged in Black, The<sup>a, j</sup>

Letter that Never Came, The<sup>a, j</sup>

Lilly of the Prairie<sup>d, †</sup>

Little Annie Rooney<sup>i, †</sup>

Little Brown Jug<sup>b, †</sup> [Combs 258]

Little Ducky Duddle<sup>g</sup>

Little Fraud (Little Friend?)<sup>c</sup>

Little Friend<sup>i, †</sup>

Little Gray Home in the West<sup>c</sup>

Little Old Log Cabin<sup>f</sup>

Little Sparrow<sup>a</sup> [Combs 188]

Liza Jane<sup>a, f</sup> [Combs 220; FMR 406-A-2; Henry 169 A-D]

Locks and Bolts (fragment)* [FMR 308-A-2; Sharp 80]

Lonesome City of Gold Where My Faith Waits<sup>c, i</sup>

Look Down, Look Down<sup>j, †</sup>

Look Down that Lane<sup>a, j</sup>

Lord Randolph, My Son (same as Oh, Randolph, My Son)<sup>a</sup> [Child 12; FMR 211-B-2; Henry 5; Sharp 7]

Lord Thomas and Fair Ellender Green (same as The Brown Girl and Fair Ellender Green)<sup>a, j</sup> [Child 73; Combs 18; FMR 208-B-2; Henry 11 A-B; Sharp 19]

Lorena<sup>a, i</sup>

Love Me and the World is Mine<sup>c, i</sup>

Love's Old Song<sup>a, i</sup>

Loving<sup>a</sup>

Lula Wall<sup>i, †</sup>

Mable Clare<sup>j, †</sup>

Man From Alexander's Town, The* [FMR 313-A]

Mansion of Aching Hearts<sup>c, j</sup>

Maple on the Hill, The<sup>c, j</sup>

Marion Gray<sup>c, j</sup>

Marvelous Eller<sup>b, †</sup>

Mary and John<sup>i, †</sup>

Mary Don't You Weep* [FMR 216-B-1]

Mexico<sup>d</sup> [FMR 405-A-1]

Michael Finnigan* [FMR 308-B-3]

Midnight Serenade (See Lady Awake)<sup>i, *</sup> [FMR 315-A-1]

Mike Maloney<sup>b</sup>

Miller's Daughter, The<sup>a</sup> [Child 10; Combs 4]

Milwaukee Fire, The<sup>c, j</sup> [*NAB* G 15; FMR 401-A-1; *KFR* 3:101]

Mishaps of a Minstrel Man[a, b]
Miss Adair Since I Came To . . [j, †]
Mocking Bird, The[a, j] [Sharp 234]
Mollie Shove the Grog Around[a, b] [FMR 207-A-4, 5]
Molly Darling (Don't Forget Me Mollie Darling)[a, i]
Monkey Married the Baboon's Sister[b, †]
Moonlight Bay[c]
My Blue Ridge Mountain Home[c]
My Gal's a High Born Lady[c, f]
My Isle of Golden Dreams[c]
My Prayer[a]
My Teacher Doesn't Think I Read So Extra Special[h]
My Yaller Gal[b] [FMR 405-A-3]
Napinee[d]
Nellie Gray (same as Dolly Gray?)[c, f]
Nellie Moore* [FMR 209-A-4]
Nellie Baron (same as Nellie Bawn?)[i, †]
Nellie Bawn (same as Nellie Baron?)[c, †] [Combs 110?; Laws O 36?]
Netty More[f] [FMR 315-B-1]
Nigger Band, The[b]
Nightingale, The (same as The Fiddlin' Soldier and While The
     Nightingale Sings)* [FMR 407-A-2; Henry 58; Sharp 145]
No Home, No Home! Cried the Orphan Girl (fragment)[a, *] [FMR 214-B-
     4]
No One Like Mother* [FMR 207-A-2]
O Captain, My Captain, Tell Me True (Sailor Boy)[i, *] [FMR 402-A-1]
Ogalala[d]
Oh, Birdie I Am Tired Now[a] [FMR 214-A-4]
Oh, Blame Me Not For Weeping (same as Oh, Shame Me Not For
     Weeping)[a]
Oh, Come Little Sister and Go With Me* [FMR 214-A-3]
Oh, How I'll Miss You Tonight[c]
Oh I feel So Awful Happy[b, †]
Oh, I Hear the Owl Go Whoo Whoo[f]
Oh, Leave Me Not I Love But Thee[i, †]
Oh, Mary, Don't You Weep[f]
Oh Me, Oh My, I Love You Dearly[i, †]
Oh Mollie Pretty Molly[i, †]
Oh, Randolph, My Son (same as Lord Randolph, My Son)[a] [Child 12;
     FMR 211-B-2; Henry 5; Sharp 7]
Oh, Sally[a]
Oh, Shame Me Not for Weeping (same as Oh, Blame Me Not for
     Weeping)[j, †]

Oh Sister, Come Kiss Me Once More[e]
Oh Sister, Let's Go Down, Down in the Valley to Pray[e, f]
Oh, Sister, Oh Sister, Let's Walk the Seashore[a]
Oh Suzy, Pretty Suzy (same as Pretty Susie)[g] [Combs 230?]
Oh, Tell Me the Story[a]
Oh, Ven She Comes[b, †]
Oh Ver, Oh Ver is My Little Dog[b, †]
Oh, Where is My Beloved?[a, j]
Oh Why Did I Get Married?[b, †]
Old Dan Tucker (fragment)[b, *] [FMR 309-A-3]
Old Love, The* [FMR 215-B-3]
Old Miss Flip Flopper (Flippleoffers)[b]
Old Man's Drunk Again, The (parody to Father, Dear Father Come
      Home)* [FMR 309-A-2]
Old New Hampshire Home[c, i]
Old Savannah Home[a, c, i]
Old Woman in Our Town, The* [FMR 406-B-2]
On a Hillside Stands a Maid[g] [FMR 405-A-2]
On The Banks of the Wabash[c, i]
Once there was a Little Mouse[b, †]
Only a Year Ago[a, i]
Only Me[c]
Only the Low Wind Wailing[a]
Our Jackie's on the Deep Blue Sea[i, †]
Out in the Moonlight[j, †]
Over the Hills to the Poor House[c, j] [FMR 406-A-1]
Over There[b, *] [FMR 314-B-1]
Owl and the Pussycat, The* [FMR 209-B-2]
Package of Old Letters[a, j] [Henry 73 A-E]
Passing Policeman[c]
Pat O'Grady[b] [FMR 216-B-3]
Pearl Bryan (or An Indiana Murder)* [Combs 63; Henry 63; *KFR* 12:1–3;
      *KFR* 21:119-20; *NAB* dF 51; FMR 402-A-2; Ann B. Cohen, *Poor Pearl,
      Poor Girl!* (Austin: American Folklore Society; University of Texas
      Press, 1978)]
Peek a Boo[b, †]
Polly Wolly Doodle[b, †]
Poor Little Thing Cried Mammy, The (fragment) [FMR 312-B-1]
Poor Old Men[a, f]
Pretty Fair Girl All in a Garden[a, i, *] [FMR 210-A-1; Henry 59 A-C]
Pretty Susie (same as Oh Suzy, Pretty Suzy)* [Combs 230?; FMR 213-B-4;
      Sharp 28]
Pretty White Horses (fragment)* [FMR 313-B-1]

Pride of the Ball<sup>c, i</sup>

Put My Little Shoes Away<sup>a</sup>

Put on Your Old Gray Bonnet<sup>c</sup>

Rambling Man, The (The Gallows Tree)* [Combs 90; Laws L 12; FMR
      314-A-2]

Red River Shore (At The Foot Of Yon Mountain)<sup>a, i</sup> [Laws N 26; FMR
      207-B-2 and 209-B-4]

Red Wing<sup>d</sup>

Riding in the Sleigh<sup>a</sup> [FMR 216-A-3]

River Rhine, The<sup>c</sup>

Roll On, Silver Moon (same as Shine On, Silver Moon?)<sup>a</sup>

Ronald and I<sup>a</sup> [FMR 207-B-3 and 306-B-1]

Row Your Boat Ashore and a Hog Eye<sup>b,</sup>* [FMR 314-A-1]

Rubber Dolly<sup>c</sup>

Said a Little Gray Mouse, "I Will Do As I Please"<sup>h</sup>

Sailor Boy (O Captain, My Captain, Tell Me True)<sup>i,</sup>* [FMR 402-A-1]

St. Louis Blues<sup>c</sup>

Sally<sup>j,</sup>* [FMR 208-A-2, 310-B-1]

Same Moon Will Shine Again, The<sup>a, c, i</sup>

Sea Song (fragment)* [FMR 307-B-2]

Seven Long Years<sup>b,</sup>† [Sharp 102]

She Rests by the Swanee River (same as Swanee River?)<sup>c, i</sup>

She Hunted Up Her Lover with Her Dog and Her Gun (same as How
      She Hunted Up Her Lovers)<sup>a</sup> [FMR 211-B-3 and 404-B-1]

She was Bred in Old Kentucky<sup>c</sup>

She was Happy Till She Met You<sup>c</sup>

She's Far From the Land where Her Young Hero Sleeps (fragment)<sup>a, j</sup>
      [FMR 215-A-2]

Shine On, August Moon<sup>c, i</sup>

Shine On Silver Moon<sup>i,</sup>†

Ship That Never Returned, The<sup>a, j</sup> [Henry 135]

Shoo Fly Don't Bother Me<sup>b,</sup>†

Sidewalks of New York<sup>c, i</sup>

Silver Bell<sup>d</sup> [FMR 316-A-1 and 402-B-2]

Silver Bells of Memory<sup>a</sup>

Silver Threads Among the Gold<sup>a, i</sup>

Sing Your Way Home* [FMR 310-A-1]

Sitting Alone in the Door<sup>a, c, j</sup>

Skip To My Lou My Darling (fragment)* [Combs 298; FMR 308-A-4]

Snow Dear<sup>d</sup> [FMR 316-B-2]

Snowflakes Glistening<sup>a, i</sup>

Spanish Cavalier, The<sup>i,</sup>†

Spanish Fandango<sup>a</sup> [FMR 208-A-1]

Springtime Flowers, Springtime Showers[g]
Starry Night for a Ramble[a, c, i]
Sunshine Valley[c]
Swanee River (same as She Rests By the Swanee River?)[a]
Sweet Birds[a, i]
Sweet Bunch of Daisies[c, i]
Sweet Evalina[a, i]
Sweet Hawaiian Moonlight Fair[c]
Ta Ra Ra Boom-de-ay[b] †
Take Back the Heart that Thou Gavest[a, i]
Take Back the Ring Young Gave Me[a, c, i]
Tatta-Tat-Tat the Coronet Went[b] [FMR 314-B-2]
Texas Ranger, The[a, i] [Combs 45; Henry 123; A-B; *KFR* 1:86; *NAB* A 8]
There was a Bold and Brave Young Farmer[i] * [FMR 212-A-1; *KFR*
     18:75–76]
There'll Come a Time Some Day[c, j]
There's a Tavern in this Town[c]
There's a Light in the Window[j] †
There's a Long, Long Trail a Winding[c]
There's Locks and Bolts to Hinder (fragment)* [FMR 214-B-1]
There's No One Like Mother to Me[a, j] [FMR 307-A-2]
They Always Pick on Me[c]
This is a Roof, See How it Slants[h]
This Old Man* [FMR 214-B-2]
This Old Man Came Rolling Home* [FMR 313-B-2]
Thou Hast Wounded a Spirit that Loved Thee[a, j]
Thou Will Come No More, Gentle Anna[a, j]
Three Perished in the Snow[a, j] [Combs 77; *NAB* G 32; FMR 212-B-3]
Together We Will (same as The Clocks Are Striking And The Hour Is
     Late) [FMR 317-B-2]
Toodlum Too[b, f] [FMR 314-B-3]
Trouble in the Land O' Canaan (fragment)* [FMR 213-B-3]
Tuck Me to Sleep in My Old Kentucky Home[c]
Turkey in the Straw[b] † [Combs 245]
Twilight[a, c]
Twilight is Stealing[i] †
Two Little Children[a, j] [FMR 318-A-2]
Two Orphans[c, j]
Two Little Girls in Blue[c, i]
Two Sisters (same as Cruel Sister)[j] * [Child 10; FMR 207-B-1; Henry 4 A-
     C; Sharp 5]
Under the Bamboo Tree[c]
Up Up in the Sky[g]

Walk In, Walk In, Walk In, I Say[b, f]
We Drifted Apart (same as Drifting Apart?) [j, †]
We Must Part[j, †]
We Never Smile as We Pass By[a]
We Sat by the Riverside[a, i]
We Saw the Smoke Arising[a]
Went Down to Sal's House[b, †]
What Has Made You Grow So Quiet[i, †]
What Were All this World Without Thee[a, i]
When I Was Twenty-One and You Were Sweet Sixteen[c]
When I'm Gone You'll Soon Forget [a, c, i]
When the Hardest [Harvest?] Days Are Over, Jessie Dear[c, i]
When the Bells Are Ringing, Mary[c]
When They Laid Sweet Kitty in the Tomb[a]
Where is My Darling Tonight?[j, *] [FMR 307-B-3 and 207-A-3]
Where is My Wandering Boy Tonight?[c, j]
Where is Now that Merry Party?[a, i]
Where the River Shannon's Flowing[c, i]
Where the Silver Colorado Wends its Way[c]
Where the Sunset Turns the Ocean Blue to Gold[c, i]
While Nature was Thinking in Stillness To Rest[a]
While the Dance Goes On[c, j]
While the Nightingale Sings (same as The Fiddlin' Soldier and The
     Nightingale)* [FMR 407-A-2; Sharp 145]
Whippoorwill[a]
Whistlin' Rufus[f] [FMR 209-A-2]
White Rose, The[j, †]
Who Comes in His Pride to the Low Cottage Door?[a]
Why Don't You Love Me in the Same Old Way[c, i]
Why Don't You Try[c]
Will You Love Me When I'm Old?[a, i]
Wind That Blew Across the Wild Moore, The[a, j] [FMR 309-B-2 and 215-A-
     4; Henry 137]
With You All Our Souls Now Let Us[i, †]
Won't You Come Back To Me? (fragment)* [FMR 307-B-1]
Won't You Come Home, Billy Bailey? (Billy Bailey)[b, c, f]
You All Have Heard the Song[b, †]
You Are My Sunshine[i, †]
You Can Find a Little Bit of Dixieland[c]
You're Welcome as the Flowers[i, †]
Young Man Who Wouldn't Hoe Corn, The[b, †] [*NAB* H 13]
Zilpha Lee[c]

# Things to Accomplish

*The following transcription represents a list of things Effie wanted to accomplish before her death. The list, in Effie's handwriting, is in an 11" x 8 1/2" wide marginal ruled notebook. On the cover at the top, written with ballpoint pen in Effie's hand, it reads: "Minutes of our Family reunion in back" and "Things I Want to do." The minutes of the reunion have evidently been removed. The last verso has several negligible notations (dates, and references). MS in the possession of Noel A. Carmack.*

[ *recto* ]

Some things I'd Like to do before I die—
Get <u>old songs published</u> —also "Ariz Diary"
A <u>Book of Poems</u> —"<u>Playthings</u> + <u>Pastimes of Pioneer</u> Children"
Get paintings collected into special groups—
*Nauvoo Sketches* + paintings—<u>Childhood pictures</u>
Faces in pencil—in trips—(on busses—trains—cars) etc
Silhouettes + sketches of my family—
Portrait of Emma Marquess Davey + another for
other frame—Aunt ^Susan^ Elizabeth ^P. Pool^ Cravens (Grmas sister)
Get photos in plastic for my records—
Marquess—Armstrong—P Pool—Carmack etc
—My Children—different families—
Get pedigrees typed + printed—
Get good boxes (<u>or binders</u>) for each family ^record^
+ make shelves to put them on–(or ones
I already have)—
Paint pictures I have promised—
And for Hazels curio store + for Mr Bruchman
(and for Fay)—and pictures
Illustrations for above books—Diaries etc
Write the letter to go with old songs—for book

Get old songs on <u>tape</u>—(<u>find</u> ones I want to
record)—
Maybe buy a "Writers Market"— ^or get it <u>at library</u>^
Resubscribe for Writers Magazine—
Record the mimic of Birds songs ^<u>on tape</u>^—
Find the Material for "Calif Mother" +^sent it^ file it—
Send Article to Ch. News of Mission—theo. teaching
songs—books, etc;— Get "My story" typed

[*verso, near the top, left portion of page*]

Sr. Berkel is typing it

# Henry Edgar Carmack

*The following biographical sketch appeared in the post-1948 portion of* Down
Memory Lane. *The sketch is published here in its entirety.*

### Edgar's Story

Henry Edgar Carmack was born July 17, 1884, [*the year was 1883*] in
Hopkins County, Kentucky, after his father and mother had separated.
His life had a sad and tragic background. His mother had been left an
orphan early in life. In the Gunn record it states that his mother's father,
Abner Gunn, died about 1848, but it doesn't say when her mother, Susan
Smith Gunn died.[5] Anyway, she was an orphan when she and Thomas G.
Carmack married, about 1883. Quite a bit of property had been left to
this orphan girl by her parents, the old Sol Smith place and the Frank
Fuller farm. Solomon Smith, her uncle, had the reputation of being a
selfish, greedy man, and he coveted the property of this orphaned niece,
and schemed how he could get it. I think he was living on the place
(which he afterward acquired) when this niece Pairlee Gunn and
Thomas Carmack were married, and she was living with them.[6]

One night shortly after they were married, there was a dance in the
neighborhood, and Sol suggested they go. The women didn't want to go,
as they had something else they had planned to do, so Sol and Thomas
went alone. When the dance was about half over, Sol said he was tired and
sleepy and was going home, and for Tom to stay as long as he wanted to.
When he got home he told Pairlee a sordid tale of Tom flirting with some

---

5.  Susan A. Smith Gunn (1826–1882), daughter of Austin P. Smith and Elmira Sisk, died
    on February 12, 1882.
6.  Parilla (Parlee or Pairlee) Gunn (1870–1887) and Thomas Green Carmack were mar-
    ried on June 8, 1883.

special girl; that he felt she had sure made a wrong move in marrying him, and from the start he was making, he was sure he would never be a good husband. But he made her promise she would not tell Tom what he had said. Next morning when the men started to work, Tom was cutting stove wood for his wife to cook with, and she came out and said she wouldn't need it, as she was leaving. Tom couldn't believe it, as they had not even had a cross word. He asked her where she was going, and why, but since she had promised Sol not to tell, she wouldn't say. When he came home in the evening she was gone, and neither Sol nor Aunt Caroline would tell him why.[7] I think she went to a sister's home in Hopkins County, Sol providing her a way to go.

Sometime later he got a letter from her, saying she was going to have a baby, and she thought they had better go back together, and for him to come down there for her. But Tom was stubborn and told her that since she was the one who left she could come back if she wanted to, but he was not coming after her. But Pairlee could be stubborn too, and she didn't come. Mr. Carmack told me one day when he was telling me of this that he had wished many a time that he had gone when she sent for him, because she later married a man who was worthless and was mean to Edgar, their baby boy, and that life with the second husband was miserable. She died when Edgar was three or four years old; I could never find exactly the date she died, but Edgar said he could remember his cruel stepfather, and how afraid he was of him. He said he remembered his mother putting her hand on his head before she died and telling him that Aunt Bettie and Uncle Moses McIntosh would come and take him to their place, where Bud Childers (the stepfather) could never lay his hand on him again.[8] She had a little daughter by Childers, named Vivian, but I don't know who took care of her after the mother died. Edgar and I went to visit Vivian when Cecil was a baby; she was married to Elgin Sisk. She looked like Edgar, so they must have looked like their mother, as Edgar did not resemble his father very much.

---

7.   This presumably refers to Solomon Smith mentioned earlier in the autobiography and possibly a first spouse, Caroline [Gunn?].

8.   According to Effie's research, Moses McIntosh was born May 13, 1850 in Hopkins County. However, three other LDS genealogists have recorded Moses McIntosh born on May 22, 1856 at Turkey Creek, Breathitt County to Henry (Henly?) McIntosh and Rachel Mays; or on October 27, 1856 at Turkey Creek, Breathitt County to William Martin McIntosh (b. ca. 1835) and Sarah (Sally?) Mays (b. ca. 1840). According to one of the researchers, Moses was married to Elizabeth Griffith (b. ca. 1853). O. A. "Bud" Childers was born in 1864.

Tom had also married again by this time, to a beautiful girl named Mattie Olivia Hale.[9] She said when the news came that Pairlee had died that Tom felt terrible, and she knew then that he still loved her.

Pairlee's sister, Elizabeth McIntosh kept her word and took Edgar, and she and her husband Moses were like a mother and father to him. He always spoke of Uncle Mosie an Aunt Bettie as if he loved them dearly. They had two girls near Edgar's age, Rilla and Lenora, that he loved as if they were his own sisters. We visited them also, and they are the ones that have helped me find the records of the family, all I have been able to get. I could still get marriage records from county seats, I think. We also visited the old McIntosh home in Mannington, a big old comfortable house with huge fireplaces, upstairs rooms and a big old kitchen.

When Edgar was seven or eight years old, his father came and took him to live with them, and I am sure Mrs. Carmack was a good stepmother. She seemed to think as much of him as she did her own children.[10] This is where he grew up.

Evert Holt and my sister Sadie bought the old Sol Smith home when they married, and Edgar and I were married there also. Later, Mr. Carmack told us that when we were married we stood on almost exactly the same spot that he and Pairlee had stood on when they were married. And Aunt Helen Marquess said the dress I wore for our wedding was almost exactly like my mother's wedding dress. It was of thin white silk with a round shirred yoke, full sleeves shirred at the wrist, leaving a narrow ruffle, and the full skirt was shirred around the hips. It seems that history really did repeat itself in our case.

---

9. Mattie Olivia Hale (1873–1961) was the daughter of John Wayland Hale and Mary Elizabeth Shepherd. Mattie had eight children with Thomas Green Carmack (1863–1946): Vivian Lee (1891–1903), Carrie Bartlie (1893–1971), Lewis Henry Dietrich (b. 1894), Mary Elizabeth (1897–1982), Myrtle Ailene (1899–1960), Thomas Ernest Carmack (b. 1901), Flora Estella (1904–1963), and Theodore Alden (1920–1974). For more on Mattie Hale, see Mattie Olivia Hale Carmack, *My Story: Mattie Olivia Hale Carmack, 1873–1961*, compiled by Donna Bess Carmack Musto (Franklin, NC: Genealogy Publishing Service, 1991); and "Mattie Carmack's Story—(Edgar's Stepmother)," in Carmack, *Down Memory Lane*, 206–208.

10. Near the end of her life, Mattie Hale Carmack wrote the following: "O i have 7 living children. O yes i am thankful for them, and they are good to me, but they cant fill his [Tom's] place. I have a nice little home and have all kinds if improvement, but thair is a empty chair, a vacant place at the table. Yes and in my hart thair is a empty spot that cant ever bee fild. He was near and dear to me, he was liked by everyone who new him. And i hope to meet him someday over on the Promised Land then thair is no partin and no more tears. Thair never to part any more. Amen and amen. Written by Mattie Hale Carmack," from Mattie Olivia Hale Carmack, *My Story*, 79. See also *Down Memory Lane*, 208.

After we married, Edgar worked on the farm with Evert for a while, and then we moved to the old Ferrell farm where my father had died. Cecil was born at that place. Then Edgar started working for Mr. Galloway at a sawmill in the Williams Hollow. We were the only two families working and living there. Then the mill was moved out in the hills east of Crofton, and we moved with it. We and the Galloways lived together in an old school house till they got our houses built. We ordered them built close together, as we were the only ones living there, and it was wild rugged country. Edgar and Hol Boyd hauled the logs for the mill. They called it "Happy Hollow." It was while we lived at this place that Cecil had pneumonia, and Dr. Croft said he had died, (about 4 o'clock one bitter cold day in February, 1906).[11] But I kept bathing him with hot water and massaging him all over, without a letup, and I made the Lord some solemn promises if He would let him come back to us; and about twenty minutes after midnight, as I rubbed down his sides, I thought I felt a slight warmth. Up until then he had stayed as cold as clay. I told Mrs. Galloway to listen and see if his heart was beating, and it was, though very weak. I continued to rub him till about four o'clock, when I fell asleep. Mary Galloway came in with a piece of bread and butter in her hand, and Cecil opened his eyes and said "bite." He wanted a bite of her bread. It was the first time he had noticed anything for days. Edgar was not a member of the Church at that time. But we started having get-togethers, mostly at our place—the Galloways, Hol Boyd, Rick Worthington, the Boss, and others.

We left the mill not long after that; Evert and Sadie and Mr. Holt's folks went to Imperial Valley, California, where Judge Holt, Evert's Uncle, had a big ranch, and we moved to the old Sol Smith place they had vacated. Then we moved various places, Violet was born, and on a momentous day in 1908 Edgar was baptized. Three years later, when Noel was a baby, we went to Utah. We lived on Frank McDonald's place in Holiday [Holladay], right at the foot of Twin Peaks. Edgar got a job with Joseph Andrus, putting up hay in Park City, where they had a big hay ranch. While Edgar was gone, I took care of the garden, picked fruit, and walked the two miles to the meeting house with the children every Sunday, carrying Noel, who by this time was as big as a calf, but I enjoyed it. I picked currants (the black variety) and irrigated [the] garden with Howard, the McDonald's teen age boy, who later became President of the Salt Lake Temple.

After the haying at the Park City ranch was over, Edgar went up the canyon to help dig a pipeline for water. It took longer than they had planned, and their food supply ran low; all they had for the last ten days was white bread, bacon and potatoes. On the way home the men were

---

11. This incident was already told in detail, beginning on page 287.

riding in the back of an open truck, got drenched with a cold rain, and the wind chilled them to the bone.

Not long after they returned, Edgar complained of his foot hurting, especially a big toe. It became swollen and red, and he finally had to lay off work, as he could not wear his shoe. Then one night he had a high temperature, and a hip also started hurting. Joseph Andrus came and said we had better call a doctor, and when he came he told us Edgar had inflammatory rheumatism. That was the first day of October, and he was not able to even sit up until January, when he was up part of one week. He then had to go back to bed, and did not get up any more till March. Someone suggested hot baths with something in the water (I can't recall what it was). He was too weak to walk, so I carried him to the bathtub and bathed him every day for a long time. He was not very heavy then, and I was young and strong, and it seemed to help him. The doctor left big bottles of tablets to make him sweat. He drank gallons of water and orange juice, and the sweat poured. The washing and drying his clothing and the bedclothes was the biggest job of all, because it was winter, and very cold.

The good people of the Ward were wonderful, doing everything they could do to help. They offered to help me take care of Edgar, but he would not let anyone do anything for him but me. When he was able to be up, we moved to Burnett's fruit ranch, where he could do light work. The rheumatism and the pills to make him sweat had caused heart trouble, and the doctor said he would never be able to do hard work any more, and advised us to go where the altitude was lower. So in the fall we went back to Kentucky. I certainly hated to leave Utah, but Bishop Larsen consoled us by saying maybe we could do more good in Kentucky than we could in Utah.

We arrived just in time for the hog-killing season, and just as the gardens and fruit was all gone. We had been used to all the fruit and green vegetables we could use, and that was mostly what we had lived on, as the doctor had recommended such a diet for Edgar. The backbones and spareribs and the sagey sausage and hot biscuits for breakfast tasted good, but I was starved for fruit, and even scratched around under the apple trees trying to find a stray apple. It never occurred to me to tell someone I wanted some fruit, or to send someone to buy it; we usually accepted what came along uncomplainingly.

I must not forget that while we were in Utah, we took our three children and went to the temple in Salt Lake.[12] Edgar often recalled how

---

12. This took place on June 6, 1912. "Went to the temple" specifically for the ordinances of sealing (marriage) for eternity; husband and wife are sealed to each other and the children to their parents. Thus Grace was the first child to be "born under the covenant" of eternal family sealing, and no such ordinance would be necessary to seal her or any subsequent children.

Building a church in Larkin, Kentucky, ca. 1915. John Robert Marquess (center with large hat and overalls), Henry Edgar Carmack (front row center), Evert Holt (front row right), Joe Keith (far right). This LDS church was called the Woodland Branch. Courtesy of Hazel Bushman.

sweet the children looked, waiting in the sealing room for us, all dressed in white. I was expecting another baby (Grace) in the spring, the first of our children to be born under the covenant.

John had started a new house between the old Holt place and the Sol Smith place. He painted it red, and they called it the Red Bungalow. We moved to this Red House before it was entirely finished, and Grace and Hazel and Bernice were born there. While we were living there, a new meeting house was finished also. Two missionaries were appointed to help on it: Orvil Udy and Elmer Brundage. We had happy times getting this church built; Edgar and John and Evert had the brunt of the expense to bear, but it was a great blessing to all when it was finished.

The Simmons family, whose farm joined the Red House farm on the north, joined the Church, and were a great help in the new branch, called the Woodland Branch. It took all of us to keep things going, and a bond of love and fellowship was formed that I am sure will last through Eternity.

Later we moved to the old Holt place where we were living when our youngest child, Harold, died from burns. That was an awful year for all of us (1922);[13] Edgar had put his tobacco crop in the Association, and got nothing for it, became discouraged and sad.[14] Then Violet ran away from High School and got married, when we were almost ready to go to Arizona. That, on top of all the other worries, was almost more than we could bear. But her marriage did not work out, and she came back home before we left, and came to Arizona with us in February. Little Rebecca was born that fall. We have often wondered how we could have done without Becky, she was the joy of our lives, and a choice spirit. She was an unusually smart baby, a beautiful and talented girl, and is now Relief Society President in one of the Wards in the Hawaiian Islands. So that first marriage for Violet proved a blessing after all, though at the time we certainly couldn't see it.

My brother John and Cecil had gone to Joseph City, Arizona, ahead of us, and Cecil had a house tent with furniture, groceries and everything ready for the children and me to go to housekeeping. Edgar had to stay a while in Kentucky to collect bills, sell a few things that were left, and to try to get something for the tobacco crop. He came later in the spring, and raised a truck garden on John Bushman's place. I taught an art class in school, and Noel and I did the janitor work at the school. David always helped his dad after he started in the dairy business, driving cows, washing bottles, and general flunky—there's plenty to do when you start operating a dairy.

Cecil was called on a mission to the Southern States from the Joseph City ward, but by the time he was released from the mission, Edgar had sold his dairy business to Irvin Tanner, and we had moved to Winslow, and were living at the rock house. What a joy to have a son return from a mission. I am sorry for any parents that have not experienced it. I forgot to say that when we first came to Winslow the only

13. Actually the date was April 10, 1923.

14. Here, Effie is referring to what most black patch farmers called the "Association." The "Association," or Planters' Protective Association (PPA), was an organized group of farmers who, in response to the monopolistic practices of the Italian tobacco trust (Regie) and the American Tobacco Company sought to maintain and control the prices of tobacco above the cost of production. See Christopher Waldrep, "Planters and the Planters' Protective Association in Kentucky and Tennessee," *Journal of Southern History* 52 (November 1986): 565–88. See also Tracy Campbell, "Organizing the Black Patch," chap. 3 in *The Politics of Despair: Power and Resistance in the Tobacco Wars* (Lexington: University Press of Kentucky, 1993), 30–52. The economic stresses of Black Patch farming were often too much to bear. Some farmers chose to leave the district rather than endure the pressures and uncertainty of the tobacco market. This was especially true during the height of the Black Patch wars in Kentucky. See Suzanne Marshall Hall, "Breaking Trust: The Black Patch Tobacco Culture of Kentucky and Tennessee, 1900–1940," 364–66.

place we could find was a little house up west of the ice plant. The noise from the plant, and from the railroad where they loaded ice into the boxcars was awful at first, but we soon grew accustomed to it, and it seemed to lull us to sleep.

Later Edgar bought a house from Bishop Campbell, out in Mahoney Addition, on the North edge of town, and again we helped in building a new chapel, which was not many blocks south of us.[15] Noel and Hazel both went on missions from this place, Noel to the Southern States, and Hazel to the East Central States. Edgar was still in the dairy business, with David helping him.

There was a time between the sale of this dairy, and the time he started working at the Wholesale Produce Company, that he went with a group of men that were excavating the Keet Seel Indian ruins, under the supervision of John Weatherall [Wetherill], who was one of the men that discovered these ruins.[16] He enjoyed his stay out there; it was a new and interesting experience, and he liked the men he worked with. His letters were always interesting, and we enjoyed the pictures he sent home.[17]

He worked for the Babbit Brothers for a while, and then for Marley's Wholesale Produce Co.[18] He lifted heavy loads of meat and produce, and finally had a bad heart attack. The doctors advised him to move to a lower altitude again, and this time we came to California, as three of our children were already out here. The doctors said again that he would never be able to work again, but by taking food supplements

---

15. Archibald Campbell (b. 1897) served as bishop of the Winslow Ward from its organization on August 21, 1927 to December 31, 1930.

16. John Wetherill (ca. 1865–1944) was one of five brothers who served as guides and traders in the Four Corners area. His brother, Richard (1858–1910), is credited with discovering many of the Anasazi ruins that are part of the Navajo National Monument. See Francis Gilmore and Louisa Wade Wetherill, *Traders to the Navajos: The Story of the Wetherills of Kayenta* (Albuquerque: University of New Mexico Press, 1953), and Frank McNitt, *Richard Wetherill: Anasazi* (Albuquerque: University of New Mexico Press, 1957).

17. For published reports on this excavation experience, see John Wetherill, "Keet Zeel," Southwestern Monuments Monthly Report, supplements for March 1934 and December 1935.

18. The four Babbitt brothers, David, Charles, George, and William, were general merchants who founded a large department store in northern Arizona. Marley's Wholesale Produce Co. was probably owned by the family of Joseph W. "Pop" Marley of Winslow. In 1912, Pop Marley and his sons, "Heck," "Clay," and "Dee," were convicted of cattle rustling. In an appellate trial, the Marleys settled out of court for $75,000. See Jim Bob Tinsley, *The Hash Knife Brand* (Gainsville: University Press of Florida, 1993), 148–54, and Stella Hughes, *Hashknife Cowboy* (Tucson: University of Arizona Press, 1984), 12–14.

Edgar Carmack (left) at the Keet Seel ruins, ca.1937. The other men have not been identified. Courtesy of Hazel Bushman.

and plenty of vitamin E, he gradually regained his strength, until before he died, he drove to a chicken plant down by Santa Maria every day, and handled as much as three thousand chickens a day, for months. Some time after the plant closed, he had another bad attack, and was never able to do hard work after that, though he still had his rabbits and chickens here at home and enjoyed working with them. And he doggedly kept cutting weeds and mowing grass and cleaning the yard when he really wasn't able to do anything.

One evening he came in tired, and when he tried to lie down, a sharp pain would cut his breath off. But he felt very well as long as he sat up. I had received a letter from a man and his wife in the midwest that were interested in the same family name as mine, and they said if I had a certain October issue of the Saturday Evening Post,[19] they had a story in it. Edgar asked me to find it and read it to him, which I did, and we enjoyed the story and read their letter again. He said I must not forget to answer it and tell them how we enjoyed their story. We sat by the fire till eleven o'clock, talking. He said now that it was too late he realized that if he had done as I asked him to do and continued with the vitamins he had

---

19. It is nearly impossible to determine which article of the *Saturday Evening Post* is referred to here.

been taking, that he might still be working. I put some pillows on one end of the couch and fixed it so he could rest without lying down. He said he felt comfortable and thought he could sleep. I waited until he had gone to sleep, and then I also went to bed, but couldn't go to sleep for a long time. I looked in on him occasionally, and he seemed to be sleeping sound. The last time I looked, he had taken part of the pillows from under his head and was lower, and still asleep. At early dawn I awoke with a start, a noise had awakened me. I hurried in to the living room, but he was not on the couch. I found him slumped on the back kitchen step, with his head in his hands, trying to call me. I tried to help him up, but couldn't. He said, "Mama, this time this is it." I ran for Bill Schleuter (living in the cottage) to come and help me, and we got him on the couch and called Dr. Walters. When he came, he said, "Take him to the hospital." Edgar didn't want to go, said he would not live to get there, to please just let him rest. But the Doctor insisted, and we took him, and he was just breathing his last as they took him in the hospital. That was early morning of February 12, 1952.

He is buried in the Atascadero, California, cemetery, beside Bernice.

# Bibliography

## Manuscripts and Collections

Buck, Dan L. "Carmack Family." Microfilm copy of MS, LDS Family History Library, Salt Lake City [film #1036284, item 1].

Carmack, Effie Marquess. "Autobiography," twelve-page autobiographical sketch, May 1971. MS in the possession of John K. Carmack, Salt Lake City.

————. "Caught in an Arizona Flood." Typescript. Copy of MS in the possession of Noel A. Carmack, Hyrum, Utah.

————. Interview with John K. Carmack. Taped recording, ca. 1969. Original in the possession of John K. Carmack, Salt Lake City.

————. "The Long Road from Winslow, Arizona to Atascadero." Typescript. Copy of MS in the possession of Noel A. Carmack, Hyrum, Utah.

————. Miscellaneous poems. Typescripts. Copies of MSS in the possession of Noel A. Carmack, Hyrum, Utah.

————. "My First Experience with the Navajos, or A Week on a Western Ranch in Navajo County Arizona." Typescript. Copy of MS in the possession of Noel A. Carmack, Hyrum, Utah.

————. "My Old Kentucky Home." Bound typescript. MS in the possession of Noel A. Carmack, Hyrum, Utah.

————. Scrapbook, Pioneer Trails Art Tour, June 6–July 23, 1936. Holograph and photographs. MS in the possession of John K. Carmack, Salt Lake City.

————. "Some Things I'd Like to Do Before I Die." Holograph. MS in the possession of Noel A. Carmack, Hyrum, Utah.

————. "Tobacker." Typescript. Copy of MS in the possession of John K. Carmack, Salt Lake City.

————. Undated recording, ca. 1958. Tape in the possession of John K. Carmack, Salt Lake City.

————. Undated recording, ca. 1970. Tape in the possession of Noel A. Carmack, Hyrum, Utah.

Fife Mormon Recordings (FMR), Fife Folklore Archives, Merrill Library, Utah State University, Logan, Utah.

Journal History of the Church of Jesus Christ of Latter-day Saints, 1830–1975. Microfilm, Library, Church Historical Department, Church of Jesus Christ of Latter-day Saints, Salt Lake City.

Larsen, Bent Franklin (B. F.). Collection. University Archives, Harold B. Lee Library, Brigham Young University, Provo, Utah.

Manuscript History of the Southern States Mission, 1832–1956. Archives and
    Manuscripts Division, Church Historical Department, Church of Jesus
    Christ of Latter-day Saints, Salt Lake City. [LR 8557 2]
New York World's Fair Collection, 1939–1940. Manuscripts and Archives Division,
    New York Public Library.

## Newspapers

*Atascadero News*, Atascadero, California
*Church News* [*Deseret News* weekly insert], Salt Lake City, Utah
*Coconino Sun*, Flagstaff, Arizona
*Deseret Evening News*, Salt Lake City, Utah
Daily Kentucky *New Era*, Hopkinsville, Kentucky
*Hopkinsville Kentuckian*, Hopkinsville, Kentucky
*Semi-Weekly South Kentuckian*, Hopkinsville, Kentucky
*Telegram-Tribune*, San Luis Obispo, California
Winslow *Daily Mail*, Winslow, Arizona
*Winslow Mail*, Winslow, Arizona

## Periodicals

*Arizona Highways*
*Art Digest*
*Desert Magazine*
*Elders Journal*
*Liahona, The Elders' Journal*
*Magazine of Art*
*The Masterkey*
*Latter Day Saints Southern Star*

## Maps

*Pleasant Green Hill Quadrangle, Kentucky-Christian County*. Reston, Va.: U.S.
    Geological Survey; Kentucky Geological Survey; Kentucky Department of
    Commerce, 1957; revised 1994. [1:24,000]
D.G. Beers & Co. *Map of Christian County, Ky*. Philadelphia: J. H. Toudy & Co.,
    1878. [1:65,000]
*Map and Guide to Historic Hopkinsville, Kentucky: Including Christian County and Fort
    Campbell*. Cincinnati: Spectrum Map Publishing; Hopkinsville:
    Hopkinsville-Christian Co. Chamber of Commerce, 1990. [1:21,750]
*Map of Trigg and Christian Counties*. Frankfort: Kentucky Geological Survey, n.d.,
    ca. 1905. [1:126,720]

## Documents

Byrne, Harriet A. "Child Labor in Representative Tobacco-Growing Areas," *U.S.
    Department of Labor Children's Bureau Publication*, No. 155. Washington, D.C.:
    G.P.O., 1926.
Scherffius, W. H., "Tobacco." *Kentucky Agricultural Experiment Station of the State
    College of Kentucky Bulletin*, No. 129. Lexington: Kentucky Agricultural
    Experiment Station, 1907.

Scherffius, W. H., H. Woolsey, and C. A. Mahan. "The Cultivation of Tobacco in Kentucky and Tennessee." *U.S. Department of Agriculture Farmers' Bulletin* 343. Washington, D.C.: G.P.O., 1909.

Smith, Florence P. "Facts About Working Women." *Bulletin of the Women's Bureau,* No. 46. Washington, D.C.: G.P.O., 1925.

U.S. Dept. of Agriculture. *Soil Survey of Christian County, Kentucky.* Compiled by Ronald D. Froedge, et al. Lexington: U.S. Dept. of Agriculture; Kentucky Dept. for Natural Resources and Environmental Protection; Kentucky Agricultural Experiment Station, 1977.

Whitney, Milton. "Methods of Curing Tobacco." *U.S. Department of Agriculture Farmers' Bulletin,* 60. Washington, D.C.: G.P.O., 1898.

## Articles And Unpublished Works

Abrahams, Roger D. "Folklore and Literature as Performance." *Journal of the Folklore Institute* 9, (August–December 1972): 75–94.

Allen, Barbara. "Family Traditions and Personal Identity." *Kentucky Folklore Record* 28 (January-June 1982): 1–5.

———. "The Genealogical Landscape and the Southern Sense of Place." In *Sense of Place: American Regional Studies.* Edited by Barbara Allen and Thomas J. Schlereth, 152–63. Lexington: University Press of Kentucky, 1990.

Archbold, Annelen. "Broommaking in Kentucky." *Back Home in Kentucky* 3 (September–October 1980): 38–39.

Arrington, Leonard J. "Mormon Beginnings in the American South." *Task Papers in LDS History,* No. 9. Salt Lake City: Historical Department of the Church of Jesus Christ of Latter-day Saints, 1976.

———. "Every Life Has Significance," a summary of the life of Effie Carmack, read at the Cannon-Hinckley Group meeting, March 19, 1991, Salt Lake City. Typescript. Copy of MS in the possession of Noel A. Carmack, Hyrum, Utah.

Baird, Nancy Disher and Carol Crowe-Carraco. "'A True Woman's Sphere': Motherhood in Late Antebellum Kentucky." *Filson Club History Quarterly* 66 (July 1992): 369–94.

Barton, Bill. "The Latchstring is Always Out to the Fellowmen of Effie Carmack." *Church News,* January 15, 1966, 5.

Bartrop, R. W., L. Lazarus, and E. Luckhurst, et al. "Depressed Lymphocyte Function After Bereavement." *Lancet* 1, no. 8016 (April 16, 1977): 834–36.

Bascom, Louis Rand. "Ballads and Songs of Western North Carolina." *Journal of American Folklore* 22 (January–March 1909): 238–50.

Berrett, LaMar C. "History of the Southern States Mission, 1831–1961." M.S. Thesis, Brigham Young University, 1960.

"Bible Divination." *Folklore Journal* 1 (1883): 333, and 1 (1884): 380–81.

Blair, Kathryn. "Swing Your Partner!," *Journal of American Folklore* 40 (January-March, 1927): 96–99.

Boatright, Mody C. "The Family Saga as a Form of Folklore." In *The Family Saga and Other Phases of American Folkore.* 1–19. Urbana: University of Illinois Press, 1958.

Bolton, Bernard. "Folk Games from Western Kentucky." *Kentucky Folklore Record* 2 (1956): 123–31.

Buice, David. "Chattanooga's *Southern Star*: Mormon Window on the South, 1898–1900." *BYU Studies* 28 (spring 1988): 5–15.

Bushman, Claudia L. "Mystics and Healers," in *Mormon Sisters: Women in Early Utah.* Edited by Claudia L. Bushman, 1–23. New Edition. Logan: Utah State University Press, 1997.

Cannon, Mike. "My Old Kentucky Home: Gospel Roots Run Deep in Region of Farms, Family and Faith," *Church News,* February 22, 1992, 8–9, 10.

Carmack, Noel A. "'The Yellow Ochre Club': B. F. Larsen and the Pioneer Trail Art Tour, 1936," *Utah Historical Quarterly* 65 (spring 1997): 134–54.

———. "'A Memorable Creation': The Life and Art of Effie Marquess Carmack." *BYU Studies* 37 (1997–1998): 101–35.

"Characteristics of Folk Art: A Study Presented at the American Psychological Association Conference" [by Jules and Florence Laffal]. *Folk Art Finder* 5 (September 1984): 2, 4.

Cheney, Thomas E. "Mormon Folksong and the Fife Collection." *BYU Studies* 3 (1960–1961): 62–63.

Coppage, Noel. "Fights, Fiddles, and Foxhunts." *Kentucky Folklore Record* 7 (1961): 1–14.

Duffy, John. "Medical Practice in the South." *Journal of Southern History* 25 (February 1959): 53–72.

Eberson, Frederick. "A Great Purging—Cholera or Calomel?" *Filson Club History Quarterly* 50 (April 1976): 28–35.

Feeley, N. and L. Gottlieb. "Parents' Coping and Communication Following Their Infant's Death." *Omega: Journal of Death and Dying* 19 (1988–1989): ´ 51–67.

Feintuch, Burt. "Dancing to the Music: Domestic Square Dances and Community in Southcentral Kentucky (1880–1940)." *Journal of the Folklore Institute* 18 (1981): 49–68.

———. "Examining Musical Motivation: Why Does Sammy Play the Fiddle?" *Western Folklore* 42 (July 1983): 208–14.

Fife, Austin E. and Alta Fife. "Folk Songs of Mormon Inspiration." *Western Folklore Quarterly* 6 (January 1947): 42.

———. "Collectors and Collections." *Western Folklore Quarterly* 7 (July 1948): 299–301.

———. "Virginia Folkways from a Mormon Journal." *Western Folklore* 9 (October 1950): 348–58.

Fife, George Buchanan. "The So-Called Tobacco Trust." *Century Magazine* 65 (March 1903): 793.

Furth, Gregg. M. "The Use of Drawings Made at Significant Times in One's Life." In *Living with Death and Dying.* Edited by Elizabeth Kübler-Ross, 63–94. New York: Macmillan Publishing Company, 1981.

Garrity, Thomas F. and J. Wyss. "Death, Funeral, and Bereavement Practices in Appalachian and Non-Appalachian Kentucky." In *Death and Dying: Views from Many Cultures.* Edited by Richard A. Kalish, 99–118. Farmingdale, NY: Baywood Publishing Co., 1980.

Glassie, Henry. "The Appalachian Log Cabin." *Mountain Life and Work* 39 (winter 1963): 5–14.

———."The Types of the Southern Mountain Cabin." In Jan Harold Brunvand, *The Study of American Folklore,* 391–420. 2nd ed. New York: W. W. Norton & Company, 1978.

Gregory, Rick S. "Desperate Farmers: The Dark Tobacco District Planters' Protective Association of Kentucky and Tennessee, 1904–1914." Ph.D. dissertation, Vanderbilt University, 1989.

————. "'The Godless Trust': The Effect of the Growth of Monopoly in the Tobacco Industry on Black Patch Farmers 1890–1914." *Essays in Economic and Business History* 10 (1992): 183–90.

————. "'Look To Yourselves': Tobacco Growers, Problems of Production, and the Black Patch War." *Essays in Economic and Business History* 11 (1993): 283–94.

Guthrie, Charles S. "Tobacco: Cash Crop of the Cumberland Valley." *Kentucky Folklore Record* 14 (April-June 1968): 38–43.

Hall, Jacquelyn Dowd and Annie Firor Scott. "Women in the South." In *Interpreting Southern History: Historigraphical Essays in Honor of Sanford W. Higginbotham.* Edited by John Boles and Evelyn Thomas Nolen, 454–509. Baton Rouge: Louisiana State University Press, 1987.

Hall, Suzanne Marshall. "Breaking Trust: The Black Patch Tobacco Culture of Kentucky and Tennessee, 1900–1940." Ph.D. dissertation, Emory University, 1989.

————. "Working the Black Patch: Tobacco Farming Traditions, 1890–1930," *Register of the Kentucky Historical Society* 89 (summer 1991): 266–86.

Hulan, Richard. "Middle Tennessee and the Dogtrot House." *Pioneer America* 7 (July 1975): 44–45.

Irwin, Harvey J. "The Depiction of Loss: Uses of Clients' Drawings in Bereavement Counseling." *Death Studies* 15 (1991): 481–97.

Ives, Sumner. "A Theory of Literary Dialect." In *A Various Language: Perspectives on American Dialects.* Edited by Juanita V. Williamson and Virginia M. Burke, 145–77. New York: Holt, Rinehart and Winston, 1971.

Jeane, D. Gregory. "Folk Art in Rural Southern Cemeteries." *Southern Folklore* 46 (1989): 159–74.

Jacobs, Adam. "American Play Stuff: Party Plays." *Theatre Arts* 15 (March 1931): 247–50.

Johnson, Jerah. "The Vernacular Architecture of the South: Log Buildings, Dog-Trot Houses, and English Barns." In *Plain Folk of the South Revisited.* Edited by Samuel C. Hyde, Jr., 46–72. Baton Rouge: Louisiana State University Press, 1997.

Jones, Agnes. "Two 1826 Letters by Cornelius Carmack." *Tennessee Genealogist and Family Historian* 1 (June 1989): 8–9, 19.

————. "I Placed My Name Foremost on the List of Volunteers." *Tennessee Genealogist and Family Historian* 1 (September 1989): 15–18.

Jones, Jacqueline. "The Political Economy of Sharecropping Families: Blacks and Poor Whites in the Rural South, 1865–1915." *In Joy and Sorrow: Women, Family, and Marriage in the Victorian South, 1830–1900.* Edited by Carol Bleser, 196–214. New York: Oxford University Press, 1991.

Lewis, E. C. "James Robertson, Nashville's Founder." *American Historical Magazine* 8 (1903): 285–94.

Lightfoot, William E. "'I Hardly Ever Miss a Meal Without Eating Just a Little': Traditional Sorghum-Making in Western Kentucky." *Mid-South Folklore* 1 (spring 1973): 7–17.

Mango, Christina. "Emma: Art Therapy Illustrating Personal and Universal Images of Loss." *Omega: Journal of Death and Dying* 25 (1992): 259–61.

Montell, W. Lynwood. "Hog Killing Time in the Kentucky Hill Country." *Kentucky Folklore Record* 18 (1972): 61–67.

————. "Cemetery Decoration Customs in the American South." In *The Old Traditional Way of Life: Essays in Honor of Warren Roberts.* Edited by Robert E.

Walls and George H. Shoemaker, 111–29. Bloomington: Trickster Press, 1989.

Moody, Thurmon Dean. "Nauvoo's Whistling and Whittling Brigade." *BYU Studies* 15 (summer 1975): 480–90.

Morgan, John. "Dark-Fired Tobacco: The Origin, Migration, and Survival of a Colonial Agrarian Tradition." *Southern Folklore* 54 (1997): 145–84.

Newell, Linda King. "The Historical Relationship of Mormon Women and Priesthood." In *Women and Authority: Re-emerging Mormon Feminism.* Edited by Maxine Hanks, 23–48. Salt Lake City: Signature Books, 1992.

Oats, Joyce Carol. "Joyce Carol Oates On Harriette Arnow's 'The Dollmaker.'" In *Rediscoveries.* Edited by David Madden, 60–66. New York: Crown Publishers, 1971.

Pullen, Carl W. "Some More Dance Songs from West Kentucky." *Kentucky Folk-Lore and Poetry Magazine* 3 (1928): 15–18.

Richards, Mary Stovall. "All Our Connections: Kinship, Family Structure, and Dynamics Among White Families in the Mid-Nineteenth Century Central South." *Tennessee Historical Quarterly* 50 (Fall 1991): 142–51.

Rolph, Daniel N. "Kentuckians and Mormonism: An Historical Overview, 1831–1931." M.A. thesis, University of Kentucky, 1985.

———. "Folklore, Symbolic Landscapes and the Perception of Southern Culture." *Journal of Southern Studies* 1 (summer 1990): 117–26.

Schliefer, S. J. and S. E. Keller, et al. "Suppression of Lymphocyte Stimulation Following Bereavement." *Journal of the American Medical Association* 250 (July 15, 1983): 374–77.

Schwab, R. "Paternal and Maternal Coping with the Death of a Child." *Death Studies* 14 (1990): 407–22.

Scott, Shaunna L. "Drudges, Helpers and Team Players: Oral Historical Accounts of Farm Work in Appalachian Kentucky." *Rural Sociology* 61 (summer 1996): 209–26.

Sessions, Gene A. "Myth, Mormonism, and Murder in the South." *South Atlantic Quarterly* 75 (spring 1976): 212–25.

Simon, Rita. "Bereavement Art." *American Journal of Art Therapy* 20 (July 1981): 135–43.

Smith, Frank H. "Dances and Singing Games." In *The Southern Appalachian Region: A Survey.* Edited by Thomas R. Ford, 271–78. Lexington: University of Kentucky Press, 1962.

Smith, John F. "Plays and Games." *Kentucky Folk-Lore and Poetry Magazine* 1 (1927): 9–14.

Stewart, Karen. "Broommaking in Western Kentucky." *Kentucky Folklore Record* 18 (1972): 46–48.

———. "Making Apple Cider in Western Kentucky." *Kentucky Folklore Record* 18 (1972): 92–95.

Stone, Sue Lynn. "'Blessed Are They That Mourn': Expressions of Grief in South Central Kentucky, 1870–1910." *Register of the Kentucky Historical Society* 85 (summer 1987): 213–36.

Stroebe, Margaret S. "The Broken Heart Phenomenon: An Examination of the Mortality of Bereavement." *Journal of Community and Applied Social Psychology* 4 (February 1994): 47–61.

Stroebe, M. S. and W. Stroebe, et al. "The Broken Heart: Reality or Myth?" *Omega: Journal of Death and Dying* 12 (1981): 87–106.

Stuart, Jesse. "Kentucky Hill Dance." *New Republic* 79 (May 16, 1934): 15–16.
Thompson, Lawrence S. "Some Notes on the Folklore of Tobacco and Smoking." *Kentucky Folklore Record* 10 (1964): 43–46.
Tyler, Pamela. "The Ideal Rural Southern Woman as Seen by 'Progressive Farmer' in the 1930s." *Southern Studies* 20 (fall 1981): 278–96.
Waldrep, Christopher. "Planters and the Planters' Protective Association in Kentucky and Tennessee." *Journal of Southern History* 52 (November 1986): 565–88.
———. "The Organization of the Tobacco Industry and Its Impact on Tobacco Growers in Kentucky and Tennessee, 1900–1911." *Mid-America* 73 (January 1991): 71–81.
West, Roy. "Pioneer Preachers: Religion in the Upper Cumberland." In *Lend An Ear: Heritage of the Tennessee Upper Cumberland.* Edited by Calvin Dickinson, et al., 21–32. New York: University Press of America, 1983.
Wetherill, John. "Keet Zeel." Southwestern Monuments Monthly Report, supplement, March, 1934.
———. "Keet Zeel." Southwestern Monuments Monthly Report, supplement, December, 1935.
Wilson, Gordon. "Singing Games or Play-Party Games." *Bulletin of the Kentucky Folklore Society* (1925): 26–30.
———. "Talismans and Magic in Folk Remedies in the Mammoth Cave Region." *Southern Folklore Quarterly* 30 (June 1966): 192–201.
———. "Traditional Aspects of the One-Roomed School–III: Playtime." *Kentucky Folklore Record* 13 (1967): 62–67.
Wolfe, Margaret Ripley. "Fallen Leaves and Missing Pages: Women in Kentucky History." *Register of the Kentucky Historical Society* 90 (winter 1992): 64–89.
Wright, Sue M. "Spotlight on Christian County: Patriarch of the Pennyrile." *Back Home in Kentucky* 8 (July-August 1985): 25–30.

## Books and Pamphlets

Abernethy, Thomas Perkins. *From Frontier to Plantation in Tennessee: A Study in Frontier Democracy.* Chapel Hill: University of North Carolina Press, 1932.
Arnow, Harriet Simpson. *The Dollmaker.* New York: Macmillan, 1954.
Axton, W. F. *Tobacco and Kentucky.* Lexington: University Press of Kentucky, 1975.
Beveridge, Albert J. *Abraham Lincoln, 1809–1858,* 2 vols. Boston: Houghton Mifflin, 1928.
Billingsley, Robin, comp. *Duncan: Fountain of the Gila River, 1883–1983.* Duncan, Ariz.: Historic Booklet Committee, 1983.
Blaine, John Ewing. *The Blaine Family: James Blaine, Emigrant, and His Children, Ephraim, Alexander, William, Eleanor.* Cincinnati: Ebbert & Richardson, 1920.
Browne, Edward T., Jr., and Raymond Athey. *Vascular Plants of Kentucky: An Annotated Checklist.* Lexington: University Press of Kentucky, 1992.
Cain, Shirley West, comp. *1880 Federal Census of Christian County, Ky.* Hopkinsville: Christian County Genealogical Society, 1992.
Campbell, Tracy. *The Politics of Despair: Power and Resistance in the Tobacco Wars.* Lexington: University Press of Kentucky, 1993.
Carmack, Effie Marquess. *Backward Glances: An Autobiography in Rhyme.* Ord, Neb.: Quiz Industries, n.d.
———. *Down Memory Lane: The Autobiography of Effie Marquess Carmack.* Atascadero, Calif.: Atascadero News Press, 1973.

Carmack, Mattie Olivia Hale. *My Story: Mattie Olivia Hale Carmack, 1873–1961.* Compiled by Donna Bess Carmack Musto. Franklin, NC: Genealogy Publishing Service, 1991.

Carr, Stephen L., ed. *Holladay-Cottonwood Places and Faces.* Holladay, Utah: Holladay-Cottonwood Heritage Committee, 1976.

Chambers, J. S. *The Conquest of Cholera: America's Greatest Scourge.* New York: Macmillan, 1938.

Christian County Genealogical Society. *Family Histories, Christian County, Kentucky, 1797–1986.* Paducah: Turner Publishing Co., 1986.

———. *Family History Book, Christian County, Kentucky.* Paducah: Turner Publishing, 1991.

Clark, James R. *The Story of the Pearl of Great Price.* Salt Lake City: Bookcraft, 1955.

Clewell, Gladys D., ed. *Lands and Peoples; The World in Color.* 7 vols. New York: The Grollier Society, 1929.

Coulter, E. Merton. *The Civil War and Readjustment in Kentucky.* Chapel Hill: University of North Carolina Press, 1926.

Cunningham, Bill. *On Bended Knees: The Night Rider Story.* Nashville: McClanahan Publishing House, 1983.

Daniels, William M. *Correct Account of the Murder of Generals Joseph and Hyrum Smith at Carthage on the 27th Day of June 1844.* Nauvoo, Ill: John Taylor, 1845.

*Deseret News 1997–1998 Church Almanac.* Salt Lake City: Deseret News, 1996.

*The Doctrine and Covenants of the Church of Jesus Christ of Latter-day Saints.* Salt Lake City: Church of Jesus Christ of Latter-day Saints, 1981.

Ellis, John. *Medicine in Kentucky.* Lexington: University Press of Kentucky, 1977.

Farquhar, S. E. *The New Human Interest Library.* 6 vols. Chicago: Midland Press, 1928.

Feintuch, Burt. *Kentucky Folkmusic: An Annotated Bibliography.* Lexington: University Press of Kentucky, 1985.

Fine, Elizabeth C. *The Folklore Text: From Performance to Print.* Bloomington: Indiana University Press, 1984.

Ford, Tennessee Ernie. *This is My Story, This is My Song.* Englewood: Prentice Hall, 1964.

Gibbs, Kenneth T. and Carolyn Torma. *Hopkinsville and Christian County Historic Sites.* Frankfort: Kentucky Heritage Commission, 1982.

Gilmore, Francis and Louisa Wade Wetherill. *Traders to the Navajos: The Story of the Wetherills of Kayenta.* Albuquerque: University of New Mexico Press, 1953.

Goodstein, Anita Shafer. *Nashville, 1780–1860: From Frontier to City.* Gainsville: University of Florida Press, 1989.

Hagood, Margaret Jarman. *Mothers of the South: Portraiture of the White Tenant Farm Woman.* Chapel Hill, 1939; reprint, New York: Arnow Press, 1972.

Hatch, William W. *There is No Law . . .: A History of Mormon Civil Relations in the Southern States, 1865–1905.* New York: Vantage Press, 1968.

Hays, Kevin J. *Folklore and Book Culture.* Knoxville: University of Tennessee Press, 1997.

Herndon, William H. and Jesse W. Weik. *Herndon's Life of Lincoln.* Edited by Paul M. Angle. Cleveland: Fine Editions Press, 1949.

Hughes, Stella. *Hashknife Cowboy: Recollections of Mack Hughes.* Tucson: University of Arizona Press, 1984.

*Hymns.* Revised and enlarged. Salt Lake City: Church of Jesus Christ of Latter-day Saints, 1948.

*Hymns of the Church of Jesus Christ of Latter-day Saints, 1985.* Salt Lake City: Church of Jesus Christ of Latter-day Saints, 1985.

Irvin, Helen Deiss. *Women in Kentucky.* Lexington: University Press of Kentucky, 1979.
Jenson, Andrew. *Historical Record: A Monthly Periodical.* Book I. Salt Lake City: Andrew Jenson, 1889.
————. *Latter-day Saint Biographical Encyclopedia.* 4 vols. 1901. Reprint, Salt Lake City: Western Epics, 1971.
————. *Encyclopedic History of the Church of Jesus Christ of Latter-day Saints.* Salt Lake City: Deseret News Publishing Company, 1941.
Kant, Candace. *Zane Grey's Arizona.* Flagstaff: Northland Press, 1984.
Kebler, John E., ed. *The Kentucky Encyclopedia.* Lexington: University Press of Kentucky, 1992.
Kephart, Horace. *Our Southern Highlanders: A Narrative of Adventure in the Southern Appalachians and a Study of Life Among the Mountaineers.* New York: The Macmillan Company, 1922.
Kingsley, Charles. *Village Sermons, and Town and Country Sermons.* New Edition. London: Macmillan and Co., 1878.
Kline, Mary-Jo. *Guide to Documentary Editing.* 2nd ed. Baltimore: John Hopkins University Press, 1987.
Kooiman, Helen. *Walter Knott: Keeper of the Flame.* Fullerton: Plycon Press, 1973.
Ludlow, Daniel H., ed. *Encyclopedia of Mormonism.* 4 vols. New York: Macmillan Publishing Company, 1992.
Lundwall, N. B., comp. *The Fate of the Persecutors of the Prophet Joseph Smith.* Salt Lake City: Bookcraft, 1952.
McNitt, Frank. *Richard Wetherill: Anasazi.* Albuquerque: University of New Mexico Press, 1957.
Manley, Roger. *Signs and Wonders: Outsider Art Inside North Carolina.* Raleigh: North Carolina Museum of Art, 1989.
Marshall, Suzanne. *Violence in the Black Patch of Kentucky and Tennessee.* Columbia: University of Missouri Press, 1994.
Masters, Edgar Lee. *The Sangamon.* The Rivers of America. New York: Farrar & Rinehart, 1942.
McConkie, Bruce R. *Mormon Doctrine.* Salt Lake City: Bookcraft, 1966.
Meacham, Charles Mayfield. *A History of Christian County, Kentucky: From Oxcart to Airplane.* Nashville: Marshall & Bruce Co., 1930.
Meador, Anna Hunsaker. *Cemetery Records, Northern Section of Christian County, Kentucky.* Hopkinsville: Author, 1976.
————. *Cemetery Records of Southern Portion of Christian County, Kentucky.* Hopkinsville: Author, 1980.
Medical Historical Research Project. *Medicine and Its Development in Kentucky.* Louisville: The Standard Printing Company, 1940.
*Melchizedek Priesthood Leadership Handbook.* Salt Lake City: Church of Jesus Christ of Latter-day Saints, 1990.
Miller, John E. *Laura Ingalls Wilder's Little Town: Where History and Literature Meet.* Lawrence: University Press of Kansas, 1994.
Miller, John G. *The Black Patch War.* Chapel Hill: University of North Carolina Press, 1935.
Miller, Nora. *The Girl in the Rural Family.* Chapel Hill: University of North Carolina Press, 1935.
Montell, William Lynwood. *Ghosts Along the Cumberland: Deathlore in the Kentucky Foothills.* Knoxville: University of Tennessee Press, 1975.
————. *Folk Medicine of the Mammoth Cave Area.* Tompkinsville, Ky.: Mammoth Cave Folklore Project, 1976.

————. *Upper Cumberland Country.* Jackson: University Press of Mississippi, 1993.

Montell, William Lynwood and Michael Lynn Morse. *Kentucky Folk Architecture.* Lexington: University Press of Kentucky, 1976.

Myres, Sandra L. *Westering Women and the Frontier Experience, 1800–1915.* Albuquerque: University of Mew Mexico Press, 1982.

Nall, James O. *The Tobacco Night Riders of Kentucky and Tennessee, 1905–1909.* Louisville: Standard Press, 1939.

Niederman, Sharon. *A Quilt of Words: Women's Diaries, Letters & Original Accounts of Life in the Southwest, 1860–1960.* Boulder: Johnson Books, 1988.

Odum, Howard W. *Southern Regions of the United States.* Chapel Hill: University of North Carolina Press, 1936.

————. *The Way of the South: Toward the Regional Balance of America.* New York: Macmillan, 1947.

Pace, Linda Garland and Hilton Smith, eds. *The Foxfire Book of Appalachian Toys & Games.* Chapel Hill: University of North Carolina Press, 1993.

Perrin, William Henry. *County of Christian, Kentucky: Historical and Biographical.* Chicago: F.A. Battey Publishing Co., 1884.

————. *County of Trigg, Kentucky: Historical and Biographical.* Chicago: F.A. Battey Publishing Co., 1884.

Pickard, Madge E. and R. Carlyle Buley. *The Midwest Pioneer: His Ills, Cures, & Doctors.* New York: Henry Schuman, 1946.

*Poetry Broadcast: An Anthology Compiled for Radio Programs.* New York: The Exposition Press, 1946.

Porcher, Francis P. *Resources of the Southern Fields and Forests.* Charleston, 1863; reprint, New York: Arno Press, 1970.

Rando, Theresa A., ed. *Parental Loss of a Child.* Champaign, Ill.: Research Press, 1986.

Rennick, Robert M. *Kentucky Place Names.* Lexington: University Press of Kentucky, 1984.

Rich, Ben E. *Mr. Durrant of Salt Lake City: "That Mormon."* Salt Lake City: George Q. Cannon & Sons, 1893.

Rolph, Daniel N. *"To Shoot, Burn, and Hang": Folk-History from a Kentucky Mountain Family and Community.* Knoxville: University of Tennessee Press, 1994.

Sauer, Carl Ortwin. *Geography of the Pennyroyal: A Study of the Influence of Geology and Physiography Upon Industry, Commerce and Life of the People.* Frankfort: The Kentucky Geological Survey, 1927.

Schiff, Harriet Sarnoff. *The Bereaved Parent.* New York: Crown, 1977.

Scott, Anne Firor. *The Southern Lady: From Pedestal to Politics, 1830–1930.* Chicago: University of Chicago Press, 1970.

Seymour, Randy. *Wildflowers of Mammoth Cave National Park.* Lexington: University Press of Kentucky, 1997.

Smith, Joseph, Jr. *Teachings of the Prophet Joseph Smith.* Compiled by Joseph Fielding Smith. Salt Lake City: Deseret Book, 1979.

Stahl, Sandra K. Dolby. *Literary Folkloristics and the Personal Narrative.* Bloomington: Indiana University Press, 1989.

Summers, Harrison B. comp. *A Thirty-Year History of Programs Carried on National Radio Networks in the United States, 1926–1956.* Columbus: Ohio State University, 1958.

Tanner, George S. and J. Morris Richards. *Colonization on the Little Colorado: The Joseph City Region.* Flagstaff: Northland Press, 1977.

Tanselle, G. Thomas. *Textual Criticism and Scholarly Editing.* Charlottesville: University Press of Virginia, 1990.

Thomas, Daniel Lindsey, and Lucy Blayney Thomas. *Kentucky Superstitions.* Princeton: Princeton University Press, 1920.

Thomas, Benjamin P. *Lincoln's New Salem.* Springfield: The Abraham Lincoln Association, 1934.

Thompson, Lawrence S. *Kentucky Tradition.* Hamden, Conn.: Shoe String Press, 1956.

Tinsley, Jim Bob. *The Hash Knife Brand.* Gainsville: University Press of Florida, 1933.

Turner, William T. *Gateway From the Past: A Pictorial History Commemorating 175th Anniversary of Hopkinsville and Christian County, Kentucky, Including Program of the Christennial Celebration, July 3–8, 1974.* Hopkinsville, Ky.: Burdine's Print, 1974.

Waldrep, Christopher. *Night Riders: Defending Community in the Plack Patch, 1890–1915.* Durham: Duke University Press, 1993.

Warren, Robert Penn. *Night Rider*, Southern Classics Series, edited by M. E. Bradford. Nashville, 1939; reprint, Nashville: J. S. Sanders & Co., 1992.

Wharton, May Cravath. *Doctor Woman of the Cumberlands: The Autobiography of May Cravath Wharton, M.D.* Pleasant Hill, TN, 1953; reprint, Nashville: Parthenon Press, 1972.

Weslager, Clinton A. *The Log Cabin in America: From Pioneer Days to the Present.* New Brunswick: Rutgers University Press, 1969.

Westover, Adele B. and J. Morris Richards. *A Brief History of Joseph City.* Winslow, Ariz.: The Winslow Mail, n.d.

———. *Unflinching Courage.* Joseph City, Ariz.: John H. Miller, 1963.

*Who's Who in the South and Southwest.* Vol. 1, 1st ed. Chicago: Larkin, Roosevelt & Larkin, 1947.

Wigginton, Elliot. *The Foxfire Book.* Garden City: Doubleday, 1972.

———, ed. *Foxfire 6.* Garden City: Anchor Press, Doubleday, 1980.

———, ed. *Foxfire 9.* Garden City: Anchor Press, Doubleday, 1986.

Willhite, A. B. *Christian County, Kentucky 1900 Federal Census.* Russellville, Ky.: A. B. Whillhite, 1996.

Willis, Laura, comp. *Christian County, Ky. Census of 1870.* Hopkinsville: Christian County Genealogical Society, 1996.

Wilson, Douglas S. *Honor's Voice: The Transformation of Abraham Lincoln.* New York: Alfred A. Knopf, 1998.

Wilson, Gordon. *Folklore of the Mammoth Cave Region.* Edited by Lawrence Thompson. Kentucky Folklore Series, No. 4. Bowling Green: Kentucky Folklore Society, 1968.

Wolfe, Margaret Ripley. *Daughters of Canaan: A Saga of Southern Women.* Lexington: University Press of Kentucky, 1995.

WPA, Federal Writer's Project. *Arizona: A State Guide.* American Guide Series. New York: Hastings House; Arizona State Teacher's College at Flagstaff, 1940.

WPA, Federal Writer's Project. *Kentucky: A Guide to the Bluegrass State.* American Guide Series. New York: Hastings House; University of Kentucky, 1939.

# INDEX

# POETICS/POLITICS

## RADICAL AESTHETICS
## FOR THE CLASSROOM

### *Edited by Amitava Kumar*

St. Martin's Press
New York

ISBN 0–312–21865–6

Library of Congress Cataloging-in-Publication Data
Poetics/politics : radical aesthetics for the classroom / edited by
    Amitava Kumar.
        p.  cm.
    Includes bibliographical references and index.
    ISBN  0–312–21865 (cloth). — ISBN  0–312–21866–4 (pbk.)
    1. Poetics. 2. Poetry—History and criticism—Theory, etc.
3. Aesthetics—Political aspects. 4. Poetics—Study and teaching.
5. Poetry—Study and teaching. 6. Radicalism in literature.
I. Kumar, Amitava, 1963–
PN1042.P578  1999
801'.93'071—dc21                                          99–22576
                                                               CIP

First edition: September 1999
10  9  8  7  6  5  4  3  2  1

# *Permissions*

# *Contents*

# *Acknowledgments*

IN THE OPENING PAGES of the Introduction to his *Culture and Imperialism*, Edward Said describes the conditions under which his book was produced: "In its writing I have availed myself of the utopian space still provided by the university. . . ."

*Poetics/Politics*, too, owes its existence to the much-threatened space of the humanities institution. In recording that debt, I also want to underline the fact that the goals of this volume are tied to that debt's repayment. It is only right, therefore, that I express my principal thanks to the contributors to this collection who are all engaged in a meaningful dialogue about the place of culture in our classrooms.

While this book was in production, I found my own toe-hold in that other endangered institution of higher education—tenure. I want to thank all those colleagues who supported me in that process. In fact, I hope this volume will be of help in diverse classrooms, and that through such uses I shall have played my part in the more oblique, and mercifully impersonal, settlement of valuable debts.

At St. Martin's Press, I want to thank Maura E. Burnett for flagging off this project. Thanks also to Amy Reading for continued assistance and to Rick Delaney for help with production. Michael Laffey at the University of Florida provided early editorial help. The General Secretary of the *desi* Politbureau Vijay Prashad gave unstinting help with the printing and xeroxing of the manuscript during two long afternoons.

This book is for my father, Ishwar Chandra Kumar. He was the first in his village to go to a city to receive higher education. The ambiguous hold that education gives us over our places of origin is a troubled structure of feeling that I must have inherited from him. A problem that worries this collection—of finding in the aesthetics of displacement a strategy of political mobilization—is *my* gift to him.

# Editor's Introduction

*Amitava Kumar*

## At the Opening . . .

As my students and I watch "The Couple in a Cage: A Guatinaui Odyssey," a recent video-documentary made by Coco Fusco and Paula Heredia, we witness with horror and undeniable fascination the corruption of high culture. We are at a museum amidst the well-shod denizens of metropolitan United States; the occasion is the opening of a show, a peculiar show, where a couple brought from an island called Guatinaui, off the Gulf of Mexico, are displayed to the audience in a cage. Someone in a museum-staff uniform announces: "If you'd like your photos with the Guatinaui, simply step up to the cage and enunciate very clearly: 'Fo-to.' They don't speak English." Those who step up to have this encounter memorialized pay a dollar; those who want a view of the male's genitalia pay five dollars. When we get to glimpse the male's sexual organs, he appears to have been castrated. A man in a suit claps. Others stand around sipping their cocktails, taking in the show.

We too are taking in the show. We have heard the staff at one of the museums declare: "This display is a part of a five-hundred-year tradition of exhibiting indigenous people, a tradition first started by Christopher Columbus." The museum receives angry phone calls from some of their members who are outraged at the way in which they have seen human beings treated, and these gentlefolk state that they are withdrawing their membership. Others seem rather amused and even experience a faint sense of patriotic pride. One young man from a group of U.S. sailors comments on the behavior of the couple: "They pick up traditions really well, like drinkin' Coca-Cola, listenin' to music, watchin' TV 'n' eatin' saltine crackers. . . . That's America for ya."

Many of my students can't believe this could be real. They are face to face with the gullibility of an American public deeply invested in a set of complicitous ideologies. These are the ideologies that support faith in the institutions of the nation-state and high culture, not to mention the concomitant faith in the implicit or explicit inferiority of a vast array of Others. The said public's inability, if not refusal, to read in the actions of Others the strategies of sly mimicry and resistance is surprising to many of my students. They, and I'd imagine other viewers, are forced to pause when at the end of the video-film, the filmmakers announce that this was a performance created by Guillermo Gómez-Peña and Coco Fusco: "The performance was conceived as a satirical comment on the past. To the performers' surprise, however, many of their visitors thought they were real."

I find this revealing. The explosion in cultural studies has rendered rather banal the assertion that the real is constructed; and yet we find again and again the persistence of the real as if this were precisely not the case. In his introductory essay in this volume, Michael Taussig writes: "We act and have to act as if mischief were not afoot in the kingdom of the real and that all around the ground lay firm." There are two related responses—and they are present in this volume before you—to this condition that Taussig names a "forgetting."

First, we need to invent, and keep inventing, in solidarity with the performances of Gómez-Peña and Fusco, those strategies that reveal the fault lines of the real. This cannot only be a traditional, academic practice of ideology critique. By insisting upon the performative, I want to underline the importance of other practices, some more private but others emphatically more public, more spectacular, sometimes more ludic, and at other times more (or less) artful. Hence, the demand for a poetics that is political. Several of the essays in this collection address precisely this point. This search is present in Eric Lott's mix of memoir and music criticism wherein he looks closely at what he calls "the political richness of sensuous human noise-making." Or in Samir Gandesha's exploration of Punk as a model of multiculturalism when mapped against the larger contradictions of the postcolonial city. And also in Paula Rabinowitz's richly textured essay in this volume in which she reveals the lines of narrative conventionality that have secured the divisions of the private and the public.

Second, our response to the condition that Taussig names "forgetting" should also include a contrary recognition: as teachers, we are indeed for most of the time engaged in elaborating a practice in which the obduracy of the real is challenged and its claims to being somehow "natural" is seriously undermined. In other words, as some of the essays assembled here show, what is being developed in our classrooms, and in the field of pedagogy, is a politics that perhaps gets practiced nowhere else so very consistently. Ira Livingston's essay about the "disavowal of power" in the canonical voices of both poetic and scientific discourses projects that kind of pedagogical practice. In a different vein, Elizabeth Langland turns her training in literary poetics to an examination of administrative politics so that we may imagine alternative futures in academia.

These essays are speculations about the material basis of our shared life as teachers. It is only right, then, that some of these deliberations should point to the limits of such practices or the presumption of communities. Sean McCann's questioning of the familiar polemicization as well as the polarization in these debates is an indictment of what he considers a kind of "forgetting"—one that is different from what Taussig had in mind—that refers to the amnesia about the history of such debates. Situating himself in another discursive domain, Michael Bibby uses the example of the poetry of the Black Panthers to posit radically divergent, and in fact opposed, public spheres. Both McCann's and Bibby's essays on the limits of consensual public spheres of communication must too, in my opinion, produce for our students a sense of the real as being fundamentally unstable because it is a site of contestation. Here, too, the real work lies not in simply asserting that the real is "constructed"; instead, this pedagogy aims to uncover how groups attempt to secure their sense of the real by articulating the interested visions of culture.

This volume makes its appearance at a time when, reeling under pressures of downsizing as well as attacks by the resurgent right in this country, the profession of teaching languages and cultural studies has been witnessing a conservative return to what Bruce Robbins has called a "'purist' aesthetic."[1] This retreat is evidenced in a broad range of phenomena: from the "back to literature" appeals of a recent MLA president like Elaine Marks to the mainstream responses to publications like David Denby's *Great Books*, from the resurgent formalism of apolitical, *New* New Critical aesthetes in prestigious journals like *Critical Inquiry* to the panicked discussion in the pages of *Profession* about our professional usefulness, rather obsolescence, in an age of a rapidly shrinking job market.

Our colleagues have responded to this general condition by addressing, sometimes with considerable zeal, the institutional conditions of our own existence. A slew of books in the past year or more by impressive writers from the left like Cary Nelson, Michael Bérubé, Stanley Aronowitz, and Randy Martin has made active links between the economy, the oppressive ruling ideologies, and pressing issues of employment.[2]

But spirited responses of another sort—those that would take back the ground of culture from those who would build high-rise towers or prisons on it—have been curiously lacking. Bérubé's *Employment of English* is perhaps more of an exception, in its deliberations on the specificity of the literary and the aesthetic, among those authors who have written most strenuously on the culture wars and its aftermath.[3] In his latest book, while providing a list of policy changes among our priorities and our goals as teachers, especially as teachers who need to reclaim the space of the humanities, Bérubé also makes a strong case for the specificity of the aesthetic and its autonomous relation to our pedagogy and our lives:

> [E]ven the most narrowly "literary" works really can defamiliarize the familiar and renew perception; compel readers to imaginative sympathy, disgust, ecstasy, terror; train young adults to attend to the subtleties of language, the rhythmic variations of verse, and the power of rhetorical hermeneutics; lengthen children's attention spans to the point at which they can finally understand how Frank Churchill's letter finally exposes Emma Woodhouse's inability to read *Emma*'s multiple subtleties of language; and, in rare cases, make undergraduates curious enough to keep reading after they graduate. And when critics on the cultural Left point out that none of this is necessarily inconsistent with the project of giving students mere ideological obfuscation or training them in quietism, my impulse is to agree—and then to suggest in return that if one desires guarantees that one's teaching and writing can never be put in the service of ideological obfuscation or quietism, one would be better off not wasting time with the humanities in the first place.

There are some fine examples, in the contemporary cultural setting, of the mobilization of oppositional aesthetics in the classroom and outside. *June Jordan's Poetry for the People: A Revolutionary Blueprint* presents the example of university students using poetry and pedagogy to proclaim resistance against capitalism and imperialism.[4] Another prize-winning book, *Spreading the Word: Poetry and the Survival of Community in America*, also provides the example of another kind of academic practice, refusing to cede culture to those who do not actively link it with community.[5] Its writer, Ross Talarico, in his contribution to this volume, spells out the agenda of teaching poetry in opposition to the corporate commercial jingle. Most recently, Randy Martin, also a contributor in these pages, published his *Critical Moves: Dance Studies in Theory and Politics*, which deploys dance as language of political mobilization to counter the notion of arrested motion that has too often, and perhaps too conveniently, served as the image of the crisis of left politics.[6] In his essay in this volume, while elucidating a classroom exercise, Martin demonstrates that the task of taking back the space of culture is, in some sense, also a matter of learning physically, sensually, *socially*, about the immediate space that bodies occupy and alter.

Of course, there is a whole history, broad and many hued, for this kind of work in this country and elsewhere. And yet, one is so often forced to speak as if poetics and politics were opposed and one is trying to invent a somehow new admixture of the two. I have in front of me an essay in which the writer comments on this reductionism and its reasons:

> My first response to the symposium topic is to wonder what brings us to this pass, where we have a meeting about "politics and poetry." Not about kinds of politics, or kinds of poetry: just "politics" and "poetry." The issue, so defined, is so *un*defined it's quite crude. Not that we're to blame for this. It's remarkable that there is even such a meeting. Ordinarily "political poetry" is considered beneath comment. Nonetheless, if we look at the historical record, at the poetry that has been kept and revered, it's astounding that there are any reservations whatever about the viability of political poetry.[7]

The "crudity" of issues that this writer laments is contested by this volume. Not so much by asserting the connection between, say, art and politics, but instead by performing the more difficult and necessary labor of elaborating a nuanced framework for judging the cooperation of those related terms. A serious attempt at exploring the complexities of subjectivities, communication, and formalism is present in Grant Kester's contribution to this anthology wherein he extends a subtle critique of the influence of Gilles Deleuze's philosophy on contemporary architecture and art. Consider also Csaba Toth's debunking of binaries in his essay in this volume. Toth's contention is that "noise" has become a pedagogical force "by building new collectivities both in aggrieved neighborhoods and college campuses." Toth effects not only a reversal of interest in "noise" over "music," but also strives for a relentless contextualization of "noise" within postmodern, postindustrial cultures of protest. He demonstrates that the stakes are always higher than can be admitted by unproductive oppositions.

There are at least two other, laudable ways of contesting the barrenness of the binary opposition between poetics and politics. One is to register the historic depth of the engagement with such questions and the multifold elaboration of specific issues in that debate. The other is to insert difference and the urgency of the pressures brought on by the work done by scholars in fields such as feminist studies, postcolonial studies, and queer studies. Let me take them up in quick succession. As far as the former is concerned, the history of the earlier debates in Marxism, principally between Brecht, Lukacs, Adorno and Benjamin, are crucial if we are to avoid a "forgetting" of our past. Fredric Jameson, a writer who is easily among those closest to those traditions of debate in the United States, provides in his essay in this volume an elaboration of a contemporary Marxist aesthetics that productively draws upon that past.[8] The second point that I raised above, about the insertion of difference, namely the difference of feminist, postcolonial, or queer scholarship, provides the general context for our reading of an essay like the one by Camilla Griggers in this volume. Griggers enters the theater of memory to recall the face of war. In the process she "performs" gendered, postcolonial identities—for instance, by morphing the faces of Madison Avenue models into those of Vietnamese women burned by napalm.

What kind of a theater is a classroom? How precisely is a critic an actor? Why, and in what manner, should we consider writing, any writing, a performance?

In his recent *Literary Theory: A Very Short Introduction*, Jonathan Culler makes at least three points that deserve comment.[9] I take them as symptomatic of the dominant self-understanding of the literary-theoretical discipline, and also of how new entrants to its fold are being introduced to its character and goals. I also want to identify Culler as another, more sophisticated, less conservative, but hardly challenging proponent of the "return to literature." I entertain his ideas about literary theory here because even though not all of the contributors to this volume would identify themselves as card-carrying literary theorists, almost all of the essays that follow are indeed broadly situated in that discourse. Also, I feel that the questions with which I opened this section as well as Culler's arguments can be used to identify those questions that await this volume.

The first point I want to note is that Culler downplays the importance of cultural studies, or at least the cultural studies that he identifies as being interested in "totality." And by that term he means any and all attempts to read cultural forms as expressions of the social context from which they derive. My second point is that against cultural studies Culler posits a notion of poetics. (What I'm also imputing here—and my reading is nothing if not tendentious—is that this is also a valorized notion in Culler's discourse.) Culler defines poetics as "the attempt to account for literary effects by describing the conventions and reading operations that make them possible." And lastly, the third point of particular interest to me in Culler's discourse is that while poetics is offered as a bulwark, if not a corrective, to the politics of cultural studies, it too is in some ways overwhelmed by the more fashionable interest in performativity. Culler is being receptive here to the work of Judith Butler; Culler's emphasis is on how language, through repetition, "gives life to the forms it repeats."

The responsibility of writing an introductory text for literary theory cannot be an easy one, and I think Culler is able to be both comprehensive and lucid. My serious quarrel with him, however, is on the grounds that he is unable to imagine a mode of analysis in which an interest in social totality can coexist with poetics. Why does Culler remain so certain that politically charged writers and teachers cannot admit the "suspension of the demand for immediate intelligibility, the willingness to work at the boundaries of meaning, opening oneself to unexpected, productive effects of language and imagination, and the interest in how meaning and pleasure are produced"? Equally egregiously, from my point of view, Culler cannot imagine the notion of performativity working not simply by repetition but also by rupture. In other words, neither his version of cultural studies nor his particular brand of poetics can engage the use of language in ways that would make unstable—even revolutionize—the world. Again, I must repeat that I have gone on at length about Culler's slim volume because I believe it is an introduction to the future of our profession. And I hope that this volume you hold in your hands will challenge Culler's binaristic vision by extending a relationship between politics and poetics that is always divided— or joined—by the more ambivalent sign of the oblique '/'. But I also hope that this sense of unstable oscillation of the two terms will engender, in specific contexts, some thinking about the performative aspects of our own critical production in our classrooms, in other public places, even in this volume. This is the context in which, perhaps, we can read H. Aram Veeser's essay on a composition student's sly mimicry of her teacher's desires, producing something disturbing and unexpected. Similarly, my article, wanting both terms of Culler's fixed, opposing binaries, asks the question: "When Barthes gushes over a letter he has received from Morocco, how does one bring to a discussion with one's students both the poetics of desire in writing and the politics of unemployment for Moroccan youth in France?"

I want to end my own very short introduction to *Poetics/Politics* by citing in its entirety a public letter written by a friend and a colleague. You will remember the days when the Unabomber, his identity still a mystery and to most a menacing one, tried to give a new twist to the slogan "publish or perish" by insisting that his manifesto be published in two main East Coast newspapers or he would attack again. The serial bomber had declared in his open letter that his targets were only academics in the "technical fields." "We would not want anyone to think," the Unabomber wrote, "that we have any desire to hurt professors who study archaeology, history, literature or harmless stuff like that." The cultural junta of this country had for the past several years assured us that those in our profession who read books in relation to race, class, gender, and sexuality were causing great harm to Western civilization. And now came this individual who, perhaps because he spent his evenings and weekends filing trigger mechanisms, dismissed us as harmless. My friend's letter was a response to the Unabomber's arrogant dismissal of language workers. I have brought this text to you as a public service announcement because it works on the limits or the borders of what it means to be public, or to use language, or, for that matter, to claim or proclaim performativity:

Dear Sir,

Before proceeding, please consider: this text is a powerful surveillance device: it tracks each movement of your eyeballs (knowing you are reading these words at this moment) and then becomes a detailed map of where your eyes have been. (Look back and see: those are the words you read just now; we have exactly the same sequence in our files.)

Are you reading this? Are you reading THIS? Well, you MUST be reading this otherwise how could you know what is written here?

This text understands and has anticipated your contempt—and your amusement at these very words—and also: the little tingle at your web's edge crossing the synapse between this page, your eyes, infected with a kind of virus that attaches to your sense of your immunity to the harmlessness of these and any words: don't worry; there's no need to read on or to stop since the explosive device has already been triggered (the syntax, length and speed of the preceding sentence was adjusted to deliver the device; go back and look; we don't think you can locate it).

These words have reached you where police have failed; you and they have sadly underestimated us; we knew you would. WE won't betray you to the Forces of Control whose tool you are already; only they and you

DON'T KNOW THIS, and all things being equal, that's the way we like it; we can even tell you so (it's what we call "the revelation of the device") without your knowing. See, we have just told you, but do you understand? That's precisely the point.

This text is just a mirror where you watch yourself explode. Your sense that you have survived the reading of this text intact will be the cue that we have gotten through (this is what your scientists call an "unfalsifiable theory"). You'll go about your work in a changed world, like a Japanese soldier hidden in a cave, living and dying and never knowing that the war had ended many years before. You and your enemies are part of a conspiracy to keep you from knowing.

Our textual virus is a version of those "small, completely autonomous units" that you have dreamt about and we have learned to manufacture. Using a self-referential technology (sometimes called "poeticity"), we are able to empty a message (such as this one) almost completely of content by turning it back on itself, producing a set of small singularities that alter the local structures of meaning.

The notion that technical specialists are distinct from nontechnical and "harmless" intellectuals (as you mentioned in your letter to the *Times*) was installed in you in the late eighteenth century by some of our predecessors. Binary Opposition technology is well known by us. If there were two kinds of people in the world, those who divide people into two kinds and those who don't, you would be one of the former. But there are not. We installed this technology ourselves; we let the Binary Virus loose, and it insinuated itself everywhere. Massive structures, including your own cognitive apparatus, were built around it and are completely dependent on it. We taught you everything you know, but we didn't teach you everything WE know (we have a saying that "the bricoleur invented the engineer"). It would be suicide for you to try to dismantle yourself and put yourself back together to extract yourself from these technologies: what would be left to put you back together when you had been dismantled? Transplanting your own brain would be simple by comparison!

Have you noticed how every sentence seems to stand on its own, as if it may or may not be connected to the surrounding sentences? That is because we have written this text around the set of the singularities that we mentioned earlier; you might say it is their phenotype, their carrier. The pattern of gaps-in-play that we have woven into this text (those little moments of blankness you have felt while reading this text, where you seemed to lose the thread for a moment) will always both enable and dis-able your dream of a world comprising "small, completely autonomous units" (which, by the way, was implemented in you by some of our double-agents: Democritus, Newton, Leibniz, Mill).

Your life and your work and your world, like those of your enemies, is like a ouija board on which one hand on the planchette may be yours, but the other is your enemy's, and the message is ours. We have responded, here, to the questions your life keeps posing you in ways you and your enemies cannot by definition comprehend; the machinic phylum crosses us all; your machines are only means but only our machines mean, and this text proclaims our monstrous victory over you and your beloved and despised technocrats.

Always,
The Unapoets

## Notes

1. Bruce Robbins, "The Return to Literature," in Amitava Kumar, ed., *Class Issues: Pedagogy, Cultural Studies, and the Public Sphere* (New York: New York University Press, 1997), 22–32.
2. Stanley Aronowitz and William Difazio, *The Jobless Future* (Minneapolis: University of Minnesota Press, 1995); Michael Bérubé and Cary Nelson, ed., *Higher Education Under Fire* (New York: Routledge, 1995); Cary Nelson, ed., *Will Teach for Food* (Minneapolis: University of Minnesota Press, 1997); Cary Nelson, *Manifesto of a Tenured Radical* (New York: New York University Press, 1997); Randy Martin, ed., *Chalk Lines: The Politics of Work in the Managed University* (Durham: Duke University Press, 1998).
3. Michael Bérubé, *The Employment of English* (New York: New York University Press, 1997).
4. Lauren Muller and Poetry for the People Collective, ed., *June Jordan's Poetry for the People: A Revolutionary Blueprint* (New York: Routledge, 1995).
5. Ross Talarico, *Spreading the Word: Poetry and the Survival of Community in America* (Durham: Duke University Press, 1995).
6. Randy Martin, *Critical Moves: Dance Studies in Theory and Politics* (Durham: Duke University Press, 1998).
7. James Scully, "Remarks on Political Poetry," in *Line Break: Poetry as Social Practice* (Seattle: Bay Press, 1988), 3–7. See p. 3.
8. See also Fredric Jameson, ed., *Aesthetics and Politics* (1977; rpt. New York: Verso, 1980).
9. Jonathan Culler, *Literary Theory: A Very Short Introduction* (Oxford: Oxford University Press, 1997).

# Chapter 1

# A Report to the Academy

Michael Taussig

*To put it plainly, much as I like expressing myself in images, to put it plainly: your life as apes, gentlemen, insofar as something of that kind lies behind you, cannot be farther removed from you than mine is from me. Yet everyone on earth feels a tickling at the heels; the small chimpanzee and the great Achilles alike.*

—Franz Kafka, "A Report to an Academy"

So what is this tickling at the heels to which Kafka's all-too-human ape would refer us all-too-apish humans? I call it the mimetic faculty, the nature that culture uses to create a second nature, the faculty to copy, imitate, make models, explore difference, yield into and become Other. The wonder of mimesis lies in the copy drawing on the character and power of the original, to the point whereby the representation may even assume that character and that power. In an older language this is "sympathetic magic," and I believe it is as necessary to the very process of knowing as it is to the construction and subsequent naturalization of identities. But if it is a faculty, it is also a history, and just as histories enter into the functioning of the mimetic faculty, so the mimetic faculty enters into those histories. No understanding of mimesis is worthwhile if it lacks the mobility to traverse this two-way street, especially pertinent to which is Euro-American colonialism, the felt relation of the civilizing process to savagery, to aping.

My way of traversing this two-way street takes me into an eccentric history that begins with the curious and striking recharging of the mimetic faculty caused by the invention of mimetically capacious machines such as the camera in the second half of the nineteenth century. This history then somersaults backward in time so as to explore a foundational moment in the equation of savagery with mimesis—namely, the experience of young Charles Darwin in 1832 on the beach at Tierra del Fuego, full of wonder at the mimetic prowess of primitives, especially as it concerns their mimicking him. This history then fans forwards in the form of other sailors setting sail from northern climes, as they appear carved in the shape of wooden curing figurines in the early twentieth-century Swedish ethnography of certain Indians of the Darién Peninsula between the Panama Canal and Colombia. Wondering about the magical possibilities in this image-making of Europeans makes me speculate first about what it might be like to live in Darién-like mimetic worlds where spirits copy physical reality, and second, what it means for me as a white man to trace a history in which an image of the white man is used by Indian men to access magical power emergent from the womb of the Great Mother. This somersaults me forward into myself from First Contact time with Darwin on the beach, through the invention of mimetic machines, to late twentieth-century Reverse Contact now-time, when the Western study of the Third and Fourth World Other gives way to the unsettling confrontation of the West with itself as portrayed in the eyes and handiwork of its Others. Such an encounter disorients the earlier occidental sympathies that kept the magical economy of mimesis and alterity in some sort of imperial balance. History wreaks its revenge on representational security as essentialism and constructionism oscillate wildly in a death struggle over the claims of mimesis to be the nature that culture uses to create a now-beleaguered second nature. And this brings me to the vexing subject of "constructionism," of making things up.

For in this history I am often caught musing as to whether the wonder of magic in mimesis could reinvigorate the once-unsettling observation that most of what seems important in life is made up and is neither more (nor less) than, as a certain turn of phrase would have it, "a social construction." It seems to me that the question of the mimetic faculty tickles the heels of this upright posture and makes it interesting once again. With good reason postmodernism has relentlessly instructed us that reality is artifice yet, so it seems to me that not enough surprise has been expressed as to how we nevertheless get on with living, pretending—thanks to the mimetic faculty—that we live facts, not fictions. Custom, that obscure crossroads where the constructed and the habitual coalesce, is indeed mysterious. Some force impels us to keep the show on the road. We cannot, so it would seem, easily slow the thing down, stop and inquire into this tremendously braced field of the artificial. When it was enthusiastically pointed out within memory of our present Academy that race or gender or nation was so much social construction, invention, and representation, a window was opened, an invitation to begin the critical project of analysis and cultural reconstruction was offered. And one still feels its power even though what was nothing more than an invitation, a preamble to investigation has by and large been converted instead into a conclusion—for example, "Sex is a social construction," "Race is a social construction," "The nation is an invention," and so forth, the tradition of invention. The brilliance of the announcement was blinding. Nobody was asking: What's the next step? What do we do with this old insight? If life is constructed, how come it appears so immutable? How come culture appears so natural? If things coarse and subtle are constructed, then surely they can be reconstrued as well? To adopt Hegel, the beginnings of knowledge were made to pass for actual knowing.

I think construction deserves more respect; it cannot be name-called out of (or into) existence, ridiculed and shamed into yielding up its powers. And if its very nature seems to prevent us—for are we not also socially constructed?—from peering deeply therein, that very same nature also cries out for something other than analysis as this is usually practiced in reports to our Academy. For in construction's place—what? No more invention, or more invention? And if the latter, as is assuredly the case, why don't we start inventing? Is it because at this point the critic fumbles the pass and the "literary turn" in the social sciences and historical studies yields naught else but more metacommentary in place of poesis, little by way of making anew?

But just as we might garner courage to reinvent a new world and live new fictions—what a sociology that would be!—so a devouring force comes at us from another direction, seducing us by playing on our yearning for the true real. Would that it would, would that it could come clean, this true real. I so badly want that wink of recognition, that complicity with the nature of nature. But the more I want it, the more I realize it's not for me. Not for you either . . . which leaves us in this silly and often desperate place wanting the impossible so badly that while we believe it's our rightful destiny and so act as accomplices of the real, we also know in our heart of hearts that the way we picture and talk is bound to a dense set of representational gimmicks that, to coin a phrase, have but an arbitrary relation to the slippery referent easing its way out of graspable sight.

Now the strange thing about this silly if not desperate place between the real and the really made-up is that it appears to be where most of us spend most of our time as epistemically correct, socially created, and occasionally creative beings. We dissimulate. We act and have to act as if mischief were not afoot in the kingdom of the real and that all around the ground lay firm. That is what the public secret, the facticity of the social fact, being a social being, is all about. No matter how sophisticated we may be as to the constructed and arbitrary character of our practices, including our practices of representation, our practice of practices is one of actively forgetting such mischief each time we open our mouths for something or to make a statement. Try to imagine what would happen if we didn't in daily practice thus conspire to actively forget what Saussure called "the arbitrariness of the sign"? Or try the opposite experiment. Try to imagine living in a world whose signs were indeed "natural."

Something nauseating looms here, and we are advised to beat a retreat to the unmentionable world of active forgetting where, pressed into mighty service by society, the mimetic faculty carries out its honest labor suturing nature to artifice and bringing sensuousness to sense by means of what was once called sympathetic magic, granting the copy the character and power of the original, the representation the power of the represented.

Yet this mimetic faculty itself is not without its own histories and own ways of being thought about. Surely Kafka's tickling at the heels, brought to our attention by the ape aping humanity's aping, is sensateness caught in the net of passionful images spun for several centuries by the colonial trade with wildness that ensures civilization its savagery? To witness mimesis, to marvel at its wonder or fume at its duplicity, is to sentiently invoke just that history and register its profound influence on everyday practices of representation. Thus the history of mimesis flows into the mimesis of history, Kafka's ape standing at the turbulence where these forces coalesce. And if I am correct in invoking a certain magic of the signifier and what Walter Benjamin took the mimetic faculty to be—namely, the compulsion to become the Other—and if, thanks to new social conditions and new techniques of reproduction (such as cinema and mass production of imagery), modernity has ushered in a veritable rebirth, a recharging and retooling of the mimetic faculty, then it seems to me that we are forthwith invited if not forced into the inner sanctum of mimetic mysteries where, in imitating, we will find distance from the imitated and hence gain some release from the suffocating hold of "construction" no less than the dreadfully passive view of nature it upholds.

# CHAPTER 2

# (Not) Going with the Flow: The Politics of Deleuzean Aesthetics

*GRANT KESTER*

> One creates new modalities of subjectivity in the same way that an artist creates new forms from the palette.
> —Félix Guattari, *Chaosmosis: An Ethico-Aesthetic Paradigm*

## INTRODUCTION

OVER THE LAST FIVE YEARS the concept of the "aesthetic" has emerged with considerable force in American and European intellectual circles. As David Beech and John Roberts note in the *New Left Review,* this "return" to the aesthetic has been staged largely by writers identified with a left political position. This is, as they argue, somewhat surprising because of the tendency in the past of writers on the left to regard the aesthetic as little more than an extension of bourgeois ideology.[1] It has typically been conservative commentators who have celebrated the aesthetic for its capacity to reveal the fortuitous correspondence between the subjective tastes of the wealthy and powerful and ostensibly universal standards of cultural excellence.[2] Beech and Roberts suggest that this new concern with beauty, bodily pleasure, and subjectivity derives in part from the anxious soul-searching of progressive academics faced with the demise of the Soviet Union (and the resultant "crisis of Marxism") and the ascendancy of political and cultural conservatism in the United States and the United Kingdom. They note in particular the recent works of neo-Marxist art historians such as Charles Harrison and T. J. Clark who have to some extent repudiated or at least reevaluated their former commitments. Harrison and Clark now consider their interest in the political and cultural context of art production to have been unduly instrumentalizing and have embraced instead the belief that art enjoys a fundamental autonomy from the social.[3]

Beech and Roberts' essay—which also examines the philosophical works of Andrew Bowie and J. M. Bernstein—reflects only one dimension of a broader interest in somatic experience that has been registered across a range of other disciplines including art practice and theory, architecture, film studies, and critical and literary theory. In the American art world, interest in the aesthetic has been linked in recent years with the seemingly inexhaustible fascination with beauty and "the body," a movement that is associated with writers such as David Hickey, Wendy Steiner, Barbara Stafford and, as I will discuss below, Gilles Deleuze.[4] Hickey's book, *The Invisible Dragon: Four Essays on Beauty,* published in 1993, precipitated a groundswell of interest in beauty and the aesthetic, especially within art schools. In *The Scandal of Pleasure* (1995) Steiner defends aesthetic experience on the basis of its subversive capacity to generate diverse and even conflicting interpretive responses. And Stafford's books, including *Body Criticism* (1994) and, more recently, *Good Looking: Essays on the Virtue of Images* (1996), have been influential in turning the attention of artists and art historians to the changing status of visual and sensual experience during the modern period. In Stafford's narrative this bodily "intelligence" has been driven underground during the post-Enlightenment period. As a result, we have come to mistrust sensory experience and surrendered ourselves instead to an "authoritarian reason."[5] A variant of this analysis can be found in recent architectural criticism. In *Architecture and the Crisis of Modern Science* (1983) Alberto Pérez Gómez contends that architecture was violently severed from its organic rootedness in the phenomenologically rich experience of physical construction by the evil abstraction of the Renaissance building plan, thus effecting a mind/body split that has reduced the contemporary architect to little more than a clerical worker.[6]

What has emerged from these works, taken in conjunction with the theoretical writings of Bernstein and others, is a generalized view of the aesthetic as an autonomous, powerfully transgressive mode of experience which places us in touch with a repository of "anexact," "subrepresentational," sensual knowledge. In the following essay I will investigate this "new" aesthetics, focusing on its significance for contemporary art practice and cultural politics. My interest in the aesthetic is based on its status as an epistemological mode, a way of knowing the world, rather than on its relevance for the evaluation of beauty *per se.* There are two interrelated aspects of aesthetic epistemology that are of particular importance for my investigation. The first is the relationship of the aesthetic to the constitution of the subject: how one comes to experience a sense of self through forms of aesthetic knowledge. The second is the question of how aesthetic forms construct or pattern our experience of the "given" world around us. The relationship "of knowledge to its Other, to that which is to be known," as Wlad Godzich has noted, is one of the primary concerns of aesthetic discourse.[7] In my view these two dimensions of research into the aesthetic—the formation of subjectivity and knowledge of the given—provide it with a particular salience for current debates over identity, community, and political transformation.

The questions of subject constitution and intersubjectivity have been elaborated with particular intensity in the works of the French philosopher Gilles Deleuze (and in Deleuze's collaborations with Félix Guattari). Moreover, Deleuze and Guattari's approach to these questions has been staged through an ongoing negotiation with the traditions of Enlightenment philosophy. The aesthetic and modes of subjectivity associated with aesthetic experience play a central role in Deleuze and Guattari's work. On the thematic level, Deleuze and Guattari have a long-standing interest in the operations of literary, cinematic, and visual works of art. Deleuze has written on the English painter Francis Bacon (*Francis Bacon: Logique de la sensation,* 1981), Marcel Proust (*Marcel Proust et les signes,* 1964), and auteur cinema (*Cinéma 1: l'Image-Movement,* 1983 and *Cinéma 2: l'Image-Temps,* 1985). And Deleuze and Guattari co-authored a study of Franz Kafka (*Kafka: pour une littérature mineure,* 1975). However, it is not simply the subject matter of art that is of concern in their work but the analytic system that they have developed, which assigns to the aesthetic a significant capacity for political agency. This centrality is explicit in one of Guattari's more recent books *Chaosmosis: An Ethico-Aesthetic Paradigm* (1995), in which he describes the "aesthetic paradigm—the creation and combination of mutant percepts and affects" as "the paradigm for every possible form of liberation."[8] The movement toward what I am calling a new aesthetics is of course quite diverse and it is important to avoid overgeneralizing about what is in fact a disparate set of approaches located across a range of different disciplines. I do, however, concur with Beech and Roberts' assessment that these approaches are united by a concern to reestablish the (relative) autonomy of aesthetic experience in response to what is seen as its unduly instrumentalized role in earlier critical theory. Deleuze and Guattari's work presents what is undoubtedly the most complex attempt to reclaim the efficacy of the aesthetic and to understand the political implications of aesthetic subjectivity.

If Deleuze and Guattari consider the artist to be in some ways an exemplary subject, artists have returned the compliment by avidly embracing their work. With the exception of Deleuze and Guattari's co-authored books *Anti-Oedipus* and *A Thousand Plateaus* and Guattari's *Chaosmosis,* it has been Deleuze's work (the *Cinema 1* and *Cinema 2* studies; *Leibniz, the Fold, and the Baroque; Difference and Repetition; The Logic of Sense; Bergsonism;* and *Expressionism in Philosophy: Spinoza,* among others), that have had the greatest influence in the arts. In fact, over the past few years Deleuze has threatened to overtake Jean Baudrillard and Jacques Derrida as the art world's French philosopher of choice. Both *Feature* and the *Journal of Philosophy and the Visual Arts* have published a number of essays on the relevance of Deleuze's thought for contemporary art practice.[9] And Deleuze's book *Leibniz, the Fold, and the Baroque* (published in 1988 and translated into English in 1993) precipitated a spate of special issues including, most notably, *New Observations* ("Art in the Folds," 110, January/February 1996) and *Architectural Design* ("Folding in Architecture," 63, 3/4, 1993).[10] Part of the attraction that Deleuze holds for artists, in addition to his rather flattering portrayal of their liberatory creative powers, is his reliance on figural terms, in part as an attempt to challenge the logocentrism of conventional philosophical discourse. I will discuss the implications of this "figuralism" in more detail below. Deleuze, who committed suicide in November of 1995 after a lingering illness, received obituaries in fashionable art magazines such as *Parkett* and *Artforum* and continues to be regularly cited and invoked by artists, architects, curators, and critics. In addition, his currently unpublished lectures and essays promise that the flow of Deleuzean discourse will continue unabated for some time.[11] I want to outline some of the ways in which Deleuze's philosophy has been taken up in the art world, but it is first necessary to describe more specifically how the aesthetic functions in his thought.

## I. THE SPECTRE OF HEGEL

Deleuze's attempts to rethink the constitution of the subject were heavily influenced by the negative example of the Hegelian tradition. During the years following the end of World War II, Hegel's thought came to dominate the French academic system, due in large part to the lectures given in Paris during the 1930s by the Russian émigré Alexandre Kojéve and to the teaching of Jean Hippolyte at the Sorbonne. By the time Deleuze was studying at the Sorbonne in the mid-1940s, Hegel was an unavoidable fact of life. For

Deleuze and his contemporaries it was necessary to move beyond Hegel, and specifically to move beyond Hegel's ontology as outlined in the *Science of Logic* and the *Phenomenology of Spirit*. There were two aspects of Hegel's ontology that Deleuze found particularly objectionable. The first was the belief that being was externally determined, that is, that it required the "recognition" of some other subject. "Self-consciousness exists" as Hegel writes, "in and for itself when, and by the fact that, it so exists for another; that is, it exists only in being acknowledged."[12] The second was that this determination unfolded through a process in which the external subject's identity was negated or destroyed. These two views are presented by Hegel in his explanation of the master/bondsman relationship in the *Phenomenology of Spirit*: " . . . one is the independent consciousness whose essential nature is to be for itself, the other is the dependent consciousness whose essential nature is simply to live or to be for another. The former is lord, the other is bondsman."[13]

The Hegelian subject requires the existence of an external agent to establish its identity. As a result of this vulnerability it emerges as an aggressive and conative entity, driven to sacrifice other subjects through the process of negation on which its own survival depends. For many French thinkers of the postwar period, Hegel's thought is set in a syllogistic chain that stretches from the psychology of the master/slave relationship to Nazi Germany to modern day state capitalism. In each case a monolithic entity attempts to mask its own external dependence by imposing its will (both conceptually and physically) through the mastery or destruction of difference (slaves, Jews, labor, or natural resources). There is a certain easy transference here between questions of ontology and questions of a political and institutional nature that is, as we shall see, a hallmark of Deleuze's writing. This set of associations was strengthened by the events of May 1968. After the inaction of the French Communist Party (PCF) following the worker and student strikes, whatever residual faith that French intellectuals such as Deleuze might have had in organized or collective forms of political struggle was extinguished. Any overarching program, identity, theory, or mode of resistance that might potentially subordinate and "negate" the specific differences of member individuals was to be deplored: any collective form (of thought, social, or political organization) was irretrievably compromised by its association with a coercive, Hegelian reason.[14]

In order to defeat this paradigm Deleuze can't simply invert the terms of Hegel's formulation and "free" the slave of dominative reason. Hegel himself has already anticipated any direct transcendence of oppositional terms through the concept of the dialectic. Thus Deleuze was driven to search through Western philosophy for alternative models of subject constitution that would be both positive and internally grounded. It is this search that leads him to Leibniz, Spinoza, Nietzsche, and Bergson. From these disparate sources he assembles a model of subjectivity that does not rely on external determination and negation. It is impossible here to convey the full detail of Deleuze's formulation. I will, however, identify two aspects of this new subject that have a direct bearing on the implications of Deleuze for a new aesthetics.

First, Deleuze's subject is determined by internal rather than external differentiation. Deleuze turns to Henri Bergson's concept of an *"élan vital"* or life force to describe a process of internal differentiation: "Being differs with itself immediately, internally. It does not look outside itself for an other or a force of mediation because its difference rises from its very core."[15] The experience of difference, of predication, that is necessary for the formation of even the most nominal form of subjectivity, is thus drawn into the interior of the subject. Deleuze is consistently attracted to models of the subject which describe it as enclosed or sealed from discursive interaction with the external world. Thus his interest in Leibniz's "windowless monad" in *Liebniz, the Fold, and the Baroque* or the "Body without Organs" of *Anti-Oedipus,* which eliminates all possible points at which the subject's desires might be organized or regulated through an intersubjective domination. On the one hand any "organ" represents a site of possible external coercion (or "territorialization") of the body's "intrinsic drives." At the same time the organs represent the demand of the body to master or consume the outside world.[16]

The second step that Deleuze takes is to expunge any residual traces of Cartesian self-identity from his monadic subject (which in some respects bears a striking resemblance to the protean and self-sufficient bourgeois individual). He turns to the concept of a "will to power," developed in Nietzsche's version of the master/slave relationship. For Neitzsche the master's will is unrestrained by reason or conscious reflection—his subjectivity is always in motion, always in the process of being produced in the act of doing. Deleuze is concerned to identify the will to power not with the personality of the master (he seeks to "de-personalize" Nietzsche, as Michael Hardt has written), but rather as a positive, creative force that works *through* the body of the master, thus resolving the problem of how to found identity without negation.[17] Only an action that bypasses our rational, conscious self can invent entirely new possibilities (new forms of art, new models of social organization). The master is able to engage in a radical self-forgetting that allows him to change from one mode of being to the next. The master doesn't depend on recognition from the Other; rather, he utterly destroys the Other, clearing the ground for an absolute break with existing values instead of the false and half-hearted Hegelian negation. The slave on the other hand is negative and reactive; burdened by resentment against the master, unable to forget, and brooding over past injustices. The slave, because he is powerless against the master in reality, must make a virtue out of his powerlessness and turn an abstract and ineffectual reason against the master, holding him accountable to an ideal standard of justice and equality that doesn't pertain in the real world. The slave's reason is simply a reaction to (and the negation of) the master's power. The slave inverts the master's values (aggression and the power to destroy and create at will) and makes them his own (passivity, the deferral of radical change for some ideal utopia).

The Nietzschean master is for Deleuze a prototypical artist. As he writes: "in Nietzsche, 'we the artists' = 'we the seekers after knowledge or truth' = 'we the inventors of new possibilities of life.'"[18] The artist is able to transcend his own subjectivity and create entirely new values. Moreover, when the artist creates it is not as an expression of his individual personality; rather, he is merely the vehicle for a greater spiritual force that moves through his body. He (and it has to be said here that Deleuze has written on few if any women artists) is literally not himself and is transported through the act of creativity to a productive mode of existence (the "being of becoming") that transcends reason and conventional self-consciousness. This experience of positive being is captured in Deleuze's discussion of Bergson's "creative emotion," which is produced "between the pressure of society and the resistance of intelligence":

> And what is this creative emotion, if not precisely a cosmic Memory, that actualizes all the levels at the same time, that liberates man from the plane (plan) or the level that is proper to him, in order to make him a creator, adequate to the whole movement of creation? This liberation, this embodiment of cosmic memory in creative emotions, undoubtedly only takes place in privileged souls. It leaps from one soul to another, 'every now and then,' crossing closed deserts ... And from soul to soul, it traces the design of an open society, a society of creators, where we pass from one genius to another, through the intermediary of disciples or spectators or hearers.[19]

Although Deleuze is anxious to downplay the "personalist" references in Nietzsche, to say nothing of Bergson's confederacy of "privileged souls," I have some question as to how fully the Deleuzean subject is differentiated from the traditional, romantic belief in creative genius. There is of course a long tradition of describing the artist as a conduit for higher forces in the *Picasso: Creator and Destroyer* genre. The concept of genius in its conventional usage refers to a form of subjectivity in which individual identity is consummated with an intelligence that transcends existing norms and values and "gives the rule" to art, in Kant's words. Just how innovative a form of being is this, given its association with the idea of a privileged elite of highly sensitive individuals who streak like comets through the dull sky of an otherwise mundane culture? In fact, Deleuze's books consistently celebrate the achievements of mostly white, male Europeans, from Artaud to Beckett to Joyce to Kafka to Proust to Ravel to the "Great Directors" of the *Cinema* books. Whether a given action or work is attributed to an impersonal "will to power," an *élan vital,* a body without organs, or a good old-fashioned "genius," the practical effect is much the same—both the effect of the work of art on a potential viewer and on the political and cultural construction of the artist and art-making. Throughout his writing Deleuze seems oblivious to the normative social and cultural function of the artistic personality, its conflicted relationship with the market, with bourgeois myths of individuality and merit, and with the complex function of symbolic capital. Moreover, he seems to assume that artists, or at least the effects produced by works of art, are necessarily progressive. This is, in part, because he is treating the artist as an ideal form of being. But what does it mean strategically and politically to celebrate a mode of being that, in its outward appearance and operation (rather than in its internal ontological condition), is so strikingly isolated and individualistic?

This may seem like a rather petty complaint to make given the grand philosophical questions that Deleuze is attempting to address, but it is related to a broader criticism I have of his work, which has to do with the status of the aesthetic itself as an organizing political principle. If the Deleuzean subject is an ideal form of being, one that is currently experienced only by a "privileged few," then it takes on a decidedly Hegelian connotation; it emerges as a teleological goal or model, a condition toward which we should aspire, assisted by the special personality of the artist. Deleuze's work is by and large based not on an explicit political or historical analysis but on the assumption of a transhistorical form of bad subjectivity. Capitalism is "bad" because it produces "bad" (dominative, binary, hierarchical) forms of subjectivity. The solution then is to establish in philosophical terms what a "good" subjectivity might be (nonhierarchical, decentered). This description is arrived at through the use of a figurative language (the body without organs, the monad/nomad couplet, the rhizome, smooth versus striated space, the fold). But what precisely is being figured? It seems clear, as I've noted above, that this mode of being is offered as something yet to be achieved. It does not currently exist, except in fragmented and dispersed forms (in art-making or schizophrenia, for example), and it requires the work of philosophy to survey these fragments and develop a framework within which their broader political significance can be established.

How might this ideal be achieved? In other words, what forms of political agency are Deleuzean monads capable of? If the Deleuzean subject is no longer required to look outside itself for a determinative moment, if it has withdrawn from all "linked and connected flows," how precisely will it make contact with other subjects?[20] Any conventional form of intersubjective dialogue, communication, or political organization is out of the question. First, because it would inevitably succumb to the dynamic of negative determination, and second, because the very concept of discourse requires a model of subjectivity that is anathema to Deleuze. The effective separation of the corporeal "body" as a potentially liberatory site and as a surrogate mode of being (if not of subjectivity *per se*) has the effect of separating the Deleuzean subject from any form of social experience based on discourse. As a result Deleuze must locate the basis of intersubjectivity or community in devices such as "cosmic memory" that perform a typically "aesthetic" function in reconciling the individual with the social, or the one and the multiple (albeit in a very atypical ontological framework). There are, in fact, distinct echoes of Schiller in Deleuze's appeal to a nature like state of unregulated bodily desire, defined by positivity, creativity, and expression, which is threatened by the hierarchical, rational, systematizing abstraction of modern life.

This aesthetic function is typified in Deleuze's treatment of Spinoza. Deleuze turns to Spinoza for an account of the possible foundation for the social organization of bodies. He develops the theory of a "univocity" of being; the idea that individual subjects are all related attributes of a larger whole or substance: "not only is being equal in itself, but it appears equally present in all beings . . ." [21] As expressive bodies we are able to sense or intuit our essential commonalty with other bodies. As Deleuze writes, paraphrasing Spinoza, "God produces things in all attributes at once. Because the attributes are all equal, there is an identity of connection between modes differing in attribute."[22] The natural harmony that exists between and among individual bodies obviates the need for any discursive rationality; as individual beings we are all united as attributes of a greater force (God for Spinoza; the aesthetic or cosmic memory for Deleuze), drawn together by the commonality of a "joyful passion."[23] Deleuze's study of Spinoza also exhibits his characteristic ontological foundationalism: his tendency to draw conclusions about social and political relationships from ontological questions with little or no mediation ("modes" become subjects, "substance" becomes roughly synonymous with the social or an underlying foundation for sociability, an ontological *conatus* becomes political or social power).

Moreover, despite his allergy to Hegelian negation Deleuze himself seems susceptible to certain binary tendencies. There is a distinctly Manichean quality to his definition of power: representation is opposed by "subrepresentation," conscious reason to the unconscious or "aconceptual ideas," hierarchical forms to rhizomatic structures, order to chaos, identity to alterity, and so on. Moreover, this same oppositional form is echoed in Deleuze's figural language, for example, the "smooth" versus "striated" spaces discussed in *A Thousand Plateaus* or in the following description of the nomad:

> On one side, we have the rigid segmentarity of the Roman Empire, with its center of resonance and periphery, its State, its pax romana, its geometry, its camps, its lines (boundary lines). Then, on the horizon, there is an entirely different kind of line, the line of the nomads who come in off the steppes, venture a fluid and active escape, sow deterritorialization everywhere, launch flows whose quanta heat up and are swept along by a Stateless war machine.[24]

Despite his concern with preserving difference against the reductive abstractions of Hegel, Deleuze also tends to speak in totalizing terms. He ascribes inherent moral or political value to given forms of power or modes of being (the rhizome, the fold, the boundary line), with little or no concern for the specific historical and political contexts in which they might operate or the effects they might produce. Along with this comes a tendency to collapse differences among and within forms of resistance under the guise of a kind of universalized bohemianism. Here is Guattari from *Chaosmosis*:

It is in an underground art that we find some of the most important cells of resistance against the steam-roller of capitalist subjectivity—the subjectivity of one-dimensionality, generalized equivalence, segregation, and deafness to true alterity. This is not about making artists the new heroes of the revolution, the new levers of History! Art is not just the activity of established artists but of a whole subjective creativity which traverses the generations and oppressed peoples, ghettos, minorities . . .[25]

The aesthetic emerges as a transhistorical political form that unites "established artists," "ghetto dwellers," "minorities," and generally "oppressed peoples" everywhere and over the generations. There are no doubt any number of "established artists" who have little or no interest in being included in the company of Guattari's "ghetto dwellers" and "minorities." The basis of this aesthetic resistance, defined through an almost total collapse of specificity and attention to context, is to be "true alterity."

Not surprisingly Deleuze provides relatively few examples of what a contemporary political practice based on his ontology might look like. The *locus classicus* is, of course, May 1968, an event that has done so much to form the political imaginations of Deleuze and his contemporaries. This is his description from *A Thousand Plateaus*:

Those who evaluated things in macropolitical terms understood nothing of the event because something unaccountable was escaping. The politicians, the parties, the unions, many leftists, were utterly vexed; they kept repeating over and over again that "conditions" were not right. It was as though they had been temporarily deprived of the entire dualism machine that made them valid spokespeople. Bizarrely, de Gaulle and even Pompidou, understood much more than others. A molecular flow was escaping, minuscule at first, then swelling, without however, ceasing to be unassignable.[26]

These are the characteristic elements of a Deleuzean political movement: it is described not as the product of a conscious agency or plan but as the spontaneous movement of an anonymous political substance that "swells" and "flows" and "escapes," like steam from a radiator. It operates not on the oppressive and generalizing level of macropolitics but on the level of individual bodies and subconscious desires, on the street and in action. As an event it entirely eludes the centralizing, teleological, and rational mindset of both the left and the right. And most importantly its meaning, like that of a work of art, can't be "assigned" or accounted for in advance. In these rare moments political struggle becomes an aesthetic event—unplanned, unadministered, unanticipated new collectivities or configurations of bodies are formed that elude the instrumentalizing grasp of political "theory," and that may break up as easily as they have congealed. Deleuze's commentators repeat this basic formulation with variations. Thus Michael Hardt, who has written one of the best general introductions to Deleuze's thought, describes "political assemblage" as "an art in that it has to be continually made anew and reinvented."[27]

Hardt attempts to read Deleuze as endorsing the general ideals of "liberalism," defined as the refusal of a specific political *telos*: "the most important single tenet of liberal democratic theory is that the ends of society be indeterminate, and thus that the movement of society remain open to the will of its constituent members.[28] While this is certainly a laudable sentiment, one could no doubt find fairly similar language in the *Congressional Record* or most high school civics classes. The difficulty comes, of course, when we attempt to define concepts like "will" and "openness" in actual political contexts. Brian Massumi, in his *User's Guide to Capitalism and Schizophrenia,* is a bit more specific, providing a list of approved Deleuzean political movements that includes, in addition to the obligatory May 1968, the French Situationists, the Yippies, the Provos in the Netherlands, "extraparliamentary Greens" in Northern Europe, the Italian autonomia movement of the 1970s, and Catalonian anarchists during the Spanish Civil War.[29] Despite his caricature of the "Standard of the European White Male Heterosexual," Massumi's list is remarkably European, white, male, and heterosexual. There is no mention of the National Welfare Rights movement, the Black Panthers, La Causa, the Dodge Revolutionary Union Movement in Detroit, post-Stonewall gay activism, the black urban rebellions that took place in American cities between 1964 and 1968, or the Lordstown, Ohio GM work-stoppages of the early 1970s, to name but a few American examples from around the same period, perhaps because these are seen as compromised by their association with concrete, "Hegelian" objectives or insufficiently Deleuzean forms of political agency.

## I. A DELEUZEAN AESTHETIC

In this section of this essay I want to explore the implications of the new aesthetics, and of a Deleuzean aesthetic in particular, for art practice and cultural politics. There are three interrelated aspects of the Deleuzean aesthetic I've discussed above that have a particular relevance for art practice. The first is what I will term a "figural formalism" ; the second is the nondiscursive, internally determined construction of the Deleuzean subject; and the third is the consequent reliance by Deleuze on the aesthetic, understood as an ahistorical force, as the basis for social or political organization.

I have already discussed Deleuze's use of the figure as a philosophical device. These terms (the monad/nomad, the rhizome, the body without organs, the fold) function not through the traditional techniques of philosophical analysis but by a compelling visual/intuitive "logic." The figure is integral to Deleuze's effort to develop a subjectless model of political power. The form of the fold or the rhizome is not simply a metaphor. Rather, it takes on a life of its own (the influence of Henri Focillon on Deleuze is evident here) and is endowed with an inherently liberatory capacity to transmit or express modes of being and of social organization. When taken up in art and architectural practice the discursive mobility that is a feature of Deleuze's figural language (the movement from the ontological to the social, or from a figural form to a political form) manifests itself in a tendency toward literalism, in which the mere presence of a folded shape in a sculpture, or a convoluted roof-line in a building, is taken as a political expression. The catalog for a recent exhibition of paintings by Kenny Scharf provides a typical example. Scharf is a painter who first gained recognition in the early 1980s as part of the East Village art scene in New York. His paintings feature jumbles of cartoon characters, pop and advertising icons, and fantastic, rubbery objects, arrayed against lurid backdrops that combine graffiti-style spray paint, washes of color, and sci-fi landscapes. In an essay contained in a brochure for the show, the exhibition's curator draws on Deleuze's concept of "smooth" and "striated" space to situate Scharf's canvases:

> Striated space, the domain of the State (the university, the military, the corporation) is hierarchical and is ruled by order, purpose, routine, and control—all attributes that cannot exist in smooth space which flourishes on anarchy and choice . . . Plumbing the surface of a Scharf painting is analogous to jumping into this "matrix of contingent connections". The cacophony and chaos of his facades activate the viewer's gaze, allowing her to embark on a smooth voyage through Scharf's fun tunnel.[30]

This statement presents a less sophisticated (or perhaps simply more laconic) expression of the characteristic Deleuzean tendency to collapse differences among modes of power. The university, the military, and the corporation are presented as interchangeable manifestations of a greater oppressive form, under the generalizing categories of "order" and "control." This ordered form is then juxtaposed to the "anarchy and choice," "chaos," and "fun" of Scharf's paintings. The "smooth" surfaces of Scharf's paintings—they are typically painted with little or no impasto and relatively fine surface detail, and with various iconic elements arranged over a field of color—become a gesture of cultural resistance against the oppressive order of the modern state.[31]

Some of the most striking examples of this literalism occur in architecture and specifically in the rarefied precincts of conceptually oriented architectural journals such as *Architectural Design* and the *Journal of Architectural Education*. In the following discussion I will refer primarily to discussions contained in the 1993 *Architectural Design* issue on "Folding in Architecture." Deleuze's work has been particularly welcomed in academic architectural circles because it provides a much needed infusion of intellectual legitimacy for a long-standing analysis of the "crisis" of modern architecture. This analysis, which previously drew on the phenomenological tradition, locates the effect of an instrumental reason in conventional forms of measurement, geometry, and representation culminating in the architectural "plan". The plan epitomizes an abstract, a priori rationality that imposes itself on the infinitely nuanced and ultimately unmappable "site" (a kind of surrogate nature). Deleuze's writing has been used to credential an updated version of this view, which again relies on a reflexive figural literalism. The response to the tyranny of the plan and traditional forms of measurement involves, predictably enough, some recourse to nontraditional forms of measurement and representation: "anexact" geometries, "proto-geometric" or "weak" forms, "viscous systems," and so forth.[32] The rigid lines and planes of the modernist bunker give way to a whole repertoire of "smooth spaces," "hybrid movements," and generally "folded, pliant, and supple" architectural forms. Thus Peter Eisenman's plan for a convention center in Columbus, Ohio, according to Greg Lynn, opens up "unforeseen connections . . . between differentiated sites and alien programs." Eisenman's approach requires "conciliatory, complicit, pliant, flexible and often cunning tactics . . . [a] multitude of *pli* [folds]."[33] "The force of . . . [the] Deleuzean schizo-analytic model" as Lynn continues, lies in "its ability to maintain multiple organizations simultaneously. In Eisenman's project the tower and grid need not be seen as mutually exclusive or in contradiction."[34] It is the relationship between formal modes within design (for instance, the grid or the tower) and their "cunning" reorganization that defines architectural practice under the auspices of a Deleuzean aesthetic.

Deleuze's reflexive analysis of being (a negative and externally determined ontology will be remedied by one that is positive and internally determined) leads, as I've argued above, to the formal reflexivity of "smooth" versus "striated" space or the fold versus the Cartesian grid. This same reflexivity is reiterated in the formal dynamic of conceptual architecture that defines bad architecture in terms of exact geometries and good architecture as "supple" and aleatory. In each case the operations of reason are hypostatized (for Deleuze reason and discourse can be experienced only as dominative, and for architects buildings based on "exact geometries" have a necessarily instrumentalized relationship to their site). Architecture's complicity with, or resistance to, oppressive forms of power is acknowledged only on the formal and technical level; in terms of the organization of space and material in response to exact or anexact aesthetic typologies. The social, cultural, or political context of habitation, the position of a given structure within a larger urban space or political economy, the privileged position of the architect him or herself within this economy are all effectively negated as areas of critique, analysis, or creative intervention.

Although there are occasional references in the *Architectural Design* issue to the creation of a "broadly empowering political space," individual projects are discussed almost solely in terms of the architect's ability to generate formal and technical expressions of anexact geometries.[35] The architect is treated throughout as a paradigmatically autonomous creative subject involved in a protean struggle with the materiality of building. Nowhere is the subject position of the architect him or herself questioned, or the underlying creative system in which an elite of well-known architects, typically supervising an office of underpaid designers, travel the globe imposing their innovative and aleatory buildings on the urban landscape. The possibility that the autonomy and hierarchy of the architectural profession itself might be subject to a Deleuzean critique is of course not considered. Nor is the possibility that the creative process might be opened out into a collaborative relationship between the architect and the residents or inhabitants who will actually work in, live near, or inhabit his "auratic, signature buildings" (as opposed to the clients who pay for them).[36] The closest that the architect comes to this kind of dialogue is to acknowledge the presence of nearby design typologies or forms in his own building. Of course even these "connections" must be carefully modulated to avoid the oppressive means/end rationality of signification. Thus Eisenman is celebrated for making vague references in his projects to the surrounding cityscape ("provisional, ad hoc affiliations" rather than scandalously full-blown "alignments").[37]

There is actually one occasion, described in the *Architectural Design* issue, in which an architect risks some interaction with the hoi polloi. It occurs while Frank Gehry is designing a chair-assembly factory and a furniture museum for Vitra in Germany. In Gehry's initial proposal he devoted most of his creative energy to the design of the museum, while making the chair-assembly factory look pretty much like the other (typically bland) industrial buildings in the area. The client expressed his "fear" that the assembly plant employees would complain that "all of the design attention was being invested in the museum, and none in the workplace." "As an afterthought" he asked Gehry to "enliven" the factory building. In response Gehry "appended" some additional design elements. The architectural effect was "dramatic," according to Jeffrey Kipnis, and "the additions knit affiliative links between the factory buildings and the museum, smoothing the site into a heterogeneous but cohesive whole."[38] This is what a Deleuzean practice comes down to, then, in architectural terms: placating workers who are concerned that their factory is not receiving an adequate proportion of Gehry's cultural capital.

Far from opening up the creative process to a dialogical interaction with the people who work in the factory, Gehry simply imposes a formal reconciliation between the two buildings. The architectural elaboration of a Deleuzean aesthetic demonstrates just how easily a conventional model of artistic individuality can be detached from any ontological claims. Throughout the essays contained in *Architectural Design* the architect is cast as that most conventional of subjects: the heroic creator assimilating complex philosophies and meeting practical demands to produce something absolutely "new." In lieu of any discursive interaction with the public, Gehry, Eisenman, and others rely on the figural itself as a kind of surrogate political mode that ostensibly enacts both dialogue and resistance even as they enjoy the privileges of a lifestyle supported by corporate capital.

Far from being viewed by Deleuze as a basis for ontology, discursive interaction is seen as a source of potential contamination which must be avoided at all costs (via an internal determination).[39] He is left, however, with the problem of how his monadic subjects might communicate or form political or social alliances. Deleuze's solution, as I've noted above, is to postulate the operation of an abstract aesthetic force that enables some form of social or political organization. But this force can operate only in rare moments of spontaneous political action. It seems to me that this is not a particularly productive way to go about developing a cultural politics since it excludes so many forms of resistance that have made political change possible in the past. Further, it discourages us from developing a strategic and critical awareness of those forms of intersubjectivity, dialogue, and discourse that we have to rely on in most actually existing political and cultural struggles (most of which bear little or no resemblance to Deleuze's volunteerist fantasy of May 1968).

Due in part to his great antipathy to Hegel, Deleuze seems to assume that external determination and negation are irrevocably linked. I would argue, however, that it is possible to develop an externally determined ontology that does not depend on negation. We can locate one resource for this model in Valentin Volosinov's work on dialogical interaction. In *Marxism and the Philosophy of Language* Volosinov provides the outline for a mode of discursive intersubjectivity that is both positive and creative.[40] "The organizing center of any utterance, of any experience," as Volosinov writes, "is not within but outside—in the social milieu surrounding the individual being."[41] Although Volosinov doesn't make an explicit appeal to ontology, his analysis of "experience" clearly has ontological implications. Thus he distinguishes the prelinguistic and individualistic "I-experience" from the "we-experience." The "we-experience . . . is not by any means a nebulous herd experience; it is differentiated. Moreover, ideological differentiation, the growth of consciousness, is in direct proportion to the firmness and reliability of the social organization. The stronger, the more organized, the more differentiated the collective in which an individual orients himself, the more vivid and complex his inner world will be."[42]

Deleuze argues that Hegel's model of being depends on the spatial relationship between a fixed and static subject and some external thing. Drawing on Bergson, he postulates instead a mode of being that is always/already differentiated and that doesn't have to search for difference in an external object. Bergson describes being as a process that unfolds over time (through "duration") and in which identity is never fixed. Thus we carry "difference" within ourselves, in all the potential forms of being that each of us contains. It is in this movement from "virtual" to "actual" forms of being that Deleuze locates the "positive," "expressive" antidote to Hegelian negation. It is notable, however, that this positive moment occurs within the subject's own ontological experience. It is this internalization that lends itself so easily to the solipsistic individualism of a conventional artistic identity.

A dialogical ontology would locate this positive moment in the subject's (external) social and discursive interactions. The concept of a dialogical ontology doesn't depend on a fixed subject; rather, it argues that being changes over time through the experience of discursive interaction. It thus operates in both a spatial register (the realm of the social and of intersubjective experience) as well as a temporal, Bergsonian register. In the context of a cultural politics, the "positivity" of this mode of being would derive from the interaction between the artist and a given community or constituency. The creative autonomy of the artist (Deleuze's "Great Directors" and "privileged souls") would be replaced by a concept of the artist as a co-participant in cultural or political struggles rooted in a specific community context. The "work of art" would emerge less as a discrete object (a novel, painting, or convention center) constructed along the lines of a figural formalism than as a process of dialogical exchange. This process would take the place of Deleuze's aesthetic force or "cosmic memory" as the basis of a positive, intersubjective creativity.

In the Gehry case mentioned above there is no indication that the work of the architect, or the act of cultural resistance, might be defined through a collaborative dialogue with the inhabitants of a given site or structure. If this were the case the outcome would be far more "spontaneous" and "unassignable" precisely because the architect can't know in advance what new forms of knowledge might be produced out of his or her interaction with a community. Instead of a reflexive formal response, the structure of the building would come into being through a process of exchange in which the autonomy of the architect/designer would be at least partially challenged. Moreover, in this way "site" would be defined in a far more complex manner. Rather than a matrix of universalized phenomenological experience, overlaid with a schematic historical sensibility, the site would be understood in terms of the complex actions and interactions of its current inhabitants and the social, economic, and political forces that pattern its present and future use. Defined in these terms the site is given the power of speech; it can talk back to the architect and respond to, modify, or critique his or her plans. It seems obvious that the tyranny of the "plan" lies not simply in the fact that one employs conventional forms of measurement but in the entire apparatus (of which the plan is merely symptomatic) in which the autonomous and self-sufficient intelligence of the architect/creator plays such a central role.

Notes

1. Dave Beech and John Roberts, "Spectres of the Aesthetic," *New Left Review* 218 ( July-August 1996), p. 105.
2. See Terry Eagleton, *The Ideology of the Aesthetic* (Oxford: Blackwell, 1990), pp. 60–61.
3. "Spectres of the Aesthetic," pp. 112–114. Also see Peter Brooks, "Aesthetics and Ideology: What Happened to Poetics?" in *Aesthetics and Ideology,* ed. George Levine (New Brunswick: Rutgers University Press, 1994).
4. Dave Hickey, *The Invisible Dragon: Four Essays on Beauty* (Los Angeles: Art Issues Press, 1993); Wendy Steiner, *The Scandal of Pleasure* (Chicago: University of Chicago Press, 1995); Barbara Maria Stafford, *Good Looking: Essays on the Virtue of Images* (Cambridge: MIT Press, 1996), and *Body Criticism: Imaging the Unseen in Enlightenment Art and Medicine* (Cambridge: MIT Press, 1994).
5. As Stafford writes "Among my several aims is to expose how the visual arts, and bodily-kinesthetic intelligence in general, were damned to the bottom of the Cave of the humanities. . . . sensory and affective phenomena continue to be treated as second-rate simulations of second-class reflections. . . . Coercive and authoritarian analogies such as the book of the world, clear and distinct truth, dissecting reason, and pure spirit became objective standards against which confused, or non-geometric, shapes and colored, or mutable, semblances were judged." *Body Criticism: Imaging the Unseen in Enlightenment Art and Medicine,* p. 2.
6. "Contemporary architecture, disillusioned with rational utopias, now strives to go beyond positivistic prejudices to find a new metaphysical justification in the human world; its point of departure is once again the sphere of perception, the ultimate origin of existential meaning." Alberto Pérez-Gómez, *Architecture and the Crisis of Modern Science* (Cambridge: MIT Press, 1983), p. 325.
7. Wlad Godzich, "Correcting Kant: Bakhtin and Intercultural Interactions," *boundary 2: an international journal of literature and culture* 18:1 (Spring 1991), p. 13.
8. Félix Guattari, *Chaosmosis: An Ethico-Aesthetic Paradigm,* trans. Paul Bains and Julian Pefanis (Bloomington: Indiana University Press, 1995), p. 91.

9. "Multiplicity, Proliferation, Reconvention," ed. Jeremy Gilbert-Rolfe and John Johnston, *Feature* (1996); *Journal of Philosophy and the Visual Arts,* No. 5 (London: Academy Editions, 1995).

10. "Art in the Folds," *New Observations* No. 110 (January-February 1996) and "Folding in Architecture," *Architectural Design* 63: 3/4 (1993).

11. See Richard Pinhas's "Deleuze Web," which includes transcripts of seminars that Deleuze gave while teaching at Vincennes (http://www.imaginet.fr/deleuze/sommaire.html).

12. G. W. F. Hegel, *Phenomenology of Spirit,* trans. A. V. Miller (Oxford: Oxford University Press, 1977), p. 111.

13. Hegel, p. 115.

14. For an useful intellectual history of the impact of May 1968, see Peter Starr, *Logics of Failed Revolt: French Theory After May '68* (Stanford: Stanford University Press, 1995).

15. Cited by Michael Hardt in *Gilles Deleuze: An Apprenticeship in Philosophy* (Minneapolis: University of Minnesota Press, 1993), p. 14.

16. "In order to resist organ-machines, the body without organs presents its smooth, slippery, opaque, taut surface as a barrier. In order to resist linked, connected, and interrupted flows, it sets up a counterflow of amorphous, undifferentiated fluids." Gilles Deleuze and Félix Guattari, *Anti-Oedipus: Capitalism and Schizophrenia,* trans. Robert Hurley, Mark Seem, and Helen R. Lane (Minneapolis: University of Minnesota Press, 1983), p. 9.

17. *Gilles Deleuze: An Apprenticeship in Philosophy,* p. 31.

18. Gilles Deleuze, *Nietzsche and Philosophy,* trans. by Hugh Tomlinson (New York: Columbia University Press, 1983), p. 103. As Deleuze writes, for Nietzsche "Art is a 'stimulant of the will to power', 'something that excites willing.' The critical sense of this principle is obvious: it exposes every reactive concept of art" (p. 102).

19. Gilles Deleuze, *Bergsonism,* trans. Hugh Tomlinson and Barbara Habberjam (New York: Zone Books, 1991), p. 111.

20. *Anti-Oedipus: Capitalism and Schizophrenia,* p.9.

21. Gilles Deleuze, *Expressionism in Philosophy: Spinoza,* trans. Martin Joughin (New York: Zone Books, 1992), p. 173.

22. *Expressions in Philosophy: Spinoza,* p. 110.

23. *Expressions in Philosophy: Spinoza,* p.240.

24. Gilles Deleuze and Félix Guattari, *A Thousand Plateaus: Capitalism and Schizophrenia,* trans. Brian Massumi (Minneapolis: University of Minnesota Press, 1987), p. 222.

25. *Chaosmosis: An Ethico-Aesthetic Paradigm*, p. 91.

26. *A Thousand Plateaus: Capitalism and Schizophrenia*, p. 216.

27. *Gilles Deleuze: An Apprenticeship in Philosophy*, p. 121.

28. *Gilles Deleuze: An Apprenticeship in Philosophy*, p. 120.

29. Brian Massumi, *A User's Guide to Capitalism and Schizophrenia* (Cambridge: MIT Press, 1992), p. 121.

30. Greg Bowen, "Rhizomatic/Schar(morphous): Scharf's (Outer)Space Fun," in *Kenny Scharf: When Worlds Collide* (University Galleries of Illinois State University, January 14 – February 23, 1997). Bowen continues: "Kenny Scharf is smooth, and I don't mean smooth as in cool or hip, although that would certainly apply. No, Kenny Scharf is smooth in a hip theoretical way. Behind the bubble gum colors and through the gaping grins of his morphed cartoon characters are the foundations for intriguing critical thought concerning our fractured contemporary existence . . ."

31. Another instance occurs in a catalog for an exhibition of paintings by Maria Nazor at Laurie Rubin Gallery in 1989. After explaining the distinction Deleuze draws between the "molar" and the "molecular," the writer goes on to assure us that "A careful glance at Maria Nazor's paintings" will reveal that "they have *absolutely nothing* to do with molar structures, nothing to do with points, positions, ordered progressions, with closed systems, templates, and grids. The absence of molar segmentarity constitutes the absolute newness of these paintings" (author's italics). Catalog for Maria Nazor exhibition, October 21 – November 18, 1989, Laurie Rubin Gallery (155 Spring Street, New York, New York 10012), text by Phillip Evans Clark.

32. The term "anexact" derives from Husserl and appears, among other places, in *Ideas: General Introduction to Pure Phenomenology,* trans. W. R. Boyce Gibson (New York: Macmillan, 1931), section 74, p. 190. For the use of this term in an architectural context, see Greg Lynn, "Architectural Curvilinearity: The Folded, the Pliant and the Supple," in *Architectural Design* 63:3/4 (March - April 1993), p. 11. The other terms cited appear in the *Architectural Design* issue cited above and in Greg Lynn, "Multiplicitous and In-Organic Bodies," *Architectural Design* 63: 11/12 (November – December 1993).

33. Greg Lynn, "Architectural Curvilinearity: The Folded, the Pliant and the Supple," p. 11.

34. Lynn, "Architectural Curvilinearity," p. 10.

35. Jeffrey Kipnis, "Towards a New Architecture," *Architectural Design* 63:3/4 (March – April 1993), p. 42.

36. Kipnis, p. 41.

37. Kipnis, p. 45.

38. Kipnis, p. 46.

39. It is on the basis of his demand for a "pure" form of ontology that Hegel criticizes Spinoza in *Science of Logic:* "Self-subsistence pushed to the point of the one as a being-for-self is abstract, formal, and destroys itself . . . It is that freedom which so misapprehends itself as to place its essence in this abstraction, and flatters itself that in thus being with itself it possess itself in its purity." G. W. F. Hegel, *Science of Logic,* trans. A. V. Miller (Atlantic Highlands, NJ: Humanities Press, 1969), p. 172.

40. There is an ongoing debate as to the actual authorship of *Marxism and the Philosophy of Language.* Some historians claim that Bakhtin wrote the book, even though it was published under Valentin Volosinov's name. Others argue that Volosinov and Bakhtin co-authored it. For stylistic economy I will simply use Volosinov's name. For a discussion of this debate, see the forum in *Slavic and East European Journal* 30/1 (Spring 1986), pp. 96–102.

41. V. N. Volosinov, *Marxism and the Philosophy of Language,* trans. Ladislav Matejka and I. R. Titunik (Cambridge, MA: Harvard University Press, 1986), p. 93.

42. *Marxism and the Philosophy of Language,* p. 88.

CHAPTER 3

# The Ambiguous Politics of Politicizing, or De-Politicizing, the Aesthetic

*Sean McCann*

*For the students of English 301*

*A never-ending inner struggle takes place in the souls of intellectuals. They are torn between a feeling of their superiority, their special mission, and a secret envy of humans whose work bears visible and verifiable results.*

—Leszek Kolakowski

*Above all else: in God's name don't think of it as Art.*

—James Agee, *Let Us Now Praise Famous Men*

I

GODFREY ST. PETER, THE EPONYMOUS HERO of Willa Cather's 1925 novel *The Professor's House,* has few doubts about the curriculum of his university. It should focus, he suggests, on "the purely cultural studies," and the reasons for his conviction are evident. From St. Peter's perspective the rival domains of inquiry and action are entirely bankrupt. Science offers not wisdom but mere comfort and a "superficial kind" of amazement. Politics has become little more than shallow democracy. The province of "the common sort," it exerts a "degrading influence" on everything it touches. And religion, which once made "a gorgeous drama" of ordinary existence, can no longer be believed. It reeks now of provincialism and prejudice. Only art retains the potential to fashion "a rich thing" of life. If, as his name seems to suggest, Cather's hero is meant to stand as the founder of a posttheological religion (a god-free Saint Peter), then the creed he embodies is clearly one in which art assumes the part once played by the church. He is the prophet of the religion of culture.[1]

At first glance, that religion looks distinctly Arnoldian. Like Matthew Arnold and his followers among Cather's contemporaries, St. Peter values art because it promises to fulfill both the inspirational and disciplinary roles once exercised by religious belief. And as for Arnold too, "cultural studies" can serve those functions in Cather's world because they are imbued with an aspirational rhetoric. Art redeems because, in its pursuit of perfection, it forces a refusal of the vulgar. Tom Outland, the character who plays Christ to Cather's St. Peter, is attractive to the Professor in good part because he "never handled things that were not the symbols of ideas" (236). The Professor's garden, where he first meets Tom and where the two spend long hours in private conversation, is a transparent symbol of such virtue. It is "walled-in," "French," "barren," and a mark of the Professor's "distinction" from his neighbors. Cultivation in this novel means, in short, an aristocratic and homoerotic removal from "the common sort" and a pursuit of "the fine, the almost imaginary obligations" against the merely "social" bonds of everyday life (51, 50).

And yet, on closer inspection, Cather's novel turns out to be not Arnoldian at all—at least not in the way we've come to use that term in recent years. The whole middle book of her three-part novel is dedicated to Tom Outland's recollection of his youthful discovery of a group of Anasazi ruins in a New Mexico mesa. And that reminiscence plays a crucial role in establishing the Professor's vision of culture, since in Tom's description the ruins come to exemplify everything that is absent from the debased world of the present. If the "higher processes of art are all processes of simplification," as Cather argued in her contemporaneous essay "The Novel Démeublé"—processes that work to make a "fastidious" order by "select[ing]" from "the teeming, gleaming stream of the present"—then the "cliff city" Tom discovers embodies her aesthetic preferences.[2] "It all hung together," Tom recalls, "seemed to have a kind of composition." Characterized by symmetry, by stark and simple geometry, and by "immortal repose," the cliff city, he remarks, is "more like sculpture than anything else" (179–180). The most significant aspect of the ruins, though, is the fact that explains their remarkable beauty. The cliff city, Tom realizes immediately, is the product of "a people with a feeling for design," and the ruins they've left mysteriously behind are a testimony to their "particular civilization." For Tom, that particularity and the beauty of the pueblo are inseparable. "It seemed," he says of the city's design, "to mark a difference" (182, 183).

Thus, if Cather's novel seems to begin with an Arnoldian view of culture, it quickly turns toward the ethnographic or anthropological perspective now commonly thought to be the opposite of Arnold's. On the mesa, "culture is ordinary," to use Raymond Williams's phrase—the "shape" of "a particular way of life."[3] And Cather's novel offers a paean to its idiosyncrasy and coherence. Standing amid the ruins of the Anasazi city, her characters can envision what Williams might call "the common life" of its people—"working out their destiny, making their mesa more and more worthy to be a home for man, purifying life by religious ceremonies and observances, caring respectfully for their dead, protecting the children" (198).[4] By implication, too, they can contrast the work of that "superior people" to the wretched conditions of the present, a world that seems debased to Cather precisely because it lacks the particular, organic culture the Anasazi represent. The problem with the Professor's society, she makes clear, is that it lacks the "difference" the Anasazi protected. The twentieth-century United States is all "teaming, gleaming stream" and no "selection" (197, 61). Moreover, the meaning of that lack of selection is far-reaching. Where the Anasazi exemplify a community of descent, "a particular people" who develop in "isolat[ion] . . . without the influence of example or emulation," the Professor's "society" lacks their "stronghold" (198, 199). It is prey to the baleful influence of the "stranger"—a figure represented for Cather by the anti-Semitic caricature of the cosmopolitan Jew.

Seen from this perspective, Cather's idea of culture looks far closer to the anthropological pluralism common to current uses of the word than it does to the universalist elitism often associated with Arnold.[5] While it wouldn't be fair to say that Cather was in any way egalitarian—the Anasazi are worthy of reverence because they are "superior," after all—she was in 1925 already a cultural relativist. Indeed, she suggests quite plainly that superiority is the ultimate product of cultural particularism. Tom Outland's story and the image of the abandoned mesa remind the Professor that the Anasazi were superior because at least for a time, they kept apart from strangers. By the same token, they suggest that modern America is weak because it allows entry to Jews. The Anasazi ruins, like Tom Outland himself, are thus a moral example to the Professor of the way one might preserve a commitment to the almost imaginary obligations of difference against the ravages of modernity. They are the image of a common culture the Professor can only admire and lament. So long as he maintains his fidelity to their memory, though, he remains connected to a source of legitimacy that lends credibility to his "distinction." He is not just a Professor, nor merely a snob, in other words, but "something quite different"—a man of culture in the fullest sense (22).

By contrast to Cather, James Agee was both universalist and egalitarian in spirit. His masterwork, *Let Us Now Praise Famous Men,* belongs to the decade following that of *The Professor's House,* and the ten years that divide the two books mark a profound shift in the American political atmosphere they aptly represent.[6] It would be difficult to imagine two literary works more antagonistic in temper. If Cather worshipped art and hoped to root its authority in a particular and organic culture, Agee claimed to see the same suffering all over the world, and he yearned to denounce every kind of arrogance and division that prevented the flow of human sympathy. That meant especially the elitism of high art. "The 'esthetic' is made hateful" by contemporary education, he complains. "It is false-beauty to begin with" (311). Truly meaningful writing, by contrast, would not accept the cloister of art but rather would force us to recognize the ideological "bondages" that lead us to fetishize the aesthetic in the first place. In that way, we might eventually return literature to its place in the continuum of culture—"the whole realm of human consciousness, action, and possibility" (308). Scorning the sophistication of the educated, then, Agee celebrates instead the beauty, the resilience, and the resistance he discovers in the practices and artifacts of the illiterate, rural poor. Indeed, he longs to dissolve the prestige of his own work in the common milieu of their life. "If I could do it, I'd do no writing at all here," he explains. "It would be photographs; the rest would be fragments of cloth, bits of cotton, lumps of earth, records of speech, pieces of wood and iron, phials of odor, plates of food and of excrement . . . A piece of the body torn out by its roots might be more to the point" (13).

In short, if Cather arrives at the sense that "culture is ordinary," Agee begins from that conviction. Yet, much as Cather's Arnoldian elitism brings her ultimately to the democratic sensibility of the anthropological perspective, Agee's professed beliefs have contradictory effects. His desire to destroy the "false-beauty" of art and to reunite literature with the whole realm of human consciousness leads him to invoke those titanic figures who in his view have already pointed in that direction—Beethoven, Kafka, Céline, Marx, and ultimately himself. In this respect, *Let Us Now Praise Famous Men* is a book that quite self-consciously cannot fulfill its announced intentions. Though Agee wants his text to be in every sense a document of ordinary life, his preoccupation is with the constraints of ideology, social organization, and personal limitation that prevent that achievement. As a consequence *Famous Men* is less an expression of ordinary culture than a jeremiad directed to the cultural elite, aimed at the realization of a common life that it cannot imagine. The paradox at the heart of the book, around which Agee relentlessly circles, is that as an avant-gardist document, *Famous Men* cannot help invoking the elitism it hopes to disavow. It must remain, like Cather's mesa, a moral example of attitudes that Agee both values and sees as hopelessly distant.

Those values differed sharply from Cather's. She was reactionary and nativist. He was, at least in his own description, "a Communist by sympathy and conviction" (249). She valued concision, clarity, and selection; his work was intentionally messy, romantic, and too willfully inclusive to tolerate any clear order. Yet the two share a problem, and it is perhaps the defining problem of twentieth-century cultural life. Each assumes that an art that remains cut off from popular experience, that is not rooted in "common life," grows pale and abstract, and each recognizes that the obvious ways of overcoming that alienation——in mass politics, commercial entertainment, or personal cultivation——threaten to empty art of whatever makes it potent, moving, and critical. Both writers are left with the determination to defend the moral examples posed by their books and a nagging question. Though they pose that question in different ways, both *The Professor's House* and *Let Us Now Praise Famous Men* ask whether a culture that seems Arnoldian—snobbish and professionalized—can become one that seems closer to the spirit of Raymond Williams, anthropological and ordinary. Put in slightly different terms, they ask: how can the institutional divide between art and the remainder of life—the whole realm of human consciousness, action, and possibility—be overcome so that the former is not empty and the latter is not blind? Significantly, each writer can only gesture toward an answer.

That question has not gone away, of course. But it is an unfortunate aspect of our contemporary debates that many of the people who raise it nowadays act as if the problem had never occurred, at least not seriously, to anybody but themselves and a few carefully chosen antecedents. Our current disputes about the need to politicize or to depoliticize the aesthetic echo the problems raised by Cather and Agee, problems that in turn recall the dilemmas worried about by many of their contemporaries and their predecessors. Yet it seems also to be a condition of such disagreements that they always appear to mark an entirely new crisis. In this essay, I'd like to suggest an explanation for the prosperity of such beliefs and to offer a description of the kinds of action they enable in the long tradition of the discourse on the aesthetic (by which I mean the tradition of philosophical and political rumination on the problematic status of art). In my view, those actions do not necessarily correspond with the beliefs held by the actors involved.

The demand that we politicize the aesthetic and the demand that we depoliticize it both cast themselves as primarily *political* arguments with instrumental ambitions. They hope to have effects, to change or defend our world. In reality, though, instrumentality tends to take a back seat in these arguments, and the often vague or distant effects such actions might have become less significant than the example posed by the actions themselves. That is so, I think, because our arguments about the politicization or depoliticization of art are not primarily political arguments at all but rather, as in Cather and Agee, claims about ethical character. They are concerned less with realizable ends than with the kinds of people we are, and their underlying demand is that we be the kind of people who care about ends that seem both enormously significant and, at bottom, all but unrealizable. Like Cather and Agee, the discourse on the aesthetic characteristically asks us to strive against ordinary constraints and toward "almost imaginary obligations," and it tends to envision the fulfillment of those obligation in the image of a common life that overcomes the tensions between the educated and the popular. Arguments about the inevitably untenable and dissatisfying status of art are thus, as I will attempt to explain more fully below, a type of ethical theater. Their fundamental mode is the kind of incomplete and evocative gesture that both Agee and Cather finally offer.

## II

The success of such a performative mode depends on the acceptance of a number of untried assumptions, the most basic of which is the fundamental opposition worried by both Cather and Agee—that between arrogant expertise and common life. In our current vocabulary that opposition is posed frequently as the conflict between "Arnoldian" and "anthropological" views of culture, in which the former signifies something like elitist aestheticism and the latter refers to the broad realm of popular meaning and invention. (The contrast is restated in Jonathan Culler's analogous distinction between "poetics" and "cultural studies" cited in the Introduction to this volume.) The common belief is that these perspectives are genuinely antagonistic and that they've been accepted as such by their proponents. The comparison between Agee and Cather suggests, however, that such an assumption is misplaced. The matter can be posed, too, in a more far-reaching way. For not only do Cather and Agee each make the division between the Arnoldian and anthropological models of culture look suspect; they point toward the fact that even for Arnold such distinctions did not hold.

Contemporary opposition to Arnold's account of culture depends more frequently on tacit agreement than it does on argument, but it is not hard to imagine how Arnold got his bad reputation. What he means by culture seems to be closer to the aristocratic ideal of civilization than any meaning for the word we now accept as valid. The celebration of the best that has been thought and written and of the touchstones of literary achievement elevates greatness over the claims of the common and the particular. It celebrates the freedom of the elite against the force of custom, and it fails to acknowledge the fact, one might say, that even high culture is cultural in the anthropological sense—that it emerges from the tradition, social practice, and shared assumptions of a particular class. Celebrating the pursuit of "perfection" and of intrinsic aesthetic worth, Arnold therefore seems to disregard the relativity of judgments of taste and appears not only to slight but to disallow a view of culture as a system of collective meaning—what Williams famously called "a whole way of life."[7]

Like his heir Willa Cather, though, Arnold is himself less Arnoldian than he's often made to seem. If one looks closely at his most important document in this line, *Culture and Anarchy,* it becomes apparent that Arnold is not especially a defender of canonical art, that he is as much a collectivist as many of his contemporary detractors, and that at least incipiently he, too, is a relativist.[8] Perhaps the most striking aspect of Arnold's celebration of aesthetic achievement is how few examples he provides. He offers in effect not a list of touchstones but the abstract idea of touchstones—not a canon but the entirely indeterminate idea of canonicity. Indeed, the most apparent feature of his claim that culture means the pursuit of "perfection" is how completely vague perfection comes to seem. In this manner Arnold echoes the rhetoric of his predecessor Friedrich Schiller (whose ideas about aesthetic education he follows closely, refurbishing them for the environment of industrial England). For Schiller, beauty was the engine of cultural development, the "highest reality." But it was also by the same token sheer "indeterminacy"—a "cipher" defined only by relation to the forces of appetite and instrumental reason it worked to check.[9] Arnold similarly sees in culture only negation—what he calls "renouncement" or "a purging effect." It is whatever resists our tendency to fall into sloth or partiality, moralism or scientism, philistinism or barbarism. In this light, culture and its goal of "perfection" appear solely as vague, counterfactual ideals, designed to prompt their adherents toward "a balance and regulation of mind which is not often attained without fruitful effort." Like the protestant ethic it emulates, then, Arnold's theory "places human perfection in an *internal* condition" and asks nothing other than that people constantly examine themselves to be certain they continue to develop. It demands "[n]ot a having and a resting" in established ideals but a constant and interminable "growing and a becoming" toward an undefined ideal condition.10

Arnold's vision of culture, in other words, is not a defense of traditional standards but a technology for personal and social movement. Such a view is comparatively unconcerned with any art or literature in itself, and it stakes no claims to particular aesthetic values. Sheer development is the only articulable goal. Moreover, for Arnold, as for Schiller before him (and Cather later), the very lack of interest in any particular art as a good in itself leads ultimately toward a collectivist and relativist idea of what culture might mean. We "are all members of one great whole," Arnold contends, and that means that "the expansion of our humanity," prompted by the pursuit of perfection, "must be a *general* expansion." Culture is a "*social idea.*" When Arnold looks for examples of the general and social, though, he is led in particular to emphasize the "*national* glow of life and thought" (62, 78, 79, original emphases). That emphasis, moreover, is integral to the direction of his argument. For if, in his famous formulation, culture is to counter the anarchy fostered by liberal freedoms (the freedom of "doing as one likes"), and if, more specifically, it is to constrain the class antagonism fostered by industrialism and nourished by education and parliamentary democracy, that will be possible only if culture can speak for what Williams calls the common life. It must be, Arnold acknowledges, not just the possession of the educated but the voice of "the collective nation" (117).

Thus Arnold resists strenuously the suggestion that "culture" is either universal or the possession of a specific class in order to claim instead that culture is *national.* It may seem, for instance, that his values belong especially to an emerging intelligentsia. Arnold acknowledges the fact, but he then argues that such champions of culture are not a social class in themselves. They are rather "aliens" to all classes and therefore the true exponents of "the fermenting mind of the nation." In "each class," he explains, "there are born a certain number of natures with a curiosity about their best self, with a bent for seeing things as they are." That tendency enables them not just to appreciate great art but more significantly to recognize the national spirit that subsists beneath class antagonisms. "Thus, an English Barbarian who examines himself will, in general, find himself to be not so entirely a Barbarian but that he has in him, also, something of the Philistine, and even something of the Populace as well. And the same with Englishmen of the two other classes" (110, 186, 109, 108). In Arnold's description, a true man of culture recognizes himself not as a member of a class *or* as a cosmopolitan but as a national representative. He is neither worker, aristocrat, nor bourgeois, but an Englishman. By extension, only the man of culture, because he rises above class distinctions, has the capacity to recognize that Englishness and thereby to represent "the collective character" of the nation in "the action of the *State*" (121, original emphasis).

Thus *Culture and Anarchy* is, on the one hand, clearly a brief for the intelligentsia and for its duty to claim governing power. On the other, Arnold is no technocrat or enlightenment universalist. He legitimizes his men of culture not by their claim to expertise or reason but because they can speak for a particularly national spirit. Fittingly, then, when he despairs of seeing such spirit recognized in Britain and believes it lost amid individual freedoms and class segmentation, he turns for inspiration to a society that gives it greater recognition—Prussia. In north Germany, Arnold notes approvingly, "the Sovereign" rises "above many prejudices and littlenesses," and the intellectuals who advise him in nation-building accordingly have an influence the English man of culture can only envy (117). Arnold's intellectual heroes in *Culture and Anarchy* are these men—not, as one might expect, the authors of his touchstones. He never celebrates any great writer or artist. Rather, he admires precisely those German intellectuals who, championing *kultur*, would become the intellectual grandparents of our current anthropological notions of culture: Lessing, Schleiermacher, Humboldt, and most revealingly, the original theorist of cultural pluralism, Herder. What makes these figures worthy of emulation, he suggests moreover, is not their brilliance or learning in particular. (In other words, they do not represent the best that has been thought and written.) They are important to Arnold as protonationalists, figures who, because they are determined to educate a people in the name of the Sovereign, "humanise" learning. In so doing, they return knowledge that is "difficult, abstract, professional, exclusive" to "the whole of society" (79).

What we see in Arnold, then, is a tendency that will blossom in Cather—not international elitism but an incipient cultural nationalism whose force comes from the democracy it envisions in a holistic, "particular way of life." It is in fact that dedication to *national,* popular education, Arnold claims, that makes "the men of culture" not elitists but "the true apostles of equality" (79). And such an appeal to the recognition and development of a collective and relative culture suggests that the habitual opposition drawn between "Arnoldian" and "anthropological" perspectives is tenuous at best. Like Cather, Arnold wants ultimately to be not abstract, professional, and exclusive but the voice of an egalitarian nation. That this equality in the common life is to come from a conservative program for the educational improvement of all Englishmen rather than from, say, the destruction of class privilege is perhaps finally less significant than the fact that collectivism is the only means he can imagine to legitimize his work. The "Arnoldian" and "anthropological" views of culture are simply not as antagonistic as they are sometimes made to seem.

It might be more accurate, then, to cast these two perspectives in a different light, to see them not as competing models of interpretation but as members of a common constellation that yokes together both elitist and egalitarian stances. In fact, each of these apparently opposite tendencies can be seen to depend on its counterpart; each validates itself by ultimately reaching out toward the opposite extreme. What such a perspective emphasizes is that even the most elite of aesthetic sensibilities turns finally to some image of popular legitimation and envisions itself as speaking for a people whose needs or spirit otherwise remain unexpressed. Likewise, even the most democratic and relativist of perspectives turns in the end to expert authorization and, as in Cather, to the invocation of superiority.

Such apparent paradoxes, I'd like to suggest, are built into modern ideas of the aesthetic, a matter that for at least some two hundred years now has seemed to all who take it seriously both fundamentally problematic and basic to the condition of "modernity" itself.[11] It may have been true that for classical or traditional aesthetics the forms and values of art seemed, in theory if not in practice, to be aspects of eternal and universal hierarchies of value.[12] At least since the late eighteenth century, though, when Kant radically refounded the operations of beauty, the place and the determination of the aesthetic have been essentially uncertain—and uncertain in a set of apparently irresolvable ways deftly outlined by Kant's theory. As a function of his "Copernican revolution" away from arguments about the structure of reality and toward claims about the structures of cognition, Kant made the judgment of taste a subjective operation that could be given no standards or rules, no a priori determinations (at the same time that he made difficult arguments for its necessity and universality). The grounds of beauty were to be found not in objective principle or exterior rule, but in the inherent unpredictability of subjective taste and genius. The explanation for that underdetermination, moreover, was the now familiar but once revolutionary claim that the judgment of taste is its own kind of faculty—autonomous from both scientific understanding and moral reasoning. It leads neither to "cognition for the understanding nor . . . [to] practice for the will" but remains as the price of its autonomy "merely contemplative."[13]

As a result, Kant pointed out, the experience of beauty depends upon a kind of constitutive mistake. We speak of it *"as if* beauty were a characteristic of the object and the judgment logical," and in truth, such experience cannot exist without the object to enable such belief. In reality, though, the experience of beauty does not produce conceptual knowledge of the world. Rather, it refers back "simply to the subject (to its feeling); the judgment is . . . [thus] far always aesthetical." Beauty, in sum, depends on empirical experience (unlike, say, Kant's moral principles). Ultimately, however, it is not empirical at all but rather an awareness of subjective capacity. The result, Kant acknowledges, is a "strange and irregular thing." For although judgments of beauty or sublimity are by his description subjective, they are not therefore personal or idiosyncratic—what we would usually mean by the word "taste" and what Kant refers to as "private conditions." To see something as beautiful or sublime at all, we must, Kant claims, "attribut[e] a similar satisfaction to everyone," claim "the agreement of all men." Thus, judgments of taste are for Kant at once subjective apprehensions that cannot be submitted to political or conceptual argument *and* demands for universal assent. They have, Kant explains in an avowedly paradoxical phrase, "a title to subjective universality."[14]

Kant went to great and perhaps unconvincing lengths to explain and justify that paradox. But he placed alongside it an equally important one whose difficulties he did not acknowledge as thoroughly—although he rested significant rhetorical and theoretical weight upon it. Just as he argued that the experience of beauty was at once subjective and universal, Kant suggested that the judgment of taste was not entirely the autonomous operation he contended. About the other two faculties of the mind, treated respectively by the first two critiques—empirical understanding and moral reason—there was no doubt. These operations depended on "two kinds of concepts" with "distinct principles of the possibility of their objects." Philosophy, therefore, could be "correctly divided into two parts," and between the two regions a "great gulf" intervened. In the third critique, as many commentators have stressed, Kant intended to address that gulf and turned to aesthetic judgment as "a means of combining the two parts of philosophy into a whole." Thus the very idea of beauty again gives rise to an apparent contradiction. It involves an autonomous cognitive operation and is "a special faculty" with its own "particular laws." At the same, the experience of beauty is the mental capacity that somehow joins up all the activities of the mind. It is "the mediating link" that unites the actions of moral awareness and scientific understanding, which would otherwise remain alien to each other.[15] For Kant, in short, the aesthetic is doubly paradoxical—at once individual and collective, island and bridge.

The underdetermination and the ambiguous place of the aesthetic have haunted philosophies of art ever since. But as Max Weber suggested when he adopted Kant's tripartite philosophy to create a sociological theory of modernity, the difficulties Kant identified have turned out to be problems of practice as well as of theory. It is often argued that in his third critique Kant created the grounds for the formalist and subjectivist aesthetics that have grown in prominence over the two centuries since he wrote. In a related claim, it is sometimes suggested that Kant's emphasis on the autonomy of aesthetic judgment served as an apologia *avant la lettre* for a social formation that didn't yet exist in 1790. The notion that beauty is its own faculty with its own laws provided a theoretical justification for the expertise eventually claimed by professional artists and critics, who needed to defend their unique abilities and who would eventually use that defense to create a near monopoly on legitimate aesthetic knowledge. Kant, one might claim, forecast the eventual autonomy of art.[16]

Importantly, though, the paradoxes basic to Kant's thought could always point in opposite directions, and that ambivalence has been constantly apparent in recurrent arguments about the status of the aesthetic. If the subjective orientation of Kant's theory of beauty seems to predict the progressive interiorization of art—its surrender of moral and cognitive significance and its attraction to antisocial hedonism—it also suggests a movement toward social responsibility in its claim that taste is not "private," that it demands assent. Beauty, Kant suggested, pointed toward a "*sensus communis*," a common nature existing apart from actual societies but also reinforcing the awareness of a basic human community. From the perspective of this appeal to "common feeling," the experience of beauty might look not at all antisocial but rather the expression of and the basis for community. Indeed, as Kant's followers, beginning with Schiller, emphasized, this "indeterminate norm" could provoke the vision of a utopian reorganization of society, of a new human fellowship based not on inherited constraints but upon mutual sentiment. The "capacity to judge" outlined by Kant in the third critique thus appears in Hannah Arendt's phrase as a "specifically political ability."[17]

The same is true also for the justification of professional expertise apparently laid out in the third critique's claim for the specificity of judgment. The simultaneous emphasis that Kant placed on the way the aesthetic unified the divided faculties of the mind points toward the dissatisfaction to which the autonomy of art would inevitably give rise. By Kant's own terms, which become still stronger in later writers like Schiller and Hegel, the notion that art would be truly and irrevocably autonomous from all other parts of life must inevitably seem like a cheat and a capitulation. Beauty, one might argue following Kant, was meant to serve a higher purpose than narrow professionalism. "It must be false that the cultivation of individual powers necessitates the sacrifice of their totality . . . we must be at liberty to restore by means of a higher Art this wholeness in our nature which Art has destroyed."[18] Rather than reify the segmentation of knowledge and experience, beauty should work in some way to counter that division.

Thus, if we do take Kant's theory as a blueprint for the development of the aesthetic, it is easy to see the way he predicted the fundamental problems of the modern art world. While that milieu has pursued its professional authority, arrogating progressively more ground to its monopoly on aesthetic expertise, it has also been forced to recognize that its own autonomy is a kind of impoverishment, and one that leaves it with a basic problem of legitimacy. At the same time that artists and intellectuals assert their professional independence, they must also court popular acknowledgment by suggesting, like the other professions, that their autonomy is good for everyone. For no other profession, though, is such a claim so lacking in credibility. (Artists can't point like scientists to advances in knowledge, or claim to make safer bridges like engineers, or even suggest that they fashion more just and efficient laws like legislators.) As a consequence, modern art is constantly impelled to overcome or disavow its own autonomy. In J. M. Bernstein's apt description, the aesthetic in its particularly modern sense is driven by an unavoidable imperative; it "must exceed its constitution"— moving to overcome the very institutional demarcation that allows it to appear as a specialized form of activity in the first place. It must become "more than merely 'aesthetic' phenomena." As it does for Arnold and Cather in other words, art and expertise constantly seek to become not *merely* art, but common culture.[19]

\*\*\*

It is clear from Kant's philosophy, then, why elitists might eventually want to become "true apostles of equality" and why the "anthropological" model of culture embraced by both Cather and Arnold is so attractive. The appeal to this vision of culture inevitably invokes a world that exists prior to the demarcations that Kant legislates—in which all the divisions characteristic of modernity (among politics, science and art, theory and practice, mental and manual labor, craft and genius) are submerged within the common life. It is also apparent, though, why the effort to invoke such authority is likely to be problematic and to culminate in fresh appeals to expertise. For, if Kant suggests in a line of reasoning fully developed only by his successors, that the aesthetic might lead toward the reintegration of both our faculties and our communities, he emphasizes more strongly that any such reunion must be incomplete, a matter of evocative impression rather than actual transformation. At its most salient for Kant, the experience of beauty can only "serve to represent" the underlying comity of our selves and our worlds that he believes we must presuppose.[20] By implication it can reassure us against the suspicion of mental dissociation and political nominalism without actually doing anything to change the arrangement of our faculties or our world.

Thus, if on the one hand the paradoxes of the Kantian aesthetic can be read as a prescient warning against the arrogance of an autonomous art, they can also be seen as a prediction of the limits of both avant-gardism and nostalgia, which share a desire to dismiss the institutional limits of the aesthetic. The very effort to imagine a utopian future or a premodern world immune to our institutional constraints will inevitably take place in the terms established by professional discipline. This is James Agee's problem in particular. Wanting not just to document but to capture and celebrate the beauty latent in the lives of the rural poor, he can turn only to the aesthetic vocabulary whose "false beauty" he distrusts. Indeed, he acknowledges that he sees the real beauty of his farmers' lives, which they cannot articulate themselves, only because of his very schooling in the false beauty they both distrust. Wanting to deny the shallow superiority of art, then, he turns the rural poor into artists of their own lives. Just as Cather celebrates the Anasazi as superior people because they are aesthetically gifted, Agee ultimately suggests not that art should truly be dismissed, but merely that we should broaden our idea of art, so that in effect tenant farmers belong among our list of the best that has been thought and written.[21]

If the paradoxes of Kant's theory do have any lasting validity it is because they help to clarify such complications. They suggest that just as it is all but impossible to be an "Arnoldian" elitist without appealing to popular legitimation, it is difficult to remain an "anthropological" egalitarian without invoking judgment and recognition. From the perspective of Kant's theory, we cannot avoid seeing their respective tendencies toward autonomy and community, superiority and democracy, high art and common life as mutually dependent and inextricable complements. By this reading of the third critique, we will be fated to regard the aesthetic as an irrevocable but imperfect part of culture. Art, along with its makers and audiences, will always seem part of a broader world, but it will never seem merely the product of its world. As modern subjects, Kant suggests, we can be satisfied neither with the thought that art is autonomous nor that it is committed, deracinated nor autochthonous.

### III

Approaching our ideas about art and culture in this fashion is useful among other reasons for the way it helps to explain the peculiar vitality of such oppositions. They remain among the last sacred binary contrasts of intellectual life, and they do so because the tension they express is both real and not amenable to solution. The very fact that such antagonisms cannot be dismissed, moreover, means that the attitudes we take toward them can assume a significance of their own. Because the problem of art's status is not one that can be solved, it becomes one in which we can imagine ideal solutions and thus display values we admire. By bringing attention to the intractable friction among independence and commitment, art and culture, autonomy and community, we can affirm our determination to move toward one side or another of these divides even in the face of insuperable difficulty. In doing so, furthermore, we show that our values are not simple and unreflective. Stressing the inextricable conflicts basic to the aesthetic, we are enabled to cast ourselves in the mode shared by the Professor and James Agee—as agonistically divided figures who, succumbing neither to antipopular elitism nor to anti-elitist reductionism, constantly balance and play off the two.

It is this story of self-fashioning I referred to earlier when I suggested that arguments over the status of art were less theoretical or political arguments (they pose no conceptual difficulty that can be resolved and they have little bearing on any policy in particular) than an ethical theater—a rhetorical mode in which, in Tony Bennett's phrase, we have the opportunity to construct an "ideal of personality."[22] This seems to be what Terry Eagleton points toward when he refers to recent manifestations of aesthetic theory as "an *ersatz* kind of ethics." The *ersatz*ness comes for Eagleton, of course, from the fact, that the "privatized hedonism" of this particular form of discourse seems poorly linked to the public, transformative politics Eagleton seeks. As Cather, Arnold, and Agee all suggest, though, that very feeling of falseness and incompletion is integral to the whole ethical theater of aesthetic thought. A major part of the *ersatz* discourse, in other words, is the suspicion of *ersatz*ness and the longing to displace it with something more authentic. "[O]ur story *should* be one of politics, not art," Susan Buck-Morss says, and that hortatory sentiment is exemplary of the whole tradition of thought. In order to take part in it, we must always claim to be moving away from the tendency to be trapped in the narrow or overly professionalized perspective that locks art away from Agee's "whole realm of human consciousness, action, and possibility." "Culture and politics," Hannah Arendt says in the same fashion, "belong together." The problem is that for some reason they always seem to be forced apart.[23]

This tendency in aesthetic discourse can be seen to proceed from one side of the paradoxes staged by Kant's theory. They draw from the sense implicit in Kant and emphasized by his successors that in order to fulfill its special destiny, the aesthetic must "exceed its constitution," moving to unify our faculties and our societies. The imperative that art not be *merely* aesthetic (or vice versa, that the aesthetic not be merely art) is thus one of the crucial set pieces of the ethical theater constituted by aesthetic discourse. There is no more common fear in that discourse than the concern that art will become trivial, just as there is no more common contention than that the aesthetic is nothing if it does not push in some ways toward personal and social transformation. This is what Arnold means for example, when he claims that learning must be "humanise[d]." The same phrase is employed by Cather, not incidentally, to describe the common life she envisions on the Anasazi mesa. And although the terminology used to describe that imperative has changed, the conviction remains strong that art must move always toward rejoining the whole realm of human consciousness. Even so earnest a defender of tradition as T. S. Eliot, for example, takes pains to point out that poetry cannot be mere "Blue-book knowledge." It must be part of "a living whole," the expression of "the mind of . . . [the poet's] own country"—a collective intelligence, the true writer learns, that is "much more important than his own private mind." In Nietzsche's directly analogous terms, culture is valuable insofar as it counters both "a scornfully remote art" and our "fragmentation into individuals" in order to move us toward "a higher community."[24]

Such convictions lead philosophical reflection on art to its most persistent commonplace: that the aesthetic is "a proto-political discourse standing in for and marking the absence of a truly political domain in modern, enlightened societies."[25] All writers working in this vein see art as both an *ersatz* ethics and as bearing the potential for something much more profound. In particular, the standard argument runs, the aesthetic is to provide the basis for a critical sensibility richer than mere opposition and a solidarity deeper than narrowly social or bureaucratic kinds of organization—"a community of subjects," in Terry Eagleton's paradigmatic formulation, "linked by sensuous impulse and fellow feeling rather than by heteronomous law."[26] From this perspective, not only will the aesthetic be redeemed by its reunion with the whole continuum of life, it will redeem as well the political world to which it returns, thus fashioning the utopian community that Schiller first envisioned as "the aesthetic State." In such a world, Schiller suggests, the cultivation by beauty of all people will return us to the "zoophyt[ic]" civilization once possessed by the Greeks—a society in which individuals are not estranged from each other but belong to a mutually dependent common whole. By the same token, aesthetic education will transform the nature of political authority. Law will not seem bureaucratic and oppressive, and government will no longer be, in Schiller's striking phrase, "alien to its citizens." Rather, the state will "carr[y] out the will of the whole through the nature of the individual."[27]

This is, of course, a utopian vision—one in which the realization of a common identity somehow obviates the possibility of conflict among individuals. But as Schiller, Eagleton, Arnold, and every other thinker operating in this mode implicitly recognizes, its importance comes not as much from the future it anticipates as from the way it licenses a unique critical attitude in the present. Just as this perspective is bound to see art as *ersatz*—an orphaned child destined for great things in the future perhaps but now inevitably weak and alienated—it casts contemporary political life as false and incomplete. Our world lacks a "truly political domain" precisely because it divides the rich realm of nonformulaic, nonlegalistic values from the sphere of public debate, government, and administration. The law thus seems inevitably "heteronomous" to our lives, our society "mechanical," and our common citizens strangers rather than companions in "fellow feeling." It becomes possible in sum to create a critical sensibility that objects to a particular state of affairs on the basis of its aesthetic impoverishment alone. As critics envisioning a Schillerian utopia, that is, we can object to the political definition of our world, not merely because it is unjust or unwise or even because it has been arrived at by undemocratic means (although these criticisms are not necessarily incompatible with such an attitude) but simply because the state is a stranger to its citizens. Against that inadequate condition we can pitch the critical authority of culture, not as an alternate set of policies or governmental methods but rather as an image of wholeness that shows up the partiality and inadequacy of every existing political arrangement.[28]

The rhetorical mode that results from such a stance is enormously productive. It enabled Schiller, writing in reaction to the French Revolution and the Reign of Terror, to suggest that potentially corrosive individual freedoms were unnecessary to political progress. For "[t]he gift of liberal principles becomes" in this mode "a piece of treachery to the whole."[29] Sixty years later, it allowed Arnold to scorn not only the "machinery" of capitalism but the critical response posed by religious moralism, parliamentary liberalism, and working-class radicalism—all of which appeared in Arnold's description as partial, one-sided, and divisive. The same habit of critical thought, too, provided later writers like Nietzsche, Eliot, and Cather with a means to distinguish merely "social" forms of organization—exemplified by sexual exchange, the capitalist market, and representative democracy—from the "true bonds" of culture. Only those almost imaginary obligations, they presumed, could draw upon the mind of the nation and relate citizens not as pathetically isolated individuals but "as representatives of the race."[30]

In all these cases, the common life of culture promises to redeem within itself the falsely divided realms of art and politics, calling forth thereby the vision of communion that Jürgen Habermas defines as "the utopia of reconciliation."[31] Nowadays we tend to be hesitant about such chiliastic visions, but the critical sensibility that inspired these utopian images remains, though muted, very much alive. Consider, for example, Susan Buck-Morss's recent writings on the question. For Buck-Morss, who draws in particular on the essays and fragments of Walter Benjamin, the aesthetic exists mainly in a badly compromised condition. Just as Schiller saw "modern humanity" trapped in "barbarity" and "enervation"—a condition created by the very "wound" inflicted by overcultivation—Buck-Morss bemoans the impoverishment of "the human sensorium." Capitalism, commodification, and mass culture have conspired to degrade the aesthetic, she suggests. Once a "cognitive mode of being 'in touch with reality,'" it now "takes the form of an *an*aesthetics," a form of "addiction" that, rather than stimulating, "paralyz[es] the imagination." Hope lies, therefore, only in the prospect of a "dialectical reversal"—what Schiller referred to analogously as "a total revolution . . . in the whole mode of perception." "[F]reed from 'art'" and cut loose from commodity fetishism, "aesthetic perception" might regain its place in a whole "anthropology" (Buck-Morss's revealing term for the holistic reunion of "critical cognition" and "somatic experience"). Following this path, she claims, we will not only free aesthetics from mere art, we will engage in a special brand of politics, "producing solidarity" that might "generate a force of collective awakening."[32]

As with her master Benjamin, Buck-Morss's is a narrative particularly engaged with the dreams and failures of socialism, but it is important to recognize that the story she tells has no necessary political affiliation. Just as writers like Eliot and Cather could adopt the Schillerian vision for a reactionary political fantasy, Buck-Morss has contemporaries who share her mode of criticism while casting it, not in the jargon of the post-Frankfurt school left but in the rhetoric of the libertarian right. Thus, for example, Libby Lumpkin shares Buck-Morss's dissatisfaction with the "dire consequences" suffered by the aesthetic in contemporary life. She, too, complains about a reified art and imagines a "full scale redemption of practice" to replace it. She does so, though, not by stressing "collective awakening" but by praising the virtues of the market against academic delusion and professional bureaucracy. Art, Lumpkin argues, has become progressively more arid and narrow over the centuries because intellectuals and experts forced "academic disinterest" upon it. As a result, the aesthetic was made into a pseudophilosophy, turned sadly into a "liberal art" and separated from its vital roots in "the vulgar arts." Here too, then, a dialectical reversal is required. The snobbery and intellectual pretense of the contemporary art world must be defeated through a rediscovery of "the arts of commerce." As her ally, the currently influential critic Dave Hickey puts it, artists and audiences must both realize that "*everyone* is interested and self-interested, and should be." They must embrace the vitality that comes from "taking risks" and "accept the obligation of taking care of themselves in pursuance of their own ends." Only through this embrace of the market will we escape the "therapeutic institution" that has imprisoned beauty and return the aesthetic toward what Lumpkin calls "the ultimate validation of art in the social economy."[33]

In short, though Buck-Morss and Lumpkin write from ostensibly opposite ends of the political spectrum, they share basic attitudes. Each wants to save the aesthetic from the constraints of art and especially from the divisions created by its ambivalent place in the capitalist economy. Buck-Morss and fellow leftists hope to purge the aesthetic of its basis in commodification; Lumpkin and her allies look to save art from the illusions of intellectual transcendence by making it *all* commodity. Each writer's theory of art is justified, too, by a compelling theory of history. There was a time, they both suggest, when our cultural practices were less harshly divided than they now seem, and both lament art's complicity in the historical creation of its own estrangement. Finally, both imagine that contemporary artists and audiences will overcome this complicity by realizing the mistakes of their predecessors so as to return their efforts to "the social economy" or the "collective." Thus for both, thinking about the aesthetic leads to a jeremiad about how art has fallen from its true mission and thereby to a narrative of anticipation. In such a mode, the current moment is always a crisis, but the future inevitably promises, if we are but strong, imminent transformation.

The most evident features of these covertly millenarian stories correspond, though, to but one side of Kant's paradoxical vision, that which stresses the role of beauty in creating a sense of social and personal holism. The contrary dimension of the third critique—that which, loosely speaking, emphasizes division and separation—tends to receive far less explicit credibility from contemporary critics. It too, though, remains a crucial component of the contemporary discourse on the aesthetic, one that even those thinkers most skeptical about its value have trouble avoiding.

This side of the Kantian vision is exemplified by perhaps the most oft-challenged notion in the entire body of aesthetic philosophy—the concept, taken by Kant from earlier eighteenth-century writers, of "disinterest." According to the third critique, disinterest is the capacity that enables appreciation without "inclination, . . . favor, or . . . respect," and it is perhaps the most indispensable feature of the subjective disposition necessary in Kant's account to aesthetical judgment. For it is the notion of disinterest that allows Kant to differentiate among the "pleasant, the beautiful, and the good," and thus what enables him to construe taste as a particular, autonomous faculty. Only what can be appreciated apart from desire or moral-political will, he contends, can be experienced as beautiful.[34]

Contemporary skepticism toward this idea follows from some entirely reasonable suspicions: that there could be no such thing as an appreciation without *some* interest (whether moral-political or appetitive) and that the idea is contradictory on its face, since by Kant's description we would seem to have an interest in being disinterested. Nevertheless, the notion continues to play an often hidden but crucial role in contemporary aesthetic discourse. Indeed, it is the feature most essential to the constitution of that discourse as an ethical theater. Before getting to that function, though, consider for the moment the sheer indispensability of the idea. Most criticisms of the concept of disinterest draw on some variety or combination of two basic tacks. Assuming that the very notion invokes an autonomous, self-determining subject (said to be an ideological chimera in itself), Kant's critics argue that disinterest serves as a *sub rosa* apology for the male bourgeois intellectual. This is roughly the position taken by Marxists, critical sociologists like Bourdieu, and some feminists. Alternatively, they claim that the appeal to disinterest demands a puritanical denial of life and bodily pleasure (roughly the stance adopted by Nietzsche, his contemporary Walter Pater, and their followers).

Yet however true such criticisms ring, and it is hard to deny their relevance, it is also hard for those critical positions to do without the very concept they seek to dismiss. Bourdieu, for example, is relentless in his irony toward Kant's idea and its role in creating a whole vision of "pure taste." Disinterest, he suggests, is the expression, "in a rationalized form, [of] the ethos of the dominated fraction of the dominant class"—that is, the "bourgeois intelligentsia." It is "nothing other than a refusal, ... a disgust for objects which impose enjoyment and a disgust for the crude, vulgar taste which revels in this imposed enjoyment." In short, disinterest is not at all a restraint from interest, but rather the deceptive legitimation of the intellectual's overweening will to power. "What is at stake ... [is] the attempted imposition of a definition of the genuinely human ... nothing less than the monopoly of humanity."[35]

Yet Bourdieu begins this denunciation of Kant by explaining his failure to take up the third critique earlier, and that explanation calls on some revealing terms. His avoidance of philosophical aesthetics, Bourdieu explains, was the result of "a deliberate refusal." Since aesthetic discourse bestows an undeserved and deceptive set of rewards on its adherents, an illegitimate sense of superiority to the impure and coarse, an accurate account of the sociology of taste requires, "above all, a sort of deliberate amnesia, a readiness to renounce the whole corpus of cultivated discourse on culture."[36] Put differently, Bourdieu acknowledges that he must be disinterested toward the seductions of disinterest and renounce the satisfactions of renunciation. And while he is certainly self-conscious in playing up the irony in this situation, that does not change the fact that the imprimatur of disinterest is fundamental to his claim to authority and legitimacy. He can only criticize Kant rightly, Bourdieu suggests, because he himself refuses to be seduced by the very attractive prospect of falling into the easy satisfactions of aesthetic discourse.

Similar paradoxes trouble the Nietzschean distaste for disinterest. "Art," Nietzsche claimed, is "fundamentally opposed to the ascetic ideal." Pursuing it "is therefore the most distinctive *corruption* of an artist that is at all possible; unhappily, also one of the most common forms of corruption." Though artists, along with the rest of us, often forget the fact, beauty is inversely related to the pathetic slave morality implied by disinterest. It is in fact a "consequence of 'interest,' even . . . a consequence of the strongest, most personal, interest . . . sexual excitation." We should reject therefore *"the impoverishment of life"* threatened by Kant's principles and instead relish the promise of satisfaction held out by art. In this way "the ascetic ideal" might be called on not to deny appetite but "to produce orgies of feeling." Yet although he praises the erotic component of art, Nietzsche is also capable of claiming that "the danger for artists, for geniuses . . . lies in women," for they seduce the artist toward the very Christian anticorporalism that art must resist.[37] To be sure, like Bourdieu, Nietzsche knowingly reverses the traditional rhetoric of aesthetic discourse. Women are dangerous to art not because they raise the threat of appetite but because as bourgeois moralists they may impose a finicky distaste for the desirous body on their lovers. Yet as with Bourdieu, the very effort to escape the chains of disinterest necessitates calling anew on the concept. For Nietzsche, the true aesthetic subject must once again *resist* the appeal of a cheap and delusional satisfaction in order to pursue a higher good. The paradox is apparent in Nietzsche's own rhetoric. The ascetic ideal exemplified by disinterest can't be done away with, he acknowledges; it must simply be turned toward "life" and "orgies of feeling" rather than away from such excesses.[38] Only in such manner can we be sure that we pursue "true cultivation" rather than the prison of "modern cultivatedness," a "new and improved *physis*" rather than "a cunning, egotistical praxis."[39]

In fact, Bourdieu, Nietzsche, and their analogues implicitly call upon disinterest for much the same purposes praised by the third critique. For Kant, disinterest is valuable because it enables autonomy from coercion. Guided by it, we can experience a *"free* satisfaction; . . . no interest either of sense or of reason, forces our assent." Nietzsche and Bourdieu likewise appeal to resistance and renunciation for the way they help to liberate us from the false promises of ideology, and in doing so they implicitly call upon a second major set piece of the ethical theater of aesthetic discourse.

This claim, which is strictly complementary to the argument that art is a protocommunal discourse, values the aesthetic for the way it enables us to resist ordinary constraints or for the manner in which it presents us with occasions on which we can exercise such resistance. The keynote of this side of aesthetic discourse is therefore not the image of reconciliation but the language of freedom. Thus, for example, Schiller praises beauty for the way it encourages us to deny "the dominion of blind necessity" along with "the formulas which State and priesthood hold in readiness." Coleridge likewise celebrates poetry for the way it counters the "chains" of "vicious phraseology that meets us everywhere, from the sermon, to the newspaper, from the harangue of the legislator, to the speech from the convivial chair." Speaking in almost identical terms, Barthes invokes the text of bliss for its capacity to denaturalize "the world's jargons" and thus to point toward "the subversion of all ideology." And Adorno sums up all these sentiments with the remark that truly worthwhile art signals our refusal of an "accommodation to the world."[40]

This collection of names could be extended indefinitely. Its point is that like the vision of reconciliation, the rhetoric of autonomy is pervasive throughout the tradition of aesthetic discourse and that it has no given theoretical or political meaning. Such language refers simply to a basic set of ethical principles that all thinkers working in this vein implicitly agree to value. Thus, if the aesthetic sometimes seems important for the way it promises to return us to a unified world and experience that we have forgotten, the theorists and critics who stress disinterest and autonomy praise the aesthetic for the way it exemplifies resistance to the constraints and solicitations that constantly surround us. From this perspective art tends to dramatize the dynamic and ever recurrent effort to deny the hold of myth, ideology, and cheap satisfaction. And just as nearly every example of aesthetic discourse makes some reference to the ultimate value of the common life, all agree at some level that such resistance is a good in and of itself. Even those who seek to cast doubt on the ideological fiction of the autonomous subject cannot avoid invoking that value. For they inevitably contend that the myth of individuality is an ideology from which we must struggle to free ourselves. Suggesting that the invocation of disinterest seduces us toward a cheap and false image of freedom, they demand that we resist the delights of renunciation for a higher liberation. We must struggle to make ourselves, that is, autonomous to autonomy.

Thus the values associated with disinterest subtly insinuate themselves into the writing of even those thinkers most repelled by the notion and most determined to return the aesthetic to the whole continuum of culture and politics. And that insinuation explains a characteristic irony of aesthetic discourse. Even at its most urgent and chiliastic, the pursuit of the utopia of reconciliation remains hortatory and lodged in a stance of deferral. The ultimate reunion of art and life, culture and politics is always something that is to take place in the near future but also a condition that must not be rushed. As Schiller's founding example has it, we must resist the "premature striving for harmony." Should we fall into such prematurity, he suggests, we will fail to achieve the reconciliation we seek—the "*absolute inclusion*" of conflicting "realities." Instead, we will be "mixing but not uniting" the faculties we desire to combine.⁴¹

In practice that means that the pursuit of reconciliation remains always in the "negative condition of sheer indeterminacy," always in preparation for a conclusion that never arrives. We are interminably "on the way towards culture."⁴² Like Schiller, those thinkers who emphasize the aesthetic's capacity to reconnect our divided lives, or who stress the necessity that it exceed its constitution, also always recognize that such reconciliation can occur prematurely, take place in negative as well as positive ways. And that recognition leads the entire discourse to a characteristic Manicheanism. If art is to rejoin life, it must do so in the proper fashion and avoid the improper fashions that constantly shadow this promise. Indeed, those negative versions of reconciliation are typically more evident than the positive ones intended to supplant them. Thus Nietzsche can envision "true cultivation" because he sees "modern cultivatedness" everywhere around him. Likewise, Buck-Morss values the connection with reality promised by the aesthetic because it seems always prevented by *an*aesthetics—the condition in which we are not "in touch" with the world but its slave—just as Lumpkin stresses a return to the "social economy" against the prison of social institutions. In Terry Eagleton's similar formulation, art serves "as an image of emancipation"*or* it "ratif[ies] domination." For all these thinkers, each of whom avowedly distrusts the ideas of autonomy and disinterest, we must first maintain our freedom so that we can anticipate an ultimate reunion of art and life, individual and society in one common life. Should we fail in this resistance, however, we will fall into the false reconciliation that produces not community but mass culture and shallow individuality.⁴³

This Manicheanism and the fear of what Peter Bürger describes revealingly as "false sublation" run all through the history of aesthetic discourse. (Think, for example, of Walter Benjamin's classic distinction between the fascist aestheticization of politics and the socialist politicization of aesthetics—mirror images differentiated only by intent.) Their effect must be to demand that we always wonder what god we are serving—to ask in our encounter with art whether we pursue cultivation or cultivatedness, whether we are drugged or engaged, whether we serve emancipation or acquiesce to domination. Exactly the same dilemma holds true, though, for those writers who stress the value of disinterest and autonomy over the appeal of reconciliation. That is, just as "false sublation" plays a crucial role in the drama of reconciliation, a vision of false resistance structures even the most stringent rhetoric of autonomy. Thus, for example, Adorno, who leveled brutal scorn at artistic "commitment" and who celebrated abstraction for its capacity to resist social domination, warns also that the autonomous aesthetic must not "conver[t] its own malediction into a theodicy"—must not turn independence from a vital struggle to a complacent habit. "[E]ven in its opposition to society," art must "remai[n] a part of it." And since it will always be difficult to distinguish between an abstract art that boldly refuses conformity and one that wallows in cynicism ("No firm criterion can draw the line between a determinate negation of meaning and a bad positivism of meaninglessness"), here, too, we must always worry about our intentions. There is no point, Adorno emphasizes, to "an assiduous soldiering on just for the sake of it."[44] Whether we seek to be disinterested or committed, it seems, we must always worry that we don't carry these ideas too far and merely soldier on—that when we are committed we are not so engaged that we forget to protect out autonomy and that when we pursue our autonomy we don't forget that it is meaningless unless tacitly committed.

## IV

The tension between disinterest and reconciliation serves, then, as a key structuring opposition that organizes the entire discursive field of aesthetic reflection. In this way it is directly homologous to the comparison between "Arnoldian" and "anthropological" ideas of culture and to the related opposition between autonomous and committed art. Together these contrary and yet mutually dependent impulses allow us to restage continually a series of crucial ethical dilemmas. Posed against each other, they enable us to see ourselves as both independent and committed, autonomous yet not alienated, politically engaged but not entangled by ideology, and as bodily figures who are not therefore reduced to blind appetite.

The entire tradition of aesthetic thought constantly replays the drama of negation and self-fashioning implied by these contrasting sets of values. And when we initiate our students into that tradition, we ask them to participate in its ethical theater as well. We suggest to them that although they may have thought it trivial, art matters because it raises and dramatizes such dilemmas, and we encourage them to be as preoccupied by the lack of resolution among them as we are. "Beauty cultivates us," Kant claimed in the third critique, and beginning with Schiller, his followers used that notion to suggest that the aesthetic was inherently pedagogical—that approaching it in the proper spirit would enable us to work upon and improve ourselves and thereby our world.[45] In the hands of Matthew Arnold and other Victorians, this notion became the platitude that art somehow improves and uplifts us—a bromide that has been badly discredited many times over. Yet, as I hope this essay has suggested, the ideas underlying it continue, though in novel garb, to exert a powerful subterranean force. For nearly every thinker who continues to work in this tradition, the aesthetic matters much as it did for Kant and Schiller. It provides an arena in which we can stage our concerns about autonomy and commitment and in which we can constantly worry over and work upon our dispositions, aiming always to be not just lovers of art or social critics but better and constantly improving people.

The sheer fact that such problems are inevitably and unendingly recurrent and that, seen in this guise, the history of aesthetic thought resembles less a developing body of knowledge than an astonishingly repetitive series of ethical imperatives might lead one to want to dismiss the whole matter. That would be impossible, of course. If we take either seriously, we cannot stop worrying about art's relation to life. Nor, to put matters in a way that may more accurately express what is at issue, can we stop worrying about our attitudes—whether we are unconsciously shaped by ideology, whether we have fallen into complacence or arrogance, whether we've let our beliefs and practices fall out of accord. These are the problems thematized by aesthetic discourse, and they are irrevocable.

What we can stop worrying about, however, is developing a philosophical or political solution to these problems. We do not need explanations of why art should be autonomous or committed, since everyone already believes it should be both, and we should not expect that the tension between these possibilities could ever be satisfactorily resolved. If the perspective I've outlined here has any merit, it suggests that the avant-gardist dream to sublate art and life, culture and politics must inevitably be incomplete. On the other hand, it also suggests that the desire to purge art of political relevance, to reduce it to timeless beauty, private satisfaction, or self-contained professional expertise will also be pointless.[46] To return, for example, to the figures with whom we began, everything that makes the work of Cather and Agee significant and moving stems from the fact that they strive against just such narrowings. And they serve in turn as a reminder that art can be neither politicized nor depoliticized *tout court*. The institution of art as such will remain in the indeterminate condition first sketched by Kant and Schiller—at once part of a whole way of life and alien to it, inevitably political and not only so. There is no utopia of reconciliation, just as there is no heaven of art, and there is little reason to think either would be desirable in the first place.

I am grateful to Minou Roufail, Tom Huhn, and David Weisberg for their helpful comments on this essay.

## NOTES

1. Leszek Kolakowski, *Modernity on Endless Trial* (Chicago: University of Chicago Press, 1990), 42; James Agee and Walker Evans, *Let Us Now Praise Famous Men: Three Tenant Families* (Boston: Houghton Mifflin, 1988), 15; Willa Cather, *The Professor's House* (New York: Vintage, 1990), 121, 53, 42, 56, 55; subsequent citations to these editions are given parenthetically in the text.
2. Cather, *Not Under Forty* (New York: Knopf, 1936), 48, 49.
3. Raymond Williams, "Culture Is Ordinary," *Resources of Hope* (London: Verso, 1989); Raymond Williams, *Keywords: A Vocabulary of Culture and Society,* (London, Oxford University Press, 1985), 90.
4. Williams, *Culture and Society, 1780 – 1950* (New York: Penguin, 1961), 285.
5. See Walter Benn Michaels account of the novel in *Our America: Nativism, Modernism, and Pluralism* (Durham: Duke University Press, 1996), 35–38, 45–48, 50–52.
6. *Let Us Now Praise Famous Men* was not published until 1941, but the bulk of the book was composed in 1936.
7. Williams, *Culture and Society,* 16.
8. Unlike many of his followers, Raymond Williams acknowledged these confusions, though he sometimes downplayed them in order to stress the divide between what he took to be "incompatible systems of thought." See *Culture and Society,* 121–36, and *Keywords,* where Williams stresses both such incompatability and "the range and the overlap of meanings" in the idea of "culture" (86, 91).
9. Friedrich Schiller, *On the Aesthetic Education of Man in a Series of Letters,* trans. Reginald Snell (Bristol, England: Thoemmes Press, 1994), 102, 103.
10. Matthew Arnold, "Culture & Anarchy: An Essay in Political and Social Criticism," *Culture and Anarchy and Other Writings,* ed. Stefan Collini (New York: Cambridge University Press, 1993), 56, 65, 59, 61, 62, original emphasis; subsequent citations to this essay are given parenthetically in the text.
11. My argument here and throughout draws from, among other sources, the following: Ferenc Fehér and Agnes Heller, "The Necessity and Irreformability of Aesthetics," *Reconstructing Aesthetics: Writings of the Budapest School,* ed. Heller and Fehér (New York: Basil Blackwell,

1986), 1–22; Geoffrey Galt Harpham, "Aesthetics and the Fundamentals of Modernity," *Aesthetics and Ideology*, ed. George Levine (New Brunswick, NJ: Rutgers University Press, 1994), 124–49; Ian Hunter, "Aesthetics and Cultural Studies," *Cultural Studies*, ed. Lawrence Grossberg, Cary Nelson and Paula Treichler (New York: Routledge, 1992), 347–72; Luc Ferry, *Homo Aestheticus: The Invention of Taste in the Democratic Age*, trans. Robert de Loaiza (Chicago: University of Chicago Press, 1993). These various arguments are not perfectly consistent with each other, nor do I follow any one of them particularly closely. All share, though, the sense that the problems of the aesthetic are an irrevocable feature of "modernity" and that they are crucially related to the way individuals form and display dispositions.

12. This is, of course, a standard argument; see, for example, Ferry, *Homo Aestheticus*, 7–32, or Matei Calinescu, *Five Faces of Modernity: Modernism, Avant-Garde, Decadence, Kitsch, Postmodernism* (Durham: Duke University Press, 1987), 13–92.

13. Immanuel Kant, *Critique of Judgment*, trans. J. H. Bernard (New York: Hafner, 1951), 28, 43.

14. Kant, *Critique of Judgment*, 46, 38, 27, 28, emphasis added.

15. Kant, *Critique of Judgment*, 7, 32, 12, 31, 33, 34.

16. A strong version of both these classic arguments can be found in Pierre Bourdieu, *Distinction: A Social Critique of the Judgment of Taste*, trans. Richard Nice (Cambridge, MA: Harvard University Press, 1984), 485–500; compare Arthur Danto, "From Aesthetics to Art Criticism," *After the End of Art: Contemporary Art and the Pale of History* (Princeton: Princeton University Press, 1997), 81–99.

17. Kant, *Critique of Judgment*, 75, 76, 77; Hannah Arendt, *Between Past and Future: Eight Exercises in Political Thought* (New York: Penguin, 1977), 221; compare Jürgen Habermas, *The Philosophical Discourse of Modernity: Twelve Lectures*, trans. Frederick Lawrence (Cambridge, MA: MIT Press, 1987), 45–50. Kant used this particular idea of a fundamental "common sense" to address the paradoxes basic to his theory of beauty. If the judgment of taste were to claim a title to subjective universality, such an apparently contradictory outcome stemmed, Kant suggested, from the double nature of human community—the split between the common humanity of all people and the actual organization of individuals in contingent and parochial associations. Because of that division, Kant claimed against empiricism that it was impossible to discover a true sense of beauty by "suffrage." An empirical survey of

what actual people thought was beautiful would only produce a compendium of custom and local prejudice, that is, "private conditions." Our presumption that all people would agree with our judgments of taste depends not on our reliance on those conditions but on our implicit appeal to a universal "common sense." Thus for Kant the experience of beauty hinted at a utopian possibility distinctly in line with his enlightenment convictions. Not only might it bridge the divided operation of our faculties, it promised a recognition of the universal qualities of mankind. It was left to Schiller to make of this possibility an influential political vision and to turn Kant's enlightenment universalism toward romantic particularism.

18. Schiller, *On the Aesthetic Education of Man,* 45.
19. Bernstein, *The Fate of Art: Aesthetic Alienation from Kant to Derrida and Adorno* (University Park: Pennsylvania State University Press, 1992), 2.
20. Kant, *Critique of Judgment,* 107.
21. Nor are these difficulties merely contingent. As Raymond Williams noted when he first began to describe the appeal of the anthropological idea of culture, its affective force came from the way it "bypassed . . . the hostility" created by high culture's association with "class distinction," while the analytic power of the idea came in the way it promised, against our experience of various forms of partiality, a "total qualitative assessment." If that description is accurate, it suggests that we value the ethnographic idea of culture in good measure because it fulfills the avant-garde dream of smashing the institutions of art. It frees the aesthetic from its imprisonment in narrow categories and enables us to discover beauty, meaning, and value everywhere. The result, as Christopher Herbert has argued, is that the very effectiveness of the anthropological idea of culture (along with its conceptual difficulties) stems from the fact that it casts everything it touches—and, in strong forms, the whole of each society it describes—as a work of art. Williams, *Keywords,* 92; *Culture and Society,* 285; Herbert, *Culture and Anomie* (Chicago: University of Chicago Press, 1991).
22. Bennett, *Outside Literature* (New York: Routledge, 1990), 166.
23. Eagleton, *The Ideology of the Aesthetic* (Cambridge, MA: Basil Blackwell, 1990), 7; Buck-Morss, "The City as Dreamworld and Catastrophe," *October* 73 (Summer 1995), 22, emphasis added; Arendt, *Between Past and Future,* 223.
24. Eliot, "Tradition and the Individual Talent," *Selected Prose of T. S.*

*Eliot,* ed. Frank Kermode (New York: Harcourt Brace, 1975), 40, 39; Friedrich Nietzsche, *The Birth of Tragedy Out of the Spirit of Music,* trans. Shaun Whiteside (New York: Penguin, 1993), 27, 20, 18.

25. Bernstein, *The Fate of Art,* 3.
26. Eagleton, *The Ideology of the Aesthetic,* 28.
27. Schiller, *On the Aesthetic Education of Man,* 40, 41, 138.
28. See Ian Hunter for an especially clear-sighted account of the prejudices and limitations of this mode of critique.
29. Schiller, *On the Aesthetic Education of Man,* 46.
30. Eliot, "Notes Toward the Definition of Culture," *Selected Prose,* 304, 305; Schiller, *On the Aesthetic Education of Man,* 138.
31. Habermas, "Modernity—An Incomplete Project," *The Anti-Aesthetic: Essays on Postmodern Culture,* ed. Hal Foster (Port Townsend, WA: Bay Press, 1983), 3–15.
32. Schiller, *On the Aesthetic Education of Man,* 35, 39, 132; Buck-Morss, "The City as Dreamworld," 8, 9; 23; Grant H. Kester, "Aesthetics after the End of Art: An Interview with Susan Buck-Morss,"*Art Journal* (March 1997), 38–46; see also Buck-Morss, "Aesthetics and Anaesthetics: Walter Benjamin's Artwork Essay Reconsidered," *October* 62 (Fall 1992), 3–41. Of course, Buck-Morss denies the commonality between her vision and that of her predecessors, claiming that "I am in no way advocating a new romanticism." But on any close inspection, it seems clear that she shares more with other examples of the aesthetic critique than she differs from them.
33. Lumpkin, "Dire Consequences: A Short History of Art as a Liberal Art," *Art Issues* 50 (November/December 1997), 23, 24, 26; Hickey, *Air Guitar: Essays on Art and Democracy* (Los Angeles: Art issues. Press, 1997), 206; *The Invisible Dragon: Four Essays on Beauty* (Los Angeles: Art issues. Press, 1993), 53; I am indebted to Minou Roufail for drawing my attention to these writers.
34. Kant, *Critique of Judgment,* 42.
35. Bourdieu, *Distinction,* 487, 488, 491, 492.
36. Bourdieu, *Distinction,* 485.
37. Nietzsche, *On the Genealogy of Morals,* trans. Walter Kaufmann and R. J. Hollingdale (New York: Vintage, 1989), 154, 104, 105, 106, 139.
38. Compare the analogous paradox created by Nietzsche's contemporary Walter Pater. Like Nietzsche, Pater slighted the appeal of disinterest and claimed that "Not the fruit of experience, but experience itself, is the end" of the aesthetic disposition. It should lead us to "[g]reat pas-

sions," a "quickened sense of life, ecstasy and sorrow of love," and "various forms of enthusiastic activity." Yet, Pater, too, praises "the charm of ascêsis." Like Nietzsche, he simply claims that good ascêsis differs from bad "Christian asceticism."*The Renaissance: Studies in Art and Poetry* (New York: Oxford University Press, 1986), 152, 153, xxxii, 142.

39. Nietzsche, "On the Utility and Liability of History for Life," *Unfashionable Observations,* trans. Richard T. Gray (Stanford: Stanford University Press, 1995), 111, 167, 116.

40. Kant, *Critique of Judgment,* 44, original emphasis; Schiller, *On the Aesthetic Education of Man,* 28, 49; Coleridge, "Biographia Literaria," *English Romantic Writers,* ed. David Perkins (New York; Harcourt Brace Jovanovich, 1967), 485; Roland Barthes, *The Pleasure of the Text,* trans. Richard Miller (New York: Hill and Wang, 1975), 30, 33; T. S. Adorno, "Commitment,"*The Essential Frankfurt School Reader,* eds. Andrew Arato and Eike Gebhardt (New York: Urizen Books, 1978), 317.

41. Schiller, *On the Aesthetic Education of Man,* 70, 88, 90, original emphasis.

42. Schiller, *On the Aesthetic Education of Man,* 98, 43.

43. Eagleton, *The Ideology of the Aesthetic,* 411.

44. Bürger, *Theory of the Avant-Garde,* trans. Michael Shaw (Minneapolis: University of Minnesota Press, 1984), 54; Benjamin, "The Work of Art in the Age of Mechanical Reproduction," *Illuminations,* ed. Hannah Arendt, trans. Harry Zohn (New York: Schocken Books, 1969), 242; Adorno, "Commitment," 317, 315.

45. Kant, *Critique of Judgment,* 107.

46. This might be taken to be the implication of not only recent middlebrow defenses of great literature, like David Denby's and Nicholas Delbanco's, but of more sophisticated responses to the problematic status of the modern institutions of art, like that in Richard Rorty's *Contingency, Irony, and Solidarity* (Cambridge, MA: Cambridge University Press, 1989), 96–121; or in David Hollinger's "The Knower and the Artificer," *Modernist Impulses in the Human Sciences,* ed. Dorothy Ross (Baltimore: Johns Hopkins University Press, 1994), 26–53.

# CHAPTER 4

# "You're not just telling us what we wanna hear, are you, boy?"

### H. ARAM VEESER

MY TITLE COMES FROM A SCENE in the film *Raising Arizona*. The warden tells the convict, "You're not just telling us what we wanna hear, are you, boy? 'Cause we don't want to hear that." Mimicry and parroting back stand at the limits between desired compliance and feared parody, not only in prison but also in higher education. I do not wish to suggest that the university resembles a penitentiary: such comparisons insult both inmate populations. Every institution straddles the gap between proper servility and ironic servility. In one of the two books I shall discuss, Richard Rodriguez proclaims himself an imitator, though a reformed one. In the other book, James Traub brands as unevolved mimic men the larger chunk of City College's underprivileged student body.

Traub's attack on mimicry is banal. As the most flagellated of the ancient pedagogical arts, mimicry takes a rough ride in Plato's *Phaedrus*. Beginning with the seventeenth century in England, fears of imitation have run wild. Thus the poet Carew flattered his mentor, John Donne, observing in Donne's poetry "the lazy seeds / Of servile imitation thrown away, / And fresh invention planted."[1] Before Carew's day the English went relatively easy on imitation, and Renaissance schoolteachers were fond of giving pupils imitation exercises, for example, finding 150 ways to say "Thank you for your lovely letter." But by 1700 the cognoscenti tended to agree that "All the art of imitation/Is pilf'ring from the first creation." Plagiarists were attacked for the first time.[2]

That brings up the topic of James Traub's best-selling appraisal of City College, entitled *City on a Hill*. Traub is a journalist who writes features for the *New York Times Magazine*. He has no particular qualifications to write about higher education. "What, no graduate work?" a professor mockingly asks him. Traub traces the story of CCNY's rocky descent into the depths of open admissions. He attends classes and marvels at the students' unserious-ness, attraction to extravagant type fonts, careless attendance habits, ego-centrism, lack of self-knowledge, and mental slowness. About halfway through the book he turns to a fairly typical unprepared student who has somehow succeeded in college. He wants to find out her secret. Traub calls his chapter about this woman "A Miraculous Survivor," and we soon find out why:

> Tammy was quiet and demure, serious, and rail thin. She sat very straight in the chair next to [her counselor] Sternglass, her books resting in her lap. Tammy wore very thick glasses that enlarged her eyes; a straight gold bar across the top obscured the view of the upper part of her face. She looked like the kind of girl you would have met at a church social. Stern-glass, smiling encouragingly, asked Tammy if writing had helped her in the learning process. Tammy brightened, struck by a happy thought. "Oh, yes," she said, "I learned to use these words like 'therefore' and 'more-over.'"
>
> "Really?" asked Sternglass. "How?"
>
> This was a topic that Tammy had given some thought to. "I learned from listening to professors," she said, her vowels stretched out with the faintest traces of a southern accent. "You know what I found out? That teachers really like it if you imitate them. Last year I had this psychology professor who said 'in that,' 'moreover,' and all that kind of thing, so I started using them in my papers. And I got an A. And then I started using those words in all my papers."

Traub's unornamented telling of this tale allows Tammy's strategy to emerge in all its glorious perversion of true education. The learning process has been, for her, not the mastery of a body of knowledge but rather the per-verse imitation of the professor's verbal tics. It's much as though she had learned to clear her throat in just the same timbre as her professor and for that received the grade of A. Traub does not need to comment. His tone says it all. His words for it? "Clever mimicry"—that is, the sort of achievement proper to a parrot or an ape. It's clear that he has just described, by his lights, a monstrous perversion of the learning process.

Traub's attack on Tammy's mimicry joins his other Orientalist asper-sions. Orientalist stereotypes such as "the lazy native" and "the exotic child" all recur frequently in Traub's text. He says that students who had little intelligence or self-application nonetheless prepared immaculate packages of their term papers, all "neatly typed, often in one of the exotic fonts available in the City College printers" (218). He views students the way sophisticated Western anthropologists tend to view Trobriand islanders or the Nuer or aboriginal Australians—that is, by looking down his nose at them. He reads a student's paper and critiques the professor who graded it, for "she had not said, 'Your writing is childish'" (220). Traub would have administered the bracing corrective. Other childish City College students abound, according to Traub. One is Joyce, of whom "It was hard to say whether she had retained the ability to conjure up a child's world or still actually dwelt in such a world" (222). City College students lack energy and are deeply lazy, we learn. But their fatal flaw is their lack of self-knowledge.

Self-knowledge ranks high in the therapized New York intellectual milieu that Traub inhabits. Among his friends and peers, a watery U.S.-patented psychoanalysis passes for deep self-knowledge. Few City College students have reposed for even one hour of their lives while they paid a psychoanalyst to hear them out and discuss their desires and defenses. More than 50 percent nestle below the poverty line ($24,000 per family per year). "And so they paddled along in their egocentricity," laments Traub (219). Traub's psychoanalytic terms—egocentricity and latent (215)—pepper the text and remain undefined. "Amelia's writing was sincere—painfully so—but not egocentric," writes Traub. "Her subject, in fact, was how the dawning of consciousness had drawn her out of herself" (216). He feels so vastly better equipped to address the challenges of anxiety, desire, and development that he can simply dismiss the "unreflective, if heartfelt, narration, the egocentrism that writing theorist Andrea Lunsford has singled out as a sign of the cognitively "immature student" (215). I wish he were misrepresenting Lunsford, but he isn't. The problem is that many compositionists belong to Traub's therapized milieu and think that it's the only life worth living.[3] The very well-meaning Marilyn Sternglass, whose book (which Traub saw in the making) won several awards, also embraces a pedagogical model that posits student-writers' naive self-expressiveness as an unformed, necessary stage on the road to mature—that is, therapeutically informed—self-analysis.[4]

By therapized I mean not the common put-down—"this class is worthless, just emotional therapy"—but rather the New York intellectuals' current common sense. Briefly, therapized means that one has taken the trouble to reflect on one's own self-deceptions, defenses, and resistances to painful truths. Usually this reflection is accomplished with the aid of a licensed psychotherapist, whose time is (as Freud expressed it) leased by the patient. "Since not every sufferer is stable enough, or intelligent enough, to sustain the rigors of the psychoanalytic situation," therapy is a badge of brains and stability.[5]

The therapy model works best for writers such as Henry Louis Gates, Jr., and Richard Rodriguez, who come from an intact nuclear family, wherein the Oedipal drama stabilizes the terms of analysis. Garden-variety, watered-down U.S. psychotherapy has more difficulty coping with the destabilizing, fractured histories that City College students tend to present. Therapy allows for mimicry. By imitating the therapist or another paternal figure, the subject of therapy takes conscious control of his life and breaks away from the family trap. Just that family drama structures *Hunger of Memory: The Education of Richard Rodriguez*. Rodriguez has withstood plenty of criticism; he was an opponent of affirmative action and bilingual education. As a consequence, the right patronized him and the left abused him. But he remained clear-sighted about the ways education transformed him and insists that most of his transformation came about through mere copying.

"I had been submissive, willing to mimic my teachers, willing to re-form myself in order to become 'educated'" (160). Rodriguez explains that mimicry enabled him to move up the social ladder. He was a first-generation scholarship student, son of Mexican parents. In referring back to his pathetic childhood self, his alienation is so great that he chooses the third person. "The scholarship boy is the great mimic," explains Rodriguez, "a collector of thoughts, not a thinker; the very last person in class who ever feels obliged to have an opinion of his own" (67). A scholarship boy's first lesson is self-loathing. Thus, Rodriguez calls himself an intellectual bracero, a stoop laborer in the vineyards of thought, a domestic in the house of European whiteness: "I vacuumed books for epigrams" (64). Even his self-loathing is wonderfully plagiarized. He is following a British sociolinguist who says of the scholarship boy that "He has something of the blinkered pony about him."[6] This like the third person contributes to his anthropological stance toward none other than himself.

One senses that Rodriguez has evolved beyond the imitative self he describes, a self that now seems even to him undeniably weird. This earlier self approximates the accents of his teachers and classmates; "odd too is the effect produced when he uses academic jargon" because "all his ideas are clearly borrowed" (66). His imitations expose him to white scoffing and brown resentment. The effect disturbs his own family although "nothing is said of the silence that comes to separate the scholarship boy from his parents" (68). Soaked in white culture, the boy loses the power to chat at home. Thus, "we tried to make our family conversation seem like more than an interview" (58) but failed. Rodriguez follows the conventional pattern, right down to therapy. He refers to self-revelations that can be made only to strangers. A version of psychoanalytic transference weans him from his family. That's the weaning effect that Traub wishes for City College students. Traub approvingly quotes the student who asks, "will [my parents] ever look into my eyes and think they are looking into the eyes of a stranger?" (222).

To return to Rodriguez, perhaps the most impressive evidence of his new therapized self-consciousness is his wish to rethink gender. "[T]here was something unmanly" about denying his ethnicity, he confesses (129). "I suspected that education was making me effeminate" (127).

Self-consciousness has replaced all these anxieties. Rodriguez thinks his earlier self pathetic. "[S]ome Hispanic students wearing serapes pass by. I needed to laugh at the clownish display. I needed to tell myself that the new minority students were foolish to think themselves unchanged by their schooling" (159). His self-conscious analysis of this "need" suggests that he's beyond such needs now. "If, because of my schooling, I had grown culturally separated from my parents, my education had also given me new ways of speaking and caring about that fact" (72). This condensed and subtle statement could stand as the credo for all of therapized New York.

With this statement, Rodriguez arrives as a therapized New York intellectual. Similar arrivals take place in Traub's therapized world: "Best to admit those limitations and remain conscious of them" (311). Self-consciousness absolves all sins. Rodriguez might well be Traub's ideal of successful therapy.

Rodriguez understands that his mimicry upsets people. The striving-to-succeed scholarship boy "ends up too much like [his teachers and white students] . . . In his pedantry, they trace their own" (69). But he makes little of the threat he himself poses.

We should be clear. Rodriguez wants to absorb and be absorbed. Describing himself in the distant third person, Rodriguez continues. "He lifts an opinion from Coleridge, takes something else from Frye or Empson or Leavis. He even repeats exactly his professor's earlier comment. All his ideas are clearly borrowed. He seems to have no thought of his own. He chatters while his listeners smile—their look one of disdain" (66). One such onlooker would be James Traub, gazing down his nose at the gibbering Tammy.

Through all this progress toward therapized self-consciousness, mimicry acts as both a ladder and a dead weight. Traub quotes a City College student: "I didn't really understand an American history course I was taking, but I got an A. Maybe I had acquired the knowledge without understanding it. And I can read sheet music, but I can't recreate a piece of music from it in my head. Can it be said that I understand the signs on the paper, or am I mimicking yet again?" (318). Mimicry has fallen low even in the mimic's own estimation. This means the mimic has arrived at selfhood.

A fully mature self-consciousness looks back on an imitative, native like childhood. That last sentence forms the template for all minority arrival narratives. It's the template of the contemporary ethnic *bildungsroman*. How did the *bildungsroman* of therapy come to replace the nineteenth-century *bildungsroman* of lost illusions?

Must the educated Western subject leave imitation behind? So it would seem. But other practices have used imitation and mimicry as marks of sophistication. The New Historicism took up modernism's struggle to come to terms with the strange, primitive, ritualistic, and remote. Eliot's *The Waste Land,* Gauguin's South Pacific, Picasso's African sculpture, Orson Welles's voodoo *Macbeth* all address barbaric rites. With Stephen Greenblatt's "Filthy Rites" and "Learning to Curse," New Historicism trumped the modernists. The modernists had either formalized the primitive or contextualized its functions but in any case remained observers paring their fingernails. New Historicism in Greenblatt participated in primitive modes of knowledge.[7] They told stories. Thus, the famous New Historicist elevation of the anecdote to a favored position of scholarly authority. Greenblatt calls himself a "salaried, middle-class shaman" and says he "began with the desire to speak with the dead."[8] Greenblatt imitated the sorcerers and medicine men of the Ojebway Indians and the Scottish Highlanders. His own effigies were of course somewhat different—texts rather than figurines. His genius was to see that the elaborate literary essay from Berkeley, California, was as magical a representation as is a voodoo doll or a Cuna mola. The gap separating Berkeley Ph.D. from the aboriginal shaman diminished, and literary criticism would never be the same again.[9]

The first great difference between mimicry and New York therapy now emerges. Therapy pretends to have unmediated access to the real, whereas mimicry acknowledges the magical properties of every representational act. "The analyst's interpretation calls the analysand's attention to what he is really saying or doing," writes Peter Gay.[10] "Psychoanalytic treatment is founded on truthfulness," wrote Freud (302). Faith like Freud's leads to a naive representational theory. Freud: "The physician should be opaque to the patient and, like a mirror, show nothing but what is shown to him" (303). Freudian practice is much more complex and nuanced than these statements might imply. Unfortunately, it is the unnuanced, simpler version that filters down to Traub and composition theorist Andrea Lunsford.

Simplicity has been triumphantly banished from contemporary literary theory. Two very different meetings of pedagogy and politics come out of Butler and Bhabha. For Butler, one learns a gender more or less as one learns to drive a car. For Bhabha, the oppressed postcolonial peoples learn both to imitate and to parody the occupier. Butler's and Bhabha's imaginative post-Freudian accounts of mirroring and identity formation reveal the less abject, more fecund side of mimicry.

Traub's example of debased mimicry, the woman Tammy, has in Bhabha's sense hit upon a profoundly subversive strategy. That strategy, sometimes called postcolonial mimicry, actually falls somewhere between mimicry and mockery. No matter how perfect the mimic's act of homage and submission to the master, mimicry is also the sign of the inappropriate, "a difference or recalcitrance which . . . poses a threat."[11] Bhabha's instances of colonial imitation "all share . . . a discursive process by which the excess or slippage produced by the *ambivalence* of mimicry (almost the same, *but not quite [the same]*) does not merely 'rupture' the discourse, but becomes transformed into an uncertainty which fixes the colonial subject as a 'partial' presence" (86). Colonial rule succeeds only when mimicry fails; were the mimicry an absolute success, the colonized and the colonizer would merge and become indistinguishable. Thus, "mimicry is at once resemblance and menace" (86). Failure at the heart of a successful practice—not just a hackneyed trope of deconstruction but also a cynosure of basic writing, composition, freshman English.

But Bhabha is referring to the way a dominating power keeps on top, and surely that is not the objective of composition teachers, most of whom are good hearted. Bhabha actually has something more complex in mind. His question is this: "How does mimicry emerge as the subject of the scopic drive and the object of colonial surveillance? How is desire disciplined, authority displaced?" (89). Mimicry flatters but also returns to the colonizer a grotesque, funhouse-mirror image of himself. To quote Bhabha again: " . . . [T]he subject of colonial discourse—splitting, doubling, turning into its opposite, projecting—is a subject of such affective ambivalence and discursive disturbance, that the narrative of English history can only ever beg the 'colonial' question" (97).

Bhabha's words might be tested hypothetically against Tammy's case: "Produced through a strategy of disavowal, the *reference* of discrimination is always to a process of splitting as the condition of subjection: a discrimination between the mother culture and its bastards, the self and its doubles, where the trace of what is disavowed is not repressed by repeated as something *different*—a mutation, a hybrid" (111). Colonial construction of the cultural (the site of the civilizing mission) "is authoritative," Bhabha says, "to the extent to which it is structured around the ambivalence of splitting, denial, repetition—strategies of defense that mobilize culture as an open-textured, warlike strategy whose aim 'is rather a continued agony than a total disappearance of the pre-existing culture'" (114).

This does seem a bit draconian if displaced to the first-year writing classroom. True, Susan Miller has shown that composition was invented at Harvard precisely to keep lower-status kids in their place.[12] But it would be too optimistic to say of composition that (using Bhabha's words) "the display of hybridity—its peculiar 'replication'—terrorizes authority with the *ruse* of recognition, its mimicry, its mockery" (115). And it would be too unfair to composition to charge that it seeks the continued agony of composition students. Composition teachers are often Robin Hoods, the salt of the earth, selfless and bold. It is much too hard on the basic writing teacher to say that "the voice of command is interrupted by questions that arise from these heterogeneous sites and circuits . . . that the colonialist is an exhibitionist, because his *preoccupation* with security makes him "remind the native out loud that these he alone is master . . ."" all this contributing to making the "settler-native boundary an anxious and ambivalent one" (116). We are not settlers in just that way. Nor are the students natives.

Despite Traub's condescension to Tammy, Tammy's mimicry charts a more nuanced, less naively realist epistemology than Traub's therapy. Just a reminder: by therapized I mean those middle-class intellectuals who, smart and self-aware, speak in the full consciousness of their own defenses and resistances—in short, a more-or-less accurate psychoanalyticese. I do not mean the put-down, "Expressive writing is just emotional therapy." Tammy's is not, however, a specifically post*colonial* mimicry. Postcolonial in Bhabha's sense overstates the ambivalence, hybridity, and destabilizing force of Tammy's innocuous discovery of "in that," "moreover," "therefore," and other pompous academicisms. Tammy's successes represent the people's ability to occupy that occult zone between anthropologist and native. Like Greenblatt, Tammy has mastered not one discourse but two. Unlike Rodriguez, she has forsaken neither the nativist idiom nor the middle-class one. Tammy's almost magical intuitions, her theatrics of language, her shamanism of images expose the inadequacies of Traub's therapeutic model and Sternglass's theory of stages. Paradoxically, Tammy's sorcererlike imitations have their sources in the monuments of Roman and Renaissance pedagogy: Quintillian and Erasmus. Unaided by Sternglass or Lunsford, Tammy had to invent her own composition pedagogy, and irony of ironies, it turned out to be canonical.

## NOTES

1. "Elegy upon the Death of Dr. John Donne," Thomas Carew, *The Poems of Thomas Carew; with his masque,* Coelum Britannicum, ed. Rhodes Dunlap (Oxford: Clarendon Press, 1957).

2. Imitation and plagiarism had an entirely positive charge in classical pedagogy from Quintilian through the Renaissance humanists. See Edward P. J. Corbett, *Classical Rhetoric for the Modern Student* (New York: Oxford University Press, 1965). Quintilian's famous *Institutes* centered writing instruction on imitation. Imitation poses some interesting problems (unless, like Traub, one is dead to subtlety). For example, the most influential pedagoue of the humanist era, Desideratus Erasmus, devised a series of exercises based on imitation. In his best-selling little book, *De duplici copia verborum ac rerum,* Erasmus gave students 150 ways to say "Your letter has delighted me very much" (*Tuae literae me magnopere delectarunt*). Some of the ways were good—"Your epistle has cheered me greatly"—and some were less satisfactory: "When your letter came, I was seized with an extraordinary pleasure." Copying prose and imitating sentence patterns are a staple of foreign language teaching. Testimonials to the value of imitation come from luminaries as varied as Benjamin Franklin, Somerset Maugham, Malcolm X, Richard Rodriguez, Judith Butler, and Homi Bhabha.

3. Lyn Worsham usefully explains why a more radical road could not be taken. See her "Writing against Writing: The Predicament of *Ecriture Feminine* in Composition Studies," *Contending with Words: Composition and Rhetoric in a Postmodern Age,* ed. John Schilb and Patricia Harkin (New York: The Modern Language Association of America, 1991), 82–104. Composition steered clear of French Feminist theories of *l' ecriture feminine* because Cixous, Irigaray, Wittig, and others had too revolutionary and political a message.

4. Marilyn S. Sternglass, *Time to Know Them: A Longitudinal Study of Writing and Learning at the College Level* (London and Mahwah, NJ: Lawrence Erlbaum Associates, Publishers, 1977). Sternglass's book was the winner of MLA's 1998 Mina P. Shaughnessy Prize.

5. Peter Gay, *Freud: A Life for Our Time* (New York and London: W. W. Norton, 1988, 1998), 295. I offer a nontechnical definition of therapy since Traub and other intellectuals, all laypeople, have a nontechnical grasp of psychotherapy.

6. Richard Rodriguez, *Hunger of Memory: The Education of Richard Rodriguez: An Autobiography* (Boston, MA: D. R. Godine, 1981). Rodriquez writes "All quotations in this chapter are from Richard Hoggart, *The Uses of Literacy* (London: Chatto and Windus, 1957), chapter 10," (p. 47, footnote).

7. See Richard Halpern, "Shakespeare in the Tropics: From High Modernism to New Historicism," *Representations* 45 (Winter 1994): 1–25.

8. Stephen Greenblatt, *Shakespearean Negotiations: The Circulation of Social Energy in Renaissance England* (Berkeley and Los Angeles: The University of California Press, 1988), p. 1.

9. See also Michael Taussig, *Mimesis and Alterity: A Particular History of the Senses* (New York and London: Routledge, 1993): "[C]an't we say that *to give an example, to instantiate, to be concrete,* are all examples of the magic of mimesis wherein the replication, the copy, acquires the power of the represented? . . . Just as the shaman captures and creates power by making a model of the gringo spirit-ship and its crew, so here the ethnographer is making her model" (16).

10. Peter Gay, *Freud: A Life for Our Time* (New York and London: W. W. Norton, 1988, 1998), 298. The Freud quotes in this chapter are taken from Gay, *Freud*; see pp. 302–3.

11. Homi Bhabha, *The Location of Culture* (New York and London: Routledge, 1994), p. 86.

12. Susan Miller, *Textual Carnivals: The Politics of Composition* (Carbondale and Edwardsville: Southern Illinois University Press, 1991), pp. 48–76. See also Gerald Graff, *Professing Literature: An Institutional History* (Chicago: University of Chicago Press, 1987), pp. 38–44.

# CHAPTER 5

# *Pulp Theory: On Literary History*

PAULA RABINOWITZ

## DILETTANTE SCHOLAR

I AM A WANNABE HISTORIAN, let me begin with this confession, but I know the profession would never have me: I was told as much by an eminent historian early in my graduate career. However, I had already divined this years before Professor von X barred me from his course on American social history. It was this knowledge that had originally sent me to American Studies classes in the 1960s, because I was a woman who loved fiction too much—couldn't imagine a history without it. I could never make up my mind which story was better—truth or artifice; and because I, like Norman Mailer, could not see how one could answer the question "Why are we in Vietnam?" without reading American history and literature together, I decided to ignore their differences. I became unfit for the disciplined rigors of the academy—interdisciplinary studies being really just a fancy way of saying dilettantism.

My essay sketches some thoughts on literary history—in both senses of the term: the history of literary works and movements, and the imaginative fictions daring to rewrite history. These are the thoughts of a dilettante, neither historian nor literary critic, who often finds herself drawn more to the marginalia and footnotes of the used books I buy than the main story. Because virtually my entire intellectual career has been enmeshed in women's studies, I focus specifically on women's literary historiography and the place of women's historical fiction in contemporary feminist political debate. The questions I explore concern the relations among feminist historiography, feminist literature, feminist theory, and feminist politics, all of which seem to be verging on collapse from intellectual exhaustion. My central question asks how fiction writes history or, to use the editor's frame: What can poetry (the literary use of language) do for politics (the social organization of people), especially now, in a context in which the terms of public discourse are severely limited to a range somewhere between "New Democrats" and the religious right and the cultural iconography to describe politics draws its force from pulp fiction? To do so, I look at the ways in which three recent novels by women who are clearly "feminist" writers have been read by mainstream critics.[1] I mean to investigate what we do when we do criticism as much as how critical parameters limit the scope of fiction, and of politics.

We want to cling to a distinction between truth and artifice—between document and fiction, between history and literature, politics and poetics. Why? On the one hand, critics want a fiction of well-rounded characters; who knows why? Perhaps because they were taught in some dreary literature (or worse, creative writing) class that this is the basis of great fiction. Contemporary novels must present plausible—that is, a plotted—psychology, psychology without an unconscious, and they must deal in recognizable subject matter, topics such as abuse, abortion, alcoholism. On the other hand, historians seek causes in changing political, economic, social formations and expect a rational story to unfold. Ho-hum. "The novel," writes Don DeLillo, "is the dream release, the suspension of reality that history needs to escape its own brutal confinements."[2] The problem of troubling categories is that the act forces a realignment in the direction of indeterminacy, a fall down the rabbit hole to a place where conventions are overturned and the training in a field found inadequate. Unless feminist pedagogy resists these disciplinary prescriptions by forcing open the messy possibilities of contradiction and overdetermination (to quote Althusser quoting Freud), it is doomed to fail dismally.

Three recent novels by American women take their subjects from historical figures and incidents—Toni Morrison's *Beloved* (1987), Frances Sherwood's *Vindication* (1993) and Joanna Scott's *Arrogance* (1990)—to circulate feminist theory within contemporary culture.[3] These books, as literary histories, allow us to think about why writing historical narratives or narrating writerly histories offers us a politics for and a history of the present. These works are all dilettantes' histories—works by those "lovers of the fine arts," those "refusers of a profession," rank "amateurs," "parasites," to quote from some of the citations found in the *Oxford English Dictionary.* Novelists are really counterfeit dilettantes (the true ones being artists or musicians and their fans), which makes them more even likely to tell the truth than those in the profession of truth-telling: "I'm suspicious about the nature of history or biography, and what really happened and what didn't happen," says Frances Sherwood. "The biographers might rely on Mary's letters, but have you ever written a letter that was a lie? I have."[4] Critics severely chastised each author—even as they praised each for her poetic erudition—for wholesale "fiction-mongering," lying, tampering with the historical record, such as it is, then meddling in the politically correct.[5] The controversies surrounding these novels point to the uneasiness with which we approach those transgressors of boundaries—be they poets, dilettantes, or feminists.

Let me begin with an earlier "second-wave" feminist excursion into literary history: Anne Stevenson's "family history in letters" (as it is subtitled) *Correspondences,* whose title plays on the doubled meaning of the word—epistles back and forth and the reverberations between one set of representatives and others. Her saga of two hundred years of New England's women's crises over family, work, money, and thwarted dreams of creative expression and sexual desire plays with an actual archival source found in the barn of her family's Vermont farmhouse. Her poems rewrite the letters she found moldering there to appear truly authentic by mimicking eighteenth- and nineteenth-century diction and including the archivist's footnotes (in the form of marginalia detailing damage by fire, water, or rodents). As the poems move into and through the twentieth century, various poetic styles are picked up and discarded as first one then another generation of women suffers humiliation at the hands of mothers and lovers, editors and husbands.

The long confessional poem dated 1954, before Betty Friedan named the problem that had no name, written by one of the last heirs of the dynasty to her mother and posted from a state mental institution, offers a typical 1950s explanation for abandoning her daughter—"they think you're to blame."[6] However, Stevenson's family history concludes with a 1972 letter from this same woman, now renamed after her divorce and an expatriate writer, to her estranged father: "It is a poem I can't continue. / It is America I can't contain" (p. 88). These private episodes of loss cannot contain the nation; yet they are precisely the stuff of 1970s feminist revisions of American political discourse.

The tradition of Marxist-feminist criticism argues for the importance of analyzing both social and literary texts as complementary, interruptive and sometimes competing narratives, suggesting that literary scholarship must never forget social relations. How could it? Even the most personal confessions, those that "can't continue . . . can't contain," failing at Whitman's democratic "I am large. I contain multitudes," seek voices, reveal nations, in caches of secret and hidden documents that are the heart of contemporary feminist historical inquiry. We write literary history not to escape or forget the troubling geography in which the clipping or the letter or the drawing now dwells but precisely to detail this climate as well as its earlier one. Situating a book in history or fancying literature from history—doing both kinds of literary history—reveals the past and so enables a close reading of the present.

When Stevenson came upon the cache of family letters in the early 1970s, women's historians were busily reinventing the discipline of history to include and understand such private forms as the diary or letter as legitimate data—seen then as a window on that supposedly separate sphere of woman: private life. Recently, Felicity Nussbaum has argued that the construction of the private self in those diaries and letters is paramountly a public and political act enabling enlightenment subjectivity and so empire, capitalist accumulation—the big stuff of politics and economics. At a time when feminist historians find the public/private split useless, is it any wonder that feminist novelists pick up history—that no longer exclusive realm of public truth—for their fiction? Or more accurately, can we be surprised that they turn again to historical fiction to argue contemporary political issues?

## BELOVED, ARROGANCE, AND VINDICATION

Toni Morrison took what had been a footnote in histories of the slave community—Margaret Garner's murder of her child (which she found in Angela Davis's citation of Herbert Aptheker's offhanded remark published in a Communist Party USA journal during the cold-war years)—as the center of her massive novel about the secret heart of the nation—slavery and racism—and spun pages and pages of sensuous description of clothing, food, work, tools, instruments of torture.[7] Certain critics faulted her for not leaving these "unspeakable things unspoken."[8] When Morrison tapped the mind of the enslaved mother she provided a counterhistory for Davis's footnote—as well as to the gap in Frederick Douglass's narrative (one of the sources for *Beloved*) about his mother's absence: "I do not recollect of ever seeing my mother by the light of day. She was with me in the night. She would lie down with me, and get me to sleep, but long before I waked she was gone. Very little communication ever took place between us . . . Never having enjoyed, to any considerable extent, her soothing presence, her tender and watchful care, I received the tidings of her death with much the same emotions I should have probably felt at the death of a stranger."[9] Morrison was savaged, much as Zora Neale Hurston had been during the 1930s, for staging a minstrel show in prose, pandering to the sensational desires of a mass white public—in this case, a white feminist one.

Because *Beloved* focuses on "what a woman suffers as a slave," motherhood and maternity—the emotions, but also the legalities of blood bonds, ownership and parental rights, and the racialist implications of reproduction and property rights—and the gothic residue of racialist sexuality became central.[10] The novel linked the history of American racism and the legacy of slavery to contemporary debates on abortion, welfare, teen pregnancy, which have galvanized the new right in its backlash against the movements for liberation among African Americans and other racial minorities and among women and gays of all races. Morrison's novel investigates questions about legitimate and illegitimate mothering, about the work of the reproductive body in the political economy of America, about the discomfort female sexuality elicits within a patriarchal culture. Its presentism, its conscious "design to placate sentimental feminist ideology," (and critical theoretical) controversies left it open to political attack. Critic Stanley Crouch denounced its "melodrama," its "biblical grandeur." Because its supernatural elements moved it out of the realm of history into that of spectacle, Crouch likened Morrison's politics and poetics to those of "P. T. Barnum."[11]

Lest it appear that only critics at *The New Republic* express outrage with a novelist who tampers with history, Margaret Forster, the feminist biographer of Daphne Du Maurier, revealed a surprisingly similar panic a few years later about Frances Sherwood's *Vindication*. Frances Sherwood's stunning 1993 novel so provoked its *New York Times Book Review* critic that she felt compelled to warn readers that the story of Mary Wollstonecraft being told by Sherwood was not verifiable. But truth is not really what was at issue. In her biography *Love, Anarchy and Emma Goldman,* Candace Falk revealed that the 1970s feminist heroine had been the love slave of Ben Reitman. Doing the work that feminist historians do, Falk had discovered a cache of letters between the anarchist and the hobo in the archives of the Bancroft Library at the University of California at Berkeley. These same sources from private life—diaries and letters—have been the means feminist historians use to place women as a subject in history. However, it seemed from the response to Falk's research that they attain value only if they reinforce "positive images" about women. With few exceptions,

Falk's disclosure about Goldman's "sexual slavery" (the title of Kathy Barry's 1978 book), coming as it did at the height of the feminist sex wars, were met with outrage by feminists.

Unlike Falk, whose facts debunked some kind of feminist hero-worship about how the personal was political, Sherwood's crime was to embellish the scanty facts and question why we think personal life corresponds to political action at all. Damned if you do, damned if you don't. Forster's concerns center around three distressing scenes in Sherwood's novel—Wollstonecraft's slippage into madness after her breakup with Henry Fusili, her pleasure as an s/m bottom, and her abuse of her first-born daughter, Fanny. None of these incidents, asserts Forster, could possibly have occurred: "Mary Wollstonecraft? Whipped? It's just as likely that she would have snatched the whip and turned it on him," she declares in a huff.[12] That Sherwood's novel takes liberties, if you will, with Wollstonecraft's life and art (Mary Wollstonecraft was after all not only a historian, political theorist, and journalist but a novelist herself) in order to discuss what the reviewer for the *Library Journal* notes as "so many trendy topics—child abuse, mental illness, homosexuality, and drug addiction—without departing from the basic facts" is precisely what makes the novel convincing as a literary history.[13] And if one takes seriously complaints about biographies and their failure to bring their subjects to life, it is clear that only novelists might be able to animate "the indirect author/hero of this mess."[14]

What else is historiography but a continual revision? Forster's sense that history is cheapened when called to serve the present as if it has sold itself like some bar maid is akin to Crouch's anger at Morrison's appeal to the "ideology . . . [of] the black woman as the most scorned and rebuked of victims." In her own justification of the liberties taken with literary decorum, however, Wollstonecraft argued, "I have rather endeavoured to pourtray [*sic*] passions than manners. . . . I could have made the incidents more dramatic [but] would have sacrificed my main object, the desire of exhibiting the misery and oppression, peculiar to women, that arise out of the partial laws and customs of society. In the invention of the *story*, this view *restrained* my fancy; and the *history* ought to be considered, as of woman, than of an individual."[15] Wollstonecraft's last piece of writing fails as a novel according to critic Moira Ferguson because it returns to her treatise on education, coming full circle to reproduce the effect of a political exhortation; in other words, it is not about a character but about a class, womankind.[16] For Wollstonecraft, however, the novel served as a pedagogical tool; another vehicle by which she could traffic in the political arguments of her day. The reviewer for London's *New Statesman and Society* ultimately champions Wollstonecraft's didactic fiction over Sherwood's fabulation: "If we are Wollstonecraft, then she is us, and the conclusion is somehow much more presumptuous than the premise."[17] But why must this be so? Both these authors narrate a feminism that complicates the picture of woman's story and history by depicting women as victims or more dangerously exonerating them as victimizers or more damning still suggesting that they may be both at the same time, constructing, as reviewer Loraine Fletcher calls it, "a feminist continuous present." By participating in contemporary political debates through literary history, Sherwood embraces Wollstonecraft's (and indeed feminism's) best history; but the slippage among genres so common in the eighteenth century is highly questionable these days.

   *Vindication* airs many of the dark corners of this continuous contradiction, such as the noncongruence between ideology and desire as played out in the sex debates of the 1980s. Until recently, with the publication of books by Nadine Strossen, Sally Tisdale, and Katha Pollitt, Sherwood's novel was one of the few mainstream publications to push a so-called pro-sex line.[18] The feminist antiporn argument received wide attention in the mass-marketed form of Andrea Dworkin's tome, *Intercourse;* it was mainstreamed by feminist slicks such as *Ms.* and rarefied by the academic credentials of Catherine MacKinnon.[19] However, the feminist anticensorship and pro-sex arguments circulated work by Pat Califia, Alice Echols, Suzie Bright, and Carol Vance only within small presses and little magazines—Cleis Press, Monthly Review Press, *On Our Backs.*[20] *Vindication* is a history of the present dressed up, in perfect period costume, as a historical fiction from the eighteenth century. If *Vindication* is a history of the present, then of course Wollstonecraft is us. Yet foremothers' names are not to be sullied; women's history celebrates remarkable and exceptional women. To suggest that an Amazon such as Wollstonecraft may have harbored a less-than-PC set of desires is troubling within today's backlash world. Sherwood's Wollstonecraft takes her cues from the current controversies about pornography, s/m, butch/femme animating, or rather rupturing, feminism.

   Joanna Scott's 1990 novel pivots on Viennese artist Egon Schiele's twenty-four day prison sentence in 1912 for "disseminating indecent drawings and endangering public morality." These charges were the only ones to stick after he was accused of abducting a young peasant girl who had posed for his life drawings of nude girls masturbating and embracing.[21] Schiele's case, tried in the village of Neulengbach, was no *cause célèbre* in pre-war Austria, but Scott effectively distills the events preceding and following his arrest to elaborate her rococo meditation on his obsessive artistic genius. The novel is narrated retrospectively by the young girl but relies often on the voice of Schiele's model and lover of the time. Taking these few weeks as the central instance in the artist's short life, Scott composes a novel which explores the political history of *fin-de-siècle* Vienna.

As in the other examples, Scott stretches a footnote into a full-length alternative history of the artist and his city.[22] Art historians usually hurry over the "tragic time" of Schiele's imprisonment, minimizing and even dismissing the grim and clearly political poetry his self-portraits made in his cell.[23] Intent on viewing Schiele as "one of the most normal" people whose life "was relatively eventless," critics declare in no way was he a "rebel" rather he was only concerned with his art, which, figurative and erotic, to be sure, is devoid of any spatial fix orienting the pictures.[24] However, as curator James Demetrios has implied, precisely because these works are aberrations in Schiele's career—they are dated and titled, and the figures appear in spatial contexts—they should be seen as significant; they interrupt the more purely formalist considerations dominating art history in general and Schiele criticism in particular.[25] These twelve charcoal, pencil, and watercolor studies of the artist curled under thin blankets on his bare cot are captioned with such inflammatory titles as "To Confine the Artist Is a CRIME, It MEANS MURDERING UNBORN LIFE" or "For My Art I Will Gladly Endure to the END."

Of course, because Scott chooses to focus on the trial and imprisonment of the artist for pornography, one can hardly miss her very contemporary references to arts' funding and censorship controversies circulating around the Cincinnati Art Museum's exhibit of Robert Mapplethorpe's photography, Andres Serrano's "Piss Christ," performance artists Karen Finley, Holly Hughes and the rest of the NEA Four, and other cases that figured so prominently in the sexual hysteria of the Reagan/Bush years. Again, Scott's exaggerated literary history provides a device for probing the present. Like the others, she pushes fiction into an argument with biography. And like them, Scott was chastised by critics who could not fault the novel's "sensuous, provocative patterns" detailed through "rich experiences, intriguing perceptions," because she failed to "bring either Schiele or his art to life" being "more . . . a treatise than a novel, it's often bulk with exposition, and perilously short on active characters and dramatic scenes."[26]

## CORRESPONDENCES

Even if critics have had a rough time recognizing the singular contributions of these women's literary histories, I hope I have made it clear that the novels borrow from a feminist literary tradition operative since Wollstonecraft. Feminist literary history emerges on the threshold between the unwritten and the rewritten.[27] Like Walter Benjamin's angel of history, this angle on history ever looks over its shoulders even as it plants itself firmly in the present only to blown forward by the storms of complaint.

Anne Stevenson's verse history reimagined America from the perspective of those just barely outside its center—middle-class WASP women—and returns the novel to its epistolary origins, even as she pushed the limits of poetic diction into everyday vernacular. The many women who write most of these letters are shown to be willful, contemptible, self-involved, racist, pathetic, anguished; they speak of money, violence, war, civil unrest, madness, sex, children and poetry, tracing how families produce and reproduce themselves. In short, they survey all the debates raging among feminists during the late 1960s and 1970s.

Unraveling family and, by extension, social history through the discovered cache of letters hanging like the Moor's shriveled head at which the young Orlando aims his make-believe lance in the chilly attic of his ancestral home formed Josephine Herbst's 1930s Trexler trilogy.[28] Herbst's one-hundred-year saga of her family's struggle to achieve and maintain middle-class stability developed from the stories Herbst heard her mother tell during long hours spent hiding in storm shelters against the tornadoes of western Iowa. Her mother's stories, retold by Anne Trexler, were kept alive through her words, but their veracity depended on the "bags of old letters hanging from the rafter like beheaded corpses as if the written works of the dead somehow pledged the family to immortality."[29] Letters in the attic, mildewed and moth-eaten, keep memory and history alive. They legitimize the secret history of any family lucky enough to possess a house, eventually becoming the sources for subsequent social histories once their location has been discovered and their secrets are deposited in the archives for future generations of scholars to peruse. The novelist has privileged access to this source of family immortality, of history—her letters may even be among those saved. Herbst obliquely makes this point by including excerpts of her own reportage, often written in the form of letters to *The New Masses* from various sites of struggle: foreclosed farms and dairy cooperatives in the Midwest; sugarcane workers' soviets in Realengo, Cuba; the anti-Nazi underground in Berlin. These documentary narratives shore up the literary history of postbellum America encapsulated in the Trexler saga.

As Woolf and Herbst knew, stealing the words of one's forebears provides fodder for exactly the kind of story most fitting for modernist narrative—internal psychic states. Hart Crane reveals her secret affair in his poem, "My Grandmother's Love Letters," which were "pressed so long / Into a corner of the roof/ That they are brown and soft, / And liable to melt as snow."[30] Discovered, we learn from his biographer, in the secret hideout Crane found for his boyhood masturbation, they let us in more on the author's desires than his grandmother's.[31] Crane's discovery of his grandmother's secret literary history, "hung by an invisible white hair," then rummaged in the family archives of the attic, updates an American Gothic convention—revealing the secret of the purloined letter or the custom house.[32] Stevenson, like Herbst, shifted the modernist focus from the secret reader of letters to the saga they narrated, returning to Hawthorne's romance, turning private dispatch into a political diatribe.

## AMONG FOOTNOTES

I came across *Correspondences* a few years ago in a small poetry bookshop in Ann Arbor, Michigan shortly after finishing Janet Malcolm's *New Yorker* piece on Sylvia Plath; Malcolm profiles Plath's "authorized" biographer, the expatriate poet Anne Stevenson.[33] In *The Silent Women,* Malcolm charges biographers with violence and theft, accusing them of wholesale self-interested fiction-mongering in the name of crass self-promotion or overbearing ideology.[34] She does not spare herself (How could she? The essay appeared in the midst of the Jeffrey Masson trial); ultimately she self-servingly links her story with Anne Stevenson's and so with Plath's, assuring her place in this pantheon. Both Stevenson and Plath were American expatriate poets living in Britain during the straitlaced 1950s and early 1960s; each deserted her children—Plath carefully stuffing the cracks under their door after depositing milk and cookies in their room before turning on the gas oven, Stevenson running off to Scotland with her lover and diving into a bottle; each forged poetry out of these crises. Only Malcolm remains clean: she was merely an envious Michigan co-ed in the 1950s, jealous of the brilliant Stevenson, who won a Hopwood Award for poetry the year their paths crossed.

As it happened, Stevenson was in residence for a week at Ann Arbor—

reading from her new volume of poetry and recounting the tribulations of doing literary biography—when I, a former Hopwood winner, happened to have been in pursuit of Stevenson's 1974 volume, to which Malcolm had alerted me. At her book signing, she told the proprietor of Shaman Drum Books that her sister still owned the barn in which the correspondences were kept and might still have few copies of the long out-of-print edition moldering there. On a trip through New England later that month he found two and kept one for himself, and I was lucky enough to buy the other. So now I, too, self-servingly can fix a place for myself in this complex web of literary fictions, histories, and biographies.

As it was meant to, *Correspondences* has led me to me and my work as a literary historian.[35] This essay examines how the literary can use history to argue (feminist) politics; I have left out the other side of the equation: how histories of literature invariably succumb to their political cultures; so let me conclude briefly with yet another literary history—my own. My attempt to rewrite the literary histories of American radicalism, women's writing, and modernism has resulted in my becoming a minor footnote in literary history: virtually no book on the 1930s can avoid noting that an enormous body of writing by and about working-class women confounds the conventional readings of literary modernism (as bourgeois) or of literary radicalism (as antifeminist) or of feminism during the interwar years (as dead); yet these concluding footnotes are often tagged on to most authors' well-developed arguments without altering them.[36] This used to trouble me greatly. Only now do I understand that it takes a long time before a footnote enters the political unconscious to generate a new (as in novel) narrative.

Undoing literary history means reinterpreting and rewriting narrative, reinscribing and reimagining history, recasting the terms that set particularity and totality apart, insisting on maintaining a divide between literature and history, poetics and politics not by revaluing one over the other but by interrupting the plot that sets the two apart. As much as history shapes lived experience, narrative structures life histories or at least their telling. We live and narrate as historical subjects: not only do we make our own history under circumstances not of our making; we tell our own stories within forms not of our invention. The divide between the literary and the historical is fluid; and it is within this permeable boundary that literary history can engage politics. When women write themselves into history and thus become political subjects, it is often through fictional devices, filling in the unspoken gaps and relying on narrative conventions learned from poetry and fiction more than from politics.

Marion Marzolf's 1970s revisionary history of women in journalism is entitled *Up from the Footnotes*—up, presumably, from the obscurity of copyediting to the bylines.[37] The title celebrates women's collective surfacing from a submerged depth—from fashion pages and Miss Lonelyhearts columns to hard news reporting. But it is among footnotes that literary invention and historical reinvention commence—footnotes being the equivalent of intellectuals' gossip columns as much as vessels for the detritus of knowledge—so the triumphant rise to visibility entails a loss when previously hidden stories surface only to become codified themselves. Still, these will inevitably generate new footnotes and with them new political movements requiring still more novel literary histories twisting the past.

## Notes

1. See Rita Felski, *Beyond Feminist Aesthetics: Feminist Literature and Social Change* (Cambridge, MA: Harvard University Press, 1989) on the various strategies feminist writers have used to enter the social.

2. Don DeLillo, "The Power of History,"*The New York Times Magazine* (September 7, 1997): 60–63, p. 62.

3. I do not want to imply that only women novelists are engaged in dilettante historiography—clearly E. L. Doctorow (*Ragtime* and *The Book of Daniel*), Gore Vidal (*Hollywood, Burr,* and the America cycle), Don DeLillo (*Libra*), and Robert Coover (*The Public Burning*), to name just a few, see "the force of history" as De Lillo puts it, as the province of fiction. However, the works I consider seem to be doing more than the already mammoth task of setting the writer's "pleasure, his eros, his creative delight in language and his sense of self-preservation against the vast and uniform Death that history tends to fashion as its most enduring work." (De Lillo, p. 63). They are allowing the psychological expansiveness of fiction not only to reanimate the past but to intervene in the present.

4. Diane Prenatt, "Interview with Frances Sherwood," *Belles Lettres: A Review of Books by Women* 10 (Spring 1995): 22–26, p. 26.

5. Emerson condemned Hawthorne's "fiction-mongering" as unworthy of the philosophical questions with which he was concerned. Thanks to Mark Penka for pointing this out.

6. Anne Stevenson, *Correspondences* (Middletown, CT: Wesleyan University Press, 1974), p. 70.

7. Davis quotes Herbert Aptheker's passing comment that "[O]ne may better understand now a Margaret Garner, fugitive slave, who, when trapped near Cincinnati, killed her own daughter and tried to kill herself. She rejoiced that the girl was dead—" 'now she would never know what a woman suffers as a slave' "—and pleaded to be tried for murder. " 'I will go singing to the gallows rather than be returned to slavery.' " Angela Davis, *Women, Race and Class* (New York: Random House, 1981), p. 21; Herbert Aptheker, "The Negro Woman", in *Masses and Mainstream* 11 (February 1948): 12.

8. Toni Morrison, "Unspeakable Things Unspoken: The Afro-American Presence in American Literature," *Michigan Quarterly Review* 28 (Winter 1989): 1–34.

9. Frederick Douglass, *Narrative of the Life of Frederick Douglass, An American Slave, Written by Himself* (1845; rpt. Garden City, New York: Dolphin Books, 1963), p. 2.

10. The vexed and strange interrelationship of fiction and history within slave women's literary cultures includes as well the research by Jean Fagin Yellin into Harriet Jacobs's *Incidents in the Life of a Slave Girl, Written by Herself,* thus authorizing it as a genuine slave narrative, not merely the sentimental fiction presumed by literary historians. Because the conventions of the sentimental novel were more clearly recognizable within Jacobs's narrative than within that of Douglass (though his tale relies on virtually every coding of the sentimental, also), her story was viewed with suspicion by generations of scholars. Hers is surely a bizarre, even gothic, story; but the tale seemed fantastic because it conformed to popular narrative forms.

11. Stanley Crouch "Aunt Medea," review of *Beloved, The New Republic* 19 (October 1987): 38–48. See also Marilyn Judith Atlas, "Toni Morrison's *Beloved* and the Reviewers," *Midwestern Miscellany* 18 (1990): 45–57, for a comprehensive reading of the various responses to the novel.

12. Margaret Forster, "This Is Sort of Your Life, Mary Wollstonecraft," *New York Times Book Review* (July 11, 1993): 21.

13. Edward B. St. John, review of *Vindication, Library Journal* 118 (March 15, 1993): 109.

14. Stendhal writing of the scandal surrounding the attempted murder of his daughter-in-law by the Baron de Pontalba and his subsequent suicide, quoted in Angeline Goreau, "A Spectacular Mess of a Marriage," review of *Intimate Enemies: The Two Worlds of the Baroness de Pontalba* by Christina Vella, *New York Times Book Review* (August 31, 1997): 6–7, p. 6. Goreau concludes her favorable review of the biography by longing "for a novelist who could explore the intricate workings of motivation, who could trace the see-sawings of power and control, who could ask the tricky question of who the 'author' of this family's story finally was" (p. 7).

15. Mary Wollstonecraft, "Author's Preface," *Maria or The Wrongs of Woman* (1798, rpt. New York: W. W. Norton, 1975) p. 7 (emphasis added).

16. See Moira Ferguson's Introduction to Wollstonecraft, *Maria,* esp. p. 20.

17. Loraine Fletcher, Review of *Vindication, New Statesman and Society* 6 (June 4, 1993): 40.

18. Katha Pollitt, *Reasonable Creatures: Essays on Woman and Feminism*

(New York: Knopf, 1994); Sallie Tisdale, *Talk Dirty to Me: An Intimate Philosophy of Sex* (New York: Doubleday, 1994); Nadine Strossen, *Defending Pornography: Free Speech, Sex and the Fight for Women's Rights* (New York: Scribners, 1995). All reviewed in *The Nation* (February 20, 1996).

19. Andrea Dworkin, *Pornography: Men Possessing Women* (New York: Putnam, 1981) and *Intercourse* (New York: Free Press, 1987); *Ms.* "Is One Woman's Sexuality Another Woman's Pornography?" (April 1985).

20. The 1980s sex debates were often far more vicious than the relatively balanced term *debate* would suggest. Some of the decades's key texts promoting the "pro-sex line" include: Angela Carter, *The Sadeian Woman and the Ideology of Pornography* (New York: Pantheon, 1978); *Heresies* #12 "Sex Issue" (1981); *Diary of a Conference on Sexuality,* "The Scholar and the Feminist," Barnard Women's Center, 1982; Sue Cartledge and Joanna Ryan, *Sex & Love: New Thoughts on old Contradictions* (London: The Women's Press, 1983); Ann Snitow, Christine Stansell, and Sharon Thompson, ed., *Powers of Desire: The Politics of Sexuality* (New York: Monthly Review Press, 1983); Carole Vance, ed., *Pleasure and Danger: Exploring Female Sexuality* (Boston and London: Routledge and Kegan Paul, 1984); Jane Root, *Pictures of Women: Sexuality* (London: Pandora Press, 1984; Varda Burstyn, ed., *Women Against Censorship* (Vancouver and Toronto: Douglas & McIntyre, 1985); Joan Nestle, *A Restricted Country* (Ithaca, NY: Firebrand Books, 1987). Note the relative obscurity of these publications. See Paula Rabinowitz, "Ethnographies of Women: *Soft Fiction* and Feminist Theory," in *They Must Be Represented: The Politics of Documentary* (London: Verso, 1994), pp. 157–175, for an account of the ways in which the sex debates played out women's experimental films. More current (and mainstream) conservative/libertarian reinventions include Camille Paglia, *Sex, Art and American Culture: Essays* (New York: Vintage, 1992) and *Vamps and Tramps: New Essays* (New York: Vintage, 1994); Katie Roiphe, *The Morning After: Sex, Fear, and Feminism* (Boston: Back Bay Books, 1993).

21. Erwin Mitsch, *The Art of Egon Schiele,* trans. W. Keith Haughan (London: Phaidon Press, 1975), pp. 34–35.

22. Michiko Kakutani's predictably less-than-enthusiastic review was entitled "Portrait of a Tortured Artist in a Tortured City," *New York Times* (July 27, 1990) Sec. C, p. 25.

23. The only critical essay on his prison work is Alessandra Comini, "Egon Schiele in Prison," *Albertina-Studien* 4 (1974): 123–137. All of the images are reproduced in Erwin Mitsch, *Egon Schiele in der Albertina* (Graphische Sammlung Albertina, 1990.

24. Serge Sabarsky, *Egon Schiele* (New York: Rizzoli, 1985), pp. 8–9.

25. James T. Demetrios, *Egon Schiele and the Human Form: Drawings and Watercolors* (Des Moines: Des Moines Art Center, 1971). After describing Schiele's coded inscriptions, however, Demetrios makes a point of not including any of the prison images in the show. It is not clear why, but the show's title stresses "form."

26. *Times'* reviewers on both sides of the Atlantic concurred in their estimations of the novel. Scott Bradfield, "Onan and Egon," *New York Times Book Review* (August 19, 1990): 14, said the first and third things quoted in this sentence. Neil Taylor, review of *Arrogance, Times Literary Supplement* (July 26, 1991): 20, said the second.

27. Nancy Armstrong and Joan Scott have jointly swept away any logical reasons for retaining the distinctions among feminist scholars. Each has laid bare the underlying assumptions shoring up women's literature on the one hand and women's history on the other. With feminist literary critics such as Felicity Nussbaum arguing that the private expressions of self by eighteenth-century bourgeois women through diaries and autobiographies helped codify middle-class subjectivity, and feminist social historians such as Linda Gordon claiming the working-class home as a central site of state formation through the organization of social welfare programs, it is difficult to see just where the private ends and the public begins or vice versa. See Felicity A. Nussbaum, *The Autobiographical Subject: Gender and Ideology in Eighteenth-Century England* (Baltimore: Johns Hopkins University Press, 1989) and Linda Gordon, *Heroes of Their Own Lives: The Politics and History of Family Violence* (New York: Viking, 1988).

28. Woolf's 1928 novel *Orlando* takes as its subject the slippage between fiction and biography as it traces the 300-odd-year lifespan of its eponymous wealthy boy-man-woman writer-hero. With its central concerns of tracing the political effects of gender and class on the bodies of individuals, *Orlando* is the gold standard for feminist literary history. *Pity Is Not Enough, The Executioner Waits,* and *Rope of Gold* are the titles of the three Josephine Herbst novels which never actually appeared as a trilogy until Warner Books reissued them together in 1985.

29. Herbst, *Rope of Gold,* (1939; rpt. New York: Feminist Press, 1984), p. 169.

30. The poem appeared in Crane's 1926 volume, *White Buildings.*

31. Hart Crane, "My Grandmother's Love Letters," in *The Collected Poems of Hart Crane* (New York: Liveright, 1933), p. 65. The poem goes on to ask, "Are your fingers long enough to play/Old keys that are but echoes." See John Eugene Unterecker, *Voyager: A Life of Hart Crane* (New York: Farrar Strauss and Giroux, 1969).

32. Perhaps the ur-text of "discovered" documents offering a source for American revisionist historiography is *The Scarlet Letter* in which Hawthorne rethinks, in light of Republican failures, his family's and his nation's sordid past through Hester Prynne's tale. This tradition is particularly important to African American women's tradition: from Harriet Jacobs waging guerrilla warfare against her master from her attic enclosure by writing a series of letters posted secretly from afar to Rita Dove narrating her grandparents' lives through lyrics culled from family letters, diaries, and mementos in *Thomas and Beulah* (Pittsburgh: Carnegie-Mellon University Press, 1987).

33. Janet Malcolm, "The Silent Woman," *The New Yorker* (August 23, 1993), pp. 84–149. See also, Janet Malcolm, The Silent Woman: Sylvia Plath and Ted Hughes (New York: Knopf, 1994).

34. See, for example, Sharon O'Brien, "My Willa Cather: How Writing Her Story Shaped My Own," *New York Times Book Review* (February 20, 1994): 3. The biographer of Mary McCarthy (not one to shy from self promotion herself), Carol Brightman, in "Character in Biography," *The Nation* 26 (February 13, 1995): 206 passim, has taken insufferable postmodernist English professors to task for their self-indulgent biographies while promoting her biography and collection of letters between Mary McCarthy and Hannah Arendt.

35. Both the original and current contexts for these remarks (a panel entitled Literature/History/Culture and a book on poetics and politics respectively) asked contributors to place themselves and their work as scholars and teachers within the paradigm provided by the invitation to speak. Hence my obligatory, and at this point clichéd, turn to myself. See Adam Begley, "The I's Have It: Duke's 'Moi' Criticism," *Lingua Franca* (March/April 1994): 54–59.

36. To offer just two examples: Near the end of his landmark study, *Repression and Recovery: Modern American Poetry and the Politics of Cultural Memory, 1910–1945* (Madison: University of Wisconsin

Press, 1989), Cary Nelson cites *Writing Red*'s "persuasive evidence" that feminism did not die out in the 1930s. Mary Loeffelholz, *Experimental Lives: Women and Literature, 1900–1945* (New York: Twayne Publishers, 1992), offers a concluding footnote mentioning Charlotte Nekola and Paula Rabinowitz, eds., *Writing Red: An Anthology of American Women Writers, 1930–1940* (New York: Feminist Press, 1987), and mentions that factors other than gender influenced women's writing.

37. Marion Marzolf, *Up from the Footnote: A History of Women Journalists* (New York: Hastings House, 1977).

CHAPTER 6

# Defrosting: Self/Poetry/Power/Science

1

ROBERT FROST FAMOUSLY CALLED POETRY "a momentary stay against confusion." Given all that dominant power and ideology render unintelligible, it is a resonant assertion. Unfortunately, "momentary" seems to suggest something isolated and punctual, and "stay against confusion" seems to imply that poetry may be the reactionary defense of an order and identity (its own, for one) against all others. I start to hear a series of counter- and counter-counterassertions echoing in the wake of Frost's definition: "a rhythmic engagement with chaos" or "a ritual flirtation with abjection and grandiosity" or maybe "a moebius membrane" or "a benign metastasis." The move from the assertion to its echoes is what I'm calling "defrosting."

Virginia Woolf famously remembered that before the First World War, "people would have said precisely the same things but they would have sounded different, because in those days they would have been accompanied by a sort of humming noise, not articulate, but musical, exciting, which changed the value of the words themselves."[1] She identified the hum with poetry; we sometimes also call it "culture" or "ideology."

This essay explores defrosted boundaries between "the words themselves" and the "sort of humming noise" that is the sum of their many crossamplifying and canceling echoes, among powers and selves asserted and disavowed, and finally among the performative powers of poetry and science.

2

Many of the canonized poems of the Western Romantic tradition revolve around the axis of what is often called The Self, a.k.a. "the subject." To be more precise, they *precess,* through countless iterations eulogizing and elegizing this Self while beating their (figurative!) breasts over its alienation, fearing and longing for its dissolution, usually finally noisily or quietly heroically coming to terms with or transcending it.

But sarcasm does not escape the orbit. Poet John Berryman, who sarcastically called such a self "Henry," professed boredom with "his plights & gripes / bad as achilles," but finally had to jump off a bridge to escape them. When I lived in Minneapolis, I often used to walk past the parking lot where (I was told) Berryman had landed. Such pathos and tragic-heroizing was what psychoanalyst Jacques Lacan hated about the existentialist self, whose "subjective impasses" he characterized as

> a freedom that is never more authentic when it is within the walls of a prison; a demand for commitment, expressing the impotence of a pure consciousness to master any situation; a voyeuristic-sadistic idealization of the sexual relation; a personality that realizes itself only in suicide; a consciousness of the other that can be satisfied only by Hegelian murder.[2]

Lacan—a kind of Berryman with a bungee—worked to redeem a more discombobulated self—or, to put it another way, served up as a delicious breakfast the "hommelette" that had been Berryman's bitter dessert. The so-called death of the subject proclaimed by "the boys in the human sciences" (as Donna Haraway put it) may be in many aspects another Master-retooling for a New World Order, but it also brings new—poetical and political—opportunities for renegotiation and resistance.

In any case, the countless poetic elaborations of Self, like the epicycles-upon-epicycles that had to be posited to shore up the model of a geocentric universe, are subject to obsolescence in the light of Other models. But this is news only where and for whom the model had been dominant: for counterexample, Chinese cosmology had not required the lynchpin of geocentrism and thus was not shaken to its roots by Copernicus, no less than that great protagonist of Western lyrics, "I," had scarcely made an appearance in a couple thousand years of Chinese lyric poetry. Not coincidentally, furthermore, for almost a thousand years of China's state education system, one was tested and gained access to political power by—yes—writing about poetry. So too, after Mao, Chinese poets' insistence on the aesthetic or nonpolitical nature of their poetry continues to be a political act, whereas American poets' insistence on the political nature of their poetry tends more to be an aesthetic gesture.

These much too neat oppositions have their reverberations. Here, too, in the West (wherever that may be), not all of us have a single, jealous god. Not all of us—gladly—bear the same cross of Self, but those who don't are usually made to bear the cost for those who do. Dominant ideologies displace their contradictions onto others; both to take them up *and* to refuse them is often a matter of survival.

3

One moonlit night in August, 1996, an old friend and I went swimming in the ocean. Along with its other charms, this event had special significance for me since night swimming had once been my particular phobia. Ten years before, I had described it as follows:

> When I swim out into a lake at night I am possessed by a terror that sends me racing back to shore. I've tried on several occasions to steel myself and keep swimming out, but the terror grips me. I begin to feel that the depths are inhabited by others, by monsters; that I will be pulled down, drowned, consumed or torn apart. I begin to feel that my body is no longer distinct from the dark inhabited water, that I am losing any sense of the boundaries between lake and shore and air, that I am just a swimming in the darkness—and that others swim in me.
>
> It occurs to me that I experience a much milder version of the same fear when I write: I find that, when the writing begins to take me up I often draw back to do some chore or errand, as if to get some perspective, to turn rather than be turned by thinking, to grasp rather than be grasped.
>
> It begins to occur to me that everything important could be characterized as a swimming out into darkness: feeling, thinking, loving, speaking, teaching, reading, driving, going to sleep, waking up, being born, dying, and so on. Perhaps the phobia condenses and displaces these fears into an easily avoidable site, localizing what otherwise might suffuse everything.

By 1996, though, I had been thinking for some time that I had unraveled the phobia, unraveled the defended self that seemed to need the phobia—or, more simply, just that "I" had unraveled. The moonlit swim seemed to show me that this was the case, but maybe there was just too much moonlight to know for sure. In any case, it was a heightened experience I wanted to write about but was embarrassed to have fixed on such a conventionally poetic occasion. It occurred to me that "Swimming in the Sea on a Moonlit Night" recalled Frost's "Stopping by Woods on a Snowy Evening," which I came to realize was a kind of "anti-poem" to the one I wanted to write. Instead of writing the poem, then, I found myself unwriting the anti-poem, as follows:

> There are three main characters in the poem; two men and a horse, also male: a classic American erotic triangle.
>
> The first man owns a house and woodland lot. His job in the poem is to make the poet look good, by failing to realize the poetic profit the poet poaches from his woods when he's away.
>
> The horse, like all subordinates, apparently, enjoys routine. His job in the poem is to make the poet look good, by (thinking, no doubt, only of his dinner) failing to understand the poet's sublimer impulses (the poet allows the horse politely to protest, and then be still), and when the poet says that "I have miles to go," the horse must pull the poet (offstage).
>
> The poet—not wanting to be caught looking at another man's property, first ascertains that he's alone (the horse don't count)—as if he were the only person in the universe (the state, apparently, to which all genius must aspire)—oversees a furtive, rigorously orchestrated fantasy about a kind of mother/mistress whose job is to be "lovely, dark and deep" ; to be more self-effacing even than the horse (you cannot even tell for sure she's there; she does her job so well); to play the roles of nature, love, and death; to be seductive and to be resisted, and by being resisted, to make the poet look good.
>
> He dreams of the supremacy of cold and whiteness over everything— a universal, uniform, unmarked collective whiteness that levels all distinctions, obliterates all darkness, transcends all properties, like dollars or democracy—the consummation and the sweet apotheosis of his frosty self.
>
> But first, we all have jobs to do.

Call it a cheap shot, if you want: scratch Norman Rockwell and find George Lincoln Rockwell? But I mean REALLY, how is "Stopping By Woods . . ." anything but the nth rewriting of the old modestly heroic self; the "White Man's Burden" all over again? What's so galling about it is its modesty; the smugness of power and privilege to efface itself and its others. That's what drove my poem, to call pleasure on its furtive and disavowed implication in power. And, in other contexts, vice versa: for example, the righteous indignation of the right; the way they GET OFF ON IT. A while ago I saw on television some footage of the young senator Al Gore gazing proudly across the committee table at his blonde wife as she testified that rap lyrics should be censored. You could just see the hard-on in his eyes. Now THAT'S what I call obscene; power that won't cop to the pleasure it takes—that gets off by disavowing the pleasure—is also punishable by poetry. And that's why I wrote a POEM instead of a somber piece of criticism: you can question the pleasure I take in calling Frost out (do I not protest too much?—yes, no doubt—and wouldn't it be better to just leave Frost alone and get on with it?—probably), but at least I have not disowned it.

Call it a stylistic difference, if you prefer. To proclaim power in pleasure and vice versa, to assert oneself too nakedly, to protest too much: these are often the putative sins of counterhegemonic arts from rap and graffiti to performance poetry. For example, listen to the *Voices from the Nuyorican Poets Cafe* (anthologized in *Aloud*): would Frost ever, like Nicole Breedlove, have to come right out and tell the reader to "make sure the / Library of Congress / is notified" of her life or like Maggie Estep flaunt her "unabashed gall" in proclaiming "I am / THE SEX GODDESS OF THE WESTERN HEMISPHERE"?[3] Or was Hattie Gossett appropriately modest when she asserted that "in jamaica & los angeles they couldnt get enough of this" or Tracie Morris when she confirmed for her "Project Princess"— against the forces of negating invisibility and negating hypervisibility— "It's all about you girl"?[4] No, says Frost, my trick is to cover my tracks, to make it all about me without saying so!

What I wanted to do, when I came to write my poem, was to make another kind of answer to Frost: from a "lost" self that gains worlds in return, plural and perverse, whose response to a "lovely, dark, and deep" ocean is—to swim in it (or as the old TV commercial used to say, "You're soaking in it"):

> Almost full moon,
> a skipped stone,
> echoing light:
>
> by You we know
> how many ways
> of being where
> One is and is
> not (round).

Swollen ocean, kneaded
by Her yeasty fingers;
sewn with Her pleats
and pearly sequins:

in You we know
how many ways
to not be flat;

among sun, moon,
earth, ocean—queer:
how many ways
the earring's earring
is the ear.

You then, stepping dripping
from the water, looking
like a movie, like
the moonlight, like the
Birth of Venus, like
*La Dolce Vita,* turning
ebbing backwards into being
real as only all that glitters is

the some of us,
unborn but living
questions how split up
we are not
we but Ouija.

The poem works for me as a momentary stay against confusion—by which I mean, a way of reminding myself that Frost's clarity is, more often than not, my confusion—something I do not insist on being admired by those in no danger of forgetting. If it is only against the expectation of an exclusive and singular self that the poem is a poem (and thus disingenuously reinforces the Self as its Other), like a CEO who sees a dominatrix on the side—I mean, insofar as the poem cannot break its orbit around its antipoem, it tries to redefine the orbit as perversely plural (it was never "the self" that was the problem, but "the" self). As it happens, the path of one body orbiting another can be traced perfectly by Newtonian calculations, but add just one more body and the calculations become impossibly, unsolvably complex: this is what is known in physics as the "Three-Body Problem." To gain Newtonian knowledge—or to gain a discrete self—how much is rendered unintelligible! That's why I decided to call the poem, "The Three-Body Problem Is No Problem."

4

Linguist Roman Jakobson defined poetry by the predominance of what he called "self-reference."[5] The term has wide implications, but basically it refers to the way poetry foregrounds itself as an artifact of language (for example, by rhyme or rhythm or diction), as opposed to referential discourse, which tends to efface its own artifice, the better to represent itself as a transparent window onto the world (a ploy also known as "realism"). The extreme form of self-reference may be where "the medium IS the message," but Jakobson's point was that all discourses and statements perform referential, self-referential, and other functions, and that each is crucial even where subordinated to others. More often than not, though, self-reference is disavowed by referential discourses; thus "self-referentiality" is usually a term of dismissal in science, just as "rhetoric" is in political discourse: in Enlightenment ideology, poetry, politics, science and religion are imagined to be organized by mutual oppositions.

Philosopher J. L. Austin identified a way of "doing things with words" he called "performativity"; neither referentiality nor self-referentiality but where they meet; where the words themselves constitute the action.[6] What does poetry perform? A love poem can perform love (the labor lavished on the artifact providing its own evidence) and power (as in the old ploy of immortalizing the beloved)—and according to the U.S. Navy code, "unwanted poetry" can even constitute, in itself, sexual harassment. African American traditional and popular forms such as "signifying" or "the dozens"—no less than the high oratory of political speeches—are rituals of identity production and exclusion, just as the "right" kind of writing or reading (or writing about) poetry can constitute cultural or countercultural "competence" or "literacy."

A performative statement cannot be evaluated according to its truth or falsity: if I say "I apologize," you can question my sincerity, but I can protest that my statement did in itself constitute an apology (arguably in some contexts even more so if I didn't "mean" it, since then it would be more of a testament of your power to wring an apology from me). Austin proposed that performative statements be evaluated according to what he called their "happiness": for a performance to be "happy" it must work within its idiom; the speaker must have the proper performative "authority." I can performatively "claim this land in the name of Queen Isabella," but only a set of relations extrinsic to the statement (how I am positioned as a historical agent) can say whether and for whom the statement is a "happy" one, whether I am celebrated or hated or taken away in a straightjacket. But this account seems prejudicially to polarize text and context (what is intrinsic and extrinsic to the statement itself), because among what statements work to perform, to constitute, to negotiate and renegotiate, are the very terms of their idiom and authority. Perhaps the extent (always partial and relational) to which statements can achieve such power is the extent to which they can be called poetic.

And what is the "extent" of poetry? How local, how "momentary" are the powers of art? Literary theorist Mikhail Bakhtin related the novel to the tradition of "carnival," in which for a specified time all power relations are turned ritually upside down (beggars dress as kings, aristocrats as highwaymen, men as women, and so on); art can be a kind of portable carnival, a way of letting off steam, a ritually contained "safety valve." How much does this safety valve protect the status quo and how much does it threaten to subvert it? How "leaky" is the valve? Perhaps it is not the ritual but what leaks from it that can be called poetic.

## 5

A subject inflicting immediate violence on an object would seem to be the most straightforward instance of power. A gun, for example, is an instrument to make power straightforward: it polarizes two people into subject and object (an act of violence in itself) according to which end each is on.

When anything more than the immediate effect of violence is considered, things get more complicated: a gun may be turned on its owner; the shooter may be jeopardized by his action; a political killing may galvanize the cause it was meant to hinder or end up discrediting the killer's cause: guns produce BACKLASH.

The power to destroy is straightforward; it is in fact the relentless straightforwardness of a fired bullet—and what happens when this is resisted—that makes it destructive. In fact, like Foucault said, where there is no resistance, there is no power: a fired bullet won't stop a swarm of gnats.

Such violence operates as simple fact: all facts, as such, are "brute facts" (as Peirce observed): it doesn't matter whether you believe in them or not or how you understand them as meaningful or not, there they are anyway. In the 1890s, the Lakota Sioux leader Kicking Bear asserted the power of the Ghost Shirt to protect its wearer from bullets, or perhaps one should say that its function was to perform this belief, but Ghost Shirt wearers were just as dead when shot, weren't they? Moreover, didn't the assertion of the power of the shirt put them in the way of bullets they might have dodged? The extension of this argument is that even if the Ghost Shirt worked well to inculcate a strategic belief in a kind of impenetrability (effective in producing brave warriors) rather than the FACT of impenetrability, facts—like bullets—eventually and inevitably triumph over faiths (or rather, performances) that run counter to them. So the story goes. Or should we say instead that the Ghost Dance as a cultural practice has truly helped keep its practitioners alive in the face of overwhelming assaults? And stay tuned: what are the consequences for Euro-American peoples of what they stole from Native Americans: gold, tobacco, sugar, alcohol, coffee, coca; not to mention lands dominated or laid to waste, species driven to extinction? The way capitalism distributes its damages has its backlash too.

Violent power is exercised not only in destruction but in production: certain entities or "raw" materials are disordered with respect to their own organization (or rather, with disrespect) and reorganized (often simultaneously); perhaps all power could be thought of as a thermodynamic transaction.

The power to persuade, to please, to teach, or to elicit recognition or love or desire—the powers of poetry, among others—clearly requires more than simple coercion. It requires dynamic engagement with another, and a certain (at least strategic) respect for the identity of the other and for the other's powers and constraints, whereas simple violence is defined as power precisely for its violation of the other. "Random violence" or "arbitrary power" are in this sense redundancies; the path of a bullet through a body is violent and powerful because it is random or arbitrary in relation to the organization of the body, regardless of the deliberateness or rationality with which it was fired. On the other hand, if I want to compel you to perform a complex and ongoing task, it will not suffice to put a gun to your head, much less to shoot you. Most likely I will have to speak to you in your language or teach you mine in order to tell you what I want; the task must be adjusted to your capacities and/or vice versa; even if I kill you at will, I may have to reckon with the fact that you may call my bluff or even prefer death to serving me; to keep you on the job, I may have to tailor rewards and punishments to your desires and fears (and/or vice versa). It is easy to see that this master/slave dynamic is a dialectical one; it becomes difficult to say whose identity and constraints end up being most definitive for the relationship; perhaps the "complex and ongoing task," as described, becomes difficult to distinguish from *love*.

And what if I want you to love me *freely*? And what if I, too, want a kind of freedom that I cannot simply seize but must work out some way to get you to *grant* to me? Is this still in the realm of power? What if I want you to retain your own constraints and desires, even where they are not in synch with mine, just so I'll know I'm in contact with another—or is it just so I can keep getting the thrill of seducing or dominating or resisting you and of being seduced or dominated or resisted in turn, the old Hegelian soap opera (yes, but a sustainable and ongoing one)?

These examples distort the operation of power by making it a relationship between two discrete agents, when it is the hegemonic and transsubjective ubiquity of power that make it powerful in the first place. Perhaps Woolf's "sort of humming noise" is POWER.

6

The controversy over anthropologist Robin Dunbar's theory of *Grooming, Gossip, and the Evolution of Language* was reported in the March 1997 *Lingua Franca*.[7] Observing that "many chimps spend up to a fifth of their waking hours" grooming each other—a rather scandalous waste of time to a functionalist—Dunbar also found that between primate species there seems to be some positive correlation between neocortex size and the size of the social group. Dunbar marshals these and other observations to support the theory that as group size increased, language evolved as a "cheap and ultra-efficient form of grooming"—"a kind of vocal grooming"—and as a kind of gossip; grooming and gossip being ways of enacting and negotiating positions in a complex web of relationships.

However, as *Lingua Franca* reports, some have criticized Dunbar for failing to account for the brain's supposedly hardwired "grammatical machinery," which evolutionist Steven Pinker is quoted as saying must have emerged "for making complex propositions like 'the wildebeest is on the other side of the lake.'" Now, it would seem to me that purely indexical communication—grunting and pointing—would suffice in this case. But notice, too, that Pinker's example typically poses an antagonistic relation with an "other" (here, another species) presumably identified as such because it is either potential predator or prey to an equally univocal "self" (one might say that the statement functions to produce this self; it is also the speaker's way of bonding with the addressee against a common enemy, a way of saying, "I'm with you"). By situating the "self" here and the "other" species "on the other side," Pinker encodes a familiar series of binary relations: the referential signifier here and its signified over there, culture/language on our side and the "wildebeest" on the other, science and the world. But maybe Pinker's statement gets closer to its meaning by changing everything into its opposite: instead of "the wildebeest is on the other side of the lake," how about, "the human is on the self side of the sign"? In any case, Pinker's statement can be seen now to be a truly complex proposition whose primary reference to its own referentiality makes it into a kind of shell game.

On the other hand, if a simple referential statement seemed at first not even to require language as such, it's hard to imagine anything but language sufficing for a truly complex proposition such as "Trog is sulking because you spent too much time grooming his cousin yesterday"—especially when you have to consider what kind of complex grooming the speaker must be doing in making the statement. Here it is clear that language is always already sub- and metalanguage; it performs linkages and distinctions that cannot simply be reduced to a binary of self-and-other but rather negotiates always PARTIAL relationships of opposition and affiliation that come around to divide self from self as both the precondition and impossibility of self.

Dunbar's theory, like the language it attempts to account for, "enacts and negotiates its position in a complex web of [discursive] relationships" relationships: the gossip and grooming functions it identifies identify it with Austin's "performativity" and against dominant referentialism.

It would be possible to find in primate grooming a kind of "symbolic" behavior in which primate society, through this excessive "cleanliness" ritual, enacts and polices its own internal boundaries on the surface of bodies; "a momentary stay against confusion," or as Bourdieu said it, a process whereby "social subjects, classified by their classifications, distinguish themselves by the distinctions they make."[8] One might emphasize here the gratuitousness of the behavior, its excessiveness or its arbitrarity vis-à-vis any Social Darwinist account. Society and culture here could be construed as realms of relative freedom: we have more "leisure time" for nitpicking, or as Marx said, to "criticize after dinner." But arbitrarity—such as the famous structuralist arbitrarity of language in linking and dividing words and things—is not itself arbitrary; or rather, arbitrarity IS the performance of difference: a chimp is a chimp mainly because it grooms other chimps and vice versa, and in fact it is the particular chimp that it is mainly because it grooms and is groomed by the particular chimps that it grooms and is groomed by. Pure arbitrarity is simple violence—the path of a bullet through a body—or the meaningless freedom of nonrelation: nods and winks to blind horses. Partial arbitrarity is the push and pull of power and meaning.

## 7

At a forum I attended in November 1996 at New York University, a panel that included cultural critic Andrew Ross, physicist Alan Sokal, and others discussed the vicissitudes of the phony science studies article Sokal managed to get published in *Social Text*. Sokal rehearsed the complaints about relativism and the rising tide of antiscientific irrationalism that had inspired his performative hoax, citing a prime example of what he kept calling "sloppy thinking" from a October 22, 1996 *New York Times* article, prejudicially entitled "Indian Tribes' Creationists Thwart Archaeologists."

The article described effects of a 1990 repatriation act, "which allows tribes to claim the remains of their ancestors": "All across the West, clues about North America's past are on the verge of being returned to the ground with little or no analysis." Archaeologist Robson Bonnichsen is quoted as saying, "Repatriation has taken on a life of its own and is about to put us out of business as a profession." On the other side, Sebastian LeBeau, repatriation officer for the Cheyenne River Sioux of South Dakota is quoted as saying, "'We never asked science to make a determination of our origins . . . We know where we came from. We are descendents of the Buffalo people. They came from inside the earth after supernatural spirits prepared this world for humankind to live here.'" The article concludes by observing that "some archaeologists have been driven close to a postmodern relativism in which science is just one more belief system." An archaeologist working for the Zuni people is quoted as saying that Zuni accounts are "just as valid as the archeological viewpoint of what prehistory is about." That phrase—"just as valid"—is what set Sokal off about "sloppy thinking."

Against the many different Native American accounts of "emergence," current archaeological theory proposes that the first Native Americans crossed the Bering Straits from Asia over a no longer extant land bridge about 10,000 years ago and then spread across the American continent. Sokal proposed that the two accounts simply be debated in an open forum, and may the truest theory win. When an NYU American Studies professor in the audience, Nikhil Singh, tried to question how blithely Sokal had assumed the power to set the terms of the metadiscourse whereby the two accounts could be judged, he was hooted down by scientists accusing him of postmodern jargon-mongering—and indeed, Sokal couldn't seem to make heads or tails of the question.

Can the "validity" of the archaeological and Native American accounts be judged? The archaeological Bering Straits narrative predictably casts a context-independent free agent setting off to colonize a new world. But (to adapt the argument made by Vine Deloria, Jr., in *Red Earth, White Lies*), this is not the story of Native American origins; it is the white man's story of HIMSELF. The Native American accounts of emergence (like the Sioux story cited above) seem to stress that their identities as peoples, indeed as people—no less than the identity of the land—is contextual, relational, ecological; that is, we were not we before we were here; we were not here before we were we; here was not here before we were. Perhaps we should begin by acknowledging the validity—and arguably the superiority—of such accounts *as theory*, at least as they seem to affirm the ecological paradigm of "co-evolution" belied by the story of the context-independent free agent.

It is prejudicial to lump the Native American accounts with fundamentalist Christian "creationism," which has different epistemological and ethical agendas: for one, a single and jealous god, the tenor of whose worship infuses scientific fundamentalism. The issue is not science versus religion but the contradictions among overlapping scientific/religious/economic social complexes. These complexes are not a smorgasbord from which we can assemble the optimum mix of scientific rationality and eco-performative sociality.

Bruno Latour has told the story of Aramis, the French mass-transit project featuring small traincars that couple and uncouple en route as needed, controlled by on-board computer chips hooked into a massive control system. These chips proved to be bones of contention in the network of relations among the various disparate scientific, technological, and governmental and other groups that had to collaborate on the project. Latour proposes that the chips must be engaged as "non-human actors"; that they do not "represent" social ties but that *They are the new social ties.*"9 By the same token, we could say that the contested bones do not "represent" the social ties or lived history of the Native American peoples or the political and epistemological struggle between peoples. The bones ARE these ties and struggles. (Although many tribes have allowed certain scientific testing of bones as long as the tests do not require too much physical violation of the bones, any negotiation that acknowledges multiple and conflicting agendas is apparently anathema to a science that proclaims, in effect, THOU SHALT HAVE NO OTHER GODS BEFORE ME.) As Latour's example was meant to suggest, to say that the bones ARE the struggle is not fetishism, or if it is, it would be useful to compare it not with rationality but with commodity fetishism on the other hand, or to compare the kind of knowledge and professional profit the scientists hope to extract from the bones with their sociopolitical functions for the Native Americans. Identity (like poetry) is necessarily a fetish, a displaced and condensed set of relations.

Jack Goody, in his book *The East in the West*—a study of why science rose as such only in the West—adduces the following example from psychologist A. R. Luria's work with Russian peasants after the revolution:

> one noncollectivized (and presumably more traditional) peasant was posed the following problem: "In a certain town in Siberia all bears are white. Your neighbor went to that town and he saw a bear. What color was that bear?" The peasant responded that there was no way for him to know what color that bear was, since he had not been to that town. Why didn't Professor Luria go to his neighbor and ask him what color the bear was? Such responses were typical . . .10

The collectivized peasants, on the other hand, are said to have "responded very much as *we* might respond" (19, my emphasis). Goody adduces the example as illustrating the nonuniversality of formal, syllogistic reasoning. But he fails to notice that the peasant in the example seems to understand the Professor's question, first and foremost, as part of a (performative) power transaction—a game with stakes—and is rightly resistant and suspicious: you can hear the peasant "winding up" the Professor: "Why didn't Professor Luria go to his neighbor and ask HIM what color the bear was?"

If you look hard enough, maybe you can even see the twinkle in the peasant's eye, which, as evanescent and undocumentable as it has always been (and, I guess, was meant to be), manages to survive as a stowaway in the Professor's account. But to this ludic twinkle, Luria and Goody seem to be blind (they fail the peasant's test, too!), as blind as Sokal is to the self-referential and performative poetics and politics of science, and for the same reason: they'd have to give up too much if they saw it; they'd have to change. It's not the poets and critics of scientific rationality who deny the pull of gravity (usual shorthand for the inescapable "reality" of the world) but the scientists who deny the gravity of language and its being of the world (which is, some go on to assert, why they keep trying to saw things apart and nail them together).

Poetry IS the performance and negotiation of power relations in language, of which what is usually called poetry is a special ritual but not necessarily a definitive case. Some science types have even gone so far as to adopt "autopoesis" as the name for what all organisms do as self-organizing systems, but in that "auto" you can hear that old internal combustion engine, the self, blithely chugging along. The private *frisson,* the shudder, the poignance of a knowledge that reverberates inside an enclosed self and an enclosed poetry, "each mind keeping as solitary prisoner its dream of a world" (as Pater put it); the "impotence of a pure consciousness to master any situation" may be sweet, but poetry, like all organisms, is all interfaces, inside and out, and an anything-but-private *friction* is also how we are moved by poetry or insist that we shall not be moved.

What color is the bear? As is known by those who find unbecoming the unbearable, funereal whiteness of being; who seek in one way and another to reject the white man's burden ("Gladly, the cross-eyed bear" in its frosty polarity), there is no way altogether to avoid being put into jeopardy by the question, but it may help to phrase an answer in the form of a question, a series of ludic echoes, even if these are nods and winks to the blind (Trojan) horse of science: What is the bear? ... Is the bear?...Is the bear "the" bear? ... How does who bears what color bear on what color the bear is? The peasant asks an important question: why DIDN'T the Professor go to his neighbor and ask him? The professor didn't really want to know. But sometimes poetry, sometimes science, and sometimes politics *does.*

## NOTES

1. Virginia Woolf. *A Room of One's Own* (San Diego: Harcourt Brace Jovanovich, 1981), p. 12.
2. Jacques Lacan. *Ecrits,* trans. Alan Sheridan (New York: W. W. Norton, 1977), p. 6.
3. *Aloud: Voices from the Nuyorican Poets Cafe,* ed. Miguel Algarin and Bob Holman (New York: Henry Holt, 1994). For Breedlove, see p. 41; for Espet, see p. 63.
4. See *Aloud.* For Gossett, p. 204; for Morris, p. 101.
5. Roman Jakobson. "Linguistics and Poetics," in *Style in Language,* ed. Thomas Sebeok, (Cambridge, MA: MIT Press, 1960), pp. 350–77.
6. J. L. Austin, *How to Do Things with Words,* 2nd ed., ed. J. O. Urmson and Marina Sbisa (Cambridge, MA: Harvard University Press, 1975).
7. Robin Dunbar. *Grooming, Gossip, and the Evolution of Language,* reviewed by Daniel Zalewski in *Lingua Franca,* March 1997, pp. 19–20.
8. Pierre Bourdieu. *Distinction,* trans. Richard Nice (Cambridge, Harvard University Press, 1984), p. 6.
9. Bruno Latour. *Aramis, or The Love of Technology,* trans. Catherine Porter (Cambridge: Harvard University Press, 1996). See also Bruno Latour, "Ethnography of a High-Tech Case: About Aramis," in Pierre Lemonnier, ed., *Technological Choices* (New York: Routledge, 1993), pp. 372–398.
10. M. Cole, et al., *The Cultural Context of Learning and Thinking,* quoted in Jack Goody, *The East in the West* (Cambridge: Cambridge University Press, 1996), pp. 18–19.

CHAPTER 7

# The Sound of One Hand Clapping, or Does Academic Administration Have a Poetics?

ELIZABETH LANGLAND

CERTAINLY, ACADEMIC ADMINISTRATION HAS ITS POLITICS. And if the institution is public, that politics begins with the state legislature and often includes whatever miscellaneous citizen/business-folk are appointed to serve on a governing board of regents. And if it's a public institution, it also exists in a state system of universities and colleges, competing for resources—need I add the redundancy "scarce"? And whatever Mount Parnassus one might imagine one's institution to sit atop is secondary to whether it is in the state capitol or the state's population centers, with hungry constituencies nipping at the heels of a herd of state legislators.

I am at the end of a three-year term as associate dean for faculty affairs in liberal arts and sciences, and I dimly remember that my profession has a poetics, the still, small voice of which is drowned out in the clamor for seats and student credit hours, the coin of the realm in the institutions governed by new accountability measures and "responsibility-centered management." In this system, colleges within a university end up competing for student credit hours in a race that too often rewards predatory instead of collegial behavior. Academic decisions about course offerings become a numbers racket. In fact, the institution is so constructed through the incredibly detailed particularity of these politics that the practices of disciplines often appear to rise in the distance, like mountain peaks, sublime and transcendent, remote and enduring.

En route to my stint as associate dean, I have already been a director of women's studies, a department chair, and a graduate coordinator. Through print and panel I have entered the dialogue on the market for our graduate students and our individual and institutional responsibility.[1] And I've penned sage advice on retaining faculty lines, recommending that chairs view lines as investments in the institution's future, an investment they need to be prepared to persuade a dean to make.[2] It's all more political than poetical, couched in the business-speak of the market: faculty lines like stocks waiting to appreciate.

And why not? Every faculty member's now a speculator, the solid, stalwart, and predictable TIAA trampled in the general stampede to CREF to experience that lovely heady rush of riding the bull. The old time-honored reliability of TIAA, like replacing a medievalist with a medievalist or a Victorianist with a Victorianist, has transmogrified into a risky venture, preyed upon by inflation, in contrast to new and exciting options and alternatives that are bound to appreciate.

Markets have permeated our institutional lives; it's hard to think outside them. Everyone has bought into the logic of the marketplace. Students are now "customers" or, more ominously, "consumers" of our product. A professional fund-raiser has told me that the most powerful argument for raising dollars from donors is our state's (or nation's) need for "information age" worker-graduates who will enable our nation-state to compete in a global economy. The unremunerated life, it seems, is not worth living, whatever we might still want to claim about the unexamined one.

Two quotations made their way insistently into my decanal life and seemed to encapsulate my administrative experiences. Laurence Sterne gave me the first, "God tempers the wind to the shorn lamb," and F. Scott Fitzgerald the second, "And so we beat on, boats against the current, borne back ceaselessly into the past." But whatever pleasure these formulations give me in dealing with the occasional haplessness of my colleagues or our seeming tendency to revisit the same issues over and over again, reflection suggests that this felt pressure of the past was a rather comforting illusion in the face of an alternative like drifting with the currents into the ever deeper waters of a widening sea. These two quotations capture my sense of personal and institutional vulnerability, and their wisdom and urbanity seem to reach out across the years to arrest my free-fall either into cynicism or into embracing the logic of free-market capitalism invading the academy. In this position, these remnants of a literary practice are fragments shored against the ruins.

What has brought us to this point? And what is the logic of this moment in which I seek to join politics with poetics? In part, "It's the economy, stupid." University administrations are under enormous pressure to control the spiraling costs of higher education. Carol Christ, provost at Berkeley, points to the many factors that contribute to these costs: the financial stress states are experiencing, the competition for public dollars, the prospect of reduced federal support for research, the cost escalation in university and college budgets that outpaces inflation, and the public resistance to tuition increases. These all impact on faculty positions because an overwhelming proportion of university budgets is tied up in faculty lines; one can't address the budget crisis without looking at tenure.[3] Thus, in part, *because of* the guarantees of tenure, we share the economic logic of the 1980s and early 1990s: downsizing, flexible staffing, elimination of full-time workers, who are replaced by part-timers and adjuncts. And also because of the guarantees of tenure, certain faculty have been spared the ravages of and fear that their own positions are in imminent peril. But this guaranteed security in a world where middle managers and white-collar workers everywhere else face a historically unprecedented vulnerability does not sit well with the public and electorate, who demand, if not the end of tenure then at a bare minimum a conception of academic responsibility to accompany claims for academic freedom. The language of accountability, therefore, penetrates the academy; there arise demands for more and better teaching, pressures to meet performance standards. And these demands for more teaching from individual faculty members and greater productivity from an entire faculty intersect with the end of mandatory retirement, burgeoning technologies that require support dollars formerly slated for tenure lines, the increasing migration into American universities of foreign students who swell the numbers of eligible job candidates, and calls for flexible staffing.[4] Suddenly, the torrent of jobs Bowen and Sosa famously projected would materialize in the late 1990s dwindles to a trickle.[5]

At the same time that revenue sources and jobs have been drying up, universities, initially buoyed up by cold war research dollars, have been building graduate programs and pressing to enter the ranks of the Research I institutions. The desirability of graduate education, which is central to that challenge and its success, and the cachet of research over teaching have shaped the attitudes, values, and identities of the academy's tenured knowledge workers, its professoriat. The federal dollars that initially fueled that buildup have increasingly been withdrawn and university tuitions have increased to cover the shortfall. Thus, for some years now, graduate students have been shouldering a burden of debt to fund the educations that no longer culminate in employment within the academy.

This is the situation in which we now find ourselves. Cary Nelson argues the inherent dishonesty of arguments that proceed from "choice": that is, if students want a graduate degree, who are we to prevent them; it's their choice, isn't it? Pointing to the vast difference between an eager undergraduate who loves literature and a trained graduate student whose identity has now been constructed as that of a professional teacher-researcher, Nelson insists our responsibility is not discharged merely by warning students about the market. And I agree with him.

However, if Nelson doesn't expect a trained graduate student to relinquish this professional identity easily, it's not clear why he excoriates a tenured faculty for failing to do so any more readily. Indeed, having lingered in the groves of academe for several years, even decades, many faculty will find that the epistemic shift now demanded is overwhelming. And if only moral and not financial imperatives are motivating the shift, well, it's easier to sleep with a bruised conscience than with a ravening fear in the gut that one's own future is imperiled by a mountain of debt and a fundamental unemployability in the area in which one has trained for years.

Furthermore, collective political action is also inimical to the research model in which that faculty were trained. Faculty in the humanities have tended to denigrate and devalue joint endeavors, such as co-authored books and articles; faculty in the sciences and social sciences have built their conception of basic or "pure" research (as opposed to instrumental research) on the foundation of the disinterested pursuit of knowledge. In short, the concepts that found the research institution have always warred with collective political action. It is true to say both that 1) politics—beliefs, values—always inform our research, and 2) the belief that the dross of self-involvement has been purged is essential to the pure or basic research ideal.

The interrelated economic, historical, and social forces now impacting the academy demand a different stance; the emergence of global capitalism makes it difficult to deny any longer the politics of our disciplinary choices and commitments. The question seems no longer whether poetics and politics coexist, but rather what are the precise conjunctions of poetics and politics and what is the political responsibility of our practice of poetics at this historical moment.

The fall of the Iron Curtain that marked the triumph of capitalism and free markets, as well as the resistless pressure of corporate downsizing, especially of middle management, has made the preserves of tenured academe seem—to return to a theme—as anachronistic as communism or socialism. Universities, like businesses, so the argument goes, need a flexible workforce so that shifts in demand for the product or falling profits can be met with a swift response, a reduction in or reassignment of the workers.

This long prolegomenon is not meant to register as a complaint, a sign of the "endemic pessimism and cynicism [that] are hard to cure, especially among academics."[6] It is intended, rather, to frame the question of whether an institution so implicated in a free-market economy can afford to ignore politics in any of its endeavors and to suggest that the seeming freedom from politics enjoyed in an earlier age was simply an illusion produced by postwar prosperity and economic stability. I note, too, that the "luxury" of funded basic research in that postwar boom has given way to dollars targeted for increasingly instrumental research efforts.[7] We can read, then, the triumph of New Criticism and its "idolatry of the text" (see Robert Alter) as the humanistic equivalent to basic research. Furthermore, one could plausibly argue that the politics of our poetics in the post - World War II cold-war era were well served by disclaiming any politics to our poetics, especially when politics often wore the very visible dress of propaganda and suppression of free speech.

And now, with scientific inquiry often in the pockets of government and corporations, humanities disciplines have a clear responsibility to investigate the tangled skeins of politics and poetics, of dollars and disinterest. There, it seems to me, is the beginning of the difference it makes that I am an academic and in an academic position. This is the beginning of a poetics of academic administration that seeks to answer the question of appropriate responses to our "current crisis" (tendentiously phrased) in the academy. My poetics, then, involves the intimate application of formal and structural analysis to the institution that houses me and gives shape to my aspirations. It means struggling against the odds to identify the terms of the archive in which I find myself. It means analyzing both the nostalgic discourse of an edenic nonpolitical past that operates like a Siren call for so many and the fracturing discourse of corporatization that threatens to structure our future. From where I sit, I can think no more valid poetics than this.

Several distinguished voices have joined the Siren chorus clamoring for returning to a purer past. In his Presidential Address to the Association of Literary Scholars and Critics in November last year, Robert Alter called for renewed respect for the literary imagination, described as "an investigation of literature free of the ulterior motives of political agendas."[8] What he understands by that notion "requires clarification," as he recognizes, but we generally understand the call as a rejection of new critical tendencies in the academy, grouped generally under the heading of studies: postmodern, feminist, gay, and cultural, to name a few. Alter explains:

> The claim that you want to turn away from politicization in the discussion of literature very frequently encounters the following objection: every-

thing is inevitably political, from reading Wallace Stevens to brushing your teeth, and so when you say you intend to talk about literature, not politics, you are merely failing to acknowledge your own implicit political values, whether bourgeois individualist or paleoliberal or neoconservative or social-democratic. The obvious rejoinder to this line of argument is that there is a world of difference between possessing political values, which no doubt in some way we all do, and fostering a political agenda, which in the most egregious instances can easily turn the classroom into an arena of indoctrination. It may be helpful to recast this question of politicization in regard to the work of literature as an object of knowledge. John Ellis has made the case trenchantly in his new book, *Literature Lost*: "Any empirical investigation requires a principled open-mindedness about the material to be studied, which may compel one to revise initial hypotheses and draw unanticipated conclusions.". . . The fundamental intellectual problem with politicized literary studies, Ellis suggests, is that the teachers and critics presume to know the real answers even before they have posed the questions. As he succinctly puts it, "If we are determined to take from literature only the attitudes that we bring to it, it ceases to have any point."

This is a tendentious description of what is variously called postmodernism or cultural studies, and it is precisely our poetics that enables us to point to the fault-lines in its argument. First, a recognition that literature, like other discursive formations, is invested in the economic, social, and political milieus that have produced it is rendered in Alter's text as "politicization in the discussion of literature"—in other words, as making literature serve a political agenda, hardly the same thing at all. Second, by rendering "everything is political" as conflating "reading Wallace Stevens" with "brushing your teeth," Alter seems to shudder in horror that the bourgeois godliness of clean teeth might challenge the green freedom of Stevens's cockatoo and late coffee and oranges in a sunny chair. And third, by "fostering a political agenda" and taking from literature only the attitudes we bring to it, Alter suggests the benighted are all plummeting downward to darkness on unextended wings.

If we are in a free-fall, however, no nostalgic invocations of a purer past are going to arrest our descent. At best, such calls may enable those facing a decade or so before retirement to anticipate the upcoming years with greater comfort, if not complacency. The institution is changing around us, the ground shifting under our feet and the transformation is being accomplished more by economic imperatives than by intellectual convictions. The logic of the free market has swept up the academy, and our insufficient responses have a persistent air of belatedness. Few who have spent any time recently in academic administration can be unaware of the sea-change. At the same time, few of the professoriat have been adequately trained to think systematically about relationships between our institutional histories and our sociopolitical and economic histories. The very specialization that crowns an original research project—the dissertation, article, or book— requires that we continue to assume the existence of an institution in which that project will be valued.

Numerous writers on the crisis in higher education begin with the implicit assumption that what is wrong with universities may be traced to self-indulgent faculty or mindless students. This is another form of seeking redemption in going back—this time to an era of greater integrity. Michael Lewis's *Poisoning the Ivy: The Seven Deadly Sins and Other Vices of Higher Education in America* is only one of the most recent attacks on the professoriat, which is frightening in its self-congratulatory and pompous hectoring of what Lewis sees as abusive faculty. Lewis's utter blindness to pernicious trends in higher education allows him to become an unwitting mouthpiece for corporate-speak and free-market economics. The "seven sins of teaching" that Lewis identifies—abandonment, harassment and exploitation, misrepresentation, special pleading, default, proud incompetence, and particularistic assessment—are all to be corrected by what he calls "individualized performance contracting."[9] Each faculty member will be given "specific performance expectations that are contractually mandated."[10] "Successful performance contracting" will require the imposition of hierarchy, reversing the trend toward democratization in the academy. Finally, Lewis recommends licensing professors, just as we license doctors, lawyers, real estate agents, accountants, or whatever other professional we might want to name.[11]

To many, these reforms might sound eminently reasonable; the very familiarity of the terms in which they are couched—contracts and performance—might enable them to masquerade as reasonable. This is the language of corporations with their productivity and performance measures, their boards of directors and management hierarchies, their credentialing and certifying modes. And Lewis does not think to question his own ready and automatic importation of the methods of the one to the concerns of the other, his conflation of the goals of intellectual life with those of professional credentialing.

To raise those questions, however, is my goal here. My long prolegomenon to this essay strove to anchor my reader in the academic-administrative experiences out of which I was writing. No one can be in academic administration for long before realizing how completely our universities and colleges are implicated in the logic of corporate life and the free-market economy. This logic is as resistless as evolution itself. And to my mind, we have only one choice: thinking our way through it to what some responsible future formation of the university might look like. Wherever we are going, at whatever unhappy place we may arrive, I cannot imagine that crawling back into the evolutionary seas that gave birth to us will deliver us into a better future.

If the faculty *has* failed, it has not done so primarily in its responsibility to students. It is in discharging duties connected with teaching and advising students that I have found faculty (with the occasional exception who proves the rule) to be most conscientious. No, members of the faculty have more often failed the institution in failing to inform themselves about its management and in absolving themselves from leadership within their departments and colleges. And this tendency to disengage from the institution in which one is employed has been exacerbated in recent years when increasing pressures for more teaching have been accompanied by decreasing rewards. If Cary Nelson laments that faculties are "ill-prepared to take collective action" on behalf of cafeteria or clerical workers (and he's right), it is both more astonishing and more disturbing to me that faculties are often incapable of seeing and furthering their narrowly conceived institutional self-interest. I've watched department after department sacrifice salary dollars, lines, research dollars, and awards because the members are so busy fighting with each other over curricula and other governance issues that they have lost the confidence of the administration. Provost Carol Christ reveals that

> When I allocate faculty positions, I use three criteria. The first and most important of these is excellence. All administrators want to invest available resources in strong units that will use them effectively. How does one judge excellence? Perhaps the most obvious way is by national rankings, by research productivity. But administrators look at other departmental attributes as well—the quality of department governance, for example. Nothing jeopardizes a department's claim on resources so quickly as factionalization.[12]

Apparently, bromides about washing one's dirty linen in public have not taken hold at the department level. Searches for a new chair are fraught with hostility and conflict; parties that should seek common cause fracture into warring factions. Mediocre individuals are advanced as compromise candidates, to the ultimate discredit of a department. "God tempers the wind to the shorn lamb"—mercifully. There are very few consensus builders in the academy. What kind of solidarity with cafeteria workers can we expect when even self-protective solidarity with one's colleagues cannot be achieved?

My point is that there is politics and there is politics: for many—maybe most—academics it is difficult to think of building the department into an effective political coalition within the institution. Or to figure out how to transcend the partisanship bred by the university's organization into departments. It is easier to lament one's purblind colleagues than to try to change them, even though one has powerful arguments from self-interest. It is easier to think in global rather than local, institutional terms, especially since leadership in the academy has increasingly devolved to an administration conceived as separate from the teaching and researching faculty. And nothing is more common, it seems, than a tendency to demonize the administration.

I have in the past read and profited from Stanley Aronowitz's work on labor and the academy and, therefore, turned to him again in writing this paper for insight into the crises that face us now. I was stunned to find he simply and uncritically replicated the banal us-versus-them binarism:

> When combined with committee work, many faculty are transformed into human teaching machines, while others, in despair, desperately seek alternatives to classroom teaching, even stooping to accept administrative positions, and not just for the money or power. The old joke that the relationship between a tenured professor and a dean is the same as that between a dog and a fire hydrant has become one of the anomalies of the waning century. Now the administrators are the cat and the faculty the catbox.[13]

Surely we need a better way to think through the present situation.

Thinking through the current logic is something Bill Readings, author of *The University in Ruins,* sets out to do, and that is why I had such a strange and curious response to reading his scholarly analysis—a breathless anxiety that I have when reading a mystery, dying to know how it all turns out. Because those of us positioned at the administrative controls of this academic machine wonder what kind of control we really have and even what kind of control we should wish to have.

Readings's story begins with the triumph of a new educational logic forged in the smithy of free-market economics. Readings argues that no longer is *culture* the goal of education, the goal that founded the "modern" university. In the postmodern university, the goal is "excellence," a term that functions to allow the university to understand itself solely in terms of the structure of corporate administration.[14] It's not that no one knows what it is but its very nonreferentiality allows it to serve as the "principle of translatability" between radically different idioms.[15] "*Everyone* has his or her own idea of what it is."[16] (32–33). In short, to achieve excellence tells you nothing because the criteria for excellence are not revealed.[17]

The first shoe falls: the University of Florida embarks on its first capital campaign in the school's history (1986 – 1991), under the motto "Embrace excellence." The University of Excellence is "another corporation in the world of transnationally exchanged culture."[18]

Excellence, in Reading's words, "exposes the pre-modern traditions of the University to the forces of market capitalism." Classic free-market maneuvers, such as the British government's decision to allow the polytechnics to rename themselves as universities, guarantee that "the only criterion of excellence is performativity in an expanded market."[19] Readings terms this an *administrative,* not an *ideological,* move because the values driving the decision are mystified and it is made to seem a mere administrative convenience.

The second shoe falls. The University of Florida enters its second capital campaign (1996 – 2000) under the banner of "It's performance that counts." It spells an even deeper commitment to so-called accountability measures that now determine the flow of resources in the institution. The fundamental confusion here is one astutely identified by Readings: accountability and accounting are not the same things. Yet they have been conflated in the administrative imagination.

Fundamentally, then, the question is this: are the things one is counting the things for which professors should be held accountable? We may begin by asking what is counted: student credit hours generated, numbers of majors, time to degree of majors, majors professionally licensed and employed upon graduation. These have been identified as some key measures of the academic product we are delivering to our customers.

The individual in charge of "product quality control" is the administrator. The professor has been replaced by the administrator as the central figure in the academy. No longer *primus inter pares* in the University of Culture, the president is now bureaucratic administrator in the University of Excellence.[20] And the University experiences a Fordist speed-up and streamlining of labor as the workforce is cut, teaching productivity is maximized, and product output of students graduated and funneled into the market is increased. If we look back to the recommendations for reforming the professoriat put forward by Michael Lewis, we see that he has missed the departure of the train from the station: administrative hierarchy has already triumphed, productivity measures rule, the syllabus is a contract, the student a consumer, and professional licensure is the measure of education. Lewis misrecognizes the imperatives of a free-market economy for the desirables of a university, and his ideological misrecognition facilitates his becoming yet another enthusiast from within the academy for the forces that are threatening the very existence of what he wants to preserve.

In this classic whodunnit, it wasn't Professor Plum in the library with the quill pen. But as I said earlier, it was for an answer to the mystery of the university's future that I engaged Bill Readings's work with such breathless anticipation. "Can another way be found," he asks, "to think the University?"[21] His answer—creating the university of dissensus, dissolving disciplinary boundaries but retaining as structurally essential the question of the "disciplinary form given to knowledges," and inculcating in our students the habit of questioning—must be built on the acceptance that the University today is a "ruined institution."[22] He anticipates the emergence of a general humanities department amid a cluster of vocational schools, which will themselves include devolved areas of expertise traditionally centered in the humanities: media and communications. But how long can anyone remain engaged by questioning the disciplinary form given to knowledge once there are no longer any disciplines? One generation, perhaps, for those who still remember when there were disciplines? And what accounting measures justify this general humanities department of the future? At the present moment, student credit hours generated by composition justify and fund our literature departments. But when composition takes place elsewhere, in a devolved area of expertise, those student credit hours will justify more composition, more communication. And with the disappearance of the research project—the fetish of the University of Culture—what will justify the practices of writing dissertations, humanities publishing, and tenure in the academy?[23] Why not hire part-time, licensed knowledge workers to teach efficient communication on the information superhighways?

I do not dispute that we need to think our way through this crisis. As I have already said, we cannot go back. Readings's thinking through is built upon the twin assumptions that the habit of questioning is a fundamental attribute of the humanities and that questioning itself will remain somehow fundamental to the university and the world it serves. That's a beginning. We are ultimately creatures whose needs cannot be answered fully by dollars and the things that dollars will buy. What we can bequeath to our students are significant bodies of knowledge, which we have broadly researched and thought deeply about because they raise and answer questions important to us. And we are responsible for cultivating in our students the same enthusiasm for inquiry that has fueled and sustained our own careers. But we can't tell them what to think or stop them from transforming the body of knowledge, which we ourselves transformed before them. A body of knowledge and a habit of engaged inquiry, this is a beginning. But a two-legged stool is even less stable than a three-legged one, and it seems that this one may fall without some propping up.

So what do I propose? I'll content myself with a proposal even more modest than cannibalizing our young, although it may seem mere *apologia pro mea vita*. Readings's "opportunism" seems right—that is, being ready for strategic interventions. We cannot see so far ahead that we can predict how the institution will turn out. But the professoriat must take on leadership if not administration, and the administration must talk to the professoriat.

If we return to Stanley Aronowitz's observation about tenured faculty and deans, pissing dogs and fire hydrants, we discover that his analogy elides, even as it reveals, the difference between universities and corporations as businesses. The further bureaucratization of the administration and hierarchization of the academy is retarded by the cycling in and out of workers from the knowledge camps. This interpenetration of management and workers is what continues momentarily to separate the university from the corporation; there's not a professional managerial class with golden handshakes and golden parachutes. That some professors have transformed themselves into professional administrators should not surprise us. That the liberal arts and science disciplines still, at some level, resist this transformation should encourage us. The dean *is* a tenured faculty member, whereas the president of a corporation is never also a blue-collar worker, although she or he may have started that way. The terms of academic success—research and teaching proficiency—that allow faculty to feel contempt for administrators are not available in comparable analogues to workers in a corporation. And there's a constant shuttling back and forth between faculty and administrators. True, some faculty make a career of administration, but many simply do a stint and return to their departments thereafter. Can one imagine a corporation in which the president (even of UPS) subsequently returns to driving a delivery truck?

This interpenetration of the faculty into the administration and the administration into the faculty creates possibilities for productive interchanges. It's certainly one way to learn intimately how the university functions. But it's not the only route. And it has become absolutely essential to create structures for such interchange because of the increasing pressures, both internal (scarce dollars) and external (public demands for accountability). In the past, these pressures were simply less acute, and although there were some tensions between administrators and faculty, there was a good deal of harmony because both were occupied with education. As Readings noted, the president was *primus inter pares.* Who would make that claim now when universities often deliberately recruit a prominent businessman to run their institutions?

Now it seems that faculty are most closely in touch with the continuing business of the university—education—whereas administrators are perforce most closely in touch with the university as a business. The rhythms informing faculty lives emphasize fostering and sustaining periods of contemplation about specific, individual projects, fostering and sustaining conversation between and among peers as well as students. The rhythms that shape administrative life are marked by a pressure to deal with the big picture and by constant interruption as long-term projects are put on hold while administrators respond to the newest budget or educational crisis. In short, the two modes are largely incompatible although, to be sure, faculty are experiencing more interruptions as their tasks multiply. Annette Kolodny's *Failing the Future: A Dean Looks at Higher Education in the Twenty-first Century,* published just as I was grappling with this essay, eloquently summarizes any faculty member's ignorance about the institution she or he serves:

> After only a few months as dean, one realization brought me up short: by joining the middle management of academic administration, I came to know the functioning of a large research university in a way that had never been available to me previously. . . . However engaged I was in campus life, as a faculty member I had had only a limited understanding of how any institution functioned, from its budget to it relationships with

different political constituencies. What I realized with a shock as dean, in other words, was how abysmally ignorant most faculty—including myself—really are about the workplace in which they function.[24]

Kolodny goes on to point out the consequences of this ignorance:

> The price we pay for such ignorance is the faculty's inability to respond effectively during periods of crisis. By not understanding how a public university is financed in any given state, faculty fail to grasp why there may be money to erect a new building but not for correcting salary compression. By not knowing about the multiple and often conflicting constituencies that compete to shape the president's agenda, faculty are at a loss to assess accurately the rationale behind some new policy move or public speech. Such ignorance makes a sham out of the concept of shared governance, and it leave faculty focusing their frustration on the dean, the provost, or the president as the closest cause for the problems they're suffering. Even more dangerous, such ignorance also leaves faculty views vulnerable to dismissal by governing boards and state legislators. In their eyes, faculty appear both uninformed and naive.[25]

In order to bridge the philosophical and experiential gaps so that the university can benefit from the joint wisdom of both, there must be conversations between the faculty and administration, a shared respect and a sharing of information.[26] One solution that Kolodny proposes might be annual faculty-administration retreats in which key members of departments meet with central members of the administration to discuss current problems and solutions.[27] Kolodny also suggests we need to restructure graduate education so that the next generation of professors is prepared to participate meaningfully in institutional change and crisis. Beyond their disciplinary specialization, our graduate students need data, knowledge of governance, organization, budgets, and decision-making processes, and an informed understanding of national educational issues.[28]

But all of these measures will ultimately fail unless we engage our poetics with our politics. What do I mean? A workable poetics cultivates and sustains rigorous processes of thought. Precisely because literature and other arts are representations, a good poetic practice will address politics. In literature, *what* is represented is as interesting as *how* it is represented. And because literature in its representative capacity engages with our worlds, both the "how" and the "what" are open for interpretation and judgment and, inevitably, engage with politics. We wouldn't want it any other way. Why would we care if literature were simply a self-enclosed system making beautiful harmonies to itself? That would be no better than finding one text simply a political blueprint for another.

But it is not only literature's representative character that interests me. It is also the corollary mode of thinking generated by its study. The study of literature accomplishes magnificently two things that interest me here: 1) it teaches one to think logically and systematically about claims to represent the world. Whose "world" is being represented, for whom, and for what purpose? 2) It sets a stringent standard for evidence. Because our students and much of the public at large believe that literature says whatever one wants, the demand for convincing "proof" (if I may so term it) is extraordinarily high. To achieve that level forces readers to develop subtle, sophisticated, and complex modes of analysis. I have become persuaded that complaints about the politicization of texts are often more properly complaints about sloppy thinking.

In short, literature and the practice of a literary poetics train one to read worlds as texts and to read those texts in their nonreducible complexity. What better practice for a citizenry or an associate dean? My literary poetics are the culmination of particular forms of thinking that have been invaluable in my current position, which itself cannot, as my entire essay makes clear, escape politics—that of academic institutions and world economies.

Where we will go depends on our continual willingness to bring the tools of our academic trade to leadership work in the academy. It demands our understanding the history of higher education in this country and our moment in that history. In my case, it means, in part, using my poetics to identify the discourse of corporatization currently governing the world of the academy so that I may communicate and act accordingly. To do that much may not be enough, but to do less is certainly to risk whatever future we may wish to imagine.

## Notes

1. See my essay "The Future of Graduate Education; or, Which Graduate Programs Have a Future?" *ADE Bulletin* 111 (Fall 1995): 28–32.
2. See my essay "Holding the Line: The Idea of the Faculty in an Age of Downsizing," *ADE Bulletin,* No. 115 (Winter 1997): 14–19.
3. Carol Christ, "Retaining Faculty Lines," *ADE Bulletin* 115 (Winter 1996): 10. Christ points out that 81 percent of the budget at Berkeley is devoted to faculty lines, 66 percent to tenured and tenure-track faculty.
4. Jack Schuster identified these numerous intersecting factors in "Speculating about the Labor Market for Academic Humanists: 'Once More unto the Breach.' "*Profession* 95 (1995): 56–61.
5. William G. Bowen and Julie Ann Sosa, *Prospects for Faculty in the Arts and Sciences: A Study of Factors Affecting Demand and Supply, 1987 to 2012* (Princeton: Princeton UP, 1989).
6. I cite the last line, which I stumbled upon while drafting this essay, of William Rubinstein's review of *Understanding Decline: Perceptions and realities of British economic performance, Times Literary Supplement,* January 23, 1998: 6, col. 4.
7. See Stanley Aronowitz and William DiFazio, *The Jobless Future: Sci-Tech and the Dogma of Work* (Minneapolis: University of Minnesota Press, 1994), pp. 247, 340.
8. For the complete text, see *TLS,* January 23, 1998: 15–16.
9. Michael Lewis, *Poisoning the Ivy: The Seven Deadly Sins and Other Vices of Higher Education in America* (Armonk, NY and London, England: M. E. Sharpe, 1997), p. 157.
10. Lewis, p. 163.
11. Lewis, pp. 170–74.
12. Christ, p. 10.
13. Stanley Aronowitz, "The Last Good Job in America," *Social Text* 51 (Summer 1997): 105.
14. Bill Readings, *The University in Ruins* (Cambridge, MA and London: Harvard University Press, 1996), p. 29.
15. Readings, p. 24.
16. Readings, pp. 32–33.
17. Readings's examples of this nonreferentiality are helpful. He notes that what makes a boat excellent are not the same things that make an airplane excellent. Or that when Cornell boasts of achieving "excellence

in parking," one has no way of knowing that the University has successfully limited the access of cars to campus rather than accommodated all the cars seeking spots (p. 24).

18. Readings, p. 43.

19. Readings, p. 38.

20. Readings, pp. 54–55.

21. Readings, p. 46. Readings also notes that there is no way back because, in what we might see as a Foucauldian paradigm of power, the discourse of excellence can accommodate even student dissent and campus radicalism as signs of the excellence of its student life (p. 150).

22. Readings, p. 169.

23. Readings comments:

> the role that the humanities are called upon to play in the University of Excellence . . . wavers between consumer service (the sense of individual attention for paying students) and cultural manicure. . . . Hence it is not the research model . . . that will save the humanities (or indeed the natural sciences), since the organization of the humanities as a field structured by a project of research no longer appears self-evident (with the decline of the nation-state as the instance that served as origin and telos for such organization). In a general economy of excellence, the practice of research is of value only as an exchange-value within the market; it no longer has intrinsic use-value for the nation-state (pp. 174–75).

24. Annette Kolodny, *Failing the Future* (Durham: Duke University Press, 1998), pp. 13–14.

25. Kolodny, p. 14.

26. Interestingly, Kolodny tried to institute information sharing at the University of Arizona to empower the faculty, but she was not highly successful. She attributes her failure in part to a group of faculty entrenched in their resistance to her from the outset of her administration. As significant, I believe, are the difficulties facing any one person trying to institute such policies unilaterally.

27. I encountered Annette Kolodny's book late in the process of drafting this article and was interested to discover that she governed her deanship at Arizona on the principle that the more information she provided to the faculty, the better the institution would become. She says, "Shaken by the recognition of what had been my own level of ignorance, in the dean's office I found myself eager to share every bit of

information with faculty, department heads, program directors, and staff. I wanted them to become informed and active partners with me in devising budget strategy and determining policy" (p. 15).

28. Kolodny, p. 16.

CHAPTER 8

# Insurgent Poetry and the Ideology of the Poetic

*Michael Bibby*

AT THE RURAL UNIVERSITY in south-central Pennsylvania where I teach, I offered a seminar in 1995 on the nature of poetry written by activists and armed insurgents in oppositional political struggles. To get some sense of the ideas and attitudes about poetry they were bringing to the class, I surveyed students at the first session. Although most of my students had taken other courses in poetry and were relatively well-read, none of them could name a poet associated with a particular political struggle or movement in the twentieth century. When asked to name any "political poetry" they knew, the students most often responded by citing the titles of famous 1960s protest songs (for example, "Blowin' in the Wind" and "We Shall Overcome"). Yet when I asked them to name poets they had read in their English classes, they listed the usual canonical names: Eliot, Pound, Frost, Keats, Shelley, Wordsworth, Milton, et al. In conversation with my students later in the course, I suggested that such poets might themselves be considered "political." Many students strongly disagreed, arguing that these great poets' art transcended mere "politics."

What I want to note here is not that these students were especially uninformed—indeed they were some of the brightest in our program and clearly had learned their lessons well. Rather what interests me is how they had been taught to regard "poetry" as apolitical. The only "poetry" they recognized as political was in song, outside what we might call the disciplinary field of the "poetic"—and what makes such poetry political for them tends to be its seemingly "outsider" status. I do not mean to suggest that this view is somehow "wrong," that the "problem with today's students" is that they have had their culture mediatized and made inauthentic. Rather I believe my students' separation of "poetry" and "political poetry" reflects their interpellation by an ideology of the poetic. Their understanding of poetry as apolitical, in fact, was so unexamined as to be foundational to their assumptions about literature and, indeed, their identities as English majors. Since at least the mid-1940s, the pedagogy of English departments and writing workshops has worked assiduously to depoliticize poetics; indeed poetry as a disciplinary field has depended on producing a poetic understood as an elevated form of aesthetic discourse beyond the reach of popular activism, a sacrosanct rhetoric unsullied by contact with the struggling masses. The depoliticization of poetry is so thorough that the openly partisan poetry of activists, for example, is widely viewed by the American academy and the literary press as simply not "poetic."[1] Even though almost every major political insurgency of the twentieth century has its own poetry, the field of literary study has been virtually silent on it.[2]

I want to suggest some ways of reading insurgent poetry not only as a step toward recuperating such work but also as a means of demonstrating the interests of power in the ideology of the poetic. By "the poetic" I mean the general aesthetic principles, evaluative criteria, and discursive norms that constitute the late twentieth-century American disciplinary field of poetry: academic criticism, university poetry workshops, major publishing houses, and reviews and articles about poetry in the mainstream press. Although such an umbrella concept runs the risk of effacing crucial differences among the various "poetics" currently practiced, it nonetheless highlights their similarities, which sustain an ideological consistency in the critical evaluation of poetry. Among some of its assumptions, the poetic favors linguistic and allusive complexity, irony, subtlety, and circumlocution; it privileges artistic "making" over ideological statement, process over product, form over content; and it understands itself in relation to a canonical, Anglo-European tradition. These broad categories are flexible enough to encompass not only "lyric-voice" writers, such as Jorie Graham or Mark Doty, but also "language" poets such as Charles Bernstein or Clark Coolidge. I do not mean to indict such poets for some sort of collusion with dominant ideology—rather I mean to suggest that the "poetic" constitutes the ideological field in which their texts are made legible and given value.

Delineating normative aesthetic boundaries, the poetic guarantees the perpetuation of "civilization" and its values. Its institutionalization from Cleanth Brooks and Allen Tate's *Understanding Poetry* to the *Princeton Encyclopedia of Poetry and Poetics* has guaranteed its status as a specialized discourse that must be learned through disciplinary training, and that once learned confers value in the academic marketplace. Training in "poetry" is regarded as an essential component of the "liberal arts" at every university and college. The uniformity of the poetic taught and its universal place in the higher education curriculum suggest that its function is indispensable to the bourgeois public sphere. It serves to exclude—to act as a means of distinguishing "good" from "bad"—forms of versification that violate the bourgeoisie's cultural norms.[3] Those who understand its rules and standards and who can apply it to their judgment of poems acquire the right to speak about poetry in the public sphere. The function, therefore, of specialized training in the poetic is to legitimate the cultural norms and values of the bourgeois public sphere.

The poetic ultimately serves to legislate critical value, rewarding texts that confirm the poetic, silencing those which do not. Insurgent poetry is therefore "outlaw," seeking to assert the right to speak from outside the bourgeois public sphere, "beyond the pale" where the "uncivilized" dwell. By "insurgent poetry" I mean verse written by partisans of oppositional political struggles, activists on the front lines, guerrillas, saboteurs, revolutionaries engaged in conflict with a ruling and oppressive political order. The very conditions for the production of insurgent poetry place it outside the poetic as a disciplinary norm. Insurgents often utilize poetry because it offers an immediate, visceral, portable, mnemonic medium, one that can be written on a moment's notice, in quick lines jotted down during lulls in the conflict or during hectic political meetings.

The ideological interests of the poetic become apparent when we consider the tropes used to delegitimate insurgent poetics. Openly partisan, insurgent poetry is viewed as a "low" form of discourse in which "content" overshadows "form." It is considered mere "reportage," "transitory," "mass language," "sloganeering," "artless," "doggerel," "agitprop," "propaganda." In contradistinction, "good" poetry—rarely critically examined—is subtle, it does not preach, it is linguistically complicated, its formal elements are finely wrought so as to support but not overshadow its content, yet its content should not overwhelm its form. While such criteria may bear value in certain contexts (as a revolt by the educated middle-class against the alienating effects of mass commercial language, for example), they may not offer much to poet-activists and their partisans in the heat of urgent political struggle. Such poets—especially during periods of armed insurrection—may find realist, didactic, and agitational rhetoric valuable and strategic.

Although explicitly propagandistic rhetoric is not the only legitimate discourse for political poetry, I want to argue that such language is not necessarily unpoetic. If Aristotle's *poiesis* implied a knowledge in making, producing, creating, then certainly insurgent poetry involves a knowledge of producing support and solidarity for ideological aims through a system of rhetorical figures, formal strategies, and symbols distinct from prose.[4] To appreciate this poetry in its contexts, however, requires rethinking poetics in relational and contingent ways: for example, rereading the value of figurative language, ambiguity, particularity, and immanence in relation to the conditions of struggle; reconsidering how direct exhortation, generalities, and the explicit may be valuable formal elements for a poetry of armed insurrection.

This essay will focus on some poems I taught in my seminar from the poetry of the Black Panthers and the GI Resistance, two American insurgencies of the Vietnam era that belie the myth that the United States is not itself a "frontline" for armed resistance. My choice here is strategic not only as an incursion into the terrain of the poetic in American criticism, but also as a critical intervention into my students' ideologically determined notions of poetics. Most of my students were first-generation college students from working-class families; all of them were white. While the mutinous writings and politics of the GI Resistance problematized their rural Pennsylvania white male working-class iconography of the Vietnam-Era veteran, the Black Panther movement directly challenged their attitudes about racial politics. Although they could readily dismiss the Panther poetry as agitprop or simply "sociological," they had more difficulty assessing the GI poetry. In both cases, though, students found the poems' messages immediately accessible but saw nothing interesting in their formal properties. My discussions with them sought to illuminate form in order to demonstrate that poetics worked tactically to convey political expressions.

## "Rip off the pigs' technical equipment": Prosody in Black Panther Poetry[5]

Synthesizing the anti-imperialist national liberation theories of Frantz Fanon, Ho Chi Minh, Mao Zedong, and Fidel Castro with indigenous black nationalist traditions, the Black Panthers envisioned art as an indispensable tool of revolutionary struggle. As Captain Crutch stated in a 1968 issue of *The Black Panther*: "the Black Panther Party is an armed body for carrying out the political tasks of revolution. . . . But we must also shoulder such important tasks as doing propaganda among the people."[6] According to Emory, the revolutionary art of the Black Panthers "enlightens the party to continue its vigorous attack against the enemy as well as educate the masses of black people. .... [T]hrough their observation of our work they feel they have the right to destroy the enemy."[7] The revolutionary art called for by the Black Panthers is an aesthetic articulated precisely as an act of war against dominant aesthetics associated with white, imperialist culture. Based in black vernacular expressive culture and inflected by the rhythms of rally chants and oratory, Black Panther poems speak to a public traditionally denied access to the modernist languages reified in American poetry criticism.

The use of didacticism, propagandizing, and imperative voice in Sarah Webster Fabio's poem "Free by Any Means Necessary" not only serves to mobilize her readers but also wages an assault on dominant poetics.

> The pen
> is a weapon;
> it can discharge
> volleys of
> meaning
> hurled toward
> the bull's eye
> of truth;
>
> it can deafen
> the ear with
> the roar of
> a people's voice
> clamoring for
> justice.
>
> It can kill
> lies emitted
> in ink from
> oppressor's presses
> making beasts
> of holy men
> justifying
> their slaughters
>
> Black people
> righteous men,

throw away
those water pistols
what we need
are stoners to
riddle America's
bastions of
bigotry

which have
kept the black
man back
the poor people
poor
the dispossessed
and isolated
estranged from
the mainstream
of life.

The pen
has always
been a white
weapon; it
must be wrested
from the oppressor's
hands by
black power.

It must blast
forth the fire
of black
consciousness,
creating new images
of our people,
by our people,
for our people;

the black panthers
are the holy men

of our time;
they are the
last practitioners
of the judeo-christian
ethic—all others
have turned their
priesthoods into a mafia
protecting, not man
but status quo.

Free Huey
Free American justice

Free Leroi
Free creativity & art

Free Rap
Free free speech

Free Bobby
Free love, respect and power

Free Eldridge
Free our souls on ice

Free black panthers.
Free humanism
Free black men
Free goodness & honor
Free Huey, now,
and Free us all.[8]

When my seminar students first encountered this poem they were repelled by its naked political address, its seeming lack of verbal subtlety, and its bombastic assertions. Some felt that it was merely a chant and not meant to be read as a poem. Although Fabio's poem violates the workshop dictum to "show, not tell," within the cultural contexts of black vernacular and Black Panther activism, "telling it like it is" is a highly prized rhetorical strategy. Yet beyond its rhetoric one can discern other formal characteristics that undermine attempts to oversimplify its poetic. Line breaks, for example, as James Scully argues, are themselves political acts; and once students took note of the poem's line lengths and its many enjambments, we discussed how Fabio's line breaks might express the urgency of the political struggle, calling attention to both the free verse literary conventions they flaunt and the immediacy of their address, their enjambments propelling the audience onward to the final stanza's repetitious imperatives for freedom. On another level, I asked students to consider how the poem depends on a central metaphor which, after Amiri Baraka's 1966 call for "poems like fists," had become a compelling trope in radical black struggle: the poem/pen as a weapon. The class at first found this simply a reiteration of the cliché that the pen is mightier than the sword; but they also noted that the text posits a writing that would in fact act as a concrete weapon against oppression. From the metaphorical language of lines 3 to 14 the poem asserts that the pen "can kill" the false language of the white-owned media. The internal rhyme of line 18 ("oppressor's presses") underscores the inherent structural relationship between racial oppression and ownership of the media. In the fourth stanza, we listen to the imperative voice calling on black people to turn away from symbolic forms of resistance ("water pistols") and take up arms. In stanza 6 the poem returns to the problem of the struggle for control of representation, fusing the figurative analogy between the pen and the gun and, in stanza 7, calls for poetry to "blast / forth the fire / of black / consciousness." Demanding freedom for the party's leaders, the poem's final repetitions not only denote revolution, they also "revolt" against the academic norms of poetic discourse and, indeed, are "revolting" to the academic listener—they violate the longing for harmony, music, and lyricism often sought in repetitious verse patterns, and instead emphasize "bombastic" chant and sloganeering.

Elaine Brown's "A Black Panther Song" similarly presents a direct assault against the ruling poetic, and in particular against the convention of the sonnet, a verse form central to the production of a white lyric "I."

> Have you ever stood
> In the darkness of night
> screaming silently you're a man
> Have you ever hoped
> That a time would come
> When your voice could be heard
> In the noonday sun?

Have you waited so long
Till your unheard song
Has stripped away your very soul
well then believe it my friends
That the silence will end
We'll just have to get guns and
be men.[9]

One early reaction from my students was that Brown's poem seems to follow a flawed sonnet form. Yet what appeared as flawed, could also be read as a subversion of the sonnet's traditional insistence on the particularities of the "lyric I" in favor of the relational position of a self-in-community. The poem's address draws the reader/listener into the recognition of a shared situation of black oppression and answers this oppression by asserting a chiasmic call to arms. The questions that propel the poem to its conclusion demand an answer that can be affirmed only through an armed insurrection against racial oppression and an assertion of black identity. Neither the poem's meter nor its rhymes conform to the traditional sonnet, and while its closing lines resemble Shakespearean form, this convention is left unsettled. Instead of a series of quatrains closed by a couplet, its opening question comprises a tercet, followed by a quatrain, followed by a tercet. Its actual "turn" occurs in line 11, which begins an off-rhymed aaaa quatrain, if we read "be men" as a separate line (as it appears in both *The Black Panther* newspaper and its reprint in the book *The Black Panther Speaks*). Reading "be men" as the fourteenth line of the poem emphasizes its call for the assertion of identity against oppression; it supports those who "scream silently" that they are men. But this last strophe could also be read as a tercet, which violates the requirement of the sonnet form. The rhymes in these final lines are also significant, emphasizing a relational chain between *friends, end,* and *men.* Appropriating the vehicle of the sonnet, Brown reasserts control over poetic expression, "rip[ping] off [the pigs'] technical equipment" and articulating an oppositional identity against the totality of white subjectivity.[10]

## (DIS)FIGURING POETICS IN THE GI RESISTANCE

Although the Black Panthers have been widely recognized as an important insurrection of the 1960s, the mutinous activism of soldiers and veterans during the Vietnam War has been almost entirely ignored.[11] The GI Resistance, as it was known, consisted of various groups of soldiers and veterans opposed to the war and to the lack of civil rights in the military. Some of these groups acted as subversive fronts for militant civilian parties (such as the Workers World Party) and were highly organized; others were much more loosely organized around shared antiestablishment values. Yet because activists in GI Resistance often sabotaged military operations, and in some cases took up arms against officers, the movement posed a threat to the Vietnam-era military and the state more profound than perhaps any other of the 1960s. One unique effect of GI organizing was that it produced an extensive network of underground newspapers, many featuring dissident poetry by soldiers. By 1971 over 144 such newspapers, often crude mimeographs, had been printed and disseminated among soldiers during the war. The poem was an important mode of expression for these soldiers, whose time for writing was severely limited by military regimentation and seriously fraught with the concrete dangers of both combat and reprisal. As many GI activists have testified, dissident writing by soldiers could result in imprisonment, transfers to hazardous duty or frontline combat, and physical attacks.

GI Resistance poetry often demonstrates an obsessive attention to the details of corporeal violence; in many ways this emphasis on injury not only expresses the soldier's concrete experiences of the war but it also acts as a discursive strategy for subverting militarism. Through images, tropes, and symbols of mutilation, GI Resistance poetry sought to "frag" the military "corps," to disfigure its masculinist paradigms.[12] Just as the geography of Vietnam was a deterritorialized zone of incoherent signs for American soldiers, the human body existed in the war as a "fragged" object—a *corps sans organes*. The U.S. military's insistence on totalities, on seamless ideological structure, could be revealed by the war's atrocities to be incoherent. As Herman Rapaport has written:

> [T]he "whole" body, that sexual and libidinized corps, is perceived by the third world as inherently castrated, and . . . for this reason it was so easy to terrify troops in the field by simply bringing up again a forgotten trauma, the lack of a phallus, the body as partial object. Enter the guerilla as schizoanalyst. Indeed, the "unity" which the Military Corps maintained was only another register of the rhizome, split down the middle by an all-or-nothing ideology, de-totalized and fragmented. The Vietnamese's ability to see the contradiction was to sight Vietnam, the Thousand Plateaus,

within the metaphysical geo-psychography of the West, to have entered our paradigms only to overcode them with theirs, to liberate from within our *machine de guerre,* in true antipsychiatric fashion, the *corps sans organes.*[13]

The return of the repressed, the primal fear of castration, resonates throughout representations of mutilation in GI Resistance poetry. According to Rapaport, "When 'Charlie' castrated the corpses of its enemy, it wasn't anything else but a sign pointing to the fact that dismemberment means a loss of sexuality, a ruining of Western man's acceptability as a man in the eyes of his peers."[14] It was precisely by representing the war's mutilation of the U.S. military's masculinist myths that GI poetry articulated a discourse of resistance.

Basil T. Paquet's "Basket Case," for example, utilizes the trope of the castrated body as a paradigm of the vet's status in American culture, a culture that fetishizes the unity of its military "corps." Although students will note that this poem is written in sonnet form, I also try to show them how it undermines the form's pastoral conventions with its brutal rendering of mutilated sexuality.

> I waited eighteen years to become a man.
> My first woman was a whore off Tu Do street,
> But I wish I never felt the first wild
> Gliding lust, because the rage and thrust
> Of a mine caught me hip high.
> I felt the rip at the walls of my thighs,
> A thousand metal scythes cut me open,
> My little fish shot twenty yards
> Into a swamp canal.
> I fathered only this—the genderless bitterness
> Of two stumps, and an unwanted pity
> That births the faces of all
> Who will see me till I die deliriously
> From the spreading sepsis that was once my balls.[15]

The images of failed fertility (the "little fish" wasted in a "swamp canal," fathering only abstract sensations of bitterness and pity, the disease that replaces the scrotum) and the association of sex and violence in the image of the mine signaled by the internal rhyme (*lust/thrust, thighs/scythes*) convey the complicated relation to sexuality that the speaker experiences. In a society in which the mutilated male cannot be sexual because mutilation is metonymic of a lack of phallic coherence, a sexual subject-position for the poem's speaker both marginalizes and transgresses the norm. He is at once male, by virtue of being a soldier, and not-male, by having lost the "equipment" that defines maleness. Here I present to students accounts of Vietnam-era basic training and note how the whole culture of military training links violence to sexual identity. As the marching chant often used in training went: "This is my rifle, this [penis] is my gun, one is for fighting, one is for fun." The failure the soldier expresses in this poem is not only sexual but military, especially since sexual potency and military prowess are made almost indistinguishable in the training of Vietnam-era soldiers.

The Paquet poem, like other representations of castration in Vietnam-era soldier literature, resonates powerfully with the military discourses inscribed on the soldier's body that make loss of the phallus equivalent to military failure and vice versa. The abject fear that the Viet Cong provoked in American soldiers by castrating corpses not only foregrounds the radically deterritorialized nature of combat in Vietnam but also signifies failure of the unit, the military, and ultimately the country. While such symbolism may operate to relegitimize masculinity—to blame the loss of the war, for example, on a lack of "balls" on the part of either the soldiers or the country—more often in GI Resistance poetry castration delegitimizes the military.[16] The Paquet poem, for example, achieves its impact in its representation of the soldier's body as the obverse of dominant cultural representations of the soldier. The macho braggadocio in the opening lines crumbles into the impotence of the final lines. The male body becomes monstrous, outside the symbolic order of phallic law, engendering only alienation and "unwanted pity."

Several GI Resistance poems use images of mutilation to symbolize the incoherence of the war and the abject fear many soldiers experienced in combat. Mutilation signifying castration renders the (male) soldier body meaningless in the symbolic order; the male body penetrated by fragments of grenades and mines, or high-velocity bullets, is transgressed in a way that defies language, that makes metaphor, symbol, and circumlocutions useless. The opening up of a body, the production of gashes and new orifices that exceed the limits of the body's coherence, defies dominant representations of the soldier as a seamless totality, an impenetrable masculinity, so that rather than being the phallic penetrator, the soldier in Vietnam became the penetrated, inverting one of America's most powerful cultural symbols of the masculine. Ronald J. Willis's ironically titled "Victory," for example, renders the penetration of the soldier's body in chilling detail:

> Bullet has muzzle velocity, so great,
> 1235 feet per second
> and 1.2 seconds later it meets Steel Helmet
> who held up as well he might Bullet
> but Bullet's force was great and he
> was melting and vaporizing and
> spiritizing out tiny blobs of lead
> as Helmet gave in
> inward bulged the steel and
> on rushed Bullet 1.204 seconds
> after leaving Muzzle—
> jagged edges behind him he met
> Hair who held him up nowise in his Journey
> Skin gave way to mushroomed Bullet and
> Bones deformed at his will
> 671 feet a second he went as he tore
> vessels too surprised to bleed
> then Bullet nosed through soft gray-white stuff
> hardly hard as butter

Teaching this poem I like to point out how Willis anthropomorphizes the bullet, helmet, and body parts, while the human body the bullet has penetrated is rendered inert, inhuman, and barely discernible. Only military gear and body parts have any agency—the whole body hardly exists. This is the poem's paradox; the minutely detailed parts describe the destruction of a whole human body—but in the incoherence of the war, the whole person has no meaning, is an illegible sign, a cipher waiting to be tallied up in the body count. As the poem narrates the soldier's death, it represents the soldier's subjective memories as objects, similar to tissue or bone, that the bullet passes through:

> First he cut through the memory of Mom
> then a small gray dog
> through a first car, a wreck but the hell
> it ran
> through a huge area of scrapped knees and

pulled pigtails then
a little bit of fear . . .

The poem proceeds through a catalog of thoughts and memories that define the human experiences of a man who is in the very process of being rendered inert, dead matter before the reader's eyes. I call students' attention to the ways in which the poem undercuts the sentimentality of the soldier's memories by focusing on the agency of the bullet; the sentimental has been made senseless by the insensitive bullet. When the bullet finally explodes out of the other side of the soldier's head, the poem follows it to a tree, where it lodges, "sitting there warmly—/duty done—/to map Hell where Paradise had been."[17] In its clinical description of the bullet's penetration of the body, "Victory" appropriates military jargon turning it against itself to demonstrate its inherent inhumanity. Further, by fragmenting the soldier's body the poem reveals the incoherence of the military "corps" as a political totality. When I present this poem within the contexts of the Vietnam-era military culture, students can appreciate how its flat, declarative style articulates an insurgency against a militaristic ideology that uses jargon to obscure the grotesque realities of its actions. In subverting this language, "Victory" also "turns the guns around."

## INSURGENT POETRY AND THE RULE OF THE SUBLIME

Viewed from the ideology of the poetic, the insurgent poetry I have been discussing is crude and lacks subtlety. Yet certain situations demand "crude" expressions, and in times of urgency, subtlety may be a precious commodity available only to the few. But as I have shown these poems do not, as some critics would claim, lack formal inventiveness; indeed, form is instrumental and strategic to the politics of the poems. Poetics constitutes an oppositional politics in these cases; and the analysis of their poetics can itself be a political act. To articulate a counterpoetics in poems reviled as primitive and unrefined is to challenge the epistemological privileges securing the cultural hegemony of dominant poetics—indeed, such reading challenges the authority of the public sphere's Kantian sublime.

Kant envisioned the public sphere as an arena for the rational exchange of discourse conducted among property-owners in a bourgeois capitalist economy. Like Kant, Habermas imagines the public sphere as a guarantee of individual civil liberties concomitantly calling upon the individual's moral duty to members of the sphere.[18] Yet clearly one's membership in the Kantian public sphere was predicated not only on economic class but also on education, training, and fluency in accepted modes of articulation. Mastering the rhetorical and philosophical arts was key, which necessarily implied understanding and acquiring the skills accepted as valuable by the bourgeois cultural hegemony. The importance placed on, for example, individuality, immanence, formal innovation, linguistic complexity, and circumlocution in poetry reflects the public sphere's need to elide its inherent contradictions and obviate its local values as universal values. Under the ideology of the poetic, poems judged "sublime"*(die Erhabenheit)* transcend their particular time and place, their historical and political contexts— which is to say that they successfully articulate the local values of a hegemonic class natural and universal. *Die Erhabenheit* poetry stands above and is elevated from the common, from the ordinary, a ruler overshadowing and silencing the vulgar masses.

Indeed the rule of the sublime polices the gates of the public sphere. Terry Eagleton has argued that the aesthetic has enabled the insertion of power into the formation of the subject, at the level of the particular and individual.[19] Privileging individual appreciation and tastes, the aesthetic serves to train individuals as subjects of a certain power, to accede to the hegemony that shapes their tastes. In order to secure the social contract, however, the aesthetic must also serve to bind individuals together. It does so through the obviation of its values, and by eliding its historical, social, and political contingencies, the aesthetic poses itself as a universally recognized realm for the appreciation of beauty and, ultimately, truth. It links citizens together through an appeal to affections, imagination, compassion, sensuous impulses as against repressive rationalism; and thus, it poses itself as an emancipation of the individual that is also concomitantly a binding together of individuals (or at least individuals who have the proper level of appreciation). The dream of liberal bourgeois humanism made manifest in the aesthetic is to present itself less as a ruling social bloc and more as a "public sphere," "a political formation rooted in civil society itself, whose members are at once stoutly individualist and linked to their fellows by enlightened social intercourse and a shared set of cultural manners" (Eagleton 32).

Proper training in the "finer arts" is central to the perpetuation of the cultural hegemony represented by the public sphere. As Oskar Negt and Alexander Kluge have argued, Habermas's public sphere acts a "mechanism of exclusion" even though it presents itself as a mechanism of demo-cratic inclusion.[20] Further, Negt and Kluge show how this bourgeois public sphere maintains its hegemony and delegitimizes alternative public spheres by imposing an educational system that privileges bourgeois modes of self-expression: "All bourgeois forms of the public sphere presuppose special training, both linguistic and mimetic. . . . This is one of the most important exclusionary mechanisms of the bourgeois public sphere."[21] The poetic is one of the key "exclusionary mechanisms" of this public sphere, a discipline requiring a specialized training and knowledge that hypostatizes the inherent values and tastes of liberal bourgeois culture. By insisting on individuality and particularity in the political poem, critics reassert the liberal bourgeois myth of a rational, free subject as an antidote to party politics.

Eagleton has written, "We live within societies whose aim is not simply to combat radical ideas—that one would readily expect—but to wipe them from living memory: to bring about an amnesiac condition in which it would be as though such notions had never existed, placing them beyond our very powers of conception" (7). The poetic serves to foster this amnesiac condition, making insurgent poetry seem not only illegitimate but almost unimaginable, keeping it, in a concrete sense, outside the realm of literary criticism and outside the classroom. Thus my students come to class unable to imagine that the nakedly ideological verse of the Black Panthers, for example, could be read as "poetry." If, as Negt and Kluge assert, pedagogy is strategic to the maintenance of cultural hegemony, then by teaching insurgent poetry we can bring reading practices to the front lines, making poetic analysis itself an act of resistance, a means of disarticulating the rule of the sublime, and perhaps creating a counter-public sphere.

## NOTES

1. See Barbara Harlow, *Resistance Literature* (New York: Methuen, 1987); Cary Nelson, *Repression and Recovery: Modern American Poetry and the Politics of Cultural Memory, 1910 – 1945* (Madison: University of Wisconsin Press, 1989); Mary DeShazer, *The Poetics of Resistance: Women Writing in El Salvador, South Africa, and the United States* (Ann Arbor: University of Michigan Press, 1994); James D. Sullivan, *On the Walls and in the Streets: American Poetry Broadsides from the 1960s* (Urbana: University of Illinois Press, 1997); and my *Hearts and Minds: Bodies, Poetry, and Resistance in the Vietnam Era* (New Brunswick: Rutgers University Press, 1996).

   Despite these attempts to recuperate activist poetry, by and large it has been consigned to "sociological" studies. Susan Schweik once told me that a famous poet scoffed at her work on a black British political poet as "merely of sociological interest."

2. The Salvadoran civil war, the Nicaraguan revolution, the Palestinian *intifada*, the IRA struggle, and the Mozambican revolution all produced significant poetry. Within the U.S. one might cite poetry of the American Indian Movement, the Chicano movement, the Puerto Rican liberation movement, and the Black Panthers. Collections of such verse are available, although their survival in the literary economy is tenuous at best. For examples of collections currently in print, see Robert Márquez, ed., *Latin American Revolutionary Poetry* (New York: Monthly Review Press, 1974); Claribel Alegría and Darwin J. Flakoll, ed. and trans., *On the Front Line: Guerrilla Poems of El Salvador* (Willimantic, CT: Curbstone Press, 1989); Maina wa Kinyatti, ed., *Thunder from the Mountains: Poems and Songs from the Mau Mau* (Trenton, NJ: Africa World Press, 1990); Simon Fuller, ed., *The Poetry of Protest* (London: BBC/Longman, 1991); and Martín Espada, ed., *Poetry Like Bread: Poets of the Political Imagination* (Willimantic, CT: Curbstone Press, 1994).

   Curbstone Press has made available a number of books by partisan poets of revolutionary movements over the past decade, including works by Roque Dalton, Otto Rene Castillo, and Tomàs Borges. Although poetry collections by political insurgents often go out of print and disappear from the market, they are usually available in libraries, which suggests that much more research could be done to recuperate this work.

Yet within the established institutional settings for poetry criticism, such as the Poetry Studies presentations at the Modern Language Association annual meetings, insurgent poetry has been almost entirely ignored.

3. For more on the critique of the public sphere as a "mechanism of exclusion" see Oskar Negt and Alexander Kluge, *Public Sphere and Experience: Toward an Analysis of the Bourgeois and Proletarian Public Sphere,* trans. Peter Labanyi, Jamie Owen Daniel, and Assenka Oksiloff (Minneapolis: University of Minnesota Press, 1993).

4. Criticism's banishment of politically agitational language from poetry is not simply an aesthetic judgment. As Barbara Harlow has argued, it serves ultimately to "deny to poetry and culture any political role or access to political power. Literary production must, for the most part, be either domesticated or else disacknowledged as 'literature.'" *Resistance Literature,* 54.

5. Much of the following two sections were delivered as "Front Lines: Poetry and Insurrection" at the Poetry and the Public Sphere conference held at Rutgers University, April 25–26, 1998. I'd like to thank my co-panelists, Jan Barry, Eliot Katz, and Lorrie Smith, as well as my audience for insightful commentary.

6. "Correcting Mistaken Ideas." *The Black Panther Speaks,* ed. Philip S. Foner (New York: Da Capo, 1995), 22.

7. "Revolutionary Art/Black Liberation," *The Black Panther Speaks,* 16.

8. In *The Black Panthers Speaks,* 20–21. This poem was originally printed in the May 18, 1968 issue of *The Black Panther.* During the 1960s, Sarah Webster Fabio was well known within black literary circles as an important poet, critic, and theorist of the Black Aesthetic. Her 1971 essay, "Tripping with Black Writing," was a key statement of the movement.

9. In *The Black Panther Speaks,* 31. Elaine Brown was an important leader of the Panthers and played a leading role in steering the party during Huey Newton's exile.

10. This quote comes from Emory, "Revolutionary Art/Black Liberation," in *The Black Panther Speaks,* 18.

11. Much of the following discussion has been adapted from my book *Hearts and Minds,* 123–172.

On the panel at which I first presented parts of this paper, my co-panelist Jan Barry, an activist in the Vietnam Veterans Against the War (VVAW) and a founding member of 1st Casualty Press (which published antiwar GI literature), argued against my reading of the GI Resistance as an armed insurrection. In Barry's view, the primary motivation for resistance was pacifism and anti-militarism, and Barry sees Vietnam-era soldier dissidence as part of a tradition of liberal pacifism. While I agree with Barry's assessment with respect to the VVAW and 1st Casualty, much of the underground GI press I discuss here was produced and supported by more militant groups, such as the Worker's World Party. As my chapter on GI Resistance in *Hearts and Minds* demonstrates, many dissident soldiers used fragmentation devices and guns in their efforts to disrupt the war and overthrow the military. A number of GI activists were originally active in civilian militant groups and enlisted for the purposes of infiltrating the military and sabotaging the war effort, hoping to precipitate revolution. There are also several accounts of dissident soldiers returning to the U.S. to join armed militant factions.

Although it is critical to respect and appreciate the pacifist tradition expressed by soldier dissidence in the Vietnam War, I also believe it is historically important to recognize the extent to which resistance within the military threatened the state. I don't mean to romanticize the militant aspects of soldier dissidence; rather I want to claim that these aspects are nonetheless historically significant and that the poetry produced in the contexts of militant, armed political struggle demonstrates a poetic anathema to the ruling poetic.

12. "Fragging" was GI slang during the Vietnam War for an assassination derived from the use of fragmentation devices.
13. "Vietnam: The Thousand Plateaus," *The 60s Without Apology,* ed. Sohnya Sayres, Anders Stephanson, Stanley Aronowitz, and Fredric Jameson (Minneapolis: University of Minnesota Press, 1984), 145, 146.
14. Rapaport, 145.
15. In *Winning Hearts and Minds: War Poems by Vietnam Veterans,* ed. Larry Rottmann, Jan Barry, and Basil T. Paquet (Brooklyn: 1st Casualty Press, 1972), 20.
16. This concept paraphrases Susan Jeffords's argument concerning how Vietnam representations attempt to "remasculinize" American culture, or regain the privileged authority of the masculine that was supposedly lost in the Vietnam War. See *The Remasculinization of America: Gender and the Vietnam War* (Bloomington: University of Indiana Press, 1989).

17. Ronald J. Willis, "Victory," *Gigline* 1, no. 4 (1969): 18. Alongside this poem in *Gigline* is a drawing of a helmet with a hole in it. When the poem was reprinted in a 1969 issue of *OM,* a graphic drawing of the limp body of a soldier, his exploded head thrown back against a rock, mouth gaping open, appeared on the same page. Underneath this drawing are lines from Sophocles: "Who is the slayer, who the victim? Speak."

18. According to Habermas, "Only property-owning private people were admitted to a public engaged in critical political debate, for their autonomy was rooted in the sphere of commodity exchange"; yet the public sphere was ideally open to "anyone who understood how to use his reason in public."*The Structural Transformation of the Public Sphere: An Inquiry into a Category of Bourgeois Society,* trans. Thomas Burger and Frederick Lawrence (Cambridge, MA: MIT Press, 1991), 109, 105.

19. See *The Ideology of the Aesthetic* (London: Blackwell, 1995). References to this work will be cited hereafter in the text.

20. *Public Sphere and Experience,* 11.

21. *Public Sphere and Experience,* 45–46.

# CHAPTER 9

# *Cognitive Mapping*

*FREDRIC JAMESON*

I AM ADDRESSING A SUBJECT ABOUT which I know nothing whatsoever, except for the fact that it does not exist. The description of a new aesthetic, or the call for it, or its prediction—these things are generally done by practicing artists whose manifestos articulate the originality they hope for in their own work, or by critics who think they already have before their eyes the stirrings and emergences of the radically new. Unfortunately, I can claim neither of those positions, and since I am not even sure how to imagine the kind of art I want to propose here, let alone affirm its possibility, it may well be wondered what kind of an operation this will be, to produce the concept of something we cannot imagine.

Perhaps all this is kind of a blind, in that something else will really be at stake. I have found myself obliged, in arguing an aesthetic of cognitive mapping, to plot a substantial detour through the great themes and shibboleths of post-Marxism, so that to me it does seem possible that the aesthetic here may be little more than a pretext for debating those theoretical and political issues. So be it. In any case, during this Marxist conference I have frequently had the feeling that I am one of the few Marxists left. I take it I have a certain responsibility to restate what seem to me to be a few self-evident truths, but which you may see as quaint survivals of a religious millenarian, salvational form of belief.

In any case, I want to forestall the misapprehension that the aesthetic I plan to outline is intended to displace and to supercede a whole range of other, already extant, or possible conceivable aesthetics of a different kind. Art has always done a great many different things and had a great many distinct and incommensurable functions: let it continue to do all that—which it will, in any case, even in Utopia. But the very pluralism of the aesthetic suggests that there should be nothing particularly repressive in the attempt to remind ourselves and to revive experimentally one traditional function of the aesthetic that has in our time been peculiarly neglected and marginalized, if not interdicted altogether.

"To teach, to move, to delight": of these traditional formulations of the uses of the work of art, the first has virtually been eclipsed from contemporary criticism and theory. Yet the pedagogical function of a work of art seems in various forms to have been an inescapable parameter of any conceivable Marxist aesthetic, if of few others; and it is the great historical merit of the work of Darko Suvin to repeatedly insist on a more contemporary formulation of this aesthetic value, in the suggestive slogan of the *cognitive*, which I have made my own today. Behind Suvin's work, of course, there stands the immense yet now partially institutionalized and reified, example of Brecht himself, to whom any cognitive aesthetic in our time must necessarily pay homage. And perhaps it is no longer the theater but the poetry of Brecht that is for us still the irrefutable demonstration that cognitive art need not raise any of the old fears about the contamination of the aesthetic by propaganda or the instrumentalization of cultural play and production by the message or the extra-aesthetic (basely practical) impulse. Brecht's is a poetry of thinking and reflection; yet no one who has been stunned by the sculptural density of Brecht's language, by the stark simplicity with which a contemplative distance from historical events is here powerfully condensed into the ancient forms of folk wisdom and the proverb, in sentences as compact as peasants' wooden spoons and bowls, will any longer question the proposition that in his poetry at least—so exceptionally in the whole history of contemporary culture—the cognitive becomes in and of itself the immediate source of profound aesthetic delight.

I mention Brecht to forestall yet another misunderstanding, that it will in any sense be a question here of the return to some older aesthetic, even that of Brecht. And this is perhaps the moment to warn you that I tend to use the charged word "representation" in a different way than it has consistently been used in poststructuralist or post-Marxist theory: namely, as the synonym of some bad ideological and organic realism or mirage of realistic unification. For me "representation" is, rather, the synonym of "figuration" itself, irrespective of the latter's historical and ideological form. I assume, therefore, in what follows, that all forms of aesthetic production consist in one way or another in the struggle with and for representation—and this whether they are perspectival or trompe l'oeil illusions or the most reflexive and diacritical, iconoclastic or form-breaking modernisms. So at least in my language, the call for new kinds of representation is not meant to imply the return to Balzac or Brecht; nor is it intended as some valorization of content over form—yet another archaic distinction I still feel is indispensable and about which I will have more to say shortly.

In the project for a spatial analysis of culture that I have been engaged in sketching for the teaching institute that preceded this conference, I have tried to suggest that the three historical stages of capital have each generated a type of space unique to it, even though these three stages of capitalist space are obviously far more profoundly interrelated than are the spaces of other modes of production. The three types of space I have in mind are all the result of discontinuous expansions or quantum leaps in the enlargement of capital, in the latter's penetration and colonization of hitherto uncommodified areas. You will therefore note in passing that a certain unifying and totalizing force is presupposed here—although it is not the Hegelian Absolute Spirit, nor the party, nor Stalin, but simply capital itself; and it is on the strength of such a view that a radical Jesuit friend of mine once publicly accused me of monotheism. It is at least certain that the notion of capital stands or falls with the notion of some unified logic of this social system itself, that is to say, in the stigmatized language I will come back to later, that both are irrevocably totalizing concepts.

I have tried to describe the first kind of space of classical or market capitalism in terms of a logic of the grid, a reorganization of some older sacred and heterogeneous space into geometrical and Cartesian homogeneity, a space of infinite equivalence and extension of which you can find a kind of dramatic or emblematic shorthand representation in Foucault's book on prisons. The example, however, requires the warning that a Marxian view of such space grounds it in Taylorization and the labor process rather than in that shadowy and mythical Foucault entity called "power." The emergence of this kind of space will probably not involve problems of figuration so acute as those we will confront in the later stages of capitalism, since here, for the moment, we witness that familiar process long generally associated with the Enlightenment, namely, the desacralization of the world, the decoding and secularization of the older forms of the sacred or the transcendent, the slow colonization of use value by exchange value, the "realistic" demystification of the older kinds of transcendent narratives in novels like *Don Quixote*, the standardization of both subject and object, the denaturalization of desire, and its ultimate displacement by commodification or, in other words, "success," and so on.

The problems of figuration that concern us will become visible only in the next stage, the passage from market to monopoly capital, or what Lenin called the "stage of imperialism"; and they may be conveyed by way of a growing contradiction between lived experience and structure, or between a phenomenological description of the life of an individual and a more properly structural model of the conditions of existence of that experience. Too rapidly we can say that while in older societies and perhaps even in the early stages of market capital the immediate and limited experience of individuals is still able to encompass and coincide with the true economic and social form that governs that experience, in the next moment these two levels drift ever further apart and really begin to constitute themselves into that opposition the classical dialectic describes as *Wesen* and *Erscheinung*, essence and appearance, structure and lived experience.

At this point the phenomenological experience of the individual subject—traditionally, the supreme raw materials of the work of art—becomes limited to a tiny corner of the social world, a fixed-camera view of a certain section of London or the countryside or whatever. But the truth of that experience no longer coincides with the place in which it takes place. The truth of that limited daily experience of London lies, rather, in India or Jamaica or Hong Kong; it is bound up with the whole colonial system of the British Empire that determines the very quality of the individual's subjective life. Yet those structural coordinates are no longer accessible to immediate lived experience and are often not even conceptualizable for most people.

There comes into being, then, a situation in which we can say that if individual experience is authentic, then it cannot be true; and that if a scientific or cognitive model of the same content is true, then it escapes individual experience. It is evident that this new situation poses tremendous and crippling problems for a work of art; and I have argued that it is as an attempt to square this circle and to invent new and elaborate formal strategies for overcoming this dilemma that modernisms as such emerge: in forms that inscribe a new sense of the absent global colonial system on the very syntax of poetic language itself, a new play of absence and presence that at its most simplified will be haunted by the erotic and be tattooed with foreign place names, and at its most intense will involve the invention of remarkable new languages and forms.

At this point I want to introduce another concept that is basic to my argument, that I call the "play of figuration." This is an essentially allegorical concept that supposes the obvious, namely, that these new and enormous global realities are inaccessible to any individual subject or consciousness—not even to Hegel, let alone Cecil Rhodes or Queen Victoria—which is to say that those fundamental realities are somehow ultimately unrepresentable or, to use the Althusserian phrase, are something like an absent cause, one that can never emerge into the presence of perception. Yet this absent cause can find figures through which to express itself in distorted and symbolic ways: indeed, one of our basic tasks as critics of literature is to track down and make conceptually available the ultimate realities and experiences designated by those figures, which the reading mind inevitably tends to reify and to read as primary contents in their own right.

Since we have evoked the modernist moment and its relationship to the great new global colonial network, I will give a fairly simple but specialized example of a kind of figure specific to this historical situation. Everyone knows how, toward the end of the nineteenth century, a wide range of writers began to invent forms to express what I will call "monadic relativism." In Gide and Conrad, in Fernando Pessoa, in Pirandello, in Ford, and to a lesser extent in Henry James, even very obliquely in Proust, what we begin to see is the sense that each consciousness is a closed world, so that a representation of the social totality now must take the (impossible) form of a coexistence of those sealed subjective worlds and their peculiar interaction, which is in reality a passage of ships in the night, a centrifugal movement of lines and planes that can never intersect. The literary value that emerges from this new formal practice is called "irony" ; and its philosophical ideology often takes the form of a vulgar appropriation of Einstein's theory of relativity. In this context, what I want to suggest is that these forms, whose content is generally that of privatized middle-class life, nonetheless stand as symptoms and distorted expressions of the penetration even of middle-class lived experience by this strange new global relativity of the colonial network. The one is then the figure, however deformed and symbolically rewritten, of the latter; and I take it that this figural process will remain central in all later attempts to restructure the form of the work of art to accommodate content that must radically resist and escape artistic figuration.

If this is so for the age of imperialism, how much more must it hold for our own moment, the moment of the multinational network, or what Mandel calls "late capitalism," a moment in which not merely the older city but even the nation-state itself has ceased to play a central functional and formal role in a process that has in a quantum leap of capital prodigiously expanded beyond them, leaving them behind as ruined and archaic remains of earlier stages in the development of this mode of production.

At this point I realize that the persuasiveness of my demonstration depends on your having some fairly vivid perceptual sense of what is unique and original in postmodernist space—something I have been trying to convey in my course, but for which it is more difficult here to substitute a shortcut. Briefly, I want to suggest that the new space involves the suppression of distance (in the sense of Benjamin's aura) and the relentless saturation of any remaining voids and empty places, to the point at which the postmodern body—whether wandering through a postmodern hotel, locked into rock sound by means of headphones, or undergoing the multiple shocks and bombardments of the Vietnam War as Michael Herr conveys them to us—is now exposed to a perceptual barrage of immediacy from which all sheltering layers and intervening mediations have been removed. There are, of course, many other features of this space one would ideally want to comment on—most notably, Lefebvre's concept of abstract space as what is simultaneously homogeneous and fragmented—but I think that the peculiar disorientation of the saturated space I have just mentioned will be the most useful guiding thread.

You should understand that I take such spatial peculiarities of postmodernism as symptoms and expressions of a new and historically original dilemma, one that involves our insertion as individual subjects into a multidimensional set of radically discontinuous realities, whose frames range from the still surviving spaces of bourgeois private life all the way to the unimaginable decentering of global capital itself. Not even Einsteinian relativity or the multiple subjective worlds of the older modernists are capable of giving any kind of adequate figuration to this process, which in lived experience makes itself felt by the so-called death of the subject or, more exactly, the fragmented and schizophrenic decentering and dispersion of this last (which can no longer even serve the function of the Jamesian reverberator or "point of view"). And although you may not have realized it, I am talking about practical politics here: since the crisis of socialist internationalism, and the enormous strategic and tactical difficulties of coordinating local and grass-roots or neighborhood political actions with national or international ones, such urgent political dilemmas are all immediately functions of the enormously complex new international space I have in mind.

Let me here insert an illustration, in the form of a brief account of a book that is, I think, not known to many of you but in my opinion of the greatest importance and suggestiveness for problems of space and politics. The book is nonfiction, a historical narrative of the single most significant political experience of the 1960s: *Detroit, I Do Mind Dying*, by Marvin Surkin and Dan Georgakis. (I think we have now come to be sophisticated enough to understand that aesthetic, formal, and narrative analyses have implications that far transcend those objects marked as fiction or literature.) *Detroit* is a study of the rise and fall of the League of Black Revolutionary Workers in that city in the late 1960s.[1] The political formation in question was able to conquer power in the workplace, particularly in the automobile factories; it drove a substantial wedge into the media and informational monopoly of the city by way of a student newspaper; it elected judges; and finally it came within a hair's breadth of electing the mayor and taking over the city power apparatus. This was, of course, a remarkable political achievement, characterized by an exceedingly sophisticated sense of the need for a multilevel strategy for revolution that involved initiatives on the distinct social levels of the labor process, the media and culture, the juridical apparatus, and electoral politics.

Yet it is equally clear—and far clearer in virtual triumphs of this kind than in the earlier stages of neighborhood politics—that such strategy is bound and shackled to the city form itself. Indeed, one of the enormous strengths of the superstate and its federal constitution lies in the evident discontinuities between city, state, and federal power: if you cannot make socialism in one country, how much more derisory, then, are the prospects for socialism in one city in the United States today? Indeed, our foreign visitors may not be aware that there exist in this country four or five socialist communes, near one of which, in Santa Cruz, California, I lived until recently; no one would want to belittle these local successes, but it seems probable that few of us think of them as the first decisive step toward the transition to socialism.

If you cannot build socialism in one city, then suppose you conquer a whole series of large key urban centers in succession. This is what the League of Black Revolutionary Workers began to think about; that is to say, they began to feel that their movement was a political model and ought to be generalizable. The problem that arises is spatial: how to develop a *national* political movement on the basis of a *city* strategy and politics. At any rate, the leadership of the League began to spread the word in other cities and traveled to Italy and Sweden to study workers' strategies there and to explain their own model; reciprocally, out-of-town politicos came to Detroit to investigate the new strategies. At this point it ought to be clear that we are in the middle of the problem of representation, not the least of it being signaled by the appearance of that ominous American word "leadership." In a more general way, however, these trips were more than networking, making contacts, spreading information: they raised the problems of how to represent a unique local model and experience to people in other situations. So it was logical for the league to make a film of its experience, and a very fine and exciting film it is.

Spatial discontinuities, however, are more devious and dialectical, and they are not overcome in any of the most obvious ways. For example, they returned on the Detroit experience as some ultimate limit before which it collapsed. What happened was that the jet-setting militants of the league had become media stars; not only were they becoming alienated from their local constituencies, but worse than that, nobody stayed home to mind the store. Having acceded to a larger spatial plane, the base vanished under them; and with this the most successful social revolutionary experiment of that rich political decade in the United States came to a sadly undramatic end. I do not want to say that it left no traces behind, since a number of local gains remain, and in any case every rich political experiment continues to feed the tradition in underground ways. Most ironic in our context, however, is the very success of the league's failure: the representation—the model of this complex spatial dialectic—triumphantly survives in the form of a film and a book, but in the process of becoming an image and a spectacle, the referent seems to have disappeared, as so many people from Debord to Baudrillard always warned it would.

Yet this very example may serve to illustrate the proposition that successful spatial representation today need not be some uplifting socialist-realist drama of revolutionary triumph but may be equally inscribed in a narrative of defeat, which sometimes even more effectively causes the whole architectonic of postmodern global space to rise up in ghostly profile behind itself, as some ultimate dialectical barrier or invisible limit. This example also may have given a little more meaning to the slogan of cognitive mapping to which I now turn.

I am tempted to describe the way I understand this concept as something of a synthesis between Althusser and Kevin Lynch—a formulation that, to be sure, does not tell you much unless you know that Lynch is the author of a classic work, *The Image of the City*, which in its turn spawned the whole low-level subdiscipline that today takes the phrase "cognitive mapping" as its own designation.[2] Lynch's problematic remains locked within the limits of phenomenology, and his book can no doubt be subjected to many criticisms on its own terms (not the least of which is the absence of any conception of political agency or historical process). My use of the book will be emblematic, since the mental map of city space explored by Lynch can be extrapolated to that mental map of the social and global totality we all carry around in our heads in variously garbled forms. Drawing on the downtowns of Boston, Jersey City, and Los Angeles, and by means of interviews and questionnaires in which subjects were asked to draw their city context from memory, Lynch suggests that urban alienation is directly proportional to the mental unmappability of local cityscapes. A city like Boston, then, with its monumental perspectives, its markers and monuments, its combination of grand but simple spatial forms, including dramatic boundaries such as the Charles River, not only allows people to have, in their imaginations, a generally successful and continuous location to the rest of the city, but in addition gives them something of the freedom and aesthetic gratification of traditional city form.

I have always been struck by the way in which Lynch's conception of city experience—the dialectic between the here and now of immediate perception and the imaginative or imaginary sense of the city as an absent totality—presents something like a spatial analogue of Althusser's great formulation of ideology itself, as "the Imaginary representation of the subject's relationship to his or her Real conditions of existence." Whatever its defects and problems, this positive conception of ideology as a necessary function in any form of social life has the great merit of stressing the gap between the local positioning of the individual subject and the totality of class structures in which he or she is situated, a gap between phenomenological perception and a reality that transcends all individual thinking or experience; but this ideology, as such, attempts to span or coordinate, to map, by means of conscious and unconscious representations. The conception of cognitive mapping proposed here therefore involves an extrapolation of Lynch's spatial analysis to the realm of the social structure, that is to say, in our historical moment, to the totality of class relations on a global (or should I say multinational) scale. The secondary premise is also maintained, namely, that the incapacity to map socially is as crippling to political experience as the analogous incapacity to map spatially is for urban experience. It follows that an aesthetic of cognitive mapping in this sense is an integral part of any socialist political project.

In what has preceded I have infringed so many of the taboos and shibboleths of a faddish post-Marxism that it becomes necessary to discuss them more openly and directly before proceeding. They include the proposition that class no longer exists (a proposition that might be clarified by the simple distinction between class as an element in small-scale models of society, class consciousness as a cultural event, and class analysis as a mental operation); the idea that this society is no longer motored by production but rather reproduction (including science and technology)—an idea that, in the midst of a virtually completely built environment, one is tempted to greet with laughter; and, finally, the repudiation of representation and the stigmatization of the concept of totality and of the project of totalizing thought. Practically, this last needs to be sorted into several different propositions—in particular, one having to do with capitalism and one having to do with socialism or communism. The French *nouveaux philosophes* said it most succinctly without realizing that they were reproducing or reinventing the hoariest American ideological slogans of the cold war: totalizing thought is totalitarian thought; a direct line runs from Hegel's Absolute Spirit to Stalin's Gulag.

As a matter of self-indulgence, I will open a brief theoretical parenthesis here, particularly since Althusser has been mentioned. We have already experienced a dramatic and instructive meltdown of the Althusserian reactor in the work of Barry Hindess and Paul Hirst, who quite consequently observe the incompatability of the Althusserian attempt to secure semiautonomy for the various levels of social life, and the more desperate effort of the same philosopher to retain the old orthodox notion of an "ultimately determining instance" in the form of what he calls "structural totality." Quite logically and consequently, then, Hindess and Hirst simply remove the offending mechanism, whereupon the Althusserian edifice collapses into a rubble of autonomous instances without any necessary relationship to each other whatsoever—at which point it follows that one can no longer talk about or draw practical political consequences from any conception of social structure; that is to say, the very conceptions of something called capitalism and something called socialism or communism fall of their own weight into the ashcan of History. (This last, of course, then vanishes in a puff of smoke, since by the same token nothing like History as a total process can any longer be conceptually entertained.) All I wanted to point out in this high theoretical context is that the baleful equation between a philosophical conception of totality and a political practice of totalitarianism is itself a particularly ripe example of what Althusser calls "expressive causality," namely, the collapsing of two semiautonomous (or now downright autonomous) levels into one another. Such an equation, then, is possible for unreconstructed Hegelians but is quite incompatible with the basic positions of any honest post-Althusserian post-Marxism.

To close the parenthesis, all of this can be said in more earthly terms. The conception of capital is admittedly a totalizing or systemic concept: no one has ever seen or met the thing itself; it is either the result of scientific reduction (and it should be obvious that scientific thinking always reduces the multiplicity of the real to a small-scale model) or the mark of an imaginary and ideological vision. But let us be serious: anyone who believes that the profit motive and the logic of capital accumulation are not fundamental laws of this world, who believes that these do not set absolute barriers and limits to social changes and transformations undertaken in it—such a person is living in an alternative universe; or to put it more politely, in this universe such a person—assuming he or she is progressive—is doomed to social democracy, with its now abundantly documented treadmill of failures and capitulations. Because if capital does not exist, then clearly socialism does not exist either. I am far from suggesting that no politics at all is possible in this new post-Marxian Nietzschean world of micropolitics—that is observedly untrue. But I do want to argue that without a conception of the social totality (and the possibility of transforming a whole social system), no properly socialist politics is possible.

About socialism itself we must raise more troubling and unsolved dilemmas that involve the notion of community or the collective. Some of the dilemmas are very familiar, such as the contradiction between self-management on the local level and planning on the global scale; or the problems raised by the abolition of the market, not to mention the abolition of the commodity form itself. I have found even more stimulating and problematical the following propositions about the very nature of society itself; it has been affirmed that with one signal exception (capitalism itself, which is organized around an economic mechanism), there has never existed a cohesive form of human society that was not based on some form of transcendence or religion. Without brute force, which is never but a momentary solution, people cannot in this vein be asked to live cooperatively and to renounce the omnivorous desires of the id without some appeal to religious belief or transcendent values, something absolutely incompatible with any conceivable socialist society. The result is that these last achieve their own momentary coherence only under siege circumstances, in the wartime enthusiasm and group effort provoked by the great blockades. In other words, with the nontranscendent economic mechanism of capital, all appeals to moral incentives (as in Ché) or to the primacy of the political (as in Maoism) must fatally exhaust themselves in a brief time, leaving only the twin alternatives of a return to capitalism or the construction of this or that modern form of "oriental despotism." You are certainly welcome to believe this prognosis, provided you understand that in such a case any socialist politics is strictly a mirage and a waste of time, which one might better spend adjusting and reforming an eternal capitalist landscape as far as the eye can see.

In reality this dilemma is, to my mind, the most urgent task that confronts Marxism today. I have said before that the so-called crisis in Marxism is not a crisis in Marxist science, which has never been richer, but rather a crisis in Marxist ideology. If ideology—to give it a somewhat different definition—is a vision of the future that grips the masses, we have to admit that save in a few ongoing collective experiments, such as those in Cuba and in Yugoslavia, no Marxist or Socialist party or movement anywhere has the slightest conception of what socialism or communism as a social system ought to be and can be expected to look like. That vision will not be purely economic, although the Marxist economists are as deficient as the rest of us in their failure to address this Utopian problem in any serious way. It is, as well, supremely social and cultural, involving the task of trying to imagine how a society without hierarchy, a society of free people, a society that has at once repudiated the economic mechanisms of the market, can possibly cohere. Historically, all forms of hierarchy have always been based ultimately on gender hierarchy and on the building block of the family unit, which makes it clear that this is the true juncture between a feminist problematic and a Marxist one—not an antagonistic juncture but the moment at which the feminist project and the Marxist and socialist project meet and face the same dilemma: how to imagine Utopia.

Returning to the beginning of this lengthy excursus, it seems unlikely that anyone who repudiates the concept of totality can have anything useful to say to us on this matter, since for such persons it is clear that the totalizing vision of socialism will not compute and is a false problem within the random and undecidable world of microgroups. Or perhaps another possibility suggests itself, namely, that our dissatisfaction with the concept of totality is not a thought in its own right but rather a significant symptom, a function of the increasing difficulties in thinking of such a set of interrelationships in a complicated society. This would seem, at least, to be the implication of the remark of the Team X architect Aldo van Eyck, when, in 1966, he issued his version of the death-of-modernism thesis: "We know nothing of vast multiplicity—we cannot come to terms with it—not as architects or planners or anybody else." To which he added, and the sequel can easily be extrapolated from architecture to social change itself: "But if society has no form—how can architects build its counterform?"[3]

You will be relieved to know that at this point we can return both to my own conclusion and to the problem of aesthetic representation and cognitive mapping, which was the pretext of this essay. The project of cognitive mapping obviously stands or falls with the conception of some (unrepresentable, imaginary) global social totality that was to have been mapped. I have spoken of form and content, and this final distinction will allow me at least to say something about an aesthetic, of which I have observed that I am, myself, absolutely incapable of guessing or imagining its form. That postmodernism gives us hints and examples of such cognitive mapping on the level of content is, I believe, demonstrable.

I have spoken elsewhere of the turn toward a thematics of mechanical reproduction, of the way in which the autoreferentiality of much of post-modernist art takes the form of a play with reproductive technology—film, tapes, video, computers, and the like—which is, to my mind, a degraded figure of the great multinational space that remains to be cognitively mapped. Fully as striking on another level is the omnipresence of the theme of paranoia as it expresses itself in a seemingly inexhaustible production of conspiracy plots of the most elaborate kinds. Conspiracy, one is tempted to say, is the poor person's cognitive mapping in the postmodern age; it is a degraded figure of the total logic of late capital, a desperate attempt to represent the latter's system, whose failure is marked by its slippage into sheer theme and content.

Achieved cognitive mapping will be a matter of form, and I hope I have shown how it will be an integral part of a socialist politics, although its own possibility may well be dependent on some prior political opening, which its task would then be to enlarge culturally. Still, even if we cannot imagine the productions of such an aesthetic, there may, nonetheless, as with the very idea of Utopia itself, be something positive in the attempt to keep alive the possibility of imagining such a thing.

## Notes

1. Dan Georgakis and Marvin Surkin, *Detroit, I Do Mind Dying: A Study in Urban Revolution* (New York: St. Martin's Press, 1975).
2. Kevin Lynch, *The Image of the City* (Cambridge: MIT Press, 1960).
3. Quoted in Kenneth Frampton, *Modern Architecture: A Critical History* (New York: Oxford University Press, 1980), pp. 276–77.

## Discussion

*Question (Nancy Fraser)*: First, I want to say something, for the record, about the implicit political gesture built into your presentation of the question of totality, which seemed to me rather irresponsible, given that there have been many discussions of the issue and that many nuanced positions have been expressed. You essentially conflated many differences and subtle positions on this question. But I do have a more constructive question to ask, because I am sympathetic to a certain kind of totalizing thought, namely, a critical social science that would be as total and explanatorily powerful as possible. Thus, I wonder why you assume that cognitive mapping is the task of the aesthetic? Why wouldn't that be a task for critical social science? Or are the two different kinds of tasks conflated in your paper?

*Jameson*: The question of the role of the aesthetic as opposed to that of social sciences in explorations of the structure of the world system corresponds, for me, to the orthodox distinction (which I still vaguely use in a somewhat different way) between science and ideology. My point is that we have this split between ideology in the Althusserian sense—that is, how you map your relation as an individual subject to the social and economic organization of global capitalism—and the discourse of science, which I understand to be a discourse (which is ultimately impossible) without a subject. In this ideal discourse, like a mathematical equation, you model the real independent of its relation to individual subjects, including your own. Now I think that you can teach people how this or that view of the world is to be thought or conceptualized, but the real problem is that it is increasingly hard for people to put that together with their own experience as individual psychological subjects, in daily life. The social sciences can rarely do that, and when they try (as in ethnomethodology), they do it only by a mutation in the discourse of social science, or they do it at the moment that a social science becomes an ideology; but then we are back in the aesthetic. Aesthetics is something that addresses individual experience rather than something that conceptualizes the real in a more abstract way.

*Question*: Your paper suggests that cognitive mapping is an avenue by which we might proceed at this point in time. Is this a tactical or a strategic choice? If it is tactical, then how do you conceive the question of strategy? And if it is strategic, what do you consider the problem of tactics today? The reason I raise such a question is that there seem to be opportunities now to create an interconnected culture that might allow real political problems to be discussed. If that's true, the question of strategy and tactics seems central.

*Jameson*: That's an important question. I would answer it by trying to connect my suggestion with Stuart Hall's paper, in which he talked about the strategic possibilities of delegitimizing an existing discourse at a particular historical conjuncture. While I haven't used it, the language of discourse theory is certainly appropriate here (along with my own dialectical language). My comrade and collaborator Stanley Aronowitz has observed that whatever the left is in this country today, it has to begin by sorting out what the priorities really are. He takes the position that our essential function for the moment is pedagogical in the largest sense; it involves the conquest of legitimacy in this country for socialist discourse. In other words, since the sixties, everybody knows that there is a socialist discourse. In the TV serials there's always a radical; that has become a social type, or, more accurately, a stereotype. So while people know that a socialist discourse exists, it is not a legitimate discourse in this society. Thus no one takes seriously the idea that socialism, and the social reorganization it proposes, is the answer to our problems. Stuart Hall showed us the negative side of this struggle as the moment in which a hegemonic social discourse finds its content withdrawn from it so that finally those things that used to be legitimate are no longer legitimate and nobody believes in them. Our task, I think, is the opposite of that and has to do with the legitimation of the discourses of socialism in such a way that they do become realistic and serious alternatives for people. It's in the context of that general project that my more limited aesthetic project finds its place.

*Question (Darko Suvin)*: First of all, I would like to say, also for the record, that I agree with your refusal to equate totality with totalitarianism. I want to remind people of the strange origins of the connotations of the word "totalitarianism." They arose after the war, propogated by the Congress of Cultural Freedom, which was associated with such names as Stephen Spender and Irving Kristol and with journals such as *Encounter*, funded by the CIA, as it turns out. This is admittedly not a conclusive argument; even people funded by the CIA can come up with intelligent ideas now and then. But it should make us wary of such an equation. So I think your rebuttal is well taken and not at all irresponsible.

Now to my question. I have a major problem with this idea of postmodernism, even though your elaboration of it is more sophisticated than Ihab Hassan's. I would like to try to suggest a way out of this problem. Rather than thinking of your three stages of capitalism—which I gather are coextensive with realism, modernism, postmodernism—as closed, Hegelian world-historical monads subsequent to each other in time, so that at some point (around 1910 or 1960) one begins and the other ends, couldn't we think of capitalism as a whole (beginning whenever you wish), and then a series of movements (such as realism, modernism, postmodernism) that have become hegemonic in a given subphase of capitalism but do not necessarily disappear. After all, most literature and painting today is still realistic (for example, Arthur Hailey). In other words, we have shifting hegemonies, although I think it is still a question of how one proves that a shift of major dimenstions (for example, the shift associated with the names Picasso, Einstein, Eisenstein, and Lenin) really occurred in the 1960s. But, in that case, postmodernism could emerge as a style, even become hegemonic in the United States and Western Europe, but not in India and Africa, and then lose its dominant position without our having to shift into a new episteme and a new world-historical monad. And you would have a subtler interplay between a simultaneously coexisting realism, modernism, and postmodernism on various levels of art and literature.

*Jameson*: The questions of periodization, coexistence, and so on are difficult and complex. Obviously, when I talk about such periods they are not sealed monads that begin and end at easily identifiable moments (beginning in 1857 and ending in 1913, or beginning in 1947 or 1958, etc.). And there are certainly survivals and overlaps. I would, however, like to say something about the problem people have with the concept of postmodernism. For me, the term suggests two connected things: that we are in a different stage of capital, and that there have been a number of significant cultural modifications (for example, the end of the avant-garde, the end of the great auteur or genius, the disappearance of the utopian impulse of modernism—about which I think Perry Anderson was both eloquent and extremely suggestive). It's a matter of coordinating those cultural changes with the notion that artists today have to respond to the new globally defined concrete situation of late capitalism. That is why it doesn't bother me too much when friends and colleagues like Darko Suvin or Perry Anderson or Henri Lefebvre find this concept of postmodernism suspicious. Because whatever Perry Anderson, for example, thinks of the utility of the period term postmodernism, his paper demonstrates that something really fundamental did change after 1945 and that the conditions of existence of modernism were no longer present. So we are in something else.

Now the relative merit of competing terms—postmodernism or high modernism—is another matter. The task is to describe that qualitatively different culture. By the same token, I trust that people who have some discursive stake in other terms, such as totality or its refusal, do not take my remarks on the subject too narrowly. For example, I consider the work of Chantal Mouffe and Ernesto Laclau an extremely important contribution to thinking about a future socialist politics. I think one has to avoid fighting over empty slogans.

*Comment (Cornel West)*: The question of totality signals an important theoretical struggle with practical implications. I'm not so sure that the differences between your position and Perry Anderson's, and those put forward by Stanley Aronowitz, Chantal Mouffe, Ernesto Laclau, and a host of others can be so easily reconciled. And it seems to me that if we continue to formulate the question in the way that you formulate it, we are on a crash course, because I think that holding on to the conceptions of totality that you invoke ultimately leads to a Leninist or Leninist-like politics that is basically sectarian, that may be symptomatic of a pessimism (though that is a question). If we opt for the position that Mouffe, Laclau, Aronowitz, and others are suggesting, the results are radically anti-Leninist as well as radically critical of a particular conception of totality. It is important to remember that nobody here has defended a flat, dispersive politics. Nobody here has defended a reactionary politics like that of the *nouveaux philosophes*. Rather, their critiques of totality are enabling ones; they are critiques of totality that is solely a regulative ideal we never achieve, never reach. And if that is the case, I really don't see the kind of reconciliation that you are talking about. I think you were very comradely in your ritualistic gestures to Chantal and Ernesto and others, but I am not so sure that we are as close as you think. Now that means we're still comrades within the left in the broad sense, but these are significant differences and tendencies within the left, and I didn't want to end the discussion with a vague Hegelian reconciliation of things when what I see is very significant and healthy struggle.

*Jameson*: I don't understand how the politics I am proposing is repressive, since I don't think I have yet even proposed a politics, any more than I have really proposed an aesthetics. Both of these seem be all in the future. Let me try to respond by expanding on the distinction that came up in the second question, the notion of tactics versus strategy. It is not a question of substituting a total class/party politics for the politics of new social movements. That would be both ridiculous and self-defeating. The question is how to think those local struggles, involving specific and often different groups, within some common project that is called, for want of a better word, socialism. Why must these two things go together? Because without some notion of a *total* transformation of society and without the sense that the immediate project is a figure for that total transformation, so that everyone has a stake in that particular struggle, the success of any local struggle is doomed, limited to reform. And then it will lose its impetus, as any number of issue movements have done. Yet an abstract politics that only talks socialism on some global level is doomed to the sterility of sectarian politics. I am trying to suggest a way in which these things always take place at two levels: as an embattled struggle of a group, but also as a figure for an entire systemic transformation. And I don't see how anything substantial can be achieved without that kind of dual thinking at every moment in all those struggles.

# CHAPTER 10

# America's New Bards: The Corporate Classroom and Its Lessons on Life

*Ross Talarico*

MY LIFE AS A POET HAS NOT BEEN EASY. In some important ways, I've been fortunate—publishing widely, my poetry fairly well-respected, reading poems to audiences throughout the country, even winning a couple of prestigious literary awards. But of course, like most poets in America, I've had to teach for a living, and in that arena too I've been fortunate, being poet-in-residence and making my way to the top professorial rank, and creating and directing a writing program to boot. So what's so wrong, one might ask.

Something is very wrong. There's something very suspicious about a system that not only tolerates poets, but subsidizes them through universities and elsewhere, the same system that has not only obliterated the true poetic sensibility in this country but that has incorporated the elements of poetry and subverted them through corporate means. What I'm saying is that every year in America poets multiply themselves with a diminishing correlative effect on community and society itself. The art gets more imitative, less distinct, more elitist, less socially, politically, and culturally aware. The poet gets more self-centered, more interested in the existential act of performance, the effect of the expression, immediate rather than reflective, the focus personality rather than the universal awareness that goes beyond personality. Poetry, in effect, for all the annual summer conferences, for all the literary magazines that continually sprout, for all the MFA programs in creative writing and all the students inhabiting them, has been subverted, like everything else in the culture of appearances and surfaces, by a system that provides, as critic Eliot Weinberger puts it, "a sealed cage with plenty of cheese."

I've always believed that at the core of poetry, of any art, was the notion of an affirmation of life—a celebration based on thorough, honest examinations of human existence and predicament, even if a resolution echoes the words of Goethe, who says, "If I have to live a life of anguish and fear, I thank God at least I have a voice to speak of it." To know that voice, to use it and share it with others is the essence of poetry, from the Greeks to Shakespeare, from Walt Whitman to . . . to . . . That's just it—something doesn't change, we need a voice, one that speaks at once to both heart and mind, something at once both immediate and universal. And that voice continues to exist brilliantly in fact, on the surface of our needs—the strong image, the musical phrase, the visual jolt, and the sound bite. It is the voice of the corporate, commercial enterprise, employing all the poetic components *except for reflection, insight, analysis*, etc., since those things are not part of the corporate operati. In other words, as we are bombarded endlessly by the provocative images and lyrical phrases of television commercials and magazine ads, edified by their apparent relevance, the recognition (if nothing more) of legitimate social themes as they tickle our subconscious, we go through the motions of literary appraisal, the brief, economic display of sound and sight, a hint of conflict, and the illusion of epiphany; but on any closer examination, we have been manipulated by an experience that helps us deny our humanistic possibilities, slick, striking, sensational campaigns that exploit our fears, anger, hostilities, and anxieties—in other words, a notion completely antithetical to the literary equivalent, that affirmation of life that leads to empathy, insight, and an understanding, that might put the true value of consumerism into proper perspective.

To make a closer examination of "perspectives," I'll take a critical look, a closer reading and analysis, of three popular, successful commercials created by the unlimited budgets of corporate enterprises—namely, McDonald's, General Motors, and Coca-Cola. These represent the work of the "new bards in America," which I allude to in the title of this essay. They also represent, there's no denying it, the brilliant effectiveness of big-business advertising in general, where no one spends one or two million dollars in production costs and air-time without a guarantee, based on numerous indicators, that the effort will more than pay for itself in consumer response. Then I'll look at three poems that correlate subject-wise and to some possible degree thematically with the three commercials. These poems were written by ordinary people, not professional writers or poets—a white male in his seventies, a white woman in her eighties, and a black teenager. The three poems were produced in community center workshops on a volunteer basis.

There was, a year or two back, a series of McDonald's commercials that served to induce in our conscious and subconscious minds the memorable, catchy, lyrical phrase, "You deserve a break today." They generally employed, not surprisingly, family scenes, images, and settings that brought us immediately to a consideration of one of the most pressing of our social dilemmas—recognition of traditional family values in a culture of dysfunctional families. The particular commercial I'll allude to begins with a scene inside a house in which a father is working on a door frame and a son about five years old approaches him as he's kneeling and obviously consumed by some repair. We are, as viewers, almost immediately edified in the sense that we are exposed to a man, a father, "taking care" of his house. It is, of course, a symbol as well as an image, the gesture representing the head of the household attending to the entranceway to the home itself. In a few seconds we will see, if we critically review the commercial, a wonderful irony emerge, one worthy of our sense of literary merit, since it is not, after all, an entrance we are to be concerned with but an exit from the home. The young boy comes up to the father and suggests some idle social activity—first playing ball, then some other activity as he approaches the dad again; but each time the father rejects the suggestion by saying no, and "Not now, I'm busy." We can all relate to that scene, and, if we had to, could add a hundred other items that, in a world of being too busy with work and thus too busy with the growing agenda of general repairs, commitments, and exhaustive responsibilities, kept us from spending the appropriate time with our children in a nourishing home environment. Again, this is edification—we recognize a theme and the commercial certainly seems to consider it. Finally—don't forget, we are seeing the entire commercial unfolding in thirty seconds or so—the boy comes up to the father and asks, "Can we go to McDonald's?" Suddenly the music swells, the expressions of both the child and the father change, and magically we are removed from the setting of hostility and noncommunication; in other words, as we begin to hear (and sing along in our mind) the lyrical music of the orchestrated phrase, "You deserve a break today," we *leave* the house. The scene that emerges as the music begins to dominate is, of course, a McDonald's restaurant, where the father and son are now cheery and talkative, sitting there, as one might in another culture in an earlier existence at a kitchen table at home, enjoying each other's company. The camera zooms back, capsulating the full environment, more families eating, laughing, ordering hamburgers and fries, all under the friendly golden-arches canopy of McDonald's. The viewer is inundated with the warmth of knowing that family values still exist, despite the frightening impact of homes without dialogue, without face-to-face family dinners, without one parent or the other, or without parents at all. We have been edified by the extraordinary power of the "poetic" elements of the commercial, the stark swift images, the economy of words sustained by music, the quick juxtaposition of conflicting emotions—the muted sadness and the concluding spectacle of animated joy, the epiphany, and the celebratory moment of the communion of souls. It leaves us feeling terribly satisfied, and why wouldn't it, since we are spared almost entirely of any personal concern whatsoever as far as the issue that certainly is the basis of the commercial in the first place, a concern that, in the hands of the "poets" of these corporate advertisers, has been totally overwhelmed, concealed, and dissipated by the end of the commercial.

But if we were to "read" the commercial, as we might a poem or a short story, we might utilize our powers of analysis and come up with the *real* message of the commercial, which is responsive to the fears and anxieties that engage us in the first place: if it is too stressful to deal with the serious issues of dysfunctional family life in America, come to McDonald's—for only at McDonald's can you experience old-time family values as you know them, smiling dads and moms cheerfully providing you with the sustenance of Big Macs. The irony I alluded to earlier is evident in a critical reading of the commercial: the doorway leads *out* of the house, not in, for *only* in the corporate world of McDonald's can family values have the opportunity to materialize. The message is sinister, a stark contrast to the mood of the viewer who is already singing along with the well-known lyric that signifies the corporate entity. Such a state of mind needs nothing more than a continual menu of neural stimuli and an assurance that everything is fine in designated shelters.

In contrast, let me share with you a poem also written on the subject of father and son, one written from a man in his seventies remembering his father. His name is Joe Pohl, and this was written in a free public creative writing workshop in upstate New York. The poem is called "Casting" and re-creates his experience as a boy fishing with his dad:

> Summer lay gently on the land that day,
> the lambent air, soft and warm
> carried, for a moment, the voice of a
> summer thrush
> over the murmuring drone of honey bees.
>
> There was no wind to disturb the morning,
> all was motionless to suit the day.

We parked and walked silently to the stream
lost in quiet anticipation.

The water, over the tumbled rocks,
gurgled with that unique sound of
all shallow streams,
a sound as ancient as the earth.
We too, as fishermen, were of this
brotherhood
of ancient things.

We assembled our rods, strung the lines
through the guides,
attached the lures, and stepped into the
water.

"I'll go up as far as the bridge" said my
father
and smiled, because he would beat me to the
first cast.
And I saw the years fall from his shoulders.

There was no gap between us now.
We were both the same age.

Certainly this poem gives us in its minute or so reciting time what a
thirty-second commercial might give us. There is a specific setting established, images that set the tone of the experience and a theme briskly established—it too examines a particular moment when father and son come
together in some timeless salute to love and companionship. The "visuals"
are established early on and throughout the poem. Of course, the power of
the poem comes through with the preciseness of the language, language
that allows us not only to see the immediate setting but to place it within the
spiritual human landscape, which gives the fishing trip a universal nature, a
connection to other men, other times—a "brotherhood / of ancient things."
There is nothing very abstract about this poem, and nothing vague. It is a
tribute to our ability to sustain memories that not only distinguish our individual lives but that define our magical abilities, our imagination and

interpretive powers, to define moments by our emotional attachments to them. It is in all the multileveled associations with the words we encounter, in fact, that not only suggest a timelessness by analysis of theme, but that alter even our time-frame regarding how we read and experience the poem: although one could recite this poem in sixty seconds, it takes much, much longer to "experience" the poem—pauses, recollections, personal and universal allusions, reflection, and of course the standard assessment of the quality of a literary experience, the urge to reread it.

Ironically, the last two lines of the poem—"There was no gap between us now. / We were both the same age,"—could easily be used as an effective "soundbite" conclusion to some commercial promoting a product with an appeal to succeeding generations: a car, clothing, cologne, exercise equipment, etc. But Joe Pohl's poem gives those lines the context they deserve, articulating a particular thought that strikes all of us deeply as we remember our parents and hold them forever in a moment that defines a feeling that can't be duplicated by a product endorsement. And that's the difference here between the million-dollar McDonald's ad, in which it's convenient to reach out for anything, even a Big Mac, to forget the fears and anxieties that are a part of our home experience, and this seventy-some-year-old man who simply worked through his inner resources to create a lasting memory of the bond that is suddenly illuminated on an afternoon spent fishing with his father. One avoids the story because it is overwhelmed by a musical phrase; the other invites analysis through its complementary lyrical invitation.

The other day my nine-year-old daughter brought a packet home from her third-grade class. It was a brochure, promotional letter, and order form for something called Sentimental Souvenirs School Days Keepsake Collection of Memories Systems, a local business, as the letter explained, "specializing in the Packaging of Memories." Here's a part of the letter, addressed "Dear Parents," that was a part of the package:

> These one-of-a-kind keepsake systems are designed to be "STUDENT FRIENDLY," allowing children from preschool through high school and even college to package THEIR OWN MEMORIES in a fun and organized way. Students have taken great pride in sorting and choosing their most treasured memories to preserve. What a wonderful way to encourage ORGANIZATIONAL AND CATEGORIZING SKILLS as they consolidate the mounds of "stuff" we all tend to collect into one compact place.

What was this "system"? It was a bunch of brightly colored three-ring notebooks and photo albums. That was it. The price? Well, of course, there were two: one retail, $59.95, and predictably the "special reduced price for students of $43.95 to $49.95! This whole scam, this embarrassing ploy to conceal blatant consumerism with an artificial regard for educational concerns, obviously was approved by both the principal of the school *and* the PTA (which is mentioned in the promotional material). I'm hoping a few teachers were outraged by this misguided promotion of the culture of consumerism—but I'm not sure if any of them brought any of the issues so obvious here to the attention of their students (or if they were allowed to). But the point should be clear: there was once "a compact place" (to quote Sentimental Souvenirs) where we decided not just what thoughts and experiences were memorable, but why experiences stayed with us, were a joy to recall, or haunted us, for that matter. That compact place used to be the mind, and its process became evident as we created meaningful essays, or journals or diaries, or short stories or poems, or even oral histories or anecdotes—and we could always keep a scrapbook, and you could get a photo album at K-Mart for five dollars and, with the encouragement of parents or teachers, decorate it yourself. This episode seemed so preposterous to me I couldn't believe it. Did any parents complain, send a note to school, or have a heart-to-heart talk with their kids about it? I don't know. All I do know is that I couldn't have *invented* a more appropriate instance to make my point about how little effort we give the essential elements of story-telling and analysis in our culture compared to the degree and extent we push our young people into a culture of consumerism that eliminates inner resources.

Let's pause for another commercial.

The most popular theme in today's world of corporate advertising is, aptly, gender hostility—commercials reflecting the confusion, resentment, and anger brewing between men and women concerning the abandonment of traditional roles, roles that are at once romanticized and ridiculed in our society, commercials often promoting reversal of gender roles. We now see the man on all fours in a garden, shirt off, smelling the flowers, while a woman looks on from an upstairs window, seductively fantasizing, and in one pants commercial actually blowing the seeds of a dandelion she holds in her hand toward him. In another, it is the man pushing the shopping cart down the aisle in a toy store, the child tagging along, held in check from throwing teddy bears and things into the cart; and it is the man who comes across what used to be his toy, a full-size Isuzu all packaged up on a shelf, and, of course, he too will have to ask mom, who's probably working in this inference, for the toy that traditionally was his to pick out and purchase—a sports-utility vehicle at that! Certainly there is no denying the existence of genuine concern in both men and women when traditional roles are challenged, basically shattering the idea altogether of men being the breadwinners in the family and women being the stable homemakers who keep the destructive, dysfunctional forces of our culture at bay. There are genuine issues here that consciously and subconsciously need to be addressed—the socioeconomic reality is that, in real-money terms, male earnings have been steadily declining over the past twenty years, probably as much as 20 percent. Women, whether agreeable or not, have been forced out of the home for many years now and, still underpaid and underemployed, find themselves slaves to the male-created consumer images of them that promote—always—style, not substance. There are serious questions to be asked; it is no wonder commercials promoting conflict between genders are edifying and engaging.

There was a popular General Motors commercial that aired over several months last year. It was an ad for a Chevrolet Camaro, and it centered on gender hostility, with a young, free-spirited woman sailing down a country road on a beautiful afternoon. Camaro, it is said in the auto business, is a "woman's car," or a car appealing to young women in their initial new car-buying experiences. And how does GM relate to this important market group? Advertisers, in many ways more than literary artists, are sensitive and responsive to the emotional makeup of social and cultural issues. The intent of a commercial such as this one is to bring us immediately to the issue, allowing us to recognize its relevance consciously and subconsciously, and, crucial to the speed and intensity of the images that flash by us, lead us to the emotional reaction that allows us to vent without rational analysis. The woman, driving fast and seemingly carefree, at first resembles the figure in many car commercials of the past in which the road and the vehicle, of course, are symbols of freedom and adventure. But a few seconds into the ad we realize there's much more to this than a simple romantic flight of fancy. She begins shifting the gear stick, thrusting it with authority through the gears. Each time she does, with the Camaro roaring responsively in a deep-throated echo of words, she firmly declares the objects of her wrath, the direction of her fury: "This," she declares, thrusting the shift into second or third, "is for my ex-boyfriend." "And this," she continues, throwing the shift forward as if delivering a knee to the groin of an intruder, "is for my boss." This combination of wrath and freedom, harmoniously coming together with each verbal thrust, gives the car enough speed to pass a truck in front of her—and, as she does so, we are given several angles of the event with a good look at the truck driver, a vile male with a perverse grin on his face. He looks at her and says something we can't make out, and then, shithead that he is, points his hand lewdly down at his crotch and says something to her as she passes. She's obviously the protagonist at this point, all the men in her life, including the truck driver, sharing the blame and being left behind. But we're not done yet. As she passes the truck, we see her coming toward us speeding down the road. She looks happy—thrilled, really, as if anger and resentment were the culture's new highs. Then, in a beautiful piece of camera-work, she reaches up through her open sun roof and gestures to the truck driver she's left behind. Is she waving? We don't know because the shot of her hand is carefully blurred, a technique that's clever and effective because by this time our own subconscious interprets the gesture for us, the only gesture appropriate for this thirty-second adventure in hostility: she's throwing the guy the finger as she makes her way down the open road. This commercial too makes effective use of the elements of poetry—the brief, immediate images and the indisputable tone of its human utterance, the clever variations of traditional symbols, and the elaboration of the open-road metaphor. The viewer, once again, is edified, but again, the issue is cleverly concealed—the product of corporate manipulators sensitive to universal needs but with no interest in understanding human predicaments. Their message: in the corporate world of General Motors, you can be delirious with revenge on others (and why shouldn't you be!), a trait not to be examined and resolved in some humanistic, empathy-producing manner but one that makes you hip and cool as a consumer, a personal triumph that eliminates the need to see any further than gender hostility as an end in itself.

Compare that effective commercial with a similar theme expressed in a poem based on an oral history from an 80-year-old woman remembering her early life in America during the depression. Katheryn Edelman told this story as a member of our senior citizen oral history workshop when I was the writer-in-residence for city government in upstate New York. We would hear the story as a group, probe for details, and I would transcribe it and write it as a personal narrative:

Convertible, 1928

Top down, eighty miles an hour,
dust rising
through the apple-scented air

of Route 104,
little George strapped down
to the brown leather cushions
of the front seat,
I aimed that Hudson toward Syracuse
and pushed my foot to the floor . . .

I saw the car
white top up one day, down the next,
in a showroom on Stone Street
in Rochester.
Every day I walked by it,
seeing myself behind the wheel,
my sunlit hair in the wind.
When I told my husband I wanted it,
he simply said, "Buy it."
but he didn't say it joyfully or eagerly.
There was a kind of resignation
in his voice;
he had wanted to go to Europe
with the money we had—I'd wanted
a house, and that's
what we bought a year earlier.

So I scraped up all the money
I could get my hands on,
about twelve hundred dollars
(including the mortgage money)
and I drove that Hudson convertible
right out of the showroom.
When I drove it around the neighborhood,
my friends thought I was a bootlegger's wife.
I took weekly trips to my mother
in Syracuse,
and I let the wind
have its way with my hair.

But the broker didn't hesitate
when our mortgage was late,

and in thirty days past due
there were locks on the doors,
and the house my husband never wanted
wasn't ours any more.
He got laid off too,
being the Depression and all.
Europe was even more distant in his eyes.

So we made our way
to my mom's farm in Syracuse,
where we had to live for a while.
Broke, we drove around
in that Hudson convertible
until even little George learned to
laugh in the modest glory
of the rumble seat.
On Route 104 there were no speed laws,
no cops,
and we drove so stylishly fast,
like a bootlegger and a bootlegger's wife.
But we were a little scared then,
not of the speed,
but because we didn't know exactly
where we were going.
(*Transcribed and written by Ross Talarico*)

Like the GM commercial, this story too involves a woman, the sense of frustration and impending freedom, and a brand-new automobile. Of course, this rendering has something most commercials studiously avoid: *context.* The individual experience serves, as literature usually does, to illuminate a prevailing social milieu, in this case a predicament that comes into conflict with personal desires. The contrast allows us to see the vital gap, in fact, between desire and reality, but it does so in a manner that gives us a fuller view of the range of human emotions—in this case, to use a phrase from Henry Miller, a kind of "hopelessness without despair." Katheryn too is resentful of the man in her life. He doesn't understand her needs and wants to retreat from it all. She, quite courageously and perhaps foolishly, is obsessed by the symbol in America that represents, even in 1928, a spirit that would be impossible to suppress in a devastated economy: the new car and the open road, speed and freedom, a new life waiting somewhere in the dusty unknown. But true to the makeup of human complexity, fear is a part of the equation—without it, the story of Katheryn would be merely quixotic, foolish, and sensational. We see the significance of the contrast between the spirit of the individual and the drudgery of the times. In the GM commercial the "victory" was superficial and hollow, the *possession* of the car the only saving grace of an individual without any resilient resources; Katheryn Edelman's "victory" is qualified, as it should be, by the emerging awareness of nothing less than her own humanity. The woman in the Camaro throws a finger and there's nothing else to consider in a world that eliminates reflection, analysis, and other possibilities. Katheryn, on the other hand, understands the consequences of her decisions and delves deeper into her own resources, accepting for a moment her ambiguous and paradoxical experience. There is, after all, plenty to be angry and resentful about in America in the nineteen twenties and thirties, people losing everything and dreams dissolving in a disillusioned awakening of social realities—there is no way to consider the individual without some perspective of the time and conditions that shape that individual. For the woman in the GM commercial, the Camaro is everything; for the woman in the narrative poem, the car is simply the vehicle (excuse the pun) through which she recognizes the conflicts, the cares, and responsibilities (especially little George in the rumble seat), the vital human capacities to worry, wonder, dream, and survive.

Let me make one thing clear. I am not writing to chastise the writers and producers of commercials. They do their jobs brilliantly, and I'll be the first to admit that and congratulate them. They manage to capture moments through their imagination and technological advancements, what poets have longed to do for hundreds of years. Their images are startling; their contextual brevity and economy of words are fascinating. They are lyrical, masters at bridging the familiar with the unique. No one can argue that. The point I want to make is that the *intention* of the commercial-maker and literary writer is fundamentally different from the very beginning of the process. Of course, no one would argue that either. What I am concerned about is the idea that we are creating whole generations now who no longer can make a distinction between a brightly produced ad and an illuminating literary moment—between, in fact, a story and a nonstory. In the 1990s it is safe to say that the emergence of the sophisticated techniques of television commercials has influenced what we see in television programming—from sitcoms to news shows to MTV. Like the commercials I am reviewing, TV programming edifies us by bringing up topics that are, it is to be hoped, of concern to us, like the sit-com *Friends* (in a society in which people tend to have fewer friends than ever), and *Martin* (in which blacks have a wonderful sense of humor about their societal plight and are given a middle-class existence for their good sportsmanship), and MTV (where teenagers think they are seeing brief visual narratives to accompany the music instead of random images that serve to eliminate completely any sense of story whatsoever). Films, in turn, now strive to imitate their television counterparts since the audience has now been trained by television. In this steady bombardment, what is lost, of course, is the ability to even recognize what a "story" consists of—because the fundamental elements of storytelling are not really essential to our idea of entertainment. Reflection, paradox, recognizing conflict and ambiguity, compromise and what T. S. Eliot called "the contentment that comes with knowing"—none of these literary components are desirable in the corporate world of selling products. Why would they be? All I'm saying is that it is time to educate ourselves, especially our educators and our children, to know the difference, to make distinctions by being able to analyze intelligently what's given us, not just in the world of books and literature but in the world of "story substitutes" that bombard us daily. No, ad-makers, television producers, and blockbuster film producers do their job and do it well. What we can't do is ignore them, pretend that what they produce is not competing with our sense of what literary awareness has become. What we need to do is not look the other way and get snobbish or elitist about what's happening to young people in America; what we have to do is take a better look, a closer look. We have to snap out of the half-daze that defines our passive yet receptive response to television. We have to approach it with the same critical tools that we use in assessing literature. We have to "read" television. We have to "read" the ads and commercials in America.

Let's "read" another one.

But before I interpret a classic commercial for Coca-Cola, I should explain an essential concept to ward off the typical insistence that there is no intended effort on the part of advertisers to engage in the exploitation of prejudice, hatred, fear, etc. I agree—no group of marketers sits in a back room somewhere figuring out how to deceive the public or to take advantage of the worst instincts of Americans. They do their best to simply produce "what works" and that's their job, without taking the time or effort or money to articulate whatever themes may or may not be inherent in their productions. A writer of literature, short stories, or poems would have that responsibility as a part of the genre and tradition in which he or she works. But commercial producers, those imaginative artists, are free to make their incessant pitches in a way that at once *attracts* an audience and keeps the product in the commercial's consciousness. Next to the highlighting of the product itself, there really are no issues that need any serious thought, no human explorations required except for initial engagement. As a matter of fact, what they do consciously is make an effort to avoid presenting any real issue that might make the viewer look either beyond the commercial itself or, worse yet, inside himself or herself to inner resources that might provide the kind of nourishment that can substitute or even ridicule the consumer yearning for the product. So there is no secret committee, no darkened back room, no cynical conspiracy— just a group of clever professionals engaged in a system that pays well and propagates itself. Since there is no story to be told, just random impressions, they just go about their jobs, not in a devious way, but seemingly immune to whatever interpretations may come from a more serious critical reading of their work.

The Coke ad begins with a black teenager getting on a bus in some urban setting. Several people get on with him, and there are a few people sitting near the front of the bus, especially in those first seats that face the aisle. The teenager looks about seventeen, I would say, and he's wearing headphones and carrying a Walkman. As he gets on the bus, he gets a curious look from the bus driver, and as he begins to walk down the aisle, he gets looks of anxiety from a couple of people sitting in the front of the bus, especially an older white woman. The young man himself is tall, good-looking, and very light-skinned, and as the music increases in volume in the commercial, we see that he is singing along with that same music, which in the visual is apparently coming from his Walkman and his earphones. So what we have so far is a variation of a stereotypical urban scene, one that is frightening to many Americans, especially white Americans: a black teenager getting on a bus in an urban setting. The looks of anxiety on the faces of those on the bus confirm this—an important image in the crux of the ongoing scenario. Should we be worried about black teenagers crossing the paths of little old white women in urban situations in America? In our stereotypical, prejudicial world, and in the context of both realities and myths about the violent, troublesome existence with young black men and boys in our inner city, the answer is yes, perhaps. And this commercial takes full account of that fear— indeed, it is the prelude to the commercial's real message, which will follow in the next few seconds. As the young black man continues down the aisle to find a seat, we see the faces of the bus riders change from anxiety to a kind of simpleminded cheer as the music swells and the volume of the young man's voice increases. We get a good look at him too—handsome, with a voice like an angel's, nothing in the least threatening about his demeanor. He is singing, aptly, the Coca-Cola song, and by this point we are all charmed by him, quite a contrast to the stereotypical reaction that caused the curious, anxious looks in the first place.

But the commercial saves its devastating message for the heavy-hitting conclusion. By the time he finds a seat, we are already convinced that he's an angel with a voice to match, and even the old white lady wouldn't have to worry if he carried her groceries home. But that's not quite enough as the commercial ends and we're singing along, feeling relieved and upbeat in a situation most suburban viewers wouldn't put themselves in for a hundred bucks. The last image is the *coup de grace*. Our final look at the young man as he sits in his seat reveals there is no one behind him—for him to sit in the last seat against the back of the bus would be, no doubt, too blatant, might indeed startle us and wake us from that half-daze so essential to television watching. But he is, by all accounts and I'm sure not left to chance, the black boy at the back of the bus—and the message is clear: in the world of Coca-Cola, in that corporate shelter where we can feel safe, there's no need for anxiety because blacks, even young, energetic, teenager blacks, take their place obediently and harmlessly—-where? *In the back of the bus, of course, where they belong!*

In contrast, let's look at a poem written by an eighteen year-old black youth in a basketball/writing program in a recreational center in upstate New York. The poem also takes place in an urban setting, and it also has a gentle quality about it, and though it lacks the catchy musical theme, the music of its words gives us a deeper understanding of what it means to be a black teenager in the midst of the inner city. Compare the difference in the viewer/reader's reaction when you finish the poem: the concern is outward after the literary experience, a concern that is based on an awareness of context and social realities—the affirmation of human nature comes from a sudden exposure to a world too often stereotyped and exploited, not from a simplistic notion that we can shelter ourselves from such exposure, denial, diversion, and corporate identity.

FATHER
*Germone Wright*

On the corner of Seward and Jefferson
I met a bum who just might be
my father.

At least he looked like
the man I once knew.
At that moment memories came to my mind.
I began daydreaming of the times
he'd take me to the park.
We'd go swimming,
and then play tag until I was
all worn out . . .
Suddenly I was back on Jefferson Avenue
and all I saw was the darker shadow
of life.
There were junkies and dope dealers
just standing around, all centered
on the same thing, some dealers, some users.
Then I thought to myself,
Which did my father do? He'd left
so sudden I couldn't follow him.
He left when I was eight
and now I'm eighteen.
As I looked up at the sky
I saw only half the moon, looking so dim.
It looked like a lightbulb about to blow.
As I looked down
the ground seemed broken up too,
cracks in the streets, glass all over.
As I looked up once more
to look around,
I could not see my father,
and I thought, there he goes again,
disappearing,
never telling me where he's going.

Something simple happens when we read a legitimate piece of literature: we learn something. Sometimes it's a reiterance or a clarification of what we already know or have suspected but have not articulated in a meaningful way; sometimes the experience of the literature provides an insight, or another way of seeing or understanding; sometimes, in the works that strike us deeply, we experience the epiphany that marks unforgettable works. In this poem by an eighteen-year-old who, to my knowledge, had never written a poem before, what comes clear to me is the irony of the role reversal at the end of the poem—the son wondering and caring about where the father has gone, and doing so in a fatherly way and with the maturity of a fatherly voice. This poem too, like the Coke ad but in a more sophisticated, referential way, acknowledges the kind of things that certainly make the inner city streets and corner no place to plan a picnic. But it doesn't dismiss them or marginalize them in a lyrical tribute to an illusionary America in which these things don't exist. In a short poem, which takes again in real time no longer to read than it takes to watch a commercial, we are taken through the complex mindframe of a youth recognizing someone who triggers a memory; we get the warmth and intimacy of that memory, the sorrow of its absence, and the sudden emptiness of a youth who has to reverse painfully the roles of boys and men. For me, it's a moving reminder of the deep psychological scars we have left on a nation, on an entire group of children growing up disadvantaged in urban America. It's not the Coke ad—and the difference is crucial: it brings us closer to reality, not further from it. We see the soul of a black teenager, not a light-skinned boy who *believe it, can really sing*! One is the voice of our true humanity, the other is another version of MTV.

So what do we do? If we leave it up to the think tanks like the one led by William Bennett a few years ago, we will probably get another bizarre list of suggestions, like making young kids read Shakespeare, from a group who, perhaps purposely, ignores the reality of the devastating impact of television and popular culture. The fact is that we cannot pretend that television is just an innocent bad habit in a country in which only the production of military arms is a business bigger than entertainment. Teachers across the country have to admit what they already know: little Johnny may or may not read an assigned chapter any given evening, but he sure as hell will watch his favorite sit-com—and all the commercials that are embedded in and frame it. No, we can't sit back and bemoan the diminishing reading and critical-thinking skills while someone making three times the pay of schoolteachers gets not only access each night to the young minds of America, but another million dollars or so in expenses to make sure the job is done effectively. So here's my suggestion.

First of all, we should begin immediately to train our teachers in this country to develop skills in critical analysis and apply those skills not only to literature but to television, advertising, and other media communications that produce the equivalent of and counterpart to the kind of reading traditionally assigned in our classrooms. This is no easy task. I am presently

Professor of Writing and Communications at a university in California that certifies more teachers than any other university in the country; and I can assure you that analysis and interpretation of writing and literature, that critical thinking itself, are not skills generally nurtured or developed in our educators. One can't begin to "read" the sophisticated techniques of a big-budget television commercial, for example, if one can't articulate the difference between subject matter and theme in a short poem, or recognize the inferred conflict or the prevailing metaphor in a short story. If we utilize literature, understanding its components, its themes, and most of all its meanings in a social and cultural context so the whole process of learning is relative and sensible, then we can apply those analytical tools to the television equivalent of poems, stories, etc., that we're given daily as a cultural initiation into the world of consumerism. And that, of course, would comprise the next part of teacher training—to apply their critical-thinking skills to television, and, for a change, take the medium seriously and confront it head-on instead of dismissing it. For a start, I'd suggest that every new teacher trained in this country be given a course, at least, in a cultural studies program in Literary Media Analysis. At that point, I can make my most important suggestion: That on any given school night, we, as educators, send five or ten million students home with the assignment to turn on the TV and write a critical analysis of *Mad About You*, or *Home Improvement*, or *Friends* or *Law and Order*, or *ER*, and certainly a couple of major commercials that grace the "programming." Encourage the students to take a close look, a "reading" of the TV material as they would a poem or a short story. Indeed, a corresponding part of the educational experience would be to find works of literature that can be compared to the TV programming, and contrast them through critical analysis, much like those examples in this essay.

Imagine the impact on television producers and advertising executives if suddenly they understand that we educators fully acknowledge their extraordinary gifts in creating programming that shapes the minds of our young people. They would be honored. And our children might begin to make a distinction crucial to developing cultures throughout the history of mankind: recognizing the difference between an affirmation of life and a hollow promise of material well-being; distinguishing between a "story," which is still the primary vehicle through which generations pass on wisdom, and a "nonstory" (psuedonarrative), in which momentary sensations eliminate the need for a general perspective and provide for a parallel existence between isolated moments and isolated individuals.

CHAPTER 11

# Leaping into the Dialectic: Etudes in Materializing the Social

*RANDY MARTIN*

ONE QUESTION FOR RADICAL PEDAGOGY is how the form our teaching takes relates to the content of what we are trying to get across. In this we ask a lot of ourselves, but what exactly are we asking from our students? We can wait for the end of the term to give exams or assign papers, but as students sit in the classroom on a daily basis, how are we to ascertain what is going on if learning and sitting still are concomitant activities? One response could be that it depends on what we are trying to teach. And if we are fundamentally committed to teaching that social change is both necessary and possible, then we might wonder whether students can learn this lesson sitting still.

Certainly the social change we have in mind must be specified, and this requires a great deal of mental activity. To pursue a marxist pedagogy, the critique of capital must be contextualized historically and grounded culturally. Methodologically speaking, how do we promote students' sense that they are part of social change, that this is a perspective, not simply an observation, and therefore their lived relation to the context that makes them and that they in turn create is tangibly in motion? The grasp of this lesson, I would suggest, is not simply a cognitive act but one that assumes that learning is also enacted, put into motion, so to speak, as performance, an embodied activity. It is not that such embodiment is avoidable as students sit through class, but the question for teaching social change is how they can learn from what could be considered the material social basis of historical activity.

Teaching social change entails offering students the opportunity to participate in the movement of learning and demonstrating that the social world is not simply an idea in their heads but the very medium in which they are embodied. My interest here is in concretizing these claims with some very simple classroom illustrations, which ask for different kinds of responses from our students than may typically be the case. Minimally, these exercises ask that we connect the form of classroom participation with the material content of the very context in which students work together. I come at these examples with a background in the performing arts, specifically jazz improvisation, modern dance, theater, and clowning. While these arts focus on the techniques of the body, they are also pedagogical staging grounds in their own right, whose lessons can be exported to other disciplinary domains. The particular setting in which I apply them is a class called Perception and Creativity, a course that both contextualizes the arts in society and deploys the arts, with their special sensitivity to the form that knowledge takes, as a means of gaining insight into the workings of society. My present posting is at Pratt Institute in Brooklyn, New York, a school of art, architecture, design, and information science (but not of the performing arts). Here, the students are inclined to give the arts the kind of intellectual weight I want to attribute to them but not necessarily more inclined to get out of their seats and move than students I have taught elsewhere. The mix of fine and applied arts at Pratt tends to draw students from diverse economic and cultural backgrounds, and the school attracts international students, who comprise nearly a third of those enrolled. I therefore want to share these particular students' affinities and resistances to my endeavors (which for me prove to be quite instructive) and then think through some possible implications for radical pedagogy.

The students have been sitting all semester, and my request that they push their chairs back and stand in the center of the room does not exactly bring them leaping to their feet. Even after they clear a space in the center of the room, they remain close to their chairs, still respecting the now widened gulf that typically separates them from the teacher and charges the latter with the power to speak and to silence them. At my prodding, they enter this newly demilitarized zone and with further encouragement disperse themselves throughout it. They are visibly agitated to be exposed in the very borderlands that otherwise lend a measure of protection and anonymity from this kind of bodily scrutiny, which, I now try to assure them, is effectively harmless.

The students are already caught up in a dilemma of radical pedagogy, namely, that they are transgressing a norm that conventionally serves not only to keep them in their place but to limit what can be demanded of them. One should expect that such mandated transgression, resting as it does on the very authority it seeks to undermine—in spatial terms, the apparent fixity of the teacher's position in class—can succeed only if it exposes the contradiction that it depends upon. For the powers gained by the left academy are not all of its own making; they are in some measure borrowed from an institutional hierarchy that allows radical teachers to operate but also renders them the objects of student resistance even when the class claims to act on the students' behalf (for which class does not?).

Faced with the dead weight of these traditions, I want to re-establish for the students the very sense of bodily security that I have just denied them, if only to set the terms for what I want them, through their own activity, to move away from. Before starting, the students are cautioned that I am about to take them through a series of simple movement exercises using various images, and if an image is confusing or ineffective for them, they should not dwell on it but see if the next one works any better. I invite them to relax, breathe, take a moment, and feel the connection of the weight of their own bodies to the floor on which they are standing. When they have settled into their new places for a bit, I offer them, in the most soothing tones I can evince, a narrative with pregnant pauses meant to allow the students to execute what I am suggesting. The narrative goes something like this:

Imagine that the inside of your entire body, from head to toe, is filled with fine, soft sand. Your feet are porous and you stand on a meshed grating under which is a hole as deep as you are tall. The sand flows gently, gradually, out from the bottoms of your feet into the hole. The smoothly polished grains of sand leave your head, your neck, the sinking sand moves past your shoulders, down your arms and out your fingers. The level of sand in your body continues to sink below the line of your chest, then your navel, your pelvis, thighs, you feel it coursing gently through your knees and calves, past your ankles, until finally the last grains have left the soles of your feet. The inside of your body is now completely hollow, unobstructed by bones or organs, and you can feel a cool breeze flowing through it. Following that breeze, a rush of effervescent spring water percolates up through the sand. The water is sucked through your feet and begins to rise through your body, filling it with millions of tiny bubbles suspended in clear liquid. Now, not only your feet but the entire surface of your body is porous. As your body cavity fills, the water continues to circulate, and as the little bubbles burst they are released through your skin into the air. The bubbles escape from every surface of your body, leaving every nook and cranny—under your armpits, between your fingers, behind your knees—fizzing and tingling. You allow this tingling sensation to be released into the room around you and as you do so, the air on every side, top and bottom, becomes dense, spongy, and gelatinous. Now all of that dynamic motion that coursed through your body fills the space in which you are suspended, and you feel it now on the outside of your skin. Standing where you are, press your body forward into this spongy mass and feel the space before you compress a little. Feel the compression evenly across the frontal length of your body, and compress and release several times. Try the same behind you. Feel the density of the space evenly along the back of your neck, the small of your back, all the way along your legs to your heels. Push to one side. Then the other. Press up above you and down through your feet. The space outside you is supporting you, it accepts your weight and returns it in perfect equilibrium. Now, without directly looking at anyone, see if you can compress the space between you and another person on the other side of the room. Try this again with a person off to the side or behind you. Maintain this sense of connection through the physical density of the space around you as you begin to walk slowly in the room. Do not worry about where you are walking, keep your attention on the changing configuration of space as you move in it. Try to remain aware of the space as a whole as it continuously changes shape. Without overfocusing on any one person, try to retain at least a vague awareness of everyone together. Continue to walk at your own pace, and keep your attention on the changing shape of the space that lies around you. Allow yourself to imagine that the openings in this space create pathways for you to walk along, which in turn open up spaces for others to be drawn to the places you have just departed from. Add to your movement repertory of weavings and changes in direction, the possibility of stopping. As you stop, sense the motion that continues to move through you as others reconfigure the space around you. When you start to move again, do so only in relation to the movement of another. See if you can register the stopping and starting of others, whether you see them or not, in your own body. Allow the movement by somebody else to act as a switch for you, bringing you to motion or to rest. Find out if it is possible to move only in relation to the stopping and starting of others. This does not mean that you commence or cease your walking every time someone else does, only that you can sense every change in the space, that whether you go or stay, no change leaves you unaffected, every movement courses through you, and you in turn contribute to every shift or traversal that transpires. In this you need not see anyone, let alone mirror his or her movement; you are attached to all that occurs at the same time that that larger occurrence leaves a constantly moving imprint on the place you happen to occupy at the moment. All right. Come to a pause together.

We begin our discussion with the students' reflection on their experience. One student observes that she maintained a certain self-consciousness that spilled over into embarrassment from time to time. We talk about the cultural boundaries around the body that sustain a sense of privacy. Another student offers that at moments he lost the sense of a fixed boundary between himself and others and began to feel that the changing space could actually move him. The gender differences here are duly noted, and we ask whether there are other social and cultural determinants of where the presumed normalcy and naturalness of the body's boundaries lie. But already it is difficult to lay responsibility with nature for what we are here calling the body, and we must turn to what was so quickly sketched among us to see how the contours of a social body, as both means and medium of activity, might make itself felt.

The question then arises, if the taken-for-grantedness of the free-willed individual securely in place within the body's physiognomy can be so quickly disturbed, and the seemingly invisible social forces that move us all so readily materialized, what maintains the static boundary between self and Other? What else is captured by this divide between what is inside and outside a body so that history appears as a series of exemplary individual's ideas rather than a contest over the context in which those ideas and the forces they refer to appear? For it is not that the students deny the existence of society but rather that their own formation as an instance of its principles of motion seems difficult to grasp. Social structure is something we discuss in class, but it is a concept that apparently refers to something abstract, fixed, and invisible. The effects of the students' own social movement, however weak, fleeting, or minor, at least materialize for the moment in the classroom, that which is constantly being referred to outside of it in so many of the lectures that have preceded this class session.

Through all of this discussion, the students have not yet sat down. They remain standing in the space they have carved for themselves out of what previously was something of a no-person's land. They literally entered the social boundary that divided teacher's and student's space, as if the former were public and on display and the latter invisible and opened up this edge both for physical occupation and critical scrutiny. One student referred to the security of watching the teacher perform lectures under the guise that the student could not be seen, a reversal of the conventional rendering of the panopticon where the subordinated and incarcerated assume they are under constant surveillance because they cannot see their jailers. But the benefits of adhering to the classroom as spectacle will be further challenged as I ask the students to come forward and perform the paper assignment I have given them.

The writing assignment also poses the question of how we study change. The problem once again as I pose it to the students is that life is constantly in motion, yet when we try to observe that process and write down what we see, we arrest that motion in the words we put on the page. Further, society, riven as it is with divisions, does not change all at once as a single piece but is comprised of different elements that move at uneven rates in relation to one another. Indeed, the tensions among these diverse elements result in what we perceive as a movement of the whole society. The performing arts, I suggest, provide a language of motion that can inspire our writing and our perception of how to grasp the internal dynamics of social change.

The students are asked to observe a social situation from the perspective of its being a performance. They are to identify five terms that define the situation: (1) the performer or focus of the activity; (2) the audience or those who bear witness to the event; (3) the text, the implicit script, codes, or rules that govern what is expected to happen in the situation; (4) scenic objects, the things or props that help focus the activity; and (5) the scenic space, what is taken by participants as the environment within which the activity occurs. After observing an actual situation—whether a street corner, an elevator, a parade, a classroom—and identifying these five terms, the students are to focus on a clear change in one of the elements and to see how it impacts upon all the others. Their papers consist of recording the observed differences between what they initially see and what transpires, and then evaluating what this teaches them about the dynamics of change. They are to pay special attention to the forces that maintain and transform the implicit social text, so that what structures the situation is rendered not only visible but fungible as well.

One reservation the students tend to voice is that social change and historical movement appear as phenomena that transpire beyond the reach of their own daily experience. Such matters may affect them, but they are hard-pressed to imagine themselves the protagonists of historical change. They express concern about finding a situation significant enough to write about. I try to assure them that their life circumstances are already replete with historical significance but that the standard means of evaluating history precludes the students' recognition of their own place within it. To illustrate how to select a situation and make use of it, I recount to them an occurrence that happened one year when I was giving the assignment. It was a balmy, late October day—Halloween in fact. As I sought to explain how scenic objects carried meanings of the social text, an anonymous passerby on the street threw an egg into the classroom. The egg sailed through the open window and landed right in front of me. Laughter. It was then possible to detail how this newly introduced prop shifted focus away from the performer, revealed the fragile boundary of the scenic space, and punctured the authority that governed that implicit classroom text. I noted my own efforts to assimilate the challenge, but the point was made.

Returning to the ethnographic present of the classroom, after the students have completed the first movement exercise, I solicit volunteers to have their papers performed. In one section of the class, students are reluctant and suggest we draw numbers to select an exemplar and then are skeptical when I announce who is closest. The model for these performances comes from the work of the Brazilian dramaturg Augusto Boal, whose book, *Theater of the Oppressed,* based on the methods of Paolo Freire, has already been discussed in the class.[1] Specifically, Boal, whose interest is in collapsing the distinction between actors and spectators that is supposed to divide protagonic action from passive absorption of the theatrical message or text, develops an exercise called form theater. His "poetics of the oppressed" is designed to get people to recognize the contingency of their own life circumstances so that they can "rehearse the revolution." In his workshops, participants enact scenes from their own lives using other participants not only as living actors but as the inanimate objects and features of the built environment, from machinery to doors to furniture. Once the scene is in motion, anyone can yell "Stop," replace an actor or prop, and change the action to alter the course of the event.

I ask the students to do this with their classmates, using the two moments in their papers as the change in destiny of the scene. Once the students have set the stage and enacted their papers, I ask them to improvise different possible outcomes, so that any student, not simply the author of the paper, can yell "Stop," intervene, and change the scene. Once again, at first the students are reluctant, especially to tell their colleagues what to do and to physically put them in their places. After several papers are enacted, their reluctance fades and they intervene more readily. They stop two cops who are detaining a student (with a pass) who has jumped the subway turnstile. They refuse to continue working under arrogant bosses. When a panhandler receives a five-dollar bill and is asked for change from the donor, she says apologetically that she has no change and leaves the subway car, applauded in her exit.

In discussions afterwards, students make two observations that strike me. One is to note that over the past hour we have enacted in class itself the very premise of the paper by changing the underlying text that governs what constitutes appropriate learning activity. The students' willingness to cooperate in an otherwise atomizing classroom setting suggests that the cement that holds them in their individuated positions may not be as strong or rigid as one might think after fifteen or more years of learning to sit still and alone in class. That even this minor form of cooperation comes so readily to the surface hints at the larger process of socialization that engenders mutual interdependence but maintains this is if it were a latency in society.

The other thing noted by the students is the difficulty of translating one medium of expression into another. Several recognized that they had not written their papers so that they could be performed, and perhaps more profoundly, some saw that the text they themselves had written rested upon mobilizing the labor of others if it was to be brought to life. The appreciation that rules, codes, and structures do not actually generate the capacity for social activity that springs from bodies working together, that what governs activity does so by taking what it does not acknowledge it has taken and depends upon, has the potential to alter the students' understanding of politics and order. When their papers are a writing assignment, it is their efforts that are ordered. When their papers become the text, the marching orders for others, they realize the gap between the power to demand and the ability to enact what the text can only imply.

Clearly the intervention I have designed for the students is quite limited in its scope and range. Students may recognize what performance can teach about the materiality of the social spaces they embody, but the single episode on display in the classroom is at best a provocation. I have taught classes that alternated between the classroom and a movement studio over the entire semester, which culminated in improvised performances done in public places. One, a shopping mall in upstate New York, elicited a furious response by the mall manager, who took us into his office and lectured us on the impropriety of distracting the shoppers and engaging in activities in the mall's common areas without his permission. Fortunately, we kept the video camera running through this encounter, and the footage made for a lively discussion the next day about public space and private property.

Privileging the performing arts pedagogically can be a lot of fun. But to do so also introduces some interesting conceptual challenges to certain sacred dualisms of mainstream social science, such as the distinctions between micro and macro, structure and process, society and self, public and private. It is tempting to see in performance either an analogy for society or a model for small-group interaction. But the most radical pedagogical possibilities lie in neither of these directions. For if the exercises I have described even point toward the internal motion that constitutes the materiality of the social, then this is nothing less than the dialectic that propels all historical activity, irrespective of its scale. The notion of a boundary that could separate the large from the small in social life, fixity from that which is in motion, the differentiated self from the socialized ensemble, however influential in the social sciences, always rested on fragile philosophical foundations.

Improvisation, which in the examples above is what concretizes the dialectic as practical activity, is neither an analogy nor restricted to the intimacy of interpersonal interaction. Improvisation is not spontaneous expression but rather the moment at which the response to a textual demand (whether implicit or explicit) overwhelms what the initial commands themselves mandated by structuring the field in which the response takes place. Students are surprised that changes in the classroom codes come so easily, even as they themselves resist these changes for reasons justified by their suspicion of what is being demanded of them by the teacher without the benefit of knowing the conditions of evaluation for what they produce. Obviously in these incidental changes, the rules, the relations of authority as such do not disappear (as if they could suddenly), but their appearance becomes noticeably contingent on the very activity that the students engage in. While the space of this essay does not permit further elaboration, I want only to say that what performance suggests in the classroom is not simply an instance of history made without choosing its conditions, but also a theory of history, the one that Marx turned to the theater to evoke.

## NOTES

1. See Augusto Boal, *Theater of the Oppressed* (New York: Urizen Books, 1979) and Paolo Freire, *Pedagogy of the Oppressed* 20th rev. ed. (New York: Continuum, 1995).

   For related reading, also see the following titles: Jacques Attali, *Noise: The Political Economy of Music* (Minneapolis: University of Minnesota Press, 1984); Michael E. Brown, *The Production of Society: A Marxian Foundation for Social Theory* (Totowa: Rowman and Littlefield, 1986); Jan Cohen Cruz, and Mady Schutzman, *Playing Boal* (New York: Routledge, 1993); Jane Desmond, ed., *Meaning in Motion: New Cultural Studies of Dance* (Durham: Duke University Press, 1997); Harold Garfinkel, *Studies in Ethnomethodology* (New York: Prentice-Hall, 1967); Erving Goffman, *Presentation of Self in Everyday Life* (New York: Anchor Books, 1959); Karl Marx, *The German Ideology*, In Karl Marx and Friedrich Engels, *Collected Works*, vol. 10 (New York: International Publishers, 1979); Karl Marx, *The Eighteenth Brumaire of Louis Bonaparte*. In Karl Marx and Friedrich Engels, *Collected Works*, vol. 11 (New York: International Publishers, 1979); Peggy Phelan, *Unmarked: The Politics of Performance* (New York: Routledge, 1993).

CHAPTER 12

# The Work of Noise and Pedagogy

*CSABA TOTH*

*There could be millions of people creating only noises.*
—Blixa Bargeld, Einsturzende Neubauten

ON MAY 21, 1980, the arched, oval-shaped roof of the Congress Hall in West Berlin, Germany, where President Jimmy Carter made an appearance during his 1978 visit, collapsed, injuring five people. About 120 persons attending a business convention at the time of the collapse escaped unhurt out the back door. "Structural fatigue" in the pre-stressed concrete edifice—constructed in 1957 by the Benjamin Franklin Institute as the American people's "gift" to West Berliners—caused the collapse of the new building. The 1,200 – seat Congress Hall located near the old Imperial Diet (Reichstag), and not far from what was then the Berlin Wall, served as the symbol of the Americanized western half of the city that overcame the devastation of World War II and defied Berlin's division.[1]

The collapse of the Congress Hall symbolically signaled the beginning of the noise/industrial movement[2] in Europe and had its (self-)destruction immortalized in the title of Einsturzende Neubauten's manifesto-like record *Kollaps*.[3] By the mid - 1980s, the movement crossed both the Atlantic and the Pacific, and sound practitioners in the United States and Japan were engaged in generating their own variant of noise and factory performance. Groups such as the Neubauten drew larger and larger crowds to their live shows in old factories, Test Department performed to massive working-class audiences in support of the heroic strike of the National Union of Miners (1984), and most recently (1997), the Burning Man festival, an annual fire-noise event, attracted over ten thousand worshippers to Nevada's Black Rock Desert.

The birth of noise culture was concomitant with the deindustrialization of the West, a development that went hand in hand with a globalizing process: the emergence of a global information network and immense transnational corporations. Saturation with consumer goods and informational simultaneity wove a web far finer and more minute than anything imaginable in the classical industrial era. The programmed, anonymous, depersonalized workplace imposed its tyranny of silence, and a domination by corporations of the urban-industrial space. The postindustrial condition cast its long shadow over those left behind in the barracks-like apartment blocks of cities across Europe, and the company towns of the United States and Japan.

In the 1980s, cities such as Manchester, parts of London, the Rust Belt in the U.S. (Pittsburgh and Cleveland) became necropolises of a deindustrializing neocapitalism, while West Berlin, home of Einsturzende Neubauten, embodied the paranoid mentality of the Cold War and came to symbolize "the decline of the West." Concomitant with industry's demise or treading through its ruins, venture capitalists heavily invested in the new wave of "cyber work," producing models such as North Carolina's Research Triangle, Seattle, Portland, Oregon, and solidifying Silicon Valley's grip over the Bay Area in Northern California.

Why generate noises of industry amidst industrial ruins? What is the "value" of noise performance for a new pedagogy? For noise practitioners, the factory, brutal as it was, made sense: the work existed and took form in a concrete, lived time. Each object was different from the others and was produced by labor that was possible to isolate in itself. The necessary labor of production was intrinsic in the product of labor. I construct noise performance as an aesthetic production that challenges social and cultural institutions, collapses genre boundaries, and has broader pedagogical implications. A certain kind of critical social theory and radical pedagogy grounded in modernist ideals and practices relates to popular cultural work disapprovingly. Critical pedagogist Ursula A. Kelly claims in her book *Schooling Desire* that while some such antagonism may be informed by a fundamentally bourgeois moral sensibility that rejects "undisciplined pleasures and desires," it is undeniable that "the anti-libidinous character of some progressive discourses positions many to feel a choice between pleasure and politics must exist."[4] A critical look at noise performance as a uniquely postmodern cultural practice within youth culture—one that builds on nomadicity, border-crossing, and chaos, among others—will examine lived engagements of media and meaning only to reveal more about how "desires, dreams, identities, and social relations are shaped."[5] An understanding and, when necessary, a critique of such cultural engagements and affective investments by practitioners and "consumers" alike are vital to a more democratic schooling project. Taking seriously the cartography of popular cultural practices will make student-teacher relations more informed and more meaningful and potentially will require a refiguring of the social, cultural positionment of the educator herself or himself. An examination of noise production is all the more intriguing since, due to its "loudness" and "atonality," it most often successfully defies (school-)disciplining or curricular "colonization."[6]

Our pedagogies, I firmly believe, will benefit from the unique and multifarious perspectives afforded by contemporary youth cultures. As cultural theorist George Lipsitz explains, "We need to explore the potential of popular culture as a mechanism of communication and *education*, as a site for experimentation with cultural and social roles not yet possible in politics."[7] The complex cultural vision of noise producers posits history as pregnant with possibilities for redeeming social practices and sets goals in the name of an alternative future that undermine the universalist (self-)defense of capital. Youth cultures in general, and industrial noise practice in particular, re-galvanize the discourse of utopian imagination. This is the discourse of the "not yet," a language, in critical pedagogist Henry Giroux's words, "in which the imagination is . . . nourished in the effort to construct new relationships fashioned out of strategies of collective resistance based on a critical recognition of both what society is and what it might become."[8] Also, if we accept the probably true assertion that most of our students attend our classes "in order to be distinguished in the labor pool,"[9] such a claim is at least not immediately relevant to noise practitioners within youth culture whose aim might be to break through walls with steam-hammers or (literally) smash our eardrums with ultrasound. This radical negation of "music," and not only music, provides at least some hope in an era when everything has been almost completely banalized by commodification.[10] The "rage" of our students manifested in noise practices is not some form of "primitive rebellion" or "machine breaking." Indeed, following Walter Benjamin, who is frequently cited by noise producers, I suggest that *their* pedagogies have a utopian force: these "destructive characters" reduce to rubble what exists "not for the sake of rubble, but for that of the way leading through it."[11]

What version of capital is contested in the decline of industrialization or the rise of industrial music? I insist that industrial/noise performance exercises a culturally coded and politically specific critique of late capital, and offers tools for undoing dominant versions of U.S. history. To be sure, noise music operates in the shadow of recontainment by the very commodity structures it intends to challenge. But resistance to such commodification continues to occur, and it appears to be true for industrial what cultural studies scholar Russel A. Potter says about hip-hop: "the recognition that everything is or will soon be commodified has . . . served as a spur, an incitement to productivity."[12] In his influential book on noise, French cultural theorist Jacques Attali maps the political economy of music as a succession of economic orders.[13] Each order is organized in relation to production, exchange, desire, and subject position. According to Attali's map, the economic order of Repetition is entering a state of decomposition and degeneration, and a fourth order—Composition—may be emerging. Though its characteristics are far from clear, Attali offers a speculative description based on treating noise within the current economic order as prophetic. This new economy is marked by the uncontrolled proliferation of noise (carnivals with unpredictable outcomes, and a "new mutation" in emancipatory technology enhancing individual power as the power of uncontrolled proliferation, are among the examples given by Attali),[14] idleness, excess exchange value cum surplus expenditure without accumulation, private pleasure, the illegitimate recomposition of use value rather than commodities produced in the exchanges between bodies through the work of noise, and finally, the merger of consumer and producer.

Noise music, in its many alterations, has fulfilled many of Attali's prophecies about a new political economy through "music." It ruptures conventional generic boundaries: it is often not music at all, but noise, or sound, or sweat (as in the case of Einsturzende Neubauten's "Sweat Song") frequently combined with visual material, and disseminated by way of video, public-access cable broadcasts, phone, and Internet performances. Due to its polymorphism, it escapes the closure of a club space or concert stage. It is often performed and disseminated outside the commercial nexus (in fact, noise arguably would not exist without the self-activity of its fans). When staged, the relation between performer and everyday person is blurred, and participation by audience members in industrial/noise events is, in many instances, a distinctive phenomenon.

It is documentable that industrial/noise has become a transnational global cultural form capable of mobilizing diverse constituencies. How do histories of industrialized nations relate to one another, what are the shared trajectories among the U.S., Britain, Germany, and Japan—countries that house expansive noise cultures? How does postcolonial noise, whether through diaspora or immigration, enter into the political economy of these countries? In my research, I distinguish between several interrelated waves in the history of industrial/noise performance. Representatives of the first wave in the early 1980s—most famously Einsturzende Neubauten from the "city-state" of West Berlin—initially rejected repetitive modes of technology, considered themselves subelectronic, and coextensively deployed sound found in a (post)industrial environment as well as the body as their chief sources of noise. British groups such as Throbbing Gristle/Psychic TV, Cabaret Voltaire, Japan's Merzbow and Null (Tokyo) and Hijokaidan and Hanatarash (Osaka/Kyoto), and, in a move of autocritique, the Neubauten themselves, shaped the transition to the second wave of noise/industrialists emerging in the U.S. at the end of the 1980s, who embraced power electronics and the use of electronic media.[15] The directions within the current, *third* wave, which, together with the pioneering noise production of the Neubauten, constitute the focus of this essay, include fire-noise (Scot Jenerik from 23five collective in San Francisco), machine performance and noise-video (Zipper Spy, who, for a number of years, worked in the Bay Area), and low-tech, ecological noise (Small Cruel Party from Seattle). These noise practitioners explore the interface between body configurations/organic materials and old as well as state-of-the-art technologies. Their noise work nonetheless situates them more proximously to the early Neubauten than to second-wave cultivators of power electronics.

In musicological terms, for first-wave practitioners of noise, repetition was equated with industrial standardization and mass production and represented a move toward a single totalitarian code. The body appeared to be the perfect vehicle to achieve nonrepeatability. On the contrary, second-wave noise performers used sonic forces that were informed by mass reproduction technology (synthesizer, computer, video, etc.). Their work defied assumptions that performers using advanced technology were "inevitably" subsumed by the larger logic of the repetitive economy of capital. By focusing on rap in her book *Black Noise,* cultural historian Tricia Rose convincingly maps alternative uses of high technology and their relationship to repetition. She stresses the multiple histories and approaches to sound organization inside commodified culture. Rose claims that in black culture, repetition means circulation and equilibrium and is not tied to accumulation and growth, as in the dominant culture.[16] That Rose's conceptualization of rap can be applicable to industrial/noise music is backed by important interactions between rap music and noise electronics. Kraftwerk, Can, and Faust from Germany influenced DJs in Kingston, Jamaica, and U.S. hip hop artists; samplings by African American noise formation Code Industry (Detroit) introduced black politics into white noise; Public Enemy toured the United Kingdom accompanied by British industrial bands; and, in Los Angeles, Death Row Records' rappers routinely work together with Interscope's industrial musicians.

The importance of the intervention by second wave noise performers was that it went beyond the model, according to which objects are simply use values that extend the body or enable its disembodiment—a model that premised its emancipatory assumption on a re-establishment of the organic interrelation between man and object and that looked to direct exchange to facilitate those relations. This new wave proposed ways in which technology can provide destabilizing strategies, problematizing some earlier concepts in noise that overdirectly identified technology with capitalist progress and social control. When the 1990s generation of noise performers in the Bay Area and the Northwest's urban aggregate entered the cultural scene, they had two models, two pedagogies, in noise to reference. As we will see, their decisions were powerfully influenced by their encounters with postmodern capital.

## THE NOISE OF COLLAPSING NEW BUILDINGS

Any history of latter-day noise must start with Einsturzende Neubauten. This German noise formation came of age in West Berlin, the symbol of a divided Europe and, for decades, playground of cold-war intrigue. Berlin's architecture as a conduit of the city's history was of pivotal significance to the Neubauten.[17] The infamous Reichstag stood beside the Wall. The ruins of the Prinz-Albrecht-Palais, which had functioned as the S.S. and Gestapo headquarters with its torture chambers, the ruins of which were now "hidden" under the construction materials of the new Berlin, also lay along the "Wall fringe."[18] Juxtaposed with these mementos of the Nazi past was the glitter of the new, high-modernist Berlin. Reputed architects such as Walter Gropius, Alvar Aalto, and Hans Scharoun replanned and redesigned the city and turned it into the shop window of late capital's consumer culture, which thus provided a daily tease for a confused populace that lived east of the Wall under existing socialism. However, for a large number of West Berliners, including Turkish workers (a third generation born there, yet without citizenship rights), students, "draft dodgers," squatters, emigrants, and exiles, daily reality meant the impersonal high-rise blocks (the so-called

*Neubauten*) built in the course of urban renewal programs, and pre-1918 "rental barracks" that survived World War II.

Berlin's "downfall mythology"[19] as the paradigmatic site for "the decline of the West," for a Europe built on "negative statics,"[20] was embodied in the Einsturzende Neubauten. The Neubauten believed that the collapse was indeed imminent, that it was no self-delusion. After their "Dance the Decline" (1980) performance at an overpass of the Berlin Autobahn, the group's singer Blixa Bargeld remarked on the prescience of that show by noting that subsequently buildings in Berlin came crumbling down: first the Congress Hall, then an unemployment bureau, and a bus depot; finally, the Deutschlandhalle (a civic center) had to be closed down due to the danger of imminent collapse.[21] "To make a building collapse," Bargeld commented wryly, "you don't necessarily need a force from the outside."[22] Their furious record of 1987 *Funf auf der nach oben offenen Richterskala* (Five on the Open-Ended Richter Scale), where, at five, an earthquake pounds even newer buildings into collapse,[23] combined a historical perspective on Berlin with ecopolitics, which resonated with the rise of leftward Green politics in Germany.

The Neubauten erased borderlines between art and labor.[24] For them, the production of noise was "physically and emotionally draining work," which called for tools and machines such as "pneumatic drill, Black & Decker, bits of girder, tangled stands of steel, lead mallets, crowbars, old radios."[25] The group reshaped the international music scene: from Budapest's Art Deco and Bp. Service to London's Test Department and Milwaukee's Boy Dirt Car, hundreds of bands were beating on industrial waste in front of large, receptive audiences. When in the course of a Neubauten concert in Bochum the audience began "spontaneously" demolishing the factory that served as the site for the event and failed to observe that the band stopped playing, Bargeld concluded, "There could be millions of people creating only noises ... real changes happen through social means. I mean it has already been a social phenomenon."[26]

In their noise video *Decoder* (1983), the Neubauten expanded a mythic Berlin into the "Western world," in which the behavior of people has been altered by "functional music." This music, the influence of which is complemented by the sophisticated surveillance techniques of the postmodern state, is concocted by corporations such as Muzak and the fast-food chains and has a particular tonal sequence that enhances the efficiency and obedience of those exposed to it. To combat "functional music" and the forces behind it, the "decoder," a computer-driven musician and disenchanted

Muzak employee, joins forces with the metal-bangers of the first generation, the anarcho-leftist *Autonomen,* and sexworkers. Significantly, the few
emancipatory moments prior to the final eruption of mass rioting originates
from the subaltern: the "decoder's" conversion experience takes place to the
melodies of Turkish music (Germany's "invisible" minority), a transformation that, in real life, was reaffirmed by musician-actor F. M. Einheit's
changing his name to Mufti.

Einsturzende Neubauten tied its noise performances to concrete social
action when it documented the huge May Day demonstrations in Berlin in
1987, perhaps the biggest crowd action in the city since 1945. The rebellion
took place in Kreuzberg, the poorest part of the city, in which fifty thousand
residents crammed into dilapidated edifices lived overwhelmingly unem-
ployed and poverty-stricken. The morning of that day, police, without war-
rant, ambushed the headquarters of local citizens' parties that were
collecting signatures against the indignities of a census directed against
squatters and illegal immigrants. These arrests added to an already strained
political climate in the city due to the noisy preparations for a forthcoming
visit by then-President Ronald Reagan, and led to some counterviolence by
the *Autonomen.* Within hours, the conflict escalated into a carnival of mass
rioting when pensioners, students, Turkish teenagers, and middle-class
women joined forces in the ensuing feast of looting. The Neubauten were
on the scene witnessing the *Autonomen*'s desperate efforts to protect
"people-friendly" businesses, and the frenzy of destruction.[27] The noises of
the insurgency were eventually released by the band in 1989 as *Haus der
Luge* (House of Lies). In the House of Lies, the floors are littered with bodies of dead angels, God shoots himself in the mouth, and the city's Master
Architect awaits the arrival of concrete at twelve sharp.

The Neubauten's other noise-video, *Man* (1985) guides the viewer
through the scrap-yards of the modern metropolis. At the high point of the
narrative, just as they did during an interrupted concert at the ICA in London some years earlier, the Neubauten hammer their way through the walls
of an old factory only to confront the menacing, concrete edifice of Corporate Headquarters. Bargeld howls, "Hai! Hai! Hai! . . . This was made to
end all parties, bye, bye . . ."[28] French syndicalism's metaphor of "boring
from within"—small "militant minorities" winning over those silenced
inside large organizations—is pictured here with Bargeld screaming into
the bullhorn and the other Neubauten beating "metal on metal." The
Neubauten make their entry, in Walter Benjamin's words, into their "'oppo-

nent's strength in order to destroy him from within.'" Their "barbarism" does not signal random destruction for its own sake. That way, literary theorist Irving Wohlfarth claims, it would be a mere mimesis of production "for its own sake, " and such "Romantic nihilism" would amount only to "a harmless by-product of the status quo."[29] Benjamin himself, whose essay "The Destructive Character" has often been referenced by Bargeld,[30] connects such cultural work to a syndicalist perspective. Wohlfarth discerns how Benjamin, excavating the effaced deep layers within the left-radical tradition, retrieved the great French syndicalist Georges Sorel in order to forge a scenario for "'divine' counter-violence."[31] Such a counterviolence simultaneously combines "modern surface and archaic depth, 'signal' and 'oracle.'"[32] The willingness to adopt a "modern surface" is a key attribute of the destructive character who thus prevents "enlightened" capital from labeling challenges to its domination as "atavistic" or "primitive."[33] For Benjamin, just as for the Neubauten, destruction must shatter the cover-up by capitalist culture regarding the violent effacement of the traces of a disappearing world of "experience," but must do so without erecting a facade of "inviolate *things*" from the past.[34]

## THE NOISE OF FIRE, WATER, AND VIDEO[35]

Contemporary noise performers assume the role of the destructive character itself. They vindicate themselves the task of waking us up, to shock us out of passivity by placing outmoded figures into a dialectical relation with the most modern modes of thought in order to break the universalizing reductions of our times. In his reading of Benjamin, literary historian David Kauffman insists that by retrieving memory in face of the empty temporality that rules capitalist modernity, we might recover indications from the past that oppression might be challenged.[36] The activation of "the arsenals of the past, ideas and practices, which disrupt the hegemony of forces of heteronomy," might shake what Adorno calls the "trance-like captivity" of capitalist culture.[37] The complex art practice of the present generation of noise performers might constitute the "retroactive force" that Benjamin, impelled as much by Sorel as by Marx, envisioned in order to contest "every victory, past and present of the rulers."[38] The "retroactive force" that noise producers activate in their art practice reflects a nuanced relationship toward both work and machinery. On the one hand, the worker as figure plays an important role in these performances as the at once forgotten and erased agent of history. Noise practitioners seek to combat this erasure by making the forgotten agent of labor visible and at least indirectly explain the structural relations of present-day capital that keep laboring bodies out of sight. Their approach is consistent with Marx's observation that the connection between the capitalist mode of production and the body's positionment within those relations is contingent, rather than natural and necessary.[39] To these performers, machine culture did not spawn a homogenous, uniform labor, an "abstract labor" that undergirded the entire capitalist economy. As they set such quantitative generalizations about labor aside, the fear of "drift[ing] into automatism"[40] in modern industrial work does not inform their attitude. In fact, as political historian Kenneth H. Tucker, Jr. suggests, syndicalists and subsequently Benjamin shared the belief that modern technology could fuse with art and could create a more democratic and aesthetically pleasing "industry."[41]

Scot Jenerik's work provides a good example for the neo-syndicalist perspective in the work of noise.[42] Founder of the 23five noise-organization in San Francisco that serves as "a think tank, resource center, and sound archive to promote an atmosphere where theoretical discourse may flourish" and as "a development site for educational projects" for schools and cultural centers,[43] Jenerik is best known for his performances with sculptural flame instruments. Living and working in the Bay Area, where high-earning "symbolic analysts"[44] chant the mantra of technoculture and take stock options in Silicon Valley's billion-dollar hardware, software, semiconductor, and network systems companies, Jenerik avoids the temptations of a Luddite aesthetic. Instead, in Benjamin's words, he "positions himself at crossroads" and destroys what is worthy of destruction but without a teleology, without knowing "what will replace what has been destroyed," and without constraining the free play of the forces of the future.[45] If we follow Benjamin's argument, it is precisely "an absent power" that lends a "positive force" to Jenerik's fire practice.[46]

In an inferno of propane and isopropanol, Jenerik sets metal and wood which are wired for sound on fire. In his performance piece "Demons Eating of My Flesh and Drinking of My Blood," Jenerik, half-nude, wears gloves, kneepads, boots, and shorts and beats with an iron rod on combusting wood and with his fists on sheet metal that is bathed in flames. His hands are encased in gloves wired with contact microphones in the fingertips—he calls his technique *faustschlag*. The inflamed sheets of steel have photocell triggers that activate other sound sources based on the height of the flame. A flame-thrower harp shooting flames several feet high and generating high temperatures introduces the performance. It instantaneously shocks audiences in enclosed spaces into the rite of labor, as was the case in Club Marx, Emeryville, California, where this author first saw the piece (1996). Jenerik characterizes his work as "a Dionysian frenzy of extreme physical exertion, direct elemental contact, and sonic percussion."[47]

One of the inspirational sources for Jenerik has been Houston-based performance artist D. E. Therrien, whose work, in cultural critic Mark Dery's words, presents "geometrized power relations and mechanized primitive rites."[48] However, Therrien often portrays "workers" as powerless subjects of instrumental technologies and "'ideological engines'"[49] and his literally high-voltage performances emaciate the laboring body on "technological ceremonial grounds."[50] In contradistinction to Therrien, Jenerik's fire rites, combining the body in flames with his artisanal tools through high-tech adjustments, echo a syndicalist understanding of production as becoming "more intense and more absorbing" and as such requiring the performer-worker and the audience to renew continually their understanding of machinery and work. Within the context of "Demons Eating of My Flesh and Drinking of My Blood," the worker is also an artist and inventor who masters new technologies and innovates constantly while creating models that help to illuminate the world in novel ways. The annual "labor of fire" festival in Nevada's Black Rock Desert called "Burning Man," one that Jenerik helps to sustain and in which thousands from temporary "industrial armies" participate appropriately over Labor Day weekend, bears testimony to the seductive pedagogy of Jenerik's performative syndicalism.

Tying labor to an aesthetic, imaginative, and poetic moment character-izes the noise work of Small Cruel Party (né Key Ransone) in Seattle. Influ-enced in the late 1980s by the high-electronics approach of noise performers in Japan, where he himself lived at a peak period of "Japanese noise," Small Cruel Party arrived gradually at a newer performative methodology that accounted for the aural interface between organic materi-als and an electronic aesthetic. Seattle is the archetypal postindustrial com-pany town, a "software town"[51] dominated by a single company, Microsoft. The predicament of this one-time timber city is symbolized by the future of its only working sawmill, Barbee. It is Microsoft's co-founder Paul Allen who wants to buy the sawmill to create "a lavish lakefront headquarters for his family [sic] of software and investment companies, with restaurants, condos, jogging trails, a marina."[52] With software start-ups backed by ven-ture capital funds sprouting up everywhere, Seattle's future might be tied to Teledisc, a plan to launch three hundred communications satellites into outer space to become the sole relayer of information among corporations globally.[53]

To confront this gestural yet all too real move by postmodern capital into both cyber- and outerspace, an act that, it hopes, successfully completes its effort to consume the totality of living labor, micropedagogies such as performances by Small Cruel Party (SCP) fuse ecoaesthetics with a low-tech approach. SCP prefers the force of live performance: acoustic and amplified sounds, some of which are electronically processed. The processing is minimal: delays, pitch shifting, reverberation or echo, and equalization. Microphones, contact or hand-held, are the main components, along with basic ecosystemic components and junkyard debris: water, metal, glass, stone, branches, and various objects. In SCP's signature performance, "The Waking of the Leafy Pools" (the title is a citation from Thoreau's journals), the formation uses water only. A bubbling jar with two aquarium pumps running in it is placed at the front of the performance space, thus becoming the acoustic visual and audio center for the audience. The piece begins and ends with that being the only sound. The rest of the piece is made of the successive build-up of expanding waves of sound created by the layering of the physical manipulation of three basic sound sources in the following order: small glass vessels, steel rings, and two pieces of iron.

The sonic forces that this seemingly minimalist approach creates are fearsome: "hearing with pain," the aural shock of bubbling water is astonishing. The (literal) liquefaction of forms is a necessary action in order to create a new aural language. SCP points into this direction when, at the end of each succession with the sound of water piercing the eardrums of audiences and shattering the ambient aura, he plays the *suling,* a flute used in Indonesian *gamelan* music. As the sound sources are layered, each begins to develop characteristics not obviously expected; certain harmonic qualities come to the fore and expand further. These characteristics are true for each material—glass, steel, and iron—although with differences: the sections could be thought of as three movements, each with a build-up and climax with the flute section closing up everything very calmly. "The Waking of the Leafy Pools," just as other work by SCP, does not deploy computers and rarely benefits from prerecorded materials since, by using delays with which to loop live sounds, he can mostly bypass the need for taped sections. The sonic qualities of the space itself, whether an art gallery in Pittsburgh or a warehouse in Takamatsu, Japan, or the studio of Radio Sauvagine in Bordeaux, France, are frequently played upon.

The work of Zipper Spy (née Maria Moran) initially engaged giant noise machines as exemplified by her eight-foot *Marimba Man* in order to face the question of simulated, absent bodies in the world of labor. By positing the question, "What replaces the disappearing laboring bodies in the age of industry's decline?", Zipper Spy's current work, a multipiece noise-video project titled *Mr. Future Vision Seer* (1997 - present), complicates a pedagogy based on the body's "inherently" disruptive powers. Her work constructs postindustrial capital as driven by the ultimate vision: the abolition of living labor. If anywhere, then in the halo of Silicon Valley the introduction of a cyborg order does not necessarily appear to be a remote possibility. Cultural critic William Bogard argues that postindustrial capital is on a transitional route from a "material productive order" to a rematerialized, informated order of simulation.[54] By combining the new cyber-technologies of simulation with revamped versions of venerably old technologies of surveillance, capital's emerging cyborg order will produce the informated, fully screened body as an updated model of the already panopticized body. Arguably, the vision of cyborg worker emerges in capital's formational repertoire at a particular historical juncture that coincides with deindustrialization in the U.S., Europe, and Japan. The postindustrial worker can be best imagined as one that inhabits the low-wage jobs in the computerized service sector of the economy. To Bogard, this new worker represents "a paradoxical figure whose future is already in one sense its history, whose code delineates every function that it *will have carried* out in advance."[55]

Zipper Spy's "Elimination of Process" noise-video opens with a black-leather-clad self-image unzipping herself and inviting the viewer on a journey through the uniform landscape of electronic impulses. Hers is a transparent body, a surface seen through, something in the process of elimination as surface/screen. What Zipper Spy documents is how the body, subject to decay and obsolescence, vanishes beneath the apparatus that watches it, only to be resurrected as simulacrum. Her use of subliminal visuals and unusual visual frequencies, a technique that intertexts with earlier experimentations by Throbbing Gristle and more contemporary work by Electronic Broadcast Network, allows a nuanced critique of the society of prosthetics. The ambivalence of the neither-human-nor-machine finds its perfect conduit in these visual frequencies, the physics of which, as the British noise group Chris and Cosey insist, can make the viewer either feel dizzy and nauseous or have an "instantaneous orgasm."[56] Zipper Spy's video takes us on a train ride, in the course of which we see neither the train nor its driver nor any passengers and are confronted only with the rails in high-speed motion. Still, this is a journey in pedagogy, a class in history about industrial capital in ruins at the century's end, smashed by its own accumulation of waste. The visual flow of the high-speed train ride is interrupted only by flashed-up (subliminal) images of rusting machines, car junkyards, and vacant, ruinous factory yards and snapshots of shaved, nude human bodies, crippled, paralyzed, or reprogrammed by medical technology. Finally, the train arrives at an empty station, itself an Eiffelesque design of steel and glass hinting at the early glory days of industrial capitalism. If some form of motion is still a clinical sign of life, beneath that, Zipper Spy suggests, we are quite dead. Her dispatches from the postindustrial frontlines warn us about capital's search for a "final solution"[57] to the problem posed by living labor, by labor as such.

Pedagogies as exemplified by the work of noise producers can tackle issues with which the traditional critique of political economy has difficulty in dealing. Their intervention into renegotiating the meanings of work in a (coming) era of self-organizing, prosthetized labor, of workplaces without "real" workers, is at the least thought-provoking. Their work may help us to avoid being caught by surprise in face of genuinely puzzling developments such as the emergence of a cyborg order with its constellation of the neither-human-nor-machine, and consider educative strategies for self- and social empowerment.

Noise ruptures universalizing versions of reason and linear notions of history and addresses "memories, traces, and voices"[58] of those who have been marginalized and silenced under the evermore sophisticated regimes of surveillance and self-surveillance instituted by capital, whether in public spaces or our schools. These practices do not stifle debate by imposing a particular version of history on their audiences; on the contrary, their uncertainties and ambivalences reopen space for dialogue, discussion, and action. Our pedagogy must engage rather than retreat from cultural practices such as noise performance, take seriously the social and cultural claims that these art practitioners make, since it is their interventions that will potentially make the arena of education, as Giroux claims, "messy, vibrant, and *noisy*."[59] Finally, we must constantly remind ourselves that a portion of our students facing us in our classrooms is very likely to belong to one or another of the "industrial armies" that I described, either as consumer or producer, or, what is most likely, in both of these capacities.

NOTES

1. *The Washington Post,* May 22, 1980, 25(A).
2. For purposes of this essay, I use the terms "noise" and "industrial" inter-changeably. "Industrial" has so many mutations—from voice to pure noise, "information" (Genesis P-Orridge from Throbbing Gristle/Psychic TV), aleatory music, environmental sound, and silence—that cover the whole sonic spectrum. In addition, and perhaps most importantly, the deployment of "industrial" as coterminous with noise gives a measure of historical specificity to post-1980 noise, which then can be theorized as a form of cultural disturbance in the postindustrial space.
3. An important early essay by Chris Bohn sensitively connects industrial music, specifically the Neubauten, to architecture and urban history. See Chris Bohn, "Let's Hear It for the Untergang Show," in *Einsturzende Neubauten: Hor mit Schmerzen, Listen with Pain,* ed. Klaus Maeck (Bonn: EME, 1989), 51–55. (Hereafter cited as *Hor mit Schmerzen.*)
4. Ursula A. Kelly, *Schooling Desire: Literacy, Cultural Politics, and Pedagogy* (New York: Routledge, 1997), 68.
5. Kelly, *Schooling Desire,* 70–71.
6. Kelly, *Schooling Desire,* 78–79.
7. George Lipsitz, *Dangerous Crossroads: Popular Music, Postmodernism and the Politics of Place* (New York: Verso, 1994), 17.
8. Henry Giroux, *Pedagogy and the Politics of Hope: Theory, Culture, and Schooling* (Boulder: Westview Press, 1997), 224.
9. Jeffrey Williams, "Renegotiating the Pedagogical Contract," in *Class Issues,* ed. Amitava Kumar (New York: New York University Press, 1997), 306.
10. Peter Hitchcock, "The Value of," in Kumar, 123.
11. Walter Benjamin, "The Destructive Character," in *Reflections: Essays, Aphorisms, Autobiographical Writings,* trans. Edmund Jephcott (New York: Harcourt Brace Jovanovich, 1978), 303.
12. Russel A. Potter, *Spectacular Vernaculars: Hip-Hop and the Politics of Postmodernism* (Albany: State University of New York Press, 1995), 8.
13. Jacques Attali, *Noise: The Political Economy of Music,* trans. Brian Massumi (Minneapolis: University of Minnesota Press, 1992). I have learned much about Attali's theory from comments given by cultural theorist and video producer Camilla Griggers at a panel on noise, in

which I participated. Painter and electronic media artist Faith Wilding convened the panel for her graduate seminar in the Art Department at Carnegie Mellon University on February 17, 1997. I have also benefited from the many e-mail messages I have exchanged about Attali, and music performance in general, with Philip Auslander in the Department of Literature, Communication and Culture, Georgia Institute of Technology, Atlanta, GA.

14. Attali, *Noise,* 142, 143.
15. I want to thank Koji Tano of the noise formation MSBR (Osaka/Kyoto, Japan) for his help on the history of noise in Japan.
16. Tricia Rose, *Black Noise: Rap Music and Black Culture in Contemporary America* (Hanover, NH: Wesleyan University Press, 1994)
17. For Berlin, see Thomas H. Elkins (with Burkhard Hofmeister), *Berlin: The Spatial Structure of a Divided City* (New York: Methuen, 1988). See also Bohn, "Let's Hear It," in *Hor mit Schmerzen.* Bjorn Gericke of Dresden provided me useful additional insights about Berlin's architects and architecture.
18. Elkins, *Berlin,* 195.
19. Bohn, "Let's Hear It," in *Hor mit Schmerzen,* 52.
20. Blixa Bargeld, interview, in Andrea Cangioli, *Einsturzende Neubauten* (Viterbo, Italy: Stampa Alternativa/Nuovi Equilibri, 1993), 39.
21. *Hor mit Schmerzen,* 21.
22. Cangioli, *Einsturzende Neubauten,* 39.
23. See Klaus Hubner, *Larm-Reise: Uber Musikalische Gerausche und Gerauschvolle Musik* (Augsburg, Germany: Sonnentanz-Verlag, 1991), 65.
24. For this insight, see Bohn, "Let's Hear It," in *Hor mit Schmerzen,* 51.
25. Bohn, "Let's Hear It," in *Hor mit Schmerzen,* 51.
26. Bohn, 52.
27. See "Schwarze Nacht," *Der Spiegel,* May 11, 1987, 57–64.
28. Blixa Bargeld, "Der Tod ist ein Dandy," in *Stimme frisst Feuer* (Berlin: Merve Verlag, 1988), 83. In English in the original.
29. Irving Wohlfarth, "No-Man's-Land: On Walter Benjamin's 'Destructive Character,'"*Diacritics* 8. 2 (Summer 1978): 54. See also Terry Eagleton, *Walter Benjamin, or, Towards a Revolutionary Criticism* (London: Verso and NLB, 1981), 31, 58–59.
30. Bargeld, interview, in Cangioli, *Einsturzende Neubauten,* 39–40, and interview, in *Liebeslieder: Einsturzende Neubauten,* dir. Klaus Maeck and Johanna Schenkel (Berlin: Studio K7 1993), videocassette.
31. Wohlfarth, "No-Man's-Land," 55.

32. Wohlfarth, 55.

33. Wohlfarth, 59.

34. Wohlfarth, 60.

35. On noise and video, see Csaba Toth, "'Like Cancer in the System': Industrial Gothic, Nine Inch Nails, and Videotape," in *Gothic: Transmutations of Horror in Late Twentieth Century Art,* ed. Christoph Grunenberg (Boston: The Institute of Contemporary Art and Cambridge, MA: The MIT Press, 1997), 91–80.

36. David Kauffman, "Thanks for the Memory: Bloch, Benjamin, and the Philosophy of History," in *Not Yet: Reconsidering Ernst Bloch,* ed. Jamie Owen Daniel and Tom Moylan (New York: Verso, 1997), 33–52.

37. Kauffman, "Thanks for the Memory, 45.

38. Walter Benjamin, "Theses on the Philosophy of History," quoted in Kauffman, 45.

39. See on this the superb reading of Marx's *Capital* in Ann Cvetkovich, *Mixed Feelings: Feminism, Mass Culture, and Victorian Sensationalism* (New Brunswick, NJ: Rutgers University Press, 1992), 165–197.

40. Georges Sorel, *Reflections on Violence,* quoted in Kenneth H. Tucker, Jr., *French Revolutionary Syndicalism and the Public Sphere* (New York: Cambridge University Press, 1996), 147.

41. Tucker, *French Revolutionary Syndicalism,* 147.

42. See Robert Neuwirth, "Dangerous Rhythms,"*Option* no. 54 (January–February 1994), 58–64; Mike Hovancsek, "Scot Jenerik's Fire Music,"*Experimental Musical Instruments* 13. 2 (December 1997): 34–36; Toth, "'Like Cancer in the System,'" in *Gothic,* 28 n. 5; and Mason Jones, "Interview with Scot Jenerik," IndustrialnatioN (forthcoming).

43. *Interference,* ed. Scot Jenerik (San Francisco: 23five Inc., 1996), 125.

44. Robert Reich, *The Work of Nations,* quoted in Marc V. Levine, "Globalization and Wage Polarization in U.S. And Canadian Cities: Does Public Policy Make a Difference?," in *North American Cities and the Global Economy: Challenges and Opportunities,* ed. Peter K. Kresl and Gary Gappert (Thousands Oaks, CA: Sage, 1995), 90.

45. Benjamin, "Destructive Character," 303 and 301.

46. Wohlfarth, "No-Man's-Land," 53.

47. Scot Jenerik, "Performance Description," portfolio, n.d. In the author's possession.

48. Mark Dery, *Escape Velocity: Cyberculture at the End of the Century* (New York: Grove Press, 1996), 171.

49. Dery, *Escape Velocity,* 177. The reference is to Therrien's performance, "Information Machine: Ideological Engines."

50. *Friction,* ed. Michael Asbill and Scot Jenerik (San Francisco: 23five and Art Com, 1994), liner notes to videocassette.

51. Mark D. Fefer, "Is Seattle the Next Silicon Valley?", *Fortune,* 7 July, 1997, 78.

52. Fefer, "Is Seattle," 78.

53. Joe Rogaly, "No Spot on Earth Will Be Microsoft-Free," *Financial Times,* Weekend, May 3–4, 1997, 111.

54. William Bogard, *The Simulation of Surveillance: Hypercontrol in Telematic Societies* (New York: Cambridge University Press, 1996), 103. Bogard prefers the term "telematic" to "postindustrial" (4).

55. Bogard, *The Simulation of Surveillance,* 103.

56. Chris and Cosey, interview, in Charles Neal, *Tape Delay* (London: SAF, 1992), 222.

57. Bogard, *Simulation of Surveillance,* 104. For further perspectives on cyborg work, see Critical Art Ensemble, *Flesh Machine: Cyborgs, Designer Babies, and New Eugenic Consciousness* (New York: Autonomedia, 1998) and Slavoj Zizek, "From Virtual Reality to the Virtualization of Reality," in *Electronic Culture: Technology and Visual Representation,* ed. Timothy Drucker (New York: Aperture, 1996), 290–295.

58. Henry Giroux, "Literacy and the Politics of Difference," in *Critical Literacy: Politics, Praxis, and the Postmodern,* ed. Colin Lankshear and Peter L. McLaren (Albany: State University of New York Press, 1993), 377.

59. Giroux, "Literacy," 376. Italics are mine.

# CHAPTER 13

# *Visualizing War*

CAMILLA BENOLIRAO GRIGGERS

*War photos are pictures of the American dream.*

—Paul Virilio

IN THE CASE OF WAR, seeing is never enough. Wars are caught up in ways of seeing that make the image of war already complicit with the act of war and the ideology of colonialist and imperialist violence. Aesthetics can never be separated from politics in the representation of war. In this article I want to discuss aesthetico-political issues that arise when we attempt to visualize a materialist reading of war violence in relation to U.S. imperial wars in the twentieth century. In addition, I will discuss some of the aesthetic and political concerns that have shaped my own experimental documentary practice in relation to *Alienations of the Mother Tongue* (1995), a video that gives a pan-Asian "face" to women casualties of war on the Pacific front, and *Memories of a Forgotten War*, a documentary on the Philippine-American War of 1899. As the daughter of a Filipino-American war orphan, I have focused my work as an academic and filmmaker on theorizing social violence. Trained as a feminist cultural and media critic, I turned in the early 1990s to video production in search of more public venues for my pedagogical practice.

Teaching war is one of the quickest ways to reach the limits of rationality. Technologies of modern warfare, beginning with cartography, flourished with Descartes's rationalization of spatial relations and the invention of Cartesian coordinates—a system for subsuming all phenomena to sets of abstract number relations that can be mapped onto geographical and social space. To see, in this territorializing way, is to conquer. For this reason, to see war "rationally" is the height of cynical reason. There must be an emotional understanding as well.

Yet to perceive the violence of war emotionally without intellectual, political, and historical understanding can be an experience of terror. This affective component to knowledge raises aesthetic questions in regard to the representation of war that cannot be divorced from political questions. What aesthetics are appropriate for war documentary then, when the goal is to visualize war in order to document violence for the public record?

## WAR AND THE POLITICS OF PERCEPTION

In *War and Cinema* (1989), military historian and cultural theorist Paul Virilio underscored the need to deconstruct the binary distinction between war and its representation: "From Machiavelli to Vauban, from von Moltke to Churchill, at every decisive episode in the history of war, military theorists have underlined this truth: 'The force of arms is not brute force but spiritual force.' There is no war, then, without representation, no sophisticated weaponry without psychological mystification. Weapons are tools not just of destruction but also of perception . . ." (5). Documenting war violence is thus, from the first instance, an aesthetico-political struggle, because one is dealing with a perceptual war machine that produces its own documents and artifacts.

Take the case of the My Lai massacre, the turning point for popular sentiment against U.S. involvement in Vietnam. The Army photographer Ronald Haeberle, assigned to Charlie Company on March 16, 1968, had two cameras. One was an army standard; one was his personal camera. The film on the army-owned camera, that is, the official camera of the State, showed standard operations—that is, "authorized" and "official" operations including interrogating villagers and burning "insurgent" huts. What the film on the personal camera showed, however, was different. When turned over to the press and government by the photographer, those "unofficial" photographs provided the grounds for a court martial. Haeberle's personal images (owned by himself and not the U.S. Government) showed hundreds of villagers who had been killed by U.S. troops. More significantly, the photographs showed that the dead were primarily women and children, including infants. These photographs exposed the fact that the "insurgents" in popular discourse about Vietnam were actually unarmed civilians. The photos made visible to viewers that the "enemy" in Vietnam was actually the indigenous Vietnamese population.

The U.S. military convicted only one soldier for the massacre at My Lai, and then paroled him after three years, demonstrating that the violence that

Haeberle's photographs documented was not an anomaly. The war in Vietnam was (un)officially a war waged against a civilian population. In fact, violence against civilians characterizes twentieth-century warfare. From the Philippine-American War of 1899 to Hiroshima and Nagasaki and the incendiary bombing of Tokyo, from the heavy artillery battle for Manila to the Vietnam and Persian Gulf Wars, the U.S. military has carried out campaigns that execute systematic violence against civilian populations.

The case of My Lai reminds us that public records of war (records of war that become public) have to compete with official state representations of war in order to become visible and to affect public perception. And if that were not complicated enough, in the case of wars that either preceded or excluded the popular dissemination of portable cameras and freelance photojournalists, war documentary must often be composed of official documents of war.

For example, during the Philippine-American War of 1899, U.S. photojournalists working for the likes of Randolph Hearst, Underwood and Underwood, and Harper's *History of the War in the Philippines* (1900) held the cameras, chose the frames, and selected the "objects" and "artifacts" to be documented. These photographs played a crucial role in rationalizing the ideology of 'benevolent assimilation' that authorized imperialist foreign policy in the Pacific. These same photojournalists were repeatedly censored by General Otis during the early years of the campaign in the Philippines. Those with cameras worked under warnings that he would not approve representations of the war that might negatively affect President McKinley's 1901 re-election campaign (Blount 347). Like photojournalists during the Persian Gulf War, photographers were actively policed by the very military forces they were documenting. And these photos in turn became the artifacts and archives that form the historical memory and amnesia that have become our knowledge of violence's past

For this reason, soldiers' letters home provide accounts of the war zone that conflict with official government accounts. This letter from a U.S. soldier, Cpl. Richard O'Brien, written during the 1901 Balangiga campaign in Samar during the Philippine-American War recounts events in the field that contradicted official representations by the U.S. Government. It would later be printed in the *Congressional Record*, May 15, 1902:

> It was on the 27th of December, the anniversary of my birth, and I shall never forget the scenes I witnessed that day. As we approached the town the word passed along the line that there would be no prisoners taken. It

meant we were to shoot every living thing in sight—man, woman or child.

The first shot was fired by the then 1st Sergeant of our company. His target was a mere boy, who was coming down the mountain path into town astride of a carabao. The boy was not struck by the bullet, but that was not the Sergeant's fault. The little Filipino boy slid from the back of his carabao and fled in terror up the mountain side. Half a dozen shots were fired after him.

The shooting now had attracted the villagers, who came out of their homes in alarm, wondering what it all meant. They offered no offense, did not display a weapon, made no hostile movement whatsoever, but they were ruthlessly shot down in cold blood, men, women, and children. The poor natives huddled together or fled in terror. Many were pursued and killed on the spot. Two old men, bearing a white flag and clasping hands like two brothers, approached the lines. Their hair was white. They fairly tottered, they were so feeble under the weight of years. To my horror and that of the other men in the command, the order was given to fire and the two old men were shot down in their tracks. We entered the village. A man who had been on a sickbed appeared at the doorway of his home. He received a bullet in the abdomen and fell dead in the doorway. Dum dum bullets were used in the massacre, but we were not told the name of the bullets. We didn't have to be told. We knew what they were. In another part of the village a mother with a babe at her breast and two young children at her side pleaded for mercy. She feared to leave her home which had just been fired—accidentally, I believe. She faced the flames with her children, and not a hand was raised to save her or the little ones. They perished miserably. It was sure death if she left the house—it was death if she remained. She feared the American soldiers, however, worse than the devouring flames. (Quoted in Francisco and Fast 313)

Private letters to individuals, however, are "unseen" by the public at large, unless recipients of letters seek out publishers willing to publish them. And that takes time, characterizing the genre with an after-the-fact temporality that can hardly compete with the speed and iterative power of the repeating images of the media.

Censoring depictions of events from the war zone is certainly one crucial function of the perceptual war machine. But as Virilio argues in *War and Cinema*, military logistics is by definition a politics of vision in a more structural way as well. Not only does military strategy require controlling representations of war, but military logistics are a perceptual logistics, from the most rudimentary military weapons to the most advanced surveillance systems (21). The "line of aim" upon which all weapon systems are built involves a "geometrification of looking, an alignment of ocular perception that corresponds to a 'rationalized' act of interpretation of the 'object' or 'data' being perceived" (2). I can't help thinking in this regard of the story commonly told in the Philippine-American War records of Filipino resistance fighters who did not know how to align the sights properly on their captured Spanish rifles. The Filipinos were known as pitiful marksmen compared to U.S. troops who in comparison were sharp shooters, some of whom had honed their skills at "taking aim" on native American tribespeople during the Indian Wars back home (the Massacre of Wounded Knee preceded the Philippine-American War by only nine years). This "technical ineptitude" partly accounted for the tremendous casualty rate among the Filipinos, the most conservative estimate being placed by the U.S. Government at the time at 16:1 (though historians now agree the ratio far exceeded that early official estimate). By the time the resistance was beaten down in the Southern Islands, culminating in the Battle of Bagsak in 1913 with 500 civilian Muslim Filipino casualties, over 25 percent of the Filipino population had died. Not only inadequate Filipino munitions and poor marksmanship skills but also U.S. heavy artillery, repeating guns, executions for "insurgency," and disease and starvation from relocation policies and slash and burn campaigns, contributed to the high casualty rate (Ileto 197, 249, 253–54). The war in the Philippines, as was that in Vietnam, was a depopulation campaign.

In spite of Filipino inexpertise with the line of aim as a perceptual concept, Filipinos were reputed to be vicious, fierce, and courageous fighters even in the face of impossible odds. It is commonly reputed that the .45 caliber pistol was invented by Colt specifically to put down Muslim Filipinos in the southern islands who were known to take a shot and still hack down their attackers with their krises (machete-like farm implements). This behavior was typically described as "crazed" and "savage" in U.S. reports, demonstrating the "barbarity" of the Filipinos, I suppose because it lacked the "civilized" rationality of drawing a line of aim from an appropriate distance and pulling the trigger. U.S. troops did just that at the Massacre of Bud Dajo in 1906, killing nearly a thousand Muslim Filipinos, including women and children, by firing heavy artillery into a volcanic crater in which an entire village had tried to hide.

Not only bullets, then, but also a type of distanced, instrumental thinking initiates the "process of derealization" which launches every war (Virilio 86). "When the press speaks of its own 'objectivity,'" Virilio points out, "it can easily make one believe in its truthfulness. For the newspaper's present superiority over a book is that it has no author, the reader taking it in as a truth that he alone knows, true because he 'believes his eyes'" (37). Given the role that rationality plays in implementing war, to make an "objective" documentary about war is to reproduce the very type of thinking that enables war violence to be enacted. The first pedagogical task in attempting to visualize war, it seems to me, is to destroy the safe distance between the perpetrator, the distant objective observer of the violence perpetrated, and the sacrificial victim (whose experience is defined not by remoteness but by proximity to the means of violence). Since "technologies of remote perception," as Virilio calls them, are a key component to military logistics, the distance of the viewer's rational objectivity must be shattered in the face of violence.

Clearly popular media comprise a highly complex system of signs regulating public expressions of race, class, and gender. And as a technology of remote perception, this system of signs also regulates public expressions of violence. In my book *Becoming-Woman* (1997), I show how the machinic production of the public face of white femininity in the mass media screens the sacrificial face of violence's victim. People don't see violence very easily, even though the U.S. media is obsessed with violent representations. In this sense, the banal question often bandied about by North American media critics and press—whether violent representations in the media can cause actual violence—is acutely symptomatic. The U.S. media is manifestly violent, as is U.S. culture. To entertain the possibility that they are not in the face of all evidence is patently delusional—no matter what logic of causality you deploy.

In *Alienations of the Mother Tongue* (1995), I attempted to visualize affectively the way remoteness screens violence in the mass media. I decided to bring the racialized face of the victim out of the war zone and closer to "home" for rational spectators accustomed to the safe distance of an objective gaze on violence. In terms of media, to bring such images "home" means to bring them into the comfort zones of mass mediated consumption in which the distance between viewing subject and viewed object are reduced as much as possible in order to stimulate a mirror effect that binds the capitalized subject to the fetished image. My idea was to set spectators up to "consume"—that is, to interiorize—images of war within the same plane of consumption as the polished and airbrushed techno-images with which they are invited by advertisers to identify. I wanted to bring the face of the war casualty, the sacrificial victim in this case culled from famous war photographs from Vietnam, into the landscape of Madison Avenue. And vice versa, I would take the technologized and reified face of fashion—with which all women in the U.S. as well as in Asia are encouraged to identify—[1] into the war zone, using war footage from the Pacific to evoke a sense of becoming in a landscape of violence and trauma (see figures 13.1–13.4).

For those viewers who already identified with the face of the sacrificial victim rather than with the objective gaze of the disembodied spectator because of their own specific historical experiences, the visual track offered a moment of public recognition of violence perpetrated. Other viewers were encouraged through the seductive images of Madison Avenue—that is, the face of the fashion model—to enter into proximity to violence, and through the experience of that proximity, to identify with the recipient of violence. For both viewers, a subjective voiceover bolstered a healing identification with the face of the sacrifice through a narrative connecting an

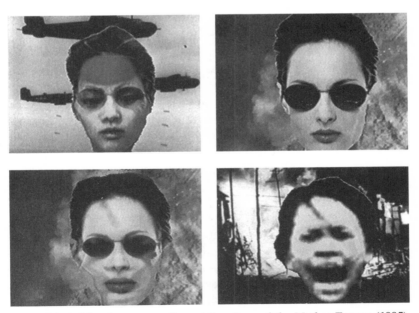

**Figs. 13.1–4: Morph sequence from *Alienations of the Mother Tongue* (1995). Produced and directed by Camilla Benolirao Griggers.**

individual experience of domestic violence, witnessed by me as the daughter of an Amerasian war orphan, to the broader social history of imperialist violence in Southeast Asia. I had two pedagogical goals: to take the viewer into the war zone (not as an observer but as a subject to trauma), and to create a social narrative (that is, a structure of knowledge) about that experience that could provide a means of recovery and healing from the trauma of violence.

The software program Morph, popularized on MTV, provided the transitional grammar to expose the hidden violence within the mass media's repeating images. That Morph had already become a cliché in popular entertainment media made it all the more appropriate as a grammar by which to distance viewers from the repeating faces of fashion that had become all too familiar. These repeating images, as Virilio reminds us, are "as devastating as repeating guns" (4). This is the power of the mass media—to flood all channels of signification in an overwhelming syncretic flow, while elsewhere in the war zones, often invisibly, violence is systematically and strategically enacted upon those who have been marked as the face of the sacrifice.

## VISION AND MEMORY

If the first pedagogical task is to shatter the safe, rational distance between the viewer and the act of violence, the second pedagogical task is to create a space in which invisible phenomena about war can be seen. This process is functionally opposite in effect to the military technique of mastering disinformation.[2] How do you make viewers see the Treaty of Paris, for example, ratified by the U.S. Congress in 1899, as an act of violence? How do you visualize economic warfare? How do you "show" viewers the violence of contract proceedings, by which every war is launched and executed from remote distances?

In the Treaty of Paris, the U.S. "purchased" the Philippines for $20 million from Spain in a contract proceeding from which the Filipinos themselves were excluded. The "sale" of the Philippine Islands to the U.S. was viewed by both contractual parties as legitimate, in spite of the fact that the government of the First Philippine Republic had already been established in Malolos, and the first President of the Philippines, Emilio Aguinaldo, had already been elected (Blount 216; Majul 166–76). In the eight months from the time of the strategic surrender of the Spanish to Admiral Dewey in

Manila Bay (rather than to Filipino nationalist troops who fought the ground war against Spanish colonialists) until the outbreak of the Philippine – American War two days before the ratification of the Treaty of Paris by the U.S. Congress on February 6, 1899, the U.S. military transported and positioned over 20,000 troops along the major roadways, railways, and waterways leading in and out of Manila in tactical preparation for war (Blount 186). Still, when firing began, U.S. newspapers reported that the war was against Filipino "insurgents" and bandits, and that the first shot had been fired by a Filipino—a claim that has now been refuted by historians on both sides. In fact, the war was tactically instigated on February 4, just two days before the ratification of the Treaty of Paris in order to push ratification through a divided Congress. Ratification of the Treaty of Paris, which authorized the "annexation" of the Philippines, was approved by a narrow margin of one vote. Without the outbreak of war and the misrepresentation of "insurgent"–led social anarchy in the Philippines, it is possible that President McKinley would not have won enough Congressional support to launch an imperialist military campaign in Southeast Asia.

Military tactics took many forms of expression in contract proceedings that orchestrated the Philippine-American War. For example, those who took up arms or advocated armed resistance against the U.S.—or who gave food or shelter to those who did—were subject to execution according to the military proclamation of December 20, 1900 put into effect by Gen. Arthur MacArthur. This proclamation authorized capital punishment for "insurgency"—the definition of which included public expressions of the opinion that the Philippines should be independent of U.S. rule. Many historians attribute the eventual success of the American occupation to this key proclamation by which most of the *illustrado* and peasant leadership fell, from the *katipunero* Macario Sakay hanged in 1907 to the religious leader Felipe Salvador hanged in 1912 (Ileto 196, Blount 319–25).[3]

These two pedagogical goals—shattering the safe distance of the rational spectator and making visible the unseen contract proceedings that enact every war—guided the design of my current video project, an independent centennial documentary of the Philippine-American War of 1899. *Memories of a Forgotten War* is an international collaboration among Filipino, Filipino American and U.S. media artists under the co-direction of myself and Manila filmmaker Sari Lluch Dalena. The project goal is to produce an easily distributed media tool for classroom use both in the U.S. and the Philippines. Marketing is directed primarily toward library acquisitions. The *Memories* project is a multimedia experiment in historical memory. It combines 16mm film, archival photographs, early films from the turn of the century, as well as digital video, computer animation, sound effects, subjective voiceover, and both analog and nonlinear editing. These multiple modalities of the historical image become a means to shatter viewers' objective distance from the (arti)fact of war. The assemblage format also facilitates the reassemblage of forgotten or fragmented collective histories. In addition, the 60-minute program attempts to provide both Filipino and American audiences with the missing historical memories of the Philippine-American war of 1899 from the multiple points of view of Filipino and Filipino American visual artists.

Little remembered in the North American national mythos, the war between Philippine nationalists and U.S. troops was one of the bloodiest military exchanges in the history of modern warfare. In the fifteen years that followed the final defeat of the Spanish in Manila Bay in 1898, more Filipinos were killed by U.S. forces than by the Spanish in 300 years of colonization. Over 1.5 million Filipinos died out of a total population of 6 million. But few in the U.S. remember any of the details of the war or why it was fought. Even in the Philippines, because of the U.S. control of the educational system, many Filipinos are not aware of the events of this history. Yet it is crucial to any historical understanding not only of the Philippines, but also of the Pacific front in World War II and the Korean and Vietnam wars, as well as the current political and economic situation in Asia, to understand what happened in the Philippines at the turn of the century, when for one short year the Philippines became the first democratic republic in Asia, only to have that nascent nationhood shattered by the violence of U.S. imperialism.

As Virilio, paraphrasing Kipling, has said, the concept of reality is always the first victim of war. This was certainly the case with the Philippine-American War, which is typically misremembered by U.S. citizens as the "annexation" of the Philippines. Disinformation about the war began in 1899, with a series of short films produced and directed by Thomas Edison. These short films are dated 1899 and labeled "Spanish–American War," even though that date is one year after Spain surrendered in 1898. The misreference is clearly to the Philippine-American War, as the films feature U.S. soldiers waving American flags and firing rifles at dark Filipino troops who are shot down in trenches. These films simulate reality—they are replete with gunpowder smoke, stamping horses, and wounded and dead soldiers—except that the landscape is New Jersey, not the tropics, and the Filipinos, who are perpetually retreating, fumbling with their rifles, and dying, are played by African Americans recruited and cast by Edison. These early silent shorts demonstrate how well the cinema lent itself to disinformation. Seeing was believing, and it mattered little if what you saw was an illusion as long as it had the look of reality—that is, visible subjects, objects, actions and continuity.

Unlike Edison's distanced approach, my own approach to the history of the Philippine-American War was traumatically marked by the proximity of colonial and imperialist domination in my biracial family. My maternal grandfather was a U.S. cavalry soldier from Oregon, stationed in Manila in 1916 just after most of the fighting had been suppressed. He married a Filipina much younger than he, whom he later abandoned, along with their three children, on the eve of World War II. My mother in her turn married a U.S. serviceman, as did her sisters, and the history repeated itself over the next generation. Add the Spanish colonial legacy to this family romance, and you get three generations of biracial marriages and three generations of mestiza daughters. "First it was the Spaniards and then the Americanos came and took the Filipina women," my great-uncle Dimas at age 84 explained to me once, sitting in the heat in the same house my mother grew up in as a child, the same house in which her mother died of tuberculosis during World War II. My maternal grandmother was half Filipino and half Spanish, her children half Filipino mestizo and half American. I, in my turn, am a third generation mestiza.

In *Memories of a Forgotten War*, I give voice to this family narrative, building an analogy between the failure of the sanctity of the marriage contract in my biracial family and the failure of the sanctity of the social contract between the U.S. and the Philippines that traces back to the originary violence of the imperial war of 1899. In subjective voiceover, I rhythmically weave personal family narratives together with historical narratives about the war, providing the context for properly "seeing" the archive of historical images about the war in the Philippines—including the exoticizing and objectifying gazes so often captured in photographs produced by U.S. photojournalists and military photographers.

The aesthetico-political process for me as the inheritor of war trauma involves a compositional model of assemblage—of looking piece by piece at fragments in multiple planes and then searching for the incommensurable correlations to see the larger frame, the larger picture. Meaning resounds by ricocheting the image as already ideologically loaded artifact off the personal and historical narrative fragments. And though it never adds up to a whole—because violence never does—it reveals to the viewer a processual model for the reassemblage of shattered meanings in the face of violence's aftermath. This method is notably Deleuzian and Guattarian, though the trauma for me precedes my affinity for their work.[4] Trauma and the experience of being not only dislocated but multiple determined my choice of Deleuze and Guattari's work as a methodological and pedagogical model. I found a correspondence between the imperialist trauma in my family narrative and Deleuze and Guattari's total negation both of oedipal family romance and Cartesian instrumental reason as imperialist. And as a media critic and theorist committed to my own practice, I was attracted to the materialist pragmatics they propose for the therapeutic reconstitution of the traumatized subject as a signifying agent. This therapeutic component in their collaborative work often goes unnoticed, but for me it was crucial, particularly the therapeutic aspects of using rhizomatics (rather than Cartesian binarism) as a compositional model for the signifying subject, as well as Guattari's insistence on the healing effects produced by connecting the lived experiences of individuals with the sociopolitical history of the group to which the individual has ties (including broken ties).[5]

In a way, the most profound pedagogical effect one could accomplish in teaching war is to get viewers to stop "seeing" just what is on the screen, where we have the illusion that memory comes at the rate of 24 or 30 frames per second. One has to overcome, overturn, or overthrow the reduction of memory to vision. The imperialism of the eye lies at the heart of Virilio's reading of vision's relation to contemporary forms of violence: "A false equation of sign-reading with knowledge, and even with the whole of knowledge . . . gave rise to the imperialism of the fourth estate—the power, that is, of press and communication media directly involved in the atypical temporality of broadcasting technology" (37). In using these very technologies to teach war, one has to first get viewers to "see" beyond disconnected events of violence so that they can comprehend the historical connectedness surrounding these events. In fact, viewers must not just see, but must understand and accept (that is, "feel" more than "visualize") their relation to that history, not only as individuals but more critically as social groups with which they may identify—since individuals are never in the end "responsible" for war. The ideology of bourgeois individualism allows people not directly affected by war violence to look the other way, so to speak, to remain unaffected, to remain distanced and disembodied historically.

It is true that sometimes the State or even the military itself will carry out criminal proceedings against individuals and hold individuals responsible for acts perpetrated during war. U.S. military courts, for example, did convict one man—Lt. William Calley—for the My Lai Massacre during the Vietnam War (though his sentence was lifted within three days by President Nixon and he served only a fraction of his sentence) (Bilton 2). But such proceedings are typically stop-gap measures with a specific representational function—to obscure the workings of the war machine at large. Calley as convicted war criminal screened the systematic violences of the war machine's strategic and tactical assemblage of economic, military, and representational power deployed in Vietnam. His trial prevented responsibility for violence from spreading across the entire corps of U.S. troops in Vietnam, if not across the entire U.S. nation-state, and at the same time reifying the Western ideological belief in the bourgeois individual as the privileged agent of history. But in order to "see" My Lai, it would be a mistake to look too closely at Calley's individual acts of racist and gendered violence in the war zone.[6] Calley can be seen and remembered properly only in the context of broadscale U.S. policies in Southeast Asia—including policies authorizing the spraying of the Vietnamese landscape with toxic defoliants like Agent Orange—which would enact a pervasive violence against the civilian population that would last for generations.

Failure to understand, or "see," such policies as violence allows the perpetuation of violence. Thus the announcement by the U.S. government in 1998 of a "coca eradication" campaign mobilizing the herbicide tebuthiuron in Colombia, supposedly in a "war against drugs," (that is, a war against the coca plant and not the general Colombian population), hardly evoked any public discussion in the U.S. media and government, though the manufacturer Dow Chemical, which faced years of lawsuits over Agent Orange, warned of uncontrollable effects including contaminated food crops and water supplies. Probably few people reading the brief article announcing the policy decision on the front page of the *New York Times* (June 20, 1998) "saw" the policy as an act of war violence against the Colombian people and their children, both born and unborn.

In this same regard, few U.S. citizens "saw" the ongoing economic sanctions against Iraq as an act of war violence against the Iraqi people, in spite of the fact that nonprofit organizations reported over 1 million Iraqi children had died by March of 1998 from sanctions cutting off food and medical supplies and reducing financial resources to such a state that drinking water was contaminated (Bruderhof Community, *Worth the Price?* 1998). Since disease and starvation typically account for the greatest number of casualties in any war, a diseased and starving child is the most common image of war violence. But such images hardly compete with the perceptual war machine's seductive representations of high-tech weaponry. From the point of view of the Iraqi civilian population, however, the U.S. bombing operation in the final days of 1998 was not another war against them launched by the U.S. military but the same war that never ended. The distinction of separate names—Desert Storm versus Desert Fox—is a functios of the perceptual war machine. Likewise, the "reasons" given for the bombing—chemical weapons violations—screen other less humanitarian determinations, such as U.S. investments in stabilizing global oil prices, U.S. interests in newly discovered oil reserves beneath the Caspian Sea, and local politics (President Clinton's impeachment).

## WAR AND MEMORY

Technologies of remote perception preempt embodied historical memory. This is what Virilio means when he writes, "If memory is science itself for those who make war, the memory in question is not like that of a popular culture based upon common experience: rather, it is a parallel memory, a paramnesia, a mislocation in time and space, an illusion of the déjà vu . . . a visual hallucination akin to dreaming" (33). "Truth" is based not on objectivity and accurateness, but on the emotional impact of the image on the viewer in a moment of embodied knowledge; it is the invisible trace of the seen image in the integrated historical memory of the viewer. Thus the third and final pedagogical goal is to connect the lived experience of the individual who suffers or perpetrates violence (either personally or historically) with the sociopolitical memory of the group. War must become a part of embodied public memory.

In *Memories of a Forgotten War*, this last goal was accomplished by shooting reenactments of events documented in the war records on location in the Philippines, casting local townspeople to act out their own history. Historical events of the past become literally embodied in the present generation through the process of production (see figures 13.5 and 13.6).

Those who know nothing of the war learn its history during production; those who know share their knowledge with the groups assembled during film shooting. Historical memory becomes a lived experience. The very process of creating public documents of the forgotten war becomes an embodied experience of integrated memory for those who participate in or witness the production. The process of remembering what was forgotten is healing. The focus is not so much on "seeing" the objective "truth" of the war as on subjectively experiencing the historical origins and aftereffects of war violence. In other words, the focus of the filmic composition is on the process of remembering rather than seeing as a historical subject who is subject to the trauma of violence (see figures 13.1–13.4).

Imaging the dead is perhaps the most difficult challenge facing the independent documentary filmmaker. People who grew up with cable television, the evening news, and Hollywood films are inured to real violence on screen. In *Memories of a Forgotten War* this problem is tackled by extending the duration of the image, allowing a space for affect to emerge. Death images are then countered with images of the living faces of resistors to the U.S. occupation.

To "give face" to Filipino nationalists and peasant resistors who "lost face," that is, lost their public image and voice, is a way of imaging a collective agency that has been forgotten, made invisible, by the workings of the perceptual war machine. This process involves resurrecting the faces of *illustrado* and peasant resistors from the historical archives of photographs of the war, digitizing them, reframing them, recontextualizing them, and then transferring them to video—a form compatible with contemporary broadcast media. In this process, I do not reify resistors to imperial violence within a discourse of bourgeois individualism, focusing on a few select individuals of heroic, epic dimension. Instead, I create the face of a general resistance to U.S. imperial occupation that crosses many social borders, including those of class, culture, and gender. These faces, engaging the camera eye defiantly, are the living faces of a Filipino resistance that continues today; they stand in stark contrast in our collective memories to the

**Figs. 13.5–6: Local amateur actors reenacting the Battle of Batac in Vigan, Ilocos Sur, Philippines, 1899, in which indigo industry workers, both men and women, resisted U.S. occupying troops and were shot down. From *Memories of a Forgotten War*, co-directed by Sari Lluch Dalena and Camilla Benolirao Griggers.**

images of the dead that they became in their own historical moment. This is the face of collective resistance to the injustice of imperial violence. This face is a memory (see figures 13.7 and 13.8).

In her address to the hundreds of thousands of people who had rallied in Manila on September 21, 1997 to commemorate the twenty-fifth anniversary of the declaration of marshal law under Marcos, former Philippine President Cory Aquino reminded the people gathered that day that historical amnesia is the first enemy of political democratization. To protect against any return of a violent past, Aquino called for memory as a guarantor of the political process. She called on the people to protest a charter change initiative to reverse term limits on elected officials in an effort by some to keep President Ramos in office past his elected term, evoking images of the past as a reminder of the dangers of historical forgetfulness:

> Twenty-five years ago, the President of the Philippines blew out the light
> of democracy and covered the nation in darkness. Congress was pad-

**Fig. 13.7: Making communal histories. On the set of the making of *Memories of a Forgotten War*, Ilocos Sur, Philippines, February 1998. Photograph courtesy of Beng Limpin.**

**Fig. 13.8:** **"Giving face" to Filipino nationalists and resistance fighters who lost face (that is, lost their public identity) in the Philippine-American War.** From *Memories of a Forgotten War*.

locked and the Supreme Court put under the gun. Journalists were picked up, newspapers were shut down. The public was blindfolded and gagged, and the country was robbed. Robbed for fourteen years, without let up or hindrance, without limit or shame. Some of the best and brightest of our youth disappeared. . . . Today, there is a dark wind blowing across our country again—the wind of ambition, a gathering storm of tyranny. We are here to shield that flame so that the light of democracy will not go out in our country again. . . . That is why we are here—to tell the people who want to stay in power, by martial law or charter change: no way and never again. Do your worst, we will do our best to stop you. And we, the people, will prevail. . . . But we are here not only to fight charter change for term extensions, we are here also to fight the amnesia that will let the old enemies of democracy ambush it again.

　　—Former Philippine President Cory Aquino at a rally commemorating the twenty-fifth anniversary of the declaration of marshal law (September 21, 1997).

Because accurate historical memory is a necessary prerequisite for political democratization, documenting war for the public record can never be a neutral act. In the case of the Philippines, historical memory was blocked by U.S. repression of accurate information about the Philippine-American War, since the U.S. civil government managed the educational system in the Philippines and set a long-standing precedent of misrepresenting the war that lasted long after Philippine independence in 1946. For these reasons, important public discussion has not yet taken place on this topic. The centennial of the war in February 1999 provides an opportune moment to bring this issue to the attention of the American and Filipino public and to encourage open discussion and debate between Filipinos and Americans on the hard facts about their violent past. The stakes are high for both countries' ability to remember the formative events of their past and the legacies of their shared histories, in order to better negotiate their futures together and separately.

In order to protect democratization, citizens of the Philippines and the U.S. need accurate and healing representations of their violent union and of the realities of U.S. imperialism in Southeast Asia. To provide one such public representation is the goal of *Memories of a Forgotten War*. Healing both victims and perpetrators from the trauma of a violent history first requires accurate memory of that history. But memory needs a body, not just an eye. For this reason, *Memories of a Forgotten War* is a pedagogical experiment in embodied public memory, an international collaboration in healing, a subjective and public exercise in freedom of speech, and a tool to facilitate public debate about the long history of U.S. imperial violence in Southeast Asia. Not an objective accounting of a war that resembles the disaffections of the evening news that are themselves functions of violent enunciation, *Memories of a Forgotten War* attempts an individual and group exercise in embodied historical memory of U.S. imperial violence in the Philippines.

## NOTES

1. Western fashion and the face of white femininity are major exports from the United States to Asian countries such as the Philippines and Japan.
2. Though it is not necessarily formally opposite in terms of aesthetics.
3. The *illustrado* class was the elite Filipino educated class; members often came from families who held minor or provincial government posts under the Spanish colonial government, or who had business interests that required commercial relations to colonial capital. *Illustrado* leaders played a key role in disseminating revolutionary ideas through their literacy and access to printing presses. Because of their elite class status and business investments, however, their interests were often in conflict with those of the disenfranchised and poverty-stricken peasant class. The *katipunan* revolutionary movement that began the revolution against Spain was an underground brotherhood whose leaders, such as Andres Bonifacio (who was betrayed by the *illustrado* leader Emilio Aguinaldo in 1897), were from among the common people. Both Sakay and Salvador were betrayed by U.S. provisional government officials who promised a reprieve if they peacefully surrendered. Both did surrender and, after imprisonment, were hanged. On the scaffold Sakay said, "Death comes to all of us sooner or later, so I will face the Lord Almighty calmly. But I want to tell you that we are not bandits and robbers, as the Americans have accused us, but members of the revolutionary force that defended our mother country, Filipinas! Farewell! Long live the republic and may our independence be born in the future! Farewell! Long live Filipinas!"
4. In the later stages of their collaboration, specifically in regard to the second volume of *Capitalism and Schizophrenia: A Thousand Plateaus* (1987).
5. One of the central postulates of Guattari's *Molecular Revolution: Psychiatry and Politics*.
6. Court testimony revealed that Charlie Company had committed rapes and random acts of violence against Vietnamese villagers prior to My Lai (Bilton 81). It would be hard to imagine that Charlie Company was the only company in the U.S. Army that engaged in these activities.

# WORKS CITED

Agoncillo, Teodoro. *History of the Filipino People*. 8th edition. Quezon City: Garotech Publishing, 1990.

Bilton, Michael, and Kevin Sim. *Four Hours in My Lai*. New York: Penguin, 1992.

Blount, James. *American Occupation of the Philippines 1898/1912*. New York: G.P. Putnam and Sons, 1913.

Bruderhof Community. *Worth the Price?* Uniontown, PA: Bruderhof Productions, 1998. (VHS 10 min.)

Deleuze, Gilles, and Félix Guattari. *A Thousand Plateaus: Capitalism and Schizophrenia*. Trans. Brian Massumi. Minneapolis: University of Minnesota Press, 1987.

Francisco, Luguiminda Bartalome, and Jonathan Shepard Fast. *Conspiracy for Empire*. Quezon City: Foundation for Nationalist Studies, 1985.

Ileto, Reynaldo Clemeña. *Payson and Revolution: Popular Movements in the Philippines, 1840–1910*. 4th edition. Manila: Ateneo de Manila University Press, 1997.

Griggers, Camilla. *Becoming-Woman*. Minneapolis: University of Minnesota Press, 1997.

Guattari, Félix. *Molecular Revolution: Psychiatry and Politics*. Trans. Rosemary Sheed. New York: Penguin, 1984.

Hurley, Vic. *Swish of the Kris: The Story of the Moros*. New York: E. P. Dutton & Co., 1936. Reprinted with a forward by Renato Constantino. Manila: Cacho Hermanos, Inc., 1985.

Majul, Cesar Adib. *Mabini and the Philippine Revolution*. 2nd edition. Quezon City: University of the Philippines Press, 1996.

Virilio, Paul. *War and Cinema: The Logistics of Perception*. Trans. Patrick Camiller. London: Verso Press, 1989.

Wilcox, Marrion, ed. *Harper's History of the War in the Philippines*. New York: Harper and Brothers Publishers, 1900.

## CHAPTER 14

# *Class of '77: Music Making History*

*ERIC LOTT*

IN 1977 THE WORLD CHANGED and I graduated from high school. This was a fortuitous rather than causal link, but because of '77 neither the world nor high school seemed the same again. The class of '77, musically speaking, included Joe Strummer and Donna Summer, Sylvester and Blondie, who lit up that year and the next few with punkish ferocity and dancy utopianism. The yearbook's theme was 7 & Seven, alcoholic enough to titillate the sophomores yet fittingly cosmological as well. The prophetic reggae group Culture produced "Two Sevens Clash." Elvis died on his throne. The whole joint was going up in smoke.

At my twentieth high school reunion last summer, more than one spliff (okay, only two) came my way. The promise of '77 seemed to hang aloft, waiting for judgment. The stud now taught elementary education; the class president had become a craps dealer; the class clown was working for Kenneth Starr (I swear); a couple of erstwhile burnt-outs bought and sold property; the Jesus freak died of cancer and the thinker, my friend, lost his mind and took his life. Only the rockers and nightlifers carried the torch. As a dim DJ spun Leo Sayer, the Eagles, and Genesis (prompting a brief exodus), I heard tales of grails followed by classmates to whom the music had been holy. Politically speaking, the revolution announced in 1977's punk and disco had screeched to a halt midway through the Carter administration, intermittently rousing itself since then to make a little noise. Culturally, the music had kept more than a few going—a social worker here and a beach-dweller there, all of whom knew enough to keep looking for the perfect beat. (A couple of kids had, alas, become cops.) I myself am locked down in the prison house of language.

If you can get work in the humanities, this is not the worst way to await and abet the changes augured in 1977. Indeed, the class of '77 is perfectly situated to understand what few recent commentators have seen fit to make clear: that political change relies on music not for propagandistic huffing and puffing or merely for an aestheticized understanding of the human mysteries politics tends to override. Political force comes from the best, most sublime music, of whatever category or type. Deep-thinking, nonacademic cultural correspondents long ago went looking for the political implications of pop, among them Ralph Ellison, LeRoi Jones/Amiri Baraka, Charles Keil, Greil Marcus, and Albert Murray; Ellison's *Shadow and Act* (1964), Jones/Baraka's *Blues People: Negro Music and American Culture* (1963), Keil's *Urban Blues* (1965), Marcus's *Mystery Train: Images of America in Rock 'n' Roll Music* (1975), and Murray's *Stomping the Blues* (1976) remain fabulous models of how to assess the status of democracy in America via American music. In the academy, too, musicologists have spent time on this pop front—Charles Hamm on Stephen Foster's blackface doodah, Wilfrid Mellers on John Philip Sousa's martial steps, Eileen Southern on New Orleans gutbucket, John Miller Chernoff on African rhythm and sensibility, and Susan McClary on Madonna's moves. Generally, though, we've missed many chances to identify the political change attendant upon harmonic changes. With '77's postpunk, postdisco generational sensibility, leftish politics, and range of pop music reference having come back to school in the form of a younger (lumpen)professoriate, the time is now to read pop life for its making of history from Watergate to Darryl Gates's L.A., from the Women's Action Coalition to ACT-UP.

Nineteen seventy-seven saw the publication in France of Jacques Attali's *Noise: The Political Economy of Music,* which not only brilliantly rewrote conventional music history's drab roll-call of geniuses by looking at societies' various ways of producing, distributing, and consuming music, but also worked against the functionalism implicit in this approach by suggesting music's predictive and even prophetic value. For Attali the elemental, bodily fact of *noise*—claps, shouts, stomps, moans, growls, knocks—is an affirmation of human existence. It is also a disturbance, an interruption of the smooth functioning of social order that music maintains by sublimating noise, submitting it to aesthetic codes analogous to social constraints. These codes, especially in the mass production and distribution of music, only distantly gesture to fundamental corporeal liberties awaiting new interjections of noise to free them up. As wary as German Marxist Theodor Adorno of the music industry's cynical manufacture of sweet sound, Attali calls for a new deal of noncommodified music—music made by everyone for his or her own joy, music beyond the buying and selling of company control, music purely for the sensuous pleasure released in and by an integrated mind and body. Writing in a moment of nascent musical upheaval, Attali had reason to believe a new era dawned. If the Sex Pistols' "Anarchy in the U.K." didn't convince, or Linton Kwesi Johnson's "Forces of Victory," or Sister Sledge's "We Are Family," or Cheryl Lynn's "Got to Be Real," or the Ramones' "Sheena Is a Punk Rocker," or X-Ray Spex's "Oh Bondage, Up Yours!"—well, then you weren't likely to be convinced by much of anything. While only a couple of these songs referenced the cold world of political struggle, they all made voice, beat, and noise announce a transformation in human relations: a new social contract between artist and audience, between ruled and ruler.

Put it this way: the day I graduated from high school was probably the last one you could listen to Led Zeppelin and believe the millennium was coming. Confronted with the deflating energies of, say, Elvis Costello's "(Angels Want to Wear My) Red Shoes," Led Zep's "Stairway to Heaven" went up like the *Hindenberg*. "Precious and Few" was my '77 senior prom theme, and if such doltish ditties didn't go away in the ensuing years, it was at least easier to ignore them in the wake of songs like Thelma Houston's big-hurted "Don't Leave Me This Way." Punk, disco, and rap changed the key of life in Anglo-America, confirming Attali's hunches and altering the grooves that governed conspicuous consumption in the West. Punk and rap assaulted and reworked ruling regimes that disco finessed in no less knowing ways, and if Reagan came along to spoil the party, the music didn't let up on the good fight. The point here is not that this music explicitly protested its political climate (though some of it did, with bells on). The point is that at the level of genre, style, address, and sonic strategy, this music decimated the oppressive banality of everyday life (memorably lampooned in Steely Dan's hilarious depiction of a bored, feuding couple: "Turn up the Eagles/the neighbors are listening" [*The Royal Scam,* 1976]). And in doing so it charted a course of distaff dissent and utopian bliss that implied a cohort of friends and summoned a collective into being. Rather than turning revolt into style, it styled insurrectionary energies that made over everyday life. Critic Simon Frith later pondered whether rock 'n' roll had in fact died in 1977—ending a twenty-year run now superseded by something else—or instead reinvented an ideal of revolt that had withered in the meantime.

Cultural studies scholar Dick Hebdige in effect provided the first popular account of this situation in his influential 1979 book *Subculture: The Meaning of Style.* One of the early studies to take advantage of continental cultural theory and contemporary sociology in its reading of British subcultures culminating in punk, *Subculture* contained many of the emphases to mark the cultural study of music in the years after its publication. Drawing on the work of Italian Marxist Antonio Gramsci and French semiotician Roland Barthes, Hebdige conceded the administered character of postwar pop culture but stressed the ability of communities of youth to construct cultures that went against the current of capital gain. Popular culture, so linked to the flow of pop music, was a battleground one entered with safety pin and Mohawk, Spandex and glitter, Adidas and Kangol cap. The shock of style meant what it said even if it didn't come out and say what it meant, and it had the capacity to give voice to the silenced, change lives, construe the world, occasionally resist the state. This was the perspective developed at the Centre for Contemporary Cultural Studies at England's University of Birmingham, popularly known as the Birmingham school, which codified the methodological scrutiny of pop-cultural production and consumption, of youth resistance through ritual, of original routes of rebellion kids invented by adapting as well as refusing their parent cultures. All of this is now the common knowledge of cultural researchers less idiosyncratic than Jacques Attali but as attuned to the political resonance of styles most tend to write off as weird, trivial, or immature.

But as often as not this line of thought has induced its own regression in listening. Subcultural theory has garnered its share of criticism—on one side for its alleged equation of dressing up with political action, on the other for its investment in insular and monolithic and often male subcultural authenticity—yet it nonetheless has governed much of the cultural study of popular music since the early 1980s. And while it has radically transformed our sense of music's place in social change, it has encouraged a neglect of the way music works on the human sensorum—music's affective charge and aesthetic force in the making of political sensibilities. There remains a stubborn Manichean tic whereby music matters either as politics or as art, and the two generally don't meet much. The tragic result, as I see it, is that this situation allows important cultural-studies interventions to be absorbed and neutralized by a general liberal cultural division between the vaporous sphere of Art and the diabolical domain of Politics. Thus in the work of facile "radical pedagogues" one encounters endless breastbeating about the political importance of pop life with little sense of the way political and aesthetic dimensions feed off each other. Or in liberal discourse, where tired celebrations of early Dylan are still cutting edge, artists like Dylan are seen as too attentive to human complexity to cater to the allegedly rigid ideologies and grimly puritanical cultures of the left. (Things get fuzzy from a distance.)

But hope for a politically attuned aesthetic sense is not lost. For one thing, recent discussions have generally shifted from relations of representation—the exhausted debates about the relative merits of high and low cultural forms, corny insider "translations" of music for outsiders, important but often uninspired "coverage" of neglected genres—to the more complex politics of representation itself: the careful exploration of what means which for whom, the embattled internal politics of even embattled genres, the angling for space on the part of women rappers, the competing aesthetics of punk and folk in white women's musical culture. Three recent pieces of work in particular raise a standard to be followed by anyone interested in the political urgency of formulated sound, and all three implicitly carry a post – '77 sensibility. Surprises await readers of this work who think they know the score when it comes to conventional canons of either taste or politics. First there is the wonderful essay on disco by Princeton scholar Walter Hughes, "In the Empire of the Beat" (in *Microphone Fiends: Youth Music and Youth Culture,* ed. Andrew Ross and Tricia Rose, Routledge, 1994), which discerns in the gay male embrace of disco and its various scions not only a cultural logic of self-preservation but also a historical rationale for its sustaining presence. With his ears trained acutely on the shapes and pleasures of the music, Hughes links its technophilia and repetitive insistence to gay men's willing acceptance of an imperial rhythm dominion that converts the everyday policing of gay desire into militant self-discipline and ecstatic self-realization. Thus is slavery to the rhythm (in Grace Jones's song) turned to the account of imperial beatitude. Where in its late – 70s beginnings disco crucially helped fashion gay identity, in the 90s it solaces a community ("don't leave me this way") confronted with the iterative horrors of an epidemic.

Then there is Joy Press and Simon Reynolds's *The Sex Revolts* (Harvard University Press, 1996), a fascinating gender reading of recent rock history in which psychoanalytic perspectives, deployed in sensitive accounts of rock music and performance, uncover often surprising political implications. The Stones' cock rock is no revelation, but the authors' account of it is; and what say you to the anti-macho resonance of all that psychedelic music (then and now) you're embarrassed to admit you love? (Both the above works, incidentally, are kin to the brilliantly speculative arguments put forward by Richard Middleton in *Studying Popular Music* [1990], where the liberatory pleasures of, say, repetitive bubble-gum music or for that matter any musical statement that depends on insistent repetition become an uncanny replay of infant bliss underwritten by the groove of the [mother's] heart, an argument with quite various political applications.) Finally, there is Armond White's extraordinary book on Tupac Shakur, *Rebel for the Hell of It* (Thunder's Mouth, 1997), a brilliant, tough-minded, passionate, and culturally wide-ranging account of the gifts as well as the fool's gold the late rapper left behind for his hip-hop constituency and anyone else alert enough to take seriously Tupac's iconic power. White calls us to a morally serious critical investigation of Tupac's life and career, from his upbringing in a revolution-ary family of Panther pedigree to his toil in the music, film, and media indus-tries; and it's White's intimate engagement with Tupac's work and the enormous areas of black feeling and understanding it calls up that makes his radical political analyses so convincing. No boilerplate progressivism obscures White's social urgency, no special pleading to mainstream igno-rance shortens his reach; you can't find a page of *Rebel for the Hell of It* without an original thought on, for instance, the "unsentimental education" given Tupac by early – 70s black pop, the instructive affinities between Tupac's 1995 "Dear Mama" and that C & W thug-lifer Merle Haggard's 1972 "Mama Tried," or the inability of clenched-voice late Tupac (as Makaveli) to capture and convey his pain in the manner of gospel vet Pop Staples or southern rapper Brad (Scarface) Jordan.

The point of all this work isn't to qualify, correct, or otherwise interrupt your pleasure. It's to observe the political stakes of that pleasure—to espy the social movement explicitly or implicitly articulated or hampered by it. Musical culture, like most cultural products, can in its wonderful commo-tion create the conditions for social motion. With Jacques Attali in mind, we might say that music and its best interpreters help create or announce the existence of a community bent on getting the respect it deserves for the social desires it lets loose.

You can see why a lot was riding on my reunion. It isolated a moment whose demands are still daunting to imagine living up to, demands the music of that time exemplifies best. For scholars of such things, there is no point in nostalgia, the faking of youth, political vanity, aestheticized com-placency. All these merely simplify, destroying the political richness of sen-suous human noise-making. Instead, the political ideal inculcated by 1977, that better time, is presence of mind—inhabiting the world as someone, to quote Walter Benjamin, "on whom nothing is lost." Presence of mind seemed rather intermittent at my reunion, though the naked fact of the pres-ent was forceful enough. Then, all of a sudden, the DJ wised up and sup-planted 70s kitsch with the Bayside Boys' mix of 1996's "Macarena." Several women immediately charged the dance floor solo until they met up and joined hands, and the class of '77 was redeemed in a disco inferno.

# CHAPTER 15

# *Punk Multiculturalism*

SAMIR GANDESHA

WHAT IS THE RELATIONSHIP between pedagogy and experience? Traditional pedagogy typically approaches experience by reducing it to a universal concept. Critical pedagogy, by contrast, begins with a fragment of experience and then traces within that fragmentary experience the social and historical mediations or relations contained allegorically within it and that make it possible in the first place. In contrast to traditional pedagogy, this approach attempts to disrupt students' expectations by leading them into an uncanny engagement with what is strange yet familiar to them. Through such an engagement it leads back to a reflection on their own experience with the world, not in an essentialist or possessive individualist manner but rather in a way that extends from the particular to questions of economy, society, and history.

The present essay is precisely such a contribution to a critical reflection on experience. Punk exemplifies the cultural contradictions of late capitalism in which, as a variety of writers such as the Frankfurt School, Walter Benjamin, and the Situationists, have suggested, the *very possibility* of experience is put in question. With the advent of what Horkheimer and Adorno call the "culture industry," or what Guy Debord calls the "society of the spectacle," genuine forms of experience become progressively colonized by a logic of commodification. For Walter Benjamin, the apotheosis of this logic was fascism, understood in his celebrated formulation as the "aestheticization of the political" in which technologically mediated violence becomes transformed into a spectacle.[1] Unlike his Frankfurt associates, however, Benjamin was somewhat more sanguine about the potential of popular culture, particularly film, for "politicizing art." In recent years, usually under the auspices of postmodernism, there has been a selective appropriation of Benjamin's dialectical vision. This involves the increasing propensity to reject the analysis of the fascistic potential of popular culture in favor of affirming its politically subversive nature. The most exemplary case of this is Madonna. While feminists have attempted to tease out the nuances of Madonna's representations of gender and sexuality, they have often turned a blind eye to the manner in which, for instance, her portrayal of Eva Peron, the wife of Argentine dictator Juan Peron, in *Evita* comes uncomfortably close to engaging in a mimesis of the actress's own megalomania. Thus inasmuch as this approach to popular culture is predicated on reified understanding of textuality—the extrication of the text from the contexts of society and history—the commodity logic of the culture industry ultimately goes unquestioned. And inasmuch as this approach of culture is often aligned with "multiculturalism," in which the deconstruction of popular culture is carried out in order to create space for hitherto marginalized forms, it actually fails to come to terms with what is most fatal for cultural difference: the commodity form in which every particular is, in principle, rendered equivalent with everything else.

Punk, in its early incarnation, is testimony that popular culture can be the basis for a critique of the culture industry or, as Adorno put it, that art and popular culture "are two halves of an integral freedom to which, however, they do not add up." The history of punk is, however, at the same time a manifestation of how fatal such a critique can actually be. In contrast to the relentless moralism of a good deal of contemporary art, the utopian vision of punk was seldom posited directly but rather emerged as a dialectical moment of its own negativity. It was precisely because punk challenged the classifying logic of capital that it was able to open up a space, however short-lived, for a genuine engagement with the other. For this reason, punk manifested an "uncanny" multiculturalism, one that reached deep down through the history of rock music to the black experience buried beneath it.

Sometime in the early 1980s I found myself at a gig by one of Vancouver's best, most infamous punk bands: DOA. The band's notoriety lay, amongst other things, in the tribute it paid to Margaret Sinclair, former wife of Pierre Eliot Trudeau and consort to the Rolling Stones, by including her on an EP cover seated on the ground wearing a skirt, knees up to her chest, without any panties on. A parody of Rod Stewart's disco hit, "Do You Think I'm Sexy," the EP was entitled "Do You Wanna Fuck?" Before Joey Shithead and the rest of the band, including legendary bassist Wimpy Roy, formerly of the Subhumans, hit the stage of UBC's SUB Ballroom, I was accosted by a young punk who took exception to the T-shirt that I was wearing at the time. Pointing to the visage of Bob Marley on the front of it, he issued the following warning: "I'd be careful if I were you, punks don't like reggae." Disconcerted more by the punk's insouciant ignorance of music history than any evident danger in declaring divided musical loyalties, I continued on with the more serious business of getting another pint.

But the young punk's reaction to the appearance of a reggae fan at the gig was not the exception but rather the rule in Canada. The notion that punk and reggae manifested *divided* loyalties owes to the manner in which punk itself, like popular culture as a whole, was so thoroughly lifted out of the context in which it first emerged. The reason for such a reification owes to the manner in which punk, perhaps more so than other forms of popular culture, was ruthlessly commodified. In fact, the band that started it all, the Sex Pistols, set out quite consciously to make itself into the purest commodity, for instance, shamelessly issuing re-releases with titles like *Flogging a Dead Horse.* Nothing, however, was to top Malcolm McLaren's film, starring none other than "the great train robber" Ronny Biggs, *The Great Rock 'n' Roll Swindle,* which offered a history of the Sex Pistols in the form of a sort of step-by-step guide to generating "cash from chaos." Such self-commodification could also be read as an attempting to beat the devil at his own game. It was an attempt to show, in the form of a parody, what usually remained hidden from sight—namely, that the culture industry's raison d'être was none other than profit. By the time of the *Filthy Lucre* tour a couple of years ago, however, the joke had worn off; we already knew the punchline.

Because punk's dissemination depended upon the very conditions of its commodification—that the experiences that it captured had to be frozen and packaged in order to be sold to kids in the U.S., Canada, Continental Europe, Japan, etc.—it was necessarily detached from the particularity of those urban landscapes of abandoned factories and damp, decrepit council flats in which different classes and ethnic and racial communities jostled for position and, I shall suggest, deeply penetrated the sensibility of the music. This is perhaps what explains the judgment of the young punk from the DOA gig. Owing to the specific nature of the Canadian city, there wasn't the same collision of cultures expressed in musical and subcultural forms. While the Canadian, particularly the once-thriving Vancouver punk scene produced extraordinarily original bands in addition to DOA such as the Subhumans, the Young Canadians, the Animal Slaves, the Modernettes, the Dirty Dishrags, the Viletones, and Martha and the Muffins, it was not provoked in the same way by black cultures that so decisively marked the British and the New York scenes. What I want to suggest is that because of this encounter, contrary to its contemporary image, punk embodied a subterranean multiculturalism.

But how radical could punk actually be? Did it not embody what Herbert Marcuse called "repressive desublimation," which is to say a form of rebellion that not only does not constitute a threat to the commodity society but actually contributes to its legitimation? Was it not the childish thumbing the nose at parental authority which, far from challenging it, only reaffirms its power? For Adorno, the fact of the lack of autonomy on the part of popular culture, that its exchange value totally dominated its use value, meant that it played an "affirmative" role; it contributed toward absorbing negative or oppositional tendencies within society. For in its commodified form, popular culture imperiled the possibility of genuine experience—rather than bringing individuals out of themselves, it simply offered them a mirror in which to glimpse their own reflections. In other words, popular culture rarely defied the expectations of its consumers. Genuine experience, in contrast, was the basis for a revolutionary imagination: there must be a glimmer of the "new" society beyond capitalism, otherwise capitalist society takes on the appearance of a natural fact: of something that has always existed and will continue to exist.[2]

At one time, the working class played the role of pointing the way forward in history; its own self-activity pointed toward a future in which the surplus product would be not privately but collectively appropriated. In other words, the development of technology, which Marx regarded as essentially progressive and liberating, would lead to a crisis in the dominant relations of reproduction in society: this was the prefiguration of a world beyond private ownership of the means of production. For Adorno, while this scenario might well have held true in the era in which Marx was writing—that of liberal capitalism—it was no longer the case in "late capitalism," which was an era of almost total administration. It was such because virtually all oppositional social tendencies, particularly the revolutionary aspirations of the working class, had been neutralized or incorporated largely owing to the emergence of the welfare state and, as suggested earlier, its counter-part: mass culture. It was in this period, in Adorno's view, that the autonomous, modern artwork became one of the last refuges of the utopian images of a society free from domination. These artworks, in showing the world in all of its contradictions and the psychological and physical suffering to which they gave rise, possessed the power to suggest a world in which suffering would no longer exist. Art, in its violence and alienated ugliness, evoked its own negation: the promise of happiness and human self-fulfillment.

While Adorno was right about many things, his understanding of the relationship between high art and mass culture was perhaps not dialectical enough. While he held that they were the flipsides of the same coin, he did not view mass culture in a nuanced enough way; he didn't allow for its ability to reflect upon the conditions of its own commodification and in the process offer the sort of utopic possibilities that he believed resided exclusively in the autonomous work of art. Indeed, Adorno has achieved a certain notoriety for his dismissal of jazz as the sadomasochistic affirmation of domination.[3] He was not, however, attentive enough to the be-bop that was emerging in the 1940s which, as Gerald Early has suggested,[4] sought both directly and indirectly to constitute a distinctive African American language attempting to circumvent easy assimilation into mainstream, white American society—a society that was still fiercely segregated and that would remain so for two decades.

Punk, I shall suggest, was also capable of reflecting on its own social and historical conditions—namely, that as soon as it was produced, it became a commodity like any other. Indeed, punk's initial shock value served not to undermine but to heighten its exchange value—a lesson well learned by artists such as Marilyn Manson. However, unlike Manson, many of the punk bands did not rest content merely with mass producing records, but sought instead to push this logic of commodification to the breaking point, to the point at which it would release hitherto repressed possibilities. As Malcolm McLaren, the man who created and managed the Sex Pistols, stated: "We wanted a situation where kids would be less interested in buying records than in speaking for themselves." Because punk was so thoroughly grounded in its own present, in contrast with the current fascination with a nostalgic and totally uninteresting repackaging of the previous decade, its ethos was, to quote Neil Young's commentary on punk, "It's better to burn out than to fade away." Which is to say, punk sought to glimpse the eternal in the transitory. In that very attempt, however, punk signed its own death certificate. This is perhaps why, like Miles Davis's own judgment about be-bop, it is not possible to listen to punk anymore, at least not in the same way as we did in the late 1970s. It also means that like many works of modern art, Punk was, contrary to all the bathroom-stall graffiti, dead at its birth. For Punk shared modernism's motto that "One must be absolutely modern." This meant that at the very moment an artwork came into being, it was already rendered obsolete by the torrential rush and flow of history. Modern art, from this view, was its own undoing.

This is perhaps one of the reasons the orthodox left has viewed artistic movements like punk with suspicion. After all, the left asked, wasn't progressive art supposed to depict society's "historical laws of motion" and in the process inform revolutionary praxis? Or, in the more contemporary idiom of identity politics, wasn't art supposed to affirm the experiences and in the process "empower" oppressed or marginalized groups? Viewed from either of these perspectives, it would appear that punk manifested a dangerous nihilism: all it could seemingly affirm was pure nothingness. To make such a claim, however, would be to ignore the fact that only in the name of another possibility could such a negation be articulated. In other words, it wasn't simply the negation of the social world for negation's sake. Rather, in its declaration that "There's no future," punk demanded that there be one. Only by bathing it in the light of redemption could punk reveal the world as a barren, desiccated landscape. As Greil Marcus puts it, punk manifested "a voice that denied all social facts, and in that denial affirmed that everything was possible."[5] In its assault on past and future, indeed, on the very structure of time itself, the experience that it fleetingly captured was nonetheless destroyed at the very moment that Vivienne Westwood established punk as a fashion statement in its own right on New York's Madison Avenue. Unlike other forms of popular culture, however, punk was, at least in its initial stages, willing to embrace and affirm such creative self-destruction—which is what makes it so interesting. But let us try to relocate ourselves, as it were, from Manhattan to another place, to the initial roots of punk within the contradictions of the postcolonial city. Maybe such a relocation can explain the strange afterlife of punk in the wake of its death. Perhaps there is a structure of experience that punk alighted upon that still might, twenty years later, have something to say to us. After all, if punk no longer exists— if one doesn't include what Iggy Pop calls the "middle-management music" of bands like Greenday, Social Distortion, and Rancid—then the social contradictions to which it bore witness certainly do.

The authoritarian populism Margaret Thatcher unleashed on the world is alive and well in Ontario, Alberta, and other provinces in Canada and continues on with a "human face" (if this is an apt description of Tony Blair's mannequin stare) in the country of its origin. And contemporary popular culture and its counterpart—an increasingly conformist cultural studies— long since relinquished any desire to speak the negative truth that now there really is "no future," particularly if you happen to be under 25. Contemporary popular culture is instead hopelessly mired in a cynical nostalgia and the "better times" it imagines takes the form of the monochromatic and aggressively banal world of *The Brady Bunch Movie.* Is it any surprise, then, that the possibility of opposition is badly fractured and fragmented across a wide spectrum of identity politics? In the face of inherently destabilizing and therefore deeply threatening processes of globalization, in which, as Marx put it in the *Manifesto,* "all that is solid melts into air," one witnesses the attempt to escape this dialectic by way of a hasty retreat into the homely, familiar, and reassuring forms of cultural particularity. Is there any greater testament to a desire for the familiar and unthreatening than the truly meteoric rise of Garth Brooks, Vince Gill, Shania Twain, and the New Country in the face of resolutely urban forms of music like hip-hop? The watch word of the 1990s is "Safe," so brilliantly captured in Todd Haynes's film of the same name. While seemingly innocuous, the desire for safety conjures up disturbing images of gated communities, of private security companies called Securicor, and panzer-divisions of luxurious sports vehicles built to withstand civil insurrection. It ultimately means being with people who look and think just like you and are unlikely to pose a threat to your identity, your values, your worldview.

Much of what passes for multiculturalism manifests a similar desire for safety. While purporting to bring about conditions in which difference is recognized and respected, multiculturalism more often than not embodies the desire for the security of the same. It typically suggests a refusal to take risks, a refusal to engage with forms of otherness or difference that represent anything more than what is officially sanctioned. In its assertion of difference, contemporary multiculturalism often ignores the very real similarities in the conditions of people who are only apparently different. In contrast, the strange multiculturalism of punk anticipates L.A. rapper Coolio's statement that "It's no longer about the difference between black and white, but about those who have money and those who don't." In contrast to the obsessive desire for "safety," punk sought out the dangerous, the risky and the provocative that it found somewhere "beyond good and evil." Rather than establishing and maintaining rigid racial, sexual, and other forms of identity, in its "ruthless criticism of all that exists," punk actively broke down and reconstituted these identities in new and often imaginative constellations and in the process manifested a form of aesthetic experience that sought to open itself up to the otherness of experience. Rather than saying simply no to the symbols of power and domination, punk appropriated, transformed, and made such symbols its own.

For instance, in her adoption of the bondage and s/m gear so prevalent in the early punk scene, Poly Styrene, lead singer of X-Ray Spex, engaged in what the Situationists called *detournement,* the deployment of a specific object or sign for exactly the opposite of what it was originally intended— for example, kung-fu movies overdubbed with Maoist revolutionary dialogue. Poly Styrene's slogan was "Oh Bondage, Up yours!" Such a strategy of detourning signs of authority and power would be crucial to punk's politics.

The strange multiculturalism of punk is due, in part, to the influence of black culture, which itself is to be located in the crucible of the proto-punk scene in New York in the mid - 1970's. This scene was heavily influenced by the style and sensibility of black culture largely because it was music that authentically expressed the essence of the "street hassle." The use of street style and language as a means of resistance to the conformity and unthinking banality of American culture itself goes back to the Beat generation's, particularly Jack Kerouac's, adaptation of the improvised idiom and riffs of be-bop culture. The Beats crucially cleared the way for the student and youth movements of the sixties by showing that the style and culture through which everyday life was lived was deeply political even when in the 1950s it was supposedly depoliticized.

But it was not just traces of black culture that appeared in the proto-punk scene, but also that of other sub-cultures, particularly the sexual outlaw cultures of the Village and the Bowery as documented, for instance, in the photography of Nan Goldin. Patti Smith, Lou Reed, Iggy Pop (from Detroit), the Ramones, Stiv Bators and the Dead Boys, Richard Hell and especially the New York Dolls reinjected into American music the sexuality, indeed the polymorphous perversity, that had existed in rock 'n' roll ever since it had been damned as the devil's music and Elvis's pelvis was censored during his famed appearance on the *Ed Sullivan Show.* But this was more than drawing out what was already surreptitiously present in popular music. The Dolls, by dressing in drag, were consciously identifying themselves with what was then—well before the likes of Ru-Paul, k.d. lang, and Dennis Rodman—a particularly marginal urban subculture.

Around the time that Elvis was found on the bathroom of Graceland, fat, drugged, and dead and consequently resurrected as the patron saint of middle America, New York bands were returning to the black experience that suffused the music of the young Elvis. The King had, so to speak, two bodies, which can perhaps be read as allegories for two different Americas: the brash, sexy body of his youth, which contributed to breaking down the racial segregation of musical styles, and the bloated corpse found on the floor of Graceland.

But things weren't quite so simple. While the New York scene drew upon the outlaw subcultures of that city, David Bowie, also deeply influenced by them, particularly through the influence of Lou Reed, was at the time valorizing Hitler as the first "superstar" (which he no doubt was, thanks to Leni Riefenstahl) and stating that what Britain needed was a dictatorship. Bowie's antics demonstrated some uncomfortable similarities between popular culture and fascism. As David Widgery has shown, Bowie even went so far as to stage a Nazi-style return to London from Berlin in a Mercedes limousine which, in the words of Widgery, "chillingly mixed rock star megalomania with Third Reich references."[6] While Bowie was later dissuaded from these coked-up histrionics by a group of Berlin socialists, there was something particularly disturbing about the manner in which he expressed a widely held sentiment. As he was to put it later: "It was that hideous thing where as an artist you kind of feel there's something in the air . . . you just sense a situation or an atmosphere and that can go into your writing."[7] Around the same time, Eric Clapton, the rock musician perhaps most deeply steeped in the tradition of Mississippi Delta blues, was publicly ruminating about the sexual endowments of black men and making statements in favor of Enoch Powell, the recently deceased right-wing Tory MP who delivered the infamous "Rivers of Blood Speech," in 1968 predicting, in what was to become very much a self-fulfilling prophecy, that if immigration didn't stop, Britain would see "rivers of blood in the streets."[8] Rod Stewart, whose own career was hugely indebted to Smokey Robinson, Sam Cooke, Aretha Franklin, and a host of black blues musicians such as Big Bill Broonzy, declared that immigrants to Britain should just pack up and go "home." Never mind that Stewart himself was living in tax exile from Britain with a succession of blonde movie stars in L.A., much to the derision of the fans of this ex-footballer, ex-gravedigger, and erstwhile working-class hero.

The specificity of punk lay in its expression of the particular accelerated dissonances of the life of the cities in which it exploded. Unlike the timelessness and repetitiveness of the country reflected in the constrained forms of twelve-bar blues, the city is the place of improvisation, of jazz. As Toni Morrison has suggested in her novel of the same name, jazz is a form deeply marked by its origins in the place where irreconcilable worlds collide. The cities that gave rise to punk as an aesthetic of collision and improvisation can be characterized as *postcolonial* inasmuch as these spaces were in the process of becoming transformed from what were once the industrial and political centers of empire into places increasingly inhabited by erstwhile colonial subjects—West Indian workers "invited" to work on British Rail and London Transport and workers from Pakistan and Bangladesh and refugees escaping racist dictatorships in Uganda and Malawi. These cities were the places where the atavistic forces of *imperium* were gathering to mount a counterattack.

For instance, on April 23, 1979, just prior to the general election that brought Margaret Thatcher to power, the fascist party the National Front attempted with assistance of the police to stage a march directly through Southall, a predominantly Punjabi section of west London, as a way of reasserting a particular set of imperial relations within the city itself. There they were met with opposition largely consisting of South Asian youth organizations but also including antiracist organizations like the Socialist Workers Party and the Anti-Nazi League. In the ensuing clash, hundreds of demonstrators were injured, a number of them were jailed, and one, a white teacher from New Zealand named Blair Peach—movingly eulogized in Linton Kwesi Johnson's "Reggae fi Peach"—was killed by a blow to the head from a police truncheon.

In the violence of its aural and visual assault, punk simultaneously reflected and reflected upon precisely this violence that it saw around it, particularly that directed at those who were considered not to belong to the "nation." Punk constituted a gilt-edged polemic aimed at those who believed, to use the words of Paul Gilroy, that "There ain't no black in the Union Jack."[9] Conscious of the manner in which blacks and Asians, particularly Rastas in their obvious attempt to break with "Babylon," actively resisted the brutal conditions under which they were forced to live, Punk consciously sought a break, through its fashion, music, and demeanor, from mainstream white society. It called for a "White Riot" as an emulation of black resistance to economic and social brutality. Punk, in other words, alienated itself from a society that dropped the hammer on those it considered aliens, a society that provided little hope for black, Asian and white youth alike in an era of deindustrialization and diminishing expectations, as the Clash put it: "What we wear is dangerous gear / It'll get you picked up anywhere / Though we get beat up we don't care / At least it livens up the air."

At very moment when the symbols of empire, in particular the Union Jack—in lethal combination with the jackboot—were becoming repoliticized, no doubt assisted by the comments of Bowie, Clapton, and Stewart, in the year of the Royal Jubilee, Punk detourned these very symbols with a vengeance. In detourning the national anthem—and this perhaps takes on added significance after the mass hysteria over the recent death-by-paparazzi of the Princess of Wales—the Sex Pistols made it into the anthem for a generation for which the "nation" either never had been or no longer was an option:

> God save the queen and her fascist regime
> it made you a moron a potential H bomb!
> God save the queen she ain't no human being
> there is no future in England's dreaming
> Don't be told what you want and don't be told what you need
> there's no future no future no future for you

This snarling commentary by Johnny Rotten, who was of Irish descent and therefore particularly abhorred the chauvinism expressed in the Jubilee celebrations, was more than simply a dressing- down of the monarchy. Rather, it constituted a critique of imperial history in its entirety; it presented a vision of history as a document not of civilization but of barbarism. It was a history that weighed like a nightmare on the minds and bodies of blacks and Asians who had to endure routine stabbings, beatings and house-bombings:

> God save the Queen cos tourists are money
> And our figurehead is not what she seems
> Oh God save history, God save your mad parade
> Oh lord have mercy all crimes are paid
>
> When there's no future how can there be sin
> We're the flowers in your dustbin
> We're the poison in your human machine
> We're the future your future

The only progress one could discern in history was that leading, as Adorno put it, from the "sling shot to the Atom Bomb"—was truly a "mad parade." The symbols of empire were therefore transformed into signs of anarchy, the glorious history of *Pax Britannica* into pure nihilism. While David Bowie and the National Front were invoking the name of Hitler, the Clash laid bare the fascism that was taking over the shop floors of whatever factories were still functioning in Britain and the U.S. in the late 1970s:

> Taking off his turban they said "Is this man a Jew?"
> We're working for the Clampdown
> They put up their posters saying we earn more than you
> We're working of the clampdown
> We'll teach our twisted speech
> To the young believers
> We'll train our blue-eyed men
> To be young believers

What is crucial is the manner in which this song reveals fascism as the murder of cultural difference—"Taken to be melted down"—something that punk confronted directly in its engagement and dialogue with black musical forms. For Hitler's political theorist, Carl Schmitt, the essence of the political is the moment when the enemy comes into view. The gesture of stripping the Punjabi worker of his turban is precisely this instance; it is the moment when Punjabi and Jew come into view as identical victims of a calculated brutality. Meanwhile, the Sex Pistols confronted the Nazis' declaration of war on memory in their suggestion that the concentration camps such as Bergen-Belsen were holiday resorts with what is perhaps their most scathing attack:

> Belsen was a gas, I heard the other day
> In the open graves where the Jews all lay
> Life is fun and I wish you were here
> They wrote Jew postcards to those held dear
> Oh dear
>
> Sergeant majors on the march
> Wash the bodies in the starch
> See them all die one by one
> Guess it's dead, guess it's glad
> So bad!
>
> So glad!
> Be a man!
> A real man!
> Join our army!
> Belsen was a gas!
> Kill a man!

Kill someone!
Kill yourself!

In addressing the resurgence of the colonial inheritance in the midst of a social crisis, the Clash asserted that "In 1977 / I hope I go to Heaven / 'cos I been too long on the dole / And I can't work at all." In 1977, the old music lost its ability to speak to the present, to the social and cultural contradictions tearing the fabric of British society. In stripping rock 'n' roll down to its roots, the Clash declared "No Elvis, no Beatles, no Rolling Stones," opting instead for the "roots" music of Prince Far-I and Mickey Dread. This is what was precisely so dynamic about punk, that is brought black and white musical forms into new constellations—each was influenced, provoked, and in some cases produced by the other. For instance, Dub-Reggae legend Lee "Scratch" Perry produced the Clash's "Complete Control," a song that addresses the "C-O-N-Control" wielded by a record company that initially promised "artistic freedom" to the band only to subordinate art to money. While deriding the violence of racist skinheads in "Crazy Baldhead," Bob Marley expressed solidarity with the punks in "Punky Reggae Party," from the album *Bus to Babylon.* The Slits, driven by the primordial drumming of Palmolive, developed a distinctive style of reggae manifesting an arresting expression of "girl power." Perhaps one of the most important links between black and white cultures was made via the work of black filmmaker Don Letts, in particular the *Punk Rock Movie,* which is an invaluable document of the early punk scene.

In contrast to the cynical appropriation of black musical forms in a way that was palatable to a white audience, many punk bands covered reggae tracks, not as a gesture of simple imitation but rather in an effort to transform a certain idiom of resistance into their own. As Gilroy points out, the Clash's hugely popular rendition of Junior Murvin's "Police and Thieves" was often heard blaring from apartment windows during pitched street battles as a kind of soundtrack. Quite unlike Eric Clapton's popularization of Bob Marley's "I Shot the Sheriff," the Irish band Stiff Little Fingers' blistering rendition of Marley's profoundly moving "Johnny Was" reinterpreted this document of random police violence in the streets of Kingston and Trenchtown, Jamaica from a perspective rooted in the equally oppressive colonial realities of the "troubles" in the north of Ireland. To quote legendary music critic Lester Bangs: "Somewhere in [punk's] assimilation of reggae is the closest thing to the lost chord, the missing link between black music and white noise, rock capable of making a bow to black forms without smearing on the blackface."[10] In the process of bringing these forms together, Punk cleared the way for the Ska and Bluebeat revival of 1979 – 1981 around the "Two-tone Label," featuring racially mixed bands like the Specials, the Beat, and the Selector. But the culmination of the encounter between black and white in punk was the massive Rock Against Racism gig in Hyde Park in 1978.

The spirit of Punk lies anywhere but in the bands that try to produce punk music today. These bands entirely miss the point that punk attempted to grasp the eternal in the transitory rather than attempting to eternalize the transitory. Punk's legacy therefore lies, rather, in the hybridity of Bhangra, Ragga, Ambient, Jungle, Acid Jazz. It can be found in grrrrl bands such as Hole, L7, and Riotgirrrls, in bands like BAD—featuring Mick Jones, formerly guitarist of the Clash and, for a time, Don Letts—with its "mix" of Chuck Berry riffs, dub, house, and its hip-hop style sampling of the films of Nicholas Roeg. It lies in the work of Jah Wobble, formerly of P.I.L., who interprets the musical languages of the Middle East and Asia through dub-heavy bass but always with the unmistakable Cockney accent of somebody who might well have been a hooligan on the football terraces.

What I have been arguing, then, is that any form of multiculturalism worth its name must come to grips with the fact that it is not so much the cultural imperialism of a dominant group within a given society that constitutes the antithesis of multiculturalism but rather the ever more powerful logic of the marketplace. Far from ensuring that cultural differences are preserved the logic of the commodity actually promotes their eradication. Punk, like be-bop before it and hip-hop after it, represented an attempt to outwit the culture industry. As we know, in all three cases they were unsuccessful; but that's not the point. The point is that there was, in these very different musical languages, stemming from very different social and historical contexts, a utopic moment: what these styles offered, if only for a fleeting moment, was the shock of the new, of coming face to face with the real otherness of experience as opposed to the tired clichés of popular culture in which the expectations of the consumer are always reaffirmed. In other words, punk offered, if only for a moment, like a firecracker in a darkened sky, the possibility of a future beyond demographic categories and control groups, beyond monolithic radio station formats and marketing strategies. Above all, these styles offered the glimpse of a vision beyond the market.

## NOTES

1. Walter Benjamin, "The Work of Art in the Age of Mechanical Reproduction," *Illuminations: Essays and Reflections,* trans. Harry Zohn (New York: Schocken Books, 1969): 241.
2. Cf. Theodor Adorno, *Aesthetic Theory,* trans. R. Hullot-Kentor (Minneapolis: University of Minnesota Press, 1997).
3. Theodor Adorno, "Perennial Fashion—Jazz," *Prisms,* trans. Samuel and Shierry Weber (Cambridge, MA: MIT Press, 1988): 121–132. For an interesting and provocative dissenting opinion on Adorno's cultural criticism, see Alex Ross's review essay "Young Adorno,"*Transition* (6. 1, 69): 160–177, in which he argues that Adorno's writings manifest a "punk, devilish" spirit.
4. See Gerald Early, *Tuxedo Junction: Essays in American Culture* (New York: Ecco Press, 1989).
5. Greil Marcus, *Lipstick Traces: A Secret History of the Twentieth Century* (Cambridge, MA: Harvard University Press, 1989): 2.
6. *Beating Time: Riot'n'Race'n'Rock'n'Roll* (London: Chatto and Windus, 1986): 41.
7. *Beating Time, 41–42.*
8. *Beating Time,* 40.
9. Paul Gilroy, *"There Ain't No Black in the Union Jack": The Cultural Politics of Race and Nation* (London: Hutchinson, 1987).
10. Lester Bangs, *Psychotic Reactions and Carburetor Dung,* ed. Greil Marcus (New York: Knopf, 1988): 238.

# CHAPTER 16

# *Teaching in the Republic of Love Letters*

*AMITAVA KUMAR*

DURING A RECENT WINTER, living alone in someone else's apartment in Brooklyn, I came across a fragment of a letter in *Roland Barthes by Roland Barthes*. I was reading the book by Barthes for a seminar entitled "Foreign Bodies" that I was teaching at the Humanities Institute in Stony Brook. The letter and Barthes's reaction made me think of writing and change, but also about the fact that I was beginning to fall in love.

Barthes has received a communication from a man in Morocco identified only as Jilali. In the letter, Jilali confesses that he wants to address "a disturbing subject." "I have a younger brother, a student in the third-form AS, a very musical boy (the guitar) and a very loving one; but poverty conceals and hides him in this terrible world (he suffers in the present, 'as your poet says') and I am asking you, dear Roland, to find him a job in your kind country as soon as you can, since he leads a life filled with anxiety and concern; now you know the situation of young Moroccans, and this indeed astounds me and denies me all radiant smiles. And this astonishes you as well if you have a heart devoid of xenophobia and misanthropy."[1]

Barthes's response—not to Jilali but to us, his readers—is characteristic for the pleasures it elicits from the text: he finds the letter's language "sumptuous" and "brilliant." Barthes goes on, one is tempted to say, gushingly, except that his ear remains discriminating: he finds the letter's language "literal and nonetheless immediately literary, literary without culture, every sentence emphasizing the pleasures of language, in all its inflections precise, pitiless, beyond any aestheticism but never—far from it—censuring the aesthetic (as our grim compatriots would have done)." The letter, Barthes sums up elegantly, "speaks *at the same time* truth and desire: all of Jilali's desire (the guitar, love), all of the political truth of Morocco." And then the concluding words: "This is precisely the utopian discourse one would want."

I make a copy of this page and mail it to my friend B., who will later decide to become my lover. I have had an argument with B., who doesn't like Billy Bragg. Before I decide that this is a matter of "musical taste" and call it quits, I offer irrefutable evidence. I tell her that Bragg used a quote from Gramsci on the sleeve of one of his records: "How many times have I asked myself whether it was possible to tie oneself to a mass without ever having loved anyone . . . whether one could love a collectivity if one hadn't loved deeply some single human beings. . . . Wouldn't that have made barren my qualities as a revolutionary, wouldn't it have reduced them to a pure intellectual fact, a pure mathematical calculation?"[2] Even in this stirring invocation of that name that made of everyone a philosopher and I'd presume a poet, my reasoning remained incomplete. I wanted to touch on love and perhaps even revolution, and yet I was saying nothing. My discourse was utopian in a sense other than Barthes meant it to be.

*Speaking at the same time truth and desire!* That is why I send B. that page from the book. Her response articulates a different kind of pleasure in the text: "Call me a grim compatriot, but corporeal unmusicality *does* seem to be one of my limitations. I don't know about censoring the aesthetic (why would we?) but how about *situating* it? . . . I have noticed, especially in recent times, that interest in the body has returned the critical gaze to the question of pleasure. But, I confess, that has always struck me as precisely a utopian kind of . . . deflection, unless one wants to assume that pleasure somehow stands outside of the usual mechanisms of social production or reproduction . . . or perhaps *because* one *wants* to assume that." Seeking perhaps a conciliation, or maybe I only want to assume that, B. writes: "Does all this boil down to the Soviets and dancing? If so, you can count me in." The letter ends with the parenthetical question to which, alas, I am unable to offer any response: "Did that bastard Barthes give Jilali's brother a job?"

The subject, whether Jilali meant it in this way or not, is indeed "disturbing." How does one teach one's students—who are reading Barthes—not to forget the difficulty of immigrants' finding jobs in France? And the threat to education that the right-wing poses in those parts? (Le Pen's National Front has ensured that in a school in Marignane only pork is served during school meals so that Jewish or Muslim children have the choice of eating that or forgetting about education. A magazine article reports that the public libraries are being forced to remove books that do not directly reflect the Front ideology: works on the French Revolution, collections of stories from North Africa, and any book showing the races mixing.)

*But*, at the same time, how to make that concern a part of imagining what Barthes calls a "utopian discourse," one that does not rely for its moral weight on a "censuring of the aesthetic?" This task would involve the clever elaboration of the role that representation, or more simply, the imagination, plays in understanding even what the right-wing calls the "bread and butter" issues. This is the zone of the aesthetic, broadly conceived, and it's crucial, especially in the domain of the everyday, because it becomes a way of recovering broad-based, popular, critical agency in a social setting in which the revolutionary future has lost its legitimacy and appeal. Thereby, an insistence on pedagogy *and* pleasure, on the politics of the text *and* the self, on the erotics of the body *and* time however defined, is also a strategy of any live political praxis. Teaching politics *and* poetics becomes a matter of negotiation: learning means to keep calling into crisis any banal fixing of the opposition between jobs for the younger brother and the inflections in the sentences written by the elder one or, for that matter, my friend B., whose letters I desire.

Bruce Robbins has written recently that the moment at which a member of the public is picked out and drawn toward the literary-discipline community is one that is touched by libidinal energy: "From the point of view of the recruit, it's a moment that has something in common with falling in love."[3] In that article, Robbins goes on to a complex and subtle reflection on the role of an aesthetic that is "mediated and impure, fraught with ethical and political difficulties"; I will touch on that myself a little later on, but first I want to return to the earlier moment of ideological reproduction in which Robbins rightly detects eroticism in the air. My question is this: should the political docility of most of our students be blamed on their being too much in love with literature—or too little?

When a University of Virginia English professor, Mark Edmundson, complains about apathetic students and the culture of consumerism that surrounds them, he can explain this by arguing that as teachers we have failed to emphasize sufficiently the idea of genius that would have offered an alternative to bland consumerism and the passive ideology of hipness. To make it worse, Edmundson adds, we are also hypocritical: "Ask a professor what she thinks of the work of Stephen Greenblatt, a leading critic of Shakespeare, and you'll hear it for an hour. Ask her what her views are on Shakespeare's genius and she's likely to begin questioning the term along with the whole 'discourse of evaluation.'" Genius, clearly for Edmundson, is the kind of love that sweeps you off your feet. Without it, you're forlorn and destined to be a loser. "A world uninterested in genius is a despondent place, whose sad denizens drift from coffee bar to Prozac dispensary, unfired by ideals, by the glowing image of the self that one might become."[4]

However, in Hanif Kureishi's novel, *The Black Album*, it is the Thatcherite depredations that are making London a despondent place, and the sad denizens are warring over the very status of genius.[5] The novel is set in the days after the *fatwa* on Salman Rushdie has been passed by the Ayatollah and portrays the rising and falling tide of "fanaticism" that grips a group of second-generation Pakistani Muslim youth. Our protagonist, Shahid, is interested in literature and he is turned on to reading and music with a fierce passion by his cultural studies lecturer, Deedee Osgood, who also quite early in the novel becomes his lover. This is a different universe from the one that Edmundson describes. Even the "bad guys" in Kureishi's novel are hardly apathetic; in fact, they are passionately moved through the act of reading, in this case, the Quran. For their principal gadfly and "our" protagonist, Shahid, too, there is a need for reading, narration, and criticism: "[Storytelling!] This is the issue! Why we need it. If we need it. What can be said. And—what can't be. What mustn't be said. What is taboo and forbidden and why. What is censored. How censorship benefits us in exile here. How it might protect us, if it can do that." What divides him from his friends is his interest in imagination, that "most magnificent but unreliable capacity . . . which William Blake called 'the divine body in every man'"— and "his friends would admit no splinter of imagination into their body of belief, for that would poison all, rendering their conviction human, aesthetic, fallible."[6]

The human, the aesthetic, and the fallible, in Kureishi's narrative, attempt to give voice to what he calls "the individual." When Riaz, the leader of the Muslims, challenges Shahid with the statement, "To me these truths about the importance of faith and concern for others are deeper than the ravings of one individual imagination," the latter's uncertain and yet emphatic response is: "But the individual voice is important, too, isn't it?"[7] It is this interest in the individual and the vision of emancipation—and not a pedagogy outfitted to a trumpeting of genius—that, at least in one Marxist interpretation, allows the aesthetic to play a privileged part. When pressed by Nancy Fraser to explain why the aesthetic rather than the social sciences should be burdened with the responsibility of "cognitive mapping," Fredric Jameson replies that the distinction between science and ideology and the space in the latter— here conflated with the aesthetic—contributes to the elaboration of the relation between the individual and the real: "Aesthetics is something that addresses individual experience rather than something that conceptualizes the real in a more abstract way."[8]

I want to use Jameson's approach to claim *The Black Album*'s protagonist's interest in writing as the reclamation not of a self-absorbed, individuated persona of an aesthete but precisely its opposite, the self finding in textual articulation the sense of its social being. At the novel's end, we find Shahid leaving his bed early to write. "Among unmarked essays, letters, and the newspaper clippings he found a fountain pen with a decent nib, and began to write with concentrated excitement. He had to find some sense in his recent experiences; he wanted to know and understand. How could anyone confine themselves to one system or creed? Why should they feel they had to? There was no fixed self; surely our several selves melted and mutated daily? There had to be innumerable ways of being in the world. *He would spread himself out, in his work and in love, following his curiosity*" (emphasis added).[9]

In an act reminiscent of Rushdie's immigrant writer Salman—who in *The Satanic Verses* rewrites the verses of the Prophet Muhammad, thereby introducing doubt in his mind—Shahid rewrites the prose poems of the leader of the "fundamentalist" group. Shahid inserts between Riaz's lines, the odor of bodies in sexual heat. Shahid's sexual fantasies find their muse in his teacher and lover, Deedee Osgood, whose masturbatory acts anoint his existence with a passion that calls into question the certainties of Riaz's ascetic passion: "Rapt, he held his breath while Deedee picked up a deodorant bottle and inserted the top into her cunt. Had Riaz ever seen such a thing? Would he want to, secretly? Maybe Deedee would give him a demonstration so he might see its humanity."[10]

A passage like this returns me to my earlier points of departure, located both in Barthes and Robbins. To Barthes because I wonder whether the moral censuring of the sexual is also a censuring of the aesthetic. To Robbins because I want to ask whether the impure aesthetics is not also what contests the purity of the preacher and represents yet another kind of entanglement with the fraught aesthetics involved in all mentoring and mediation. But beyond Barthes and Robbins, the line about Shahid from Kureishi's novel, "He would spread himself out, in his work and love . . ." returns me to my friend B., who in her own fraught role as mediator between love and its loss, provides me a fragment from another kind of letter: "Here is Paul Feyerabend (at seventy) speaking of what it meant to meet Grazia (at sixty): 'From her I learned that there are strong inclinations after all, that they are not about abstract things such as solitude but about living beings. At last I have learned what it means to love somebody, the long days with Grazia turned me from an icy egoist into a friend, a companion, a husband.' Just this evening I tripped over that in, of all places, the *New Left Review*."

I cite this letter from my friend B. in the same way that Barthes cited Jilali's, to remove the false opposition between aesthetics and the everyday world of letters, or between politics and love. But this still leaves unanswered the question "Did that bastard Barthes give Jilali's brother a job?" Or, arriving late where I left off at the end of the last paragraph, we are still faced with the question of the "utopian discourse" or at least the utopian possibility for lovers as well as teachers: "Did you ever become like Grazia? Did someone say to you that 'I need to grasp that learning from someone is not the same as being taught'?" Or, to put this differently, "How to 'teach' or simply transfer into the space of another person, or a collective like a classroom, what Paul Feyerabend calls in that moving fragment 'strong inclinations'?"

In an open field of celebration that the unexamined aesthetic often becomes, a question like the one posed to Barthes by B.'s letter returns us to the limits of the utopian discourse. Political artists wrest the utopian from the merchants of capital by not being forgetful about limits. Recently, when invited to a dinner at the White House to accept a National Medal for the Arts, Adrienne Rich said no, writing in her letter to Jane Alexander, the chair of the National Endowment of the Arts: " . . . I could not accept such an award from President Clinton or this White House because the very meaning of art, as I understand it, is incompatible with the cynical politics of this administration. . . . There is no simple formula for the relationship of art to justice. But I do know that art—in my own case the art of poetry—means nothing if it simply decorates the dinner table of power which holds it hostage. The radical disparities of wealth and power in America are widening at a devastating rate. A president cannot meaningfully honor certain token artists while the people at large are so dishonored."[11]

Here, as in Barthes's reading of Jilali, Rich speaks at the same time truth and desire. All of Rich's desire (poetry, justice), all of the political truth of America. Especially in the world of poetry, which is often protected by some of its practitioners from politics, Rich's has been a voice heralding history in our midst:

But the great dark birds of history screamed and plunged
into our personal weather
They were headed somewhere else but their beaks and pinions drove
along the shore, through the rags of fog
where we stood, saying *I*[12]

This voice interrupts a private code of poetry and joins other efforts that in other ways lead to a questioning of the institutions that limit, with their narrower, interested definitions of the aesthetic, not only poetry but also the lives and the people behind that poetry. Some recent efforts include the literary campaign undertaken by Robert Hass, the 1996 Poet Laureate of the United States, and more remarkably, the community-pedagogical efforts of Ross Talarico, recounted in the award-winning book *Spreading the Word: Poetry and Community in America*.[13] Another great model of what she calls "poetry for the people" has been collectively—and successfully—developed by June Jordan. A set of guidelines for workshops and readings is provided in her book *June Jordan's Poetry for the People: A Revolutionary Blueprint*.[14] More recently, in an article in *The Nation*, Jordan wrote of the letters that had been left at her door. These were poems by what Jordan called her "student-revolutionaries," who were writing about the passage of the Proposition 209 in California that abolished affirmative action.[15] Jordan's appreciation is not misplaced because, apart from challenging cynical appraisals of the so-called slacker generation, the activism of the students replaces the ideology of cult with the cultures of dissent. In their small, unremitting, and even public articulation of protest, instead of being forced to accept a few public intellectuals, we catch sight of the outlines of a public culture of a true democracy.

Jordan's article in *The Nation* was accompanied by three poems by her students. I would like to end by quoting three of my own undergraduate students who participated in a poetry-performance outreach program in a class I taught. We entered into a partnership with two local high schools and performed in classrooms; my students also gave feedback to the high school students on their writing and performance. This partnership was about aesthetics being sharpened as communication and politics emerging as pedagogy. Learning was no longer only about constituting the self in private contemplation of letters; it was a type of teaching in which we were trying very hard to learn to do better to say "you" and "we" instead of "I." I do not want to invest any secrets in that school of thought that says teaching is as mysterious as love; I do want to say, however, that one of the pleasures it affords is the surprising discovery of one's students' "strong inclinations." Let me present you, then, my letters from the field.

Wanting to motivate the young audience to write, Lori Young said:

> . . . And if I don't write my story, the best thing that will happen is it won't get written. The worst thing that could happen is that someone else will write it. Look at this guy here. Baggy pants riding low, gotta beeper somewhere? Unlaced hightops. Sitting back in his chair wrapped in his arms and his attitude.
>
> Probably deals drugs.
>
> Do you see the problem here? I just wrote his story. And if he doesn't write it, then mine's the one out there, and no one's ever gonna know about how pissed off he was the last time he walked into a Lil Champ on the west side of town and the clerk got nervous because he looked like he was gonna do something dangerous—like buy a Doctor Pepper or a pack of cigarettes or something.
>
> I write because no one's *ever* gonna tell my story.

Noah Kaufman makes a point about presenting a loud performance in which he would use his language to mock those around him:

> . . . And recently, the owner of the restaurant where I am employed told me a story which no doubt found amusing as he repeated it three times within the course of an afternoon. The anecdote involved his brother and his brother's fiancé, who are also red-necks. Apparently, these two possess a predilection for Thai food and the story centers around a restaurant by the name of THAICOON, just like that, one word T-H-A-I-C and Pat I'd like to buy an O and Jim looks like there's two and I think I'll solve the puzzle.
>
> The Thai place was in the poor section of whatever town they were visiting, or rather in the Black part of town, and so this restaurant proves, at least for my employer, that Black people can laugh at themselves, and that they yes, can act responsibly when they want to. The punch line, and I say punch line because it was delivered in a very dead comedic style, was simple and to the point: The funny thing is, the food was great.

The high school students, needing no prompting from their teachers, join Anthony Lamar Rucker when he turns on the music and begins to recite a rap song entitled "A Lament for Hip-Hop" he has written for the students in the guise of "B-graff":

Where in the hell did the hip-hop go?

It wasn't that far back in time
when it was common practice to drop science in rhyme
conscious rap, uplifting the masses
Elevating minds while elevating asses

with the help of a old school beat
revamped and remixed and released back to the street
with a message for you and your boyz to all chew on
these days you it's bout getting lifted with your crew on
the ave sporting new Hilfiguz
not knowing a year he said he hated niggers

yes something's changed, it must be the air
throw on a rap record these days and I will dare you
to find something to activate the intellect
pardon me one moment while I just reflect on
the golden age of rap
when it was black america's cnn
and not an easy way to make a quick million

We've gone from nation to Millions to hold us back
To ignoring conscious rappers and calling them wack

jumping off the far side
to claiming "Wessyde"
knowing all the while that we are on the outside
of the power structure.
There is a structure
to how the black community's been set up to fully rupture

CIA and crack are the newest proofs
but for 400 years it's been war on black youths

underfunded education
increasing incarceration
are just some more blockades in path of our liberation

but while affirmative action dies a quiet death
all you hear these days is the latest about Meth
Can't you see This has got to stop
these bullshit Tomming rappers heard around the clock

I used to love her, now she's gone completely
tell me if I'm crazy or has rap been so neatly
bought out by the big businesses
where only profit matters and not human interest

we're so quick to prop snoop and biggie
yet when you break it down there is no diggety
doubt
of what they're all about
they want the cream the honeys and false gangsta clout

not realizing while they're fantasizing
that their role playing is costing black lives
and
my community's still filled with pain
while jay-z, nas, and rae just pop more champagne

how can we improve this situation
of wack-ass booty rappers ruining the black nation

it's up to you to raise the game
write rhymes to resist, and not just for the fame
the power of the word is unmatched by any
Just take a look around you you'll see that you've got
plenty
of topics on which to rail
to see the fat-cat ruling class straight to hell
the power's in your hands you've got to use it
hook it with a beat and people can't refuse it

Liberate yourselves, while you've got time
With you kicking your rhymes and me kicking out mine
we're sure to rise victorious
and when that day comes. . . . GLORIOUS!

B-graff on the mic one two represent
I woulda gone longer but my time is all spent.
Peace.

# NOTES

1. Roland Barthes, *Roland Barthes by Roland Barthes*, trans. Richard Howard (New York: Farrar, Straus, and Giroux, 1977). See p. 111.
2. I have by now lost the sleeve of the Bragg tape. I found the Gramsci quote again, some years later, in Teresa de Lauretis, *Technologies of Gender* (Bloomington: Indiana University Press, 1987), p. 87.
3. Bruce Robbins, "Return to Literature," in Amitava Kumar, ed., *Class Issues: Pedagogy, Cultural Studies, and the Public Sphere* (New York: New York University Press, 1977), pp. 22–32. See p. 24.
4. Mark Edmundson, "On the Uses of Liberal Education: As Lite Entertainment for Bored College Students," *Harper's Magazine*, September 1997, pp. 39–49. The quotes appear on pp. 48–49.
5. Hanif Kureishi, *The Black Album* (New York: Scribner, 1995).
6. See Kureishi, p. 143.
7. See Kureishi, p. 195.
8. See Fredric Jameson, "Cognitive Mapping," in this volume.
9. See Kureishi, p. 285.
10. See Kureishi, p. 129.
11. Adrienne Rich, "Letter to Jane Alexander," in *Extra!*, September–October 1997.
12. Adrienne Rich, Extract from "In Those Years,"*Dark Fields of the Republic* (New York: W. W. Norton and Company, 1995), p. 4.
13. Ross Talarico, *Spreading the Word: Poetry and the Survival of Community in America* (Durham: Duke University Press, 1995).
14. Lauren Muller and the Blueprint Collective, ed., *June Jordan's Poetry for the People: A Revolutionary Blueprint* (New York: Routledge, 1995).
15. June Jordan, "Affirming Action," *The Nation*, April 28, 1997, pp. 29–31.

# Contributors

MICHAEL BIBBY, an Assistant Professor of English at Shippensburg University, is the author of *Hearts and Minds: Bodies, Poetry, and Resistance in the Vietnam Era* (Rutgers University Press, 1996) and articles on antiwar poetry. He is the recipient of the NEH Fellowship (1997–98). He is currently working on a book-length study of black poetry and racial discourses in postwar America, 1945–1955.

SAMIR GANDESHA received his Ph.D. in political science at York University, Toronto, in 1996. From 1995–97 he was a visiting scholar in the Department of History at the University of California at Berkeley. He has published articles in *Philosophy and Social Criticism* and *The European Legacy* and is completing a book entitled *Enigmatic Enlightenment: Tragedy, Vision and Ethics from Plato to Adorno and Beyond.*

CAMILLA BENOLIRAO GRIGGERS is Distinguished Chair of Women's Studies at Carlow College in Pittsburgh. She is the author of *Becoming-Woman* (University of Minnesota Press, 1997) and founding editor of the e-journal *Cultronix* on the World-Wide Web. She has produced and directed several videos including *Alienations of the Mother Tongue* (1995), *The Micropolitics of Biopsychiatry* (1996), and *Memories of a Forgotten War* (in progress).

FREDERIC JAMESON is the William A. Lane Jr. Professor of Comparative Literature and Chair of the Literature Program at Duke University. His latest books are *Brecht and Method* (Verso, 1998) and *The Cultural Turn: Selected Writings on the Postmodern, 1983–1998* (Verso, 1998).

GRANT KESTER is an Assistant Professor of modern art history and theory at Washington State University. He is the editor of *Art, Activism and Oppositionality: Essays from Afterimage* (Duke University Press, 1998) and "Aesthetics and the Body Politic," College Art Association *Art Journal* (Spring 1997). His current book project is entitled *Writers Without Hands: Discourse and Counterdiscourse in Modern Art.*

AMITAVA KUMAR, currently a Fellow at Yale University, teaches English at the University of Florida. He is the author of *No Tears for the N.R.I.* (Writers Workshop, Calcutta) and *Passport Photos* (University of California Press, forthcoming). His writing has appeared in *Critical Inquiry, minnesota review, Race and Class, Rethinking Marxism*, and *The Nation*. Kumar has recently completed an award-winning, collaborative documentary film, "Pure Chutney."

ELIZABETH LANGLAND, Professor of English and Dean at the University of California-Davis, is the author, most recently, of *Nobody's Angels: Middle-Class Women and Domestic Ideology in Victorian Culture* (Cornell University Press, 1995). Her observations in this essay spring from her experiences from 1995–98 as associate dean for faculty affairs in the College of Liberal Arts and Sciences at the University of Florida.

IRA LIVINGSTON teaches English at the State University of New York at Stony Brook. He is the author of *Arrow of Chaos: Romanticism and Postmodernity* (University of Minnesota, 1997) and the editor, with Judith Halberstam, of *Posthuman Bodies* (Indiana University Press, 1995). He is the author of the open letter to the Unabomber included in the editor's Introduction in this book.

ERIC LOTT is the author of *Love and Theft: Black Minstrelsy and the American Working Class* (Oxford University Press, 1995).

RANDY MARTIN teaches at Pratt Institute and has recently published *Critical Moves: Dance Studies in Theory and Politics* (Duke University Press, 1998) and *Chalk Lines: The Politics of Work in the Managed University* (Duke University Press, 1999).

SEAN MCCANN is an Assistant Professor of English and American Studies at Wesleyan University. He is at work on a book about hard-boiled crime fiction and the New Deal order. He has published essays in *American Quarterly*, *ELH*, and *Radical History Review*.

PAULA RABINOWITZ is Professor of English at University of Minnesota. She also teach in the programs in American Studies, Women's Studies and Cultural Studies. Her most recent book is *They Must Be Represented: The*

*Politics of Documentary* (Verso, 1994). She is currently working on two books: one on film noir, the other on three women painters.

Ross Talarico is the author of *Spreading the Word: Poetry and the Survival of Community in America* (Duke University Press, 1995), which won the MLA's Mina P. Shaughnessy Prize.

Michael Taussig is Professor of Anthropology at Columbia University. He is the author, most recently, of *The Magic of the State* (Routledge, 1997).

Csaba Toth is Associate Professor and Chair in the History Department at Carlow College. He is currently working on a book, *American Utopianism in an Atlantic Frame, 1880–1905*. He has most recently published an essay in *Gothic: Transmutations of Horror in Late Twentieth Century Art*, ed. Christoph Grunenberg (The M.I.T. Press, 1997). His writings have also appeared in *Utopian Studies* and *American Quarterly*.

H. Aram Veeser is Associate Professor of English at City College of CUNY. He has published in *minnesota review*, *Biblical Interpretation*, and *The Nation*. He has edited several well-known collections, *New Historicism* (Routledge, Chapman and Hall, 1990), *The New Historicism Reader* (Routledge, 1993), *Confessions of the Critics* (Routledge, 1996), and *Stanley Fish Reader* (Blackwell, 1998).

# Index